New England Open-House
Cookbook

NEW ENGLAND OPEN · HOUSE
Cookbook

SARAH LEAH CHASE

Food Photography by **MATTHEW BENSON**

WORKMAN PUBLISHING · NEW YORK

Library of Congress Cataloging-in-Publication Data is available.

ISBNs 978-0-7611-5519-5 (pb); 978-0-7611-8496-6 (HC)

COVER LETTERING AND INTERIOR DESIGN: Jean-Marc Troadec

COVER AND FOOD PHOTOGRAPHY: Matthew Benson

AUTHOR PHOTOGRAPH: © Terry Pommett Photography

FOOD STYLIST: Chris Lanier

PROP STYLIST: Sara Abalan

ADDITIONAL PHOTOGRAPHY: See page 388

ILLUSTRATIONS: James Williamson

Workman books are available at special discounts when purchased in bulk for premiums and sales promotions as well as for fund-raising or educational use. Special editions or book excerpts can also be created to specification. For details, contact the Special Sales Director at the address below or send an email to specialmarkets@workman.com.

WORKMAN PUBLISHING COMPANY, INC.
225 VARICK STREET
NEW YORK, NY 10014-4381
WORKMAN.COM

WORKMAN is a registered trademark of Workman Publishing Co., Inc.

Printed in the United States of America

First printing May 2015

10 9 8 7 6 5 4 3 2 1

DEDICATION

To the men in my family who have anchored my life in New England:

My husband, Nigel, for being the oyster opener, griller, and lobster cooker in our house and for bringing me that first cup of strong black coffee in bed most mornings.

My father, Dr. Raymond Chase, for his love of both the land and sea, Seth Thomas clocks and Eric Sloane barns, and for educating me in the finest of New England schools.

My brother, Jonathan, for being my closest comrade in all things related to food and family.

My son, Oliver, for telling me a chicken dinner I served him at the age of three was "fabulous" and for luring me to soccer matches, Little League games, tennis tournaments, and skiing adventures in nooks and crannies of New England I otherwise would have never explored.

My uncle, Paul Madden, for teaching me about whirligigs and weather sticks and always sharing the most engaging and amusing stories about people, places, things, and of course memorable meals.

ACKNOWLEDGMENTS

At this moment I cannot begin to express my great thanks without thinking of the popular adage "a picture is worth a thousand words." All five of my previous cookbooks published by Workman were charmingly illustrated by artists. While I have written many thousands of words to accompany the recipes in this book, it is the food photography and colorful New England snapshots that truly make the recipes and the locales that inspired them sparkle in ways that enchant far beyond what words can convey. Great gastronomic gratitude and appreciation goes to food photographer Matthew Benson and the highly talented team assisting him—chef and food stylist Chris Lanier, prop stylist Sara Abalan, and Workman's photo director Anne Kerman. My longtime photographer friend Cary Hazlegrove has sometimes harked back to her Southern upbringing by calling me *girlfriend*. I must now return the favor, for Cary is indeed a *girlfriend* of the finest kind and one whose exquisite photos of Nantucket and places hither and yonder never fail to bring me and so many others profound joy. Cary's generosity garners boatloads of thanks with additional tugboats going to her Nantucket Stock Photography colleagues.

The words, recipes, and photography that have gone into conveying my love of New England could not accurately reflect my heartfelt sentiments were they not pleasingly and palatably organized. Mind you, such in no mean feat, but one that was indeed ingeniously executed by designer Jean-Marc Troadec.

I might still be lost in my opening chapters or up to my neck in a fine kettle of Portuguese Kale Soup were it not for having Apple wizard Scott Reyburn come to my technical rescue time and time again at a moment's notice.

A host of fellow New England food lovers, family, and friends contributed to the recipes in this cookbook and I have sung your praises in the extensive headnotes and sidebars peppered throughout *New England Open-House*. In the limited space I have here, I wish to give a shout-out to those whose time and expertise is unsung: production editor Carol White, copy editor Barbara Mateer, typesetter Annie O'Donnell, and photo researcher Michael Di Mascio. When all is said, done, designed, proofed, and published—a book must sell and another huge round of thanks needs therefore to be bestowed on Workman's marketing and publicity team, most notably Jessica Wiener, Selina Meere, Molly Kay Upton, John Jenkinson, and Jack Masterson, and the whole sales staff.

The person with whom I have worked most closely throughout the entire cookbook writing process—going from my kitchen's chopping block to professionally printed page—is my editor, Suzanne Rafer. There has been a ton of upheaval in the world of publishing since my career in cookbook writing began in 1985 and I am as lucky as I am awed to have had Suzanne Rafer as my steadfast editor and friend for thirty years! Sometimes, I wonder how Suzanne does it all and would be remiss if I did not mention how fortunate we both are that the lovely Sarah Brady is Suzanne's assistant.

Finally, the world of food is one filled with enormous fun, indulgences, and lively friendships among colleagues. My culinary and personal life has most certainly been so enriched through my kinship with Ina Garten. Simply put, I must thank the warm and wonderful Ina for just being Ina.

CONTENTS

FOREWORD

By Ina Garten

I will always remember the first time I met Sarah Chase. It was the late 1980s and I owned a specialty food store in East Hampton, New York, called Barefoot Contessa. At the end of the summer, my husband, Jeffrey, and I took a little vacation to Nantucket. The thing that excited me most about that trip was that we could visit a specialty food store on the island that I'd heard so much about— Que Sera Sarah.

We walked into this charming store with all the smells of warm muffins and freshly baked pies that you would imagine wafting from the kitchen. There was—and I remember this as though it were yesterday—a beautiful young blonde woman at the counter, standing behind an enormous bowl of homemade granola. Jeffrey just happened to be wearing a Barefoot Contessa sweatshirt, and Sarah recognized the name. She introduced herself and I think we both knew at that moment that we had found a kindred spirit. We've been great friends ever since.

Sarah's amazing *Nantucket Open-House Cookbook* and *Cold-Weather Cooking* were published in 1987 and 1990, and I loved them from the moment that I opened them. All the recipes are both simple and elegant, which is what I admire in cooking, and each had a wonderful twist to make it special. Every recipe is something you *really* want to eat—Soft Scrambled Eggs with Lobster, French Bistro Chicken, and Orzo and Roasted Vegetable Salad. All the ingredients were easy to find, and when you prepared a recipe, it came out perfectly every time. What else could you want from a cookbook? These were the cookbooks of my dreams.

After we got to know each other, Sarah came to visit me in East Hampton. I took her on a tour of my world— the specialty food stores, cheese shops, and farmstands. She particularly loved the farmstands with local produce and took lots of Long Island corn back to Nantucket. We spent hours discussing the best way to make scones and what we look for in chicken soup. We swapped stories of catering private parties—the good, the bad, and the harrowing days that any caterer has. I always love our time together because Sarah is lovely and smart, and we share a lifelong love of cooking. I've been cooking for forty-five years—thirty-five of them professionally—and I haven't lost any of my passion for it. Clearly, neither has Sarah! Her later cookbooks, *Pedaling Through Provence Cookbook* and *Pedaling Through Burgundy Cookbook*, are both equally extraordinary and I cherish the personal stories and the recipes.

Those of us who love Sarah and her recipes have waited for this New England cookbook for years. Her roots are in Connecticut, Massachusetts, and Maine, and her passion is clearly in this cuisine. Each chapter is filled with stories about all the extraordinary local ingredients available in New England—of course, the fresh lobster, clams, and oysters we associate with the seaside, but also Sarah's own particular favorites along the coast. She introduces us to a local lamb farm in Barnstable on Cape Cod, a creamery in Narragansett that makes a unique Salty Sea Feta, and all the gorgeous New England farmstands that she loves. The recipes in *New England Open-House Cookbook* are familiar and yet totally original to Sarah. This is exactly the food that you want to cook at home— delicious, satisfying, earthy food that your friends and family will love. I'm very happily cooking my way through the book!

How Long Does It Take to Write a Cookbook?

"New England has a harsh climate, a barren soil, a rough and stormy coast, and yet we love it, even with a love passing that of dwellers in more favored regions."—Henry Cabot Lodge

"New England is a remarkable region for food. From our rocky coasts come the greatest variety and best quality of shellfish in America. From the rivers, bays, and ocean come an abundance and a multitude of species of fish that are also unrivaled. The rolling hills and valleys of New England are home to some of America's oldest fruit orchards, vegetable, grain, meat, poultry, and dairy farms. Almost all of the world's cranberries come from New England and the beach plums and wild berries can be found in every corner. . . . The woodlands are abundant in sugar maples, wild mushrooms, and fiddleheads. Other treats you will find are freshly milled flours, handmade cheddars, cob-smoked hams, apple cider, and old-fashioned fruit wines. The list goes on and on."—Jasper White, introduction to *Jasper White's Cooking From New England*

Originally, it was not my idea to write a cookbook about New England food and it was most certainly not my intention to take more than five years to compile it. When Peter Workman, the ingenious founder of the eponymous and wonderfully inventive publishing company, first suggested the topic to me, I resisted and insisted that I was not a New England cook. Although I have lived in New England my entire life and cannot imagine calling any other place home, my attitude toward what constituted authentic New England cooking was at the time tainted by an acceptance of the bleakness expressed by Henry Cabot Lodge rather than elevated by the optimism exuded by Jasper White.

However, my resistance to Peter Workman's New England vision began to wane when my very wise agent, Doe Coover, reminded me of all the

New England experiences I already had going for me. She cited my growing up in Connecticut, summering in Maine, attending colleges in Vermont and Boston, living and running a business on Nantucket for several years, and now making my home on Cape Cod. Certainly, Doe reasoned, I could easily fill in the missing New Hampshire and Rhode Island components. I listened and realized that I could indeed write a cookbook about the way I cooked every day, year round, with prized New England ingredients in my New England kitchen. Bushels of briny oysters, legions of lively lobsters, pails of wild beach plums, rashers of apple wood-smoked bacon, and wedges of Clothbound Cheddar later, I owe a tremendous debt of gratitude to both Peter and Doe for allowing me to discover there truly is no place like home. I am only very sad and sorry that Peter is not present to enjoy the fruition of the seed he planted.

I wrote or co-authored six cookbooks between 1985 and 1995. In my mind, this was a glorious time of cookbook writing because Americans in general were becoming much more passionate about home cooking and a cookbook's acclaim rested on merit and integrity rather than celebrity. Much has transpired since *Pedaling Through Provence* and *Pedaling Through Burgundy*—my last two cookbooks—were published by Workman in 1995. On a personal level, the way I used to conduct my life has been turned upside down by what I have come to refer to as the three m's: marriage to my husband, Nigel, in 1995; motherhood with the birth of our son, Oliver, in 1997; and our move from Nantucket Island to mainland Cape Cod at the end of 1999. These three m's meant I could no longer devote a week exclusively to planning and executing a thematic dinner party menu, dine out in Nantucket's truly terrific restaurants several times a month, fly some place chic and/or foreign for culinary and cultural inspiration at the drop of a hat, or write an entire cookbook from cover to cover in the two-year time span it used to take me.

Living on Cape Cod and in close proximity to the Kennedy summer compound in Hyannisport translated into reading something about the members of the former First Family on a steady basis. When I learned that Jacqueline Kennedy Onassis had once stated, "If you bungle raising your children, I don't think whatever else you do matters very much," I took the advice very much to heart.

Representing New England

Besides all the travel, research, shopping, schlepping, slicing, dicing, cooking, eating, and cleaning up that has gone into the many, many recipes contained in this cookbook, there are other underlying principles guiding the recipe selection. As much as I adore visiting modern New England cities like Boston, Providence, and Portland, I took care not to impart too much of an urban vibe to my recipe selection for fear that the dishes would end up reflecting a sophistication that could come from any major metropolis in the country and not represent the good rural New England home cooking I have come to admire and love. Growing up in New England has made me realize that many of its inhabitants take to a certain place or region with a passion that never diminishes. This in turn inspired me to select a favorite area in each of the six New England states to anchor my recipe research. Because I have been going to Nantucket since I was thirteen and have lived on Cape Cod now for fifteen years, there was no question that the Cape and Islands would be my chosen area of concentration in Massachusetts. Maine was pretty easy too because so many of my family members continue to live or summer on the Blue Hill peninsula in the Penobscot Bay area, though I couldn't resist expanding this realm to include the scenic and culinarily vibrant neighboring stretch of coast spanning from Rockland to Belfast. At one point when we were in the process of moving off Nantucket, we entertained living in Bristol, Rhode Island. Although the offer we had made on a house fell through somewhat nefariously, research for this book has allowed me to experience what direction our life might have taken had we settled in the historically and nautically rich Newport and Bristol pocket of the Ocean State.

Despite being born and raised in central Connecticut, I opted to focus my Connecticut research in the northwestern part of the state in the area often referred to as the Litchfield Hills. My love affair with this breathtakingly beautiful rural area of sprawling farmland, stone walls, and babbling brooks and rivers began when I was working on the *Silver Palate Good Times Cookbook* in Manhattan with cofounder Sheila Lukins and retreated to work weekends at the Lukins' vacation home in Kent, Connecticut. A few years later, after the publication of my own *Nantucket Open-House Cookbook*, Ruth and Skitch Henderson invited me to teach cooking classes at the enchanting Silo Cooking School situated on their rambling Hunt Hill Farm estate in New Milford. I continued to teach for several years at the Silo and my appreciation of the Litchfield Hills lifestyle increased with each and every visit. Some years later, my son attended boarding school at the Rumsey Hall School in Washington Depot and his two remarkable years there represented a high point for all in our immediate family and engendered many new layers of enthusiasm for this exquisite area of Connecticut.

Homing in on specific parts of Vermont and New Hampshire presented more of a challenge. Portsmouth was the place I was most familiar with in New Hampshire but I felt the bent of my book was already quite heavily coastal. So, I opted to further explore the lush inland countryside of the Upper Connecticut River Valley as I had friends with homes in Grantham and Hanover, and had become quite enamored of the towns of Plainfield and Cornish when I was assigned to write a magazine article on the charming and cozy Home Hill Inn on the River Road in Plainfield. Vermont, needless to say, did not present any coastal conflicts but instead brought on the difficulty of trying to confine my research to one area. As I explored the Green

Mountains, I seemed to develop a particular penchant for the food I found in towns beginning with a W. No family skiing trip to Vermont could be complete without a provisioning stop at the Woodstock Farmers' Market on the outskirts of the quintessentially quaint village of Woodstock, and then there was the fabulous Hen of the Wood restaurant in Waterbury, the rustic American Flatbread barn in Waitsfield, and the sublime Pitcher Inn in the tiny town of Warren. At the same time, visits to Stowe, Stratton, Dorset, Manchester, and Quechee proved to be equally satisfying, so I had to throw care and guidelines aside and simply embrace all of Vermont—an easy task and sensible decision if you are as much of a connoisseur of Vermont's superb dairy products as I am.

While this *New England Open-House Cookbook* is bursting with some 300 recipes, I know there are great New England people, places, and foods not included on these pages. I welcome hearing about them because the process of writing this book has taught me my zeal for New England idiosyncrasies and indie undertakings is alive and well enough to consider a sequel. In the meantime, I invite you to join me in cooking and savoring a few or hopefully many of my current favorite New England recipes, running the gamut from Hot Olive Whirligigs and "Fig N Pig" canapés to Simple Steamers, Fish Chowder, My Favorite Classic New England Lobster Roll, Cast-Iron Skillet Roast Chicken, Steak in the Coals, Smashed Potatoes, Cape Cod Corn Canoes, Toby's Blueberry Cheesecake, and a warming and attitude-adjusting mug of Mount Mansfield Mulled Wine. These recipes are but a small handful of the tasty treats that have graced my table and been formatted and filed on my laptop over the course of the past five years. If truth be told, it has actually taken a lifetime of my living in New England to be able to put together a collection of recipes representative of my personal philosophy about the finest kind of feasting on New England soil.

Harbingers

> "It won't be warm till snow gets off the mountain,
> and the snow won't get off the mountain till it gets warm."
> —*Old New England proverb*

Although we now live in an age of around-the-clock cable TV weather channels and have the ease of being able to surf the Internet for up-to-the-minute forecasts in almost every locale on the planet, many people I know in New England still prefer to glean their weather cues from Mother Nature. Seasoned yachtsmen and fishermen alike trust the time-honored proverb: "Red sky at night, sailor's delight. Red sky in morning, sailor's warning." Whether or not Punxsutawney Phil sees his shadow on the second day of February in distant Pennsylvania has little bearing on predicting when our sometimes brutal New England winters will yield to a flirtation with spring. I personally hedge my hopes for winter loosening its icy grip on my first sighting of tiny pristine and pendulant snowdrop flowers emerging against all odds from the frozen soil surrounding our Cape Cod home on any given sunny day in late February. I know bright purple and yellow crocuses cannot be far behind, along with a day or two when our woodstove will scarcely need a log to warm our family's Jack Russell Terrier, Latte.

Likewise, I sense summer's best beach days are soon to become a memory when clear Nantucket night skies in August begin to sport enough shooting stars to rival the oohs and aahs of the often fogged-in Fourth of July fireworks extravaganza. Later on, when a first frost kisses pumpkins destined to become jack-o'-lanterns, the sad time has come to savor that last lingering vine-ripened tomato. While nature's harbingers tend to bring a mixed bag of delight and despair, culinary harbingers—my term for a myriad of delectable New England nibbles that tease and awaken appetites—are always cause for joy, raised glasses, and usually a smidgen of local pride.

New Englanders have long had a reputation for being frugal and I have actually been a guest at crusty old anglers' clubs and small town yacht clubs where happy hour consists of stiff libations I can scarcely stomach and an open jar of peanut butter surrounded by a sleeve of Ritz crackers. While I am truly glad such places still exist and continue to thrive, today's New England food scene offers too many fine products not to share the wealth by proffering appetizers with the titillating tastes of artisanal cheeses, smoked native seafood, and just-picked backyard vegetables—all of which serve to set the stage and foretell of more fine fare to follow.

As far as I am concerned, good New England hors d'oeuvres are equally appreciated whether plain or fancy. In fact, I honestly have a difficult time deciding whether I am more impressed by the welcoming basket of freshly baked warm bread and cultured local butter placed on every table at Hen of the Wood restaurant in Waterbury, Vermont, or the over-the-top Caviar Coupes served at Nantucket's most glamorous soirees. Then again, offer me a dilly bean or a tiny sea salt tumbled tomato and I am also one happy Yankee.

Bountiful bunches of locally grown carrots brighten the artful produce display at Vermont's Woodstock Farmers' Market.

Woodstock Farmers' Market Carrot Dip

I almost never plan a trip to Vermont without figuring out a way to include a stop at the Woodstock Farmers' Market located along Route 4 on the outskirts of the charming village of Woodstock. The place is not a farmers' market in the traditional weekly open-air market sense of the word, but rather an enclosed specialty grocery store with a well-researched mix of local foods and international ingredients no good cook should be without. I tasted the store's unique signature cilantro and ginger laced carrot dip on my very first visit and have been hooked ever since.

The recipe here is my adaptation from the customer-requested recipes posted on the Woodstock Farmers' Market website. Serve this vibrant carrot dip with your favorite crackers, layer it into sandwiches, or even dollop a few spoonfuls on a plate as a bright and delicious side salad accompaniment to lunch and dinner entrées. Purchasing a pre-shredded bag of carrots will make the dip a breeze to make, but locavores can of course start with whole carrots from the backyard or a nearby farm. MAKES ABOUT 2½ CUPS

1 bag (10 ounces) shredded carrots, or
   4 to 5 whole carrots, trimmed, peeled,
   and cut into 1-inch pieces

3 scallions, both white and tender green parts,
   trimmed and minced

3 tablespoons finely minced peeled fresh
   ginger

⅓ cup minced fresh cilantro

⅓ cup mayonnaise, Hellmann's or homemade
   (page 129), or more as needed

1½ tablespoons rice vinegar

1 tablespoon tamari or soy sauce, or
   more to taste

½ teaspoon Asian (dark) sesame oil

1 tablespoon toasted white or black sesame
   seeds (optional; see Note)

1 Place the shredded carrots or carrot pieces in a food processor fitted with the metal blade. Pulse

Preserved Lemons Pronto

Even though preserved lemons are an ingredient essential to Moroccan cooking, and New England and Moroccan cuisine have little if anything in common, preserved lemons have garnered a place of respect in the kitchens of many modern New England cooks. And, rightfully so, since preserved lemons are nothing more than lemons pickled in salt to silky tenderness, and both ingredients are at the center of New England coastal cooking.

The traditional method of preserving lemons requires at least a month's patience, but quicker methods have recently come into vogue and such will work fine if you want the instant gratification of making My Mother's Crabmeat Dip over the next day or two, rather than next month or two. Here's my pronto technique: Scrub 1 whole lemon, preferably organic, and cut it lengthwise into 8 sections. Place them in a small saucepan and toss with 1 tablespoon coarse sea salt. Pour in ³/₄ cup water and bring to a boil. Cover the pot, reduce the heat, and simmer until the lemon skins are very soft, about 30 minutes. Let cool, transfer the lemons and their liquid to a small jar, and store in the refrigerator. The preserved lemons are ready to use immediately. Rinse briefly, if desired, to reduce the saltiness, and then mince the skin as called for in recipes. Jarred preserved lemons are also sold in specialty stores and online at sites such as Amazon.

the machine several times until the carrots are uniformly finely chopped. You should have about 2 cups. Transfer the carrots to a mixing bowl and toss them with the scallions, ginger, and cilantro.

2 Place the mayonnaise, rice vinegar, tamari or soy sauce, and sesame oil in a small bowl and whisk together until thoroughly combined. Pour the mayonnaise mixture over the carrots and toss to coat evenly. Taste for seasoning, adding a splash more tamari or soy sauce if the dip is not quite salty enough or a spoonful of mayonnaise if it is too dry.

3 Transfer the carrot dip to a decorative serving bowl and refrigerate it, covered, for at least 3 hours to marry the flavors. Serve the dip chilled, garnished with the toasted sesame seeds, if desired. The dip is best when served within 2 days of making it.

NOTE: *I buy my sesame seeds already toasted. However, if you want to toast your own, place the seeds in a small skillet set over medium heat and cook, shaking the pan back and forth, until fragrant, 60 to 90 seconds.*

My Mother's Crabmeat Dip

My parent's house in Blue Hill, Maine, is across the street from a family who picks and sells local crabmeat. We can literally walk up our long driveway, cross the street, and treat ourselves to incredibly fresh, just-picked crabmeat. My mother feels it is a crime to do too much to this delicacy, so she keeps her crabmeat dip very simple but unique among most Maine crabmeat dip recipes by adding a scant teaspoon of preserved lemon rind, which she makes herself and keeps on hand during the summer months. This is a dip that should only be made with very fresh peekytoe or lump crabmeat. Canned crabmeat, in this instance, will not cut it. MAKES ABOUT 1 CUP; SERVES 4 TO 6

8 ounces fresh Maine peekytoe crabmeat, carefully checked for stray bits of shell and/or cartilage

1 teaspoon finely minced preserved lemon rind (see page 3)

1 teaspoon finely minced peeled shallot, scallion, or chives

1 tablespoon minced fresh dill

2 to 2½ tablespoons mayonnaise, Hellmann's or homemade (page 129)

Sea salt and freshly ground black pepper (optional)

Plain water or pita crackers, for serving

PLACE THE CRABMEAT in a mixing bowl and, using the tines of a fork, gently flake and aerate it. Fold in the preserved lemon rind, shallots, and dill. Add just enough mayonnaise to bind the mixture lightly together. You can add a little salt and pepper if desired but take care not to mask the delicate flavor of the fresh crabmeat. The crabmeat will already have the salty savor of the ocean and the preserved lemon is also quite salty. Transfer the dip to a decorative serving crock or bowl and refrigerate it, covered, for at least 30 minutes to marry the flavors. Serve the dip on the day it is made, chilled and surrounded by plain crackers.

Hot Crabmeat Dip

I have never been a big fan of the mayonnaise-laden hot artichoke dip, which seems to appear in every Junior League cookbook from Connecticut to California. However, I am extremely fond of a Down East–inspired antidote I came up with using nary a teaspoon of mayonnaise and instead lots of fresh Maine crabmeat, a subtle splash of cream sherry, Swiss cheese, and a topping of crunchy almonds. This hot dip really hits the spot on chilly autumn and winter nights and is a great way to kick off festive gatherings of family and friends. If you don't have access to peekytoe crabmeat, fresh backfin, Jonah, or Dungeness crabmeat may be substituted. MAKES ABOUT 2½ CUPS; SERVES 8 TO 10

Butter, for greasing the gratin or pie dish

6 ounces (¾ cup) cream cheese, at room temperature

1 tablespoon light cream or whole milk

2 tablespoons cream sherry

8 ounces fresh Maine peekytoe crabmeat, carefully sorted through for stray bits of shell and/or cartilage

1¼ cups (about 5 ounces) freshly shredded mild Swiss or Jarlsberg cheese

2 scallions, both white and tender green parts, trimmed and minced

2 tablespoons minced jarred pimientos

¾ teaspoon crumbled dried tarragon

¾ teaspoon sea salt

¼ teaspoon freshly ground white or black pepper

3 tablespoons sliced almonds

Sweet paprika, for sprinkling over the top of the dip

Toasted rounds of French bread, crackers, or corn chips, for serving

1 Preheat the oven to 375°F. Lightly butter a 9-to-10 inch oven-to-table gratin or ceramic pie dish.

2 Place the cream cheese, cream or milk, and sherry in a medium-size mixing bowl and beat with an electric mixer until smooth. Using a rubber or silicone spatula, gently but thoroughly fold in the crabmeat, 1 cup of the Swiss cheese, and the scallions, pimientos, tarragon, salt, and pepper.

3 Spread the crabmeat mixture evenly in the prepared dish. Sprinkle the almonds and remaining ¼ cup

Swiss cheese evenly over the top and then dust with a sprinkling of paprika. Bake the dip until browned and bubbly, about 30 minutes. Place the hot dip on a trivet along with a spreading knife. Serve with toasted French bread or crackers or corn chips.

Community Cookbook Crab Spread

A fair amount of my research for this cookbook has been centered on combing through spiral-bound community cookbooks, old and new, that I find during my travels throughout New England. I have noticed that Maine community cookbooks in particular tend to title what I would normally consider to be a dip a spread and almost all these books contain similar recipes for crab spreads with a mixed cream cheese and mayonnaise base. The following is my interpolation of these ubiquitous crab spread recipes. The addition of cream cheese makes for a sturdier combination than the delicacy of My Mother's Crabmeat Dip (page 3) and I like the suggestion I have come across in some books for serving the spread with cucumber slices as well as crackers. MAKES 2 CUPS; SERVES 8 TO 10

4 ounces (½ cup) cream cheese, at room temperature

3 tablespoons mayonnaise

1 tablespoon freshly squeezed lemon juice

12 ounces fresh Maine peekytoe crabmeat, carefully checked for stray bits of shell and/or cartilage

3 scallions, both white and tender green parts, trimmed and minced

1½ tablespoons minced fresh dill or tarragon

Few drops of Tabasco sauce, or pinch of cayenne pepper

Sea salt and freshly ground black pepper

Thinly sliced cucumber and/or water or pita crackers

1 Place the cream cheese, mayonnaise, and lemon juice in a mixing bowl and, using a hand-held electric mixer, beat together until smooth.

2 Using a rubber or silicone spatula, fold in the crabmeat, scallions, dill or tarragon, and Tabasco sauce or cayenne. Season with salt and pepper to taste. Transfer the crab spread to a decorative serving crock or bowl and refrigerate it, covered, for at least 30 minutes but no longer than 12 hours to marry the flavors.

3 Serve the chilled crab spread surrounded by cucumber slices, crackers, or both.

Fresh Cranberry Salsa

I am not sure which came first, my attraction to Cape Cod and its islands or my love for its native tart cranberries, but I do know the two go hand in hand. I tend to brake for everything bog and this vibrant cranberry salsa discovery was an unanticipated treat at a holiday crafting workshop my industrious and talented friend Helen Baker hosted in her interior design business in Harwich on Cape Cod. Most guests brought nibbles to share and fuel the dizzying array of handcrafting opportunities Helen had laid out before us. Somewhere in between scrapbooking all my own gift tags and handprinting wrapping paper, I discovered this cranberry salsa served over a block of cream cheese that had been contributed by a working mother with several young children. I was immediately wowed by its rich colors and perk-me-up mix of tingling flavors.

The salsa may of course be served surrounded by an assortment of tortilla chips, but I sometimes like to spoon it over a long log of creamy Vermont goat cheese as opposed to cream cheese. Fresh Cranberry Salsa may also replace ho-hum cranberry relishes and jellied sauces as a spicier accompaniment to the Thanksgiving turkey, or any autumnal roast for that matter. I have played around with subtle variations when making this cranberry salsa and the recipe here is the rendition I personally like the best. MAKES ABOUT 2½ CUPS

12 ounces (1 package) fresh cranberries

⅔ cup sugar

2 tablespoons freshly squeezed lime juice

1 teaspoon finely grated lime zest

1½ tablespoons finely grated or minced peeled fresh ginger

1 small crisp apple, peeled, cored, and cut into small dice

6 scallions, both white and most of the green parts, trimmed and thinly sliced

1 to 2 jalapeño peppers, stemmed, seeded, and minced (adjust the amount according to the hotness of the peppers and your own palate)

⅓ cup minced fresh cilantro

Pinch of sea or kosher salt

1 Place the cranberries in a colander and rinse them well under cold running water. Discard any stems and mushy or bruised berries. Drain the cranberries and transfer them to a food processor fitted with the steel blade. Pulse the machine several times to chop the cranberries but take care not to pulverize them into a puree. Put the chopped cranberries in a mixing bowl.

2 Toss the cranberries with the sugar and then stir in the lime juice and zest, ginger, apple, scallions, jalapeño(s), cilantro, and salt, mixing well. Taste for seasoning adding more salt, if desired. Cover the salsa with plastic wrap and place it in the refrigerator for at least 4 hours before serving. The salsa can be refrigerated, covered, for up to 4 or 5 days.

North of the Border

I bought my first and only authentic *molcajete*—a Mexican stone mortar and pestle for making guacamole—at a fellow caterer's yard sale on Nantucket many years ago. At the time, you were lucky to find fresh cilantro at any mainstream supermarket in New England and there didn't seem to be much interest in Mexican cooking. How times have changed!

These days I can buy New England–grown cilantro almost everywhere and Nantucket, along with several other New England culinary hot spots, has its own pretty terrific Mexican restaurant, Corazón del Mar. I reason that Yankees have come to realize that eating good Mexican food infuses life in a cold climate with surrogate sunshine and warmth during the bleakest times of the year. Why else would there be so many tasty Mexican food joints in Vermont?

Seaside Guacamole

Once my son's Little League schedule began taking me over to Martha's Vineyard for baseball games, I quickly discovered Nantucket's rival island had much to offer and it was there that I came across the idea of adding grilled local corn to my guacamole during the summer months. To heighten the smoky flavor of the corn kernels, I season this guacamole with smoked sea salt. My husband's seasoning company, Coastal Goods, markets a smoked salt under the name of Sea Smoke and the Maine Sea Salt Company sells two smoked Maine sea salts, apple smoked and hickory smoked. Go with regular sea salt if you can't get your hands on a jar of smoked, but do be sure to make this seasonal guacamole because it is just the thing to tide you and lots of hungry friends over until dinner after a summer day lazed away at the beach. And, it also pairs nicely with any number of New England's microbrewed beers, the frostier the better.

If you really want to gild the coastal lily, scoop some Seaside Guacamole onto tortilla chips and top each off with a whole cooked shrimp or a spoonful of fresh crab or lobster meat. MAKES 5 CUPS; SERVES 8 TO 10

2 ears fresh corn, preferably local and just picked

Olive oil, for basting the corn

5 ripe Hass avocados

2 medium-size vine-ripened tomatoes, seeded and diced

1 small red onion, peeled and chopped

2 jalapeño peppers, stemmed, seeded, and minced

⅓ cup freshly squeezed lime juice

2 teaspoons (or a bit more) smoked sea salt or regular sea salt

⅓ cup minced fresh cilantro

Assorted tortilla chips, for serving

1 Set up a charcoal or gas grill and preheat it to high.

2 To grill the corn: Remove the husks and silk from the ears of corn and brush the kernels lightly all over with olive oil. Arrange the ears on the grate a few inches above the heat. Grill the corn, turning the ears, until the kernels are all nicely browned and slightly blistered, 5 to 7 minutes. Baste the corn with additional olive oil if the kernels appear to be getting too dry. Remove the corn from the grill and, when cool enough to handle, cut the grilled kernels off the cobs and set aside briefly. Discard the cobs.

3 Peel and pit the avocados and coarsely mash the pulp in a mixing bowl or *molcajete*. (If you don't own a *molcajete*, a potato masher or wire whisk will work well to produce a coarse mash.) Add the grilled corn kernels, tomatoes, red onion, and jalapeños and gently mix until thoroughly combined. Stir in enough lime juice and smoked salt to suit your palate. Fold in the cilantro and serve the guacamole at once with tortilla chips.

Tiny Tumbled Tomatoes

These addictive sea salt and herb dusted tomatoes have become the signature way in which my husband, Nigel, lets customers sample the flavored Sarah's Sea Salts he sells through his Coastal Goods specialty food company. I make them all the time at home in lieu of labor-intensive crudités platters and tumble any available or seasonal mixture of bite-size tomatoes ranging from cherry and grape to baby heirlooms in either our company's Mediterranean or Tuscan salt blends. The more varieties of tomatoes the merrier the presentation but grape tomatoes work just fine when availability is limited. Feel free to use any of your favorite artisanal salt blends, as there are many available these days. For a DIY version, simply blend two teaspoons of a good crunchy sea salt such as *fleur de sel* with a tablespoon of herbes de Provence or mixed Italian herbs.

Rinsing the tomatoes in a colander under cold running water leaves just enough residual moisture to make the sea salt and herbs cling to the tomatoes. People are often tempted to use olive oil in place of the water or to puncture the tomatoes and macerate them in vodka but I believe this ruins the easy, finger food appeal of the recipe. I usually serve my tumbled tomatoes at room temperature but during especially sultry summer weather, I'll chill them in the refrigerator for an hour or two to make for an extra refreshing nibble. MAKES 2 PINTS; SERVES 6 TO 8

Tiny Tumbled Tomatoes with Refrigerator Dilly Beans (page 10) and Woodstock Farmers' Market Carrot Dip (page 2) »

2 pints ripe grape, cherry, or baby heirloom tomatoes, preferably a mix of colors

1 tablespoon herb-blended sea salt

4 to 6 small sprigs fresh herbs, such as parsley, rosemary, thyme, or baby basil

PLACE THE TOMATOES in a colander and rinse under cold running water, sorting through the tomatoes and discarding any bad ones. Shake or drain most of the water off the tomatoes. Leave the tomatoes in the colander and sprinkle them with the herb-blended sea salt, tossing gently to coat evenly. Mound the tomatoes in a decorative serving bowl (I like to use a pedestal-type serving dish) and garnish them by tucking the sprigs of fresh herbs in between the tomatoes. Serve the tomatoes as finger food, although you can provide toothpicks for larger or less intimate gatherings.

Refrigerator Dilly Beans

Dilly beans are wonderfully crisp pickled green string beans and have long been popular throughout the state of Maine. They hold a favored place in both my pantry and refrigerator. I am fond of serving dilly beans as a light and healthy predinner nibble, well chilled and straight from the clear glass jelly jars in which the beans are most commonly packed. Often I'll accompany the beans with a few other favorite vegetable hors d'oeuvres such as Tiny Tumbled Tomatoes (page 8) and Woodstock Farmers' Market Carrot Dip (page 2) to make a colorful and tasty vegetable antipasto. Dilly beans can also add tangy contrast to a wedge of sharp cheddar cheese and are the perfect Down East embellishment for a Bloody Mary.

I included a recipe for traditionally pickled dilly beans in the *Saltwater Seasonings* cookbook

I coauthored with my brother, Jonathan, two decades ago but have recently gravitated to the less scientific, trendier, and certainly more instantly gratifying way of making dilly beans as a quick refrigerator pickle. However, I still insist on going through the somewhat painstaking labor of nestling each and every green bean snugly in a glass canning jar since the resulting old-fashioned farmstand look cannot be beat when it comes to serving the beans. MAKES 6 PINTS OF BEANS

For the dilly beans

Ice

Kosher salt

2 pounds very fresh and tender green string beans, stem ends trimmed

4 cups cider vinegar

2 cups water

3 tablespoons kosher salt

1½ teaspoons dill or fennel seeds

1½ teaspoons mustard seeds

1 teaspoon hot red pepper flakes

4 cloves garlic, peeled and cut into coarse slivers

Several sprigs fresh dill, or 4 fresh dill blossoms

You'll also need

Four 1½-pint wide-mouth glass canning jars

1 Have a large bowl of ice water ready. Bring a large pot of salted water to a boil then add the trimmed green beans and blanch them for exactly 1½ minutes. They will still be quite crisp. Drain the beans and then immediately plunge them into the bowl of ice water to stop the cooking and set the bright green color. When the beans are cool, drain them again. Carefully pack the beans upright (stem ends down, tail ends up) and snugly into four 1½-pint wide-mouth glass canning jars. Other glass jars can be used if you wish to recycle ones lying about but the 1½-pint jars are the best size for packing and serving the beans.

2 Combine the cider vinegar, 2 cups of water, 3 tablespoons of kosher salt, dill or fennel seeds, mustard seeds, and hot red pepper flakes in a nonreactive saucepan and let come to a boil. Let the vinegar mixture boil until the flavors blend, about 1 minute, then remove it from the heat.

3 Tuck the garlic slivers and dill sprigs between the beans in each jar. If you are using dill blossoms instead of dill sprigs, place 1 blossom on top of the beans in each jar. Carefully pour the hot vinegar mixture directly over the beans in the jars to come within 1/4 inch of the top. Take care to distribute the spices evenly among the jars.

4 Let the beans cool to room temperature then refrigerate them, covered, for at least 24 hours before serving. The beans will keep for 2 to 3 weeks in the refrigerator.

Jeweled Olives with Cranberries and Walnuts

Youthful travels in Provence are most likely the reason I'm a diehard olive aficionado, and I have often offered olives in some fashion or another to kick off the cocktail hour at my dinner gatherings in New England. A few years ago, my aunt Diane Madden got me hooked on a divine, California-inspired combination of olives roasted with red flame grapes and walnuts, a signature hors d'oeuvre at many of her Cape Cod extravaganzas. As hard as I tried, I could not justify including this rustic and fabulous hot hors d'oeuvre—without a trace of a single native New England ingredient—in this cookbook. Then I came up with the idea of changing the flavor profile somewhat to include cranberries. A heavenly marriage between the olive

groves of the Mediterranean and the cranberry bogs of Southeastern Massachusetts was born.

The jewel-like combination of olives laced with port-soaked dried cranberries, flecks of orange zest, walnuts, and fresh rosemary sprigs is truly beautiful to behold and equally thrilling to dive into when the dish emerges sizzling and intoxicatingly aromatic from a quick roast in a hot oven. Feel free to use any favorite combination of colorful Mediterranean olives or simply feature green ones mixed with ruby-colored cranberries for a striking Yuletide salute. MAKES 2½ CUPS; SERVES 6 TO 8

½ cup dried cranberries

⅔ cup ruby port

12 ounces (1½ cups) mixed imported Mediterranean olives with pits, such as Cerignola, Gaeta, kalamata, Nyon, or picholine

2 teaspoons minced orange zest

2 teaspoons coarsely chopped fresh rosemary, plus rosemary sprigs, for garnish

½ teaspoon fennel seeds

⅓ cup extra virgin olive oil

Juice of 1 orange (about ¼ cup)

½ cup coarsely chopped walnut halves

1 Combine the dried cranberries and port in a small saucepan. Let come to a boil over medium heat. Remove the pan from the heat and let the cranberries stand for about 30 minutes to plump the fruit.

2 Preheat the oven to 400°F.

3 Combine the olives, cranberries and port, orange zest, chopped rosemary, and fennel seeds in a shallow and attractive 1-quart gratin dish that can go from oven to table. Toss the ingredients gently with a wooden spoon to combine. Drizzle the olive oil and orange juice evenly over the olive mixture. Tuck the walnuts here and there in between the olives and cranberries.

4 Bake the olives until the walnuts are toasted and the liquid is sizzling, 15 to 20 minutes. Remove the

gratin dish from the oven, let the olive mixture cool for a few minutes, then garnish it with sprigs of fresh rosemary. Serve the olives hot, warm, or at room temperature directly from the gratin dish, offering small plates to scoop portions of the olive mixture onto and little bowls for discarding the olive pits.

Goat Cheese Crostini with Honey and Black Pepper

These four-ingredient crostini are easy proof that you only need a few top-notch ingredients to make something taste compellingly divine. In this case those ingredients are creamy local farmstead goat cheese (Vermont Creamery and Maine's Seal Cove Farm are two of my favorites), flavorful honey from bees that pollinate in locales like cranberry bogs or blueberry barrens, and aromatic black pepper. I am nepotistically partial to the special Tellicherry black pepper my husband Nigel's seasoning company imports from India. However, the success of the recipe does not hinge on this esoteric but exquisite pepper. MAKES 16 CROSTINI

4 ounces creamy fresh goat cheese,
   at room temperature

16 slices (⅓ inch thick) French bread,
   lightly toasted

¼ cup honey, preferably from New England

Freshly ground black pepper

SPREAD THE SOFTENED goat cheese over each slice of toasted French bread, mounding the cheese slightly in the middle. Arrange the crostini on a platter. Drizzle about ½ teaspoon of honey over each crostini and top it with a generous grinding of black pepper. Serve the crostini at once.

"Fig N Pig"

Melissa Kelly's Primo restaurant in Rockland, Maine, is the sort of fabulous, philosophically anchored farm to table establishment that begs to be visited time and again. Reservations used to be incredibly difficult to secure but since the upstairs walk-in "Counter" and "Bar" rooms opened in 2010, I'll come up with almost any excuse to dash to the midcoast of Maine and dine at Primo. It was there that I fell instantly in love with a signature bruschetta called "Fig N Pig," combining a blue cheese and onion compote base with roasted fresh figs and the restaurant's own in-house raised and cured pancetta.

The recipe here is my own easier home-cook rendition recreated from memories and cravings for this heavenly appetizer. If you wish to stay true to its New England roots, use a local blue cheese in the recipe. Vermont has several delicious blue cheeses such as the Boucher Family Farm's Green Mountain Blue Cheese, Lazy Lady Farm's Lady in Blue, and Jasper Hill Farm's renowned Bayley Hazen Blue. You can also use imported European or other domestic blue-veined cheeses. MAKES 20

2 ounces thinly sliced pancetta

2 tablespoons sliced almonds

6 ounces creamy blue cheese,
   at room temperature

2 ounces mascarpone, preferably from
   Vermont Creamery

1½ tablespoons cream sherry

5 fresh black figs, stemmed and quartered
   lengthwise

20 rounds of French bread sliced ¼ inch thick
   from a skinny baguette, lightly toasted

1 Preheat the oven to 375°F. Line 2 baking sheets with heavy-duty aluminum foil or parchment paper.

2 Arrange the pancetta slices on a prepared baking sheet in a single layer. Arrange the almonds on the second prepared baking sheet. Bake the pancetta until nicely crisped, 10 to 12 minutes. The almonds will have to be watched more closely and will take a few minutes less time. Transfer the pancetta slices to a paper towel lined–plate to drain. Set the almonds aside. Increase the oven temperature to 400°F.

3 Place the blue cheese, mascarpone, and sherry in a small mixing bowl and mash them together with a fork until thoroughly combined. Spread the cheese mixture generously over each toasted bread round and arrange the rounds on a fresh parchment-lined baking sheet. Nestle a fig quarter into the cheese mixture in the center of each toast round. Crumble the crisp pancetta into small shards and stick the shards and the almonds into the cheese surrounding each fig quarter, as if you were making imaginary porcupine quills. Bake the toast rounds until the cheese is bubbling, 4 to 5 minutes. Serve hot or warm.

Hot Olive Whirligigs

In the process of researching this cookbook and striving to strike a blend between forgotten New England fare and modern innovations, I combed through numerous out-of-print community cookbooks. These books were usually plucked from the shelves of favorite libraries or unearthed from the haphazard disarray of musty thrift shops, weekend yard sales, or flea markets. Certainly one of the most charming of my finds is the 1974 publication *A Cook's Tour of Nantucket*, compiled and edited by Sue Vallett. While the whimsical illustrations of whales spouting chef's toques were enough to win me over instantly, many of the handwritten recipes—named after special places on Nantucket—also beckoned and none more so than these Hidden Forest Hot Olive Whirligigs.

I have updated the type of olives pinwheeled into the flaky cheddar pastry from domestic canned and pitted ones to imported Mediterranean ones and find these edible whirligigs to be as uniquely alluring as the imaginative folk art whirligigs my uncle once sold through his Nantucket antiques business. MAKES ABOUT 2 DOZEN

⅔ cup unbleached all-purpose flour, plus flour for the work surface

1 cup freshly shredded sharp Vermont cheddar cheese

¼ teaspoon fine sea salt

Pinch of cayenne pepper

4 tablespoons (½ stick) chilled unsalted butter, cut into small pieces

¾ cup pitted and finely minced black olives, such as kalamata or oil-cured Provençal olives

1 Combine the flour, cheddar, salt, and cayenne in a food processor and pulse the machine to combine evenly. Add the butter and continue to pulse the machine until the mixture balls up into a dough.

2 Flatten the dough into a disk and place it on a lightly floured work surface. Using a rolling pin, roll the dough into a rectangle about ⅛ inch thick and measuring approximately 6 by 10 inches. Sprinkle the olives evenly over the dough, pressing them gently into the dough with the rolling pin. Beginning from one long end, roll up the dough like a jelly roll to form a compact log. Wrap the log of dough in plastic wrap and chill it in the refrigerator for at least 1 hour and up to 3 days.

3 When ready to bake, preheat the oven to 400°F. Line a large baking sheet with parchment paper.

4 Unwrap the chilled pastry log and, using a sharp knife, cut it crosswise into slices about ¼ inch thick. Arrange the whirligigs in rows 1 inch apart on the prepared baking sheet. Bake the whirligigs until lightly browned, about 10 minutes. Serve them hot, warm, or at room temperature. The whirligigs taste best when eaten the same day they are baked.

Clothbound Cheddar Cheese Wafers

While cheese wafers, cheese straws, and cheese balls may seem like an hors d'oeuvre genre from our parents' or even grandparents' era, I believe the ever-growing abundance of top-notch artisanal cheeses throughout New England cries out for a revival of such cheese-anchored treats. Cabot Creamery's Clothbound Cheddar epitomizes la crème de la crème of success in the artisanal cheese movement and immediately elevates the typical cheese wafer from a tasty nibble to an extraordinary one.

The basic cheese wafer is usually a simple combination of butter, flour, freshly grated cheese, and sometimes a hint of cayenne pepper for heat. While toasted pecans are a frequent and excellent addition, I have grown fond of using finely chopped smoked almonds in my Clothbound Cheddar Cheese Wafers and then further accenting this subtle smokiness with ground chipotle pepper powder instead of cayenne pepper. The wafers are always a welcome and fast-disappearing accompaniment at the cocktail hour and pair particularly well with cider, regular or sparkling. MAKES ABOUT 4 DOZEN

½ cup smoked almonds, such as Blue Diamond
   Smokehouse almonds

8 tablespoons (1 stick) unsalted butter,
   at room temperature, cut into 8 pieces

6 ounces Cabot Clothbound Cheddar cheese,
   shredded

1 cup unbleached all-purpose flour

⅛ to ¼ teaspoon ground chipotle pepper
   (adjust the amount to suit your preference
   for heat)

1 Place the smoked almonds in a food processor and process until finely chopped but not ground.

Cellared Cheddar

Clothbound Cheddar bears scant resemblance to the usual array of Cabot's Vermont cheddar cheese varieties proliferating in almost every New England supermarket. What sets clothbound cheddar radically apart from Cabot's other cheddars is that it is made by a collaboration between the big, commercially viable Cabot Creamery and the cult-revered cheese makers at Jasper Hill Farm in Vermont's Northeast Kingdom.

Thirty-five pound wheels of this buttery rich and nutty cheddar are first made at the Cabot Creamery and then trucked to a specially designed cheese-aging facility known as the Cellars at Jasper Hill. There the wheels are bound in muslin, painted with lard to form a natural and breathable shield, and then left to age in the climate-controlled cellars for ten to fourteen months. The result is an English-style cheddar that is truly exquisite in both texture and flavor and that deservedly garnered the best of class award at the 2010 World Championship Cheese Contest. Clothbound cheddar used to be rather hard to find outside of Vermont but is now carried in many Whole Foods Markets across the country.

2 Combine the butter, cheddar, and finely chopped almonds in the bowl of a stand mixer or in a medium-size mixing bowl. Beat to blend, using the paddle attachment of the stand mixer or a hand-held mixer. Add the flour and chipotle pepper and continue beating until the mixture comes together to form a stiff dough. Shape the dough into a 1-inch-diameter log, wrap it tightly in plastic wrap, and refrigerate the log for at least 4 hours. The log may be refrigerated for up to 5 days or frozen for up to 2 months if you are

a do-ahead type. If frozen, thaw the log in the refrigerator for at least 6 hours or overnight.

3 When ready to bake, place a rack in the center of the oven and preheat the oven to 350°F. Line 2 baking sheets with parchment paper.

4 Unwrap the chilled log and, using a sharp knife, cut it crosswise into slices about ⅛ inch thick. Arrange the slices in rows ½ inch apart on the prepared baking sheets. Bake the wafers until golden brown, 12 to 15 minutes. Let the wafers cool for a few minutes on the baking sheets and then, using a metal spatula, carefully transfer them to a wire rack to cool completely. Serve the clothbound cheddar wafers arranged on a pretty platter or tucked in a shallow basket. Leftovers may be stored in an airtight container at room temperature for up to 3 days.

Cheddar *Gougères*

While a hard cider industry once thrived in New England in Colonial times, making hard cider has only recently come back into vogue and the beverage is not yet thriving with anywhere near the same success enjoyed by burgeoning local beer breweries. I have been picking up attractive bottles of hard cider whenever I come across them in my travels throughout New England, but I did not become truly enamored of this mildly alcoholic quaff until Tim Dempsey, the talented and passionate bartender at The Pitcher Inn in Warren, Vermont, introduced me to Farnum Hill Ciders from neighboring New Hampshire. One effervescent sip of Farnum Hill's Farmhouse cider instantly persuaded me to take a cue from the Burgundian custom of starting evenings off with a kir cocktail and warm *gougères*, and initiate a New England–rooted pairing of flutes of hard cider with a stylized rendition of the popular French cheese puffs tweaked to highlight a local cheese.

These very tasty cheddar *gougères* are the result, with a good sharp cheddar from Vermont replacing the customary Gruyère cheese. Should you be inclined to doctor your flute of hard cider into a more kir-like aperitif, I find a splash of cranberry juice complements the apple base of the cider better than the traditional French addition of cassis. If you are one who enjoys serving apple pie with a wedge of cheddar, then the combination of hard cider and cheddar *gougères* will likely be your ticket to cocktail hour nirvana. MAKES ABOUT 3½ DOZEN GOUGÈRES

1¼ cups water

8 tablespoons (1 stick) unsalted butter

1¼ cups unbleached all-purpose flour

4 large eggs

2 teaspoons grainy Dijon mustard

¾ teaspoon fine sea salt

¼ teaspoon freshly ground white pepper

¼ teaspoon grated nutmeg, preferably freshly grated

2 cups freshly grated sharp cheddar cheese (I am partial to Grafton Village's 2-year-old cheddar)

1 Place a rack in the center of the oven and preheat the oven to 375°F. Line 2 large baking sheets with parchment paper.

2 Combine the water and butter in a medium-size saucepan and let come to a boil over medium-high heat. Once the butter is completely melted, remove the pan from the heat and gradually stir in the flour until it is completely incorporated and smooth. Place the pan over medium-low heat and cook, stirring constantly, until the batter is quite thick and beginning to pull away from the side of the pan, 3 to 4 minutes.

3 Remove the pan from the heat and beat in the eggs, one by one, beating well after each addition and preferably using a handheld electric mixer to make the process easier. Beat in the mustard, salt, pepper, and

The first step that goes into producing effervescent hard ciders at Farnum Hill in New Hampshire is harvesting the apples in early fall.

nutmeg. Using a spoon, stir in the cheddar until thoroughly incorporated. The batter may be made ahead and refrigerated, covered, for up to 24 hours before baking.

4 Drop the batter by rounded heaping teaspoons onto the prepared baking sheets leaving ½ inch to 1 inch between each. Bake the *gougères* until puffed and golden, 20 to 25 minutes. Serve the *gougères* warm, nestled in a napkin-lined basket or arranged on a serving tray.

Caviar Coupes with Cape Cod Potato Chips

While there is no caviar native to New England, we are lucky enough to have one of the premier purveyors of some of the world's finest caviars, Browne Trading Company, in Portland, Maine. Tuitions and general inflation have put a serious dent in my consumption of imported caviars, but the upside is that I have become a huge fan of Browne Trading's more affordable spoonbill (aka American paddlefish) caviar from wild freshwater sturgeon swimming in the Mississippi and Tennessee rivers.

Caviar indulgences are by no means the norm at most New England gatherings, unless of course by chance you happen to be a guest at one of Laurie and Bob Champion's Nantucket Christmas Stroll extravaganzas in early December. I catered several of these tented island galas for the Champions years ago and was recently privileged to be a guest at a much smaller and more intimate Sunday Stroll dinner party with eight guests. Laurie kicked off the evening in inimitable fashion by serving each guest a hefty glass goblet brimming with sour cream topped off lavishly with a thick layer of osetra caviar and a sprinkling of chopped red onions—all surrounded shockingly but irresistibly with bowls of ridged Lay's potato chips for scooping into the sour cream and caviar! Needless to say, I couldn't wait to "borrow" this outrageous idea.

I have toned down the Champions' original caviar coupes by using smaller four-ounce miniature clear glass pedestal goblets, purchased at a nearby Pier 1 Imports store. Since I find raw red onion can overpower delicate caviar eggs, I flavor my sour cream with minced chives rather than sprinkling minced red onion over the top of the layer of caviar. Sometimes, if the mood strikes, I'll garnish the coupes with a sprinkling of sieved hard-boiled egg yolks and whites, but this is by no means necessary. Since I live within a few miles of the Cape Cod Potato Chips factory, I feel obliged to use our highly acclaimed local chips, though Lay's ridged chips do make for a sturdier scooping vehicle. Browne Trading's spoonbill caviar is my top choice for these decadent coupes, but in less flush times I have been known to use Browne Trading's even more affordable Alaskan salmon roe or golden whitefish roe. SERVES 6

2 cups sour cream

2½ tablespoons minced fresh chives

7 ounces spoonbill (also called American paddlefish) caviar

1 bag (8 ounces) Cape Cod original kettle cooked potato chips or harvest gold kettle cooked potato chips

MIX TOGETHER THE sour cream and minced chives. Spoon ⅓ cup of the sour cream mixture into the bottom of each of six 4-ounce clear glass goblets. Top the sour cream with a generous 1-ounce layer of the spoonbill caviar. Place the goblets in the center of attractive serving plates and surround them with the potato chips for dipping and scooping.

Swordfish Salsa

Sometimes I think I could easily live on raw food alone since I constantly crave sushi and sashimi and can never resist dishes like steak tartare, ceviche, and carpaccio on menus when I am dining out in restaurants. However, since I know that not everyone shares this passion, when entertaining at home I often try to come up with dishes that marry the vibrant flavors of raw specialties with cooked components. Hence this terrific and unique Swordfish Salsa (as opposed to ceviche), utilizing wine-poached swordfish as a base. Serve this most refreshing flaked fish and chopped vegetable combination in a clear glass bowl so that its sparkling colors can be seen and surround it with an assortment of scooping chips such as tortilla, pita, and plantain. MAKES ABOUT 3 CUPS; SERVES 6 TO 8

1 center-cut swordfish steak (1 to 1¼ inches thick, 1½ pounds)

½ cup dry white wine

4 ripe plum tomatoes, seeded and diced

½ red bell pepper, stemmed, seeded, and diced

½ yellow bell pepper, stemmed, seeded, and diced

2 jalapeño peppers, stemmed, seeded, and finely minced

4 tablespoons minced fresh cilantro

½ cup freshly squeezed lime juice

2½ tablespoons extra virgin olive oil

¾ teaspoon ground cumin

¾ teaspoon dried oregano, preferably Greek oregano, crumbled

Sea salt and freshly ground black pepper

Lime wedges, for serving

Assorted chips, for serving

1 Place the swordfish in a large shallow, straight-sided nonreactive skillet and add the white wine and enough water to cover the fish completely. Let come to a boil over medium-high heat, reduce the heat to medium, cover the skillet, and let the fish simmer until it flakes easily with a fork, 7 to 9 minutes. Remove the skillet from the heat and let the fish cool in the cooking liquid for about 10 minutes. Carefully transfer the fish to a plate and let cool until comfortable to handle, 10 to 15 minutes longer.

2 Flake the poached swordfish into bite-size pieces and place these in a mixing bowl, discarding the skin and any dark pieces of fish. Add the tomatoes, bell peppers, jalapeños, and cilantro and toss all gently together to combine evenly.

3 Place the lime juice and olive oil in a small bowl and whisk to mix. Stir in the cumin and oregano. Pour the lime juice mixture over the salsa ingredients, tossing to coat. Season the salsa with salt and black pepper to taste.

4 Transfer the Swordfish Salsa to a decorative serving bowl and chill in the refrigerator for at least 1 hour and up to 1 day before serving. When ready to serve, garnish the salsa with lime wedges and surround with assorted chips for scooping.

Potted Maine Shrimp

There are quicker ways to drive from Cape Cod to my parents' house in Blue Hill, Maine, but once I get into the state and past the Freeport outlet diversions I almost always opt to mosey farther Down East on the slower and sometimes traffic-jammed coastal Route 1 because I enjoy the incomparable scenic views and serendipity of happening upon roadside trucks selling whatever is in season—from summer's wild blueberries to winter's petite fresh Maine shrimp. These tiny shrimp can seem like a lot of tedious work for those accustomed to ordering impressive jumbo shrimp cocktails in fancy restaurants. Yet, I celebrate and herald them as the only fresh shrimp readily available in New England.

A small paperback book entitled *The Original Maine Shrimp Cookbook*, published as a collaboration between the Midcoast Fishermen's Cooperative and the nonprofit Island Institute, established to protect and preserve the Gulf of Maine's ecosystem, broadened my thinking on ways to cook with Maine shrimp. But, I ended up veering off on my own fleeting culinary instincts and cravings to make this British-inspired recipe for potted shrimp, as well as a New Orleans–influenced recipe for BBQ shrimp (see page 22), using my most recent winter cache and bounty of fresh pink Maine shrimp. The smaller ramekins of potted shrimp make a welcome hostess gift. MAKES ABOUT 2 CUPS

6 tablespoons (¾ stick) unsalted butter,
   at room temperature

3 medium-size shallots, peeled and minced

½ pound peeled fresh Maine shrimp (see Note)

Pinch of hot red pepper flakes

2½ tablespoons brandy

4 ounces (1 cup) whipped cream cheese,
   at room temperature

2 tablespoons minced fresh flat-leaf parsley

1½ tablespoons minced fresh chives

½ teaspoon sweet paprika

Pinch of freshly grated nutmeg

Sea salt and freshly ground white or
   black pepper

Toast points, melba toasts, or plain crackers,
   for serving

1. Melt 2 tablespoons of the butter in a medium-size skillet over medium heat. Add the shallots and cook until softened, about 4 minutes. Add the shrimp and hot red pepper flakes to the skillet and stir to coat with the butter and shallots. Pour in the brandy and remove the skillet from the heat and away from anything flammable. Carefully ignite it with a match. Once the flames subside, continue cooking until the shrimp are just cooked through, about 2 minutes. Remove the skillet from the heat and let the shrimp mixture cool to room temperature.

2. Once the shrimp mixture has cooled, transfer it to a food processor. Pulse the machine several times until the shrimp are finely chopped. Transfer the shrimp to a bowl.

3. Place the whipped cream cheese and the remaining 4 tablespoons of butter in the food processor and puree until smooth. Return the shrimp to the processor and add the parsley, chives, paprika, and nutmeg. Process until thoroughly combined and almost smooth. Season with salt and pepper to taste. Transfer the shrimp mixture to four small 4-ounce crocks or ramekins, two 8-ounce crocks or ramekins, or one 16-ounce crock or ramekin and refrigerate it, covered, overnight to let the flavors mellow.

4. Let the potted shrimp stand to soften for about 30 minutes at room temperature before serving it with a small palette knife for spreading on toast points, melba toast, or crackers. Potted shrimp will keep in the refrigerator, covered, for at least a week.

NOTE: *Maine shrimp are only about an inch long and too tiny to devein.*

BBQ Maine Shrimp

BBQ shrimp is not a New England dish but a beloved garlicky and butter-laden New Orleans specialty. As it turns out, the shrimp in the recipe title aren't even barbecued and the preparation itself is often the subject of heated arguments down in Cajun country. Thankfully, I am not striving to be authentic or controversial here because I am using wimpy but succulent and sweet Maine shrimp in an unconventional way in this recipe and my sole goal is to share an appetizer that is really fun but messy to eat, and sinfully delicious to boot. I can't imagine anyone objecting to butter, garlic, and rosemary. SERVES 4 TO 6

1 lemon, scrubbed and thinly sliced

8 tablespoons (1 stick) unsalted butter, preferably Kate's butter from Maine (sold in many supermarkets)

¼ cup extra virgin olive oil

3 cloves garlic, minced

½ teaspoon hot red pepper flakes

1½ tablespoons coarsely chopped fresh rosemary

½ tablespoon coarsely cracked black peppercorns

2 teaspoons Worcestershire sauce

2 to 2½ pounds fresh shell-on Maine shrimp (see Note on page 21)

2 bay leaves

Lots of crusty bread, for serving

1 Preheat the oven to 475°F.

2 Arrange the lemon slices over the bottom of a 13-by-9-inch baking dish.

3 Melt the butter in the olive oil in a large saucepan over medium heat. Once the butter is melted, stir in the garlic, hot red pepper flakes, rosemary, cracked peppercorns, and Worcestershire sauce. Remove the pan from the heat and add the shrimp, tossing to coat well.

4 Spread the shrimp mixture over the top of the sliced lemons in the baking dish. Tuck the bay leaves into the dish. Bake the shrimp until the butter is sizzling and the shrimp are cooked through, 10 to 12 minutes. Remove and discard the bay leaves. Serve the shrimp hot from the oven family style with plenty of napkins and crusty bread to sop up the delicious garlic and herb butter. Have a dish handy for discarding the shells after peeling.

Roasted Garlic, Rosemary, and Blue Cheese Fondue

When I ran my Que Sera Sarah specialty food shop on Nantucket in the 1980s many customers would often stare incredulously at a platter brimming with whole heads of roasted garlic gracing my counter display of room temperature fare. A favorite client from Texas referred to the garlic bulbs as "mother-in-law breath fresheners," but people gradually caught on to the delectable but messy pleasure of squeezing the soft and caramelized cloves of garlic from their skins onto a chunk of fresh bread or blob of soft goat cheese. Roasting garlic has now become quite commonplace, and here is my evolved version in which the heads of garlic roast slowly in a bath of chicken stock and dry pear wine made by my friends Bob and Kathe Bartlett in Gouldsboro, Maine. Once the garlic is soft and the liquid concentrated in flavor, I swirl crumbled blue cheese into the dish and then place it back in the oven to melt into a fondue.

I especially like serving this fondue alfresco on summer evenings when I can pluck ripe cherry or teardrop tomatoes from my patio planters to pair with chunks of ciabatta and swish through the gooey melted mix of blue cheese, fresh rosemary, and pear wine—all topped off with a lush clove or two or three of roasted garlic. SERVES 6

6 whole heads garlic

2 tablespoons (¼ stick) unsalted butter, cut into 6 slices

¾ cup chicken stock or broth, or more if needed

¾ cup Bartlett Maine Estate Winery French oak dry pear wine, or ¾ cup dry white wine such as sauvignon blanc or viognier, or more if needed (see Notes)

10 ounces mild and creamy blue cheese, crumbled into small pieces (about 2 cups; see Notes)

1½ teaspoons coarsely chopped fresh rosemary

Chunks of fresh French bread or ciabatta, for serving

Vine-ripened cherry and/or teardrop tomatoes (optional), for serving

1 Preheat the oven to 375°F.

2 Trim the tops off the garlic heads to expose the tops of the cloves. Place the garlic in a 9- or 10-inch oval or round baking (gratin) dish. Top each head of garlic with a slice of butter. Pour the chicken stock or broth and wine into the dish to surround the heads of garlic. Roast the garlic cloves, uncovered, until they are tender and are beginning to ooze from their papery skins, about 1 hour. By this point the chicken stock and wine should have reduced to ⅓ to ½ cup. If there is less liquid, add a splash more of either chicken stock or wine.

3 Scatter the crumbled blue cheese and rosemary in between the roasted heads of garlic. Return the dish to the oven to bake until the blue cheese has melted and formed a smooth sauce with the liquid, about 10 minutes.

4 Serve the fondue hot from the oven in the baking dish, providing small plates for guests to place a roasted head of garlic and a scoop or two of the melted cheese on. Accompany the fondue with a basket of bread chunks and some small tomatoes, if desired. Eat the fondue by dipping a bread chunk or tomato into the melted cheese and topping it with a clove or two of the roasted garlic squeezed from its skin. Have plenty of napkins handy.

NOTES: *Since Bartlett's sophisticated fruit wines can be hard to come by outside of Maine, you can substitute a crisp and fruity sauvignon blanc or viognier if need be for the dry pear wine.*

Green Mountain Blue Cheese from the Boucher Family Farm in Vermont and Berkshire Blue from Massachusetts are good cows' milk choices for this recipe if you are able to lay your hands on them. If not, use another creamy and mild blue cheese.

Melted Brie and Mushroom Fondue

I like to bake this decadent and incredibly delicious fondue in a pretty fluted ceramic pie dish and serve it as a prelude to special occasion beef or lamb dinners. While Brie and Camembert cheeses are first and foremost associated with France, Vermont cheese makers have succeeded in making a few excellent cheeses in this rich and runny style. A first whiff of these bloomy rind cheeses is often quite mushroomy, making them excellent choices for this wonderful recipe. Brie-style cheeses to look for include Blythedale Farm's Vermont Camembert or Vermont Brie and Willow Hill Farm's La Fleurie. La Fleurie is made with the farm's own rich Brown Swiss cows' milk and aged in an underground cave featuring a back wall of natural Vermont bedrock, which imparts the cheese with subtle flavors of indigenous flora and fauna. SERVES 6

Pictured here are Vermont Creamery's most luscious cheeses—Bonne Bouche, Coupole, and Cremont (my personal favorite).

1½ tablespoons unsalted butter

1 tablespoon extra virgin olive oil

1 shallot, peeled and minced

3 cloves garlic, peeled and minced

4 ounces shiitake mushroom caps, thinly sliced

4 ounces cremini mushrooms, trimmed and thinly sliced

3 tablespoons cream sherry, such as Harvey's Bristol Cream

Sea salt and freshly ground black pepper

1 wheel (7 to 8 ounces) Brie or Camembert cheese, well chilled

4 to 5 fresh thyme sprigs

2 tablespoons minced fresh flat-leaf parsley

Chunks or slices of your favorite artisanal bread or crackers, for serving

1 Preheat the oven to 375°F.

2 Melt the butter in the olive oil in a medium-size skillet over medium heat. Add the shallot and garlic and cook until quite soft, about 5 minutes. Stir in the shiitake and cremini mushrooms and continue cooking until the mushrooms have released their juices, 3 to 4 minutes. Add the sherry and salt and pepper to taste, and cook, stirring frequently, until all but a tablespoon or so of liquid remains in the skillet, 4 to 5 minutes. Remove the skillet from the heat.

3 Using a sharp knife, slice the top bloomy rind off the wheel of chilled Brie or Camembert, leaving the side and bottom rind intact. Place the wheel, bottom rind down, in the center of a 7-to-8-inch round oven-to-table baking dish. Spread the mushroom mixture over the top and around the wheel of cheese. Strew the thyme sprigs randomly over the top.

4 Bake until the cheese has melted and run completely over the dish, 15 to 20 minutes. Remove the baking dish from the oven and sprinkle the parsley on top. Serve the cheese hot with small hors d'oeuvre knives to spread the melted cheese and mushroom mixture onto chunks or slices of your favorite bread or crackers.

"Eggplant Sandwiches"

When my husband and I travel to New York City we always try to allow time on the drive back to Cape Cod to stop off in Providence, Rhode Island, and either grab a bite to eat or stock up at the Italian specialty stores on Atwells Avenue in Federal Hill. Rhode Island Italian cooking bears little semblance to that which we have experienced in our travels to Italy but we admire, adore, crave, and appreciate it nonetheless. I have been making these tasty "Eggplant Sandwiches" for years and they epitomize the style of antipasto I associate with Rhode Island. MAKES ABOUT 5 DOZEN BITE-SIZE HORS D'OEUVRES, IF CUT INTO QUARTERS

2 large, firm eggplants (about 1½ pounds each), the narrower the better

Sea or kosher salt

4 ounces Genoa salami, thinly sliced

6 ounces aged provolone cheese, thinly sliced

1 small bunch fresh basil

3 large eggs

1 cup dry Italian-seasoned bread crumbs

½ cup freshly and finely grated Parmesan cheese

3 tablespoons finely chopped fresh flat-leaf parsley

Extra virgin olive oil

1   Remove the stems from the eggplants and slice each eggplant crosswise into rounds that are ⅓ inch thick. Lightly salt each slice and stack the slices in layers in a colander placed in a large bowl or sink to drain. Place a layer of paper towels, then a weight, such as a large can, on top of the slices to aid in the draining. Let the eggplant stand for about 1 hour. Rinse the slices and pat them dry with paper towels.

2   Preheat the oven to 375°F. Line 2 large baking sheets with parchment paper.

3   Match the eggplant slices into pairs of a similar size. Sandwich a single layer of salami, provolone cheese, and a whole basil leaf or two between each pair of eggplant slices. Trim away any salami or cheese that overhangs the edge of the "sandwich."

4   Beat the eggs in a shallow dish, such as a pie pan. Mix together the bread crumbs, Parmesan cheese, and parsley and spread this mixture out in another shallow dish. Dip each eggplant sandwich first into the beaten egg and then into the bread crumb mixture to coat it evenly on both sides. Arrange the sandwiches on the prepared baking sheets and drizzle a generous teaspoon of olive oil evenly over the top of each sandwich.

5   Bake the sandwiches, turning them once, until the crumbs are golden brown, 30 to 35 minutes. Let the sandwiches cool for at least 10 minutes before slicing them in half or quarters. Arrange the sandwiches on a platter and serve warm or at room temperature. The sandwiches may also be baked up to 1 day ahead, refrigerated, covered, and then reheated in a 350°F oven for 7 to 10 minutes.

Quesadillas with Smoked Vermont Cheddar and Pumpkin Seed Pesto

Thrifty New Englanders have long saved the seeds from carving their Halloween jack-o'-lanterns and roasted them in the oven for a seasonal snacking treat. Unhulled pumpkin seeds tend to be rather chewy and fibrous. In our house the novelty of munching on them usually wears off after a few days and we end up feeding the rest to the large squirrel colony leaping from branch to branch in the many towering old oak trees surrounding our Cape house. Over the past few years, however, I have noticed that hulled pumpkin seeds, or *pepitas*, have become quite the rage in local restaurants and you can now buy *pepitas* in most supermarkets rather than seeking them out in a health food store. This has prompted me to revive a uniquely tasty quesadilla recipe I had originally created years ago as a Southwestern appetizer.

Several New England companies make good tortillas (Massachusetts-based Maria and Ricardo's Tortilla Factory is a well established and long standing favorite of mine) and Vermont's smoked cheddar cheeses are always excellent. These quesadillas say autumn to me and are well suited to being served during seemingly endless marathon football watching weekends or more festive occasions such

as Halloween and Thanksgiving parties. MAKES
32 QUESADILLA WEDGES

For the pumpkin seed pesto

½ cup extra virgin olive oil

1 jalapeño pepper, stemmed, seeded, and
   minced

2 cloves garlic, peeled and minced

2 cups dry roasted pumpkin seeds
   (Eden Organic is a popular brand)

½ cup freshly squeezed lime juice

½ cup minced fresh cilantro

1 teaspoon cumin seeds

Sea salt

For the quesadillas

8 flour or corn tortillas (8-inch diameter)

2 cups freshly shredded smoked Vermont
   cheddar cheese

2 tablespoons extra virgin olive oil

1   Make the pumpkin seed pesto: Heat 2 tablespoons
of the olive oil in a small skillet over medium-high
heat. Add the jalapeño and garlic and cook until softened, about 2 minutes. Transfer the jalapeño mixture
to a food processor fitted with the steel blade, add the
pumpkin seeds, and process to make a thick paste.
With the machine running, pour the lime juice and
remaining 2 tablespoons of olive oil through the feed
tube to make a smooth puree. Add the cilantro and
cumin seeds and process until incorporated. Season
the pesto with salt to taste. Store the pesto in a covered container in the refrigerator until ready to use.
It will keep for up to 1 week.

2   Make the quesadillas: Preheat the oven to 200°F.

3   Spread all 8 tortillas on one side lightly all over
with the pumpkin seed pesto. (You won't use all of
the pesto but you can use any left over as a dip,
sandwich spread, or to make additional quesadillas.) Sprinkle ½ cup of the smoked cheddar over the
pumpkin seed pesto on 4 of the tortillas. Top with
the remaining 4 tortillas, pesto side down, and gently
press them together to make 4 round sandwiches. Film
a medium-size skillet lightly with olive oil and heat it
over medium heat. Fry a quesadilla individually in the
skillet, turning it once, until golden on both sides, 2½
to 3 minutes per side, then transfer the quesadilla to
a baking sheet and place it in the warm oven. Repeat
the process with the remaining quesadillas, adding a
bit more olive oil to the skillet as necessary.

4   Cut each quesadilla into 8 triangular wedges,
arrange them on a platter, and serve warm.

Fine Kettles and Potent Pots

"For New Englanders, and those who would be ones, chowder is a sea swell of the soul. A bowl of chowder (never a cup) evokes a forgotten day years ago, a slanted shaft of light on a wooden table. A stove-top pot steaming as the languorous hours of an autumn afternoon drift toward revelation. Chowder recalls a breeze-swept shore, a celebration of friends and walkers-by decked out in rain gear and wool, seasoned with salt and sand and shocks of briny kelp."
—*Robert S. Cox and Jacob Walker*, A History of Chowder: Four Centuries of a New England Meal

My pine-needle-green coated cast-iron Dutch oven and well-seasoned eleven-inch black cast-iron skillet are the two most used cooking vessels in my New England kitchen. The heavy pot is in such constant use for three quarters of the calendar year—simmering soups, braising meats, or baking beans—that I joke I do culinary aerobics as I lift it between the stovetop, oven, and sink.

I wouldn't think of making a chowder, bisque, or seafood stew in any other pot, as it unfailingly yields the finest kettles of clams, oysters, scallops, and fish I have ever tasted. When the weather is chilly, I'll often have two Dutch ovens simmering away at the same time because such is the perfect pot for almost every recipe in this chapter—running the gamut from My Favorite Clam Chowder to hearty soup supper favorites such as Kale Soup and October Chili.

So many of the recipes in this chapter have become staples in my repertoire of favorite family meals because they are versatile and richly flavored keepers that also coincidentally happen to keep well and even improve in complexity of taste

Taking Stock

When I first started cooking as a teenager, there were only a couple of brands of chicken and beef stock carried in supermarkets and these brands tasted like a watery murk of salt and artificial flavors. The conventional culinary wisdom was to make your own stocks from scratch at home in much the same way as restaurants did. Fortunately, the stock market has improved greatly over the past few years and I daresay the stocks currently sold in the aisles of better supermarkets are far more reliable than those sold on Wall Street. There's a wealth of organic and salt-free brands and vegetable, seafood, and veal stocks are now as readily available alongside chicken and beef stock. While I sometimes still make stocks from scratch, I find no need to apologize for relying on the convenience of high-quality store-bought cartons of stock. Two of my favorite brands are More Than Gourmet and Kitchen Basics. I always have a carton or two of the latter's seafood and veal stock in my pantry.

When I do make stock from scratch, it is usually either chicken or lobster stock (see recipe, page 138). My chicken stock is not so much a recipe as it is an instinct. Whenever I have served a whole roasted chicken for dinner, I'll take the carcass and put it into my trusty Dutch oven, cover it amply with tap water and maybe add a splash or two of white wine if there happens to be a bottle on the counter. I'll then root through my vegetable drawers and add a stray carrot or two, some celery stalks, a halved onion, and a few sprigs of parsley, thyme, or rosemary. I bring the pot to a boil, reduce it to a simmer, and usually let it all cook slowly, covered, over low heat while I snooze the night away.

In the morning, the kitchen smells heavenly and I'll strain the stock, give our dog any stray bits of meat as a treat, and have good stock on hand in the refrigerator to go into a pot of dinner soup or risotto. This type of stock will keep for 3 or 4 days in the refrigerator, though I usually use up mine within the first 24 hours of making it.

over the course of a few days. My husband is the sort of person who likes to sit down to a hot bowl of soup every day for lunch, whether it is July or January, so when I am cleaning up after a summer dinner of Swordfish Posole or winter pot of Split Pea and Portobello Soup, he is already plotting and salivating over the upcoming lunch leftovers that will sustain him for a few days to come. To a died-in-the-wool New Englander any lovingly made soup can work magic and this is why I consider the recipes in this chapter to be as potent as they are fine, whether you treat yourself to a cup or make a meal of a bowl.

My Favorite Clam Chowder

I imagine I may get a bit of flack for not including a recipe in this book for the creamless clam chowder known as Rhode Island clam chowder, served regionally throughout Rhode Island as well as along some parts of the Connecticut shore. While I'll order and enjoy this type of chowder when visiting these states, I don't love it enough to want to replicate it at home. Furthermore, I won't dare broach the subject of Manhattan clam chowder, even if I am one of those very rare Massachusetts residents who happens to be a New York Yankees fan.

Many dozens of fresh littleneck clams are a key ingredient for putting together a really fine New England clam chowder.

mahogany clams. No matter which type of clam is used, the bountiful six dozen called for in this recipe will definitely yield an unmistakably clammy (and sumptuous) clam chowder. Like my recipe for Fish Chowder (page 36), this recipe relies on the old Yankee wisdom of using canned evaporated milk for some of the dairy in the chowder. SERVES 8

6 dozen medium-size steamer clams in
    the shell, or 6 dozen small littleneck or
    mahogany clams in the shell and rinsed well

¼ cup cider vinegar (optional)

3 cups cold water

8 slices bacon, preferably apple wood-smoked

6 tablespoons (¾ stick) unsalted butter

1 very large onion, peeled and diced

3 large ribs celery, leaves included, trimmed
    and thinly sliced

3 tablespoons unbleached all-purpose flour

3 medium-size (about 1½ pounds) Maine
    potatoes, or Yukon Gold or Red Bliss potatoes,
    peeled and cut into ½-inch chunks

2 cans (12 ounces each) evaporated whole milk

2 cups half-and-half

Sea salt and freshly ground black or white
    pepper

3 tablespoons minced fresh flat-leaf parsley,
    for serving

Sweet paprika, for serving

Manhattan is not New England and my chowder loyalties have been and always will be with cream-based chowders.

Still, this is not to say I am an advocate of those wallpaper paste thick and gloppy clam chowders that somehow manage to take top honors at every chowder fest I have ever attended in New England. How the Brant Point Grill's uniquely delicious clam chowder topped with a whole fried belly clam didn't manage even to garner an honorable mention at a chowder fest I attended on Nantucket Island has me mystified enough to give up attending chowder fests altogether.

When I get the craving to make and eat clam chowder (which is quite often), I almost always make some slight variation of the Maine Clam Chowder featured over twenty years ago in my brother's and my *Saltwater Seasonings Cookbook.* This is my Platonic ideal of chowder. The original recipe called for whole steamer clams and I use them only when I am positive they will not be laden with stubborn sand. On Cape Cod, I often make this chowder with Cape Cod's pristine cultivated littlenecks and every once in a while I'll use

1 If you are using steamer clams, soak them in a large container with water to cover and the cider vinegar until they expel their sand, 20 to 30 minutes. Place the cleaned clams in a large, sturdy stockpot and add the 3 cups of water. Cover the pot and cook the clams over high heat until the shells have opened, 8 to 10 minutes. Transfer the clams to a large bowl to cool, discarding any clams that have not opened. If the broth left in the pot is sandy or gritty, strain it through a cheesecloth-lined fine mesh strainer. Set the clam broth aside.

2 Place the bacon in a Dutch oven or other large, heavy pot and cook over medium heat until nicely crisped, 7 to 9 minutes. Transfer the bacon to a paper towel–lined plate to drain. Discard all but about 2 tablespoons of the bacon fat from the pot. Add the butter and cook over medium heat until melted. Add the onion and celery and cook until they begin to soften, 5 to 7 minutes, taking care not to let them brown. Add the flour and cook, stirring constantly, until it loses its raw taste, about 2 minutes. Slowly stir in the reserved clam broth and continue stirring for a minute or two until it thickens slightly. Add the potatoes and let simmer, partially covered, until the potatoes are tender, 25 to 30 minutes.

3 While the potatoes are cooking, remove the clams from their shells and discard the shells (or save them to crush and add New England style to a pathway or driveway). If you are using steamer clams, be sure to remove and discard the dark black sleeve covering the neck of each clam.

4 When the potatoes are tender, add the cooked clams, evaporated milk, and half-and-half to the pot. Let the chowder come to a simmer and season it with salt and pepper to taste (the chowder may not need salt if the clams and bacon are very salty). Cook the chowder until it is evenly heated through, 10 to 12 minutes.

5 Ladle the hot clam chowder into large bowls and crumble a slice of bacon over the top of each serving, followed by a sprinkling of parsley and paprika.

Corn and Clam Chowder

My all-time favorite literary passage referencing Nantucket Island is the "Chowder" chapter in Herman Melville's *Moby-Dick*. The narrator and Queequeg are headed off for a typical island dinner at the Try Pots restaurant. The joint is wonderfully described by Melville as the "Fishiest of all fishy places . . . for the pots there were always boiling chowders. Chowder for breakfast, and chowder for dinner, and chowder for supper, till you began to look for fish-bones coming through your clothes."

The narrator pronounces both the clam and cod chowders "surpassingly excellent." To this day, I always strive to achieve similar descriptive hyperbole whenever I undertake the making of New England chowder. The following corn and clam combination yields a great end of summer or early autumn chowder. I accompany large, steaming bowls with crusty and chewy loaves of Nantucket's famed Portuguese bread rather than the more common oyster crackers. SERVES 4 TO 6

4 ounces best-quality slab or thickly sliced apple wood–smoked bacon, cut into ⅓-inch dice

2 tablespoons (¼ stick) unsalted butter

1 medium-size onion, peeled, and cut into ¼-inch dice

1 red bell pepper, stemmed, seeded, and cut into ¼-inch dice

1 tablespoon fresh thyme leaves

3 tablespoons all-purpose unbleached flour

5 cups fish, clam, or vegetable broth

1 pound (2 medium-large) all-purpose potatoes, peeled and cut into ½-inch dice

4 ears fresh, tender local corn, husked and kernels cut from the cobs

1 pint fresh chopped clams, with their juices

1 cup whole milk

1 cup heavy (whipping) cream

Sea salt and freshly ground black or white pepper

Minced fresh chives, for garnish

1 Place the bacon in a Dutch oven or other large, heavy pot and cook over medium heat until nicely browned and crisp, 7 to 8 minutes. Transfer the bacon to paper towels to drain and set it aside. Pour off all but 1½ tablespoons of the bacon fat remaining in the pot.

2 Add the butter to the pot and melt it over medium heat. Stir in the onion, bell pepper, and thyme and cook until tender but not browned, about 8 minutes. Add the flour and cook, stirring constantly, until the flour has lost its raw taste, 2 to 3 minutes.

3 Slowly add the broth to the pot, stirring constantly so it thickens slightly with the flour and doesn't lump. Add the potatoes, let come to a simmer, and cook until the potatoes are almost tender, about 20 minutes. Add the corn kernels and the clams, with all of their juices, to the pot and let simmer until the corn is very tender, about 10 minutes.

4 Stir in the milk and heavy cream, blending thoroughly. Season with salt and black or white pepper to taste. Cook the chowder over medium-low heat until it is just heated through, 7 to 8 minutes. Take care not to let the chowder boil or it may curdle.

5 Ladle the hot chowder into bowls and garnish each serving with some of the reserved crispy bacon and a scattering of minced fresh chives.

Barnstable Harbor Oyster Stew

My husband, Nigel, and I recently got a family permit to go oystering just down the road from our Cape Cod home on the shores of Barnstable Harbor. Nigel likes to joke that it takes him longer to suit up in his extremely awkward waders than it does to gather the half-bushel of oysters allowed for the weekly limit. Indeed, Barnstable oysters tend to be that plentiful and I have to say harvesting them is one of the more invigorating activities I love most about living on Cape Cod. Another oyster adjective that comes to mind immediately with "plentiful" is "utterly delicious" and since securing our license, my oyster cookery has expanded tenfold. This elegant, mushroom-laden oyster stew is but one noteworthy example. SERVES 6 TO 8

For the mushroom stew

1 pound cremini mushrooms, cleaned, trimmed, and thinly sliced

½ pound other interesting mushrooms, such as maitake (hen of the woods), shiitake, chanterelle, or oyster mushrooms, cleaned, trimmed, and thinly sliced

4 shallots, peeled and thinly sliced

1 small fennel bulb, trimmed, cored, and sliced thinly into 1-inch-long slivers

2 cloves garlic, peeled and minced

¼ cup extra virgin olive oil

2 tablespoons freshly squeezed lemon juice

Sea salt and freshly ground black pepper

8 ounces bottled clam juice

3 cups vegetable stock, homemade or good-quality store-bought

3 tablespoons cream sherry

1½ cups heavy (whipping) cream

For the oysters

2½ tablespoons unsalted butter

½ teaspoon sweet paprika, plus paprika for garnishing the soup

30 freshly shucked oysters, with their juices

3 tablespoons minced fresh dill

2 tablespoons minced fresh flat-leaf parsley

1 Preheat the oven to 375°F.

2 Make the mushroom stew: Place all of the mushrooms and the shallots, fennel, and garlic in a roasting

pan and stir to mix. Drizzle the olive oil and lemon juice over the mushroom mixture and toss gently together to coat everything lightly. Season the mushroom mixture with salt and pepper to taste. Bake, stirring occasionally, until the vegetables are very tender, 45 minutes to 1 hour. Remove the pan from the oven and let cool for a few minutes.

3 Transfer half of the roasted mushroom mixture to a blender or food processor. Add the clam juice and puree until very smooth. Pour the pureed mushrooms into a Dutch oven or other large, heavy pot. Stir in the remaining roasted mushroom mixture and the vegetable stock and sherry. Let the stew come to a simmer over medium heat and then let simmer until the flavors are blended, about 15 minutes, stirring occasionally. Stir in the cream and continue cooking the stew until it is nicely heated through, about 10 minutes. Do not let the stew boil or it may curdle.

4 Once the mushroom stew is heated through, prepare the oysters: Melt the butter in a medium-size skillet over medium heat. Swirl in the ½ teaspoon of paprika. Drain any juices from the oysters and add the juices to the mushroom stew. Place the oysters in the skillet and cook until the edges begin to curl, 2 to 3 minutes. Using a spatula, gently scrape all of the oysters into the pot with the mushroom stew and stir in the dill and parsley. Serve the stew at once, garnishing each serving with a little dusting of paprika.

Mussel Bisque

Ever since my siblings and I were little kids we have been gathering mussels at low tide from the rocky shorefronts of various family homes on Blue Hill Bay in Maine. While delicious, these mussels tend to be quite large and their shells are often speckled with sharp barnacles. For a while, I became a bigger fan of the smaller mussels a friend

of mine was gathering from Tuckernuck Island, a small island off of Nantucket. Then these wild mussels became infested with pesky little crabs and my friend stopped harvesting them. Nowadays the mussels that never disappoint me, and in fact thrill me, are the rope-cultured Casco Bay ones sold by the Browne Trading Company in Portland, Maine. These pristine mussels do not require much in the way of debearding or scrubbing and the meats are very tender and sweet. I'll order pounds of them when hosting *moules et frites* dinner parties and they are the best mussels to use in this lovely bisque, one of the few hot soups I serve during the summer months because the flavors remind me of both Maine and the sun-drenched French Riviera. SERVES 6 TO 8

2 cups water

3 cups dry white wine

3 pounds mussels, preferably small ones, scrubbed and debearded if necessary

6 tablespoons (¾ stick) unsalted butter

1 medium-size onion, peeled and chopped

2 leeks, well rinsed, trimmed, and minced

2 carrots, peeled and cut into small dice

4 cloves garlic, peeled and minced or grated on a Microplane

3 small vine-ripened tomatoes, seeded and cut into ¼-inch dice

1½ cups light cream or half-and-half

¾ cup heavy (whipping) cream

Sea salt and freshly ground black pepper

2 tablespoons minced fresh dill

3 tablespoons finely slivered fresh basil

1 Pour the water and 1 cup of the wine into a Dutch oven or other large, heavy pot. Add the mussels, cover the pot, and cook over high heat until the mussel shells open, 6 to 8 minutes. Discard any mussels that do not open. When cool enough to handle, remove the mussels from their shells and set the mussels aside,

Colorful wooden skiffs add their poetry to a peaceful Casco Bay cove in southern Maine.

discarding the shells. Strain the mussel cooking liquid through a fine mesh sieve into a large measuring cup and set it aside. Wipe out the pot.

2　Melt the butter in the Dutch oven over medium heat. Add the onion, leeks, carrots, and garlic and cook until they begin to soften, about 5 minutes. Reduce the heat to low, cover the pot, and slowly cook the vegetables without browning them until very tender, 20 to 25 minutes, stirring them occasionally to prevent them from sticking to the bottom of the pot. Add the tomatoes and cook until they soften and cook slightly, about 5 minutes.

3　Add enough of the remaining 2 cups of wine to the strained mussel cooking liquid to measure 5 cups and pour this into the pot with the vegetables. Let come to a simmer and simmer, uncovered, until the flavors blend and strengthen, about 15 minutes.

4　Add the light and heavy cream and the mussels to the pot. Season the bisque with salt and pepper to taste. You may not need much salt, depending on how salty the mussels are. Cook the bisque, stirring it occasionally, until it is heated through, 7 to 8 minutes. Just before serving, add the dill and basil to the

bisque. Serve the bisque hot but not piping hot, ladled into wide, shallow soup bowls.

Down East Diver Scallop Stew

My brother, Jonathan, a chef and specialty food shopkeeper in Maine, makes this simple but sublime scallop stew when he gets a winter cache of super fresh diver-harvested sea scallops plucked from the frigid surrounding waters. It is considered heresy to cook with anything but bay scallops in my Nantucket neck of the woods but I do honestly adore sea scallops and am crazy about this stew. It really wouldn't work with the smaller bay scallops but I have had success making the recipe with the larger scallops harvested off of Cape Cod, marketed as Chatham scallops. Like every old-fashioned New England seafood stew, this improves and intensifies when allowed to age overnight and then be gently reheated. When Jonathan wants to make this stew even more elegant, he'll add a couple of tablespoons of chopped lobster meat and a teaspoon of room temperature truffle butter to each bowl of scallop stew. SERVES 4 TO 6

1½ pounds very fresh jumbo sea scallops

Coarsely ground sea salt and freshly ground black pepper

6 tablespoons (¾ stick) unsalted butter

3 tablespoons shallots, peeled and minced

¾ cup dry white wine

½ cup dry sherry

3 cups whole milk

1 cup light cream or half-and-half

2 tablespoons chopped fresh flat-leaf parsley, for serving

Sweet paprika, for serving

1   Remove the tough side nibs from the outside edge of the scallops. (This is done purely for aesthetic reasons and I usually pop the nibs directly into my mouth as a quirky form of Down East sashimi.) Place the scallops on a baking sheet and season the tops generously with salt and pepper.

2   Melt 3 tablespoons of the butter over medium heat in a large skillet (both Jonathan and I use heavy stainless steel or glazed cast-iron and advise against using nonstick pans). When the butter begins to foam, working in 2 batches place the scallops seasoned side down in the skillet and season the unseasoned tops with additional salt and pepper. Do not crowd the scallops. Cook the scallops until well browned, about 90 seconds. Avoid the temptation to shake the skillet, as the scallops are likely to stick at the start of the cooking process but will release once they are sufficiently browned. Using tongs, turn the scallops over and cook them on the second side until browned, 30 seconds to 1 minute. Transfer the scallops to a plate. Repeat the process with remaining 3 tablespoons of butter and the remaining scallops.

3   Add the shallots to the skillet in which the scallops were browned and cook them over medium heat until they begin to brown, about 2 minutes. Add the white wine and sherry, scraping up any browned bits clinging to the bottom of the skillet. Let cook until the liquid is reduced by two thirds and then scrape the contents of the skillet into a Dutch oven or other large, heavy pot.

4   Add the milk and cream to the pot and heat over medium heat until very hot but not boiling, 5 to 6 minutes. Meanwhile, cut the seared scallops vertically in half. Remove the milk and cream mixture from the heat. Add the scallops to the milk mixture with any juices they have rendered. Let cool, then cover and refrigerate the stew overnight.

5   When ready to serve, fish the scallops out of the milk mixture and set them aside. Heat the milk mixture over medium heat to just below the boiling point, 8 to 10 minutes. Add the scallops to the milk mixture and let cook until just heated through, 1 to 2 minutes.

6   Ladle the stew into heated bowls, dividing the scallops evenly among the bowls and garnishing each with a sprinkling of chopped parsley and paprika.

Swordfish Posole

A dozen or so years ago I was hired to consult on various food-related topics for a truly extraordinary high-end cookware and tabletop shop with locations in Santa Fe and Dallas, Texas. The Dallas store also had a prepared food department and I was entrusted with teaching its talented chef Fraser Ellis to make a bunch of the dishes that had once been big sellers in my own take-out food shop on Nantucket. Fraser flew north to Cape Cod where we spent a wonderful week cooking together and I learned as much from Fraser as he learned from me.

I showed Fraser some of my favorite swordfish recipes and he in turn introduced me to canned hominy. Fraser then proceeded to make the most delicious New England meets New Mexico posole using some leftover grilled swordfish, our just-purchased hominy, and a hodgepodge of other lingering ingredients. It was love at first spoonful and now I'll buy swordfish specifically to make this bastardized but brilliant posole whenever the mood strikes.

If you are not using leftover, grilled swordfish in your posole, cook the steaks by placing them in a straight-sided pan with water to cover. Bring the liquid to a full boil, cover the pot, remove from the heat and let the swordfish poach in the hot liquid undisturbed for 15 minutes. The fish will be just cooked through, moist, and flake easily. SERVES 6 TO 8

3 tablespoons extra virgin olive oil

1 large onion, peeled and minced

1 poblano pepper, stemmed, seeded, and diced

1 yellow bell pepper, stemmed, seeded, and diced

1 jalapeño pepper, stemmed, seeded, and finely minced

5 cloves garlic, peeled and minced

1 teaspoon cumin seeds

1 teaspoon medium-hot chile powder, such as ancho or chipotle

1 tablespoon minced fresh oregano, or 1 teaspoon dried oregano

1 can (10 ounces) Ro-Tel Diced Tomatoes & Green Chilis

6 to 7 cups seafood stock, homemade or good quality store-bought (see Note)

1 can (7 ounces) salsa verde, preferably Herdez brand, which has no preservatives (optional but definitely adds an extra nuance)

2 cans (15 ounces each) white hominy, rinsed and drained

1 can (about 15 ounces) pinto beans or black beans, rinsed and drained

1½ pounds cooked swordfish steaks, skin removed and fish flaked

Sea salt and freshly ground black pepper

½ cup minced fresh cilantro

Lime wedges, for serving

1 Heat the olive oil over medium heat in a Dutch oven or other large, heavy pot. Add the onion and cook until beginning to soften, about 5 minutes. Add the poblano pepper, bell pepper, and jalapeño and cook until they are slightly softened, about 5 minutes. Stir in the garlic, cumin seeds, chile powder, and oregano and cook, stirring, until fragrant, about 2 minutes.

2 Add the tomatoes, 6 cups of the seafood stock, and the salsa verde, if using. Let come to a simmer over medium heat. Stir in the hominy, beans, and swordfish. Season with salt and black pepper to taste. Reduce the heat to medium-low and let the posole simmer until the flavors marry, 15 to 20 minutes. If the posole seems too thick, thin it to your liking with the remaining 1 cup of seafood stock.

3 Serve the posole hot in shallow, wide soup bowls and sprinkle each serving generously with the cilantro. Garnish the rim of each soup bowl with a lime wedge or two for squeezing into the soup.

NOTE: *If neither is available, bottled clam juice is an acceptable alternative.*

Fish Chowder

When my brother and I were writing our Maine cookbook, *Saltwater Seasonings*, we discovered that the first chapters of many old-time Maine cookbooks started off with chowders rather than today's more standard appetizer fare. Our research also taught us that the secret to many of the best Maine chowders we tried and tested was to use canned evaporated milk for some or all of the dairy. Ever since, my pantry has never been without a supply of evaporated milk and I continue to use and favor it in many of my New England chowder recipes. While clam chowder is now undoubtedly more popular than fish chowder throughout New England and across the country, I cannot rave enough about this perfected fish variation featuring an abundant amount of local cod, scrod, or haddock along with that coveted can of rich and creamy evaporated milk. A fabulous fish chowder tends to be far easier to assemble than its clam cousin, making it one of my favorite meals to serve on busy weeknights. SERVES 6

⅓ pound salt pork, cut into fine dice

2 medium-size onions, peeled and minced

3 large all-purpose potatoes, peeled and cut into ⅓-inch dice

3½ cups water

½ cup dry white wine

2½ to 3 pounds fresh, firm, white fish fillets, such as cod, scrod, or haddock, skin and bones removed

1 can (12 ounces) evaporated whole milk

2 to 3 cups whole milk

Sea salt and freshly ground black or white pepper

½ cup minced fresh flat-leaf parsley

Paprika, for garnish

Vermont Common Crackers (optional; see Note), for serving

1 Scatter the salt pork over the bottom of a Dutch oven or other large, heavy pot and cook over medium-low heat, stirring occasionally, until lightly browned and crisped, 6 to 8 minutes. Using a slotted spatula or spoon, transfer the salt pork to paper towels to drain, then set it aside.

2 Add the onions to the fat remaining in the pot and cook them until soft and translucent, 5 to 7 minutes. Add the potatoes, water, and white wine. Let come to a boil and then simmer, uncovered, until the potatoes are almost tender, about 15 minutes.

3 Place the whole fish fillets on top of the potatoes, cover the pot, and let the fish poach over medium heat until just cooked through, 8 to 10 minutes. Add the evaporated milk and 2 cups of the whole milk to the chowder. Stir gently to flake the poached fish into bite-size chunks. Season the chowder with salt and pepper to taste and continue cooking until the chowder is heated through, 5 to 7 minutes longer.

4 Ladle the hot chowder into large bowls and garnish each serving with a generous sprinkling of the reserved salt pork, the parsley, and some paprika.

Accompany the chowder with a basket of common crackers, if desired.

NOTE: *If you can't find Vermont Common Crackers, substitute smaller round oyster crackers.*

Spring Chicken Soup

In my household we tend to favor a good home-made chicken potpie to chicken soup. However, I'll occasionally make a pot of chicken soup in the springtime because it just seems like the right and healthy thing to serve after a long winter of simmering thick soups that can stick to your ribs in a manner that does not actually become the upcoming beach season. SERVES 6

2 carrots, peeled and minced

2 tablespoons finely minced peeled fresh ginger

10 cups chicken stock or broth, homemade or good-quality store-bought

½ cup dry white wine

1 tablespoon finely grated orange zest

1½ cups mini bow tie pasta or another small fancifully shaped pasta

2½ cups bite-size chunks cooked chicken breast meat, torn by hand

Salt and freshly ground black pepper

6 scallions, trimmed, white and light green parts thinly sliced on the diagonal

½ pound fresh baby spinach leaves, rinsed and stemmed, if necessary

½ cup whole fresh flat-leaf parsley leaves

1 Place the carrots, ginger, chicken stock or broth, white wine, and orange zest in a Dutch oven or other large pot and let come to a boil over medium-high heat.

2 Stir in the pasta and cook until the pasta is al dente, usually 6 to 7 minutes. Stir in the chicken and season with salt and pepper to taste. Add the scallions, spinach, and parsley and cook until the greens are wilted, 4 to 5 minutes. Serve the soup at once.

Turkey Tortilla Soup

Lou's Restaurant and Bakery in Hanover, New Hampshire, is a beloved local institution known for serving mighty tasty and generous portions of breakfast and lunch fare. Once you see their tortilla soup being served at lunchtime, you immediately have to order a big bowl for yourself as it is an architectural marvel of homemade chicken broth heaped high with sliced jalapeño and bell peppers, onions, grilled chicken, crunchy tortilla chips, shredded cheese, and guacamole. When my inquiries to share the recipe in this cookbook were not acknowledged, I set out to make my own version of the soup.

My Turkey Tortilla Soup is actually nothing like Lou's but don't let that stop you from making it because it has become my very favorite post-Thanksgiving-feast turkey soup. This really says something since over the years I have made countless different turkey soups as part of a decade-long stint I did as a spokeswoman for the Butterball turkey company. I also make this soup at times of the year other than Thanksgiving, either with the usual turkey or the remains of a roast chicken dinner. SERVES 4 TO 6

3 tablespoons canola or other neutral vegetable oil

1 large onion, peeled and minced

5 cloves garlic, peeled and minced

1 large jalapeño pepper, stemmed, seeded, and minced

3 round stone-ground corn tortillas (6-inch diameter), torn into small (1-inch) pieces

1½ teaspoons ground cumin

1 teaspoon ground coriander

1 teaspoon dried oregano

½ teaspoon chipotle chile powder, or more if you want it hotter

1 can (10 ounces) Ro-Tel Diced Tomatoes & Green Chilis

4 cups turkey or chicken stock or broth, homemade or good-quality store-bought

1½ cups frozen corn kernels

1 can (about 15 ounces) black beans, rinsed and drained

2½ cups shredded leftover cooked turkey or chicken

¾ cup heavy (whipping) cream

4 ounces mild cheddar cheese, freshly shredded (1¼ to 1½ cups)

2 to 3 tablespoons freshly squeezed lime juice

Sea salt and freshly ground black pepper

3 scallions, trimmed, white and light green parts minced

½ cup minced fresh cilantro

1 Heat the oil in a Dutch oven or other large, heavy pot over medium heat. Add the onion, garlic, and jalapeño and cook until softened, 5 to 7 minutes. Stir in the tortilla pieces and cook until softened and beginning to fall apart, about 5 minutes. Stir in the cumin, coriander, oregano, and chipotle powder and cook until fragrant, about 1 minute. Add the tomatoes and stock or broth. Let the soup come to a boil, then reduce the heat and simmer, uncovered, until the flavors are blended, about 15 minutes. Remove the pot from heat and let the soup base cool for at least 10 minutes.

2 Working in batches, puree the soup base in a blender or in the pot with an immersion blender until smooth. Return the soup base to the pot and place

Woolly sheep cozy together to graze peacefully in their stalls at a local lamb farm.

over medium heat. Add the corn, black beans, and turkey or chicken and cook, stirring occasionally, until heated through, 10 to 12 minutes. (You can make the soup several hours ahead to this point. Cool and refrigerate, covered. Reheat over medium-low heat.)

3 Stir in the cream and cheddar and cook, stirring, until the cheese has melted smoothly into the soup, 4 to 5 minutes. Season the soup with lime juice, salt, and black pepper to taste. Just before you are ready to serve the soup, stir in the scallions and cilantro. Ladle the hot soup into bowls and serve at once.

Border Bay Junction Scotch Broth

Cokie and Greg Hamm are energetic and multi-talented Cape Cod neighbors who own a lamb farm in West Barnstable and also train and board a variety of pooches in a deluxe rural setting. Our family lovingly refers to their Border Bay Junction Kennel as "The Baa Spa" because every time our Jack Russell Terrier pays a visit to the lamb farm she comes home looking extra svelte, as if she had spent a week at Canyon Ranch. When Greg isn't busy mixing fish scraps from a local sushi restaurant into the food he feeds to their own herd of Border Collies and Cokie's assorted rescue dogs, he makes a mean and very potent Scotch broth, thriftily utilizing lamb scraps on the one hand but counterbalanced on the other by an expensive splash of Islay single malt Scotch. SERVES 8 TO 10

4 pounds meaty lamb bones from the neck, shoulder, or shank, cut into 2-inch pieces

20 cups (5 quarts) water

1 tablespoon fine sea salt, or more as needed

20 black peppercorns, cracked, or more as needed

¾ cup barley

2 cups (3 large) peeled and finely diced carrots

2 cups (2 medium-size) peeled and minced onions

2 cups (3 plump) well rinsed, trimmed, and finely diced leeks

2 cups (4 large ribs) finely diced celery

1 cup (1 small) peeled and finely diced rutabaga

1 tablespoon finely peeled and minced garlic

¾ cup minced fresh flat-leaf parsley

Islay single malt Scotch or another coveted single malt Scotch (optional), for serving

1 Place the lamb bones in a large, sturdy stockpot and add cold water to cover. Let come to a boil over high heat, then reduce the heat slightly and continue cooking at a low boil, about 2 minutes. Drain the lamb bones well and rinse them under cold running water until cooled down. Drain the bones again then place them in a clean stockpot and add the 20 cups of water. Add the salt and cracked peppercorns. Let come to a boil again over high heat, cover the pot, reduce the heat to medium-low, and let simmer until

the lamb is tender but not yet separating from the bones, about 2 hours.

2 Add the barley, carrots, onions, leeks, celery, rutabaga, and garlic and cook until everything is tender, 1 hour to 1¼ hours. Remove the lamb bones from the soup, pull off all the meat, trim away and discard the gristle, and cut it into bite-size morsels. Add the meat to the soup. Discard the bones. Stir in the parsley. Taste the soup for seasoning, adding more salt and/or cracked peppercorns, if needed. Ladle the hot soup into wide bowls and add a generous splash (1½ to 2 tablespoons) of single malt Scotch to each serving, if desired. Serve at once. If making in advance, cool and refrigerate, covered, for up to 5 days. Reheat over medium-low heat.

Polish Mushroom and Barley Soup

I am very proud of my Polish heritage from my father's side of the family and have had a fascinating time revisiting the Polish section of New Britain, Connecticut, close to the area where our family and a long list of Polish cousins with z's and ski's in their last names were raised. I am embarrassed to say I have difficulty communicating with most of the merchants in this truly old world neighborhood because they all still speak only Polish and I am merely capable of uttering a phrase or two of badly pronounced Polish. Someday I hope to rectify this and pay a visit to Poland. In the meantime, I sate my Polish sensibilities by dabbling in Polish cooking. This mushroom and barley soup is hearty but healthy; grains replace the usual potatoes and the soup has no cream. Sometimes, if I have farro in my pantry, I use it in place of the barley, as it imparts an even more pronounced nutty wholesomeness to this sturdy but delicious soup. SERVES 6 TO 8

1 ounce dried porcini or oyster mushrooms

2½ cups water

2½ tablespoons unsalted butter or olive oil

1 large onion, peeled and minced

2 cloves garlic, peeled and minced

2 carrots, peeled and cut into small dice

2 small purple-top turnips, peeled and cut into small dice

12 ounces cremini or white button mushrooms, cleaned, trimmed, and thinly sliced (3 cups)

¾ cup pearl barley

8 to 10 cups beef or vegetable stock or broth, homemade or good-quality store-bought

Salt and freshly ground black pepper

¼ cup minced fresh flat-leaf parsley or dill

1 Place the dried mushrooms in a medium-size saucepan, cover them with the water, and let come to a boil over medium-high heat. Let the mushrooms simmer until softened, about 5 minutes and then remove from the heat and let them cool.

2 Heat the butter or olive oil over medium heat in a Dutch oven or other large, heavy pot. Add the onion, garlic, carrots, and turnips and cook until the onion is translucent and the other vegetables have begun to soften but are not yet tender, about 10 minutes. Add the sliced cremini or button mushrooms and cook until the mushrooms have released their juices and the juices have pretty much evaporated, 7 to 10 minutes.

3 Drain the dried mushrooms, straining the soaking liquid through a fine mesh sieve if it is sandy. Set the mushroom soaking liquid aside. Coarsely chop the soaked mushrooms and add them to the pot along with the soaking liquid. Stir in the barley and pour in 8 cups of the stock or broth. Season with salt and pepper to taste. Let the soup come to a boil over high heat, partially cover the pot, reduce the heat to medium-low, and let simmer, stirring every now and again, until the barley is very soft and plump, 50 minutes to

1 hour. If the barley has thickened the soup too much, thin it to your liking with more stock.

4 Stir in the parsley or dill just before serving. Ladle the hot soup into soup bowls and serve at once. If making in advance, cool and refrigerate, covered, for up to 4 days. Reheat over medium-low heat.

Split Pea and Portobello Soup

Lots of New Englanders believe that split pea soup should be "as thick as fog." As one who spends a lot of frustrating time in foggy places like Nantucket Island and the rocky coast of Maine, I personally would rather not have a good bowl of pea soup remind me of fog. This is my updated version of split pea soup that favors textural flavors over foglike consistency. I had read somewhere that parboiling split peas before adding them to the soup pot makes for a silkier texture. I've employed this method here. A sauté of minced baby portobello mushroom caps and apple wood-smoked Canadian-style bacon from one of my favorite smokehouses—North Country Smokehouse in Claremont, New Hampshire—replaces the more traditional addition of a ham bone or smoked pork hocks. A final optional but wonderful flourish is to serve the soup with a crumble of a pungent New England blue cheese, such as Berkshire Blue or Jasper Hill Farm's Bayley Hazen Blue, dappled over the top. SERVES 6

1 pound split green peas

10 cups water, or more as needed

4 tablespoons extra virgin olive oil

1 large onion, peeled and minced

2 large carrots, peeled and minced

2 ribs celery, minced

4 cloves garlic, peeled and minced

1 teaspoon fresh thyme leaves

1 bay leaf

Sea salt and freshly ground black pepper

1 pound small portobello mushroom caps or cremini mushrooms, wiped clean and tough lower stems trimmed

½ pound apple wood-smoked Canadian bacon, cut into ¼-inch dice

3 tablespoons cream sherry

½ cup minced fresh flat-leaf parsley

6 ounces (1½ cups) crumbled blue cheese (optional)

1 Place the split peas and water in a large pot. Let come to a boil over medium-high heat and blanch, about 2 minutes, skimming away and discarding any foam that rises to the top. Remove the pot from the heat and let the split peas stand for about 1 hour. Do not drain the split peas.

2 Heat 2 tablespoons of the olive oil in a Dutch oven or other large, heavy pot over medium heat. Add the onion, carrots, and celery and cook until softened, about 5 minutes. Add the garlic and thyme and cook until fragrant, about 2 minutes. Add the split peas and their cooking liquid to the pot. Drop in the bay leaf and let come to a simmer, stirring occasionally. Let the soup simmer, partially covered, stirring every once in a while, until the peas are very tender, about 1 hour. If the soup starts to become "as thick as fog," thin it to a more desirable consistency with a bit more water. Season the soup with salt and pepper to taste.

3 Cut the mushrooms into ½-inch chunks and place them in a food processor fitted with a steel blade. Pulse the machine on and off several times until the mushrooms are finely chopped. (You may also chop the mushrooms by hand but using a food processor is much easier and faster.)

4 Heat the remaining 2 tablespoons of olive oil in a large skillet over medium heat. Add the Canadian bacon and cook until just beginning to crisp a bit, 2 to 3 minutes. Add the chopped mushrooms and cook,

stirring frequently, until the mushrooms have released their liquid and the liquid has evaporated, 7 to 10 minutes. Stir in the sherry, scraping the skillet to release any browned bits clinging to the bottom. Cook the mushroom mixture until it has absorbed most of the sherry, about 2 minutes. Remove the skillet from the heat and stir in the parsley. Add the mushroom mixture to the pot of pea soup, stirring well to combine. Taste the soup for seasoning, adding more salt and/or pepper as needed.

5 Serve the soup hot, ladled into soup bowls. Scatter some of the crumbled blue cheese over each bowl of soup, if desired. If making the soup in advance, don't add the cheese yet. Cool and refrigerate the soup, covered, for up to 3 days. Reheat over medium-low heat, stirring occasionally. Scatter the cheese as noted above.

Double Tomato Bliss

New England has many coveted culinary delights whose fleeting growing seasons I love to celebrate, but no single one more so than late summer's local vine-ripened tomatoes. A great August or September tomato can transport sensibilities instantly to the Mediterranean and make one temporarily forget that mud season is a mere six or seven months away on the New England calendar. When I have had my summer fill of sliced tomato salads (something that rarely happens), I allow my locavorism to fuse with my passion for simple Italian dishes and set to making a stylized backyard version of the humble, but oh so comforting, Tuscan tomato soup known as *pappa al pomodoro*. I double my tomato bliss by topping this bread-thickened tomato soup with another famed Tuscan tomato treat—a garlicky and basil-laced tomato bruschetta. Chianti meets Cape Cod, tomato consumption soars, and I am one happy camper. SERVES 6 TO 8

For the soup

⅓ cup extra virgin olive oil

1 medium-size onion, peeled and minced

8 cloves garlic, peeled and minced

½ teaspoon hot red pepper flakes

3 pounds large, local, vine-ripened tomatoes, seeded and coarsely chopped

½ cup coarsely chopped or torn fresh basil leaves

Pinch of sugar

¾ cup dry white wine

4 to 5 cups vegetable stock or broth, homemade or good-quality store-bought, or water

Sea salt and freshly ground black pepper

½ pound stale Italian-style bread, such as ciabatta, broken into coarse chunks (3 cups loosely packed)

For the tomato bruschetta topping

3 cups seeded and diced (¼-inch dice) local, vine-ripened tomatoes (can be a mixture of varieties and heirlooms)

2 cloves garlic, peeled and finely minced or grated on a Microplane

¼ cup slivered fresh basil

⅓ cup high-quality extra virgin olive oil, preferably from Tuscany, plus olive oil for serving

Sea salt

6 to 8 slices (½ inch thick) Italian-style bread, such as ciabatta, toasted or grilled

3 ounces (scant 1 cup) freshly grated Parmigiano-Reggiano cheese

1 Make the soup: Heat a Dutch oven or other large, heavy pot over medium heat. Pour in the olive oil and add the onion, 8 cloves of minced garlic, and the hot red pepper flakes. Cook, stirring occasionally, until the onion is soft and translucent, 5 to 7 minutes. Add the coarsely chopped tomatoes, chopped or torn basil leaves, and sugar. Let come to a simmer and cook,

stirring frequently, until the tomatoes have broken down and thickened, about 20 minutes. Add the white wine and 4 cups of the stock, broth, or water. Season with salt and black pepper to taste and let come just to a boil.

2   Begin adding the bread, a few chunks at a time, stirring constantly, so that the bread breaks down and thickens the soup to the consistency of a porridge. You'll have to strike a balance between the amount of bread and any additional broth or water you add at this point in order to achieve a fairly thick but spoonable soup and a consistency that personally pleases you. Keep the soup warm over low heat or let cool to room temperature should the weather happen to be too hot to serve a warm soup. If making the soup in advance, cool and refrigerate, covered, for up to 3 days. Reheat over low heat or bring to room temperature.

3   Make the tomato bruschetta topping: Combine the diced tomatoes, 2 cloves of minced garlic, and slivered basil in a mixing bowl. Add the olive oil and toss gently. Season with salt to taste. Let the tomato mixture marinate at room temperature for about 30 minutes.

4   To serve the soup, ladle it warm or at room temperature into wide, shallow bowls. Float a slice of toasted bread (the bruschetta base) in the center of each serving. Spoon a generous amount of the tomato mixture on top of each slice of bread. Drizzle another swirl of olive oil over the top of each serving (there's no such thing as too much olive oil in Tuscany nor at my own stateside table) and then add a final generous scattering of the freshly grated Parmigiano-Reggiano.

Roasted Tomato Soup

I love homemade tomato soup and for years now come September I have been making at least one big batch of the Nantucket tomato soup recipe you'll find in the So Long, Summer chapter of my *Cold-Weather Cooking* cookbook. The only problem with

this recipe is that it is quite labor-intensive and I once received a handwritten ornery letter from a would-be fan complaining about all the chopping and dicing required. While I still firmly believe some of the best tasting tomatoes in the entire world are grown on the salt-misted shores of Nantucket Island, I am open-minded. In fact, I created this far less labor-intensive roasted tomato soup with some surprisingly flavorful vine-ripened tomatoes I purchased at Beth's Farm Market in Warren, Maine, and Chase's Daily (no relation, I'm sorry to say) in Belfast, Maine, during a lovely late September foray Down East. SERVES 6

3 pounds vine-ripened local tomatoes, all beefsteak or a mix of beefsteak and heirloom tomatoes

1 large onion, peeled, cut in half lengthwise, and cut into ¼-inch-wide crescent slices

8 cloves garlic, peeled

½ cup extra virgin olive oil

Sea salt and freshly ground black pepper

4 cups chicken stock or broth, homemade or good-quality store-bought

½ cup dry white wine

1 cup heavy (whipping) cream

½ cup slivered fresh basil leaves, plus slivered basil leaves for serving

2 ounces Parmigiano-Reggiano cheese

1   Preheat the oven to 425°F.

2   Core the tomatoes and cut them into either quarters or sixths, depending on how large they are. Combine the tomatoes, onion, and garlic in a large, shallow roasting pan. Drizzle the olive oil over them and season them with salt and pepper to taste. Toss well to coat evenly with the olive oil. Roast the vegetables until tender and beginning to caramelize and char in spots, 40 to 50 minutes.

3   Transfer the roasted vegetables to a Dutch oven or other large, heavy pot and add the chicken stock or broth and white wine. Let the soup come to a simmer

Chase's Daily in Belfast, Maine, grows an extraordinary variety of heirloom tomatoes and I can't resist buying one of every kind in late August and early September.

over medium heat and simmer, uncovered, stirring occasionally, until slightly thickened, about 30 minutes. Stir in the cream and ½ cup basil and cook until warmed through, about 5 minutes.

4 Using an immersion blender, puree the soup in the pot until smooth. Taste for seasoning, adding more salt and/or pepper as needed. (You can puree the soup in batches in a blender but using an immersion blender makes it easier.) Serve the soup hot, warm, or at room temperature. Ladle the soup into bowls. Top each serving with a scattering of slivered basil leaves. Use a vegetable peeler to shave the Parmigiano-Reggiano cheese and scatter the shavings over the top of the soup. Savor the fleeting pleasure of real tomato soup. If making the soup in advance, leave off the toppings. Cool and refrigerate, covered, for up to 3 days. Reheat over low heat or bring to room temperature. Scatter the toppings as noted above.

Butternut Squash and Cider Soup

Come autumn, almost every restaurant in New England feels obliged to put a butternut squash soup on the menu and the stakes between chefs get quite competitive with everyone trying to outdo one another. This has led in my opinion to some pretty absurd renditions. Truth be told, I like a butternut squash soup that is simple and straightforward and have been making one variation or another of this soup for years. Lately, I have been using fresh ginger and have added a tasty garnishing swirl of cider cream to dress up this otherwise simple and creamless soup. The soup is a breeze to make if you take the shortcut, as I always do, of buying butternut squash that is already peeled and seeded. SERVES 6

4 tablespoons (½ stick) unsalted butter

1 large onion, peeled and minced

1½ tablespoons minced peeled fresh ginger

4 cups cubed (1-inch chunks) peeled and seeded butternut squash

6½ cups apple cider

1½ cups vegetable stock or broth, homemade or good-quality store-bought, or water

½ cup crème fraîche or sour cream

Salt and freshly ground black pepper

3 tablespoons store-bought dry-roasted pumpkin seeds (optional)

1 Melt the butter in a Dutch oven or other large, heavy pot over medium heat. Add the onion and ginger and cook until the onion is quite soft, about 10 minutes. Add the butternut squash, 6 cups of the cider, and the vegetable stock or water to the pot. Let come to a boil over high heat, then reduce the heat to medium and let the soup simmer, uncovered, until the squash is tender, about 30 minutes.

2 Meanwhile, pour the remaining ½ cup of cider into a small saucepan, let it come to a boil over high heat, and cook until reduced to about ¼ cup, 3 to 4 minutes. Let the cider cool to room temperature.

3 Place the crème fraîche or sour cream in a small bowl and whisk in the cooled cider until thoroughly combined. Refrigerate until ready to use.

4 Working in batches, puree the soup in a blender until smooth. Return the pureed soup to the pot and reheat it over medium-low heat. Season the soup with salt and pepper to taste (see Note). Serve the soup hot, ladled into bowls. Place a generous spoonful of the cider cream in the middle of each serving and swirl it over the top of the soup with the tip of a knife to make an attractive marbleized pattern. Sprinkle the toasted pumpkin seeds over the top, if desired, and serve.

NOTE: *If making in advance, cool and refrigerate, covered, at this point. It will keep for up to 3 days. Reheat the soup over medium-low heat, stirring occasionally, until warmed through, 20 to 25 minutes. Continue with the recipe.*

Spring Pea Soup with Roasted Pancetta and Mint

My many years of living on Nantucket Island and vacationing in remote areas of Maine, where the nearest grocery store can be miles away, have taught me to keep a well-stocked pantry, freezer, and refrigerator and to be able to make delicious dishes from relatively common ingredients. Seasonal storms or hurricanes can mean no ferry service to Nantucket for days and thus truly pathetic produce aisles in island stores and if you have ever popped into a lone general store in a place like Brooklin or Deer Isle, Maine, you'll immediately understand why this recipe is a handy one.

Since my husband was born in England, we enjoy keeping up with the British food scene and even subscribe to Jamie Oliver's terrific monthly food magazine, where the inspiration for this recipe originated. I call the soup spring pea to distinguish it from split pea soup, but don't just relegate the recipe to rainy April nights because it hits the spot year-round and can for the most part be easily made any time. Feel free to substitute fresh parsley or basil leaves if mint hasn't taken over your herb garden as it has mine. SERVES 4 TO 6

For the pancetta and mint topping

2 cups coarsely diced or torn day-old ciabatta, French, Portuguese, or sourdough bread

3 ounces thinly sliced pancetta, coarsely chopped (you can substitute thinly sliced bacon but pancetta is preferable)

24 to 30 whole fresh mint leaves

3 tablespoons extra virgin olive, plus olive oil for serving

For the pea soup

3 tablespoons unsalted butter or extra virgin olive oil

2 fat leeks, mostly white parts with just a bit of green, well rinsed, trimmed, and minced, or 1 medium-size onion, peeled and minced

1½ tablespoons slivered fresh mint leaves

1 package (16 ounces) frozen green peas, preferably petits pois

4 cups chicken stock or broth, preferably homemade or low-sodium and/or organic store-bought

Sea salt and freshly ground black pepper

½ cup heavy (whipping) cream

Sour cream, crème fraîche, or thick Greek-style yogurt

1 Preheat the oven to 375°F.

2 Make the pancetta and mint topping: Place the bread, pancetta, and mint leaves in a shallow roasting pan just large enough to hold everything in a single layer. Drizzle the olive oil over the top, tossing to coat everything evenly. Bake the topping, stirring occasionally, until browned and crisped, 20 to 25 minutes. Remove the roasting pan from the oven and set it aside.

3 Make the pea soup: Heat the butter or olive oil in a Dutch oven or other large, heavy pot over medium heat. Add the leeks and cook, stirring frequently, until quite soft, 8 to 10 minutes. Add the slivered mint and cook until it just begins to wilt, about 30 seconds. Add the frozen peas and chicken stock or broth and let come to a boil. Reduce the heat to medium, season the soup with salt and pepper to taste, and let simmer until the peas are tender, 10 to 12 minutes. Stir in the cream and let simmer until heated through, about 5 minutes.

4 Using an immersion blender, puree the soup in the pot until very smooth. Taste for seasoning, adding more salt and/or pepper as needed. (You can also puree the soup in batches in a blender, but using an immersion blender is much easier.)

5 Ladle the hot soup into soup bowls and scatter a generous handful of the pancetta and mint topping over each serving. Spoon a generous dollop of sour cream, crème fraîche, or Greek yogurt into the center of each serving and then drizzle a swirl of extra virgin olive oil on top. Serve at once.

Kale Soup

A large Portuguese immigrant population has made kale soup one of the most popular soups throughout Southeastern Massachusetts, Cape Cod, Nantucket, and Martha's Vineyard. Everybody seems to have an opinion about how it should be made and who makes the best version. Here is my entry based on Azorean influences and my own personal preferences. Portuguese sausage is essential and Gaspar's and Amaral's are two respected brands sold throughout New England. Both companies make *linguiça* and *chouriço*, and I usually put both types of sausage in my kale soup for good measure. Red kidney beans are the bean of choice in every bowl I have ever been served. However, since I have never been a fan of red kidney beans, I succumb to my love of the color pink and use a combination of pink beans and white cannellini—and yes I use canned beans for convenience and because cooking the beans from scratch in this instance doesn't make a significant difference in the final tasty outcome. Replacing the customary white potatoes with sweet potatoes adds another layer of vibrant color to my soup.

Traditional fresh curly kale can often be rather tough, even after removing the ribs, and I have found adding this namesake ingredient can sometimes ruin an otherwise excellent bowl of soup. Portuguese friends on Nantucket recently let me in on one of their secrets: They use frozen chopped kale in place of the fresh and I can confirm that this is an excellent option. A second fine option is to use the far more tender fresh Tuscan or lacinato kale, which has been showing up more and more frequently in markets such as Whole Foods.

One more great trick for making especially hearty kale soup is to add a couple of cups of cooked and shredded beef, pork, chicken, or turkey to the pot, if you happen to have leftovers from one roast or another lurking in your refrigerator. Speaking of leftovers, kale soup always improves with a day or two of ageing and Fall River–born David Leite, author of *The New Portuguese Table*, suggests reheating a couple of ladlefuls for breakfast on a cold New England morning, claiming his father taught him "it'll hold you better than oatmeal." SERVES 6 TO 8

2 tablespoons olive oil

8 ounces Portuguese chouriço, cut into ¼-inch rounds (see Note)

8 ounces linguiça, cut into ¼-inch rounds

3 cups peeled and minced onions (about 1½ large Spanish onions)

4 cloves garlic, peeled and minced

¼ teaspoon hot red pepper flakes

4 cups homemade or good-quality store-bought beef stock or broth (I prefer the all natural Kitchen Basics brand)

4 cups water

1 can (14½ ounces) diced tomatoes

½ cup dry red wine

1 bay leaf

3 cups peeled and cubed (½-inch) sweet potatoes

1 can (15½ ounces) pink beans, rinsed and drained

1 can (15½ ounces) cannellini beans, rinsed and drained

2 cups cooked and shredded leftover pork, beef, chicken, or turkey (optional)

Salt and freshly ground black pepper

1 package (16 ounces) frozen chopped kale, or 16 ounces fresh Tuscan (lacinato) kale, center ribs removed and leaves cut into ½-inch-wide strips

Tomato juice or additional water

1   Heat the olive oil in a large, sturdy stockpot over medium-high heat. Add the *chouriço* and *linguiça* and cook until nicely browned on both sides, 5 to 7 minutes. Using a spatula, remove the sausages from the pot and set them aside. Add the onions to the pot and cook over medium-low heat, stirring frequently, until lightly caramelized, about 20 minutes. Add the garlic and hot red pepper flakes and cook until fragrant, about 2 minutes.

Vibrant wildflowers are ablaze in a field surrounding a barn nestled into the foot of a mountainside in rural Massachusetts.

2   Add the beef stock, water, tomatoes, red wine, bay leaf, and sweet potatoes and let come to a boil over medium-high heat. Reduce the heat to medium-low and let simmer, covered, stirring every once in a while, until the sweet potatoes are tender, 15 to 20 minutes. Stir in the pink beans and cannellini beans and cook just enough to warm, about 5 minutes.

3   Ladle 2 cups of the hot soup into a food processor or blender and puree to a paste. Stir the paste back into the soup pot to lightly thicken the soup. Return the browned sausages to the soup and add the shredded meat, if using. Taste the soup for seasoning and season with salt and black pepper to taste (the sausages are already quite flavorful and the soup probably will not need much salt). Add the frozen or fresh kale to the pot and continue cooking, stirring occasionally, until the kale is cooked and the soup is piping hot, 12 to 15 minutes.

4   Once all the ingredients are in the pot, the soup will likely need a bit of thinning. My husband likes his kale soup on the tomato-y side, so I often thin

the soup with tomato juice but water will also work fine. Remove and discard the bay leaf. Serve the soup hot, ladled into big deep bowls. If making the soup in advance, cool and refrigerate, covered, for up to 4 days. Reheat over medium-low heat.

NOTE: *If the Portuguese-style* chouriço *is not available, you can use an additional 8 ounces of* linguiça.

My Brother's Baked Beans

My brother, Jonathan, and I have long been enamored of the old Maine tradition of baking beans in a dirt hole dug into the ground to produce what Mainers call bean hole beans. A few years ago I was able to attend a bean hole bean supper that was scheduled as a part of a celebration of Maine foodways in Camden, Maine. When I saw the size of the hole that had been dug in the ground and the heft of the giant cast-iron bean pot, I was relieved that my first experience with bean hole beans was going to be through the hard labor of others. When I tasted the beans, I have to honestly say that they did not blow my socks off. Food historian Sandy Oliver was speaking at this event and I took to heart two things she said: (a) "New Englanders like to make hard work of a good time" and (b) "Little beans are for Bostonians, big beans are for Mainers."

Needless to say, I am no longer seduced by the rustic romance of baking my beans in a dirt hole, especially when I can enjoy my brother Jonathan's more domesticated oven-baked Maine soldier beans. Naturally, soldier beans are big beans because Jonathan lives in Maine. SERVES 6 TO 8

1 pound dried soldier beans, or other favorite large dried beans, such as pinto or cannellini

4 cups cold water

1 tablespoon kosher salt

⅓ cup pure maple syrup

2 tablespoons dark brown sugar

3 tablespoons Dijon mustard, preferably Maille or Fallot

4½ cups boiling water

1 medium-size onion, peeled

6 whole cloves

2 pieces (each ¾ inch long) fresh ginger

2 smoked ham hocks (each about ½ pound)

Sea salt

1   Place the beans in a colander and rinse them thoroughly under cold running water. Sort and discard any stray particles that may have gotten mixed in with the beans. Place the beans in a large bowl and pour the 4 cups of cold water over them. Stir in the kosher salt, stirring until dissolved. Cover the bowl with plastic wrap and let the beans soak overnight, at least 8 hours but no longer than 12 hours.

2   Preheat the oven to 300°F.

3   Drain the beans and rinse them thoroughly. Place the beans in a large clean bowl. Place the maple syrup, brown sugar, and Dijon mustard in a heatproof bowl and add the 4½ cups of boiling water, stirring until the brown sugar dissolves. Pour the maple syrup mixture over the beans.

4   Cut the onion in half and stud each half with 3 whole cloves. Ladle about 1 cup of the beans with some of their liquid into a Dutch oven or other large, heavy pot. Place the onion halves and ginger on top of the beans. Ladle more beans into the pot to cover the onions. Add the ham hocks. Add all of the remaining beans and their liquid to the pot, cover it, and bake the beans until not quite tender, about 2 hours.

5   Taste the beans for seasoning, adding sea salt to taste. Add a little water if the beans seem to be getting too dry. Return the pot to the oven and bake the beans, uncovered, until they are completely tender, 30 to 45 minutes.

During the summer months, Camden Harbor is one of the busiest ports of call for avid sailors cruising along the coast of Maine.

6 Remove the ham hocks, ginger, and clove-studded onion halves from the beans, discarding the ginger and onion. Let the ham hocks cool until easy to handle. Remove and shred any meat from the ham hocks and stir it into the beans. Reheat the beans, if necessary, over medium-low heat for 5 to 7 minutes. Serve the beans at once.

Judy's Easy Baked Beans

Judy and Walter Kaess live across the street from us on Cape Cod and they are the best neighbors and friends imaginable. They sponsored us for membership at the decidedly quirky, hundred-plus-year-old, no electricity Barnstable Yacht Club, located on Cape Cod Bay just down the road from both of our homes. The yacht club is only open during the summer and its big social events are the Fourth of July and Labor Day picnics, where members either bring designated dishes or help with the staging of the event. "Bean warming" is one of the tasks one can sign up for at every picnic, but Judy was never one to just warm the beans provided to her. Instead, she would make this easy but tasty recipe, doctoring reliable cans of New England's B&M brand baked beans. SERVES 8

Butter, for greasing the casserole dish

2 cans (16 ounces each) B&M Original baked beans

¾ cup packed light brown sugar

1 teaspoon dry mustard

½ cup ketchup

6 slices bacon, cut into ½-inch pieces

1 Preheat the oven to 325°F. Grease a 2-quart casserole dish with butter.

2 Empty 1 can of the baked beans into the prepared casserole dish. Combine the brown sugar and dry mustard in a small bowl. Sprinkle half of the brown sugar mixture over the beans. Top with the remaining can of baked beans. Sprinkle the rest of the brown sugar mixture over these beans. Spread the ketchup evenly over the top of the beans and dot them with the bacon pieces.

3 Bake the beans, uncovered, until the sauce is thickened and bubbling and the bacon is crisped, 2 to 2½ hours. Serve the beans hot or warm.

Savory Baked Beans

When my wood-burning Tuscan oven was installed in my Cape Cod kitchen, it came with an earthenware bean pot and even though I live a mere seventy miles from the city everyone calls Beantown, I never make sweetened Boston-style or

« My Brother's Baked Beans with Pumpkin Corn Bread with Maple Pecan Butter (page 298)

New England-style baked beans in this pot. Rather, I adhere to the romantic Italian tradition of letting a pot of cannellini beans laced with sage and olive oil simmer slowly overnight in the dying embers of the evening's wood fire. I have adapted and embellished the basic recipe here for cooking in a traditional oven and gilded the lily by enriching the beans with both diced and sliced pancetta, onions, garlic, tomatoes, lacinato kale, and plenty of fresh sage. Lacinato kale, sometimes called dinosaur or Tuscan kale, used to be somewhat difficult to find, but now that the health benefits of kale are so widely touted, I am able to purchase lacinato kale, organically grown in Vermont, at my local Whole Foods Market on nearly a year-round basis.

For a total pork-fest and contemporary "bean supper," pair these beans with a platter of Truelove Pork Blade Steaks (page 229). SERVES 6

For the beans

1 pound dried cannellini beans

2½ tablespoons extra virgin olive oil

3 ounces finely cubed pancetta (⅛-inch cubes)

1 medium onion, minced

4 cloves garlic, minced

1 can (14.5 ounces) diced tomatoes, preferably San Marzano, undrained

2 tablespoons coarsely slivered fresh sage leaves

3½ to 4½ cups vegetable stock or water

Sea salt and freshly ground black pepper to taste

For finishing and topping

1 bunch lacinato kale, center ribs and lower stems removed, leaves cut into ½-inch-wide strips

3 ounces thinly sliced pancetta

8 to 10 whole fresh sage leaves

1 Place the beans in a colander and rinse under cold running water, sorting through the beans and discarding any stray particles that may be mixed in. Place the beans in a large bowl and add enough cold water to come 2 inches above the beans. Cover with plastic wrap and let soak for at least 6 hours or overnight. Drain the beans and set aside briefly.

2 Preheat the oven to 350°F.

3 Heat the olive oil in a large sturdy pot or Dutch oven over medium heat. Add the finely cubed pancetta and sauté until just beginning to crisp, 5 minutes. Add the onion and continue sautéing until softened, 5 minutes. Stir in the garlic and cook until fragrant, 1 minute more. Add the drained beans to the pot and toss to coat with the other ingredients. Add the tomatoes, sage, and 3½ cups vegetable stock or water. Season with salt and pepper. Raise the heat to medium-high and as soon as the liquid in the pot has begun to boil, remove the pot from the burner, cover it, and transfer to the oven.

4 Bake the beans, covered, in the oven until they are tender, 2 to 2½ hours. The amount of time will depend on the age of the dried beans. Check the beans occasionally to make sure there is enough liquid around them for them to cook without sticking to the pot. Add more stock or water if the beans appear to become too dry. Once the beans are tender, remove the pot from the oven.

5 Raise the oven temperature to 400°F.

6 Add the kale to the beans in handfuls, stirring and folding so that the heat of the beans begins to wilt the kale. Once all of the kale has been incorporated, layer the slices of pancetta over the top of the beans to cover them completely. Scatter the sage leaves randomly over the pancetta. Return the beans to the oven and bake, uncovered, until the beans are bubbling and the pancetta and sage leaves have crisped, 25 to 30 minutes. For the most dramatic presentation, bring the bean pot to the table and serve hot, family-style.

October Chili

I have to confess that I am elated that my son's years of agonizing over Halloween costumes and going trick-or-treating with friends are now a thing of the past. This means my life doesn't have to center around remedying last-minute costume malfunctions, procuring candy, and monitoring its intake. Instead, I can do more pleasurable things like lovingly putting together a pot of Halloween chili laced with pumpkin and black beans. This festive chili would also hit the spot at any autumnal football tailgate gathering. I tend to go overboard with my chili embellishments and top my own bowl with almost everything but the kitchen sink. Feel free to choose any or all of the suggestions listed below—or to even add a few more of your own. SERVES 6

2 tablespoons extra virgin olive oil

1 medium-size onion, peeled and chopped

3 cloves garlic, peeled and minced

1 large yellow bell pepper, stemmed, seeded, and diced

1 poblano pepper, stemmed, seeded, and diced

1 jalapeño pepper, stemmed, seeded, and finely minced

1½ teaspoons ground cumin

1½ teaspoons ancho chile powder

1½ teaspoons dried oregano

3 cups chicken or turkey stock or broth, homemade or good-quality store-bought

3 tablespoons cream sherry

1 can (15 ounces) solid-pack pumpkin, preferably organic

1 can (14½ ounces) diced tomatoes

1 can (about 15 ounces) black beans, rinsed and drained

3 cups cooked turkey, chicken, or roast pork, cut into bite-size chunks

This pretty picture is testament to why quaint Vermont villages are among the most popular autumn leaf-peeping destinations in all of New England.

Salt and freshly ground black pepper

Sliced scallions, diced avocado, minced fresh cilantro, shredded sharp orange cheddar cheese, and/or sour cream, for serving

1 Heat the olive oil in a Dutch oven or other large, heavy pot over medium heat. Add the onion, garlic, and the bell, poblano, and jalapeño peppers. Cook until quite soft, 8 to 10 minutes. Stir in the cumin, chile powder, and oregano and cook until fragrant, about 1 minute.

2 Add the stock or broth, sherry, pumpkin, and tomatoes, stirring until evenly combined. Stir in the black beans and meat and season with salt and black pepper to taste. Let the chili simmer, partially covered, over medium-low heat until all the flavors have melded harmoniously, 45 minutes to 1 hour.

3 Serve the chili hot, ladled into wide shallow bowls to allow plenty of surface space for topping with your favorite chili accoutrements. If making the chili in advance, cool and refrigerate, covered, for up to 3 days. Reheat over medium-low heat.

It is easy to succumb to clever signage and the invitation to pop into a tasting room and sample the local quaff when meandering the New England back roads.

Vermonster Chili

Although I have never ventured to enter a chili cook-off or contest, making a big pot of chili is something I really enjoy doing. My enthusiasm is twofold, geared first to the ingredients I put into the pot and then shifted to the number of embellishments I can offer to top off the chili in an attempt to elevate it to over-the-top status. While I have on occasion made Texas-style chili with cubed meat, I do really prefer chili made with ground meat and this is the type of chili that is most prevalent throughout New England. Having been raised in the land of baked beans and bean suppers, I wouldn't dream of not adding beans to a pot of chili. Furthermore, I discovered I really like the flavor, texture, and visual contrast a can of hominy imparts to chili, even if such an addition is not common in my neck of the woods.

While I don't always make my chili with beer, its addition is a good way to sample intriguing craft beers from New England breweries. Likewise, I find the heartier, headier, hoppier, darker beers better suited to the pot than a pilsner. In this recipe, I have used Vermont's Rock Art Brewery Vermonster barley wine beer as some of the cooking liquid. The beer is indeed a monster of a beer with a dark mahogany color and an earthy, malty, and boozy flavor I think to be excellent for cooking but not terribly palatable for sipping. There are many other New England craft beers that would also work well in this recipe and I encourage you to seek out local breweries. One particular beer I have had equal success with is Allagash Black, brewed in Portland, Maine. This Belgian-style stout is brewed with chocolate malt, a great complement to the many Mexican seasonings in the chili. For an even heartier meal, serve the chili over white or brown rice. SERVES 6 TO 8

For the chili

2½ tablespoons extra virgin olive oil

1 large onion, peeled and minced

4 cloves garlic, peeled and minced

1 red bell pepper, stemmed, seeded, and cut into ¼-inch dice

1 yellow bell pepper, stemmed, seeded, and cut into ¼-inch dice

1 poblano pepper, stemmed, seeded, and cut into ¼-inch dice

1 large jalapeño pepper, stemmed, seeded, and minced

2½ pounds ground beef sirloin

2 tablespoons mild chili powder

1 teaspoon chipotle chile powder

2 teaspoons dried oregano

2 teaspoons ground cumin

1 teaspoon cumin seeds

1 can (28 ounces) crushed tomatoes

1½ cups (12 ounces) Vermonster beer or other malty, dark beer

1½ to 2 cups beef stock or broth, homemade or store-bought

Sea salt and freshly ground black pepper

1 can (about 15 ounces) black beans, drained

1 can (about 15 ounces) pinto or cannellini
beans, drained

1 can (15½ ounces) hominy, drained

Your choice of chili embellishments
(the more the tastier)

Freshly shredded sharp Vermont cheddar
cheese

Sliced scallions

Tons of minced cilantro

Seeded and diced tomatoes

Sour cream

Diced avocado

Hot sauce

Lime wedges

Tortilla chips

1   Make the chili: Heat the olive oil in a Dutch oven
or other large, heavy pot over medium heat. Add the
onion, garlic, red and yellow bell peppers, poblano
pepper, and jalapeño pepper and cook, stirring occasionally, until quite soft, about 10 minutes.

2   Add the ground sirloin and cook, breaking the
meat into smaller pieces with the back of a wooden
spoon, until the meat has lost its pink color and is just
beginning to brown, 5 to 7 minutes. Stir in the mild
chili powder, chipotle chile powder, oregano, cumin,
and cumin seeds and cook, stirring, to blend in the
spices, about 2 minutes. Add the crushed tomatoes,
beer, and 1½ cups of beef stock or broth and stir to
blend. Season with salt and black pepper to taste.
Let the chili come to a simmer, reduce the heat to
medium-low, cover the pot with the lid slightly ajar,
and simmer gently, stirring occasionally, until fragrant and richly flavored, about 1 hour.

3   Uncover the chili and add the beans and hominy,
stirring to incorporate them evenly. If the chili seems
too thick, thin it with up to ½ cup additional stock
or broth. I like my chili to be a bit on the soupy side
but not brothy. Let the chili simmer, uncovered, stirring occasionally, until the beans and hominy absorb
the chili flavors, about 15 minutes. Taste for seasoning,
adding more salt and/or black pepper, if needed.

4   Arrange an array of any and all of the embellishments for the chili you wish to offer at the table. Ladle
the hot chili into wide bowls and let everyone top off
the bowls of chili with the embellishments, according
to personal preference and delight.

Salad Days

> "To remember a successful salad is generally to remember a successful dinner; at all events, the perfect dinner necessarily includes the perfect salad."
> —George H. Ellwanger, *The Pleasures of the Table* (1902)

The making of salads, whether a simple leafy green affair or a labor-intensive chopped extravaganza, is my greatest culinary passion. If I didn't have a family to feed or cookbooks to write containing chapters above and beyond salads, I personally would eat salads for lunch and dinner almost every day of the week, year round. If you haven't brushed up on your Shakespeare recently, you may not know that the etymology of the term *salad days* can be traced, not to globally-warmed hot and humid summer days or fad diets, but to the great "Bard of Avon" who coined the phrase in the play *Antony and Cleopatra*, eons ago in 1606. When Cleopatra's servant Charmion questions the intensity of her love for Antony, noting that the beautiful Egyptian queen had once expressed the same emotions for Julius Caesar, Cleopatra dismisses the concern explaining: "My salad days, / When I was green in judgment: cold in blood, / To say as I said then." While this reference could perhaps tempt one to try to bestow some sort of credit on William Shakespeare for the existence of Caesar Salad as well, Googling galore easily convinces one that Italian restaurateur Caesar Cardini invented the now wildly popular Caesar Salad at his restaurant in Tijuana, Mexico, in the 1920s.

But I digress. Fortunately the meaning of *salad days* has changed over centuries of time from denoting foolish youth and naiveté to signifying, far more positively, a time when one is at the peak of his or her abilities—which is exactly how I feel whenever I indulge in my passion for making, presenting, and savoring salads. The salads in this chapter are ones I toss to serve as a separate salad course or to accompany many a New England chowder, soup, stew, and alfresco summer meal as a side enhancement. Don't despair over the chapter's relative brevity because there are plenty more substantial salad recipes tucked throughout this book in chapters such as For the Love of Lobster, Bivalve Bliss, and Picnic Pastimes & Tailgating Traditions.

In the meantime, I invite you to swoon seasonally along with me over Summer's Best Tomatoes with Burrata and Basil and Fresh Corn Salad on a warm August evening or to make a winter steak night all the more memorable with an abundant bowl of my favorite Winter Chopped Salad or The Pitcher Inn's Brussels Sprout Caesar Salad.

My Mother's Cucumber Salad

When I first started cooking, I felt compelled to add trendy ingredients to some of my mother's tried-and-true recipes. Now that I have been cooking for more than thirty years and have seen numerous culinary fads come and go, I have developed a greater respect for the uncomplicated delectability of many of my mother's recipes, and none more so than this terrific cucumber salad. I have never seen a cucumber salad made quite this way, but at the same time, I have never tasted one I love as much. You can make this salad with either Greek-style plain yogurt or sour cream and I have found I personally like a 50/50 combination of the two. If you grow your own cucumbers or can get unwaxed cucumbers from a local farm stand, by all means use them because then you can leave on pinstripes of skin to further enhance the salad's cooling visual appeal. SERVES 6 TO 8

4 firm cucumbers

1 small red onion, peeled, halved, and cut into crescent slivers

1 tablespoon kosher salt

⅓ cup cider vinegar

1 cup sour cream or plain Greek yogurt with at least 2 percent fat, or a combination of the two

3 tablespoons minced fresh dill

Freshly ground black pepper

Why settle for a single cucumber when you can buy them by the pretty pink bushel to make a host of cooling summer salads!

1   If the cucumbers are waxed, peel them completely. If the cucumbers are unwaxed, peel them in stripes, leaving 3 or 4 pinstripes of skin intact. Thinly slice the cucumbers.

2   Combine the cucumbers and red onion in a large, shallow mixing bowl, sprinkle them with the salt, and toss to coat evenly. Let stand for 20 minutes. Add the vinegar, toss again, and let stand for an additional 20 minutes.

3   Drain off the liquid by placing everything in a colander in the sink. Press gently on the cucumbers and onion to extract as much liquid as possible. Transfer the cucumber mixture to a mixing bowl and add the sour cream or yogurt and dill, tossing well to coat the cucumbers evenly. Season the cucumber salad with pepper to taste, transfer it to a serving dish, and refrigerate it, covered, for at least 1 hour before serving. Serve the cucumber salad chilled. The salad is best served the day it's made, but will keep for up to 3 days, covered, in the refrigerator.

Summer Cucumber and Tomato Salad

During the summer months, I usually make a big Greek salad at least once a week. When I want something simpler or perhaps a cucumber salad without the dairy in my mother's recipe, I make this attractive and very tasty salad. You can vary the fresh herb accent according to your menu, whim, or herb garden bounty. Basil, dill, and mint are all good options. Sometimes, but certainly not always, I'll throw in a handful of pitted kalamata olives. SERVES 4 TO 6

4 medium-size ripe tomatoes (red, yellow, heirloom, or a combination), cored and each cut into 6 to 8 wedges

2 firm cucumbers, peeled if waxed, unpeeled if unwaxed

1 small red onion, peeled and sliced into thin rings

3 tablespoons coarsely torn fresh basil or mint leaves, or 2 tablespoons minced fresh dill

2½ tablespoons red or white wine vinegar

⅓ to ½ cup extra virgin olive oil

Sea salt and freshly ground black pepper

1　Place the tomatoes in a glass or ceramic salad bowl. Cut the cucumbers in half lengthwise and then slice them into ½-inch-thick half-circles. Add the cucumber slices to the tomatoes along with the red onion and herb of choice.

2　Drizzle the wine vinegar and enough olive oil to suit your taste over the tomatoes and cucumbers. Season with salt and pepper to taste. Let the salad stand at room temperature for 30 minutes before serving or refrigerate it, covered, for 30 minutes to 1 hour if it is a hot night and you would like to have a cold salad.

Tomatoes San Gimignano

While this may not sound like a quintessentially New England recipe, I learned to make this splendid salad when I arranged a lunch at a Tuscan farmhouse and winery in San Gimignano owned and run by friends of mine from Nantucket. The gathering was planned for members of a Butterfield & Robinson bicycle tour I was leading, and everyone swooned over hostess Pam Jelleme's platter of lush and garlicky chopped tomatoes and basil speckled with crunchy ciabatta croutons and crumbles of creamy blue cheese. Pam confessed that there was nothing especially Italian about the salad but that she had invented it to indulge in her love of blue cheese.

I now make the salad all the time, often to highlight a New England blue cheese, but mostly because it tastes just as spectacular in southern Massachusetts as it did in San Gimignano and never fails to garner instant fans. SERVES 6 TO 8 AS A SALAD, 12 TO 15 AS AN ANTIPASTO

¾ cup extra virgin olive oil

2 cups ciabatta or other rustic country white bread cut into ½-inch cubes

2½ pounds cherry, grape, or other small tomatoes, cut in half

5 cloves garlic, peeled and minced

1½ tablespoons balsamic vinegar

Sea salt and freshly ground pepper

½ cup slivered fresh basil leaves

8 to 10 ounces crumbled Gorgonzola, Roquefort, or a creamy New England blue cheese, such as Berkshire Blue, Green Mountain Blue, and Bayley Hazen Blue (1¾ cups)

1 Heat 4 tablespoons of the olive oil in a medium-size skillet over medium heat. Add the bread and toss it to coat on all sides with the oil. Reduce the heat to medium-low and cook, stirring occasionally, until the bread is golden on all sides, about 20 minutes. Remove the skillet from the heat and keep the croutons in a dry place, such as a cold oven with the door shut, until ready to use.

2 Place the tomatoes, garlic, balsamic vinegar, and remaining ½ cup of olive oil in a mixing bowl and stir to mix. Season the tomatoes with salt and pepper to taste and then gently fold in the basil. Let the tomato salad sit at room temperature for at least 1 hour or up to 3 hours.

3 Thirty minutes before serving, transfer the tomato salad to a large and attractive, shallow serving dish. Sprinkle the blue cheese evenly all over the tomatoes and then dot them evenly with the croutons. Toss all very gently so that the blue cheese and croutons pretty much remain on top of the salad but manage to get splashed with some of the salad juices. Let the tomato salad stand for 30 minutes at room temperature, then serve it as a salad or part of a larger antipasto assortment.

Heirloom Tomato and Watermelon Salad

In my family, we are huge fans of the traditional Greek salad known as *Horiatiki Salata*—a combination of chunky tomatoes, peppers, cucumbers, and red onions, accented with oregano, crumbled feta cheese, and black olives. One hot July evening when my husband, Nigel, was testing an experimental Greek seasoning blend on grilled lamb to add to a newly envisioned line of "one-shot-seasonings" for his Coastal Goods specialty food company,

I decided to do a variation on our go-to Greek salad. Everyone raved about the resulting and extraordinarily refreshing combination of tomatoes, cucumbers, watermelon, and mint contrasting with briny crumbled feta cheese and earthy kalamata olives. A new favorite summer salad was born. Dicing a combination of different types and colors of heirloom tomatoes makes this modern salad as appealing to the eye as it is to the palate, especially during the hottest spells of New England summer weather. SERVES 6

4 medium-size, vine-ripened heirloom tomatoes, cored and cut into ¾-inch chunks

1 large cucumber, peeled, halved lengthwise, seeded, and cut into ¾-inch chunks

3 cups seedless watermelon, cut into ¾-inch chunks (measured after dicing)

½ cup pitted and halved kalamata olives

2 tablespoons thinly slivered fresh mint leaves

2 tablespoons minced fresh cilantro

2 tablespoons fresh lemon juice

3 tablespoons extra virgin olive oil

Sea salt and freshly ground black pepper

4 ounces (1 cup) crumbled feta cheese

1 Toss together the tomatoes, cucumbers, watermelon, and kalamata olives in a large, shallow serving bowl. If you wish to serve the salad chilled (optional, but extra-refreshing if very hot), cover and chill in the refrigerator for 1 hour.

2 When ready to serve, scatter the mint and cilantro over the top of the salad and drizzle with the lemon juice and olive oil; toss gently until all the ingredients are evenly combined and lightly coated with the lemon juice and olive oil. Season with salt and pepper to taste, erring on the lighter side as the feta will be adding salty flavor as well. Scatter the crumbled feta cheese evenly over the top of the salad and serve at once.

Summer's Best Tomatoes with Burrata and Basil

I have been making this simple but sensational tomato salad for years, but only recently have I been able to take it to the next and ultimate level by replacing the more customary fresh mozzarella with its far richer and irresistibly creamy and oozy cousin, burrata. Indeed, New England has gone seemingly burrata crazy over the past couple of years. Maplebrook Farm in Bennington, Vermont, paved the way in putting burrata on our New England map when they hired a cheese maker from Puglia to make burrata for them. Maplebrook Farm's burrata went on to garner all sorts of awards and is now widely distributed throughout New England. Fiore di Nonno in Somerville, Massachusetts, is yet another good source for this coveted Italian cheese.

Years ago, I was scolded by an Italian woman for putting balsamic vinegar on my sliced tomato salads and told in no uncertain terms that Italians use only olive oil on their tomato salads. I am not sure if this is actually 100 percent true but I have never used any vinegar since on my Caprese-style sliced tomato salads and believe my tomato salads, which I make almost every single summer evening when tomatoes are in season, are all the more perfect for this admonishment. Don't even think of making this salad unless you have the very best ingredients on hand. Your tomatoes need not be heirlooms but they must be the lushest, local vine-ripened tomatoes you can get your hands on. Mine usually come from my backyard, Bartlett's Farm on Nantucket, Hart Farm on Cape Cod, or Chase's Daily in Belfast, Maine. SERVES 4 TO 6

3 very large vine-ripened summer tomatoes, heirloom, beefsteak, or any combination of favorites

Small handful of vine-ripened cherry and/or pear tomatoes (optional)

4 to 6 tablespoons best-quality extra virgin olive oil, possibly a bit more

Fleur de sel or other crunchy sea salt and freshly ground black pepper

6 large fresh basil leaves, thinly slivered, plus basil leaves or sprigs for garnish

8 to 12 ounces burrata cheese

1 Core the tomatoes and cut them crosswise into slices ½ inch to ¾ inch thick. Arrange the slices in an overlapping pattern on a large platter. If you are using cherry and/or pear tomatoes (I almost always have them growing on my deck), cut them lengthwise in half and scatter them, cut sides facing down, over the larger sliced tomatoes. Drizzle 4 tablespoons of the olive oil evenly over the tomatoes.

2 Season the tomatoes generously with *fleur de sel* and pepper and sprinkle the slivered basil leaves over the top. Break the burrata into small, oozy, bite-size blobs and arrange these evenly over and in between the tomatoes. Drizzle at least 2 more tablespoons of olive oil over the entire salad, adding even more if deemed necessary or you are simply in the mood.

3 Garnish the tomato platter in an artistically pleasing fashion with whole basil leaves or small top sprigs and blossoms. The salad can be served at once but I usually let it stand for 15 to 30 minutes before serving. If there are any leftover tomatoes, I cover them, leave them overnight at room temperature, and tuck them into a BLT, or other sandwich the following day.

Fresh Corn Salad

This is the salad to make when local summer corn is at its tastiest and most abundant. The ingredients are few but of high quality to do justice to the sweet savor of the corn kernels. I like to serve the salad at alfresco lobster dinners as a counterbalance to the messy process of dissecting the lobsters at the table. It also pairs wonderfully with all manner of grilled fish. SERVES 6 TO 8

Ice

1 tablespoon kosher salt

8 ears very fresh local corn, husked

3 tablespoons white wine or Champagne vinegar

½ cup extra virgin olive oil

½ cup minced fresh chives

½ cup minced fresh dill

⅓ cup toasted pine nuts (see Box, page 70)

1½ ounces (⅔ cup) freshly grated Parmigiano-Reggiano cheese

Sea salt and freshly ground black pepper

1   Have a large bowl of ice water ready. Bring a large pot of water to a boil, add the salt, and cook the ears of corn until the kernels are crisp-tender, about 3 minutes. Drain the corn well and immediately immerse the ears in the ice water to stop the cooking and set the color. When the corn has cooled, cut the kernels from the cob, breaking any clumps of kernels apart with your fingers as you work.

2   Place the corn kernels in a large mixing bowl and add the vinegar and olive oil, tossing well to coat all the kernels. Stir in the chives, dill, pine nuts, and Parmesan cheese. Toss the salad again and season it with salt and pepper to taste. If desired, refrigerate the salad, covered, for a few hours before serving or serve it at room temperature right after making.

Broccoli Salad with Dried Cranberries and Toasted Almonds

I have long been drawn to eating raw food. Ceviche, carpaccio, and oysters on the half shell rank extremely high on the list of foods I adore. I never really thought of putting vegetables in this raw addiction category until I started playing around with this popular potluck raw broccoli salad. More often than not it is made poorly with bacon that has lost its crispiness and contains way too much mayonnaise. This rendition is the antithesis of every bad raw broccoli salad I have ever sampled and is one that I dream about when it is not on hand in my refrigerator. SERVES 6 TO 8

For the broccoli salad

1½ to 2 pounds fresh broccoli

¾ cup shredded peeled carrots

6 scallions, both white and tender green parts, trimmed and sliced thinly on the diagonal

¾ cup dried cranberries

¾ cup skin-on sliced almonds, lightly toasted (see Box, page 70)

½ cup fresh cilantro leaves, coarsely chopped

For the sesame vinaigrette

3 tablespoons apple cider vinegar

1 tablespoon pure maple syrup

1½ tablespoons soy sauce, or more to taste

Pinch of hot red pepper flakes

½ cup vegetable or canola oil

1½ tablespoons Asian (dark) sesame oil

1   Make the broccoli salad: Trim away and discard the tough lower stems of the broccoli. Break the

broccoli into bite-size florets and cut the remaining tender stems into ⅓-inch-thick slices. Place the broccoli in a large mixing bowl, add the carrots, scallions, dried cranberries, almonds, and cilantro and toss to mix.

2 Make the sesame vinaigrette: Place the cider vinegar, maple syrup, soy sauce, and hot red pepper flakes in a small bowl and whisk to mix. Gradually whisk in the vegetable and sesame oils to make a light emulsion.

3 Pour the vinaigrette over the broccoli salad, tossing to coat well. Taste the broccoli salad for seasoning, sprinkling more soy sauce over it if it is not salty enough. Refrigerate the broccoli salad for at least 1 hour before serving. The salad can be refrigerated, covered, for up to 3 days.

When leaving Nantucket by ferry, it's a long-standing tradition to toss a penny overboard as you round the Brant Point lighthouse to insure a return visit.

Poppy Seed Coleslaw

I used to teach this coleslaw recipe in the summer series of cooking classes I hosted during the 1990s on Nantucket. I had pretty much forgotten about it until some of my former students told me how much they had loved the coleslaw and went on to report that they were still making it to rave reviews many years later. I recently tweaked the original recipe to make it slightly less sweet and have added a few vegetables to heighten the contrasting colors. The coleslaw makes a bright and excellent accompaniment to all manner of grilled fare. SERVES 8 TO 10

1 medium-size head green cabbage, cored and thinly shredded

1 large red onion, peeled and sliced into thin rings

1 red bell pepper, stemmed, seeded, and cut into thin strips

1 yellow bell pepper, stemmed, seeded, and cut into thin strips

1 orange bell pepper, stemmed, seeded, and cut into thin strips

2 large carrots, peeled and cut into thin 3-inch-long strips, or shredded on the large holes of a box grater or with the shredding blade of a food processor

½ cup sugar

⅔ cup canola or vegetable oil

⅔ cup cider vinegar

1 tablespoon dry mustard

3 tablespoons poppy seeds

1 tablespoon kosher salt

⅓ cup heavy (whipping) cream

Freshly ground black pepper

Red cabbage leaves (optional), for serving

1 Place the cabbage, red onion, bell peppers, carrots, and sugar in a very large mixing bowl and toss to mix.

2 Place the oil, cider vinegar, dry mustard, poppy seeds, salt, and cream in a nonreactive saucepan and whisk to mix. Let come to a boil over medium-high heat, whisking constantly. Reduce the heat to medium-low and let simmer until the flavors blend, about 2 minutes. Pour the hot dressing over the coleslaw, tossing very well to coat. Season the coleslaw with freshly ground pepper to taste and toss again. Cover the coleslaw and refrigerate it for at least 12 hours to let the flavors mellow. Serve the coleslaw chilled, arranged atop a bed of contrasting whole red cabbage leaves, if desired. The coleslaw will keep, covered, in the refrigerator for up to 4 days.

The outer beaches of Cape Cod can be as beautiful in the winter as they are popular during the height of the summer season.

Winter Chopped Salad

Whenever too much winter weather begins to wreak havoc with my general culinary enthusiasm, I know it is time to lift spirits by having a great steak for dinner, accompanied by this Italian-American-style steak house salad. The salad is winter's equivalent to a summer Greek salad—chockful of vegetables but vegetables that are for the most part easily procured in the winter produce aisles of well-stocked New England supermarkets. While the tomatoes in the salad are never going to be as tasty as summer tomatoes, those tomatoes now sold year-round on the vine will work perfectly fine because they become infused with the bold flavors of the salad's olives and anchovies. SERVES 4 TO 6

2 cloves garlic, peeled and finely minced

6 oil-packed anchovy fillets, drained and finely minced

¾ teaspoon crumbled dried oregano, preferably Greek oregano

2 tablespoons red wine vinegar

2 tablespoons freshly squeezed lemon juice

1 large red, yellow, or orange bell pepper, stemmed, seeded, and cut into ½-inch chunks

½ small red onion, peeled and cut into ¼-inch-wide slivers

2 to 3 medium-size decent winter tomatoes, cut into ½-inch chunks

2 ribs celery, preferably with leaves, cut on the diagonal into ⅓-inch-wide slices

½ cup imported green or black olives, or a combination of the two, pitted and coarsely chopped

About 6 tablespoons extra virgin olive oil

Sea salt and freshly ground black pepper

1 romaine lettuce heart, chopped into ½-inch pieces

2 cups baby arugula or watercress leaves

1 ripe Hass avocado

1   Place the garlic, anchovies, oregano, red wine vinegar, and 1 tablespoon of the lemon juice in a large salad bowl and whisk together. Add the bell pepper, red onion, tomatoes, celery, and olives and stir to mix. Drizzle 3 tablespoons of the olive oil on top, toss well, and season with salt and black pepper to taste. The salad may be prepared up to this point 30 to 40 minutes in advance; let it stand at room temperature.

2   When ready to serve, add the romaine and arugula or watercress to the salad mixture. Peel, pit, and cut the avocado into ½-inch chunks. Drizzle the remaining 1 tablespoon of lemon juice over the avocado and add it to the salad. Toss the salad to mix and then add enough of the remaining 3 tablespoons of olive oil to finish the dressing and balance the flavors. Serve the salad at once.

Mood-Enhancing Winter Salad

No matter how upbeat a person you are, winters in New England with their biting chill and sunlight challenged hours, can take a toll on cheeriness. What used to be called the winter blues now goes by the fancier name of seasonal affective disorder and medically vetted cures include light therapy and prescription medications. Having spent many winters out on Nantucket Island, aptly nicknamed the Grey Lady of the Sea, I would find myself suffering more from a pervasive winter gray mood than blue, and was lucky enough to discover a culinary cure one February evening when my friend Toby Greenberg first served me this salad, employing exceptionally tasty Florida oranges she had ordered to support a Nantucket Public School fund-raising effort. The salad, like so many of Toby's truly terrific recipes, has been in her repertoire for decades.

The vibrant tried-and-true combination, for me, beats anything the doctor would have ordered. Since I find the taste of any citrus such an instant winter pick-me-up, I have added an extra orange to my version of Toby's recipe. SERVES 6

For the sherry vinaigrette

2 tablespoons red wine vinegar

2 tablespoons dry sherry

¾ teaspoon fine sea salt

¼ teaspoon freshly ground black pepper

½ cup extra virgin olive oil

For the salad

2 romaine lettuce hearts

1 small red onion, peeled and sliced into thin rings

3 navel oranges, peeled, pith removed, and sliced into sections

¾ cup pitted kalamata olives, sliced

Sea salt and freshly ground black pepper (optional)

1   To make the sherry vinaigrette: Whisk together the vinegar, dry sherry, salt, and pepper in a small bowl. Slowly whisk in the olive oil to make a light emulsion. Set aside.

2   Tear the romaine hearts into bite-size pieces and place them in a large salad bowl. Add the red onion, orange sections, and olives and toss to combine. Drizzle enough dressing over the salad to coat everything lightly and evenly, tossing well. Taste for salt and pepper and add a bit more of each, if desired. Divide the salad among 6 salad plates and serve at once. If there is leftover vinaigrette, it will keep in the refrigerator, covered, for a week, a good thing since you will likely want to make a few more private servings of the salad to keep spirits up through the week. Bring the vinaigrette back to room temperature before using.

Grilled Romaine Hearts with Blue Cheese and Bacon

It is hard to imagine a salad tastier than a well-made Caesar, but this kindred, warm salad of grilled romaine hearts topped with a creamy blue cheese dressing and crisp bacon is a worthy contender. SERVES 6

For the creamy blue cheese dressing

1 shallot, peeled and finely minced

1 clove garlic, peeled and finely minced

2 tablespoons freshly squeezed lemon juice

1 cup mayonnaise, Hellmann's or homemade (page 129)

½ cup sour cream

1¼ cups (4 ounces) crumbled creamy blue cheese, preferably from New England, such as Berkshire Blue or Green Mountain Blue

Sea salt and freshly ground black pepper

For the grilled romaine salad

12 slices New England apple or hardwood-smoked bacon

3 romaine lettuce hearts, preferably organic

½ cup extra virgin olive oil

3 oil-packed anchovy fillets, drained and finely minced

1 clove garlic, peeled and finely minced

Sea salt and freshly ground black pepper

1   Make the creamy blue cheese dressing: Combine the shallot, 1 clove of garlic, and the lemon juice in a small bowl. Whisk in the mayonnaise and sour cream until very smooth. Stir in the blue cheese and season the dressing with salt and pepper to taste. Store the dressing, covered, in the refrigerator until ready to use. It will keep for at least 1 week.

2   Make the grilled romaine salad: Set up a charcoal or gas grill and preheat it to medium-high.

3   Place the bacon in a skillet and cook over medium heat until nicely crisped, 7 to 9 minutes. Transfer the bacon to a paper towel–lined plate to drain. Cut the romaine hearts in half lengthwise and trim away any limp or unruly outer leaves. Trim the tough lower parts of the bases but leave enough of the core to keep the lettuce leaves attached and intact.

4   Place the olive oil, anchovies, and 1 clove of garlic in a small bowl and whisk to mix. Arrange the romaine heart halves on a flat tray, cut side up, and brush them all over with the olive oil mixture. Season the romaine with salt and pepper to taste.

5   Place the romaine heart halves, cut sides facing up, on the grill grate. Grill the romaine until the outer leaves have begun to char, 2 to 3 minutes. Flip the hearts over and continue grilling until the lettuce is heated through, 2 to 3 minutes more.

6   Transfer the grilled romaine to individual serving plates, placing 1 half heart cut side up on each plate. Spoon a few tablespoons of the blue cheese dressing over each half. Crumble the bacon and top each romaine half with a generous sprinkling of the crumbled bacon. Serve the salad warm.

Chopped Kale with Cranberries and Feta

Mixed salads with dried cranberries, toasted nuts, and crumbled blue cheese or goat cheese are immensely popular throughout New England. The Harrisville General Store in New Hampshire makes an extra healthy variation of this

combination by substituting shredded raw kale for the more traditional mixed greens, and the salad has purportedly become a favorite with *Yankee* magazine staffers who have offices nearby. In my version of the salad, I like to use a mix of shredded kale and savoy cabbage to lend both color and textural contrast and I favor using Narragansett Creamery's unique Salty Sea Feta—an old-world-style feta that boasts being "brined in the ocean," only fitting for a cheese made in the Ocean State of Rhode Island.

The salad makes a colorful, slawlike side to serve with luncheon soups or sandwiches and keeps quite well in the refrigerator for two to three days. SERVES 6 TO 8

For the dressing

1½ tablespoons sherry vinegar

1½ tablespoons freshly squeezed lemon juice

¾ teaspoon sea salt

1 small shallot, peeled and finely minced

½ cup extra virgin olive oil

For the salad

4 cups finely hand-shredded curly green kale leaves, tough ribs discarded

3 cups finely hand-shredded savoy cabbage leaves

½ cup dried cranberries

½ cup coarsely chopped toasted walnuts (see Box, page 70)

4 ounces (1 heaping cup) crumbled feta cheese, preferably Narragansett Creamery's Salty Sea Feta

Sea salt and freshly ground black pepper

1 Make the dressing: Place the sherry vinegar, lemon juice, salt, and shallot in a small mixing bowl and whisk to mix. Let the vinegar mixture stand for about 10 minutes to soften the shallot and mellow its pungency. Slowly whisk in the olive oil to make a light emulsion. Set the dressing aside briefly.

2 Make the salad: Place the kale and savoy cabbage in a large mixing bowl and toss to combine evenly. Mix in the dried cranberries, walnuts, and feta cheese and toss again.

3 Pour the dressing over the salad and toss to coat all the ingredients evenly. Taste for seasoning, adding salt and pepper to taste. Serve the salad at once or refrigerate it, covered, for up to 3 days.

The Pitcher Inn's Brussels Sprout Caesar Salad

The white clapboard Pitcher Inn in the tiny village of Warren, Vermont, is the sort of place that makes guests feel as if they have died and gone to heaven in New England. The themed guest quarters pay homage to Vermont history and offer luxurious comfort and respite after you have engaged in any of the area's many outdoor pleasures.

Chef Susan Schickler's food is some of the heartiest and most delicious in all of New England, somehow magically managing to reflect a seductive feminine touch in every bite. This unique brussels sprout salad captures the essence of what I admire about the creativity Sue fuses to the most basic seasonal New England ingredients. Sue humbly insists that the salad "is not something I thought of but just a dish I had at a friend's house." The pedigree of the ingredients makes the combination sing, so be sure to use the best extra virgin olive oil and authentic Parmigiano-Reggiano and Pecorino Romano cheese imported from Italy. At the Inn the salad is placed in ring molds and then unmolded onto salad plates, but I nestle it onto cabbage or radicchio leaves as a less fussy home option. Serve the salad fireside on a cold winter evening to re-create The Pitcher Inn's warmth and romantic ambience. SERVES 4

3 tablespoons freshly squeezed lemon juice

Sea salt and freshly ground black pepper

½ cup extra virgin olive oil

12 ounces brussels sprouts, stems trimmed and any yellow outer leaves discarded

1½ ounces (⅔ cup) freshly grated Parmigiano-Reggiano cheese, plus a bit more shaved for serving

1 ounce (⅓ cup) freshly grated aged Italian Pecorino Romano cheese

½ cup chopped walnuts, lightly toasted (see Box, below)

4 whole cabbage or radicchio leaves (optional), for serving

1 Place the lemon juice, 1 teaspoon of salt, and ½ teaspoon of pepper in a small bowl and whisk to combine. Slowly whisk in the olive oil to make a light emulsion. Set the lemon vinaigrette aside briefly.

2 Slice the brussels sprouts crosswise as thinly as possible, either by hand with a sharp knife or by using a mandoline. Place the brussels sprouts in a large mixing bowl and add enough of the vinaigrette to coat the brussels sprouts lightly all over but not drench them. Add the Parmigiano-Reggiano and Pecorino Romano cheeses and ⅓ cup of the walnuts. Toss gently until all of the ingredients are evenly combined. Taste for seasoning, adding more salt and/or pepper as needed.

Techniques for Toasting Nuts

I frequently call for lightly toasted and toasted nuts in my recipes because toasting dramatically enhances a nut's nutty flavor. While toasting nuts is a simple task, I always caution students in my cooking classes that unwatched nuts will usually end up as burned nuts, a costly and cuss-invoking mistake when nuts such as pine nuts and hazelnuts are called for in a recipe.

More often than not, I toast nuts by spreading them in a single layer in a ceramic baking dish or metal baking tray and then pop them into a 350°F to 375°F oven. Depending on the nut and its size, toasting can take as few as 7 or 8 minutes or as long as 15 minutes. A toaster oven may be used for small batches if you prefer not to heat up your primary oven. The key with either appliance is to keep your eye tuned to the toasting process. It is recommended to give the nuts a stir or two while toasting to ensure even toasting results. The nuts are done when they are intoxicatingly fragrant and crisped to a light golden brown.

If you are the sort of cook who can become easily distracted, I suggest toasting nuts via the stovetop method, as it requires your undivided attention. Heat a skillet, small or large enough to hold the designated amount of nuts in a single layer, on a burner over medium heat. No oil will be needed because the nuts will release their own oils as they toast. Spread the nuts in the hot skillet and stir diligently and constantly with a wooden or silicone spatula until the nuts are intoxicatingly fragrant and turn an even light golden brown in color. I find this technique takes a bit less time than toasting in the oven because the heat is more direct. Just be sure to transfer the toasted nuts from the hot skillet to another dish or tray so they do not continue to toast and possibly burn in the hot skillet.

When toasting nuts with skins, such as hazelnuts, the skins can be easily removed after toasting. Let the nuts cool for a few minutes and then enclose them in a clean cloth dishtowel. Rub the nuts vigorously with the palms of your hands and most of the skins should slip off. A few stubborn bits of skin may remain, but do not drive yourself nuts trying to remove every last bit because consuming a bit of the skins is perfectly safe.

3 To serve, line 4 salad plates with either a cabbage or radicchio leaf, if desired. Divide the salad among the 4 plates, nestling it attractively on the leaves, if using, then sprinkle a few shavings of Parmigiano-Reggiano and the remaining walnuts over and around each salad. Serve at once.

Green Garden Pea and Arugula Salad

This very green and tasty salad makes a seasonally pleasing late spring or early summer first course. Seal Cove Farm's Olga is one of New England's most unique cheeses—a washed-rind cheese made from a blend of raw cow and goat milk. It's named after a young student from the Ukraine who worked at the farm in Maine from 2006 to 2007 and who encouraged experimentation with mixed-milk cheeses. If you are unable to procure a wedge of Olga, Manchego makes a decent substitute, although the flavor profile will shift slightly to that of sheep's milk. SERVES 6

Ice

3 cups water

1½ cups freshly shelled green peas

6 cups baby arugula, rinsed and spun dry

¼ cup slivered fresh mint leaves

1½ tablespoons freshly squeezed lemon juice

2 tablespoons extra virgin olive oil

Sea salt and freshly ground black pepper

2 to 3 ounces Seal Cove Farm Olga cheese or Manchego

1 Have a large bowl of ice water ready. Bring the 3 cups of water to a boil in a medium-size saucepan. Add the peas and cook them until just barely tender, 2 to 3 minutes. Drain the peas and then plunge them into the bowl of ice water to preserve their bright green color. Drain the peas again and pat them dry.

2 Place the peas, arugula, and mint in a salad bowl and toss to mix. Add the lemon juice and olive oil, season with salt and pepper to taste, and toss well.

3 Using a vegetable peeler, shave the cheese into thin shards and scatter them over the top of the salad. Serve at once.

Warm Goat Cheese Salad with Beach Plum Balsamic Glaze

This is my Cape Cod spin on the warm goat cheese salad Alice Waters made famous years ago at her Chez Panisse restaurant in Berkeley, California. I always seem to have an ample supply of beach plum jelly in my pantry since many of my friends on Nantucket and Cape Cod make an annual event out of picking wild beach plums in top secret locations and then making batches of jams, jellies, chutneys, and cordials for gift giving. This salad delectably takes beach plum jelly from the breakfast table to the dinner table and is one salad I enjoy featuring on wine tasting dinner menus, since unlike many salads, this one pairs harmoniously with fruit-forward red wines.

For those who do not have access to picking wild beach plums or are not inclined to making jams and jellies, the charming and historic Green Briar Jam Kitchen a few miles down the road from me in Sandwich sells all of its Cape Cod products, including beach plum jelly, via mail order. The website, thorntonburgess.org, proffers a wide array of jams, jellies, marmalades, chutneys, and sun-dried fruit butters, all expertly crafted on the nature center premises. SERVES 4

⅔ cup toasted walnuts or skinned hazelnuts (see Box, page 70), finely chopped

1 log (6 ounces) creamy goat cheese, cut into 4 equal rounds

½ cup beach plum jelly

2 tablespoons balsamic vinegar

1 tablespoon finely minced peeled shallot

5 tablespoons extra virgin olive oil

4 to 5 cups baby greens or mesclun

Fleur de sel and freshly ground black pepper

1 Spread the toasted nuts out on a small plate and dredge each round of goat cheese in the nuts, pressing gently on the cheese to coat it on all sides. Refrigerate the cheese until you are ready to assemble the salads.

2 Preheat the oven to 350°F. Line a baking sheet with parchment paper.

3 Combine the beach plum jelly and balsamic vinegar in a small nonreactive saucepan over medium heat and let come to a boil, stirring until the jelly melts, 2 to 3 minutes. Stir in the shallot and let simmer until softened, about 3 minutes. Reduce the heat to low and whisk in 4 tablespoons of the olive oil. Keep the glaze warm over low heat.

4 Place the goat cheese rounds on the prepared baking sheet and bake them until warmed throughout but not oozing, 7 to 8 minutes. Meanwhile, toss the greens with the remaining 1 tablespoon of olive oil to coat them ever so lightly and evenly all over. Season the greens with *fleur de sel* and pepper to taste.

5 Divide the greens among 4 salad plates. Nestle a warm round of goat cheese in the center of each salad. Drizzle the glaze generously over the cheese and sparingly over the greens. Serve the salads at once.

Broad Street Beet Tartare

I have a lot of friends who, like myself, are fond of beets. If there is a beet salad on a dinner menu when we are out at a restaurant together, usually 75 percent of the table will order it, even when the game plan is to sample as many diverse dishes as possible.

My very favorite beet salad in the world is the wonderfully unique and delicious Beet Tartare on the menu at Le Languedoc restaurant on Nantucket. This Broad Street restaurant has been run by Alan and Ann Cunha and the Grennan brothers for almost four decades and it has remained tops on my Nantucket restaurant list throughout this time, whether I happened to be working there as a waitress, baking desserts behind the scenes in the kitchen, chatting at the tiny but animated bar, or dining as a guest in the intimate downstairs café or in one of the more formal upstairs rooms. Chef Neil Grennan's cuisine is rooted in classic French cooking, but he takes enough poetic license to keep things updated and vibrant as evidenced by this innovative chilled beet salad—assembled just like the beef tartare featured in bistros all over Paris—but with finely diced roasted beets brilliantly standing in for the red meat.

Roasting beets wrapped individually in aluminum foil is my favorite method of cooking beets and can be used any time you want to add freshly roasted beets to a salad, such as in the deservedly popular mixed green salad with beets, walnuts, and blue cheese. Le Languedoc uses brioche for its toast points but toasted rounds from a baguette will work, too. Sometimes, I press the hard-cooked eggs through a sieve and sprinkle them like confetti over the salad. However you choose to serve your beet tartare, you will be happy. SERVES 6 TO 8

A window view into one of my long-standing favorite places to dine on Nantucket—the cozy and casual downstairs bistro at Le Languedoc, not far from the island's ferry terminal.

4 medium-size red beets, tops and roots discarded and dirt scrubbed from the skins

1 shallot, peeled and finely minced (about 2 tablespoons)

1 tablespoon brine-packed capers, drained and coarsely chopped

5 cornichons, drained and finely chopped

1½ tablespoons snipped fresh chives

1 tablespoon finely minced fresh flat-leaf parsley

1 tablespoon Dijon mustard, preferably Maille or Fallot

½ teaspoon Worcestershire sauce

A few drops Tabasco or other hot sauce

Approximately 1 tablespoon mayonnaise, Hellmann's or homemade (page 129)

Sea salt and freshly ground black pepper

Mixed greens, for serving

3 hard-cooked eggs, for serving

Toast points, for serving

1 Preheat the oven to 400°F.

2 Wrap each beet individually in a piece of heavy-duty aluminum foil and arrange the beets in a small roasting pan. Bake the beets until they are tender when pierced with the tip of a sharp paring knife, at least 1 hour but sometimes as long as 1½ hours. Remove the roasting pan from the oven and loosen the foil around the beets to expose them. Let the beets stand until cool enough to handle.

3 Working in the sink to avoid the possibility of staining your countertops, peel and discard the skin from the beets and then rinse them briefly under cold running water. Place the peeled beets on a cutting board and cut them into very fine dice, a somewhat laborious process but necessary and well worth the time and effort.

4 Place the diced beets in a mixing bowl and add the shallot, capers, cornichons, chives, parsley, Dijon mustard, Worcestershire sauce, and Tabasco sauce. Stir until evenly combined. Add just enough mayonnaise to bind the ingredients. Err on the side of caution because the idea is for the mayonnaise to serve as a light binder but not dilute the brilliant red color of the beets. Season to taste with salt and pepper. Refrigerate the beet tartare, covered, for at least 1 hour or as long as 24 hours before serving.

5 When ready to serve, line 6 to 8 salad plates with the greens. At Le Languedoc, the beet salad is pressed into a 2½-to-3-inch ring mold and then unmolded in the center of the plate. I have found that packing the beet mixture gently into a round biscuit cutter and then pressing the contents gently onto the plate also works quite well. Or you can use an ice cream scoop but the patty shape is more elegant than a mound. Garnish each serving of beet tartare with 2 or 3 thin, center slices of hard-cooked egg and accompany with toast points.

When summer vegetable stands brim with leafy lettuces and juicy red tomatoes, I feel compelled to make at least a salad a day.

Our House Salad Vinaigrette

This seemingly straightforward salad dressing recipe is *the recipe* for which my husband Nigel claims he married me. I learned how to make it while doing research in France in the 1990s for my *Pedaling Through Burgundy Cookbook*. Key to the recipe's success is using a good strong Dijon mustard imported from France and a neutral tasting oil to allow the mustard's pungency to shine through rather than be overpowered, as it would be by using all olive oil. I personally like to impart a faint olive oil flavor to the vinaigrette, but this is not usually the practice in France. Nonetheless, the little hint of olive oil appeals to the salad-loving New England palates in my circle.

I use this vinaigrette on all manner of leafy green salads and sometimes legume-based salads, too. Because it is difficult to achieve the perfect balance of salt and pepper in the vinaigrette itself, I almost always season my green salads, once dressed, with additional crunchy sea salt, such as *fleur de sel*, and freshly cracked black pepper. This vinaigrette makes everything shine, from the most basic heads of Boston and Bibb lettuce to the trendier mesclun blends currently popular with many local growers. The vinaigrette tastes best when used up within five days of making it and should be applied with restraint to coat salad greens lightly and not drench them. MAKES 1 GENEROUS CUP VINAIGRETTE

1 large organic egg yolk, as fresh as possible (see Note)

1 heaping tablespoon Dijon mustard, preferably Maille or Fallot

1 clove garlic (optional), peeled

¾ teaspoon fine sea salt or kosher salt

¼ teaspoon freshly cracked black peppercorns

2½ tablespoons white wine or Champagne vinegar

¾ cup vegetable, canola, or grape seed oil

¼ cup extra virgin olive oil

PLACE THE EGG yolk and mustard in a small deep bowl. If using the garlic, mince it together with the salt and pepper on a cutting board to make a paste and add it to the bowl. If not using the garlic, simply add the salt and pepper to the bowl. Pour in the vinegar and whisk to combine well. Gradually whisk in the vegetable oil followed by the olive oil, pouring them slowly in a thin steady stream to form an emulsion with the consistency of thin mayonnaise. Store the vinaigrette in the refrigerator, covered, for up to 5 days if you are not using it within the hour. Use as needed to dress salad greens.

NOTE: *The egg yolk used remains uncooked, so make this vinaigrette only with very fresh, refrigerated organic eggs.*

Tomato Vinaigrette

This is a good all-purpose summer vinaigrette to make at the peak of the tomato season. It can be used to dress heartier greens as well as simply steamed, roasted, or grilled garden vegetables. Because I believe more is more when it comes to the topic of vine-ripened summer tomatoes, I'll occasionally dress my ubiquitous platters of sliced summer tomatoes with this tomato-laced vinaigrette for the ultimate tomato whammy. And yes I am aware this is heretical to my rule of never using any vinegar when making sliced tomato salads. I guess being in the throes of raising a teenager has enlightened me to that age-old adage: "Rules are made to be broken." MAKES ABOUT 1 ¼ CUPS

2 large cloves garlic, peeled

¾ teaspoon sea salt

2 medium-size vine-ripened tomatoes, seeded and cut into small dice

1 tablespoon balsamic vinegar

1 tablespoon sherry vinegar

¼ teaspoon dried oregano, preferably Greek oregano, crumbled

½ cup extra virgin olive oil

1 Mince the garlic and salt together on a cutting board to make a paste. Add the diced tomatoes and continue chopping to make a coarse paste. Transfer the tomato mixture to a mixing bowl.

2 Stir the balsamic and sherry vinegars and the oregano into the tomato mixture. Slowly whisk in the olive oil to make a lightly emulsified vinaigrette. If you are not using the vinaigrette within a couple of hours refrigerate it, covered, but let it return to room temperature before using. It will keep for up to 3 days.

Bivalve Bliss

"As I ate the oysters with their strong taste of the sea and their faint metallic taste that the cold white wine washed away, leaving only the sea taste and the succulent texture, and as I drank their cold liquid from each shell and washed it down with the crisp taste of wine, I lost the empty feeling and began to be happy and to make plans."
—Ernest Hemingway, *A Moveable Feast*

When I was in college, I reveled in reading everything I could about Paris in the 1920s. I dreamed about cultivating a fascinating array of writers and artists as friends and hosting soirees like Gertrude Stein had on Saturday evenings at her home on the Left Bank, only mine would take place in Cambridge or on Nantucket. However, somehow along the way I took a turn more in the direction of Alice B. Toklas than Ernest Hemingway. I cannot say I have any regrets because I have come to realize that I don't need to live in Paris to experience a Hemingway-esque oyster epiphany. I can be at a gathering in my Barnstable neighborhood on a sunny September afternoon savoring the differences between just shucked oysters from three separate farmers all growing oysters in Barnstable Harbor, pondering whether Sandy Neck oysters are better than Moon Shoal oysters and/or whether either is best chased with a sip of local Cape Cod beer poured from a growler or a chilled French Muscadet swirled in a wine glass. I need only to continue praying that Barnstable's very first and fabulous Oysterfest becomes an annual event.

I had initially toyed with the notion of calling this chapter Happy as a Clam. Yet, once I began acquiring my own shellfish licenses and picking up some helpful tips from BARS (the Barnstable Association for Recreational Shellfishing), I realized that the full sense of the expression "happy as a clam at high tide" was geared to the well-being of the bivalves and not those of us in their pursuit. Being able to gather my own oysters and clams not far from my home on Cape Cod or score Nantucket bay scallops directly from the back door of an island shanty does indeed make me very happy. Then again, the taste of a Maine Moosabec mussel, Rhode Island cherrystone, Connecticut razor clam, or wild Wellfleet oyster makes me equally happy, even if I have not personally had the thrill of harvesting the shellfish with my own two hands. I guess you could say that's why I have opted to call this chapter Bivalve Bliss.

One of the most well known quotes from Gertrude Stein's writing is: " A rose is a rose is a rose." By contrast, I have learned an oyster isn't an oyster isn't an oyster, nor is any other bivalve like another, for that matter. Wine has *terroir* and bivalves have *meroir* and this is why most of the recipes in this chapter are not terribly complicated. They don't need a lot of other ingredients, if any at all, to taste sublime. Yes, I adore oysters Rockefeller and clams casino but I do make a point of first discerning what that Chatham littleneck or Maine Spinney Creek oyster tastes like unadorned before I decide whether or not to adorn it. The industrious couple who started the small family-run Barnstable Oyster aquaculture operation have a clever marketing slogan that captures the essence of my bivalve sensibilities: "Practice shellfishness."

Sea Sauces

Hosting a cocktail party with a raw bar component has been popular on the island of Nantucket ever since I can remember, no matter what the season or occasion. During my catering years on the island I relied confidently and relentlessly on a colorful character known to all by his nickname of "Spanky" to tend to my raw bar needs with his trademark ice-filled dinghy serving as the bar for bushel upon bushel of briny oysters and clams opened to order. Spanky's Raw Bar business continues to go great guns and has subsequently garnered him some pretty posh raw bar gigs all over the country. Meanwhile, raw bars have become increasingly popular throughout New England and are now added as a welcome feature to many restaurants or are in fact their entire raison d'être. A few of my favorites are The Mooring restaurant in Newport, Rhode Island, Boston's Neptune Oyster Bar and Island Creek Oyster Bar, and the Eventide Oyster Co. in Portland, Maine.

I am good at quite a few culinary tasks, but I am not good at opening clams and oysters. Fortunately, my husband, Nigel, will rise to the occasion, now that I have outfitted him with the proper knife, a French designed wooden oyster holder, and sturdy stab-proof gloves. Good fish markets throughout New England will often open bivalves for a small fee.

While I don't let DIY pride interfere with how I obtain my fill of bivalves on the half shell, I draw the line when it comes to their embellishment and insist on making any accompanying sauces from scratch. Sometimes a squeeze of fresh lemon is all I want on the freshest local raw oysters, littlenecks, cherrystones, or bay scallops. Other times, when entertaining or staging my own New England version of the fabulously French *plateau de fruits de mer*, I'll offer an array of complimentary sauces. Here are the sauces I frequently make at home.

Classic Mignonette

If I am putting any sauce on oysters on the half shell, be they popular and well-known oysters from Cape Cod and Duxbury Bay, Massachusetts, or cult ones from Connecticut, Rhode Island, and Maine, I want it to be the classic French sauce known as mignonette. The vinegar most commonly used in making mignonette sauce should be Champagne, white wine, or red wine vinegar of decent quality, but good old-fashioned New England cider vinegar will work as well. If you really want to gild the lily, you can top your mignonette sauce off with a generous third cup or so of whatever sparkling wine you might happen to be sipping, a trick I learned

Colorful striped umbrellas take command at the popular Jetties Beach on Nantucket on a dazzling and typical summer beach day on the island.

from Barbara Lynch whose B&G oyster bar is but one thriving establishment in her highly acclaimed and burgeoning Boston restaurant empire.

The amount of black pepper you add to your mignonette will depend on personal taste. My husband is a pepper fiend, so I usually err on the side of more. On the other hand, I have been served oysters in Paris with a mignonette made only of vinegar and shallots with a pepper mill alongside, allowing pepper to be ground to taste as you slurp. I encourage you to think of Shakespeare and make the world your local oyster in whatever way suits. MAKES ABOUT 1 CUP, ENOUGH FOR 48 OYSTERS OR CLAMS

2½ tablespoons minced shallots

¾ cup Champagne, white wine, red wine, or cider vinegar

2 teaspoons to 1 tablespoon freshly cracked black peppercorns

Sparkling wine (optional)

PLACE THE SHALLOTS in a small mixing bowl and pour in the vinegar. Add freshly cracked pepper to taste. Use the sauce at once or store it in a covered container in the refrigerator until ready to use. Mignonette sauce keeps well for at least a week and can actually improve a bit with age. If you opt to top off the mignonette with sparkling wine, it should be added just before serving. Spoon the mignonette sauce rather sparingly, no more than a teaspoon per bivalve, over freshly opened oysters and clams on the half shell.

Jetties Beach Mignonette

Many moons and tides ago when as a teenager I worked on Nantucket as a mother's helper, I'd spend summer afternoons watching my young cousin Parke and his friends frolic at Jetties Beach. Years later, it became a favorite beach destination for my own son Oliver. Now, I still love going to the Jetties out of nostalgia. Furthermore, what used to be a rather average beach snack bar has recently morphed into a raw bar, the one and only thing that can lure me momentarily away from swimming and soaking up the sun (against my dermatologist's orders) on a cloudless August day. Hence the discovery of this mignonette sauce, unlike any other I have ever tasted.

Chef Bruce Yancy told me he invented it when customers began to ask for mignonette sauce at the raw bar. Yancy found the traditional mignonette sauce far too acidic for his palate and decided to moderate the acidity from the vinegar with honey. Purists may cringe, but the sauce delights me. Yancy makes the sauce in large quantities and I have scaled down his recipe for home use. MAKES ABOUT 1¼ CUPS, ENOUGH FOR 5 DOZEN OYSTERS OR CLAMS

2 tablespoons minced shallots

1 tablespoon freshly squeezed lemon juice

1½ tablespoons clover or orange blossom honey

1 cup red wine vinegar

Salt and freshly cracked black peppercorns

COMBINE THE SHALLOTS, lemon juice, and honey in a small mixing bowl. Add the red wine vinegar and stir to combine. Season the sauce sparingly with salt and generously with pepper. Use the sauce at once or store it in a covered container in the refrigerator until ready to use. Stir to recombine before serving. The sauce will keep well for at least 1 week.

Chatham Bars Inn Bloody Mary Sauce

The Chatham Bars Inn is definitely one of the most exquisite high-end destination resorts on Cape Cod, as well as in all of New England. While I enjoy relishing the sprawling, expertly tended grounds and splendid seaside location at any time throughout the year, I'm most inclined to make the forty-five minute trek from my home in Barnstable to Chatham in the warmer months when I can dine alfresco at the inn's seasonal Beach House. The sand-fringed, smack-dab beachfront location cannot help but induce raw bar cravings and CBI's prized local littlenecks on the half shell sauced with executive chef Anthony Cole's signature Bloody Mary cocktail sauce make braving summer traffic and crowds on Routes 6 and 28 totally worthwhile.

The recipe is a good one to have on hand for large parties as it yields a bountiful quantity of one of the best cocktail sauces to pair with raw oysters and clams and cooked shrimp you'll ever taste. Brands are important when making cocktail sauce. I always use Heinz ketchup and chili sauce, Gold's or Heluva Good! prepared horseradish, Lea & Perrins Worcestershire sauce, and Coastal Goods celery salt (which is made by my husband's company and, nepotism aside, is the best celery salt I have ever tasted). MAKES ABOUT 3½ CUPS, ENOUGH FOR 15 DOZEN OYSTERS, CLAMS, AND SHRIMP

1 cup unflavored vodka

2 cups chili sauce, preferably Heinz

1 cup ketchup, preferably Heinz

4 ounces (½ cup) hot prepared horseradish, preferably Gold's or Heluva Good!

2 tablespoons Worcestershire sauce

6 tablespoons Tabasco sauce

3 tablespoons coarsely cracked black peppercorns

3 tablespoons celery salt

3 tablespoons freshly squeezed lemon juice

3 tablespoons minced fresh dill

1   Pour the vodka into a medium-size saucepan and let come to a boil over medium-high heat. Let the vodka boil until it is reduced to ½ cup, 5 to 7 minutes. Add the chili sauce, ketchup, horseradish, Worcestershire sauce, Tabasco sauce, and cracked black peppercorns; reduce the heat to medium-low and let simmer until the flavors are blended, about 20 minutes, stirring occasionally. Stir in the celery salt, lemon juice, and dill. Cook 5 minutes more, then remove the sauce from the heat.

2   Once the sauce has cooled to room temperature, puree it in small batches in a powerful blender until smooth. The Chatham Bars Inn uses a high-performance Vitamix blender, but most decent home blenders will get the job done. The sauce should be quite thick. Store the sauce in the refrigerator in an airtight container; it will keep for at least 2 weeks.

Barnstable Bloody Mary Sauce

Once I had tasted the Chatham Bars Inn Bloody Mary sauce, I became so obsessed with this vast improvement on ordinary cocktail sauce that I grew impatient waiting to get the recipe from the Inn.

Back home in Barnstable, I started to think about how Bloody Mary cocktails have innumerable variations in this day and age of craft libations and reasoned that a Bloody Mary cocktail sauce was equally deserving of being personalized to specific tastes. My Barnstable Bloody Mary Sauce differs in technique from the Chatham Bars Inn recipe and is prepared in a manner more akin to the way traditional cocktail sauces are made, except with extra add-ins. My recipe also yields a smaller quantity and allows for further personalization. For example, I like lime in a Bloody Mary, but if you like lemon, go for it. I prefer the heat in a Bloody Mary to be on the mild side and to emanate from horseradish alone. If you like more fiery flavors, be my guest and spike this Bloody Mary sauce with your favorite hot sauce or a ground chile powder, such as chipotle. The sauce is not designed to cure a hangover but rather to thrill the taste buds and garnish all manner of shellfish in easygoing seaside style. MAKES ABOUT 1 CUP, ENOUGH FOR 4 DOZEN OYSTERS, CLAMS, AND SHRIMP

½ cup ketchup, preferably Heinz

⅓ cup chili sauce, preferably Heinz

2½ tablespoons hot prepared horseradish, preferably Gold's or Heluva Good!

1½ tablespoons unflavored or citrus-flavored vodka

1½ tablespoons freshly squeezed lime or lemon juice

½ teaspoon finely grated lime or lemon zest

1 teaspoon Lea & Perrins Worcestershire Sauce

½ teaspoon celery salt

¾ teaspoon coarsely cracked black peppercorns

Hot sauce or hot chile powder (optional)

PLACE THE KETCHUP and chili sauce in a small mixing bowl and stir until thoroughly combined. Stir in the horseradish, vodka, lime or lemon juice and zest, Worcestershire sauce, celery salt, and cracked black peppercorns. I think the sauce tastes perfect at this point, but add hot sauce or chile powder to taste, if you must. It will keep in an airtight container in the refrigerator for up to 2 weeks.

Corazón del Mar's Salsa Macha

Nathaniel Philbrick is a Nantucket author who rose to considerable national fame with the millennial publication of *In the Heart of the Sea: The Tragedy of the Whaleship Essex*, a mesmerizing historical account of a Nantucket whaling crew's fight for survival in the nineteenth century in the South Pacific. Corazón del Mar is a Latin-themed restaurant located in downtown Nantucket, a stone's throw from the Nantucket Whaling Museum, and its name is a clever riff on Philbrick's bestselling book while also befitting the sublime seafood creations offered at the restaurant.

Corazón del Mar is owned by the dynamo island couple Angela and Seth Raynor. Angela and Seth also run the very popular and fancier Boarding House and Pearl restaurants on the next street over. Personally, I think Seth seems happiest when he is tending to the raw bar at Corazón and I am always thrilled to score a coveted stool at the bar and watch Seth work his ceviche magic. Seth's most famous raw bar sauce is his fiery "krack sauce," but that's a secret recipe that the Raynors are hoping to bottle and market in the near future.

Slightly lower on the radar but no less memorable for me is this *salsa macha*, an unusual chile and peanut sauce that Seth serves with quaveringly fresh, thinly sliced sea scallops. I've only experienced the peanut version, but Seth likes to change things up from time to time by substituting Marcona almonds for the peanuts and/or adding lemon or lime juice or zest to the sauce. I am able to purchase the dried arbol chile peppers required for the recipe in the international aisle of larger New England supermarkets, such as Shaw's. MAKES ABOUT 2 CUPS, ENOUGH FOR MANY DOZENS OF SCALLOPS

1 cup dried arbol chile peppers

4 cloves garlic, peeled

1 tablespoon kosher salt

1 cup skinned, raw, unsalted peanuts

½ cup extra virgin olive oil

1   Place the arbol chile peppers in a heavy skillet or a Mexican *comal* and, stirring occasionally, roast them very slowly over the lowest heat setting until the peppers sound hollow, about 15 minutes. Take care not to burn the peppers. When the roasted peppers are cool enough to handle, shake out and discard as many seeds as possible. Set the pulp aside.

2   Place the garlic and salt in a large mortar and, using a pestle, crush them to form a coarse paste. Add the roasted arbol chile pulp and continue crushing into a coarse paste. Add the peanuts and crush them until the nuts resemble broken grains of rice.

3   Transfer the chile mixture to a food processor and add the olive oil. Pulse the machine on and off a few times to incorporate the olive oil. Do not overprocess the mixture. You do not want to achieve a smooth, nut butter consistency, so process the salsa very minimally. Serve the *salsa macha* at room temperature as an accompaniment to all manner of thinly sliced raw fish and scallops. The sauce will keep in an airtight container in the refrigerator for a week but must return to room temperature before using.

Sushi-Style Spicy Mayonnaise

One of my very favorite things to eat on Cape Cod and perhaps in the world are the spicy scallop hand rolls prepared at Inaho, a Japanese restaurant in Yarmouth Port, a scenic ten-minute drive from my Cape Cod home. As popular as sushi bars have become throughout New England, I had to draw the line at putting sushi and sashimi in this cookbook, since most people I know tend to eat these out in specialized restaurants, rather than prepare them

at home. While making sushi rice can be finicky and toasting nori a chore, putting together the spicy mayonnaise used in most Japanese restaurants' hand rolls is a cinch plus an unexpectedly welcome sauce addition to any home-fashioned raw bar.

Many believe that this basically two-ingredient sauce should be made with Kewpie mayonnaise, imported from Japan. I actually have no problem finding Kewpie mayonnaise locally or online, but I do sometimes think twice about using it when I see MSG listed as a prominent ingredient. The only other choice for me is to use my favorite commercial mayonnaise, Hellmann's, and compromise on a bit of authenticity. I do both, depending on the circumstances, and often go so far as to spike the spicy mayonnaise with a generous amount of chopped cilantro since the sauce is one that tends to disappear quickly, as opposed to linger in unknown parts in the back of my refrigerator. Use this spicy mayonnaise as a dip for the freshest raw New England scallops—bay, sea, or diver harvested—and by all means treat yourself to Inaho's spicy scallop hand rolls if you are in the neighborhood. MAKES ABOUT ¾ CUP, ENOUGH FOR MANY DOZENS OF SCALLOPS

¾ cup Hellmann's or Japanese Kewpie mayonnaise

About 1 tablespoon sriracha hot chile sauce (I use Huy Fong Foods brand with the rooster on the squeeze bottle)

1 tablespoon freshly squeezed lime juice

2 tablespoons finely minced fresh cilantro (optional)

PLACE THE MAYONNAISE and sriracha in a small mixing bowl and whisk to mix. I find one tablespoon of sriracha sufficient but feel free to add less or more to suit your own taste. Blend in the lime juice and cilantro, if using. Refrigerate the mayonnaise, covered, for at least 1 hour before using. Serve the mayonnaise chilled. In addition to using the mayonnaise as a dip for raw scallops, the spicy mayonnaise is excellent drizzled over

Making Opening Easy

In working on this cookbook, I have come to believe that there is no need to go through the hassle of opening oysters and clams in a raw state if they are going to be cooked later. Walter Kaess (see Oysters "Clark Rockefeller" on the facing page) agrees and we have taken to steaming our oysters in a little water or wine or a combination of the two until they just begin to open, allowing for the top shells to be pried off easily while keeping the oysters almost but not quite raw. If you are into special equipment, there's a company in Rhode Island called Gilchrist's Great Grates (greatgrate.com) that distributes a specially designed metal rack for holding shellfish in a way that retains their juices when grilling them open over an outdoor grill or on top of a gas stovetop. Walter and I both own shellfish grillers, but cooking the oysters briefly in a little liquid in a pot gets the job done just fine.

any thinly sliced raw fish plated in the style of carpaccio and is quite tasty with cooked shrimp as well. The mayonnaise is best if used within a week.

Ashby's Angels on Horseback

Ashby is a wonderful part of the extended family on Cape Cod with whom I'll often celebrate holidays, or any occasion for that matter, running the gamut from birthdays to pig roasts. Ashby lives with her husband Tom in Harwich and the two raise cows, goats, chicken, ducks, wayward family pets, Cape League baseball players, tomatoes, and sundry other items on a large piece of property they proudly call the Funnie Farm.

Most of our get-togethers are potluck extravaganzas and Ashby, without fail, is always asked to contribute these sinfully rich oysters. Sometimes, if Tom has been out scalloping rather than oystering, she'll substitute Cape bay scallops for the oysters. The recipe makes extra lemon sauce, which Ashby recommends using up as a tasty complement to cooked vegetables. MAKES 32; SERVES AS FEW AS 4 OR AS MANY AS 12 PEOPLE

For the oysters

½ cup minced fresh flat-leaf parsley

2 tablespoons finely minced peeled onion

2 teaspoons finely minced peeled garlic

16 slices thinly sliced bacon, cut in half crosswise

32 freshly shucked oysters

8 slices thin white bread, such as Pepperidge Farm, crusts removed

For the lemon sauce

3 tablespoons freshly squeezed lemon juice

½ cup heavy (whipping) cream

½ pound (2 sticks) chilled unsalted butter, cut into tablespoons

Fine sea salt and freshly ground white or black pepper

1 Prepare the oysters: Place the parsley, onion, and garlic in a small bowl and stir to mix. To make each angel on horseback, place a half slice of bacon on a work surface, sprinkle it with a bit of the parsley mixture, and add an oyster. Roll the bacon tightly around the oyster to enclose it and then secure it with a toothpick. Repeat with the remaining bacon and oysters. Place the assembled oysters on horseback on an aluminum foil–lined baking sheet, spacing them about ¾ inch apart. The recipe may be made up to this point

No matter how I count the many ways I adore eating and preparing oysters, simply iced oysters on the half shell never fail to make me ecstatic.

and continue broiling until the bacon is evenly crisped all over, 2 to 4 minutes longer.

6   Remove the toothpick from each oyster, then place each on top of a toast point. Spoon a generous teaspoon of the warm lemon sauce over the top of each bacon-wrapped oyster (see Note). Serve hot and soon and expect the angels on horseback to disappear very quickly.

NOTE: *Any extra lemon sauce will keep covered in the refrigerator for up to 4 days. It should be reheated over low heat until just warm, then spooned over hot green vegetables.*

and the oysters stored on the baking sheet wrapped in plastic wrap in the refrigerator for a few hours before baking.

2   Toast the bread slices until lightly golden. Cut each toasted slice into 4 triangles to serve as toast points and set them aside.

3   Make the lemon sauce: Place the lemon juice in a small nonreactive saucepan, let come to a boil over medium-high heat, and cook until reduced to about 1 tablespoon, 1½ to 2 minutes. Reduce the heat to medium, pour in the cream and cook at a gentle boil until the cream is reduced by half, about 10 minutes. Reduce the heat to medium-low and stir in the butter, tablespoon by tablespoon, waiting for each to be incorporated before adding the next, to make a light emulsion. Season the lemon sauce with salt and pepper to taste and keep warm over very low heat.

4   When ready to serve the angels on horseback, preheat the broiler to high, positioning an oven rack about 5 inches underneath the heat source.

5   Broil the oysters until the bacon is crisp on top, about 3 minutes. Use tongs to turn the oysters over

Oysters "Clark Rockefeller"

I used to pride myself in making an elaborate production out of preparing the recipe for famed oysters Rockefeller until my neighbor, Barnstable Harbor oystering instructor and congenial companion, Walter Kaess, introduced me to his utterly divine and embarrassingly simple riff on the recipe. Now, I almost never go to the trouble of making real oysters Rockefeller and simply could not resist naming Walter's faux recipe after Boston's notorious and nefarious Rockefeller imposter.

Don't fret over the fact that the recipe relies on Birds Eye's frozen creamed spinach. Once you make these oysters, you will no longer find it a crime. The convenience is balanced out by the fact that it is imperative to use real Pernod in the recipe. Walter's cheese of choice for the recipe is Trader Joe's Quattro Formaggio blend of shredded Parmesan, Asiago, fontina, and provolone cheeses. If you don't live near a Trader Joe's or want further to assuage any frozen creamed spinach guilt, substitute freshly grated Parmigiano-Reggiano cheese. MAKES 2 DOZEN; SERVES 6

Rock salt (optional)

24 fresh oysters in the shell

Dry white wine and/or water

1½ tablespoons unsalted butter

3 tablespoons minced peeled shallots

2 tablespoons Pernod or other French pastis, such as Ricard

1 package (9 ounces) Birds Eye frozen creamed spinach, thawed

2 to 3 tablespoons heavy (whipping) cream (optional)

Sea salt and freshly ground black pepper

2 ounces freshly grated Parmigiano-Reggiano or Trader Joe's Quattro Formaggio cheese blend (about ¾ cup)

1 Line 2 baking sheets with aluminum foil or rock salt (rock salt holds the oysters upright in place better than the foil but you can get away with not using it). Set aside.

2 If the oysters have assorted marine life clinging to their shells, scrub them clean under cold running water. Pour white wine and/or water to a depth of 1 inch in a large pot. Add the oysters, cover the pot, and let the liquid come to a boil over medium-high. Cook the oysters until the shells just begin to pop open, 3 to 5 minutes. Immediately remove the pot from the heat. Should an oyster refuse to open, discard it. When the oysters are cool enough to handle, remove the top shells, taking care to retain as much liquid as possible in the bottom shell containing the oyster. (You can discard the shells but in New England many people save the shells to plant with spring bulbs as a calcium enrichment or crush them for use on driveways and

Avoiding a Clam Calamity

As much as I adore the relaxing feeling induced by walking barefoot at the beach and feeling sand filter between my toes, I abhor crunching down on sand when I am feasting on a bowl of clams. This problem occurs primarily with soft-shell steamer clams since their necks or siphons often protrude from the edge of the shells allowing for sand to linger inside the clam's shell. An excellent way to purge steamers of their sand is to soak them in a bowl of ice water laced with ½ cup cider or distilled white vinegar for 20 to 30 minutes. The steamer clams are not fond of the vinegary water and react by naturally purging themselves of any sand. After soaking, drain the clams and give them an extra rinse under cold water before cooking.

I usually do not find it necessary to soak harder shelled littleneck, cherrystone, quahog, and mahogany clams or sharp-edged razor clams. Should you nonetheless be worried about sand, soaking in acidulated ice water will not harm the clams, but these varieties are usually already purged of sand when sold in fish markets. At the same time, I always rinse all clams well, no matter what type, under plenty of cold running water to remove any sand or grit that may be embedded on the exterior of the shells. Should the shells be especially gritty on the outside, gentle scrubbing with a clean dish brush may be required.

All fresh clams, with the exception of steamers, should have tightly closed shells. Should you notice the shell on any hard-shell clam you are about to cook to be ajar, give it a quick squeeze back together. If the clam shell remains closed after squeezing, it is fine to toss into the pot and eat. If the shell remains ajar, the clam is likely past its prime and should be discarded. Following these basic guidelines will put you well on your way to achieving bivalve bliss.

pathways.) Using a small sharp paring knife, pry each oyster from the muscle holding it in place and then nestle it gently back into the shell, still taking care to retain the oyster juices. Arrange the oysters on the prepared baking sheets and set aside.

3 Melt the butter over medium heat in a medium-size skillet. Add the shallots and cook until softened and just beginning to color a bit, 4 to 5 minutes. Add the Pernod, scraping up any browned bits clinging to the bottom of the skillet, and cook until the liquid is reduced by half, 1 to 2 minutes. Add the creamed spinach and stir to combine with the shallots. If the mixture seems dry, add a bit of cream and cook until it is absorbed, 1 to 2 minutes. Season the spinach with salt and pepper to taste and remove it from the heat.

4 When you are ready to serve the oysters, preheat the oven to 450°F.

5 Top each oyster with a generous tablespoon of the spinach mixture, spreading it to cover the oyster completely. Sprinkle about a teaspoon of cheese over the top of each oyster. Bake the oysters until the spinach topping is bubbling and the cheese is melted and lightly browned, 5 to 6 minutes. Let the oysters cool for a minute or two and then serve them hot on small plates with cocktail forks.

Barnstable Harbor Oysters "Pepin"

This recipe ranks very high in my to-die-for category. Sometimes, when a recipe is that great, you have to go to extraordinary lengths to get it. My request began with Martha Kane, who serves a littleneck clam version at her excellent Cape Cod restaurant, Fin. Martha said she couldn't share the recipe with me because she had learned it from a chef named Gil Pepin, who used to run another fine restaurant on the Cape. Pepin had closed his restaurant, become a private chef, left the Cape, and Martha had no idea how to get in touch with him. All I can say is: "Thank God for Google!" I found a Gil Pepin working for a Colorado Meat Board, called them, and begged them to pass my message and request on to Chef Pepin.

A week or so later, Gil Pepin and I began a fun phone and email exchange that ended with my procuring his recipe and learning that he used to make his creation with the very same oysters I gather in season from Barnstable Harbor. The recipe does require a fair amount of labor, a bit of which I have simplified for home cooking, but I am confident you will find the sinfully delicious results worthy of the effort. MAKES 24

For the oysters

4 ounces pancetta, finely diced

1 shallot, peeled and minced

1 pound fresh baby spinach leaves, rinsed and patted or spun dry

3 to 4 cups rock salt

24 fresh Cape Cod oysters or other favorite meaty oysters, shucked (see Note)

For the butter sauce

1 shallot, peeled and minced

2 tablespoons Champagne or white wine vinegar

¼ cup fresh lemon juice

1 cup dry white wine

½ teaspoon minced fresh lemon thyme or regular thyme

¼ cup heavy (whipping) cream

½ pound (2 sticks) chilled unsalted butter, cut into 16 pieces

1 Preheat the oven to 400°F.

2 Place the pancetta in a medium-size skillet and cook over low heat until the pancetta is crisp, 8 to 10

minutes. Remove the pancetta from the skillet. Reserve 3 tablespoons of the fat in a large skillet or wok.

3   Heat the reserved pancetta fat over medium heat. Add the shallot and cook until it just begins to soften, 1 minute. Add the spinach and increase the heat to high. Using tongs, toss the spinach to coat the leaves with the hot fat and to help them wilt, about 2 minutes. Transfer the spinach to a platter and let cool to room temperature.

4   Line 2 baking sheets with a half-inch-thick layer of the rock salt. Embed the oysters in their half-shells in the salt in a manner that keeps them level and secure. Divide the cooled spinach mixture among the 24 oysters, placing about 1½ tablespoons of the wilted spinach on top of each raw oyster to cover it.

5   Begin making the butter sauce: Combine the minced shallot, vinegar, lemon juice, white wine, and thyme in a medium-size saucepan and bring to a boil over high heat. Cook until the liquid has reduced to a scant ¼ cup, 7 to 9 minutes. Stir in the cream and immediately reduce the heat to low.

6   Place the oysters in the oven and bake until the oysters are just cooked through and piping hot, 10 to 12 minutes.

While the oysters are baking, finish making the butter sauce. Whisk the chilled butter, 1 piece at a time, into the reduction, waiting until each piece is incorporated before adding another. Once all the butter is incorporated and the sauce has formed an emulsion, stir in the reserved pancetta. As soon as the oysters emerge from the oven, spoon 1½ to 2 tablespoons of the butter sauce over each. Using tongs, carefully transfer the hot oysters in their shells to serving plates, allowing 2, 4, or 6 oysters per person, depending on the rest of the menu and the level of oyster enthusiasm. Serve at once with cocktail forks.

NOTE: *If you're not adept at shucking, ask your fishmonger to open the oysters for you within 2 hours of preparing the recipe. Reserve the shells separately.*

While specific color schemes are used to brand the buoys of lobstermen, many New Englanders find lobster buoys to be as decorative as they are functional.

Rhode Island–Style Clams Casino

In theory, clams casino would be precisely the type of storied recipe I enjoy putting in a cookbook, particularly this one. The legend that so often accompanies the recipe dates back to 1917 and the Narragansett Pier Casino in Rhode Island. Supposedly a wealthy socialite asked the casino's maître d' if the kitchen could prepare something extra special for her table of friends. She ended up so enjoying the bacon, clam, pepper, and bread crumb appetizer that was presented she dubbed the dish "clams casino."

What is there not to love about the tale except that many swear that any authentic recipe for clams casino must contain bell peppers, usually green ones, and I have discovered I personally cannot stand this combination, no matter how much bacon is in the recipe. I also realized that none of the clams casino I recalled appreciating over the years contained peppers, even the ones I had eaten in Rhode Island. What most good clams casinos I remembered did share in common was having the clam be of decent size, cherrystone rather than littleneck, a filling that was garlicky without being too densely bready, and the generous use of really flavorful bacon. Furthermore, I realized that Ritz cracker crumbs needed to be a key ingredient, but found that mixing them with lighter panko bread crumbs yielded a more modern yet still Rhode Island–rooted rendition of the recipe—and one that I could now proudly include in this cookbook. MAKES 20

20 fresh cherrystone clams in the shell

5 slices high-quality apple wood or cob smoked New England bacon, each slice cut crosswise into 4 pieces

3 tablespoons unsalted butter

3 cloves garlic, peeled and minced

4 scallions, trimmed, both white and tender green parts minced

About 8 Ritz crackers, crushed with a rolling pin or in a food processor (½ cup crumbs)

⅔ cup Italian-style panko bread crumbs

2 tablespoons minced fresh flat-leaf parsley

2 tablespoons finely slivered fresh basil leaves

Sea salt and freshly ground black pepper

Rock salt (optional)

⅓ cup freshly squeezed lemon juice

⅓ cup dry white wine

2 ounces freshly grated Parmesan or Asiago (about ¾ cup) cheese

Lemon wedges, for serving

1 Rinse the clams under cold running water to dislodge any grit clinging to the shells. Should they be especially gritty, give them a gentle scrubbing with a clean dish brush. Line 2 baking sheets with aluminum foil or rock salt (rock salt holds the clams upright in

place better than the foil and makes for a great nautical presentation but is not absolutely necessary).

2 Pour water to a depth of 1 inch in a large pot. Add the clams, cover the pot, and let the water come to a boil over medium-high heat. Cook the clams until the shells pop open, 4 to 6 minutes. Remove the pot from the heat and let the clams cool until easy to handle. Discard any clams that have not opened.

3 Meanwhile, heat a medium-size skillet over medium heat and cook the bacon until it is just beginning to crisp ever so slightly (it will finish crisping in the oven later), 4 to 5 minutes. Transfer the bacon to paper towels to drain. Discard all but 1 tablespoon of the bacon fat remaining in the skillet. Add the butter to the bacon fat and heat over medium-low heat until melted. Add the garlic and scallions to the skillet and cook until softened, about 3 minutes.

4 Stir the Ritz cracker crumbs and panko together in a mixing bowl. Add the garlic and scallions to the crumb mixture and toss to combine evenly and moisten the crumbs with the cooking fat. Add the parsley and basil and stir to combine evenly. Taste for seasoning, adding a bit of salt and pepper if desired.

5 Remove the top shells of the clams and discard them. Using a small sharp paring knife, cut each clam away from the muscle holding it in place and then nestle the clam back into its shell, taking care to retain any juices in the shell. Arrange the clams on the prepared baking sheets. Spoon a little bit of lemon juice and a little bit of white wine over each clam to moisten it. Spoon a scant tablespoon of the crumb mixture over each clam, then top it with a piece of bacon and a scattering of the grated cheese. The clams casino may be prepared ahead to this point. Wrap the baking sheets in plastic wrap and refrigerate for up to 6 hours before cooking.

6 When ready to cook, preheat the oven to 450°F.

7 Bake the clams until piping hot, 8 to 10 minutes or a bit longer if they have come directly from the refrigerator. If the bacon has not crisped sufficiently

to your liking, run the clams under the broiler for a minute or two to finish them off. Serve the clams on small plates with lemon wedges for squeezing over the top (do not omit the lemon as it really enlivens everything at the end) and cocktail forks. For a more substantial appetizer, serve 4 or 5 clams per person on larger plates.

Clams Oreganata

My husband spent many years living along the Jersey Shore and tends to gravitate to making clams oreganata over clams casino since the former has long been favored by New Jersey's large Italian-American population. This is not to say that we don't find clams oreganata on New England menus and my husband has easily managed to convince me of their merit. Clams oreganata are spicier than clams casino and a wee bit lighter since they have no bacon in the filling. I pretty much follow the way my husband makes them but opt for using panko rather than the more traditional dried Italian bread crumbs. MAKES 2 DOZEN; SERVES 4

24 fresh littleneck or Manila clams in the shell

2 tablespoons (¼ stick) unsalted butter

¾ cup water

½ cup dry white wine

5 tablespoons extra virgin olive oil

3 cloves garlic, peeled and minced

½ teaspoon hot red pepper flakes

1¼ cups Italian-style panko bread crumbs

⅓ cup fresh, finely grated Parmigiano-Reggiano cheese

2 ripe plum tomatoes, seeded and cut into ¼-inch dice

3 tablespoons minced fresh flat-leaf parsley

1 teaspoon dried oregano, crumbled between your fingers

Lemon wedges, for serving

1 Preheat the oven to 425°F.

2 Rinse the clams under cold running water to dislodge any grit clinging to the shells. Should they be especially gritty, give them a gentle scrubbing with a clean dish brush. Set the clams aside briefly.

3 Melt the butter over low heat in a large pot. Pour in the water and white wine and then pile the clams into the pot. Cover the pot, let the liquid come to a boil over medium-high heat, and cook the clams until the shells pop open, 4 to 5 minutes. Remove the pot from the heat and let the clams cool until easy enough to handle. Discard any clams that have not opened.

4 Meanwhile, heat 4 tablespoons of the olive oil in a small skillet over medium-low heat. Add the garlic and hot red pepper flakes and cook until the garlic softens, about 2 minutes. Place the panko in a small mixing bowl, add the garlic mixture, and toss to moisten the crumbs evenly with the olive oil. Stir in the Parmigiano-Reggiano cheese, tomatoes, 2 tablespoons of the parsley, and the oregano. Set the bread crumb mixture aside briefly.

5 Line a sieve with a coffee filter. Remove the clams from the pot and strain ¾ cup of the cooking liquid through the sieve into a 9-by-13-inch baking dish. This will remove any sand or debris. Set the remaining cooking liquid aside. Scatter the remaining 1 tablespoon of parsley over the cooking liquid in the baking dish. Remove the top shells of the clams and discard them. Using a small sharp paring knife, cut each clam away from the mussel holding it in place and then nestle the clam back into its shell, taking care to retain any juices in the shell.

6 If the bread crumb mixture seems a little too dry, moisten it with a few tablespoons of the remaining cooking liquid (strain it, if necessary). The bread crumb mixture should not be soggy but moist enough to adhere loosely together. Mound about 1 tablespoon

Stuffed quahogs or stuffies are especially popular in Rhode Island and it is common to see boatloads of quahogs being harvested along Rhode Island's ample and craggy coastline.

of the bread crumb mixture over each clam, packing it slightly with a spoon or a butter knife. Arrange the clams in a single layer on top of the liquid in the baking dish. When all of the clams have been packed into the baking dish, drizzle the remaining 1 tablespoon of olive oil over the top. Bake the clams until the pan juices are bubbling and the bread crumb topping is golden, 13 to 15 minutes.

7 Using tongs, place 6 hot clams on each of 4 serving plates. Spoon some of the pan juices around the clams but not over them (you do not want to make the crispy crumbs soggy). Garnish each plate with 1 or 2 lemon wedges and serve at once with cocktail forks.

Sal's Stuffies

Stuffed quahogs are a really big deal in Rhode Island and several communities stage yearly competitions to determine who makes the best stuffed quahogs, otherwise known as "stuffies."

Sal Amato is an incredibly sweet man of Sicilian decent and a vital member of my Cape Cod book group, as he has decades of juicy and riveting Cape Cod restaurant tales to share. Sal lives in a very special retro enclave on the scenic Bass River in Yarmouth, where he makes the best stuffies I have ever tasted. He was initially shy about sharing the recipe with me because one of his secret ingredients is Pepperidge Farm herb-seasoned stuffing crumbs. When I assured Sal that I myself was quite fond of this stuffing, he set about making a batch of stuffies, and could not resist commenting: "Came out really good if I say so myself!"

Stuffies, as the name screams, are all about stuffing and I am determined to let the big stuffed quahog shells take the place of traditional turkey stuffing next time I plan a Thanksgiving dinner in a coastal locale. MAKES 1 DOZEN

6 fresh quahogs in the shell

2 cups water

1 medium-size onion, peeled and coarsely chopped

½ cup coarsely chopped yellow or green bell pepper

½ cup coarsely chopped red bell pepper

½ pound chouriço or linguiça, casing removed and meat coarsely chopped

2 tablespoons extra virgin olive oil, plus more olive oil for drizzling

2 cups Pepperidge Farm herb-seasoned stuffing

2 cups panko bread crumbs

Sea salt and freshly ground black pepper

Lemon wedges, for serving

1 Rinse the clams under cold running water to dislodge any grit clinging to the shells. Should they be especially gritty, give them a gentle scrubbing with a clean dish brush.

2 Pour the 2 cups water into a large pot and add the quahogs. Cover the pot, let the water come to a boil over medium-high heat, and cook the quahogs until

Digging for Dinner

When I was a child spending summer weeks in Blue Hill, Maine, with my family, grandparents, and numerous cousins, we frequently went digging for steamer clams. As much I enjoyed the digging and gathering, it took me a long time to actually go through the ordeal of eating my first clam. I guess I must have been eleven or twelve, and we were steaming the clams we had dug that afternoon over an outdoor campfire. Yes, I'll confess, I was totally grossed out by the process of having to remove the slippery black skin from the clam's neck but, then again, I have been eating steamers ever since.

the shells have opened, 7 to 9 minutes. Remove the quahogs from the pot to cool and set aside the cooking liquid. Discard any quahogs that have not opened.

3 Once the quahogs are cool enough to handle, remove the meat from the shells (set aside all of the shells). Using a pair of sharp scissors, cut the meat into small pieces (about 1/3 inch). Place the diced quahog meat in a large mixing bowl. Strain the cooking liquid through a sieve lined with a coffee filter in case there is any sand or debris, setting the liquid aside in another bowl.

4 Place the onion, bell peppers, and *chouriço* or *linguiça* in a food processor. Pulse the machine on and off several times until everything is finely chopped but not pureed. Heat the 2 tablespoons olive oil in a medium-size skillet over medium-high heat. Add the chopped sausage mixture and cook, stirring, until the onions and bell peppers have softened, 5 to 7 minutes. Add the sausage mixture to the bowl with the quahogs and stir to combine.

5 Place the herb stuffing and panko in the food processor and pulse it on and off to make fine crumbs.

Add the crumbs to the quahog mixture and mix well. Pour in enough of the strained cooking liquid, 1 1/2 to 1 3/4 cups, to moisten the stuffing sufficiently to make it gather easily into a mound. Taste for seasoning, adding salt and/or black pepper, if needed.

6 Divide the stuffing among the 12 quahog shell halves, filling each shell generously and mounding the mixture slightly in the center. The stuffies may be prepared up to this point and refrigerated, covered with plastic wrap, for up to a day before baking or even frozen for up to 2 months.

7 When ready to cook, preheat the oven to 350°F.

8 If the stuffies have been refrigerated, let them come to room temperature before baking; if frozen, thaw them in the refrigerator overnight. Place the stuffies on a large baking sheet or 2 baking sheets, if necessary. Drizzle olive oil rather generously over the stuffed shells. Bake the stuffies until piping hot and lightly golden on top, 25 to 30 minutes. Serve hot with lemon wedges.

Simple Steamers

Whenever my husband and I go to one of our favorite Maine lobster pounds, the Trenton Bridge on the Bar Harbor Road, we begin our feast with bowls of steamers. I had always thought of steamers as a prelude to lobster until one day when I ferried over to Martha's Vineyard to watch my son play in a Little League game, I sat down to a terrific lunch of just steamers at a rustic shanty called Coop de Ville overlooking the harbor in Oak Bluffs. Steamers, I gleaned, do indeed deserve to stand alone, especially if you can score ones labeled "sandless steamers." Otherwise, you'll have to soak most steamers in lots of cold water with either vinegar or cornmeal added to encourage the bivalves to disgorge their sand. However, I personally have

never found either method to be 100 percent successful and this must be why steamers in New England are always served with a side of broth for further rinsing. Plus, you can always think of a few grains of sand as adding fiber to your diet.

Lately, there's been a tendency for people to feel the need to cook steamers in beer or wine rather than plain old water. I refuse to jump on this bandwagon because I want my steamers to taste of the sea, and not some microbrewery or vineyard. It is much better to sip a frosty craft brew or crisp glass of white wine on the side. If you absolutely cannot leave well enough alone, I have discovered that adding the tiniest little splash of Italian limoncello liqueur to the cooking water can pleasantly enhance the lemon flavor of the dipping broth. Use Kate's brand salted butter as the accompanying melted dipping butter, if you can. SERVES 2 AS A MAIN COURSE, 4 AS AN APPETIZER

3 pounds fresh steamer clams in the shell

½ cup cider vinegar (optional)

1¼ cups water

1 small white onion, peeled and thinly sliced

½ teaspoon coarsely cracked black peppercorns

1 lemon

6 tablespoons (¾ stick) butter, melted, preferably Kate's salted butter

1½ tablespoons coarsely chopped fresh flat-leaf parsley

1 If the steamer clams are not sandless, soak them in a large container with water to cover mixed with the cider vinegar until they expel sand, 20 to 30 minutes.

2 Pour the water into a heavy nonreactive medium-size pot. Add the onion and cracked peppercorns. Cut the lemon in half lengthwise, cut one of the halves into thin half-circle slices, and add them to the pot. Cut the other lemon half into wedges and set them aside for serving.

3 Add the clams to the pot, cover it, and let the water come to a boil over medium-high heat. Cook the clams until the shells open, 6 to 8 minutes. Using tongs, divide the clams between 2 to 4 serving bowls (2 bowls if you are serving the clams as a main course, 4 if as an appetizer). Discard any clams that have not opened. Strew a few pieces of onion and lemon from the cooking water over each serving.

4 Strain the broth through a cheesecloth-lined fine mesh sieve and divide it between 2 to 4 glasses or cups (I usually use small glass juice tumblers). Divide the melted butter between 2 to 4 other small dipping cups. Scatter the parsley over and in and around the steamers. Serve the clams quickly with the side cups of broth and butter. Place the reserved lemon wedges on the table along with a bowl for discarding the clam shells. Plenty of napkins or a roll of paper towels will come in handy as well.

Summer Stew with Maine Mahogany Clams, Corn, and Fingerling Potatoes

As much as I love clam and fish chowders, I almost never make or eat them during the summer months unless it is an unusually cold or rainy day. Instead, I prefer to make a lighter sort of deconstructed chowder with less rich and creamy liquid and more vivid vegetable accents. Usually when *chouriço* or *linguiça* is called for in a New England recipe it refers to the widely available reddish-orange Portuguese sausages. However, in this instance I opt to use the dried chorizo sausage imported from Spain because I love it and it has become popular enough to find easily. The Palacios brand is the one I usually purchase.

A Maine company by the name of Moosabec Mussels has recently begun distributing really tasty mahogany clams from the Gulf of Maine to supermarkets throughout New England in netted two-pound bags, perfect for this recipe. I use beer to make the stew's light broth, and I encourage the use of any local ale you happen to like, especially seasonal summer brews that will have a slight lemony flavor profile. SERVES 4

2 pounds fresh Maine mahogany or littleneck clams

12 fingerling potatoes

3 tablespoons extra virgin olive oil

4 ounces Spanish chorizo, cut into ¼-inch dice

1 medium-size onion, peeled and chopped

4 cloves garlic, peeled and minced

Kernels from 2 ears fresh local corn

8 ounces local lager-style beer

2½ tablespoons minced fresh cilantro, flat-leaf parsley, or slivered basil

1   Rinse the clams under cold running water to dislodge any grit clinging to the shells. Should they be especially gritty, give them a gentle scrubbing with a clean dish brush. Set the clams aside briefly.

2   Place the fingerling potatoes in a small pot and add water to cover. Let come to a boil over medium-high heat and then let the potatoes simmer until tender, 12 to 15 minutes.

3   Meanwhile, heat the olive oil in a large, straight-sided skillet over medium heat. Add the chorizo and cook until slightly crisp, about 5 minutes. Add the onion and garlic and cook until the onion is soft and translucent, about 7 minutes. Add the corn and cook until crisp-tender, 3 minutes.

4   Once the fingerling potatoes are tender, drain them, cut them in half lengthwise, and add them to the skillet with the chorizo. Pour in the beer and give everything a stir.

5   Arrange the clams (no need to soak them) evenly over the top of the chorizo mixture, cover the skillet,

increase the heat so the beer comes to a gentle boil, and cook the clams until they open, 5 to 6 minutes. Discard any clams that have not opened, then scatter the herb of your choice in and around the clams. Serve the stew at once in shallow bowls.

Littlenecks with Baby Arugula and Garlicky Bruschette

My culinary life is such that it can sometimes be challenging to put favorite family recipes on the dinner docket due to other recipe testing and development demands. However, this recipe for littlenecks—a simple one—is one that manages to make it into regular rotation. SERVES 4

40 fresh littleneck clams in the shell

6 tablespoons extra virgin olive oil

2 large shallots, peeled and minced

6 cloves peeled garlic, 4 cloves minced and 2 cut in half

½ teaspoon hot red pepper flakes

½ cup dry white wine

4 ounces (6 cups) baby arugula, rinsed and spun dry

4 slices (½ inch thick) ciabatta or other rustic bread

1   Rinse the clams under cold running water to dislodge any grit clinging to the shells. Should they be especially gritty, give them a gentle scrubbing with a clean dish brush. Set the clams aside briefly.

2   Heat 2 tablespoons of the olive oil in a Dutch oven or other heavy pot over medium heat. Add the shallots, minced garlic, and hot red pepper flakes and cook

until the shallot is softened, about 5 minutes. Add the white wine and clams, cover the pot, and let come to a boil. Cook the clams until they open, 5 to 6 minutes. Discard any clams that have not opened.

3 While the clams are cooking, divide the arugula evenly among 4 shallow bowls. Toast or grill the ciabatta slices. Immediately rub a half clove of garlic over the surface of each toasted ciabatta slice and center a piece of toast on top of the arugula in each serving bowl. Drizzle 1 tablespoon olive oil over each slice of toast.

4 Pile the steamed clams on top of the toast and arugula, allotting an equal number of clams per bowl. Spoon 1/3 to 1/2 cup of the hot cooking broth over the arugula in each bowl to begin to wilt it. Serve at once with an empty bowl to hold the discarded clam shells.

Less Is More Spaghetti with Clams

My household is a huge fan of spaghetti or linguine with clams. The name of the pasta shape has never been as important to me as the recipe itself. Over the years, I have tried numerous recipes with the goal always being to create a dish that comes closest to ones I have savored in such coastal towns in Italy as Civitavecchia and Forte dei Marmi. This recipe is the one that resembles them most and I discovered it when I was reviewing Scott Conant's *Bold Italian* cookbook for the weekly food column I write for the Nantucket newspaper. While I do frequently use wine when cooking clams, I took notice when Conant wrote: "I hate wine in a clam sauce. This may stem from my days in a restaurant kitchen where we had a box of cheap wine near the stove. When we cooked clams we'd put the pan under the wine spout and, using tongs to flick the tap, were encouraged to let the wine flow into the pan. The alcohol never cooked off, and the dish always tasted more of cheap wine than clams." How could I not give Conant's method a whirl? It is simple and excellent, though my pasta still ends up tasting more New England than Italian because the local littlenecks I use are not anything like the small clams found in Italy. SERVES 2 OR 3

24 to 30 fresh littleneck clams in the shell
Salt
½ pound dried spaghetti
5 tablespoons extra virgin olive oil
3 cloves garlic, peeled and very thinly sliced
¼ to ½ teaspoon crushed hot red pepper flakes
⅓ cup chopped fresh flat-leaf parsley

1 Rinse the clams under cold running water to dislodge any grit clinging to the shells. Should they be especially gritty, give them a gentle scrubbing with a clean dish brush.

2 Bring a large pot of water to a boil, then stir in the salt. Add the spaghetti and cook until just shy of being al dente, following the cooking time recommendations on the package. Set aside about 1 cup of the pasta cooking water, then drain the spaghetti.

3 While the spaghetti is cooking, make the sauce. Heat 4 tablespoons of the olive oil in a large, straight-sided saucepan over medium heat. When hot, add the garlic and take the pan off the heat. Add the red pepper flakes and swirl the garlic around in the pan to prevent it from overcooking. Add ¾ cup of the reserved pasta cooking water to the pan and bring it to a boil over medium-high heat for 1 minute to create an emulsion. Add the spaghetti and clams, cover the pan, and cook until the clams open up and the pasta is al dente, adding more water if needed, about 5 minutes. Discard any clams that have not opened.

4 Add the parsley to the pan and toss to mix. Drizzle the remaining tablespoon of olive oil over the spaghetti, taste for seasoning, adding salt if needed, and serve immediately.

More Is More Spaghetti with Clams

This is my husband's preferred version of spaghetti with clams. This is also the first time I have actually written down the recipe because I have been winging it for several years, following a prose description related in Bill Buford's *Heat*—a funny and candidly written book chronicling an amateur's far-flung adventures as a kitchen slave in a worldly array of culinary venues. In this instance, Buford was slaving away in New York City at the pasta station in Mario Batali's Babbo restaurant, where he happened to notice that the sort of people hired to test recipes for Mario's cookbooks "have very white kitchens with carefully calibrated ovens and computerized weighing devices and are the despots of the written recipe."

For better or worse, I am not one of those types and, truth be told, I sometimes find measuring to be the bane of my culinary existence yet I do (rest assured) force myself to do it. Babbo's version of *linguine alle vongole* breaks all of Scott Conant's rules (see Less Is More Spaghetti with Clams on page 95) and blasphemes other Italian rules for cooking seafood, but nonetheless still manages to wow us every time we make it, which is often. One additional note: We frequently add the fresh minced quahog clams, that come in plastic pint containers almost anywhere fish is sold, along with the little-necks in the shell because we believe extra clams are a very good thing. SERVES 4

36 fresh littleneck clams in the shell

Salt

1 pound dried spaghetti or linguine

4 tablespoons extra virgin olive oil, plus olive oil for drizzling

2 ounces thinly sliced pancetta, minced (½ cup)

½ cup minced peeled red onion

5 cloves garlic, peeled and minced

½ teaspoon hot red pepper flakes (or a bit more for extra heat)

4 tablespoons (½ stick) unsalted butter, at room temperature

Generous ⅓ cup dry white wine

12 ounces minced fresh clams (optional)

3 tablespoons minced fresh flat-leaf parsley

1 Rinse the clams under cold running water to dislodge any grit clinging to the shells. Should they be especially gritty, give them a gentle scrubbing with a clean dish brush. Set the clams aside briefly.

2 Bring a large pot of water to a boil, then stir in the salt. Add the pasta and cook until just shy of being al dente, following the cooking time recommendations on the package.

3 Meanwhile, heat the olive oil in a large straight-sided skillet over medium heat. Add the pancetta and cook until just beginning to crisp, about 3 minutes. Add the red onion, garlic, and hot red pepper flakes and cook until the onion is soft and translucent, 4 to 5 minutes. Reduce the heat to low, and add the butter and white wine, stirring so the butter melts slowly and emulsifies with the wine, 1 to 2 minutes. Add the minced clams now, if using.

4 Once the pasta has been cooking for 2 minutes, add the whole clams to the skillet with the pancetta mixture, arranging them in a single layer on top of all the other ingredients. Cover the skillet, increase the heat to high, and cook until the clams open up, 4 to 5 minutes. Discard any clams that have not opened.

5 Using tongs, remove the slightly undercooked pasta from the pot, with some of the starchy pasta cooking water clinging to it, and transfer it directly to the skillet with the clams, swirling it gently to mingle everything together. If the sauce seems a bit dry, splash more of the hot pasta cooking water into the skillet to increase the liquid. Reduce the heat to

medium-low and continue cooking and swirling everything together for 1 or 2 minutes to finish cooking the pasta. Sprinkle in the parsley, drizzle a tablespoon or two of olive oil on top, and serve at once, mounding the wonderful tangle of pasta and clams into shallow pasta bowls. Provide bowl for discarding the shells.

Pantry Linguine with Clams

When I was beginning my vast cookbook collection, Nancy Verde Barr's cookbook *We Called It Macaroni*, published in 1990 and filled with anecdotes about growing up as an Italian American in Rhode Island, was one of my foundation books. The book still holds a place of prominence in my kitchen today. Years later, I would occasionally run into Nancy on Nantucket. She had come to the island because she had fallen in love with local artist Roy Bailey, who had coincidentally charmingly illustrated another one of my favorite cookbooks, Gwen Gaillard's *Recipes with Love*.

Nancy published a second Italian cookbook in 2002 called *Make It Italian* where she included a recipe for Roy's spaghetti with white clam sauce and wrote: "I was quite happy when I learned my fiancé liked to cook, but I blanched when he reached into the cupboard to prepare his version of one of my grandmother's best dishes, pasta with white clam sauce. Canned clams? Not just any canned clams; according to Roy, they must be Geisha or Cora brand of whole baby clams. They are from Thailand and are very small, tender, and sweet. And butter in place of olive oil? And cheese! All I can tell you is that it is delicious."

I naturally made the recipe at once and immediately agreed with Nancy. The recipe is a good one to have handy if you do not live in a coastal area where fresh clams are readily available or if you

Rose-covered, shingled summer cottages are as prevalent as tourists on Nantucket Island throughout the warm summer months.

like to hibernate in remote New England cabins far away from food markets. The one thing I do differently from the original recipe is cut the amount of fennel seeds in half to 1½ tablespoons from 3 tablespoons. SERVES 4

Salt

2 cans (10 ounces each) whole baby clams, preferably Geisha or Cora brand

6 tablespoons (¾ stick) unsalted butter

1½ tablespoons fennel seeds

½ teaspoon hot red pepper flakes

¼ cup dry white wine

3 tablespoons freshly squeezed lemon juice

Freshly ground black pepper

1 pound dried linguine, spaghettini, or capellini (Roy's preference is the finer capellini)

2 tablespoons minced fresh flat-leaf parsley

Freshly grated Parmesan cheese, for serving

1 Bring a large pot of water to a boil, then salt the water generously. You will add the pasta when the sauce is almost finished.

2 Drain the clams, setting aside the clams and clam juice separately. You should have about 2 cups of clams and 1⅓ cups of clam juice.

3 Melt the butter in a very large nonreactive straight-side skillet over medium-low heat. Once the butter is melted, crush the fennel seeds and hot red pepper flakes between your fingertips and drop them into the skillet. Cook, stirring, until fragrant, about 2 minutes. Pour in the white wine, lemon juice, and the reserved clam juice. Increase the heat to medium-high and let come to a boil. Cook until the liquid is reduced by half, 5 to 7 minutes. Taste for seasoning, adding a bit of salt and/or black pepper if needed.

4 Meanwhile, add the pasta to the pot of boiling water and cook it to a stage of just shy of being al dente, following the cooking time recommendations on the package. Remove 1 cup of the starchy pasta cooking water from the pot and keep it nearby. Stir the drained clams into the skillet with the sauce. Drain the pasta in a colander and add it to the skillet. Cook over medium-low heat until the pasta becomes al dente, 1½ to 2 minutes, tossing the pasta to coat it with the sauce. Add some of the reserved pasta water if necessary to make the sauce a bit silkier and help it coat the pasta. Sprinkle in the parsley.

5 Serve the pasta at once in shallow bowls with a bowl of Parmesan cheese on the table.

Basic Steamed Mussels

I grew up gathering mussels at low tide on the rocky beach in front of my family's summer home in Maine. The mussels were quite large, heavily bearded, and often speckled with barnacles. I have always liked mussels and for several years these were the only mussels I ever ate. When I was running my food shop on Nantucket in the 1980s, a friend of mine was gathering mussels offshore on the island of Tuckernuck. These mussels were small, tender, and pristine and I quickly became a convert to this type of mussel. Then, as I noted earlier in the book, the Tuckernuck mussels became infested with tiny crabs and my friend stopped harvesting them.

For a long time thereafter, cultured mussels from Prince Edward Island in Canada became the mussels served throughout New England in most restaurants as well as sold in seafood markets. I have nothing against PEI mussels, but I have since discovered cultured Maine mussels that I find superior in flavor and quite reminiscent of the Tuckernuck mussels I had once adored. Now, whenever I have serious mussel cravings, I make the effort to seek out the Bangs Island mussels sold by Browne Trading Company in Portland, Maine, or the Moosabec Maine mussels carried by Whole Foods Markets east of the Mississippi. Both are rope-cultured mussels that require little if any scrubbing and debearding.

As much as I rail against cooking steamer clams in wine or beer, for reasons I cannot exactly pinpoint I have absolutely nothing against cooking mussels with wine or beer. In fact, I favor such preparations, as clearly illustrated in this basic recipe. SERVES 3 OR 4

3 tablespoons extra virgin olive oil

2 large shallots, peeled and minced

4 cloves garlic, peeled and minced

1 cup dry white wine

3 small sprigs fresh thyme or lemon thyme

3 pounds mussels, scrubbed and debearded if necessary

2 tablespoons minced fresh flat-leaf parsley

Crusty bread, for serving

1 Heat the olive oil in a large nonreactive pot over medium heat. Add the shallots and garlic and cook until softened, 4 to 5 minutes. Pour in the white wine and scatter the thyme sprigs on top.

2 Pile the mussels in the pot, cover it, and let the liquid come to a boil. Cook the mussels until they open, 6 to 8 minutes, stirring them once or twice. Divide the mussels among 3 or 4 shallow bowls, discarding any that have not opened. Ladle some of the cooking liquid into each bowl, sprinkle each with parsley, and serve at once, with some crusty bread alongside to soak up the garlicky juices. Have an empty bowl on hand for discarding the mussel shells.

Mountaintop Mussels with Fennel and Tomatoes

I used to be the sort of skier who would try to pack as many runs into the day as possible and never bother to eat until the lifts had shut down in the late afternoon. That all changed when we started skiing as a family with our son in Vermont at Stowe and discovered the Cliff House restaurant teetering at the top of Mount Mansfield. Now, my son tends to be the one who skis all day without pause, while my husband and I enjoy the Cliff House too much not to plan our skiing day around having a leisurely and always terrific lunch. The restaurant is part of The Vermont Fresh Network and everything I have ever eaten there has been excellent. For some counterintuitive reason, I order the mussels more than any other dish on the menu and am always struck by how satisfying they taste in a place so far away from the sea. Perhaps, the altitude has something to do with it. Then again, the dish is also equally appealing when I attempt to re-create it at sea level back in my own Cape Cod kitchen. Sometimes, I will add some *linguiça* or *chouriço* to the fennel and tomatoes, although the Cliff House always serves the mussels without the addition of any meat. SERVES 4

4 tablespoons extra virgin olive oil

1 medium-size onion, peeled and coarsely chopped

5 cloves garlic, peeled and minced

1 small fennel bulb, cored and sliced lengthwise into thin slivers

½ teaspoon saffron

¼ teaspoon hot red pepper flakes

½ teaspoon sea salt

1 tablespoon Pernod or other French pastis, such as Ricard (optional)

1½ cups seeded and coarsely diced tomatoes (canned are fine when decent fresh tomatoes are not available)

¾ cup dry white wine

3 pounds mussels, scrubbed and debearded if necessary

2 tablespoons minced fresh flat-leaf parsley or slivered fresh basil leaves

Crusty bread, for serving

1 Heat the olive oil in a Dutch oven or other large, heavy pot over medium heat. Add the onion, garlic, and fennel and cook until tender, 7 to 8 minutes. Add the saffron, hot red pepper flakes, salt, and Pernod, if using. Let steep for about 1 minute. Add the tomatoes and cook until softened (if using fresh) or heated through, 3 minutes. Pour in the white wine and cook until heated through, 1 to 2 minutes.

2 Pile the mussels in the pot, cover it, and let the liquid come to a boil. Cook the mussels until they open, 6 to 8 minutes, stirring them once or twice. Heap the mussels, vegetables, and resulting sauce into shallow bowls, discarding any that have not opened. Scatter the parsley or basil over the top. Serve at once with a basket of crusty bread for mopping up the sauce. Have an empty bowl on hand for discarding the mussel shells.

Frequent foggy days along the rocky New England coastline can give a whole new meaning to the phrase—"fifty shades of grey."

Mussels with Woodchuck Hard Cider and Crème Fraîche

Quite a few companies are currently making hard cider in New England. One of the most seasoned cideries with wide distribution is Vermont's Woodchuck Cider, so named because the company prides itself in its independent spirit and "woodchuck" happens to be the nickname for the Vermontiest of Vermonters. Amber hard cider was the first hard cider Woodchuck began producing more than twenty-two years ago and it is still its most popular, though hard cider aficionados should definitely check out the many other handcrafted, small batch varieties now offered. I like making these cider-steamed mussels in chillier months and will sometimes take a cue from the beloved Belgian combo of *moules et frites* and serve the mussels with french fries piled into napkin-lined straw baskets or cone-shaped parchment-lined glasses. Years ago, when I had all the time in the world to fuss over every morsel I put in my mouth or served to others, I would painstakingly fry my own french fries. Currently, there are too many potential distractions in my life and I've learned the hard way that frying french fries, steaming mussels, and thickening a sauce can be akin to trying to pat your head and rub your stomach simultaneously. So here is my secret, which I feel is more time-savingly clever than dirty: I order take-out french fries from restaurants who serve ones I admire and recrisp them in the oven while my mussels are steaming away. Trust me, it works and the kitchen fills up with the smell of cider and mussels, rather than nasty hot oil. SERVES 4

3 tablespoons unsalted butter

3 shallots, peeled and sliced into thin rings

1 bottle (12 ounces) Woodchuck Amber hard cider, or other not terribly sweet hard cider

1 heaping tablespoon Dijon mustard, preferably Maille or Fallot

2 teaspoons fresh thyme leaves

2 pounds mussels, scrubbed and debearded if necessary

½ cup crème fraîche, preferably from Vermont Creamery

Sea salt and freshly ground black pepper

Crusty bread and/or french fries, for serving

1 Melt the butter in a Dutch oven or other large, heavy pot over medium heat. Add the shallots and cook until beginning to soften, about 2 minutes. Add a splash of the hard cider and the mustard and stir until incorporated. Pour in the rest of the cider and sprinkle in the thyme.

2 Pile the mussels in the pot, cover it, and let the liquid come to a boil. Cook the mussels until they open, 6 to 8 minutes. Using a slotted spoon or tongs, transfer the mussels to a bowl, discarding any that have not

opened, and cover the bowl to keep the mussels hot. Swirl the crème fraîche into the liquid in the pot and cook over high heat until the sauce is slightly reduced and thickened, 3 to 4 minutes. Taste for seasoning, adding salt and pepper to taste.

3 Dump the mussels back into the pot and toss gently to coat evenly with the sauce. Alternatively, you can divide the mussels among 4 shallow bowls and pour the sauce over them. Serve at once with either crusty bread or french fries.

Wood-Roasted Mussels with Garlic Butter

When I designed the kitchen for our Cape Cod home, my husband and I were still glowing from the honeymoon we had spent in Tuscany and thought it would be the greatest thing in the world to have a wood-burning Tuscan oven as a focal point in the kitchen. The aforementioned oven required a massive chimney, which we managed to get approval for from the Barnstable Historic District Commission. Little did we know that the oven needed to reach a temperature of 750°F to cook a pizza properly, making firing up the beast feasible only in the frostiest depths of winter. Additionally, little did we know that a few years later the downhill topography of our property would cause the chimney to sink and separate from the house and that the only masons who would agree to fix the problem were those who had been hired to stabilize the Leaning Tower of Pisa!

Mussels may be inexpensive but cooking them in our Tuscan oven is now a luxury. If you are not as foolish as I am to have an indoor Tuscan oven, you can cook these mussels in your outdoor Tuscan oven (wishful thinking!) or anything you can heat to

500°F, such as a regular oven or a large outdoor grill with a cover. However, I should add a wood fire does make this dish extra good. SERVES 4 TO 6

8 tablespoons (1 stick) unsalted butter, at room temperature

3 cloves garlic, peeled and finely minced

1 shallot, peeled and finely minced

2 tablespoons finely minced fresh flat-leaf parsley

1½ tablespoons freshly squeezed lemon juice

1 teaspoon finely grated lemon zest

½ cup dry white wine

3 pounds mussels, scrubbed and debearded if necessary

Freshly ground black pepper

2 tablespoons thinly sliced scallions, both white and tender green parts

Crusty bread, for serving

1 Preheat to 500°F or set up a large charcoal or gas grill and preheat it to high.

2 Place the butter in a small mixing bowl and evenly blend in the garlic, shallot, parsley, lemon juice, and lemon zest. Set the garlic butter aside.

3 Place the white wine in a wide, shallow, ovenproof pot that has a tight-fitting lid. Add the mussels to the pot, spreading them out evenly. Cover the pot and place it in the oven or on the grill. Roast the mussels until they open, 5 to 6 minutes. Use your most heat-proof oven mitts to remove the pot from the oven or grill, place it on a heatproof surface, uncover it, and toss the mussels with the garlic butter to coat them all over.

4 Divide the mussels and their buttery juices among 4 to 6 shallow serving bowls, discarding any mussels that have not opened. Grind a bit of pepper over each serving and scatter the scallions on top. Serve the mussels at once with plenty of bread to soak up the garlicky butter and juices.

Warm Smoked Mussel Salad with Sherry and Seal Cove Chèvre

My brother invented this salad over two decades ago when he was running his restaurant, Jonathan's, in downtown Blue Hill, Maine, and it remains one of my all-time favorite recipes. The salad is best when made with ingredients sourced not too far from Blue Hill—smoked mussels from Grindstone Neck of Maine and fresh and creamy goat cheese from Seal Cove Farm in Lamoine. However, if you come from "away" as they say in Maine, you may have to be content using the more widely distributed Ducktrap smoked Maine mussels and any creamy goat cheese that is readily available in your neck of the woods. SERVES 6

For the mussels and smoky sherry vinaigrette

1 cup extra virgin olive oil

¼ cup red wine vinegar (do not use balsamic vinegar)

¼ cup cream sherry

1 clove garlic, peeled and minced

1 shallot, peeled and minced

¼ teaspoon dried thyme

6 ounces smoked mussels

For the salad

8 ounces mixed seasonal baby greens

2 tablespoons extra virgin olive oil

6 ounces creamy goat cheese, cut into 1-ounce disks

¼ cup toasted pine nuts (see Box, page 70)

2 ounces (1 cup, loosely packed) fresh pea shoots (optional)

Freshly cracked black peppercorns

1 Preheat the oven to 350°F.

2 Prepare the mussels and smoky sherry vinaigrette: Heat the 1 cup of olive oil and the wine vinegar, sherry, garlic, shallot, and thyme in a small nonreactive saucepan over medium heat. Once the mixture begins to bubble and boil, in 3 to 4 minutes, reduce the heat to low and add the smoked mussels. Let the pan sit over low heat for between 5 and 10 minutes to allow the mussels to impart their smoky flavor into the vinaigrette.

3 Meanwhile, make the salad: Divide the greens among 6 medium-size salad plates. Drizzle 1 tablespoon of the olive oil over the bottom of a small baking dish and arrange the goat cheese rounds on top. Drizzle the remaining 1 tablespoon of olive oil over the top of the cheese rounds. Bake the goat cheese until it is just beginning to melt, 3 to 4 minutes. Remove the baking dish from the oven and immediately use a spatula to place one warm round of goat cheese in the center of each salad.

4 Using a slotted spoon, remove the smoked mussels from the vinaigrette and divide them equally among the 6 salads. Whisk the warm vinaigrette remaining in the saucepan to recombine and drizzle it evenly over the salad greens. The heat of the vinaigrette will begin to wilt the greens. Scatter a few pine nuts over each salad and top the salads with a little mound of pea shoots, if using. Serve at once and offer a peppermill at the table.

Scallop Puffs Que Sera

This is the recipe for which I am best known. In fact, I am so well known for it that I see it published all the time in other cookbooks, mostly community ones. I invented it when I ran my Que Sera Sarah shop and catering business on Nantucket in the 1980s. When I built a house on the island in the nineties, I embellished the exterior with scalloped shingles and named the house "Scallop Puff," as it is a longstanding Nantucket tradition to give your house a clever name. I have probably made and served over a million scallop puffs. Others have likely done the same, though I rarely encounter a scallop puff that tastes exactly like my original recipe.

Truth be told, I was not going to include the recipe in this book because it was already published in my *Nantucket Open-House Cookbook*. However, people come up to me all the time and say if I'm writing a new book, I have to include the recipe because it is so good and there is a whole new generation of cooks out there that need to have scallop puffs in their entertaining repertoire.

Now that my arm has been twisted, I should let the new generation know that you do not need to make this recipe with the priciest, freshest, most pedigreed scallops. No, I am certainly not encouraging the use of nasty calico scallops or their ilk, but I have lots of friends, myself included, who make the puffs with scallops they have frozen during scallop season and find lingering in their freezer six months later with the Cryovac seal still intact. MAKES ABOUT 8 DOZEN

2½ tablespoons unsalted butter or olive oil

1¼ pounds bay or sea scallops, side muscles removed if desired, scallops chopped into ¼-inch dice

3 cloves garlic, peeled and minced

1 tablespoon finely grated lemon zest

⅓ cup minced fresh dill, plus dill sprigs for garnish

2 cups freshly shredded mild Swiss or Jarlsberg cheese

2 to 2½ cups mayonnaise, preferably Hellmann's

Sea salt and freshly ground black pepper

8 dozen rounds (each 1½ or 2 inches) cut from good-quality commercial white bread, lightly toasted

Sweet paprika

Lemon slices, for garnish

1 Heat the butter or olive oil in a medium-size skillet over medium-high heat. Add the scallops, garlic, and lemon zest. Cook, stirring frequently, until the scallops are just barely cooked through, 2 to 3 minutes. Add the minced dill and cook until fragrant, about 30 seconds. Let the scallops cool to room temperature.

2 Add the cheese and enough mayonnaise to moistly bind all the ingredients together. Season the scallop mixture with salt and pepper to taste. Refrigerate the scallop mixture, covered, for at least 2 hours, but not longer than 3 days, before using.

3 When ready to cook, preheat the broiler to high, positioning an oven rack 4 to 5 inches underneath the heat source. Line as many baking sheets as you own with parchment paper. You'll be making the puffs in batches.

4 Arrange the toast rounds in rows ½ inch apart on the prepared baking sheets. Top each toast round with a mounded spoonful of the scallop mixture and then sprinkle the top of each lightly with paprika.

5 Broil the puffs in batches until puffed, bubbling, and lightly golden, 2 to 3 minutes. (Watch them carefully!) Transfer the puffs to decorative serving platters, garnish them with lemon slices and dill sprigs, and pass at once. The puffs always disappear quickly. Repeat the process with the remaining scallop puffs.

Pan-Seared Scallop Salad

This rosy, mixed seafood salad is my pared-down version of a far more elaborate Italian *insalata di frutti di mare*. I serve it warm when it is chilly outside and at room temperature during

the warmer months. I often make it when I know my guests may not be as big of a fan of ceviche as I am. SERVES 6 TO 8

8 sun-dried tomato halves

1 pound fresh sea scallops, cut in half, or 1 pound Nantucket bay scallops

½ cup extra virgin olive oil

3 plump cloves garlic, peeled and cut into thin slivers

¼ to ½ teaspoon hot red pepper flakes

1 teaspoon dried oregano, preferably Sicilian or Greek

1 pound medium-size (16 to 20 count) shrimp, peeled and deveined

½ cup dry white wine

½ cup pitted and coarsely chopped kalamata or oil-cured black olives

5 scallions, trimmed, white and tender green parts thinly sliced

3 tablespoons freshly squeezed lemon juice

Finely grated zest of 1 lemon

Sea salt and freshly ground black pepper

3 tablespoons chopped fresh cilantro

3 tablespoons slivered fresh basil leaves

1 Place the sun-dried tomatoes in a small saucepan, add water to cover, and let come to a boil over medium-high heat. Reduce the heat to medium and let the tomatoes simmer until softened and plump, about 5 minutes. Remove the pan from the heat and let the tomatoes cool. When cool enough to handle, cut the tomatoes into thin slivers and set them aside.

2 Remove the tough side muscles, the nibs, from the outside edge of the scallops. (This is done purely for aesthetic reasons.) Heat 3 tablespoons of the olive oil in a large skillet over medium heat. Add the garlic, hot red pepper flakes, and oregano and cook until fragrant, 1½ to 2 minutes. Add the shrimp and cook until partially cooked, about 2 minutes. Stir in the scallops

and continue cooking until both the shrimp and scallops are just barely cooked through in the center, 2 to 3 minutes. Add the white wine to the skillet, scraping up any browned bits clinging to the bottom of the skillet, and cook until warmed through, about 1 minute. Remove the skillet from the heat and let the seafood mixture cool for 10 minutes.

3 Transfer the seafood mixture to a shallow bowl and stir in the slivered sun-dried tomatoes and the olives, scallions, lemon juice, and lemon zest. Add the remaining 5 tablespoons of olive oil and season with salt and black pepper to taste. Gently fold in the cilantro and basil.

4 Present the salad in a decorative bowl placed in the center of a table, surrounded by small serving plates and cocktail forks. Serve warm or at room temperature.

Seared Maine Diver Scallops with Shallots and White Wine

Since most people I know find it less than tempting to go swimming in the ocean in Maine, even on the hottest days of the summer, it is hard not to applaud appreciatively the rough and tough Down East fishing souls who don wet suits in the winter months and dive into the ocean in order to hand pluck the choicest sea scallops from the depths of frigid waters at their most frigid. Maine's diver scallops are a true winter luxury, requiring ingredient restraint and a specific cooking technique. This recipe may also be applied to other New England sea scallops, but I think those heroically harvested from colder Maine waters are the jewels in the crown. SERVES 4

20 jumbo diver-harvested sea scallops
  (1¾ to 2 pounds)

1½ teaspoons coarse sea salt

2 tablespoons (¼ stick) unsalted butter

1 tablespoon extra virgin olive oil

1 tablespoon peeled minced shallot

¾ cup dry white wine

1 tablespoon chopped fresh flat-leaf parsley

Lemon wedges, for serving

Freshly ground black pepper (optional)

1 Preheat the oven to 200°F. Place a wire rack on top of a baking sheet and set it aside.

2 Remove the tough side muscles, the nibs, from the outside edge of the scallops. Pat the scallops dry with a dish cloth or paper towels. Place the scallops on a large plate and sprinkle the sea salt evenly over the tops of the scallops. Season only one side of the scallops. Let the scallops stand for about 10 minutes.

3 Warm a large skillet over medium-high heat; it is important *not* to use a nonstick or cast-iron skillet; stainless steel (such as All-Clad) is the best choice. Place 1 tablespoon of the butter and 1½ teaspoons of the olive oil in the skillet.

4 When the butter has melted and the mixture begins to foam, add 10 of the scallops, salted side down. Sear the scallops until they are golden brown on the underside, 2 to 2½ minutes. Resist the temptation to move the scallops around because they will stick to the skillet if they are not left in place to sear. Turn the scallops over and turn off the heat. Transfer the scallops to the wire rack on top of the baking sheet and cover them loosely with aluminum foil. Place the baking sheet in the warm oven.

5 Add the remaining 1 tablespoon of butter and 1½ teaspoons of olive oil to the skillet. Repeat the searing process with the remaining 10 scallops. Transfer these scallops to the wire rack with the first batch. Cover all of the scallops with the aluminum foil and place the baking sheet back in the warm oven.

6 Add the shallots to the skillet and cook over medium heat until softened, 2 minutes. Add the white wine, increase the heat to high, and cook, scraping up any browned bits clinging to the bottom of the skillet, until the liquid is reduced by one third, 2 to 3 minutes. Add the parsley and turn off the heat.

7 Divide the scallops evenly among 4 medium-size plates. Spoon the pan sauce over the scallops, garnish with lemon wedges, and serve at once. Pass a peppermill for anyone who may wish a grind or two.

Rosemary Skewers with Prosciutto-Wrapped Sea Scallops

Bacon-wrapped scallops are a ubiquitous New England preparation and I regret to say I have never had one that sent me into orbit. The scallops are usually overcooked and rubbery and the bacon undercooked, fatty, and unappetizing. Even though I am not the sort of recipe sleuth who documents a zillion different ways to rectify a recipe, I did believe I could tap into my scallop sensibilities to improve upon a recipe whose flavor profile was clearly winning. This recipe represents a few things I discovered.

Sea scallops are a better choice than bay scallops for this preparation and southern New England sea scallops tend to have both the right price point and size. I usually go with scallops from Chatham or New Bedford, Massachusetts. Prosciutto works better than bacon as a wrapper, a marinade keeps the scallops flavorful and moist, and fresh rosemary skewers will make for a far more aromatic and seductive presentation than ho-hum toothpicks. Those rosemary skewers are optional, however, because I realize fresh rosemary branches may not be available each and every time you want to make

Scallop Savvy

I have been privileged throughout my scallop-eating life to have direct, local access to hours-young bay scallops harvested from Nantucket Sound. These world-renowned scallops are most often marketed as Nantucket Bay Scallops but they may also come from Nantucket Sound locations surrounding Martha's Vineyard and the southern shores of Cape Cod. During the many years I lived on Nantucket, I swore exclusively by scallops harvested by Nantucket buddies, but I have recently become more open-minded after eating bay scallops harvested on Martha's Vineyard and Cape Cod and finding their flavor, price, and cachet in every way equal to scallops that proclaim Nantucket as provenance.

The commercial bay scallop season runs from November to March, but harvesting may only take place when the temperature is above 28°F in order to prevent dredged scallops from freezing and dying on the scallop boat's culling board during the sorting process. I always buy my bay scallops fresh in season and never frozen during other times of the year. I do occasionally freeze part of my own procurement, but only when I know the scallops were harvested and shucked within twenty-four hours of my purchasing them. Frozen bay scallops never quite rival fresh ones and I make sure to use them within six months of their freezing.

Maine diver-harvested scallops are another extraordinary winter delicacy. These scallops account for less than 1 percent of all New England scallops harvested and are literally plucked by far bolder hands than mine from the frigid Maine ocean floor by professional fishermen who are also licensed scuba divers. Maine diver-harvested scallops are indeed precious ocean jewels and less is more when cooking them. I favor a simple but precisely executed pan-sear (see page 105).

The most affordable and accessible New England scallops are sea scallops and the ones I usually cook come from Chatham on Cape Cod or New Bedford on the southeastern shore of Massachusetts. When purchasing sea scallops, make doubly sure to purchase "dry" scallops, a term that may sound counterintuitive, but is a culinary mandate for cooking the sea scallops in this chapter. When scallops are labeled "dry," it means they have been shucked immediately upon harvesting on the fishing vessel and placed directly into a container without any further additives. By contrast, "wet" scallops, while also shucked directly onboard the fishing boat, are placed into containers with water more often than not laced with unpronounceable preservative chemicals. "Wet" scallops will never sear properly and are by treatment less fresh and vastly less tasty than "dry" scallops.

this recipe. Opt for skinny bamboo skewers whenever necessary. SERVES 4

4 branches (10 to 12 inches each) fresh
  rosemary, or 4 bamboo skewers
  (8 to 10 inches each)

20 jumbo fresh sea scallops (1¾ to 2 pounds)

2½ tablespoons extra virgin olive oil

2½ tablespoons freshly squeezed lemon juice

¼ teaspoon fine sea salt

2 plump cloves garlic, peeled and finely minced
  or grated on a Microplane

1 tablespoon finely minced fresh rosemary

3 to 4 ounces thinly sliced prosciutto

Freshly cracked black peppercorns

Vegetable oil, for oiling the grill grate

1 lemon, cut in half crosswise

1 About an hour before you plan to assemble and grill the scallops, prepare the skewers. If you are using rosemary branches, strip the needles off the bottom three quarters of each branch, setting aside some of the needles to chop for the marinade and reserving the rest for another use. Place the rosemary branches upright in a tall glass and fill it with enough water to soak the stripped portion of the branches. This will prevent them from burning on the grill. If you are using bamboo skewers, place them in a flat dish and cover them with water. Let the branches or skewers soak for at least 45 minutes. Drain, when ready to use.

2 Remove the tough side muscles, the nibs, from the outside edge of the scallops. Place the scallops in a nonreactive baking dish just large enough to hold them in a single layer. Place the olive oil, lemon juice, salt, garlic, and minced rosemary in a small nonreactive bowl and whisk them together. Pour the marinade over the scallops, tossing them gently to coat evenly. Let the scallops marinate at room temperature for about 30 minutes (any longer and they will begin to "cook" ceviche-style).

3 Set up a charcoal or gas grill and preheat it to medium-high.

4 Cut the prosciutto slices lengthwise in half to make strips that are about 1 inch wide. Remove a scallop from the marinade and wrap it with a strip of prosciutto. The prosciutto should wrap around the scallop 1½ to 2 times. Thread the scallop on the skewer through the prosciutto to hold the prosciutto in place. Remove another scallop from the marinade. Thread this scallop on the skewer *without* wrapping it in prosciutto. Wrap the next scallop in prosciutto and thread it onto the skewer, followed by another *unwrapped* scallop. Wrap a fifth scallop in prosciutto and thread it on the skewer. The scallops should just touch one another but not be mushed together.

5 Repeat the process to make four skewers, each with 5 scallops, 3 that are wrapped in prosciutto and 2 that are not. Place the skewers on a platter and grind a bit of black pepper over each one. Set aside

any marinade from the scallops for brushing on them as they grill.

6 Lightly oil the grill grate. Place the scallop skewers on the grate and grill them until lightly browned on the undersides, about 3 minutes. At the same time, place the 2 lemon halves cut side down on the grate and grill them until burnished, 2 to 3 minutes. Turn the scallop skewers over, brush them with any remaining marinade, and grill them 1 to 2 minutes longer. The edges of the prosciutto should be crispy, the tops of the rosemary branches, if using, charred, and the scallops just barely cooked through. Serve the skewers hot off the grill with a squeeze of charred lemon.

First of the Season Nantucket Bay Scallops

Family scalloping season on Nantucket begins in October and the commercial season at the beginning of November. No matter which you participate in, having the first scallops of the season is always a big deal. Basically, you want to do as little as possible to the scallops because they are so perfect tasting in and of themselves. In fact, I was once invited to a friend's island home in Dionis at the onset of the family season and served the first haul simply shucked and raw on the half shell.

Most people, however, prefer to cook their scallops and this is pretty much the go-to recipe on the island. I always remove the side muscle or nib because it makes the finished dish look more aesthetically pleasing, though some people prefer not to bother with the process. The muscle is edible and I always pop them directly into my mouth like sashimi. SERVES 4

1½ pounds fresh Nantucket bay scallops

3 tablespoons unsalted butter

1 tablespoon olive oil

Sea salt (fleur de sel if you have it) and
  freshly ground white or black pepper

2 to 3 cloves minced garlic

2 tablespoons freshly squeezed lemon juice

2 tablespoons dry vermouth or white wine

2 tablespoons minced fresh flat-leaf parsley

1   Remove the tough side muscles, the nibs, from the outside edge of the scallops. Melt 2 tablespoons of the butter in the olive oil over medium-high heat in a large heavy nonreactive skillet. Season the scallops with salt and pepper to taste. When the butter and olive oil begin to sizzle, add the scallops to the skillet and cook until they're just beginning to brown, about 2 minutes without stirring. Give a stir to turn the scallops over and continue cooking them until they are just barely cooked through, about 1½ minutes longer. Transfer the scallops to a plate or platter and cover them loosely with aluminum foil to keep warm.

2   Add the garlic to the skillet and cook until softened and fragrant, about 1 minute. Add the lemon juice and vermouth or white wine to the skillet, stirring to scrape up any browned bits clinging to the bottom of the skillet. Let bubble until slightly reduced, about 1 minute. Reduce the heat to low and swirl in the remaining 1 tablespoon of butter. Return the scallops to the skillet and toss gently to coat with the sauce. Sprinkle in the parsley and serve at once.

Bumper-to-Bumper Bay Scallops

G inger Heard was a warm and ebullient woman whose joie de vivre epitomized the essence of Nantucket when I began living there. Ginger's husband, Hammie, shared his terrific Bloody Mary recipe with me in my *Nantucket Open-House Cookbook*. Now, I am thrilled to feature this equally wonderful recipe of Ginger's and regret she could not have seen it in print in her lifetime.

Ginger provided me with a page of notes to guide me through this essentially simple but brilliant preparation. Foremost, she advised: "The most important part of the preparation is finding the right dish!!! Once you have this in your pantry you must never lose it. One round 8-to-9-inch Pyrex-type pie plate may become your best friend. It will hold a pound of scallops nicely. B U M P E R - T O - B U M P E R. That means placing the scallops neatly next to each other with sides touching each other but not overlapping." SERVES 4

2 cloves minced garlic

1 pound fresh Nantucket bay scallops

1 tablespoon Wondra flour

3 tablespoons unsalted butter, melted

Sea salt and freshly ground black pepper

1   Preheat the broiler to high, positioning an oven rack 4 to 5 inches underneath the heat.

2   Scatter the garlic over the bottom of an 8-to-9-inch broiler-safe pie pan. Remove the nibs from the scallops. Arrange the scallops on the garlic next to each other so the sides touch but do not overlap.

3   Place the flour in a small, fine-mesh strainer and sift it lightly and evenly over all of the scallops. Drizzle the melted butter slowly, carefully, and evenly over the scallops. Ginger had further noted: "This is what makes them deliciously crispy on top when broiled." Season the scallops with a sprinkling of salt and a few grinds of pepper.

4   Place the pan underneath the broiler and broil the scallops until the butter is sizzling and the scallops are randomly spotted brown, 5 to 7 minutes. Eat at once, as Ginger suggests, "on a toothpick or by the forkful. There is nothing else quite like a Nantucket bay scallop."

Bay Scallops with Sage Brown Butter and Spaghetti Squash

When I first came to Nantucket as a teenager the White Elephant hotel was famous for its extravagant Sunday brunch buffet. At some point the brunches fell by the wayside and many years later the hotel started sponsoring an off-season culinary series featuring chefs from around the country cooking with Nantucket ingredients. This delicious recipe was demonstrated in November of 2008 when chef Bob Iacovone from Cuvée restaurant in New Orleans paid a visit to the island during scallop season. It won me over instantly and I have adapted it and made it many times since. SERVES 4 TO 6

1 medium-size spaghetti squash
   (about 3 pounds)

8 tablespoons (1 stick) unsalted butter

2½ tablespoons coarsely torn sage leaves

Sea salt and freshly ground black pepper

1½ pounds fresh Nantucket bay scallops

2 tablespoons canola or grape seed oil

2 tablespoons pumpkin seeds, toasted
   (see Box, page 70)

1 Preheat the oven to 375°F.

2 Cut the spaghetti squash in half and scrape out all the seeds. Pour water to a depth of ¼ inch in a roasting pan large enough to hold the squash halves. Place the squash halves, cut side down, in the pan and bake them until tender, 30 to 40 minutes. Let the squash cool in the roasting pan for 10 minutes.

3 Meanwhile, melt the butter in a large straight-sided skillet and continue to cook over medium to medium-high heat, stirring frequently, until it begins to smell like roasted nuts and turn brown but not burn (tend it carefully), 2 to 3 minutes. Once the butter is browned, remove it from the heat and stir in the sage. The leaves should sizzle a bit and become crisp.

4 Use a fork to remove the spaghetti squash pulp in strings from the shell and place it in the skillet with the browned butter and sage. Heat over medium-low heat until hot, 5 to 7 minutes, tossing occasionally to coat with the browned butter. Season the squash with salt and pepper to taste.

5 Remove the nibs from the outside edge of the scallops. Heat the oil in a separate large skillet over medium-high heat. Season the scallops with some salt and pepper. When the oil is hot, add the scallops and sear without stirring until the undersides are brown, about 2 minutes. Stir to turn the scallops over and continue cooking until they are just barely cooked through, 1 to 2 minutes more.

6 Divide the spaghetti squash among 4 to 6 dinner plates and arrange some seared scallops on top of each squash serving, dividing them evenly. Sprinkle the pumpkin seeds on top and serve at once.

Christmas Eve Bay Scallops

After we moved from Nantucket to Cape Cod we began a lovely tradition of spending Christmas Eve together with our neighbors Walter and Judy Kaess. We enjoyed the fact that we only had to walk across the street to one another's festooned homes and that there was never any shortage of fine food and special occasion wine. Sometimes we collaborated on elaborate soirees celebrating the Feast of the Seven Fishes. Other times, we would opt for simplicity, especially when the Kaesses' three small grandchildren started to travel from their home in Paris to spend the holidays with the family.

A bushel of prized Nantucket Bay scallops is strewn with eel grass from the dredging process and awaits shucking in a shanty before being sold for use in both raw and cooked recipes.

3 Bake the scallops until bubbling and lightly browned on top, no more than 25 minutes. Take care not to overcook the scallops or they will turn rubbery. Serve the scallops scooped onto dinner plates with lemon wedges on the side.

Whether we dine on one or seven fishes, this recipe of Judy's is always on the menu. It is yet another incredibly simple yet stellar scallop dish. Sometimes, I add a little splash of cream sherry to the melted butter that moistens the Ritz cracker crumbs, but the choice can be yours. The recipe doubles easily and can also be made in individual ramekins or porcelain scallop shells. SERVES 4

1 pound fresh Nantucket bay scallops

About 15 Ritz crackers, crushed with a rolling pin or in a food processor (1 cup crumbs)

1½ tablespoons cream sherry (optional)

6 tablespoons (¾ stick) unsalted butter, melted

Lemon wedges, for serving

1 Preheat the oven to 375°F.

2 Remove the nibs from the outside edge of the scallops. Layer the scallops and crumbs alternately in a 1-quart casserole or soufflé dish. If you are using the sherry, stir it into the melted butter. Drizzle the butter evenly over the top of the scallops, letting it seep down between the layers.

Thanksgiving Ceviche

This is purposely not a very elaborate ceviche recipe. I keep it minimal because I consider Thanksgiving to be still part of the beginning of the local bay scallop season and I want the flavor of the scallops to shine through loud and clear. SERVES 6 TO 8

1½ pounds fresh Nantucket bay scallops

½ cup freshly squeezed lime juice

2 tablespoons extra virgin olive oil

1 jalapeño pepper, stemmed, seeded, and minced

½ red bell pepper, stemmed, seeded, and cut into small dice

4 scallions, trimmed, both white and tender green parts thinly sliced on a diagonal

¼ cup minced fresh cilantro

Sea salt

1 Remove the nibs from the outside edge of the scallops. Place the scallops in a shallow nonreactive bowl and toss with the lime juice and olive oil. Gently fold in the jalapeño pepper, bell pepper, scallions, and cilantro. Cover the ceviche and let marinate in the refrigerator for at least 3 hours or as long as overnight before serving.

2 When ready to serve, give everything a stir, taste for seasoning, and add a pinch of salt if needed. Transfer the ceviche to a decorative serving bowl. Serve chilled with small plates and cocktail forks alongside.

Christmas Stroll Ceviche

I have several good friends from Texas who own homes on Nantucket and I never cease to be enthralled by the way they entertain. This ceviche is the curative result when their houseguests had a bit too grand a time one night during a Christmas Stroll weekend on the island. In a gesture of magnanimity, an invitation was issued to several people for a ceviche and Champagne gathering the following day at their home on Main Street. Houseguest José Kuachi was early to rise the next morning in order to assemble his prized Mexican recipe for ceviche. I imagine that José must have been feeling a bit under the weather because the resulting ceviche was certainly hot enough to make one and all forget anything that might be ailing from prior excesses. José's ceviche inaugurated an annual Christmas Stroll tradition within the reveling group and it is now presented every year in an exquisite, specially engraved commemorative crystal pedestal bowl.

José encourages: "The goal in making ceviche is to express the attitude of the cook and if possible those who are going to partake of the ceviche, so tangier, spicier, and more flavorful is better." José also recommends "A dry white wine, like a Sancerre, should be served if the economy is bad; a white Chablis or one of the Montrachets if things are okay; and a rosé Champagne if things are really good." SERVES 6

1½ pounds fresh Nantucket bay scallops

15 to 20 very fresh unblemished limes

2 to 4 fresh green serrano peppers

2 medium-size tomatoes, preferably tomatoes-on-the-vine (see Note)

1 small yellow onion

1 handful fresh cilantro leaves

Sea salt and freshly cracked black peppercorns

4 tablespoons ketchup, preferably Heinz

2 teaspoons extra virgin olive oil

1½ teaspoons Maggi Seasoning Sauce

½ cup cold water

2 tablespoons or more bottled Mexican hot sauce (Valentina is a good brand)

3 ripe avocados (optional), halved, pitted, and peeled, for serving

Saltine crackers, José's choice for serving

1   Remove the nibs from the outside edge of the scallops. Place the scallops in a single layer in a shallow 9-by-13-inch glass or ceramic baking dish. Use a juicer to squeeze the juice from the limes and pour the juice over the scallops. Take care not to get any rind or oil from the limes into the juice or it will make for a bitter taste. Marinate the scallops for 1 hour in the lime juice, turning them with a spatula every 10 minutes so that the juice touches all surfaces of the scallops.

2   Meanwhile, seed and mince the serrano peppers. Mince the tomatoes, onion, and cilantro and place them in a large mixing bowl. Season with salt and pepper to taste and stir in the ketchup, olive oil, Maggi seasoning, cold water, and Mexican hot sauce. Mix all together very well.

3   Using a slotted spoon, gently remove the scallops from the baking dish and transfer them to the bowl with the tomato mixture, trying to minimize the amount of lime juice you transfer. Mix gently, taking care not to break the scallops, stir to mix. Cover the bowl with plastic wrap and refrigerate the ceviche until it's slightly chilled, about 30 minutes. Stir one last time before serving.

4   Serve the ceviche in small bowls, spooned over half an avocado if desired. Accompany the ceviche with saltine crackers on the side.

NOTE: *Given the time of the year, local gorgeous tomatoes won't be available, but tomatoes-on-the-vine most likely will be at your local supermarket.*

For the Love of Lobster

"Lobsters are scavengers. They are also cannibals. They are essentially a bottom-living animal, using their powers of swimming only in an emergency. Caught lobsters seem sluggish, but in their natural element lobsters are agile, wary, pugnacious, capable of defending themselves against larger enemies, and on occasion and for short distances they exhibit surprising speed."—T. M. Prudden, *About Lobsters*

While fancy lobster preparations may be revered in the rarified world of haute cuisine, in New England the eating of lobsters is more often than not an informal and messy undertaking requiring bibs, mallets, melted butter, specialized forks, napkins galore, and a modicum of anatomical savoir faire. Paraphernalia and expense notwithstanding, loving lobster is a New England birthright and one that inspires serious envy in places not blessed with our bounty.

If pressed, I might concede that the best lobsters I have ever eaten have been enjoyed outdoors in the rough in Maine. On the other hand, I also could be just as easily persuaded to say that the best lobster was the last one I ate and that lobster may well have been grilled over an open fire in Guilford, Connecticut; spooned into a billowy popover in Bristol, Rhode Island; butter poached in a trendy Boston restaurant; served four ways at the intimate forty-seat Company of the Cauldron on Nantucket; tucked into an après-ski bowl of macaroni and cheese in the mountains of New Hampshire or Vermont; or merely plucked from a steaming bed of seaweed in my own Cape Cod backyard.

In all fairness, I should also confess that I don't really like to cook live lobsters and imagine this is due to my Piscean sensibilities battling and winning over my Yankee birthright. When I do personally have to plunge live lobsters into a pot for steaming or boiling, *sans* husband or other source of macho support, it helps if I read about the nature of lobsters as T. M. Prudden depicted them in the quotation above. If you would rather not wrestle with the irony of having to hate live lobsters in order to love them cooked, I highly recommend the option of having your local fishmonger cook your lobsters for many but not all of the recipes in this chapter. Fishmongers in general do not seem to be bothered by any questions of morality or mortality when it comes to lobsters and often times their commercial steamers do a superior job of cooking these cannibalistic crustaceans.

If you are going to cook live lobsters at home, make sure you have the large sort of blue enamel or stainless lobster pot that comes with almost every coastal rental property in New England, and use seawater or sea-salted tap water for either steaming or boiling. I have never taken any sides on the issue of steaming vs. boiling and prefer to devote my energies to not overcooking those lobsters I do manage to put into the pot in my own home. This is usually nine to ten minutes for lobsters that weigh one pound to a pound and one quarter.

Finally, I tend to be rather opinionated about how best to highlight that coveted and loveable New England lobster flavor and therefore do not like to get sidetracked with lots of fancy preparations. In fact, I don't even bother clarifying the butter into which I dip simply steamed or boiled lobsters because I have discovered that the hand-churned butter from Maine, sold as Kate's sea salted butter throughout stores in New England and beyond, tastes the way melted butter should taste when paired with so many of the lobster recipes in this chapter.

Yes, I would be tempted to order a lobster soufflé if dining in a fine French restaurant, but at home there is nothing and I meaning *nothing* better than enjoying a homemade lobster roll or feasting on a cast-iron skillet of Lobster Fried Over Cold. See page 120 for an overview of preparing lobsters.

Simple Stovetop Lobster Bake

If there were his/hers, Mars/Venus lobster bakes, this would definitely be hers and mine, while the macho backyard wheelbarrow lobster bake undertaking on page 116 could be gleefully ceded to my husband. What I love about this indoor stovetop recipe is that it is easy, pretty, tasty, and can be made at any time of the year, providing that local summer corn isn't vital to your lobster bake enjoyment. I have often assembled this stovetop lobster bake in the snowy depths of winter, and it really hits the spot as a welcome interlude to a steady cold weather diet of thick soups and stews. SERVES 4

16 to 20 fingerling potatoes

2 medium-size white or yellow onions, peeled and cut into sixths

4 plump cloves garlic, peeled and cut in half

1 bottle (12 ounces) lager, such as Stella Artois, Samuel Adams, or any local brewery favorite

1 cup bottled clam juice, or 1 cup seafood stock or Lobster Stock (page 138)

8 whole black peppercorns

1 pound kielbasa or linguiça

4 live lobsters (1 to 1¼ pounds each)

36 fresh littleneck clams in the shell

8 tablespoons (1 stick) unsalted butter, melted

1 Place the potatoes, onions, garlic, lager, clam juice, and peppercorns in a large, sturdy stockpot. Bring to a boil over medium-high heat and parboil for 5 minutes. Add the sausage, lobsters, and clams, cover the pot, and let cook over medium-high heat until the clam shells open and the lobsters are cooked through, 15 to 17 minutes.

2 Divide the lobster bake ingredients among 4 large plates, discarding any clams that have not opened. Strain the cooking broth through a fine-mesh sieve and pour it into 4 small mugs or tea cups. Pour the melted butter into 4 small ramekins and serve both the broth and butter for dipping placed next to each serving of lobster bake.

Nigel's Backyard Wheelbarrow Lobster Bake

Maine's Trenton Bridge Lobster Pound, a family-run operation for over five decades, cooks top-notch lobsters and clams in huge pots of seawater heated by rustic wood fires.

My parents' house in Blue Hill, Maine, sits on one of the most picturesque stretches of rocky Down East coastline imaginable. One summer, about five or six years ago, during our annual summer visit to Maine, my husband, Nigel, got the idea that my parents' beach needed to be christened with a true Down East lobster bake, nestled into the shoreline's jagged rocks replete with driftwood fires burning and tended to throughout the entire day. How could any member of our family argue with such a seductive and generous proposition? Beverages flowed to fuel this extended extravaganza, fabulous family photos were snapped, and the long awaited feast was indeed everything we dreamed it would be. However, my dear mother ended up spending the next week picking up after Nigel's grand lobster bake.

Since Nigel's other favorite lobster undertaking when visiting Maine is to drive forty-five minutes to the Trenton Bridge Lobster Pound set alongside the busy road to Bar Harbor and order bowls of steamers and huge lobsters cooked over the pound's birch wood–fueled fire, I suggested that the next time Nigel mentioned the Trenton Bridge Lobster Pound my mother jump on the invitation without hesitation and pray that Nigel never again feels the urge to have a lobster bake on her beach.

Truth be told, Nigel has not staged another lobster bake until recently and this time our own Cape Cod backyard was the lucky recipient and yours truly the designated cleaner-upper. It all started when I gave Nigel a copy of Francis Mallmann's Argentine grilling cookbook *Seven Fires* as a Christmas present. He adored the book and became particularly enamored of Mallmann's recipe for *curanto*, in which a couple of different cuts of lamb are cooked pit style in a metal wheelbarrow. Nigel began to mumble about plans to do something similar, except with lobster, in our own metal wheelbarrow in our own backyard. I began to cringe mildly, knowing that summer and the season for backyard gatherings was still a few months away. Well, Nigel didn't forget or let go of his idea to stage this lobster bake in our only wheelbarrow once summer arrived. In all fairness, I must admit Nigel's second lobster bake attempt ended up being a big success plus a great way to bring the savor of the seashore to land, though I'm not sure the effort extended was any less than that used to stage his initial lobster bake on my parents' beach. One bright note, however, is that this style lobster bake is pretty much contained to the confines of the wheelbarrow and my clean-up chores only took a couple of hours.

Do try this nifty lobster bake at home if you are adventuresome and willing to devote a day to toiling over a unique and irresistibly New Englandy backyard event for six lucky lobster-loving guests. And you have a completely safe area in which to stage it. You will of course need a metal wheelbarrow plus three hefty cement cinder blocks, eighteen large rocks, one hundred pounds of sand (available in bags in stores like The Home Depot if you don't want to or can't cart it from a nearby beach), a good supply of aged firewood, a couple gallon buckets of seaweed, a new canvas drop cloth (sold in paint stores). After you finish with this list, don't forget the lobsters, clams, mussels, sausages, potatoes, ears of corn, lots of melted butter, lobster-eating paraphernalia, piles of napkins, patience, and stamina! SERVES 6

Special supplies

Metal wheelbarrow (6 cubic feet in size)

3 large cement blocks (6 to 8 inches tall)

100 pounds sand (two 50-pound bags)

18 large rocks (8 to 10 inches in diameter), well rinsed if dirty and well dried

20 to 24 pieces of aged firewood

Shovel

1 unused canvas drop cloth (about 8 by 4 feet)

2 gallons fresh seaweed

6 lobster crackers and lobster forks

For the lobster bake

2 pounds small Red Bliss potatoes, scrubbed, and boiled in water for 7 minutes, then drained

6 small yellow onions, unpeeled

6 live lobsters (1 to 1¼ pounds each), rubber claw bands removed

2 pounds fresh steamer clams in the shell, soaked if necessary to remove sand (see Box, page 84)

2 pounds mussels, scrubbed and debearded if necessary

2 pounds kielbasa or linguiça

6 to 12 ears fresh local corn, husks left on (the number depends on appetites and passion for corn on the cob)

1 pound melted butter, preferably Kate's salted butter

Sea salt and freshly ground black pepper

1 Get a good night's sleep, eat an early lunch, and begin preparations between noon and 1 p.m. on the day of your lobster bake. If you don't own a metal wheelbarrow you will need to have borrowed or bought one earlier. On a gravel or other nonflammable surface that is away from anything flammable, set up the lobster bake. Remove the wheels and prop the wheelbarrow up off the ground on 3 large cement cinder blocks. Make sure the wheelbarrow balances securely on the blocks.

2 Pour sand to a depth of 3 inches in the bottom of the wheelbarrow to serve as insulation. Place the rocks on top of the sand. Make sure the rocks are dry as wet or damp rocks can explode when exposed to a hot fire. Build a wood fire on top of the rocks, light it, and let the fire burn for the next 4 to 5 hours, adding more logs as necessary to keep the fire glowing, but not blazing.

3 Thirty minutes before adding the lobster bake ingredients make sure the logs have burned down to glowing coals. Rake the coals evenly among the rocks. Remove any large chunks of wood and dispose of them safely to avoid any fire hazards. Shovel another 2 inches of sand over the top of the hot rocks and coals.

4 Spray the canvas drop cloth with water from an outdoor hose to dampen the entire cloth. Arrange the damp drop cloth so that half of it sits on top of the

A pretty summer window box blooms with patriotic pride in honor of the Fourth of July.

trip to a local lobster pound, where most of the hard work is done for you, but bask for the time being in a sense of admirable accomplishment.

NOTE: *Have a large metal bucket close to the lobster bake in which to shovel the layer of sand. Be sure to wear heavy grill gloves when handling the drop cloth.*

layer of sand and the rest hangs over the wheelbarrow. Top the drop cloth in the wheelbarrow with the seaweed and then layer the lobster bake ingredients over it. Begin with the potatoes and nestle the onions between them. Top these with the lobsters, followed by the clams and mussels. Add the kielbasa or *linguiça* and top these with the ears of corn. Fold the overhanging damp drop cloth over the top of the food so it covers it completely. Shovel another 2-inch layer of sand on top of the drop cloth. Relax and let the lobster bake do its magic for the next 1¼ to 1½ hours.

5   Carefully peel back an edge of the drop cloth to check the ingredients for doneness after the first 1¼ hours of cooking. Assess the progress and either serve the lobster bake at once or continue cooking until everything is tender, possibly 15 minutes longer (see Note).

6   Divide all of the lobster bake ingredients among 6 large and sturdy serving plates, discarding any clams or mussels that have not opened. Serve with individual small pots of melted butter, salt and pepper, lots of napkins, and large bowls for discarding all the shells, cornhusks, and cobs. Dream of your next

Grilled Lobster with Decadent Champagne Butter

This recipe made its debut in the Private Grilling chapter of my *Nantucket Open-House Cookbook*. Shortly thereafter, I was asked by a Boston television station to demonstrate the recipe on the waterfront deck of a friend's Nantucket home for the station's Fourth of July programming. The filming ended up going splendidly and much to my amazement, the station proceeded to repeat the segment for at least the next five summers come every Fourth of July. I recently revived and revamped the recipe for a private cooking class I was asked to give in honor of a client's sixtieth birthday. Since the class was to take place on Nantucket in an unfamiliar kitchen, I decided I didn't want to go through the unpleasant task of splitting live lobsters while everyone was jovially gathered in the kitchen enjoying an aperitif glass of good wine.

I remembered that Mark Bittman had written about grilling lobsters for his column in *The New York Times* and had recommended the seemingly humane step of parboiling the lobsters before splitting them and putting them on the grill. I went one step further and asked my favorite fishmonger on Nantucket to do the lobster parboiling and splitting for me, thereby eliminating the possibility of anything even resembling an *Annie Hall* moment. I highly recommend others follow this same route as it will add ease to the overall enjoyment of this sensational preparation. Finally, the smell of lobsters grilling over hardwood charcoal is one of the most sublimely aromatic seaside elixirs, worthy of the decadent Champagne reduction butter that sauces the charred crustaceans. SERVES 6

6 live lobsters (2 to 2½ pounds each)

1 bottle (750 milliliters) brut Champagne or Prosecco

Leafy tops of 3 ribs of celery

2 shallots, peeled and finely minced

16 tablespoons (2 sticks) chilled unsalted butter, cut into tablespoons

¼ cup heavy (whipping) cream

Sea salt and freshly ground black pepper

2 large lemons, each cut into 6 wedges

Extra virgin olive oil, for brushing on the lobsters

1   The first step of parboiling and splitting the lobsters may either be done at home or by your trusty local fishmonger, no longer than 4 hours in advance. Refrigerate the parboiled lobsters until you're ready to grill them. If you want to parboil the lobsters yourself, bring a very large pot of salted water to a boil. Have a large bucket of ice water ready. Add the lobsters to the pot and cook them until they turn red, about 5 minutes. Remove the lobsters from the pot and plunge them immediately into the bucket of ice water to stop the cooking and keep them cool until ready to grill.

2   To prepare the lobsters for grilling, cut each lobster in half: Start at the head and cut between the eyes, making one long cut until the lobster is completely split in half through the end of the tail. Scrape away and discard any green tomalley but leave the roe intact on any female lobsters. Crack the claws by pounding them with a mallet or hammer.

3   Set up a charcoal grill, if possible, and preheat it to high. Otherwise, preheat a gas grill, if that is the only option.

4   Place the Champagne, celery leaves, and shallots in a heavy medium-size saucepan and let come to a boil over medium-high heat. Reduce the heat to medium-low and continue to cook at a low boil until the liquid has reduced to a mere ¾ cup, 15 to 20 minutes. Fish out the celery leaves and discard them. Reduce the heat to low. Whisk in the chilled butter, tablespoon by tablespoon until all the butter is melted, to make a light emulsion, similar to a beurre blanc. Swirl in the cream (this helps to stabilize the emulsion and keep it from separating). Season the Champagne butter with salt and pepper to taste and keep it warm over very low heat.

5   Squeeze a wedge of lemon over the exposed meat of each split lobster. Brush the shells and meat lightly all over with olive oil.

6   Working in batches if necessary, place the lobsters shell side down on the grill. Close the lid of the grill after the first minute or so and cook the lobsters until the shells begin to become charred and lightly blackened in random places, 4 to 5 minutes. Turn the lobsters over and grill them meat side down until the tail meat is just cooked through and tender, 3 to 5 minutes more (keep in mind that the claws take 1 to 2 minutes longer than the tail). See page 121 for using an instant-read thermometer to test lobsters for doneness.

7   Serve the lobsters hot off the grill with the warm Champagne butter lavished over them.

Lobster Lessons

Having spent much of my life living and/or vacationing in coastal pockets like Nantucket, Cape Cod, the Connecticut shore, and Down East Maine, I have come to take cooking and eating New England lobsters on a regular basis pretty much for granted. In all these picturesque places, I am readily able to procure lively lobsters from numerous nearby sources, and often at prices that would be the envy of a New Yorker or Californian, not to mention lobster lovers living in the vast landlocked places in between. For those not as geographically fortunate or as lobster literate as I am, I am pleased to share the following guidelines for enjoying the recipes in this chapter.

Purchasing Lobsters

The best place to purchase lobster is either directly from a lobster fisherman (or woman—thank you Linda Greenlaw) or pound or fish market specializing in selling freshly caught lobsters from a tank visible to buyers. Lobsters should be purchased as close as possible to the time you intend on cooking them. Animated flapping of tails and general friskiness is not cause for alarm but reassurance of freshness. If you must store your lobsters before cooking them, wrap them individually in dampened newspaper and place them in the coldest part of your refrigerator, ideally for no longer than 4 to 6 hours.

Size really doesn't matter, unless you are like my husband, who believes that no lobster weighing less than 2 pounds is worth the effort it takes to eat it. I and many others, on the other hand or claw, opt readily for lobsters weighing between 1 and 1¼ pounds, often labeled "chicken" lobsters, when the lobster is a component of a larger feast, such as in my recipes for Simple Stovetop Lobster Bake (page 114) and Nigel's Backyard Wheelbarrow Lobster Bake (page 116). Larger 2- to 2½-pound lobsters are in order when you want a showstopping lobster extravaganza in instances like the recipe for Grilled Lobster with Decadent Champagne Butter (page 118). I also opt for large lobsters, when I'm cooking lobsters for their meat for use in lobster rolls or salads. Since this can be a time-consuming and not especially fun task, I'll often splurge and buy freshly picked lobster meat from a reputable source, if the price is right, factoring in that the yield of meat from a 1-pound lobster is generally only a meager 4 ounces. In the latter part of the summer and into early autumn, soft- or new-shell lobsters are prevalent since lobsters shed their shells and grow new ones when the weather is warmer. The higher water content makes these lobsters messier to eat, but also easier to eat because the shells are very soft and a cinch to crack.

Cooking Lobsters

When I cook lobsters at home, I generally use three methods: boiling, steaming, and grilling. Ideally the water for either boiling or steaming should be ocean water because cooking lobsters in the medium they inhabit yields superior flavor. When saltwater from the ocean is not a possibility, the next best option is to salt tap or spring water generously with ¼ cup of sea salt per gallon of water.

When boiling lobsters, a very big pot is in order because you need to allow 3 quarts of water for every 2 pounds of lobster in the shell. This may account for the reason that every coastal rental home in New England comes equipped with a large tin pot, usually speckled dark blue with a steamer insert, and universally referred to as a lobster pot.

Steaming is easier than boiling because less water is involved and it is less traumatic to place live lobsters in a steamer than it is to plunge them head first into boiling water. The lobsters cook more gently over steam, and once cooked, they can be held warm in the steamer until ready to serve. When steaming lobsters, you need only fill the bottom of the pot with ocean water or salted tap water to a depth of 1 inch. If you do have access to ocean water, you may also want to gather some seaweed at the same time to add to the steaming bed for even more authentic ocean savor. Once the water comes to a boil, the lobsters are placed in the steamer insert, the top is put on the pot, and the rest is pretty much magic, except for paying enough attention to rearrange the lobsters in the pot halfway through steaming if they are not in a single layer. Use long, hinged metal tongs to do the rearranging and take care not to get burned by the steam rising from the pot.

Cooking charts for lobsters abound and the general consensus is that lobsters weighing between 1 and 1¼ pounds take 8 to 10 minutes to cook, the lesser amount of time if boiling and the longer amount of time if steaming. A few of the recipes in this chapter err on the side of slight under-cooking because the meat is exposed to additional heat after being removed from the lobster. Lobster Fried Over Cold (page 127) and Penne with Spicy Lobster-Vodka Sauce (page 122) are two examples. If you fall into my husband's camp, you may find it handy to know that a 2-pound lobster needs to boil for about 15 to 16 minutes or steam for 17 to 18 minutes.

Charts notwithstanding, there's a more surefire way to test a lobster for doneness than assuming such charts are entirely accurate or subscribing to the conventional old-wives'-tale wisdom that a lobster is done either when its shell is bright red or its antennae can be easily removed. Enter the instant-read thermometer! I spent nearly a decade acting as a culinary spokeswoman for the Butterball Turkey Company and cannot count the thousands of times I instructed nervous Thanksgiving cooks to test their turkeys for doneness by using a meat thermometer. So, when I happened to read the same method worked like a charm with lobsters in an article in the *Huffington Post*, I immediately embraced the method of aiming for a 140°F reading on an instant-read thermometer stuck into the meatiest part of the lobster's tail as a fail-proof way of testing for doneness. I now recommend this method to any and every insecure cook seeking lobster perfection.

One of the most intoxicating smells in the world for me is that of lobster being grilled out-doors and this is a technique I use in this chapter, and one that requires the sub-technique of parboil-ing the lobsters. Parboiling lobsters simply means intentionally undercooking the lobsters, in this case to allow for the meat to finish cooking while being licked by the flames of the grill. When I parboil lobsters, I like to cook them to the point of being almost halfway cooked.

Another recently trendy way of cooking lobster is to butter-poach the meat. Butter-poached lob-ster meat is as sublime as it sounds but the method requires first parboiling the lobsters for a mere 1 to 2 minutes. Trust me when I say such severely undercooked lobster meat is not a delight to work with in a home kitchen and this is why I now confine my butter-poached lobster experiences to dining in fine restaurants and stick to fine-tuning long-standing New England lobster traditions at home when sharing the king of crustaceans with family and friends.

Cape Codder Stuffed Lobster Tails

I brake for any and all fish markets I come across during my travels throughout New England and thus have now ended up frequenting quite a variety of different ones for varying needs and cravings. I'm most certainly glad I braked for a little gray shingled fish market in West Yarmouth on Cape Cod. Set back from the road and edging Nantucket Sound, the inviting shack was situated on an otherwise ugly and commercial stretch of Route 28. As it turns out, the Cape Codder Seafood Market oozes old-time seaside charm, stocks an impressive array of fresh local seafood, and has reasonable prices to boot. Owner Mark VanBuskirk has worked in some fine restaurant kitchens and his talents shine through in the prepared seafood he makes to sell in the market. I became an immediate fan of his old-fashioned Ritz cracker stuffed lobster tails. Mark graciously shared the recipe. SERVES 4

8 tablespoons (1 stick) unsalted butter

4 ounces sea scallops, cut into ¼-inch dice

4 ounces raw shrimp, peeled and deveined, cut into ¼-inch dice

4 ounces fresh crabmeat, carefully checked for stray bits of shell and/or cartilage

2½ tablespoons dry sherry

2 cups Ritz cracker crumbs (from about 30 crackers), crushed with a rolling pin or in a food processor

Sea salt and freshly ground black pepper

4 split (butterflied) lobster tails (8 to 10 ounces each), thawed if frozen

1 Preheat the oven to 375°F.

2 Melt 2 tablespoons of the butter in a medium-size skillet over medium heat. Add the scallops, shrimp, and crabmeat and cook until the scallops and shrimp just begin to turn translucent, about 3 minutes. Add the sherry and cook the seafood mixture until the sherry has mostly evaporated, about 2 minutes.

3 Transfer the warm seafood to a mixing bowl, add 1½ cups of the Ritz cracker crumbs, season with salt and pepper to taste, and toss to mix. Melt the remaining 6 tablespoons of butter and add 4 tablespoons to the crumb and seafood stuffing to moisten it. Toss the remaining 2 tablespoons butter with the remaining ½ cup of Ritz cracker crumbs.

4 Arrange the split lobster tails in a baking dish and divide the stuffing evenly among the 4 tails. Sprinkle the remaining buttered cracker crumbs over the top of the stuffing on each lobster tail. Bake the lobster tails until the lobster tail meat is cooked and the stuffing is a buttery golden brown, 20 to 25 minutes. Serve hot.

Penne with Spicy Lobster-Vodka Sauce

I don't think I know anyone who doesn't adore the Italian-American pasta dish known as *penne alla vodka*. The only thing better than the original is this indulgent lobster variation. In tinkering with the recipe, I discovered using brandy in place of the vodka gives the dish a decidedly French flair, which may appeal to some but dismay those accustomed to the less pronounced vodka nuances. To be honest I like both versions and might diplomatically recommend using vodka when making the pasta during warmer months and brandy when Jack Frost is nipping at either the door or your bottle of brandy.

For the lobster meat in this recipe, I use the technique I learned years ago from legendary lobsterman Dana Holbrook of cooking the lobsters ahead of time and then refrigerating the whole lobsters overnight in the shell to intensify the flavor of the meat when it is picked the following day. SERVES 4 TO 6

2 live lobsters (1½ pounds each)

Salt

1 pound penne pasta

2 tablespoons (¼ stick) unsalted butter

2 tablespoons extra virgin olive oil

1 large shallot, peeled and minced

3 cloves garlic, peeled and minced

1 jalapeño pepper, stemmed, seeded, and finely minced

¾ cup vodka or brandy

2 cups tomato puree

1 cup heavy (whipping) cream

Freshly ground black pepper

2 tablespoons minced fresh flat-leaf parsley

1   The day before you plan to serve the pasta, boil or steam the lobsters for 9 to 10 minutes (see page 120). It's okay if they are slightly undercooked. Drain the lobsters, let them cool, and then refrigerate them in their shells overnight. The following day, pick all of the meat from the lobsters, cut it into bite-size chunks, and set it aside. If your lobster has roe, finely chop it and add it to the sauce, if desired. Discard the shells.

2   Bring a large pot of water to a boil. Add the salt and the penne and cook according to the package directions until al dente.

3   Melt the butter in the olive oil in a very large skillet over medium heat. Add the shallot, garlic, and jalapeño pepper and cook until softened, 2 to 3 minutes. Remove the pan from the heat, add the vodka or brandy, and carefully ignite it with a long match. When the flames subside, return the pan to medium heat, add the tomato puree, and let come just to a boil. Reduce the heat to medium-low so the sauce simmers and stir in the cream. Cook the sauce until it is heated through and creamy, about 5 minutes, then season it with salt and black pepper to taste.

> "Let me straighten all readers out on one point. Lobsters are known in other parts of the world besides New England. But they are a sad mistake and poor imitation of the New England kind."—Robert P. Tristram Coffin, *Mainstays of Maine*

4   Add the lobster meat to the sauce a minute or two before you anticipate the pasta being done and cook it just long enough to heat through, about 2 minutes. Drain the pasta and add it to the sauce in the skillet, tossing gently so all the penne gets coated evenly with the sauce. Serve the penne hot spooned into wide, shallow bowls and garnish each serving with a sprinkling of parsley.

Maine Lobster Mac and Cheese

I see lobster mac and cheese listed on the menus of countless plain and fancy restaurants throughout New England. I've had my hands on many lobster mac and cheese recipes but they have either been far too complicated for home cooking or just not

Here, the typical speckled blue enamel steamer pot—an essential component in every New England coastal kitchen—brims with an enviable pile of just-cooked lobsters.

2 tablespoons (¼ stick) unsalted butter

1 tablespoon extra virgin olive oil

1 plump clove garlic, peeled and minced

½ cup panko bread crumbs

1 tablespoon minced fresh flat-leaf parsley

1 tablespoon minced fresh chives

1 teaspoon finely grated lemon zest

2 tablespoons freshly grated Parmigiano-Reggiano cheese

Sea salt and freshly ground black pepper

For the pasta and cheese sauce

Salt

1 pound medium-size shell pasta

6 tablespoons unsalted butter

4 tablespoons unbleached all-purpose flour

2 cups light cream

12 ounces mascarpone cheese, preferably from Vermont Creamery

1 heaping cup (4 ounces) shredded sharp white Vermont cheddar cheese

Sea salt and freshly ground white pepper

2 shallots, peeled and minced

1 pound cooked lobster meat, freshly picked from the shell and cut into ½-inch chunks

stellar enough. Since I was never a great fan of mac and cheese in the first place, I could have easily lived with not including a recipe for lobster mac and cheese in this cookbook. Somehow that all changed when, while attending a Fancy Food Show, I was given a bite of the lobster mac and cheese made in Maine by the Hancock Gourmet Lobster Company. Immediately, I knew I had to include this recipe in my cookbook. Fortunately, I was easily able to glean the mascarpone and panko crumb secrets of this truly superb recipe because company owner Cal Hancock's recipe beat Bobby Flay's recipe in one of those Food Network throwdowns I never manage to see but can find splattered all over the Internet afterward.

If you find yourself short on time or daunted in general by cooking, you can always order this fabulous lobster mac and cheese to be shipped frozen from the Hancock Gourmet Lobster Company in Topsham, Maine, along with a host of the company's other equally fabulous lobster and seafood creations. However, this is the one mac and cheese recipe I truly enjoy making, serving, and devouring at my own home. SERVES 4 TO 6

1 Make the crunchy panko topping: Melt the butter in the olive oil in a small skillet over medium heat. Add the garlic and cook until fragrant, 1 to 2 minutes. Add the panko, parsley, chives, and lemon zest. Cook, stirring frequently, for 3 to 4 minutes. Remove the skillet from the heat. Stir in the Parmesan cheese, season with salt and pepper to taste, and set the topping aside.

2 Prepare the pasta and cheese sauce: Bring a large pot of water to a boil, add the salt and pasta, and cook it according to the package directions until al dente.

3   While the pasta water is coming to a boil, make the cheese sauce. Melt 4 tablespoons of the butter over medium heat in a large saucepan or Dutch oven. Whisk in the flour and cook, whisking constantly, until well blended, about 2 minutes, taking care not to let the roux brown. Slowly whisk in the cream, stirring to make a smooth white sauce. Continue cooking over medium to medium-low heat until thickened, 4 to 5 minutes. Stir in the mascarpone cheese until it is thoroughly incorporated. Add the cheddar cheese, stirring until it melts. Season the cheese sauce with salt and white pepper to taste. Keep the sauce warm over low heat.

4   Melt the remaining 2 tablespoons of butter in a medium-size skillet over medium heat. Add the shallots and cook until softened, about 2 minutes. Add the lobster meat, toss to coat it with the shallots and butter, and cook until the lobster meat is warmed through, 1 to 2 minutes. Stir the lobster mixture into the cheese sauce.

5   Drain the pasta well and immediately add it to the cheese and lobster sauce. Mix well to combine and coat all the pasta shells with the sauce. Spoon the lobster mac and cheese into shallow pasta bowls and sprinkle each serving lightly all over the top with the crunchy panko crumb topping. Enjoy at once.

Autumn Pappardelle with Lobster, Mushrooms, Shallots, and Cream

Every lobster lover in America should own a copy of Jasper White's *Lobster at Home* cookbook. It has been a staple in my kitchen since it was published in 1998. I have made almost all of the pasta dishes in the book, and the following is a rendition of my favorite pasta recipe in the book. SERVES 4 AS A FIRST COURSE OR 2 AS A RICH MAIN COURSE

1 ounce dried porcini mushrooms

½ cup water

4 tablespoons (½ stick) unsalted butter

2 large shallots, peeled and minced

8 ounces cremini or oyster mushrooms, trimmed and sliced about ⅓ inch thick

¼ cup dry white wine

½ cup heavy (whipping) cream

1¼ pounds cooked lobster meat, freshly picked from the shell and cut into bite-size chunks

Sea salt and freshly ground black pepper

8 ounces dried pappardelle (available in Italian specialty stores and some supermarkets)

⅓ cup minced fresh flat-leaf parsley

1   Place the dried porcini mushrooms in a small saucepan and cover them with the water. Let the mixture come to a boil over medium-high heat. Turn off the heat and let stand for at least 15 minutes but no more than 1 hour. Drain the porcini mushrooms, straining the cooking liquid through a fine-mesh sieve if it is sandy. Set the cooking liquid aside and coarsely chop the mushrooms.

2   Melt 3 tablespoons of the butter in a large skillet over medium heat. Add the shallots and cook until softened, about 3 minutes. Stir in the fresh mushrooms and cook until they soften and release their juices, 4 to 5 minutes. Add the drained porcini mushrooms, their reserved cooking liquid, and the white wine and cream. Increase the heat to medium-high and let come to a boil. Reduce the heat to medium-low and simmer until the sauce has thickened slightly, about 3 minutes. Stir in the lobster meat and toss to coat it with the sauce. Cook until the lobster meat is just warmed through. Season the sauce with salt and pepper to taste and keep it warm over very low heat.

3 Meanwhile bring a large pot of water to a boil. Add the salt and papparadelle and cook according to package directions until al dente. Drain the pasta well and immediately transfer it to the skillet with the sauce. Add the remaining 1 tablespoon of butter and mix thoroughly over medium heat until the pasta is nicely coated with the sauce. Stir in the parsley and serve at once.

Lobster Fried Over Cold

This simple and utterly delectable two-ingredient combination is my most prized lobster recipe. I love it so much that I insisted it be served as the dinner entrée when my husband, Nigel, and I were married in Maine in September of 1995. Credit for the recipe goes to Dana Holbrook, the legendary Bucks Harbor lobsterman I once interviewed. During our interview, Dana quickly put to rest the ill-founded rumor that lobstermen never eat their catch when he got onto the topic of his favorite lobster preparation—"lobster fried over cold"—something far easier to make than to decipher when elaborated on with a thick Maine accent. Dana explained that sometimes he liked to boil up three or four lobsters from his daily catch and then refrigerate them in their shells overnight as a means of intensifying the meat's flavor.

The following day Dana would pick out the cold meat in fairly sizable chunks and "fry it over cold in a black spider [cast-iron skillet] womped with butter." Dana's only accompaniment? "A mess of biscuits," though I personally prefer crusty rolls and occasionally do something unthinkable to a Mainer and "womp my spider" with a touch of truffle butter. Sometimes I'll even toss a handful of fresh Nantucket bay scallops in with the lobster meat and let the warmth of the melted butter,

truffle or regular, just barely cook the scallops while heating the lobster meat.

Gild the lobster as you wish; I find it only proper to write the recipe as originally given to me by Dana more than twenty years ago. Dana always prepared his Lobster Fried Over Cold in a large nine- to ten-inch cast-iron skillet, but I invested in smaller five-inch cast-iron skillets for individual servings at my wedding and continue today to use these small skillets when I make the recipe. SERVES 4

4 live lobsters (1¼ pounds each)

8 tablespoons (1 stick) unsalted butter

Warm biscuits, crusty rolls, or baguettes

1 The day before you plan to serve the lobsters, boil or steam them until just barely done, 8 to 10 minutes (see page 120). Drain, cool, and then refrigerate the lobsters in their shells overnight.

2 The following day, pick all of the meat from the lobsters, leaving it in fairly large chunks. Discard the shells but save the roe from any female lobsters, if desired, and add it to the lobster meat, if desired.

3 Melt the butter in a large cast-iron skillet over medium heat. For individual servings melt 2 table-spoons of butter in each of four 5-inch cast-iron skillets. Add the lobster meat and cook it until the meat is piping hot, 6 to 8 minutes. Serve the lobster at once with warm biscuits, crusty rolls, or baguettes.

My Favorite Classic New England Lobster Roll

I have eaten lobster rolls at shacks, shanties, pounds, dives, and even upscale restaurants all over coastal New England. Many hundreds of

dollars later, I have finally come to the conclusion that the best lobster rolls are hands down always the ones I make at home. A really good lobster roll is actually one of the easiest things in the world to make as long as you choose every single component with care. The lobster meat must be very fresh and tender. The mayonnaise must be either homemade or else Hellmann's. The celery should be minimal and minced rather finely. The seasoning must be sparse and relegated to only salt, pepper, and a tablespoon or so of freshly minced dill or snipped chives. The hot dog roll must be a New England–style roll (slit down the top, not through the side and certainly not whole wheat!!!) in order to allow for sautéing the outside to a toasty golden brown. Even the brand of butter makes a difference and whenever I use Kate's "batch churned" sea-salted butter from Maine, I am rewarded with the lobster roll of my dreams. Fortunately, this terrific butter is sold in many supermarkets throughout New England and increasingly elsewhere.

The one nontraditional nuance I have recently come to embrace after years of making lobster rolls without deviating much from the recipe is a minor ingredient addition I picked up from Barbara Lynch, a terrific Boston-based chef for whom I have the utmost respect. Lynch calls for adding a teaspoon of the popular Asian hot sauce sriracha to the mayonnaise she makes for her lobster rolls to impart a bit of spicy heat. When I gave the idea a test run, I elatedly discovered that the sriracha adds a very subtle and appealing undertone of heat, but even more impressive was the fact that the ketchup-colored sriracha turns the mayonnaise a pretty pale shade of coral to match the color of the lobster meat itself. I know that many a dyed-in-the-wool New Englander will balk at adding something foreign, hot, and hard to pronounce to their beloved lobster rolls, so please rest assured that the sriracha is definitely optional and that Hellmann's mayonnaise can deliver a perfectly fine-tasting and very acceptable lazy man's binder for the lobster filling if you prefer not to make your own mayonnaise from scratch. SERVES 4

1 generous pound cooked lobster meat, freshly picked from the shell and cut into meaty chunks (2 cups chunks)

1 tablespoon freshly squeezed lemon juice

1 rib celery, cut into ¼-inch dice

1 tablespoon minced fresh dill or chives

⅓ to ½ cup mayonnaise, Hellmann's or homemade (recipe follows)

3 to 4 tablespoons butter, preferably Kate's salted butter, at room temperature

4 New England–style, top split hot dog buns

1   Place the lobster meat in a medium-size mixing bowl, add the lemon juice, and toss to coat lightly. Add the celery and dill or chives, stirring gently to combine. Fold in just enough mayonnaise to bind the ingredients together. The filling should be moist but not soupy. If you are not using the lobster salad immediately, store it in the refrigerator, covered, for no more than a few hours.

2   When ready to serve, generously butter the outside of each hot dog bun and then brown the buns in a skillet, one side at a time (and not the bottom or insides) over medium-low heat, until the outsides become golden brown, 2 to 3 minutes. Spoon the chilled lobster salad down the center of each toasted hot dog bun, mounding the filling somewhat sumptuously. Serve at once, as the temperature contrast between the warm, buttery hot dog buns and the cold lobster filling is an essential component of the whole wonderful lobster roll experience.

Homemade Mayonnaise

This is my basic recipe for homemade mayonnaise and, yes, the use of an uncooked egg yolk is what gives it its exceptional homemade quality. If you have reason to worry about eating raw foods, then you should probably skip this recipe and opt to use the only brand of commercial mayonnaise I ever use, Hellmann's. The sriracha option is specific to making this mayonnaise for use in lobster rolls and should be omitted if your aim is to make an all-purpose homemade mayonnaise. MAKES ABOUT 1¼ CUPS

1 extra-large very fresh egg yolk

1 teaspoon Dijon mustard

2 tablespoons freshly squeezed lemon juice

Fine sea salt and freshly ground black pepper

¾ cup vegetable or canola oil

¼ cup extra virgin olive oil

1 teaspoon sriracha (optional)

PLACE THE EGG yolk, mustard, and 1 tablespoon of the lemon juice in a small mixing bowl. Add ¼ teaspoon of salt and a pinch of pepper and whisk to combine. While continuing to whisk, pour in the vegetable and olive oils in a very slow steady stream until all has been incorporated and the mixture has formed a thick emulsion. Whisk in the remaining tablespoon of lemon juice and the sriracha, if using. Taste for seasoning, adding more salt and/or pepper as needed. Store the mayonnaise, covered, in the refrigerator until ready to use. The mayonnaise can be refrigerated for up to 5 days.

Connecticut-Style Lobster Rolls

Even though I was born and raised in central Connecticut, I spent summers in Maine with my family, a footnote most likely responsible for my never having tasted a Connecticut-style lobster roll until I began working on this cookbook. While I remain partial to the more popular mayonnaise-based lobster rolls sold almost everywhere

Weathered and barnacle-encrusted wooden lobster traps and tangled buoys are a common sight in New England's coastal fishing villages.

else throughout New England, I have to admit the Connecticut-style lobster roll, in which a toasted hot dog bun is stuffed with lobster meat soaked in hot butter, is a fine creation and one that actually reminds me of my all-time favorite New England Lobster recipe—Lobster Fried Over Cold (see page 127). My recipe here is modeled after the lobster rolls I have enjoyed at Lenny & Joe's Fish Tale restaurant in Westbrook, Connecticut, a sprawling family seafood establishment.

I believe most Connecticut-style lobster rolls are made by heating the lobster meat filling in clarified butter, but I have discovered that warming the lobster meat in Kate's sea-salted butter from Maine heightens the overall New England savor just that much more. Lobster rolls, whether hot or cold, are almost always served with a side of potato chips. If you are up for a bit of adventure, go for Cape Cod kettle cooked sea salt and vinegar chips or Lay's dill pickle chips. SERVES 4

10 tablespoons butter (1¼ sticks), preferably Kate's salted butter, at room temperature

1 generous pound cooked lobster meat, freshly picked from the shell and cut into meaty chunks (2 cups chunks)

Pinch of sweet paprika

4 New England–style, top-split hot dog buns

4 lemon wedges (optional), for serving

1 Melt 8 tablespoons of the butter in a medium-size skillet over medium-low heat. Add the lobster meat, stirring gently to coat it with the butter. Let the lobster meat cook until heated through, 4 to 5 minutes. Sprinkle the lobster meat with a very light dusting of paprika.

2 While the lobster meat is heating, smear the remaining 2 tablespoons of butter over the outside of the hot dog buns and then brown them in another medium-size skillet, one side at a time (and not the bottom or insides), over medium-low heat, turning once and cooking until both sides of the buns are golden brown, 2 to 3 minutes.

3 Divide the hot buttered lobster meat among the 4 toasted buns, mounding the meat down the center of the buns. Serve the lobster rolls at once with a lemon wedge for spritzing over the hot lobster meat, if desired.

Little Lobster Rolls

These stylized and scrumptiously rich little lobster rolls are representative of the way in which I like to modernize and tweak time-honored, traditional New England recipes. I tend to make them when I'm catering or hosting fancy summer cocktail parties. Skinny French baguettes known as *ficelles* replace the traditional hot dog buns, while the lobster meat filling is bound by a homemade Lemon Aioli laced with crispy crumbled bacon and minced fresh herbs. Once assembled the little lobster rolls are sautéed in butter and served warm—a welcome and indulgent counterbalance to the sunset sea breeze chill of many coastal alfresco cocktail party gatherings in my neck of the woods. MAKES 20 TO 24

1¼ pounds cooked lobster meat, freshly picked from the shell and cut into small dice (2½ cups diced)

Lemon Aioli (recipe follows)

6 slices best-quality bacon (North Country Smokehouse in New Hampshire is a favorite brand), cooked until crisp, drained, and then crumbled

Freshly ground black pepper

2 tablespoons minced fresh flat-leaf parsley or dill or slivered fresh basil

2 ficelles

6 tablespoons (¾ stick) unsalted butter, or more as needed

1 Place the lobster meat in a mixing bowl and add enough Lemon Aioli to bind the meat loosely together (⅔ to ¾ cup; save the rest of the Lemon Aioli to use as a sandwich spread or dip for crudités). Gently mix in the crumbled bacon and season with pepper to taste. Fold in your choice of fresh herb.

2 Cut the *ficelles* in half lengthwise and then scoop out as much of the soft interior as possible (save the bread for making bread crumbs, if desired). Slice the hollowed-out *ficelles* into 3-inch lengths. Pack each length with enough lobster salad to fill it without mounding it above the bread.

3 Melt 2 tablespoons of butter in a large skillet over medium heat and, working in batches, cook the lobster rolls, filling side down, until the edges of the bread have turned golden, 3 to 4 minutes. Repeat the process, melting more butter as needed. Serve the lobster rolls warm with cocktail napkins.

Lemon Aioli

This lovely, garlicky aioli is another mayonnaise-style dressing that uses a raw egg. If this worries you for any reason, simply stir the garlic and lemon zest into 1 cup commercial mayonnaise, preferably Hellmann's. MAKES ABOUT 1¼ CUPS

2 cloves garlic, peeled

¾ teaspoon crunchy sea salt or fleur de sel

2 large very fresh egg yolks

1½ tablespoons freshly squeezed lemon juice

1 teaspoon finely grated lemon zest

½ cup vegetable oil

½ cup extra virgin olive oil

MINCE THE GARLIC and salt together on a cutting board to make a paste. Place the garlic paste in a small mixing bowl and whisk in the egg yolks, lemon juice, and lemon zest until thoroughly combined. Slowly whisk in the vegetable and olive oils, tablespoon by tablespoon, until all has been incorporated and the mixture has formed an emulsion. Store the aioli in the refrigerator, covered, until ready to use. The aioli will keep for up to 4 days in the refrigerator.

Lobster Club Sandwiches

My first foray into the world of writing cookbooks was back in the 1980s when I worked with Sheila Lukins and Julee Rosso on the *Silver Palate Good Times Cookbook*. One day, Sheila treated me to lunch at her friend Anne Rosenzweig's newly opened Arcadia restaurant on Manhattan's Upper East Side. I ordered a lobster club sandwich and the experience was definitely one of the top ten food epiphanies in my life. Rosenzweig's lobster club sandwich went on to become so famous that she later opened a second more casual restaurant called The Lobster Club. While both Anne's lobster club sandwich and restaurant have since become the stuff of fond but distant memories, I couldn't resist reviving the incredibly delicious club sandwich and adding my own little spin to it all these years later. The recipe here is a cross between Anne's original lobster club and another one of my all-time favorite sandwiches, Chris Schlesinger's grilled shrimp BLTs with smashed avocados. Schlesinger wrote the groundbreaking *The Thrill of the Grill* cookbook back in 1990 and opened the acclaimed East Coast Grill in Cambridge, Massachusetts, in 1986.

The bread used in the original lobster club was brioche made from scratch in Rosenzweig's restaurant, but even with today's proliferation of good local bread bakeries, brioche can be hard to come by so I make my lobster clubs with a more readily available rustic country white bread, such as ciabatta. At the same time, Anne's original homemade lobster club lemon mayonnaise is an absolute must, with many bonus uses to boot. This mayonnaise is fabulous as a quick marinade and moisture enhancer for grilled fish, a dressing for leafy salad greens, a fish sandwich slather, and a binder for lobster meat if you are in the mood for a super lemony lobster roll. MAKES 2 LARGE CLUB SANDWICHES; SERVES 2 IF EXTREMELY HUNGRY OR 4 IF WILLING TO SHARE

6 thick slices smoked New England bacon, such as Nodine's Smokehouse, Vermont Smoke and Cure, or North Country Smokehouse

1 pound cooked lobster tail meat, freshly picked from the shell and cut into ½-inch thick slices

Lemon Mayonnaise (recipe follows)

6 large thin slices, rustic country white bread, toasted

16 to 20 fresh basil leaves

1 large, vine-ripened tomato, sliced

1 small ripe avocado, pitted and sliced

Sea salt and freshly ground black pepper

1   Cook the bacon in a skillet over medium heat until crisp, 7 to 9 minutes. Transfer the bacon to a plate lined with a paper towel to drain.

2   When ready to assemble the sandwiches, place the sliced lobster tail meat in a small mixing bowl and toss it with 2 to 3 tablespoons of the Lemon Mayonnaise to coat the lobster meat very lightly all over. Spread a thin layer of the Lemon Mayonnaise over 2 slices of the toasted bread. Scatter 4 or 5 fresh basil leaves on top of the mayonnaise on each piece of toast, followed by the tomato slices. Top each sandwich with 3 slices of bacon followed by another slice of toasted bread. Arrange the avocado slices on top and mash them gently into the toast with the tines of a fork. Season with salt and pepper to taste.

3   Divide the lobster between the two sandwiches and scatter 4 or 5 more fresh basil leaves over the top of each sandwich. Spread a thin layer of lemon mayonnaise over the remaining 2 slices of toast and then place these on top of each sandwich, mayonnaise side facing down. Cut the club sandwiches in half and serve at once.

Lemon Mayonnaise

A sandwich as perfect as a Lobster Club needs the perfect dressing—mayonnaise with a bracing citrus punch. Be aware that it uses a raw egg, like the other scratch recipes in the chapter. MAKES 1¼ CUPS

1 extra-large very fresh egg yolk

1 teaspoon Dijon mustard

Sea salt and freshly ground black pepper

3 tablespoons freshly squeezed lemon juice

1 cup vegetable or canola oil

2 teaspoons finely grated lemon zest

COMBINE THE EGG yolk, mustard, ½ teaspoon of salt, ¼ teaspoon of pepper, and 2 tablespoons of the lemon juice in a small, deep mixing bowl. Whisk to combine. Add the oil in a slow, thin, and steady stream, whisking constantly, to form a thick emulsion. Stir in the remaining tablespoon of lemon juice and the lemon zest. Taste for seasoning, adding a bit more salt and/or pepper, if necessary. Store the mayonnaise in the refrigerator, covered, until ready to use. The mayonnaise will keep for up to 4 days in the refrigerator.

Lobster Grilled Cheese

Grilled cheese cook-offs and contests have recently become very popular. Bartlett's Farm on Nantucket hosts a grilled cheese competition every March, and a lobster grilled cheese sandwich recently won the title of Best Sandwich in Sandwich during a June competition in Cape Cod's oldest village—Sandwich! This inspired me to make my own version and I daresay this lobster grilled cheese is indeed one of the best (and most caloric!) sandwiches ever to grace my lunch table. I highly recommend indulging in one when you need to console yourself on a dreary March day after enduring too much New England winter weather and yearn for summer by the seashore. The lobster and melted brie combination is outrageous and made even more outrageous if you are able to get your hands on a four-ounce round of Vermont's Champlain Valley Creamery's Organic Champlain Triple Brie-style cheese (often stocked at many Whole Foods markets in the Northeast and you can order it from the Creamery). MAKES 4 SANDWICHES

1 pound cooked lobster meat, freshly picked from the shell and cut into ½-inch dice (about 2 cups dice)

1 tablespoon freshly squeezed lemon juice

4 ounces rich double or triple cream Brie-type cheese, rind removed if very bloomy or thick, cheese broken into small blobs

2 tablespoons minced fresh chives

3 sun-dried tomato halves, reconstituted if necessary, finely diced

¼ to ⅓ cup mayonnaise, preferably Hellmann's or homemade (page 129)

Sea salt and freshly ground white or black pepper

4 to 6 tablespoons butter, preferably Kate's salted butter, at room temperature

8 slices best-quality white bread

4 ounces thinly sliced, mild Swiss or Jarlsberg

1   Place the lobster meat in a medium-size mixing bowl, add the lemon juice, and toss gently to coat. Add the blobs of cheese, chives, and sun-dried tomatoes. Add only enough mayonnaise to bind the ingredients together. You want to err on the side of a light hand with the mayonnaise. Season the lobster mixture with salt and pepper to taste.

2   Generously butter one side of each bread slice. Place 4 slices of bread on a large griddle or in 2 large skillets, buttered side down. Divide the lobster mixture evenly among the 4 slices of bread, spreading it to cover the entire surface of the bread in an even layer. Top each sandwich with one quarter of the sliced cheese, followed by the remaining bread slices, buttered side up. Press gently on the top slices of bread to sandwich everything together.

3   Cook the sandwiches over medium heat, turning them once and pressing down on the sandwiches occasionally with the back of a flat spatula, until they turn a buttery golden brown on both sides and the cheese is melted and beginning to ooze, 3 to 4 minutes per side. Slice the sandwiches in half on the diagonal and serve at once.

An assortment of lobster buoys, floats, and traps enliven the dark, weather-beaten wood shingles on a rustic sea shanty.

Lobster Omelet

While I have never been much of an omelet maker or eater, this is the *one* recipe that could easily alter my breakfast, brunch, lunch, or even late night dinner patterns. In short, it is perfection, and heaven, too. SERVES 1 (ELEGANTLY)

1 tablespoon plus 2 teaspoons unsalted butter

3 scallions, both white and tender green parts, trimmed and thinly sliced

2 very fresh extra-large eggs, preferably organic

1 tablespoon half-and-half or light cream

Sea salt and freshly ground white or black pepper

⅓ pound cooked lobster meat, freshly picked from the shell and cut into meaty chunks, at room temperature

2 heaping tablespoons mascarpone

1 Melt 1 tablespoon of the butter in a 6- to 7-inch omelet pan. Add the scallions and cook over medium heat until just wilted, about 2 minutes.

2 Place the eggs and half-and-half in a small bowl and whisk them until evenly blended. Add the remaining 2 teaspoons of butter to the omelet pan with the scallions and let it melt over medium-high heat. Once the butter has melted, add the egg mixture, swirling the pan to distribute it evenly. Cook the omelet, lifting the edges with a silicone spatula to let the uncooked egg flow underneath, until almost set, about 2 minutes. Season the omelet with salt and pepper to taste, scatter the lobster meat evenly over one half of the omelet and top the lobster with dollops of the mascarpone. Cook the omelet for 20 to 30 seconds more to warm the lobster and set the eggs completely. Fold the plain side of the omelet over the filling and immediately slide the omelet onto a warm serving plate. Indulge at once.

Lobster Niçoise Salad

When you live in a place where lobsters are plentiful and sometimes even a bargain, you come across a lot of crazy lobster recipes. Over the years, I have come to develop rather strong opinions about where I feel lobster belongs and doesn't belong. For example, even when I can buy lobsters for as little as $3.99 a pound, I wouldn't think of putting the meat on a pizza or in a Bolognese sauce. On the other hand, when the price for lobster is up there at $10 or more per pound, I would definitely prioritize its use in this spin on France's classic *niçoise* salad, in which lobster meat serves as an excellent and luxurious stand-in for the customary canned tuna fish. I guess I may have global warming to thank for making this Lobster Niçoise Salad a family favorite during summer heat waves. SERVES 4

10 small (about 1 inch in diameter) red-skinned new potatoes

Ice

½ pound thin green beans, often sold as haricots verts, stem ends trimmed, tails left intact

1 roasted red bell pepper (store-bought is fine if you don't want to broil your own), seeded and cut into thin 1-inch-long strips

2 tablespoons brine-packed capers, drained

Niçoise Dressing (recipe follows)

1 bunch scallions, both white and tender green parts, trimmed and thinly sliced on the diagonal

4 medium-size, vine-ripened tomatoes, cored and cut into ¾-inch-thick wedges

1½ pounds cooked lobster meat, freshly picked from the shell and cut into ½-inch chunks

5 ounces baby arugula or mesclun greens, rinsed and spun dry

Sea salt and freshly ground black pepper

4 large hard-cooked eggs, peeled and quartered

1 Place the potatoes in a medium-size saucepan and add water to cover. Bring to a boil and cook the potatoes until they are fork-tender, 12 to 15 minutes. Drain the potatoes and set them aside.

2 Have a large bowl of ice water ready. Bring another saucepan of water to a boil then add the green beans and blanch them until crisp-tender, about 2 minutes. Drain the beans and immediately plunge them into the bowl of ice water to stop the cooking and set the bright green color. When the beans are cool, drain them again and pat them dry. Place the beans in a large salad bowl.

3 Cut the potatoes in half while still warm and add them to the salad bowl. Add the roasted red pepper strips, capers, and 3 tablespoons of the Niçoise Dressing and toss to mix. Let stand until the potatoes have cooled to room temperature, about 10 minutes.

Two Maine lobstermen ready themselves for a long day on the water. Each licensed lobsterman is allowed to set 800 traps and there are about 3,000 full-time lobstermen in Maine.

PLACE THE ANCHOVY paste, mustard, garlic, basil, lemon juice, lemon zest, and salt in a small food processor. Process until pureed. Add the olive oil and process again until smooth. The dressing can be refrigerated, covered, for up to 1 week. Let come to room temperature and stir to recombine before using.

4 Add the scallions, tomatoes, lobster meat, and greens to the salad bowl. Add enough of the remaining dressing to coat all of the ingredients without drenching them. Taste for seasoning adding salt and/ or pepper, as needed. Divide the salad among 4 large dinner plates. Garnish the edge of each salad with 4 hard-cooked egg quarters. Serve the salad at once.

Niçoise Dressing

MAKES ABOUT 1 CUP

1 tablespoon anchovy paste

1 tablespoon Dijon mustard

2 cloves garlic, peeled and coarsely chopped

3 tablespoons shredded fresh basil leaves

2½ tablespoons freshly squeezed lemon juice

1 teaspoon finely grated lemon zest

1 teaspoon sea salt

⅔ cup extra virgin olive oil

Maine Lobster Stew

An authentic Maine-style lobster stew is as simple as it is rich and rather like the liquid cousin to Lobster Fried Over Cold (page 127). It is much easier to make than lobster bisque and I find it just as delicious. The secret to making a great lobster stew is lots of lobster meat and having the patience to let the stew age. SERVES 4

4 live lobsters (1¼ pounds each)

10 tablespoons (1¼ sticks) butter, preferably Kate's salted butter

2 teaspoons sweet paprika

4 cups whole milk, at room temperature

1 cup heavy (whipping) cream, at room temperature

1 Boil or steam the lobsters until slightly undercooked, 8 to 10 minutes. Drain the lobsters and let them cool until easy enough to handle, about 10 minutes. Remove all of the meat from the shells, working over a bowl to catch the juices. Cut the meat into fairly sizeable chunks and finely chop any roe, if you happen to have some female lobsters.

2 Melt the butter in a Dutch oven or other heavy pot over medium heat. Add the lobster meat, reserved juices, and any roe, and stir to coat with the melted butter. Sprinkle in the paprika and cook, stirring frequently to saturate the butter with the flavor of the lobster, 8 to 10 minutes. Slowly add the milk and

cream in ¼ cup increments, waiting for each to heat but not boil before adding the next. When all the milk and cream has been added, continue to cook the stew, without letting it boil, over low heat to blend the flavors, about 10 minutes.

3   Remove the stew from the heat and let it cool to room temperature. Cover and refrigerate the stew for at least 24 hours but no more than 36 hours. When ready to serve, gently reheat the stew over low heat, until heated through, about 15 minutes. Serve the stew hot, ladled into ceramic mugs or deep bowls.

The Ebb Tide's Lobster Bisque

The Ebb Tide Restaurant in Dennisport on Cape Cod is a nostalgic and sprawling old New England restaurant. The McCormick family has run it for more than fifty years and they pride themselves on serving unfussy but delicious regional New England fare paired with gracious helpings of hospitality. Paul McCormick is a man of many talents. He runs the restaurant, serves as a local selectman, teaches culinary classes at the community college, and still finds plenty of time to be a wonderful family man. Paul also happens to be an excellent addition to the food and travel themed book club I belong to on Cape Cod. I honestly think we do more eating than reading in this book club and Paul always brings The Ebb Tide's luscious lobster bisque to our holiday gathering—an excellent measure of the quality of food, if not literature, our group enjoys. While many people think lobster bisque should be laced with large pieces of lobster meat, Paul prefers finely processing the lobster he adds to thicken his bisque. The result is a silkier yet very flavorful bisque in which the lobster meat acts as a thickener. SERVES 8 TO 10

16 cups water, or more as needed

1½ cups dry white wine

3 live lobsters (1¼ pounds each)

2 medium-size onions, peeled and coarsely chopped

4 large carrots, peeled and coarsely chopped

1 rib celery, coarsely chopped

2 bay leaves

¼ teaspoon whole black peppercorns

6 sprigs fresh flat-leaf parsley

1 cup canned or fresh chopped tomatoes with their juice

3 cloves garlic, peeled and minced

¼ cup tomato paste

1 teaspoon sweet paprika

10 tablespoons (1¼ sticks) unsalted butter

6 tablespoons unbleached all-purpose flour

3 cups light cream

½ cup dry sherry

Sea salt and freshly ground white or black pepper

1   Pour the water and white wine into a large stockpot and bring to a boil over high heat. Plunge the lobsters into the pot, head first, and bring the liquid back to a boil. Cover the pot and simmer the lobsters until bright red and thoroughly cooked, about 10 minutes. Remove the lobsters from the stockpot but reserve their cooking liquid in the pot. Let the lobsters cool until easy enough to handle, about 10 minutes. Working over a bowl to catch the juices, twist off the tails and claws. Remove the meat from the tails and claws and set aside in the refrigerator, covered.

2   Throw the lobster shells and bodies back into the stockpot along with any accumulated juices. Add the onions, carrots, celery, bay leaves, peppercorns, parsley, tomatoes, and garlic. Let come to a boil over medium-high heat and then reduce the heat to medium-low. Place a lid slightly ajar on top of the pot and let the stock simmer and cook down a bit for

approximately 1 ½ hours. Add more water if the level of the stock falls below the lobster shells.

3 Strain the lobster stock through a fine mesh sieve and discard all the solids. Return the stock to a clean pot and let simmer over medium heat until reduced to about 5 cups, 30 to 45 minutes. Stir in the tomato paste and paprika. Keep the stock hot over medium-low heat.

4 Melt 6 tablespoons of the butter in another large pot over medium heat. Whisk in the flour and cook, stirring constantly, until well blended, about 2 minutes. Take care not to let the roux brown. Gradually whisk in the hot stock, cup by cup, until all has been added and the stock is smooth and thickened. Whisk in the light cream and sherry, stirring until evenly blended. Season with salt and pepper to taste.

5 Place the reserved lobster meat in a food processor and process until finely minced. Stir the minced lobster into the bisque and cook until the bisque is heated evenly throughout, 5 to 7 minutes. Just before serving add the remaining 4 tablespoons of butter, stirring until melted. Ladle the bisque into warmed serving bowls. If you are not serving the bisque right away and want to reheat it, do so in a double boiler to prevent the possibility of curdling. It will keep covered in the refrigerator for up to 3 days.

Lobster Stock

When we eat lobster at my parents' house in Blue Hill, Maine, we usually dispose of the shells by throwing them back into the bay, which is right in front of the house. On Cape Cod, I am not as lucky to have saltwater lapping at my doorstep and my conscience and olfactory sensibilities tend to demand that if I've served up a lobster dinner to at least four people, I shouldn't throw all those shells into the trash. So, I make lobster stock, guided by my own intuition and a few tips from one of my favorite Boston chefs, Jody Adams, who just so happens to spend time in the summer with her family in our Cape Cod village of Barnstable. MAKES 6 TO 8 CUPS

3 tablespoons olive or vegetable oil

1 large onion, peeled and coarsely chopped

2 carrots, peeled and coarsely chopped

3 ribs celery, leaves included, trimmed and coarsely chopped

2 tablespoons tomato paste

Shells and bodies from 4 to 6 cooked lobsters, broken into coarse pieces

1 cup dry white wine

1 lemon, preferably organic, cut in half

8 whole black peppercorns

Several sprigs fresh flat-leaf parsley

1 bay leaf

1 Heat the oil in a large, sturdy stockpot over medium-high heat. Add the onion, carrots, and celery and cook until softened and just beginning to brown, 12 to 15 minutes. Reduce the heat to medium and stir in the tomato paste. Add the lobster shells and cook, stirring constantly, to coat the shells with the vegetable and tomato paste mixture, about 5 minutes.

2 Pour in the white wine and add enough water to the pot to completely cover all the shells by at least 4 inches. Add the lemon, peppercorns, parsley, and bay leaf to the pot. Let come to a boil over medium-high heat. Reduce the heat to medium-low, place a lid slightly ajar on top of the pot, and let the stock simmer until full-flavored, about 1 hour.

3 Let the stock cool to room temperature. Strain the stock through a fine mesh sieve and discard all the solids. Taste and if you wish a more concentrated flavor, return it to a clean pot, bring it to a boil, and boil until reduced to the desired strength. The stock can be refrigerated, covered, for up to 3 days and frozen for up to 2 months. Let thaw before using.

Gone Fishin'

> "You can observe a lot just by watching."
> —Yogi Berra

Even though my husband keeps on his bureau an old picture of me in a pink sweater holding a formidable freshly caught bluefish, I currently prefer to fish for compliments—culinary ones. I am fine leaving the slimy bait, hooks, rods, reels, gutting, goring, and filleting to the men in my family. It is not that I don't or won't go fishing. Rather, I just happen to be more adept at packing the cold drinks, snacks, sunblock, swimsuits, and foul weather gear for fishing adventures. And, believe me, ever since my son, Oliver, developed a penchant for seeking out fishing charters in locales that were either remote or pricey or both, fishing is always an adventure. In fact, I had to give up doing the Sunday crossword puzzle in *The New York Times* because untangling Oliver's fishing lines offered more of a challenge.

I am not complaining because the benefits far outweigh the hassles and maybe even the expenses, too. From a cook's point of view, once you have tasted fish just caught by someone you love, even if that fish more often than not is bluefish, you are spoiled for life. A good fishmonger, and there are several throughout coastal New England, can also be a godsend when you eat fish as often as we do in our family. Sometimes I think there are not enough letters in the alphabet or days in the week to contain all the local species I cook or can't wait to cook. So yes, this chapter does begin with four bluefish recipes, but it is also bursting at the seams with cod, salmon, sole, striped bass, swordfish, and calamari. And then there are the ones that got away . . . hope you become as hooked as I am.

Fish Finder's Favorite Bluefish

David Goodman and I have both been writing columns for Nantucket's weekly newspaper, *The Inquirer and Mirror*, for a very long time. David actually writes two columns and his "Fish Finder" one is infinitely less controversial than his other one, entitled "Goodman's Gam." While David is very opinionated about many topics and island dwellers are likewise opinionated about him, everyone seems to concur that this bluefish recipe, created by David's lovely mother, Joyce Chase, is

a keeper. Since my son, like many others who fish the waters surrounding Cape Cod and the islands, catches more bluefish than any other type of fish, I believe you can never have enough go-to bluefish recipes, and this terrific recipe is usually the one that comes first to mind when bluefish is, once again, the catch of the day. SERVES 4 TO 6

3 tablespoons extra virgin olive oil

1 very fresh skinless bluefish fillet
(about 2 pounds)

Sea salt and freshly ground black pepper

2 medium-size vine-ripened tomatoes, seeded
and coarsely chopped

1 small red onion, peeled and coarsely chopped

3 scallions, both white and light green parts,
trimmed and sliced ½-inch thick on the
diagonal

⅓ cup diced yellow bell pepper (⅓-inch dice)

⅓ cup diced red bell pepper (⅓-inch dice)

⅓ cup imported black olives, such as niçoise or
kalamata, pitted and coarsely chopped

Finely grated zest and juice of 1 lemon

1½ tablespoons minced fresh flat-leaf
parsley, or 1½ tablespoons slivered fresh
basil leaves

1   Preheat the oven to 400°F.

2   Use 1 tablespoon of the olive oil to film the bottom of a baking dish large enough to hold the bluefish fillet. Place the fillet, skinned side down, in the dish. Season the bluefish fillet with salt and black pepper to taste.

3   Place the tomatoes, red onion, scallions, yellow bell pepper, red bell pepper, olives, and lemon zest in a mixing bowl. Add the remaining 2 tablespoons of olive oil and the lemon juice and toss well to combine and coat all of the vegetables evenly. Season the vegetables with salt and black pepper to taste. Spoon the vegetable mixture evenly over the bluefish fillet.

Dramatic bluffs, sensuous sand dunes, and crashing waves lure surfers, skimboarders, and nature preservationists alike to Marconi Beach on Cape Cod's National Seashore.

4   Bake the bluefish until it is cooked through and the flesh flakes easily when tested in the center with a fork, 25 to 30 minutes. Scatter the parsley or basil over the top and serve at once.

Bluefish Flambéed with Gin

When I first started going to Nantucket in the 1970s, this method of cooking bluefish was all the rage. I was just beginning to become interested in cooking and the recipe struck me as incredibly avant-garde but also very Nantucket. These days, I never hear anybody talk about flambéing bluefish with gin, but since there are so many craft distilleries in New England now making gin, I decided the recipe was due for a revival. While I have never been a gin drinker, this does not deter me from enjoying the herbal nuances it imparts to the bluefish. If you are one who enjoys sipping gin and tonics, you will likely covet the recipe.

I use Greylock gin from Berkshire Mountain Distillers in Great Barrington, Massachusetts, because it is what I keep on hand. Feel free to use gin from other craft distilleries, such as Maine's Alchemy or Cold River. For a total Nantucket experience, opt for Gale Force gin from the island's Triple Eight Distillery. SERVES 4

3 tablespoons unsalted butter

3 tablespoons extra virgin olive oil

1 very fresh skin-on bluefish fillet
  (1¾ to 2 pounds)

Sea salt and freshly ground black pepper

2 tablespoons freshly squeezed lime juice

1 teaspoon finely grated lime zest

1 plump shallot, peeled and minced

½ cup gin

1½ tablespoons minced fresh flat-leaf parsley
  or cilantro

Lime wedges, for serving

1 Position an oven rack about 4 inches underneath the heat source and preheat the broiler to high.

2 Melt 2 tablespoons of the butter in 1 tablespoon of the olive oil in a large, heavy, ovenproof skillet, such as a cast-iron one, over medium-high heat. Once the butter has melted and is hot, place the bluefish fillet, skin side down, in the skillet. Immediately season the top of the fillet with salt and pepper to taste, then drizzle the lime juice over it. Scatter the lime zest and shallot evenly over the fillet. Once the skin has begun to brown and the outer edges of the fillet are starting to turn opaque, about 3 minutes, remove the skillet from the heat. Drizzle the remaining 2 tablespoons of olive oil over the fillet. Place the skillet underneath the broiler and broil the bluefish until it has browned on top and the flesh flakes easily when tested in the center with a fork, 4 to 5 minutes.

3 Meanwhile, combine the gin and the remaining 1 tablespoon of butter in a small saucepan and heat over medium-low heat until the butter melts and the gin is warm, 1½ to 2 minutes. Remove the skillet from the oven. Pour the warm gin over the bluefish and carefully ignite it with a long match away from anything flammable. Once the flames have subsided, sprinkle the parsley or cilantro over the bluefish. Cut the fillet into serving pieces and serve it with the pan juices spooned on top and lime wedges on the side. The skin will have separated from the fillet and I tend not to serve the bluefish with its skin.

Broiled Bluefish with Garlicky Herb Garden Butter

Boston-based chef Jasper White has been on my culinary radar for most of my cooking life. When I was in college, he opened an acclaimed and novel-for-the-time, formal New England–themed restaurant with the eponymous name of Jasper's. These days, he is a partner in the antithetically casual Summer Shack restaurants. I own all of Jasper's cookbooks and his *Cooking from New England, 50 Chowders,* and *Lobster at Home* all continue to hold places of honor on my cookbook shelf. This bluefish recipe, however, is inspired by Jasper's most recent *The Summer Shack Cookbook: The Complete Guide to Shore Food.* I fell in love with the photograph of the recipe when I first purchased the book and then I started making my own version of Jasper's garlic butter but retained his method of scoring and broiling the bluefish. More love followed. SERVES 6

2 tablespoons olive oil

6 very fresh skin-on bluefish fillets
  (6 to 8 ounces each)

Sea salt and freshly ground black pepper

Garlicky Herb Garden Butter (recipe follows)

Lemon wedges, for serving

1 Position an oven rack 5 to 6 inches beneath the heat source and preheat the broiler to high. Line a large, rimmed baking sheet with heavy-duty aluminum foil.

2 Brush 1 tablespoon of the olive oil over the prepared baking sheet. Place the bluefish fillets, skin side down, on the foil. Using a sharp knife, score the bluefish flesh in a crosshatch pattern, cutting about 1/2 inch into the flesh and spacing the diagonal cuts about 3/4 inch apart. Brush the remaining 1 tablespoon of olive oil over the tops of the fillets to coat them lightly. Season the fillets with salt and pepper to taste. Broil the bluefish fillets until partially cooked, about 5 minutes.

3 Meanwhile, remove the herb garden butter from the refrigerator and cut the cylinder into 12 equal rounds. After the bluefish fillets have broiled for 5 minutes, place 2 rounds of the herb butter on top of each fillet, spacing the rounds about 3/4 inch apart. Return the bluefish to the oven and continue to broil it until the butter is sizzling, the fillets are lightly browned and crisp, and the flesh flakes evenly when tested in the center with a fork, 3 to 4 minutes longer.

4 Serve the bluefish with plenty of the delicious butter spooned over it and garnish it with lemon wedges.

. . . .

Garlicky Herb Garden Butter

. . . .

Should you be pressed for time and want to go directly to broiling without making my flavored butter recipe, consider using the herbal garlic butter marketed by the Nantucket Butter Company. Owner Inez Hutton is a longtime Nantucket acquaintance and I have enjoyed watching her business grow over the past few years. MAKES 1 1/2 CUPS

1 plump shallot, peeled and minced

1/2 cup dry white wine

12 tablespoons (1 1/2 sticks) unsalted butter,
   at room temperature

3 cloves garlic, peeled and minced

2 teaspoons minced fresh tarragon

1 tablespoon finely slivered fresh basil leaves

1 tablespoon minced fresh flat-leaf parsley

1/2 teaspoon finely grated lemon zest

1 Place the shallot and white wine in a small saucepan over medium-high heat. Let the shallot mixture come to a boil and continue to cook until only about 1 tablespoon of liquid remains, 3 to 4 minutes. Remove the pan from the heat and let the shallot mixture cool.

2 Place the butter in a mixing bowl and add the garlic, tarragon, basil, parsley, and lemon zest. Mix, either with a spoon or with a hand-held mixer, until evenly combined. Once the shallot mixture has cooled fold it into the herb butter.

3 Tear off a 12-inch-long piece of sturdy plastic wrap and spread the flavored butter in a log about 8 inches long, positioning it 1 inch from one edge of the plastic wrap. Using the plastic wrap as an aid, form the butter into a compact cylinder, about 1 1/4 inches in diameter. Wrap the cylinder of herb butter completely in the plastic and refrigerate it for at least 1 hour. The herb butter will keep well in the refrigerator for at least 5 days.

Baked Bluefish with Bay Leaves and New Potatoes

This is yet another popular way of cooking bluefish in the coastal areas of New England. The potatoes impart a quintessentially thrifty Yankee essence to the recipe and I did in fact come across the preparation in one of the saltiest of old salt seafood cookbooks, *Cooking the Catch* by Cape Cod fisherman Dave "Pops" Masch. Masch, however, claims his recipe inspiration came from Marcella Hazan's *More Classic Italian Cooking* cookbook. Provenance aside, Masch considers this to be "the world's best bluefish recipe." Perfection can sometimes, though not always, be improved upon, and I add my two cents by introducing bay leaves into the mix and I'll often use a variety of different small or fingerling potatoes, depending upon what's available locally. As always, it will be the freshest bluefish and/or the adventure of catching it that will make this recipe truly sing. SERVES 4 TO 6

1½ pounds new potatoes, scrubbed of any dirt

3 bay leaves, preferably fresh

⅔ cup extra virgin olive oil

4 cloves garlic, peeled and coarsely chopped

⅓ cup chopped fresh flat-leaf parsley

Sea salt and freshly ground black pepper

2 very fresh skin-on bluefish fillets (about 1 pound each)

Lemon wedges, for serving

1   Place a rack in the upper third of the oven and preheat the oven to 450°F.

2   Slice the potatoes into ⅛-inch-thick rounds. Put the sliced potatoes in a 13-by-9-inch baking dish. Add the bay leaves, ⅓ cup of olive oil, half of the garlic, and half of the parsley and toss to mix. Season the potatoes with salt and pepper to taste. Bake the potatoes, stirring once or twice, until they are about two thirds of the way cooked, 12 to 15 minutes.

3   Arrange the bluefish fillets on top of the potatoes and drizzle the remaining ⅓ cup of olive oil over the fillets and then scatter the remaining garlic on top. Season the bluefish with salt and pepper to taste. Bake the bluefish for 10 minutes, then baste it with any juices that have accumulated around the potatoes. Move the potatoes around in the baking dish by gently nudging them with a metal spatula to keep them from sticking and/or burning. At the same time, you do want the potatoes to become browned and crisp, as this is a large part of the appeal of the dish. Continue cooking the fish until it is cooked through and the flesh flakes easily when tested in the center with a fork, 7 to 10 minutes longer.

4   Remove the fillets from the oven and sprinkle the remaining parsley over them. Cut the bluefish fillets into serving portions and surround each with potatoes. Garnish each serving with a lemon wedge.

"Almost Italian" Salt Cod Salad

For several years running now, I have been letting my Polish pride and heritage take a back seat on Christmas Eve and opting instead to orchestrate a stylized version of the Italian Feast of the Seven Fishes. I always feel obliged to adhere to the constraints of the tradition and therefore have insisted that one of the seven fishes be some sort of salt cod preparation. Each and every time I have hosted this piscatorial extravaganza, the salt cod ends up being the one dish left over. No matter what the reason, this is somewhat tragic when you live

Packing cod fillets in salt adds unique flavor and texture to the fish and connoisseurs have been known to refer to salt cod as "the prosciutto of the sea."

in Southeastern Massachusetts and are trying to write a New England cookbook. In fact, I have been reminded on more than one occasion that there is an old-time salt cod preparation called Cape Cod turkey, a mushy but memorable-to-some combination of creamed salt cod and potatoes accented with bits of crispy salt pork and garnished with sliced hard-boiled eggs. I thought of trying this recipe one Christmas Eve, but I knew, even when offering it on Cape Cod, I would still have an unfathomable amount of leftovers.

Enter my older sister, Holly, and her companion, Skip Lombardi, who divide their time between the Connecticut shore and Sarasota, Florida. My sister has long been a whirling dervish, literally and figuratively, and a recent undertaking required her to travel frequently between the Connecticut shore and Cape Cod, with many an esoteric food provisioning stop in between. This salt cod salad is the result of a *baccalà* pit stop in New Bedford. Holly and Skip have collaborated on publishing an e-book entitled *Almost Italian: A Cookbook & History of Italian Food in America* and this recipe is included in their book. I am delighted to share their colorful and vibrantly flavored salad here as well, because I

know it to be the one salt cod recipe that can make fellow feasters of the seven fishes swoon. Bear in mind that preparation for the recipe needs to start two days in advance of serving it. SERVES 8 AS AN ANTIPASTO

1 pound boneless salt cod, sometimes labeled baccalà

2 cups water

2 large dried bay leaves

¼ large red onion, peeled and sliced into thin rings, rings quartered

2 cloves garlic, peeled and thinly sliced

½ cup thinly sliced celery

3 tablespoons brined capers, drained

Finely grated zest and juice from 1 large lemon, plus extra juice if needed

3 tablespoons extra virgin olive oil, or more as needed

½ teaspoon hot red pepper flakes

Freshly ground black pepper

½ cup thinly sliced strips of red or yellow bell pepper

½ cup finely chopped fresh flat-leaf parsley, plus sprigs of parsley for garnish

Lettuce leaves, for serving

Lemon wedges, for serving

1 Two days in advance of serving the recipe, rinse the salt cod under cold running water for 3 to 4 minutes. Place the fish in a bowl or dish that has sides at least 3 inches high. Add cold water to cover, making sure the salt cod is completely submerged. Cover the bowl or dish with plastic wrap, place it in the refrigerator, and let the salt cod soak for 10 to 12 hours but no longer or else the fish will become mushy. Replace the soaking water 2 or 3 times during the soaking period.

2 Drain the salt cod and then tear or cut it into 3- or 4-inch chunks. Place the 2 cups of water and the bay leaves in a medium-size saucepan and let come to a boil over medium-high heat. Add the salt cod

chunks, reduce the heat, and let simmer, until the cod just begins to flake, about 5 minutes. Remove the salt cod and bay leaves from the pan. Discard the cooking water. Feel the chunks of salt cod for any stray pin bones and, using tweezers, remove any bones you find. Set the salt cod aside briefly.

3 Place the reserved bay leaves, red onion, garlic, celery, capers, lemon zest, lemon juice, and olive oil in a mixing bowl. Add the salt cod and hot red pepper flakes and season with black pepper to taste. Toss gently to combine the salad evenly. The salad can be refrigerated at this point for up to 3 days, but for at least 12 hours for the flavors to meld.

4 Remove the salad from the refrigerator about 30 minutes prior to serving. Add the bell pepper strips and chopped parsley and toss gently to incorporate. Taste for seasoning, adding more lemon juice, olive oil, black pepper, and/or parsley . Serve the salad spooned onto a bed of lettuce leaves and garnish it with lemon wedges and sprigs of parsley.

Beyond Boston Baked Scrod

Technically, scrod is supposed to designate young cod or haddock weighing less than two pounds, but I find any fish—be it cod, haddock, pollock, or hake—is called scrod when used in the classic Boston preparation of a flaky white fish baked with buttery, paprika-laced cracker or bread crumbs. When the recipe is done right, it epitomizes classic and timeless New England cooking. At home, I tend to modernize the preparation and borrow a few flavors from my go-to French recipe for escargots. While this may not be the original recipe of Boston Brahmins, it is a favorite in my family. SERVES 4

5 tablespoons unsalted butter, at room temperature

2 cloves garlic, peeled and finely minced

1 plump shallot, peeled and finely minced

2 tablespoons finely minced prosciutto

1½ tablespoons lightly toasted slivered almonds (see Box, page 70), finely chopped

1½ tablespoons minced fresh flat-leaf parsley

2 tablespoons freshly squeezed lemon juice

Sea salt and freshly ground black pepper

2 tablespoons canola oil

4 fresh skinless cod or haddock fillets (6 to 8 ounces each)

½ cup panko bread crumbs

Lemon wedges, for serving

1 Preheat the oven to 400°F.

2 Place the butter in a mixing bowl and, using a fork to mash and fold simultaneously, add the garlic, shallot, prosciutto, almonds, parsley, lemon juice, and ½ teaspoon each of salt and pepper. Once everything is evenly incorporated set the butter mixture aside briefly.

3 Heat the canola oil in a large ovenproof skillet over medium-high heat. Season the fish fillets lightly all over with salt and pepper. Place the fillets in the skillet, skinned sides facing down, and sear the fish until the undersides are lightly browned, 2 to 2 ½ minutes. Remove the skillet from the heat and spread the butter mixture evenly over the top of each fillet. Sprinkle the panko crumbs evenly over the top of the butter, pressing them gently into the butter with a palette knife or the back of a spoon.

4 Place the skillet in the hot oven and bake the fish until the butter mixture is sizzling and the fillets are browned on top and just cooked through in the center, 8 to 10 minutes. Serve the fish with any remaining pan juices poured over the top and lemon wedges alongside.

Victory Garden Battered Haddock

I learned much of what I know about cooking fish from Marian Morash's *The Victory Garden Fish and Vegetable Cookbook*. Marian was a vital personality on the Nantucket food scene during many of my own years cooking on the island, as she was the chef at the Straight Wharf restaurant and one of television's early culinary personalities as the host of the PBS series *The Victory Garden*, produced by her husband Russell.

This recipe cleverly reverses the usual order of battering fish and is one Russell says he would select if ever asked to choose his last supper. If there is a better recommendation, I can't think of one. I've adapted it a bit, preferring the lighter texture imparted by Wondra flour. SERVES 4

½ cup Wondra flour

Sea salt and freshly ground black pepper

2 large eggs beaten with 2 teaspoons water

4 tablespoons grapeseed oil

4 fresh skinless cod or haddock fillets
   (6 to 8 ounces each)

1 tablespoon finely minced fresh flat-leaf
   parsley, for garnish

Lemon wedges, for serving

Lemon Caper Tartar Sauce (page 150;
   optional), for serving

1 Place the flour in a shallow dish, such as a pie plate, and season it generously with salt and pepper. Place the beaten eggs in another shallow dish.

2 Heat the grapeseed oil over medium heat in a skillet large enough to hold the fish in a single layer without crowding. Dredge the fish first in the seasoned flour, shaking off any excess, then dip it into

Whether the tide is low, as in this photo, or high, the lobster-red boat house at Canary Cove is a favorite scenic spot en route from my parent's house to the village of Blue Hill, Maine.

the beaten egg mixture, again letting any excess drip off. Fry the fish, keeping the heat at medium, until the bottom coating is golden, 3 to 4 minutes. Carefully turn the fish over and continue cooking until golden on the other side, 3 to 4 minutes longer depending on the thickness of the fish.

3 Serve the fish at once, dusting each serving with a sprinkling of parsley and with lemon wedges on the side. You may also accompany the fish with tartar sauce, if desired.

Buck's Baked Haddock

My brother, Jonathan, is the executive chef at Buck's restaurant in the tiny but exceptionally picturesque Maine town of Buck's Harbor. This recipe is his invention and is a favorite with

Although Acadia National Park on Mount Desert Island in Maine is very popular with tourists, solitude is also in abundance as seen at the Bass Harbor Head Lighthouse.

customers. Jonathan notes that the dish also works well when made with halibut, cod, bluefish, or pollock and cautions to avoid using fresh haddock from midspring to midsummer, since the species goes through a spawning phase making the fish somewhat difficult to fillet and hence rather mushy. Halibut or pollock are better choices during this period. SERVES 4

5 tablespoons unsalted butter, melted

4 fresh skinless haddock fillets (6 to 8 ounces each)

Sea salt and freshly ground black pepper

½ cup dry white wine

⅓ cup Garlic Balsamic Mayonnaise (recipe follows)

1 cup coarse bread crumbs, made from a day-old baguette or similar crusty white bread

3 tablespoons finely chopped flat-leaf parsley

2 teaspoons finely grated lemon zest

Lemon wedges, for serving

1 Place a rack in the center of the oven and preheat the oven to 400°F.

2 Brush 1 tablespoon of the butter over the bottom of a 13-by-9-inch nonreactive baking dish.

3 Season both sides of the haddock fillets generously with salt and pepper. Place the fillets in the baking dish, tucking the tail ends underneath themselves so each piece has a relatively even thickness from end to end. Pour the white wine over the fish. Brush the tops of the fillets with 1½ tablespoons of the melted butter. Smear the Garlic Balsamic Mayonnaise evenly over the top of the haddock fillets.

4 Place the bread crumbs, parsley, and lemon zest in a small bowl and stir to mix. Add the remaining 2½ tablespoons of melted butter and stir to mix. Evenly distribute the buttered crumbs over the top of the fillets.

5 Bake the haddock until the crumb topping just begins to brown and the fillets are just cooked through in the center (they will flake easily when tested with a fork), 15 to 20 minutes. Remove the fillets from the oven and let them rest for 5 minutes.

6 Transfer the haddock fillets to 4 warm dinner plates. Pour the juices that have accumulated in the baking dish over the fillets. Garnish the haddock with lemon wedges and serve at once.

Garlic Balsamic Mayonnaise

Extra mayonnaise can be used on sandwiches and is especially good with BLTs or roast beef. It keeps well in the refrigerator, covered, for up to two weeks. MAKES ABOUT 2 CUPS

6 large cloves garlic, peeled

1 tablespoon extra virgin olive oil

2 cups mayonnaise, Hellmann's or homemade (page 129)

2 tablespoons balsamic vinegar

1 Preheat the oven or a toaster oven to 400°F.

2 Place 3 of the garlic cloves in a small ramekin and drizzle the olive oil over them. Bake the garlic until it is soft and golden brown, 8 to 10 minutes. Take care not to let the garlic burn.

3 Place the roasted garlic with its olive oil and the remaining 3 cloves of raw garlic in the bowl of a food processor, a mini food processor if you have one, fitted with the steel blade. Add the mayonnaise and balsamic vinegar and process until smooth. The mayonnaise can be refrigerated, covered, for up to 2 weeks.

Down East Fish Sandwiches

L obster rolls and fried clams may be the fare that comes first to mind when thinking of making a pilgrimage to a New England seafood shanty, shack, restaurant, or dive. However, in my family, many of us are equally partial to the sort of fried haddock sandwiches served at places like the Fisherman's Friend Restaurant in Stonington, Maine, or the Bagaduce Lunch in Penobscot. When traveling the distance is a deterrent but cravings persist, this is how to make a really good fried fish sandwich at home. SERVES 4

4 fresh skinless haddock fillets (4 to 6 ounces each)

Sea salt and freshly ground black pepper

½ cup unbleached all-purpose flour

¼ cup cornmeal

1 teaspoon baking powder

1 large egg

½ cup whole milk

Canola or vegetable oil, for frying

4 large hamburger, bulkie, or kaiser rolls

2½ tablespoons unsalted butter, at room temperature

4 large Boston lettuce leaves

4 large slices ripe tomato

Lemon Caper Tartar Sauce (recipe follows)

1 Season both sides of the haddock fillets with salt and pepper. Place the fillets on a wire rack set on top of a baking sheet and let the haddock come to room temperature, about 30 minutes.

2 Place the flour, cornmeal, and baking powder in a shallow dish, such as a pie plate, and stir to mix. Beat the egg and milk together in another shallow dish.

3 Pour oil to a depth of 2 ½ inches in a Dutch oven or other large, heavy pot. Begin to heat the oil over medium heat. Increase the heat to medium-high and continue heating the oil until it registers 370°F on a deep-fry thermometer.

4 Preheat the oven to 200°F.

5 Heat a griddle or cast-iron skillet over low heat. Split the rolls and butter each half. Toast the rolls, buttered-side down until golden brown, about 3 minutes. You may have to do this in batches; if so, place the first batch of rolls, loosely covered with aluminum foil, in the warm oven.

6 While the rolls are browning, dip each haddock fillet, one at a time, in the egg and milk mixture, allowing the excess to drip off. Next, dip the fillets in the flour mixture to coat them evenly all over, then shake off any excess. Place the battered fish back on the wire rack.

7 Working in 2 batches if necessary, gently place the haddock fillets in the hot oil, setting a spatter screen on top of the Dutch oven. Cook the fillets until golden, about 4 minutes. Gently turn the fillets over and cook them until golden, about 3 minutes. Remove the fillets from the oil and transfer them to drain on paper towels. Lightly salt the fillets right after they come out of the oil. Loosely cover the first batch of fillets and put them in the preheated oven to keep them warm.

No summer jaunt to Maine is complete in my book without a scenic drive to the fishing village of Stonington at the tip of Deer Isle. The water views are spectacular.

8 Place a toasted roll on each of 4 plates, putting a lettuce leaf and tomato slice on the top half of the roll. Place a fried haddock fillet on the bottom half. Dollop the fish with the Lemon Caper Tartar Sauce or serve it in a bowl alongside so each person can add the amount that suits her or his liking before closing up the sandwich.

Lemon Caper Tartar Sauce

Tartar sauce is an excellent complement to many fish preparations and this homemade version is far tastier than any jarred sauces sold commercially. MAKES ABOUT 1 CUP

2 tablespoons brined capers, drained

2 tablespoons peeled and minced shallots

1½ teaspoons finely grated lemon zest

1½ tablespoons freshly squeezed lemon juice

1 tablespoon Dijon mustard

1 heaping cup mayonnaise, Hellmann's or homemade (page 129)

Pinch of cayenne pepper (optional)

1 tablespoon minced fresh dill or flat-leaf parsley (optional)

Freshly ground black pepper

PLACE THE CAPERS, shallots, lemon zest, lemon juice, mustard, and mayonnaise in a mixing bowl and stir to combine evenly. Fold in the cayenne and dill or parsley, if using. Season with black pepper to taste. The tartar sauce can be refrigerated, covered, and will keep for at least 5 days.

Halibut Pan Roast with Clams and Linguiça

Halibut is the meatiest of all the flatfish species found in New England waters. Much of it comes from the Gulf of Maine. Since it can be quite costly, I strive to make my preparation of it extra special and am very fond of this Portuguese inspired combination of the fish surrounded by flavorful clams and *linguiça*. While littleneck and mahogany clams both work well in this recipe, if you can get your hands on some razor clams, add them to the mix also. They recently started popping up at fish markets on Cape Cod and friends have told me that they are able to gather them locally. Razor clams are far richer than littlenecks and a few go a long way as a terrific looking accent in a dish like this. SERVES 6

4 tablespoons fresh white bread crumbs

About 4 tablespoons chopped fresh flat-leaf parsley

4 tablespoons extra virgin olive oil

8 ounces linguiça, sliced into thin rounds

1 small onion, peeled and coarsely chopped

3 cloves garlic, peeled and minced

1 teaspoon fresh thyme leaves

¼ teaspoon hot red pepper flakes

½ cup dry white wine

1 can (28 ounces) crushed tomatoes in tomato puree, preferably San Marzano tomatoes

Sea salt and freshly ground black pepper

6 fresh skinless halibut fillets (5 to 6 ounces each)

2 pounds fresh clams in the shell, preferably a combination of littlenecks or mahogany clams and 6 razor clams, scrubbed

Crusty rolls or grilled slices of ciabatta or other rustic bread, for serving

1　Place a rack in the center of the oven and preheat the oven to 400°F.

2　Place the bread crumbs, 1½ tablespoons of the parsley, and 2 tablespoons of the olive oil in a mini food processor. Pulse the machine on and off to moisten the crumbs evenly with the olive oil and tinge them green with the chopped parsley. Set the bread crumb mixture aside.

3　Heat the remaining 2 tablespoons of olive oil in a large ovenproof, straight-sided skillet over medium heat. Add the *linguiça* and cook until lightly browned, about 5 minutes. Add the onion, garlic, thyme, and hot red pepper flakes to the skillet and cook until the onion is soft and translucent, 5 to 7 minutes. Pour the white wine into the skillet and cook, scraping the skillet to release any browned bits clinging to the bottom, until the wine has reduced to about ¼ cup, 3 to 4 minutes.

4　Add the tomatoes, let the sauce come to a simmer, and cook, stirring occasionally, until the flavors blend, about 10 minutes. Taste for seasoning, adding salt and black pepper to taste, going light on the salt since the clams will soon be releasing their salty juices into the sauce. Remove the sauce from the heat.

5　Arrange the halibut fillets in the skillet, embedding them in the sauce. Spoon a bit of the sauce over the top of each fillet. Sprinkle about 2 teaspoons of the parsley and the bread crumb mixture evenly over the top of each halibut fillet, pressing the crumbs gently with your fingertips to help them adhere to the halibut. Arrange the clams, hinged sides facing down, in and around the fish fillets.

6　Place the skillet in the oven and bake the halibut until it is just cooked through in the center, the clams have opened, and the bread crumbs are golden, 25 to 30 minutes. Remove the skillet from the oven, discard any clams that have not opened, and then sprinkle the remaining 1½ tablespoons of parsley over the halibut. Present the skillet at the table set on a hot plate. Serve 1 halibut fillet per person, accompanied by plenty of sauce and an assortment of clams. Serve a basket of crusty rolls or grilled slabs of ciabatta or other rustic bread on the side. Have an empty bowl handy for the clam shells.

Campfire Mackerel

My son, Oliver, caught the fishing bug early in life, around the age of five or six, when my brother took him out on Blue Hill Bay in Maine in an old Boston Whaler that has been in our family for decades. They went trolling for mackerel, the mackerel were prolific, and Oliver has been fishing ever since, although not always with his beginner's luck success. In our family, we always cook the mackerel we catch in the same way, over an outdoor campfire within hours of catching the fish. A clean, lightly oiled, hinged grilling basket will make easy work of turning the fish and avoid the possibility of the oily little tinker mackerel sticking to the grilling grate when you flip it.

If building a campfire is not feasible, a Weber kettle or any backyard charcoal grill will do just fine. Just be sure to use "all natural" lump charcoal that can be mixed with any of the hardwoods you choose. Should you have leftover mackerel, it can be used in place of store-bought smoked mackerel in the recipe for Smoked Mackerel Rillettes (page 273). SERVES 4

4 tablespoons vegetable oil

2 lemons, each cut into 6 to 8 wedges

8 just-caught tinker mackerel (4 to 6 ounces each after gutting and cleaning)

1 Build a small wood fire in a campsite fireplace enclosed by large stones. Use only such hardwoods as birch, maple, apple, oak, and/or alder for the fire. Allow the fire to burn down to a bed of coals with just a little bit of flame. Place a grate across the stones, leveling it as best you can. The grate should be approximately 6 inches above the coals. Place a hinged grill basket on top of the grate to heat. Place the vegetable oil in a small bowl. Roll up a couple of paper towels and grasp them with a pair of tongs. Dip the paper towels in the oil and rub the inside surfaces of the grill basket. This will help to keep the mackerel from sticking.

2 Toss the lemon wedges in the remaining oil and coat them thoroughly. Thread the lemon wedges onto 1 or 2 metal skewers (if you don't have metal skewers, you can use wooden skewers that have been soaked in water for at least 30 minutes). Grill the lemons over the coals, turning them once to make sure they are charred on both sides. Set aside the lemons for squeezing over the cooked mackerel.

3 Open the grill basket and place the mackerel on the lower surface. Close the grill basket and cook the mackerel over the coals until the skin just begins to char, 3 to 4 minutes. Turn the basket over and grill the mackerel on the second side for 3 to 4 minutes.

4 Place 2 mackerel on each of 4 plates. Garnish with the charred lemons and serve at once.

Family Gathering Gravlax

There are designated drivers and designated gravlax makers, and in my family the latter undertaking and culinary honor falls to my aunt, Diane Madden. My aunt always makes her coveted cured Scandinavian-style salmon for Easter gatherings and her beautifully presented platters of gravlax often make encore appearances at our Thanksgiving, Christmas, and New Year's celebrations. Needless to say, everyone adores Diane's gravlax recipe as well as its sweet and tangy accompanying mustard dill sauce. While gravlax is usually served as an appetizer, I'll happily make a lovely light meal of sliced gravlax on rye bread as an antidote to too many rich holiday foods. While pairing gravlax with a mustard dill sauce is traditional and superb, I sometimes opt to dollop the rosy slices of salmon with Vermont Creamery crème fraîche mixed with a bit of minced fresh dill and squeeze of fresh lemon juice.

You'll need to plan ahead when making the recipe, as the fish needs to cure in the refrigerator for three days. My aunt prefers to make her gravlax with Norwegian salmon and I also recommend using Shetland Island's salmon, as both are sustainably farmed and sold by conscientious fishmongers. SERVES 8 TO 10

For the gravlax

1 side (2 pounds) fresh salmon, skin on, pin bones removed

½ cup kosher salt

½ cup sugar

1 bunch fresh dill

For the mustard dill sauce

¾ cup imported Dijon mustard

¼ cup cider vinegar

¼ cup sugar

⅓ cup honey

3 teaspoons dry mustard

½ cup extra virgin olive oil

½ cup minced fresh dill

Sliced rye bread for serving

1   Place the fish on a cutting board and cut it crosswise in half so that you have 2 fillets of equal size. Combine the salt and sugar in a small bowl and stir together to mix evenly. Rub half of the mixture evenly over the flesh of the first fillet and then top with half of the bunch of fresh dill (stems included). Rub the rest of the salt and sugar mixture over the flesh of the second salmon fillet. Place this fillet, flesh side down, directly on top of the first salmon fillet as if you were making a big salmon sandwich. Arrange the rest of the dill on top of the salmon skin that is facing up. Wrap the sandwiched fillets first in plastic wrap and then wrap again in heavy-duty aluminum foil. Place the wrapped fillets in a Pyrex baking dish and weight them down with a large brick or a few heavy, unopened cans. Refrigerate for 3 days, turning the fish over and then replacing the weights, once every day.

2   To make the mustard dill sauce: Whisk the Dijon mustard, vinegar, sugar, honey, and dry mustard together in a mixing bowl until thoroughly combined. While continuing to whisk, slowly pour in the olive oil to make an emulsion. Fold in the dill. You will have 1½ cups of sauce. Store in the refrigerator until ready to use. The sauce will keep for at least 3 weeks.

3   After 3 days, unwrap the salmon and rinse the fillets under cold running water to remove the salt and sugar cure. Pat the fillets dry with paper towels, and then refrigerate, loosely covered with plastic, for at least 3 hours. When ready to serve, slice the chilled gravlax thinly on the diagonal with a long sharp knife. Arrange the slices on a serving platter and accompany with rye bread and the mustard dill sauce. The gravlax is best when consumed within 3 days of curing.

Many a New England town celebrates the Fourth of July with a parade down Main Street in the morning and a splendid display of fireworks in the evening.

Frenchie's Fourth of July Salmon

This recipe is named after my friend Michel Becaas (you can read about him in the box on page 156). I make salmon *à la Frenchie* all the time. Because Michel isn't standing by in my kitchen, I do things a bit more my way than his. Since I have yet to have success growing lovage, I use lemon verbena in its place and find its flavor equally delicious. Also, I am not sure whether or not Michel grilled his salmon on both sides, but I prefer to grill my salmon skin side down the entire time because we all love crispy salmon skin in my house and it can sometimes be tricky to flip the fish without it breaking apart. Restaurant quality grill marks can be lovely, but then again we are cooking at home. Finally, I often serve this salmon with an American-style cucumber sauce, "Frenchified" by using crème fraîche in place of the usual sour cream. SERVES 6

Fourth of July in many small New England towns is marked by a homespun parade and plenty of flag-flying patriotism.

1 whole side (about 3 pounds) skin-on salmon fillet, pin bones removed

¼ cup white wine, rice, or cider vinegar

¼ cup olive oil, plus extra for oiling the grill grate

Sea salt and freshly cracked black peppercorns

2 tablespoons coarsely chopped fresh lemon verbena or lovage

Cucumber Sauce (optional; recipe follows)

1 Place the salmon fillet in a nonreactive baking dish large enough to hold it in a single layer. Place the vinegar and olive oil in a small nonreactive bowl and whisk to mix. Pour the vinegar mixture over the salmon. Season the salmon generously with salt and pepper and scatter the lemon verbena or lovage evenly all over the top. Let stand at room temperature for 30 minutes.

2 Meanwhile, set up a charcoal grill for indirect grilling with hardwood charcoal on one side of the grill and preheat it to medium-high.

3 When ready to cook, oil the grill grate. Remove the salmon from the baking dish and arrange it, skin side down, so that it is not directly over the coals. Set aside any remaining marinade to spoon over the fish as it grills. Cover the grill and cook the salmon until the skin is crispy and the flesh is either just barely cooked through in the center or slightly less if you like rare salmon, about 20 minutes, depending on the thickness of the fish and heat of the fire, basting the salmon once or twice with the reserved marinade. Carefully remove the salmon using 1 very large or 2 shorter spatulas to support the fillet as best you can.

4 Cut the salmon into serving pieces. Serve the salmon with or without the skin. If you are using the Cucumber Sauce, dollop it atop each serving or offer it in a serving bowl at the table.

Cucumber Sauce

Although this type of cucumber sauce is most often paired with poached salmon, I enjoy it equally on salmon that has been grilled. The sauce needs to be made at least an hour in advance of serving to allow it to chill and firm up in the refrigerator. MAKES 2 CUPS

1½ tablespoons unsalted butter

1 plump shallot, peeled and minced

2 tablespoons minced fresh dill, or 1 tablespoon minced fresh tarragon

½ cup crème fraîche, preferably from Vermont Creamery

½ cup mayonnaise, Hellmann's or homemade (page 129)

1¼ cups peeled and seeded cucumber, cut into ¼-inch dice

Sea salt and freshly ground black pepper

1 Melt the butter in a small skillet over medium heat. Add the shallot and cook until softened, 2 to 3 minutes. Remove the skillet from the heat, stir in the dill or tarragon, and let the shallot mixture cool to room temperature, about 10 minutes.

2 Meanwhile, place the crème fraîche and mayonnaise in a small bowl and whisk to mix. Blot the diced cucumber with a thick paper towel or clean dishcloth to absorb any extra liquid. Fold the cucumber into the crème fraîche and mayonnaise until evenly incorporated.

3 Stir the cooled shallot mixture into the cucumber mixture and season the sauce with a bit of salt and pepper to taste. Refrigerate the sauce, covered, for at least 1 hour before using to firm it up and blend the flavors.

Slow-Roasted Salmon à la Ritz

In this particular recipe the word *Ritz* refers not to the beloved crackers that make many a New England recipe sinfully delicious, but to the venerable Ritz-Carlton hotel in Boston. It is not that I am a frequent habitué of the hotel, though my aunt and uncle did throw me a splendid party there when I graduated from Harvard. The first house I owned on Nantucket also had the same address as the Ritz-Carlton in Boston—15 Arlington Street—and every once in a while my packages got delivered to the hotel rather than my humble island abode. In any event, I have long been attracted to dishes with either Ritz crackers or Ritz-Carlton in the title. My signature chicken salad during my Que Sera Sarah shop-keeping days on Nantucket was inspired by my aunt and uncle's (the same ones who threw me the party) description of the chicken salad served at Boston's Ritz. I can't actually remember how this salmon recipe made it into my repertoire, but I do know I have been making it and enjoying it ever since my Arlington Street days. The slow roasting imbues the salmon with a meltingly tender texture. SERVES 6

1 cup fresh white bread crumbs, made from a baguette or similar crusty white bread

⅓ cup coarsely chopped fresh flat-leaf parsley

1 tablespoon imported grainy Dijon mustard

2 teaspoons finely grated lemon zest

1 tablespoon freshly squeezed lemon juice

2 teaspoons honey

3 tablespoons unsalted butter, at room temperature

2 tablespoons extra virgin olive oil

Sea salt and freshly ground black pepper

6 skinless salmon fillets (about 6 ounces each), pin bones removed

Lemon wedges, for serving

1 Place a rack in the center of the oven and preheat the oven to 300°F.

2 Place the bread crumbs, parsley, mustard, and lemon zest in a food processor and process until the parsley is more finely chopped and the mixture is evenly combined. Add the lemon juice and honey and process again until well blended. Add the butter and 1 tablespoon of the olive oil and process to moisten the crumbs evenly. Season the bread crumb mixture with salt and pepper to taste.

3 Use the remaining 1 tablespoon of olive oil to film a roasting pan that is large enough to hold the salmon fillets in a single layer. Arrange the salmon fillets, skinned side down, in the roasting pan. Gently pat a layer of the bread crumb mixture evenly over the top of each fillet, pressing gently on the bread crumbs to make them adhere. Bake the salmon fillets until they are done to your liking, just barely cooked through in the center or slightly less if you like rare salmon, 25 to 30 minutes. Serve the salmon at once, garnished with lemon wedges.

Salmon with Wasabi Crème Fraîche

In my household salmon has become much like chicken when it comes to planning weeknight meals. We eat it almost once a week. Scottish salmon and Norwegian farm-raised salmon are good choices and can readily be purchased at top seafood markets throughout New England and beyond. If you can find wild Pacific salmon by all means feel free to use it. I am especially fond of this preparation because it is an easy way to enjoy sushi-style flavors without having to go through the fuss associated with rolling your own sushi at home. The salmon skin will not get crispy, so you have the option of using either a skin-on or skin-off fillet. SERVES 4

1 tablespoon canola or vegetable oil

1 salmon fillet with or without skin (about 2 pounds), pin bones removed

Sea salt and freshly ground black pepper

½ cup crème fraîche, preferably from Vermont Creamery

2 teaspoons freshly mixed wasabi paste, or more to taste (see Note)

4 scallions, both white and tender green parts, trimmed and thinly sliced on the diagonal

3 tablespoons coarsely chopped fresh cilantro

1 Preheat the oven to 425°F.

2 Use the oil to film the bottom of a nonreactive baking dish large enough to hold the salmon fillet. Place the salmon in the baking dish with the skin or skinned side facing down. Season the salmon with salt and pepper to taste.

3 Place the crème fraîche and wasabi paste in a small bowl and whisk until well combined. Taste for seasoning, adding a bit more wasabi if you are a wasabi

A Fourth of July French Lesson

Serving salmon and peas on the Fourth of July is a longstanding New England tradition. However, if you happen to be the guest at a Frenchman's home on the Fourth and that Frenchman is a former chef, then you will be obliged, and happily so I must add, to have your salmon prepared according to French sensibilities. Truth be told, I discovered what has now become one of my favorite ways to cook salmon when I was invited to celebrate the Fourth with a few close friends at the Nantucket home of Marina Cholaki and Michel Becaas. This circle of friends often endearingly calls Michel "Frenchie" because even after spending decades in America he remains steadfastly and incorrigibly French.

I had to calm myself with a glass of wine, French of course, when I saw Michel using vinegar in the simple marinade he was making for the salmon. I myself had always used lemon or sometimes another citrus juice when marinating fish and never would have dreamed of using vinegar. Michel assured me that the vinegar was necessary to counterbalance the fattiness of the salmon. He also added some olive oil, salt, pepper, and lovage plucked from his backyard to the marinade. When Michel's grilled salmon masterpiece was presented at the table, I had to toast him with another glass of wine, French of course, because it was the most delicious grilled salmon I had ever tasted. For the recipe, see page 153.

fiend. Spread the crème fraîche mixture evenly over the salmon. Sprinkle half of the sliced scallions on top of the salmon.

4 Bake the salmon fillet until it is done to your liking, either just barely cooked through in the center or

slightly less if you like rare salmon, 15 to 20 minutes. Remove the salmon from the oven and sprinkle the rest of the scallions and the cilantro over the top. Divide the salmon into 4 portions and serve at once.

NOTE: *To make this paste, you'll need a jar of wasabi powder. Instructions for mixing the paste are on the jar.*

Maple-Glazed Salmon

Despite the Asian flavors in this recipe, this is a popular way of cooking salmon in New England due to the use of maple syrup. After trying many different variations, I have settled on this recipe as my personal favorite. I like to crisp the salmon skin on the stovetop and then finish cooking the fish in a hot oven. However, the recipe can also lend itself to grilling in hotter summer months. SERVES 4

⅓ cup soy sauce

⅓ cup pure maple syrup

2 tablespoons rice wine vinegar

2 teaspoons Asian (dark) sesame oil

1 tablespoon finely minced peeled fresh ginger

¼ to ½ teaspoon hot red pepper flakes

4 skin-on salmon fillets (6 to 8 ounces each), pin bones removed

1 tablespoon canola oil

3 scallions, both white and tender green parts, trimmed and thinly sliced

3 tablespoons coarsely chopped fresh cilantro

1 Place the soy sauce, maple syrup, rice wine vinegar, sesame oil, ginger, and hot red pepper flakes to taste in a small bowl and stir to mix. Place the salmon fillets in a shallow nonreactive dish and pour the marinade over them, turning to coat them evenly. Let the salmon marinate for 30 minutes at room temperature.

2 Place a rack in the center of the oven and preheat the oven to 425°F.

3 Remove the salmon from the marinade, pour the marinade into a small saucepan, and set the saucepan aside. Film a large, heavy, ovenproof skillet, such as a cast-iron one, with the canola oil and heat over medium-high heat. Add the salmon fillets, skin side down, and cook until the skin is crispy and golden brown, 3 to 4 minutes. Transfer the skillet to the oven and bake the salmon fillets until they are done to your liking, either just barely cooked through in the center or slightly less if you like rare salmon, 8 to 12 minutes.

4 While the salmon is baking, let the reserved marinade come to a boil over medium-high heat and simmer until reduced to the consistency of a glaze, 3 to 4 minutes. Serve the salmon with some of the glaze spooned over each fillet and a generous sprinkling of scallions and cilantro on top.

Classic Connecticut Shad Roe

I grew up in Connecticut where certain folks, my parents included, revered the early spring delicacy of shad roe, vermillion-hued lobes of fish eggs harvested from female shad fish who swim up rivers to spawn. Shad roe festivals still take place today along the banks of the Connecticut and Housatonic rivers and they tend to strike me as a throwback to a bygone era. I like shad roe but I don't love it. Yet, I am easily persuaded to indulge in cooking it during the fleeting spring season when I see it touted by connoisseurs as the foie gras of fish. I prepare shad roe exactly as I remember my parents did—with lots of butter and bacon. The texture of shad roe is described by some as similar to quinoa, making it a great canvas for all that smoky bacon and creamy butter. SERVES 2

Come springtime, shad swim up the Connecticut River to freshwater spawning grounds in rippling brooks such as this one spanned by the Chatfield Hollow covered bridge.

4 slices cob or apple wood-smoked bacon, or another favorite New England bacon

10 tablespoons (1¼ sticks) unsalted butter (see Note)

½ cup unbleached all-purpose flour or Wondra flour

¾ teaspoon fine sea salt

½ teaspoon freshly ground black pepper

2 pairs shad roe (each weighing about ½ pound)

1 tablespoon finely minced fresh flat-leaf parsley

Lemon wedges, for serving

Balsamic vinegar (optional), for drizzling

1 Place the bacon in a medium-size skillet and cook over medium heat until nicely crisped. Transfer the bacon to a paper towel–lined plate to drain. Wipe out the skillet.

2 Melt the butter in a saucepan and skim off and discard all the foam and milky white solids.

3 Pour the butter into the medium-size skillet and heat over medium heat for 1 minute. It may seem like

quite a bit of butter but the secret to cooking shad roe is almost to poach it in butter.

4 Combine the flour, salt, and pepper in a shallow dish, such as a pie plate. Dredge the shad roe in the seasoned flour to coat it evenly all over, shaking off any excess. Place the shad roe in the skillet and immediately reduce the heat to low. Partially cover the skillet and cook the roe until lightly browned, about 6 minutes. It is important to keep the heat low because if it is too hot the roe will start to pop out of the membrane containing it. Gently turn the roe over, taking care not to rupture the sacks, partially cover the skillet, and continue cooking the shad roe over low heat until just opaque and firm when pressed gently with a fingertip, 6 to 8 minutes.

5 Remove the roe from the pan and dab it with a paper towel to absorb any excess butter. Place one pair of roe on each serving plate and sprinkle it with parsley. Cross 2 slices of bacon over the top of each serving and accompany them with lemon wedges. The lemon tempers the richness of the roe and these days it has also become popular to drizzle the roe with a few drops of good balsamic vinegar.

NOTE: *This butter will be clarified in Step 2. Some stores sell butter that is already clarified and you can certainly use this in place of making your own. If you do, you'll only need 7 tablespoons of already-clarified butter.*

Sautéed Sole with Lemon and Capers

This is one of those dishes I make when I can't think of anything else I want to make or eat, and I'm always happy with the choice, as the preparation is as timeless as it is tasty. I usually use grey sole, yellowtail flounder, or plaice and sometimes call the recipe poor man's Dover sole. The recipe may be doubled, but because sole fillets are so delicate and don't hold up all that well when cooked in batches, I prefer to make the recipe to serve two. SERVES 2

½ cup unbleached all-purpose flour or
   Wondra flour

Fine sea salt and ground black pepper

5 tablespoons chilled unsalted butter

1 tablespoon extra virgin olive oil

4 fresh sole fillets (about 6 ounces each)

½ cup dry white wine

1½ tablespoons brined capers, drained

½ lemon, thinly sliced

1 to 2 tablespoons freshly squeezed lemon juice

2 tablespoons minced fresh flat-leaf parsley

1 Preheat the oven to 200°F.

2 Combine the flour, ¾ teaspoon of salt, and ¼ teaspoon of pepper in a shallow dish, such as a pie plate, and stir to mix.

3 Melt 1 tablespoon of the butter in the olive oil in a large, heavy skillet over medium heat. Dredge the sole fillets in the seasoned flour to coat them evenly on both sides, shaking off any excess. Add the fillets to the skillet and cook until lightly browned on the underside, 2 to 2½ minutes. Carefully turn the fillets over and cook them until opaque in the center, about 2 minutes longer. Transfer the sole fillets to 2 ovenproof dinner plates, placing 2 fillets on each plate. Keep the fillets warm in the oven while making the sauce.

4 Add the white wine, capers, and lemon slices to the skillet. Let the wine mixture come to a boil and simmer until the wine is reduced to about ¼ cup, about 3 minutes. Reduce the heat to low and stir in the remaining 4 tablespoons of butter, 1 tablespoon at a time, allowing each tablespoon to melt before adding the next, to make a light emulsion. Taste for seasoning, adding lemon juice, salt, and pepper, to taste. Spoon the

sauce generously over the warm sole fillets, sprinkle the parsley over them, and serve at once.

Grilled Striped Bass

So far, my son has only caught one striped bass in his fishing career, but I am fortunate to have a cousin and a few generous friends who have had better striper fishing luck. No matter what the source, having striped bass for dinner is a cherished summer event, and basically I cook it the same way every time—simply marinated and grilled. SERVES 4

⅓ cup dry white wine

2 tablespoons freshly squeezed lemon juice

1 plump shallot, peeled and finely minced

4 tablespoons extra virgin olive oil, plus extra
   for oiling the grill grate

1 tablespoon minced fresh flat-leaf parsley

1 tablespoon coarsely chopped fresh tarragon

4 fresh skin-on striped bass fillets
   (6 to 8 ounces each)

Sea salt and freshly ground black pepper

Lemon wedges, for serving

1 Combine the white wine, lemon juice, and shallot in a small nonreactive bowl. Let stand until the shallot softens, about 10 minutes. Whisk in the olive oil, parsley, and tarragon.

2 Place the striped bass fillets in a shallow nonreactive baking dish large enough to hold them in a single layer. Season the fillets with salt and pepper to taste and pour the marinade over them, turning the fillets to coat them evenly. Let the bass fillets marinate at room temperature for about 30 minutes.

3 Set up a charcoal or gas grill and preheat it to medium-high.

4   When ready to cook, oil the grill grate. Remove the bass fillets from the marinade and place them flesh-side down on the grill grate. Grill the bass fillets until cooked through in the center (they will flake easily when tested with a fork), 3 to 4 minutes per side, turning them once and basting them once or twice with any marinade remaining in the dish. Serve the bass hot off the grill with lemon wedges.

Swordfish Oreganata

We have several garden banks with varying sun exposure surrounding our house on Cape Cod. At times, I have struggled to get ivy, myrtle, and/or pachysandra to take a thriving hold on these banks, yet surprisingly I have no problem on my sunniest bank getting oregano to come back year after year in great wild profusion. Needless to say, I am always trying to find ways to use my oregano bounty and this Italian-inspired recipe may well take the prize.

For decades I used to grill swordfish in the manner I had first learned on Nantucket—slathered in mayonnaise to keep it moist. While this has always been a great way to cook swordfish, I yearned to try something new and adapted this recipe from another fish cookbook I adore in my collection—Evan Kleiman's *Cucina del Mare: Fish and Seafood Italian Style*. I believe the book is now out of print but that doesn't make me crave Kleiman's oregano-accented Sicilian sauce called *salmoriglio*, spooned over summer's best and freshest harpooned swordfish, any less. SERVES 6

For the salmoriglio (oregano sauce)

1 cup extra virgin olive oil

½ cup hot tap water

5 tablespoons freshly squeezed lemon juice

1 teaspoon finely grated lemon zest

3 cloves garlic, peeled and finely minced

1½ tablespoons minced fresh oregano

1½ tablespoons minced fresh flat-leaf parsley

For the swordfish

6 fresh center-cut swordfish steaks (8 ounces each and at least 1 inch thick)

3 tablespoons extra virgin olive oil, plus extra for oiling the grill grate

2 tablespoons freshly squeezed lemon juice

Sea salt and freshly cracked black peppercorns

1   Make the *salmoriglio:* Pour the 1 cup of olive oil into a 1-quart glass or stainless steel mixing bowl. Run tap water until it feels quite hot to the touch and then fill a measuring cup with a pouring spout with ½ cup of the hot water. Slowly pour the hot water into the olive oil in a very thin stream, whisking constantly. The mixture will look like a slightly emulsified vinaigrette. Whisk in the 5 tablespoons of lemon juice and the lemon zest, then stir in the garlic, oregano, and parsley. Let the *salmoriglio* stand at room temperature for at least 30 minutes and up to 3 hours to blend the flavors.

2   Prepare the swordfish: Set up a charcoal or gas grill and preheat it to medium-high.

3   Place the swordfish steaks on a large platter and brush them lightly all over with the 3 tablespoons of olive oil and 2 tablespoons of lemon juice. Season the swordfish steaks generously on both sides with salt and pepper. Let the swordfish steaks stand at room temperature for 10 to 15 minutes.

4   When ready to cook, oil the grill grate. Place the swordfish steaks on the grill grate, cover the grill, and partially cook the swordfish for about 5 minutes. You can give the steaks a quarter turn after 2½ or 3 minutes if you want the swordfish to have nice grilling marks. Turn the swordfish steaks over and continue grilling them until just cooked through in the center, 4 to 6 minutes more, depending on the thickness of the steaks.

Many consider swordfish caught in the waters surrounding Block Island to be the best in New England. The island also offers excellent sweeping coastal vistas, here the North Light.

5 Transfer the swordfish steaks to dinner plates. Give the *salmoriglio* a quick stir to re-emulsify it and spoon a generous ¼ cup of the sauce over each swordfish steak. Serve at once.

Swordfish Baked in Rhode Island Red Wine

Rhode Island is the perfect size state for tootling and that is exactly what I was doing—tootling between Newport and Little Compton—when I decided to pay a visit to Sakonnet Vineyard on a beautiful early fall afternoon. I purchased a few bottles of their wine to sample once home and no longer tootling and even got a souvenir wine glass with a red rooster on it, which is now my preferred little glass to sip from while in the mad throes of cooking dinner.

While I have long known salmon pairs splendidly with pinot noir, I had never thought of pairing swordfish, though meaty, with red wine. Somewhere, however, I had recalled seeing a recipe that suggested such and since I had also purchased some fresh Block Island swordfish along with a bottle of Sakonnet's Rhode Island Red wine, I figured there would be more to gain than lose. My hunch was right and this is indeed a perfect way to cook swordfish when chillier weather sets in in the fall. Should you happen to see fish labeled "pumpkin" swordfish in the fall, buy it, because it will add to the pretty autumnal hues of the preparation. Pumpkin swordfish gets its unique pale orange/coral tint from the swordfish having fed on shrimp, or so I have been told. SERVES 4

2 tablespoons extra virgin olive oil

1 fresh center-cut swordfish steak (1½ to 1¾ pounds and at least 1 inch thick)

Sea salt and freshly cracked black peppercorns

1¼ cups Sakonnet Vineyard Rhode Island Red wine or another fruity red wine such as Beaujolais, or more as needed

2 shallots, peeled and thinly sliced into rings

1 tablespoon coarsely chopped fresh rosemary

8 sprigs fresh thyme

1 Preheat the oven to 450°F.

2 Brush 1 tablespoon of the olive oil over each side of the swordfish steak, season both sides generously with salt and pepper, and let the swordfish stand at room temperature for about 15 minutes.

3 Pour the wine into a baking dish or gratin dish large enough to hold the swordfish comfortably but somewhat snugly, with no more than an inch or two of space around the sides. Scatter the shallots and rosemary over the wine. Transfer the swordfish to the baking dish. The wine should come about halfway up the sides of the fish. If not, add more wine. Spoon a bit of the wine over the top of the swordfish. Strew the thyme sprigs over the top of the fish.

4 Bake the fish until just cooked through in the center, 20 to 25 minutes. Remove the swordfish from the oven and let it rest in the wine bath for about 5 minutes. Divide the swordfish into serving portions and serve with a few tablespoons of the cooking liquid spooned over the fish.

Swordfish Piccata

I first made this swordfish when I was catering a dinner on Nantucket for the owners of the Horchow catalog in the 1980s. I unearthed the recipe some years later and was thrilled when it became one of my son's favorite dinners. While it is somewhat reminiscent of the recipe for Sautéed Sole with Lemon and Capers on page 158, swordfish holds up better to sautéing so this preparation is good for feeding more than two. SERVES 4

⅔ cup unbleached all-purpose flour

1 tablespoon coarsely cracked mixed
   peppercorns (see Note)

1½ teaspoons sea salt, or more if needed

1 fresh center-cut swordfish steak, skinned
   and thinly sliced (2 pounds, sliced about ⅓
   inch thick) to resemble veal scaloppine

4 tablespoons (½ stick) unsalted butter

3 tablespoons extra virgin olive oil

4 cloves garlic, peeled and minced

½ cup dry white wine

⅓ cup freshly squeezed lemon juice

⅓ cup minced fresh flat-leaf parsley

Lemon slices, for serving

1 Combine the flour, peppercorns, and salt in a shallow dish such as a pie plate. Dredge the swordfish slices in the flour mixture and shake off any excess.

2 Melt 1 tablespoon of the butter in the olive oil in a large skillet over medium-high heat. When hot, working in batches so as not to crowd the pan, add the slices of swordfish and cook until browned on the underside, 2 to 3 minutes. Turn the fish over and cook until browned on the second side and just barely cooked through the center, 2 to 2½ minutes. Transfer the cooked swordfish to a platter and cover it loosely with aluminum foil to keep warm. Repeat the process with remaining swordfish slices.

3 Add the garlic to the skillet and cook over medium-high heat until fragrant, 30 seconds to 1 minute. Add the white wine and lemon juice to the skillet, scraping up any browned bits clinging to the bottom of the skillet. Let the liquid come to a boil and cook until reduced slightly by about one third, 2 to 3 minutes. Reduce the heat to low and slowly swirl in the remaining 3 tablespoons of butter 1 tablespoon at a time. Taste the sauce for seasoning, adding more salt, if needed. Return the swordfish to the skillet and let it cook for a minute or two more to absorb the flavors of the sauce. Sprinkle the parsley over the swordfish and serve at once with lemon slices.

NOTE: *Although you can use all black peppercorns in this recipe, a mixture of black, white, green, and pink—sometimes marketed as rainbow pepper—is much prettier.*

Yellowfin Tuna Tartare

I am guessing I am not the only one crazy about tuna tartare since it appears on tons of restaurant menus all over the country. Unfortunately, not all tuna tartares are created equal and if you really want to gorge on this wonderful concoction while simultaneously resting assured of its freshness, then definitely take a stab at making it at home.

There are a few secrets to the tuna tartare I make at home. First and foremost, you must be absolutely sure that the tuna is super fresh and never consider using frozen, even if the packaging proclaims it is "sushi grade." Yellowfin tuna is the tuna I am able to get most reliably on Cape Cod, but this will vary in other regions. My next secret is using a few products made by my long-time Armenian pal, John Boyajian, at his Canton, Massachusetts, plant—namely wasabi sesame oil and pure lime oil. For many years, I have not been able to live without Boyajian lime oil, but the wasabi sesame oil has now become a pantry staple as well. Tuna tartare looks and tastes best if consumed within a few hours of assembling, but can be eaten on the sly for up to twenty-four hours. There are several ways to serve tuna tartare. Restaurants are fond of piling it into a martini glass, and I like serving it mounded into an avocado half for lunch or a first course at a sit-down dinner. For less formal occasions, place the tartare in a bowl, surround it with rice crackers, and offer it as a help-yourself appetizer, one that will disappear quickly. SERVES 4 AS A FIRST COURSE OR LUNCH, 6 TO 8 AS AN APPETIZER

1 pound very fresh skinless yellowfin tuna, trimmed of all dark meat and sinew

2½ tablespoons freshly squeezed lime juice

1 tablespoon tamari, plus more if needed

1 teaspoon finely grated lime zest

2 tablespoons canola oil

2 tablespoons Boyajian wasabi sesame oil

2 scant drops Boyajian lime oil

1 jalapeño pepper, seeded and finely diced

1½ teaspoons finely grated or minced peeled fresh ginger

4 scallions, both white and tender green parts, trimmed and minced

2½ tablespoons minced fresh cilantro

Toasted sesame seeds (optional), for garnish

1 Using a sharp knife, cut the tuna into ⅛-inch dice and place it in a medium-size mixing bowl.

2 Place the lime juice, tamari, and lime zest in a small bowl and whisk to mix. Whisk in the canola oil, wasabi sesame oil, and lime oil. Pour the lime juice mixture over the diced tuna and toss gently to coat it evenly. Add the jalapeño pepper, ginger, scallions, and cilantro and toss again until all of the ingredients are evenly combined. Taste for seasoning and add a splash or two more of tamari if a saltier taste is desired. (You can also add a few pinches of sea salt if you don't want to add more tamari.)

3 Refrigerate the tuna tartare, covered, for at least 45 minutes for the flavors to meld. Serve the tuna tartare chilled with sesame seeds lightly sprinkled over the top, if desired.

Fennel and Coriander Crusted Tuna Steaks with Red Wine Béarnaise

These days, I eat more raw tuna than I do cooked but this is the one cooked recipe that never fails to excite me. It is my adaptation of a wonderful dish served years ago at Nantucket's Sconset Café, when Pamela McKinstry was the chef-owner. The tuna is prepared almost like steak au poivre, with fennel and coriander seeds being mixed in with the peppercorns to lend truly sublime flavor. On Nantucket, the tuna was sauced with a ginger beurre blanc, but I like to pick up on the "steak" theme by pairing my tuna with a rich red wine béarnaise. SERVES 6

The village of Sconset on Nantucket is renowned for its summer colony of absolutely spectacular rose-covered cottages.

¼ cup fennel seeds

3 tablespoons whole coriander seeds

2 tablespoons mixed whole peppercorns (see Note, page 163)

6 fresh yellowfin tuna steaks (about 6 ounces each and ¾ to 1 inch thick)

2 large shallots, peeled and minced

2 tablespoons minced fresh tarragon

⅔ cup dry red wine

3 tablespoons balsamic vinegar

2 large egg yolks

3 to 4 tablespoons canola or grapeseed oil

12 tablespoons (1½ sticks) unsalted butter, at room temperature, cut into tablespoons

Sea salt

1 Place the fennel seeds, coriander seeds, and peppercorns in a mortar. Using a pestle, grind them until coarsely ground. Coat the tuna steaks on both sides with the spice mixture, place them on a platter, and refrigerate them for about 30 minutes.

2 Meanwhile, combine the shallots, tarragon, red wine, and balsamic vinegar in a saucepan. Let come to a boil over medium-high heat and let boil until all but 2 tablespoons of liquid remain. Remove the saucepan from the heat and whisk in the egg yolks, one at a time. Set the saucepan aside briefly.

3 Heat 2 to 3 tablespoons of the oil in a large, heavy skillet over medium-high heat. Cook the tuna steaks until crusted brown on the undersides, 3 to 4 minutes. Turn the tuna steaks over and continue cooking to the desired degree of doneness, anywhere from 2 minutes for rare tuna (my preference) to 5 minutes for tuna cooked evenly all the way through. Add a bit more oil to the pan if the tuna appears to be sticking.

4 While the tuna is cooking, finish making the béarnaise sauce. Return the saucepan with the red wine mixture to low heat and whisk for a minute to rewarm. Slowly whisk in the butter, 1 tablespoon at a time, until all of it is absorbed and the sauce is thickened, 7 to 8 minutes.

5 To serve, season the tuna steaks lightly on top with a sprinkling of sea salt. Transfer the tuna steaks to dinner plates and nap them generously with the béarnaise sauce. Serve at once.

Elaine's Tuna Confit

Elaine Baird and her husband, Julian, have a well-equipped fishing boat and once treated my son and his buddies to an informative and successful fishing expedition offshore from where they live—in the Cape Cod waters between Orleans and Chatham. The Bairds also have neighbors who fish even farther offshore for tuna. When the catch is good, this is how Elaine likes to preserve her windfall of the freshest tuna imaginable. Elaine says the recipe is inspired by a Molly Stevens piece that

appeared in *Fine Cooking* magazine a few years ago. She has shared her tuna confit with our fellow book club members on occasion and I think it is absolutely brilliant. Elaine notes that she has also made the same recipe successfully with striped bass. SERVES 6 TO 8

For the tuna confit

1 clove garlic, peeled

1 teaspoon kosher salt

1 tablespoon coarsely chopped fresh rosemary

4 to 6 cups extra virgin olive oil

6 ultrafresh tuna steaks (2½ to 3 pounds total and each 1 inch thick)

For the vinaigrette

½ cup fresh flat-leaf parsley or cilantro leaves, or a combination of the two

2 tablespoons brined capers, rinsed and drained

6 kalamata olives, pitted

2 cloves garlic, peeled and coarsely chopped

1 tablespoon freshly squeezed lemon juice

¼ teaspoon sea salt

½ teaspoon freshly ground black pepper

¼ teaspoon sugar

⅓ cup extra virgin olive oil

1 Make the tuna confit: Place the garlic clove, 1 teaspoon of kosher salt, and the rosemary in a mortar and, using a pestle, grind them to a coarse paste. If you do not have a mortar and pestle, chop the ingredients together with a chef's knife on a cutting board. Moisten the garlic mixture with 1 to 2 teaspoons of the olive oil to make a spreadable paste. Rub the paste over the tuna steaks and let them stand at room temperature for 1 hour. There will not be a lot of paste; it is meant to just season the tuna lightly.

2 Place a rack in the center of the oven and preheat the oven to 225°F.

Elaborating on Elaine

Elaine Baird is a lovely and talented member of the Cape Cod book club to which I belong. She is well read on a vast number of topics and an inherently inventive cook. Should chowder be the topic in an assigned book, Elaine will cook up at least three different chowders, running the gamut from classic to obscure. Recently our group was reading a book set in the 1950s with scarcely a mention of food. Elaine was the designated host and decided her only choice was to orchestrate a menu of fifties food replete with a Jell-O–style dessert, only Elaine's gelatin was made from beach plum juice. Of course, she had picked the beach plums herself and extracted their juice. It was the only "Jell-O" I have ever enjoyed in my entire life.

3 Pour olive oil to a depth of 1 inch into a very large straight-sided ovenproof skillet. Heat the olive oil over medium-low heat until it registers 120°F on a deep-fry thermometer. Slip the tuna steaks in a single layer into the warm oil. Transfer the skillet to the oven and bake the tuna until the centers of the steaks turn rosy and small white droplets begin to rise to the top of the oil, about 25 minutes. Remove the skillet from the oven and let the tuna cool to room temperature. If you are not serving the tuna right away, store it in a covered container in its olive oil in the refrigerator until needed. Let the tuna come to room temperature before serving. The tuna will keep well for at least a week.

4 Make the vinaigrette: Place the parsley or cilantro, capers, olives, chopped garlic, lemon juice, ¼ teaspoon of sea salt, pepper, sugar, and ⅓ cup of olive oil in a blender and blend until smooth. Use the vinaigrette at once or refrigerate it, covered, until ready to use. It will keep for up to 5 days. Let the vinaigrette return to room temperature before using.

5 When ready to serve, remove the tuna confit from the olive oil and slice the steaks ½ inch thick. Arrange 4 to 5 slices on each plate and drizzle the vinaigrette on top.

Ode to Rhody Oven "Fried" Calamari

I have never been much of a fan of fried seafood. I'll eat an order of fried clams or oysters at most once every two years. However, fried calamari is a whole different story. I brake for squid of any sort and will almost always order it whenever I see it on a restaurant menu. And, there is probably no better place in the world to eat fried calamari than in Rhode Island, or Little Rhody as the state is often called. In fact, if I were in charge of promoting Rhode Island tourism, I would design a license plate with a squid or two on it, in the same vein that a Maine license plate sports a lobster or a Florida one an orange. But, alas, I am not in charge of Rhode Island tourism and furthermore I am not terribly keen on deep fat frying calamari in my own home.

Fear not fellow calamari *fritto* lovers. This cheater's version, baked in the oven comes close to some of the best fried calamari I have ever eaten, plus you don't have to suffer through a side of marinara dipping sauce, a Rhode Island custom that has never floated my boat. An accompanying squeeze of lemon is quite good, or a bowl of silky Homemade Mayonnaise (page 129) or homemade Lemon Aioli (see page 132) even better. SERVES 2 AS A MAIN DISH, 4 TO 6 AS AN APPETIZER

1½ pounds cleaned fresh squid, both bodies and tentacles

2 tablespoons freshly squeezed lemon juice

3 tablespoons extra virgin olive oil

½ teaspoon finely grated lemon zest

2 cloves garlic, peeled and coarsely chopped

2 teaspoons fresh oregano leaves, coarsely chopped

2 tablespoons fresh flat-leaf parsley, coarsely chopped

¾ cup loosely packed small fresh French bread cubes

⅔ cup panko bread crumbs

¾ teaspoon sea salt, plus additional for serving

¼ teaspoon hot red pepper flakes

Lemon wedges, for serving

1 Place a rack in the center of the oven and preheat the oven to 425°F. Line a large rimmed baking sheet with parchment paper or aluminum foil.

2 Cut the squid bodies into ⅓-inch-wide rings and leave the tentacles whole. Place the squid in a shallow nonreactive dish, add the lemon juice, 2 tablespoons of the olive oil, and the lemon zest, and toss to mix.

3 Place the garlic, oregano, and parsley in a food processor, preferably a mini one, and pulse the machine on and off a few times to chop them more finely. Add the bread cubes, panko, salt, and hot red pepper flakes. Process until the bread cubes have become crumbs and all the ingredients are thoroughly combined. Add the remaining 1 tablespoon of olive oil and pulse to moisten the crumbs lightly. Transfer the bread crumb mixture to a large shallow bowl.

4 Add the squid rings and tentacles to the bread crumb mixture and toss gently with your hands to coat the squid evenly with the crumbs. Arrange the breaded squid in a single layer on the prepared baking sheet. Bake until the squid are tender and the bread crumbs are crisp and golden, 10 to 12 minutes. Remove the baking sheet from the oven, dust the squid with a bit more sea salt, and serve it hot with lemon wedges.

People flock to Wellfleet to enjoy tasty oysters and great fish markets as well as to spend an old-fashioned evening at the town's famous drive-in movie theatre.

Grilled Cape Cod Calamari

I fell in love with Wellfleet shortly after moving from Nantucket to Cape Cod at the end of 1999. Although, the town is about an hour away from my location on the mid-Cape, the drive on the Old King's Highway is a scenic one and always worthwhile because Wellfleet lures with its famous oysters, funky drive-in movie theater, quirky shops, terrific restaurants, stunning beaches, engaging inhabitants, and on and on and on. While I shop at many different fish markets on the Cape and each has its own merits, the family-run Hatch's Fish Market in Wellfleet is a destination like no other for its stunning and esoteric array of impeccably fresh and local seafood. The prices are as high as the quality, so often it is Hatch's just-caught Provincetown calamari that beckons as the most affordable option, but what an option!

Grilled squid ranks up there as one of my top ten favorite foods and when the squid is superfresh, this recipe cannot be beat. While the dish exudes summer, I'll also make it at other times of the year because the warm feta cheese in the Greek salad I often pair with grilled calamari can brighten a cozy winter dinner as much as an alfresco August one. SERVES 4

2 pounds cleaned fresh squid, both bodies and tentacles

¼ cup freshly squeezed lemon juice

1 teaspoon sea salt

4 cloves garlic, peeled and grated on a Microplane

¼ teaspoon freshly ground black pepper

¼ teaspoon hot red pepper flakes

1 tablespoon chopped fresh oregano, or 1½ teaspoons dried oregano

1½ teaspoons finely grated lemon zest

½ cup extra virgin olive oil, plus 1 to 2 tablespoons olive oil for serving

2½ tablespoons minced fresh flat-leaf parsley

Greek Salad with Warm Feta (recipe follows)

1 lemon, cut into wedges

1 If the squid are large, cut the bodies in half lengthwise so that the bodies can lie flat; otherwise leave them whole. Using the tip of a sharp knife, lightly score the bodies with crosshatch cuts spaced about ½ inch apart. Place the squid bodies and tentacles in a large, shallow, nonreactive dish.

2 Place the lemon juice, salt, garlic, black pepper, hot red pepper flakes, oregano, and lemon zest in a small nonreactive bowl and whisk to combine. Slowly whisk in the olive oil to make a light emulsion. Pour the lemon juice mixture over the squid, tossing it gently to coat and let it marinate at room temperature for 30 to 40 minutes.

3 Meanwhile, set up a charcoal or gas grill and pre-heat it to medium-high. Have ready a grilling basket or fine mesh grid to place the squid on so it doesn't slip through the grill grate.

4 Remove the squid from the marinade, discarding the marinade. Place the squid in the grilling basket or on the fine mesh grid and then place the grilling basket or grid directly over the heat. Grill the squid, turning once, until opaque and randomly charred, 1½ to 2 minutes per side. Transfer the squid to a serving platter, immediately drizzle 1 to 2 tablespoons of olive oil over it, and sprinkle the parsley on top.

5 Divide the Greek salad and grilled squid among 4 dinner plates and garnish each serving with a lemon wedge or two for squeezing over the squid. Enjoy at once.

Greek Salad with Warm Feta

If you are as much of a fan of Greek salad as I am, you won't be disappointed by this variation with its surprising and seductive cubes of warm feta cheese. SERVES 4

2 shallots, peeled and thinly sliced

Ice water

1 small English (hothouse) cucumber

1½ tablespoons freshly squeezed lemon juice

1½ tablespoons red wine vinegar

1 clove garlic, peeled and grated on a
 Microplane

Sea salt

½ cup extra virgin olive oil

5 small ripe tomatoes, such as Campari
 tomatoes, cut into ½-inch chunks

1 yellow or orange bell pepper, stemmed,
 seeded, and cut into ½-inch dice

½ cup pitted and coarsely chopped kalamata
 olives

1½ teaspoons dried oregano

6 ounces feta cheese, cut into ½-inch cubes
 (about 1 cup cubes)

2 cups baby greens

Freshly ground black pepper (optional)

1 Preheat the oven to 375°F.

2 Place the sliced shallots in a small bowl and cover them with ice water. Let the shallots stand for 5 to 7 minutes, then drain them.

3 Peel the cucumber in stripes, leaving pinstripes of skin intact. Cut the cucumber lengthwise into 4 spears and then cut each spear into ½-inch chunks.

4 Place the lemon juice, wine vinegar, garlic, and ¾ teaspoon of salt in a large salad bowl and whisk to mix. Whisk in ¼ cup of the olive oil. Add the tomatoes, bell pepper, cucumber chunks, drained shallots, olives, and 1 teaspoon of the oregano. Toss everything gently together to coat with the dressing and let the tomato mixture stand at room temperature.

5 Place the feta cheese in a baking dish or a gratin dish, leaving a bit of space between each cube. Drizzle the remaining ¼ cup of olive oil over the cheese and sprinkle the remaining ½ teaspoon of oregano on top. Bake the feta until the cheese is heated through and just beginning to melt, 5 to 6 minutes.

6 Add the baby greens to the salad bowl along with the warm cubes of feta cheese and toss everything together. Taste the salad, adding a bit of the remaining warm olive oil from the baking dish with the feta cheese and some salt and black pepper, if desired.

Calamari Ragu

Over the past decade making a Bolognese-style pasta sauce with lobster rather than red meat has become trendy. I could never bring myself to do this with lobster but was willing to attempt it with far less expensive calamari, which I figured would be better suited to withstanding the long simmering time needed to make a flavorful ragu. The bet was a good one and this sauce, though somewhat unconventional, is delicious served with a wide pasta like papparadelle or a short stocky shape, such as rigatoni. MAKES ENOUGH SAUCE FOR 2 POUNDS OF PASTA; SERVES 8

3 tablespoons extra virgin olive oil

½ cup minced peeled carrots

½ cup minced celery

½ cup minced peeled red or yellow onion

4 large cloves garlic, peeled and minced

¼ teaspoon hot red pepper flakes, or more to taste

Sea salt

1 can (6 ounces) tomato paste

1 cup dry white wine

1½ pounds cleaned fresh squid, coarsely chopped

1 can (28 ounces) whole tomatoes, preferably San Marzano

Finely grated zest of 1 lemon

3 tablespoons freshly squeezed lemon juice

Freshly ground black pepper

1   Heat the olive oil in a Dutch oven or other large, heavy pot over medium-low heat. Add the carrots, celery, onion, garlic, hot red pepper flakes, and ½ teaspoon of salt to the pot and cook, stirring frequently until the vegetables begin to soften, about 10 minutes. Do not let the vegetables brown.

2   Add the tomato paste, stir to incorporate, and cook until the vegetable mixture begins to caramelize on the bottom of the pot, about 5 minutes. Add the white wine, scraping up any browned bits clinging to the bottom of the pot. Increase the heat to medium-high so the vegetable mixture comes to a boil and then reduce the heat to medium so that it simmers.

3   Meanwhile, place the squid in a food processor. Pulse several times and then process the squid until it takes on the consistency of somewhat shimmery mashed potatoes.

4   Coarsely crush the tomatoes with your hands and add them along with the juices from the can to the pot. Let come to a boil over medium-high heat and add the squid. The proteins in the squid will seize and the squid will miraculously separate into the consistency of the ground meats of a classic Bolognese sauce. Reduce the heat to medium-low, partially cover the pot, and let simmer, stirring occasionally, until the sauce is richly aromatic and flavorful, 1½ hours.

5   Add the lemon zest and lemon juice. Taste for seasoning, adding more salt and black pepper to taste. The sauce is now ready to serve over pasta. It will keep in the refrigerator, covered, for 3 days or can be frozen for up to 2 months.

Home on the Free Range

> "If I hadn't started painting, I would have raised chickens."
> —Grandma Moses

> "Classics can be phenomenal when done right. A simple roast chicken dish could be the best thing you ever eat."
> —Joe Bastianich

I grew up in Southington, Connecticut, hearing embellished but endearing stories about my maternal grandmother's youthful trials and tribulations corralling her family's chickens from roaming about the barnyard grounds back into the safety of their chicken coops. The tale I still remember to this day entails all the chickens escaping from their coops during a torrential rainstorm and my grandmother expressing her wrath by canning the whole flock the following day. Even though I have never actually been exposed to an old-fashioned canned chicken, the story serves as a reminder that I had failed to taste a really exemplary chicken on New England turf until the early 1990s when I discovered I could mail order superb French-breed chickens from D'Artagnan in New Jersey. Fast forward to current times and tasty free-range and organic poultry is now readily raised and available throughout New England. Old Ackley Farm chickens pop up on many a menu on Maine's Blue Hill peninsula, while Vermont has its birds from Misty Knoll Farms and Rhode Island garners renown for its pastured broilers from Pat's Pastured and Aquidneck Farms. Wychwood Farm in Stonington, Connecticut, has elevated our Thanksgiving turkey from the expected to the extraordinary. Miss Scarlett's Blue Ribbon Farm raises all sorts of free-range animals on Cape Cod and even the more commercial but nonetheless excellent tasting Bell & Evans air-chilled chickens are sold at my town's local Barnstable Market, less than a half mile from my house.

We have friends on Nantucket and neighbors on Cape Cod who raise chickens for both eggs and eating. Whenever a glossy *Martha Stewart Living* magazine or Williams-Sonoma catalog arrives in our mailbox with spreads on architecturally stunning chicken coops for the backyard, my husband gets inspired to raise our own chickens. I have to remind him that our Jack Russell Terrier barks at

chickadees on the bird feeder and that life would be far from peaceful with chickens running around our property. I win the argument because I am able to cook many a fine chicken dinner without our having to raise our own hens, let alone herd them back into coops endowed with more stylish pizzazz than our own abode. "Home on the Free Range" for me means Cast-Iron Skillet Roast Chicken for a midweek dinner, Chicken Potpie any day of any week, Chicken Thigh Osso Buco to celebrate a spring daffodil festival, Brined Turkey Thighs on a summer night in Maine, and making Speedy Duck Confit for my husband on Valentine's Day.

Cast-Iron Skillet Roast Chicken

This terrific recipe is one of my friend Toby Greenberg's favorite weeknight "little chicken dinners." It quickly became one of my family's favorites after Toby invited us to her cozy Milk Street home to share this chicken with her on a quiet and cold off-season night on Nantucket. I make the recipe frequently and will sometimes change up the fresh herbs or substitute an herb-infused sea salt for plain sea salt but I always employ Toby's nifty nuance of perching the whole chicken atop a bed of thickly sliced red onion rings as it is placed in the cast-iron skillet. The onion rings cook down, become caramelized, and are delicious spooned over the pieces of carved chicken. SERVES 3 OR 4

2 tablespoons extra virgin olive oil

1 large red onion, peeled and sliced into ⅓- to ½-inch thick rings

1 chicken (3½ to 4 pounds), preferably organic and/or free-range

1 whole lemon

Several sprigs fresh thyme

Flaky sea salt and freshly cracked black peppercorns

1 Place a rack in the center of the oven and preheat the oven to 425°F.

2 Drizzle the olive oil over the bottom of a large cast-iron skillet. Separate the onion rounds into about a dozen rings and arrange them in an overlapping fashion in the center of the skillet to make a slightly elevated perch for the chicken. Balance the chicken on top of the onion rings.

3 Prick the lemon all over with the tip of a sharp paring knife and stuff the lemon into the chicken's cavity along with the thyme sprigs. Season the chicken generously inside and out with salt and pepper. Tie the legs of the chicken together with kitchen twine.

4 Roast the chicken for 30 minutes, then reduce the oven temperature to 375°F and continue roasting the chicken until the skin is beautifully browned and an instant-read meat thermometer inserted into a thigh registers 185°F (be sure the thermometer does not touch a bone), 20 to 30 minutes longer.

5 Let the chicken rest for 7 to 10 minutes before carving it into serving portions. Be sure to spoon some of the caramelized onion rings over each serving.

Kill Kare Kamp Poule au Pot

Kill Kare Kamp on Walker Pond in Sedgwick, Maine, offers everything a lover of uncomplicated Maine living could desire and then some. The same family has owned the shingled cottage since 1917, when it was skillfully built into the rocks on a densely wooded lakefront property as a place to retreat and "kill your cares." We did exactly that early one September when we rented the cottage to celebrate a significant birthday of my husband's. I had stopped for provisions en route at Chase's Daily in Belfast and was laden with some of the most fabulous vegetables I honestly have ever seen or eaten in my entire life. Friends from Nantucket were joining us and they graciously added chickens raised by their daughter on the island to our "kamp" larder. Since my husband had once courted me over a dinner at a favorite restaurant in London called La Poule au Pot, it seemed only fitting to make a spontaneous *poule au pot* to inaugurate our first evening at Kill Kare Kamp. It was a most memorable event and your re-creations of this rustic feast will of course vary, depending on access to great local vegetables and lovingly raised chickens. Feel free to improvise as need be to suit your own circumstances, pleasures, and vegetable preferences. SERVES 4 TO 6

1 plump roasting chicken (5 to 5½ pounds), preferably organic and/or free-range

Several sprigs fresh thyme

Several sprigs fresh rosemary

2 heads garlic

1 lemon

6 tablespoons extra virgin olive oil

Sea salt and freshly cracked black peppercorns

⅔ cup dry white wine

1 pound baby rainbow carrots, peeled only if necessary, tops trimmed to ½ inch

1 pound fingerling potatoes, scrubbed of any dirt

8 baby artichokes, stems trimmed

1 Place a rack in the center of the oven and preheat the oven to 425°F.

2 Place the chicken in the center of a large roasting pan. You can place the chicken on a small flat rack resting in the roasting pan but this is not necessary.

Place several sprigs of thyme and rosemary and a whole head of garlic inside the cavity of the chicken. Cut the lemon in half and squeeze the juice over the chicken, removing any seeds as you squeeze. Tuck the lemon halves into the chicken cavity and tie the legs of the chicken together with kitchen twine. Rub 2 tablespoons of the olive oil evenly over the chicken skin and season it generously with salt and cracked peppercorns. Pour the white wine into the roasting pan. Roast the chicken for 45 minutes.

3 Meanwhile, place the carrots and potatoes in a mixing bowl, add the remaining 4 tablespoons of olive oil, and toss to coat. Separate the remaining head of garlic into cloves but do not peel them. Add the garlic cloves to the carrots and potatoes. Season the vegetables with salt and cracked peppercorns to taste. After the chicken has roasted for 45 minutes, scatter the vegetables in the roasting pan around the chicken. Strew the remaining thyme and rosemary sprigs over the vegetables. Continue roasting the chicken for another 40 minutes. It will be just about cooked.

4 Meanwhile, place the artichokes in a steamer basket set in a pot over enough boiling water to come just below the base of the steamer basket. Cover the pot and steam the artichokes over medium-high heat until barely tender, 10 to 15 minutes, depending on their size. Cut the artichokes lengthwise in half and scrape away the chokes if there are any. Add the artichoke halves to the vegetables in the roasting pan, toss well, and continue roasting until the vegetables are tender and an instant-read thermometer inserted into a thigh registers 185°F (be sure the thermometer does not touch a bone), 10 to 20 minutes longer. If the chicken is done before the vegetables are tender, transfer it to a cutting board and tent it loosely with aluminum foil to keep warm. In any event, the chicken should rest for about 10 minutes before carving.

5 Carve the chicken into serving pieces, place them on serving plates, and surround the chicken with plenty of roasted vegetables. Be sure everyone knows to enjoy the soft sweet garlic cloves by squeezing them from their skin.

Maine-based Green Bee Soda makes excellent craft sodas that are botanically based and sweetened exclusively with honey in an effort to support the declining honey bee population.

Artisanal Soda Can Chicken

Beer-can chicken has become a wildly popular guys' grilling recipe over the past decade. However, I recently read that a study had confirmed that the beer itself does not impart any beer flavor to the chicken but does instead create a moist and succulent grilled bird. With apologies to six-pack grillers, I have concluded there is no reason to make beer-can chicken with beer. The truth of the matter is that water or juice could replace the beer in the can that is inserted into the chicken's cavity, but why use such ho-hum liquids when there are so many burgeoning artisanal soda makers in New England? The minute I discovered and tasted the Lemon Sting soda, flavored with rosemary and honey, made by Maine's Green Bee natural soda company, I knew what the liquid of choice would be in my revamped "beer-can" chicken from here on in. If you aren't in New England and don't have access to Green Bee soda, feel free to experiment with another intriguingly flavored, artisanally crafted soda. An iced bucket filled with bottles of the soda used to cook the chicken makes a fun kid-friendly, as well as adult-savvy, picnic-style accompaniment to the chicken.

Many grilling supply stores now carry specially designed, inexpensive metal beer-can chicken roasting racks complete with a reusable can that can be filled with the liquid of your choice. These gadgets can be very handy, since most artisanal sodas are sold in bottles and the contents will need to be transferred to a can to grill the chickens.

SERVES 6

2 cups apple wood chunks

2 chickens (3 to 3½ pounds each), preferably organic and/or free-range

Sea salt and freshly cracked black peppercorns

12 sprigs fresh rosemary, plus rosemary sprigs for garnish

2 bottles (12 ounces each) Green Bee Lemon Sting soda or another artisanally crafted soda

2 lemons, cut in half

1 Soak the apple wood chunks for 1 hour in enough water to cover. Meanwhile, set up a charcoal grill for indirect grilling with natural hardwood lump charcoal on one side of the grill. Close the lid and adjust the vents to preheat the internal temperature of the grill to 300° to 325°F. Drain the wood chips and scatter half of them over the charcoal just before placing the chickens on the grill. Reserve the rest to add to the fire as the chicken cooks.

2 Generously season each chicken, inside and out, with salt and cracked peppercorns to taste. Place 3 rosemary sprigs in the cavity of each chicken. Open the soda bottles and pour the soda into 2 empty 12-ounce metal cans. Fill each can three-quarters full and make another hole or two in the top. Tuck 3 sprigs of rosemary into each can.

For some who live on the back roads of New England, bicycling to town for provisions such as flowers, fruits, and vegetables can be the favored, fair-weather means of transportation.

rest for about 10 minutes. Some juices will collect on the baking sheet. Carefully remove the chickens from the cans (potholders may be needed), transfer to a cutting board, and either carve the chickens or cut them into serving pieces. Squeeze the lemons into the accumulated juices on the baking sheet, adding any juices from the cutting board. Arrange the chickens on a serving platter, pour the juices over them, garnish them with rosemary sprigs, and serve.

The chickens should balance comfortably on the cans, but if desired, place the cans in metal holders specially designed for cooking beer-can chicken. Insert a can and holder, if using, into the cavity of each chicken; the chickens will have the tail end facing down and the wings facing up. Place the chickens upright on the grill grate so that they are not directly over the coals. Close the grill lid and roast the chickens for 1 hour, adjusting the vents and/or adding more charcoal and the remaining wood chips as necessary to keep the temperature constantly between 300° and 325°F.

3   Open the vents of the grill to increase the temperature to 450°F. Place the lemon halves, cut sides down, on the grill grate and grill until lightly charred, 3 to 4 minutes. Remove the lemons from the grill. Continue cooking the chickens with the lid closed until the skin takes on a deep brown color and an instant-read thermometer registers 180° to 185°F when inserted into a thigh (be sure the thermometer does not touch a bone), 10 to 15 minutes longer.

4   Transfer the chickens on their cans and the lemons to a rimmed baking sheet and let the chickens

Greek Girlfriend Baked Chicken and Orzo

I met Olga Drepanos when I was first opening my Que Sera Sarah food shop on Nantucket in the early 1980s. She approached me about sharing kitchen space in order to bake cookies for a shop she was launching on Steamboat Wharf. Our friendship has lasted eons longer than her business, since there was a great deal of truth to the signage byline of Olga's Cookies: "What a Crumby Life for a Greek Princess!"

Olga is not only my best Greek girlfriend but also one of my very best girlfriends, as well as godmother to my son, Oliver. She is a vivacious and spirited traveling companion, be the destination Castine, Maine, or Italy's thermal baths in Saturnia. Furthermore, she always has a bed ready in her Boston condo for me and any number of close or vague acquaintances who may be catching a Red Sox game at Fenway or an early flight out of Logan airport. Olga has a passion for languages, literature, earthy food, grappa, knitting, and mangle irons. When Olga cooks, her dishes are usually tried-and-true comfort food classics such as her mother Freda's baked chicken with orzo. Olga says the family recipe is reproduced over and over again by daughters and granddaughters until they get it right—or just like Mom's. However, Olga did give me permission to add my own flourishes. Originally I was not going to change anything until I discovered how delicious some fresh baby spinach, feta cheese, and kalamata olives were folded into the pan-roasted orzo. Should this be heresy to Greek tradition, consider my additions optional. SERVES 4

⅓ cup freshly squeezed lemon juice

2½ tablespoons extra virgin olive oil

1½ tablespoons crumbled dried oregano, preferably Greek oregano

Sea salt

½ teaspoon freshly ground black pepper

1 chicken (3½ to 4 pounds), preferably organic and/or free-range, cut into 8 serving pieces

1½ to 2½ cups chicken stock or broth, homemade or good-quality store-bought

1½ cups orzo

4 to 6 ounces (3 to 4 cups) fresh baby spinach leaves (optional)

½ cup coarsely chopped pitted kalamata olives (optional)

3 ounces crumbled feta cheese (about 1 cup)

1 Preheat the oven to 375°F.

2 Combine the lemon juice, olive oil, oregano, 1½ teaspoons of salt, and the pepper in the bottom of a 13-by-9-inch roasting pan, stirring to combine. Add the chicken pieces, turning each one over in the olive oil mixture to coat it evenly. Pour ½ cup of the chicken stock or broth into the roasting pan. Roast the chicken pieces until the skin is nicely browned, the meat is tender, and an instant-read thermometer inserted into a thigh registers 180° to 185°F (be sure the thermometer does not touch a bone), 45 to 55 minutes.

3 Meanwhile, bring a large pot of salted water to a boil. Add the orzo and cook it for 3 minutes less than the time given in the package directions. Drain and refresh the orzo under cold running water. Set the orzo aside.

4 Remove the chicken from the roasting pan and keep it warm by tenting it loosely with aluminum foil. Reduce the oven temperature to 350°F. Add the orzo to the roasting pan and stir to coat it with the pan drippings. Pour in 1 cup of the remaining stock or broth. Return the roasting pan to the oven and bake the orzo until it is tender, 10 to 15 minutes. Add up to 1 cup more stock or broth, if needed, to cook the orzo until tender. Olga says her mother would cook the orzo until it was very dry. I prefer to have it moist with about ½ cup liquid remaining in the pan. If using, fold the spinach and olives into the orzo, stirring until the heat of the orzo has wilted the spinach. Sprinkle the feta cheese over the top.

5 Divide the orzo among 4 serving plates and top each with 2 pieces of chicken. Serve hot.

Baked Chicken Breasts with Window Box Herbs

In the last three homes I have owned, including the current one, my kitchen has been located on the second level of the house, prompting me to keep several window boxes planted with fresh herbs on the decks adjacent to the kitchen so I need not traipse up and down stairs to the garden every time, which is almost all the time, I am in need of a sprig of this or a sprig of that. This recipe, which I usually make at least once a month, is perfect as a confirmation of the wisdom of my window box practices.

For reasons I have yet to grasp, skin-on, bone-in chicken breasts are never as easy to come by as skinless, boneless chicken breasts, so I stock up

whenever I can on the flavorful, skin-on Amish raised chicken breast halves sold at Whole Foods Markets specifically to make this recipe. SERVES 4

3 tablespoons extra virgin olive oil

2 tablespoons (¼ stick) unsalted butter

2 teaspoons minced fresh oregano

2 teaspoons minced fresh thyme

2 teaspoons minced fresh rosemary

2 teaspoons minced fresh chives

⅓ cup dry white wine

4 skin-on, bone-in chicken breast halves (8 to 10 ounces each)

Sea salt and freshly cracked black peppercorns

12 shallots, peeled

16 cloves garlic, peeled or unpeeled (see Note)

1 Preheat the oven to 400°F.

2 Place the olive oil and butter in a roasting pan large enough to hold the chicken breast halves with about 1½ inches in between each breast. Place the roasting pan in the hot oven to melt the butter, 4 to 5 minutes.

3 Remove the roasting pan from the oven and swirl the olive oil and butter together to combine. Stir in the oregano, thyme, rosemary, chives, and white wine. Dip each chicken breast half into the herb mixture, turning to coat the breasts generously with the mixture. Arrange the chicken breasts in the roasting pan, skin side up, spacing them 1½ inches apart. Season the chicken with salt and cracked peppercorns to taste. Scatter the shallots and garlic cloves in between and around the chicken breasts.

4 Bake the chicken until the skin is browned and crisp and the shallots and garlic are very tender, 50 minutes to 1 hour, basting it 2 or 3 times with the juices in the roasting pan. Serve the chicken breasts hot, surrounding each breast with some roasted shallots and garlic.

NOTE: *If you don't peel the garlic when you serve the chicken the cloves will have to be squeezed out of their skins when you eat, which I personally find to be part of the fun of this chicken.*

Go-To Grilled Chicken Breasts

Whenever I make these simple grilled chicken breasts, they never fail to delight. In fact, I'll often grill extras because the leftover chicken is great sliced cold the next day for sandwiches. While I prefer to make this recipe with the skin-on, boneless chicken breast halves, the recipe is also one of the best ways I know to prepare ubiquitous skinless and boneless chicken breasts. SERVES 4

⅓ cup freshly squeezed lemon juice

⅓ cup extra virgin olive oil

3 cloves garlic, peeled and minced

1 tablespoon coarsely chopped fresh rosemary

1 tablespoon coarsely chopped fresh oregano

1 teaspoon sea salt

¼ teaspoon hot red pepper flakes

4 large skin-on or skinless, boneless chicken breast halves (2½ to 3 pounds total)

Freshly cracked black peppercorns

Vegetable oil, for oiling the grill grate

1 Set up a charcoal or gas grill and preheat it to medium-high.

2 Place the lemon juice, olive oil, garlic, rosemary, oregano, salt, and hot red pepper flakes in a small nonreactive bowl and whisk to mix. Arrange the chicken breast halves in a snug single layer in a nonreactive dish and pour the marinade over them, turning the breasts to coat them evenly. Grind some black

peppercorns over the chicken breasts and let them marinate at room temperature for 20 to 30 minutes.

3   When ready to grill, brush the grill grate with vegetable oil. Place the chicken breasts on the grate and grill the chicken until the meat registers between 160° and 165°F on an instant-read thermometer inserted through the thickest part of a breast, 4 to 5 minutes per side. If desired, give the breasts a quarter turn after 2 minutes on each side to make crosshatch grilling marks. Let the chicken breasts rest for about 5 minutes before serving. The breasts may be served whole but I like to slice the meat on a diagonal into ½-inch-thick slices.

Chicken Thigh Osso Buco

Osso buco was one of the first fancy sounding foreign dishes I learned to master as a teenager. At one point, while growing up in Connecticut, I worked part-time doing various domestic chores for a couple in the fashion design business who lived in a neighboring town. Sometime along the way, I made an osso buco for them for dinner and thereafter I was always on call to pop over and put together another osso buco. While the name osso buco denotes bones with a hole in the center—that would be the veal shanks traditionally used to make an authentic Italian osso buco—I recently discovered that chicken thighs lend themselves wonderfully to the same preparation, if you are willing to let slide the whole shank/marrow bone bit, and also save yourself significant sums of money in the process.

In particular, I like to make this dish to celebrate any of several spring daffodil festivals held throughout New England because hearty flavors readily combat the chill of April showers. Serve with rice (or in the traditional Italian manner,

with a simple saffron risotto) and a sprinkling of gremolata to create a lovely daffodil-hued dinner.

SERVES 6

For the chicken osso buco

3 to 4 tablespoons extra virgin olive oil

12 skin-on, bone-in chicken thighs (about 4 pounds), trimmed of excess fat

Sea salt and freshly ground black pepper

2 fat leeks, well rinsed, trimmed, white and tender green parts minced

4 carrots, peeled and cut into ¼-inch dice

1 small onion, peeled and minced

4 cloves garlic, peeled and minced

1 can (14½ ounces) diced tomatoes, preferably San Marzano tomatoes

1 cup dry white wine

1 cup chicken stock or broth, homemade or good-quality store-bought

1 bay leaf

For the gremolata

½ cup finely minced fresh flat-leaf parsley

Finely grated zest of 1 lemon

3 cloves garlic, peeled and minced

½ cup freshly and finely grated Parmesan cheese

1½ tablespoons lightly toasted pine nuts (see page 70), optional

Steamed or boiled rice, or saffron risotto, for serving

1   Make the chicken osso buco: Heat 2 tablespoons of the olive oil in a Dutch oven or other large, heavy pot over medium-high heat. Season the chicken thighs generously with salt and pepper. Working in batches so as not to crowd the pot, add the chicken thighs to the pot and brown them on all sides. Transfer the chicken thighs to a platter. Add more olive oil to the pot as needed.

2 Preheat the oven to 300°F.

3 Add the leeks, carrots, onion, and 4 cloves of garlic to the pot, reduce the heat to medium, and cook until softened, 8 to 10 minutes. Add the tomatoes, white wine, and chicken stock or broth, stirring to blend. Return the chicken thighs to the pot and add the bay leaf. Let come to a simmer, cover the pot, and place it in the oven. Bake the chicken until it is very tender and beginning to fall off the bone, 1 to 1 1/4 hours.

4 While the chicken is in the oven, make the gremolata: Combine the parsley, lemon zest, 3 cloves of garlic, Parmesan cheese, and pine nuts, if using, in a small bowl, stirring until evenly mixed.

5 When ready to serve, discard the bay leaf from the osso buco. Taste the sauce for seasoning, adding salt and pepper, if needed. Serve the osso buco hot over rice, preferably saffron risotto, allowing 2 chicken thighs per person. Be sure to spoon a plentiful amount of the delicious vegetable sauce over the thighs. Sprinkle a generous tablespoon of the gremolata over the top of each serving. Extra gremolata may be passed at the table. Because the osso buco improves with a bit of age, it may be made ahead and reheated the following day in its pot in a 300°F oven for 45 minutes to 1 hour. Make the gremolata as the osso buco reheats.

Chicken Potpie

Everyone in my family, including our Jack Russell Terrier, loves chicken potpie and I love making it because store-bought chicken potpies, even from highly acclaimed sources, invariably disappoint. I have perfected this recipe over the years and the things I believe contribute to elevating it to a comforting standout are plenty of meaty chicken chunks (turkey may be substituted if it is the day after Thanksgiving), no potatoes but ample celery and carrots, plus frozen and only frozen peas, a hint of sherry as well as cream, and a flaky crust crafted from scratch. Nothing makes a home smell more welcoming that a chicken potpie baking in the oven, unless of course you follow it up with a homemade apple pie or apple crisp. SERVES 6

For the parsley pastry crust

1½ cups unbleached all-purpose flour, plus flour for dusting the work surface

½ teaspoon kosher salt

1½ tablespoons coarsely chopped fresh flat-leaf parsley

8 tablespoons (1 stick) chilled unsalted butter, cut into small pieces

4 tablespoons (½ stick) chilled unsalted margarine, cut into small pieces

3 to 4 tablespoons ice water

For the potpie filling

2 tablespoons extra virgin olive oil

1 medium-large onion, peeled and minced

3 large carrots, peeled and cut on a slight diagonal into ⅓-inch-thick slices

3 ribs celery, preferably with some leaves, cut on a slight diagonal into ⅓-inch-thick slices

2 cloves garlic, peeled and minced

1 tablespoon chopped fresh tarragon

4½ cups cooked chicken breast chunks (1- to 1½-inch chunks)

3½ tablespoons unsalted butter

4 tablespoons unbleached all-purpose flour

2 cups chicken stock or broth, homemade or good-quality store-bought

¾ cup milk

½ cup heavy (whipping) cream

2½ tablespoons cream sherry

Sea salt and freshly ground black pepper

1 cup frozen peas

1 egg, beaten with 1 tablespoon water or milk

1 Make the parsley pastry crust: Place the 1½ cups of flour, ½ teaspoon of kosher salt, and the parsley in a food processor. Process to combine and mince the parsley as finely as possible. Add the 8 tablespoons of chilled butter and the margarine and pulse the machine on and off several times until the mixture resembles coarse meal. Sprinkle in 3 tablespoons of ice water and continue to pulse the machine on and off until the pastry begins to form a ball. Add an additional tablespoon of ice water if needed to make the pastry stick together. Shape the pastry into a flat disk, wrap it in plastic wrap, and refrigerate it for at least 1 hour or as long as 24 hours.

2 When you are ready to bake the potpie, place a rack in the center of the oven and preheat the oven to 375°F.

3 Make the potpie filling: Heat the olive oil in a large skillet over medium heat. Add the onion, carrots, celery, garlic, and tarragon. Cook, stirring occasionally, until the vegetables are slightly shy of being tender, 8 to 10 minutes. Meanwhile, place the chicken in a large mixing bowl. Add the cooked vegetables to the chicken, tossing to combine. Set the chicken and vegetable mixture aside.

4 Melt the 3½ tablespoons of butter in a medium-size saucepan over medium heat. Stir in the 4 tablespoons of flour and cook, stirring constantly, until the mixture is well blended, about 1½ minutes. Gradually pour in the chicken stock or broth, whisking as you pour, to make a smooth and lightly thickened sauce. Gradually add the milk, cream, and sherry, whisking, then let the sauce cook, stirring it occasionally, until it is smooth and thickened, 6 to 8 minutes. Season the sauce generously with salt and pepper to taste. Pour the sauce over the chicken and vegetables, stirring to bind all of the ingredients loosely together. Add the peas, give the filling another stir, and then scrape it into a 13-by-9-inch baking or gratin dish.

5 Lightly flour a work surface. Roll the pastry crust out to a size approximately 1 inch larger than the baking dish, trimming the dough as needed. Carefully transfer the pastry to the top of the potpie and crimp the edges decoratively. Using the tip of a sharp paring knife, make 3- or 4-inch-long slashes over the top of the crust to serve as steam vents as the potpie bakes. If desired, any leftover scraps of dough can be rerolled, cut out with cookie cutters, and used to decorate the top of the potpie. I frequently put a chicken, or hearts, or stars on the top of my potpies. Brush the pastry all over with the egg wash and place the baking dish on a rimmed baking sheet in the oven.

6 Bake the chicken potpie until the crust is golden and the filling is bubbling, 50 minutes to 1 hour. Let the potpie rest for 5 to 10 minutes before serving.

Seared Duck Breasts à l'Orange

This is my easy New England riff on the classic and labor-intensive French duck à l'orange. I use the wonderful duck from Lac Brome in Canada, which I discovered during a ski trip to Quebec's Eastern Townships some years ago and can now purchase in many better New England supermarkets. Since duck is rich in and of itself and is made even richer in this recipe with a glossy glaze of maple syrup, orange marmalade, and rosemary, I find three standard half-pound Lac Brome duck breasts sufficient to serve four. For added pizzazz, accompany the sliced duck breasts with a mounded spoonful of Baked Cranberry Conserve (page 192) or Cranberry Citrus Relish (page 193). SERVES 4

3 skin-on, boneless duck breasts halves (8 to 10 ounces each)

Sea salt and freshly cracked black peppercorns

¼ cup pure maple syrup

2 tablespoons orange marmalade

3 tablespoons freshly squeezed orange juice

1½ teaspoons grated orange zest

1½ teaspoons coarsely minced fresh rosemary

1   Preheat the oven to 375°F.

2   Using a sharp paring knife, score the skin of the duck breasts in a crisscross pattern, taking care not to cut deep enough to reach the meat. Season the duck breasts generously on both sides with salt and cracked peppercorns to taste. Heat a large cast-iron or other heavy ovenproof skillet over medium heat. Place the breasts skin side down in the skillet and sear them slowly to brown and crisp the skin, taking care to keep the heat moderate enough not to burn the skin. This should take 7 to 10 minutes.

3   While the duck is browning, place the maple syrup, orange marmalade, orange juice, orange zest, and rosemary in a small measuring cup with a pouring spout and whisk to mix the glaze.

4   Once the duck skin is beautifully browned, turn the breasts over, skin side up, and sear the second side for 2 minutes. Remove the skillet from the heat and pour off all but 2 tablespoons of the rendered fat. Save the duck fat for another use such as sautéing potatoes. Pour half of the glaze evenly over the skin of the duck breasts and place the skillet in the oven.

5   Bake the duck breasts until the glaze starts to caramelize, 5 to 7 minutes and then drizzle a bit more glaze over them. Return the skillet to the oven. The duck is done when it registers between 130° and 140°F on an instant-read thermometer, 5 to 7 minutes more. I prefer to cook my duck to at least 140°F (just pink inside) but if you like it quite rare, go with 130°F. Remove the duck from the oven. Add any remaining glaze to the skillet and let the duck rest for 5 to 10 minutes before slicing. Slice the duck breasts on a diagonal into ¼-inch-wide slices and fan 5 or 6 slices out on each serving plate. Spoon any glaze remaining in the skillet over the duck. Serve the duck hot.

Duck Breasts with Fennel and Rosemary

The flavors in this divine duck recipe take their cue from the famous Tuscan *porchetta*—a roasted whole suckling pig aromatically infused with garlic, rosemary, and fennel. Duck breasts make for a more elegant and manageable rendition and the recipe is one I am fond of serving at dinner parties. SERVES 6 TO 8

8 skin-on, boneless duck breast halves
    (about 8 ounces each)

Sea salt and freshly cracked black peppercorns

6 cloves garlic, peeled and minced

2½ tablespoons minced fresh rosemary

1 tablespoon coarsely crushed fennel seeds

2½ tablespoons olive oil

1 small onion, peeled and minced

8 ounces cremini mushrooms, trimmed and
    thinly sliced

½ cup vin santo (an Italian sweet wine),
    Marsala, or medium-dry sherry

¾ cup chicken stock or broth, homemade or
    good-quality store-bought

3 tablespoons cold unsalted butter, cut into
    tablespoons

1   Place the duck breast halves, skin side down, on a work surface. Season them with salt and cracked peppercorns. Place the garlic, rosemary, and fennel seeds in a bowl, add 1 tablespoon of the olive oil, and stir to mix. Smear the mixture under the skin of the breasts. Place 1 breast on top of another, skin sides out, to make 4 sandwiched breasts. Using kitchen twine, tie the breasts together in a couple of places. Season with additional salt and pepper. The breasts can be prepared ahead up to this point and refrigerated, covered, for up to 24 hours.

2 Preheat the oven to 400°F.

3 Heat the remaining 1½ tablespoons of olive oil in a large, heavy skillet over medium heat. Add the tied duck breasts and cook, turning, until the skin is nicely browned on both sides, 8 to 10 minutes per side. Transfer the duck breasts to a roasting pan and bake them to the desired degree of doneness, 15 to 20 minutes for medium-rare meat, or longer for more well-done meat. My preference is to cook the meat to medium: When done to this degree it will register 140° to 145°F on an instant-read thermometer.

4 Meanwhile, pour off and discard all but 1 tablespoon of the rendered fat from the skillet. Add the onion to the remaining fat and cook over medium heat until softened, 2 to 3 minutes. Add the mushrooms and cook until they begin to release their juices, about 2 minutes. Add the *vin santo*, Marsala, or sherry and let come to a boil. Add the chicken stock or broth and let simmer until the mixture is slightly reduced and thickened, 5 to 7 minutes. Reduce the heat to low and swirl in the butter, 1 tablespoon at a time, to make an emulsion. Taste the mushroom sauce for seasoning, adding salt and/or cracked peppercorns if needed, and keep the sauce warm over very low heat.

5 When the duck is cooked to your liking, remove it from the oven and let it rest for at least 5 minutes. Remove and discard the twine and slice the layered breasts into ½-inch-thick slices. Fan the slices of duck out on serving plates and nap them with the mushroom sauce. Serve the duck at once.

Speedy Duck Confit

Duck confit is like good crisp bacon. I don't know anyone who can resist it. My husband absolutely adores duck confit and the first time I made it, I cured the duck for two weeks in a cold

Sandy Neck is a picturesque barrier beach and cherished destination for boaters, beachcombers, naturalists, hikers, and horseback riders residing or visiting on the bay side of Cape Cod.

crawl space in the eaves of my then Nantucket salt-box home. These days I tend not to have the time for such ambitious undertakings and am therefore delighted to have discovered Melissa Clark's recipe for Really Easy Duck Confit (Really!), first published in *The New York Times* and then in Melissa's book *In the Kitchen with a Good Appetite*. I had worked with Melissa briefly during her collaboration on *The Nantucket Restaurants Cookbook: Menus and Recipes from the Faraway Isle*. Trust me, none of the recipes in that book were nearly as easy as Melissa's recipe for duck confit.

Melissa's duck confit takes less than thirty hours to make and very little of that time is hands-on. At the same time, the duck turns out just as crispy as that which has been traditionally preserved in its fat for two weeks. I prepare my confit adaptation with duck legs from Lac Brome in Canada because they are readily available at my local Stop & Shop and yield terrific results. I tend to season my duck confit more aggressively than Melissa and also use fresh thyme rather than dried thyme. I usually pair the crispy duck confit legs with potatoes sautéed in leftover duck fat and a dollop of Sandy Neck Beach Plum Chutney (page 191). SERVES 6

1 tablespoon kosher salt

1½ teaspoons freshly cracked black peppercorns

1 tablespoon fresh thyme leaves

1½ teaspoons minced fresh rosemary

6 duck legs (about 12 ounces each)

1 Place the salt, cracked peppercorns, thyme, and rosemary in a small bowl and stir to mix. Rub the seasoning blend evenly all over the duck legs and arrange the legs in a single layer in a shallow baking dish. Cover tightly with plastic wrap and refrigerate the duck legs for 24 hours.

2 Preheat the oven to 325°F.

3 Place the duck legs in a single layer, skin side down, in a very large ovenproof skillet. Use 2 skillets if you do not have 1 skillet large enough to contain the legs in a single layer. Begin cooking the duck legs over medium heat until the fat starts to render. When ¼ inch of fat has accumulated in the skillet(s), after 20 to 25 minutes, turn the legs over, cover the skillet(s) tightly with aluminum foil, and transfer the skillet(s) to the oven. Bake the duck legs until very tender, about 2 hours. Remove the foil and continue baking them until golden brown and very crispy, 1 hour longer.

4 Let the duck legs cool in the fat, then transfer them to a covered container, and refrigerate in the fat for up to 1 week.

5 When you are ready to serve the duck confit, preheat the oven to 375°F.

6 Remove the duck legs from the fat, place them in a shallow roasting pan, and cook them until crispy-skinned and piping hot, 25 to 30 minutes. Alternatively, the meat can be removed from the legs, shredded, and used in salads and other recipes calling for duck confit.

Brined Turkey Thighs with Cranberry Barbecue Sauce

My mother is an attractive woman who has long been known for her great legs. Now that she is in her eighties, she has managed to garner an equally exuberant claim-to-fame for her thighs— that is, the turkey thighs she grills during summers in Maine. Use your favorite barbecue sauce for the base of the cranberry and pale ale infused sauce that accompanies the thighs. SERVES 6

9 cups water

¼ cup sea salt

2 cloves garlic, peeled and crushed

2 cinnamon sticks (each 3 to 4 inches long)

4 bay leaves

12 black peppercorns

2 whole cloves

6 bone-in turkey thighs (10 to 12 ounces each)

2 teaspoons herbes de Provence

Vegetable oil, for oiling the grill grate

Cranberry Barbecue Sauce (recipe follows), for serving

1 Place the water, salt, garlic, cinnamon, bay leaves, peppercorns, and cloves in a nonreactive pot and let come to a boil over high heat. Reduce the heat to medium and let simmer gently until spices flavor the brine, about 10 minutes. Remove the brine from the heat and let cool to room temperature.

2 Place the turkey thighs in a nonreactive container and pour the cooled brine over them, making sure that all of the thighs are submerged in the liquid. Cover the container and refrigerate for at least 4 hours or up to 12 hours. Remove the turkey thighs from the brine and

discard the brine. Rinse the thighs under cold running water and pat them dry with paper towels. Sprinkle the herbes de Provence evenly over the thighs.

3 Set up a charcoal or gas grill for indirect grilling. Close the lid and adjust the vents to preheat the internal temperature of the grill to 300° to 325°F.

4 When ready to grill, brush the grill grate with vegetable oil. Place the turkey thighs on the grate so they are not directly over the fire, close the grill lid, and cook the thighs until an instant-read thermometer registers 160°F when inserted into the thickest part of the meat but not touching a bone, 1½ to 2 hours. Open the vents to increase the heat to 400° to 450°F, adding more charcoal if necessary. Continue cooking the turkey thighs until the skin crisps to a deep golden brown and the meat registers between 180° and 185°F on the instant-read thermometer, 10 to 15 minutes longer.

5 Remove the turkey thighs from the grill and let them rest for 10 to 15 minutes before serving. Accompany the thighs with a bowl of Cranberry Barbecue Sauce to spoon over the meat.

Cranberry Barbecue Sauce

A maple-flavored barbecue sauce, such as Pemberton's, made in Maine, is a particularly tasty choice for this accompaniment to grilled turkey thighs. MAKES ABOUT 3 CUPS

½ cup dried cranberries

1 bottle (12 ounces) pale ale, such as Geary's from Maine

1½ cups tomato-based barbecue sauce

PLACE THE DRIED cranberries and ale in a saucepan and bring to a boil over medium-high heat. Reduce the heat to medium and let the cranberries and ale simmer until plumped, about 5 minutes. Add the barbecue sauce and let simmer until the sauce is warmed through, about 5 minutes. Let the sauce cool to room temperature before serving. It can be refrigerated, covered, for up to 2 weeks.

Grilled Turkey Under a Cinder Block with Oyster and Swiss Chard Dressing

Throughout the 1990s, I spent most of the month of November working as a spokesperson for the Butterball turkey company. I appeared on *The Joan Rivers Show* with live turkeys, awaited air time in green rooms with Martha Stewart and Julia Child, removed a drumstick from an eighteen-pound roasted turkey with my knees knocking together and hands trembling live on the *Today* show at Bryant Gumbel's unscripted insistence, and swooned with delight when CBS morning host Harry Smith ripped off a piece of crispy turkey skin and hand fed it to me during a carving segment. Those were some of the noteworthy highlights, but most of my time was spent instructing people on how to roast the perfect Thanksgiving turkey via the preferred Butterball method (at a simple and steady 325°F), which I still swear by to this day.

Now that I no longer represent Butterball, I tend to cook turkey for occasions other than Thanksgiving and in innovative ways. The absolute best-tasting turkeys I have ever cooked in my life were raised at Wychwood Farm in Stonington, Connecticut. The farm unfortunately may soon stop breeding turkeys, but this recipe was born out of the fact that we almost always would buy an extra turkey during our annual Thanksgiving pickup, cut it in half in order to fit it into our freezer, and then cook it at a later date in some nontraditional fashion. In this instance the recipe's inspiration comes from the popularity of the Italian method of cooking chicken under a brick, or *al mattone*, only the turkey's size in comparison to a chicken requires a cement cinder block rather than a brick to weight it down during grilling. (Feel free to skip your bicep workouts at the gym whenever making this recipe.) You'll also need to have a pair of heavy duty grilling mitts handy to tackle the lifting of the hot cinder block throughout the grilling process.

The recipe is perfect for a late summer or early autumn Sunday dinner with family and/or friends. Plainville Farms is a trusted brand of humanely raised turkeys and they have recently begun selling half turkeys, like that called for in this recipe. SERVES 6 TO 8

½ cup dry white wine

½ cup freshly squeezed lemon juice

½ cup extra virgin olive oil

4 plump cloves garlic, peeled and minced

1 tablespoon chopped fresh rosemary

1 tablespoon chopped fresh oregano

1 tablespoon slivered fresh sage leaves

½ teaspoon fennel seeds, lightly crushed

½ teaspoon hot red pepper flakes

2 teaspoons sea salt

½ teaspoon freshly cracked black peppercorns

½ young turkey (7 to 8 pounds), backbone and
   rib bones removed

Vegetable oil, for oiling the grill grate

Oyster and Swiss Chard Dressing
   (recipe follows)

1 The day before you plan to grill the turkey, make the marinade: Place the white wine, lemon juice, and olive oil in a medium-size nonreactive mixing bowl and whisk them together. Add the garlic, rosemary, oregano, sage, fennel seeds, red pepper flakes, salt, and cracked peppercorns and stir well to combine.

Put the half turkey in a jumbo (2½ gallon) zip-closure plastic bag and then place the bag on a baking sheet. Carefully pour the marinade into the bag, seal it, removing the air, and tip the bag every which way to coat the turkey evenly with the marinade. Place the turkey on the baking sheet in the refrigerator and let it marinate overnight, at least 12 hours and up to 36 hours.

2 Set up a charcoal or gas grill for indirect grilling and preheat it to medium-high. Wrap a large cinder block in heavy-duty aluminum foil.

3 Remove the turkey from the marinade and pour the remaining marinade into a nonreactive bowl. Brush the grill grate with vegetable oil and place the turkey, skin side down, directly over the heat. Place the cinder block on top of the turkey half to weight it down and help it to lay flat. Grill the turkey until the skin has crisped, 12 to 15 minutes. Wearing heavy-duty grilling mitts, remove the cinder block and turn the turkey over. Baste the turkey with some of the marinade, place the cinder block back on top, and grill the underside until lightly browned, 12 to 15 minutes.

4 Move the turkey so it is not above the heat, placing it with the skin side up and the meatiest portion closest to the direct heat. Put your grilling mitts back on and remove the cinder block, baste the turkey one more time with the marinade, and then discard any remaining marinade. Place the cinder block back on top of the turkey, close the lid of the grill, and cook the turkey over indirect heat, maintaining a steady temperature of approximately 325°F, until an instant-read meat thermometer inserted in the meatiest portion of the breast registers between 160° and 165°F, about 2 hours.

5 Transfer the grilled turkey to a large carving board and let it rest for about 10 minutes. Slice the turkey and serve it with the Oyster and Swiss Chard Dressing alongside.

Oyster and Swiss Chard Dressing

This oyster dressing is far less rich than the usual Thanksgiving stuffing and is a local nod to the many excellent oysters harvested year-round on Cape Cod. SERVES 6 TO 8

12 freshly shucked oysters

2 tablespoons freshly squeezed lemon juice

2 tablespoons (¼ stick) unsalted butter

1 bag (10 ounces) rinsed and chopped
   Swiss chard

4 ounces pancetta, cut into small cubes
   (¾ cup cubes)

2 tablespoons Wondra or all-purpose flour

3 cloves garlic, peeled and minced

1 rib celery, cut into ¼-inch-wide slices

2 shallots, peeled and minced

1 tablespoon finely slivered sage leaves

1 teaspoon chopped fresh thyme leaves

¼ cup heavy (whipping) cream

Sea salt and freshly ground black pepper

1¼ cups cubed (⅓ inch) French or sourdough
   bread

1½ ounces freshly grated Parmesan cheese
   (about ½ cup)

1 Preheat the oven to 350°F.

2 Place the oysters, along with any accumulated juices, in a small nonreactive bowl. Add the lemon juice, cover the bowl, and place it in the refrigerator while you continue with the recipe.

3 Melt the butter in a large cast-iron skillet over medium heat. Add the Swiss chard and cook until wilted, 3 to 4 minutes. Transfer the Swiss chard to a medium-size bowl. Add the pancetta to the skillet and continue cooking over medium heat, turning occasionally, until crisp, 7 to 9 minutes. Using a slotted spatula, transfer the pancetta to paper towels to drain.

4 Add the flour to the skillet and stir until thickened into a paste or roux, about 1 minute. Continue cooking the roux, stirring constantly, until lightly browned, 3 to 4 minutes. Add the garlic, celery, and shallots to the roux and cooked until softened, 5 to 7 minutes.

5 Add the sage, thyme, and cream to the skillet and cook until slightly thickened, about 2 minutes. Return the cooked Swiss chard to the skillet, stirring to combine, and remove the skillet from the heat. Taste for seasoning, adding salt and pepper to taste. Let cool for about 10 minutes.

6 Fold the cubed bread, oysters, and all of their juices evenly into the Swiss chard mixture. Sprinkle the Parmesan over the top. (You can make the dressing up to 8 hours in advance up to this point. Refrigerate, covered, until ready to use.) Place the skillet in the oven and bake the dressing until it is bubbling and lightly browned on top, 25 to 30 minutes.

Fruity Poultry and Pork Accompaniments

While scurvy is not a disease one hears much about these days, I am convinced maritime explorers and New England sea captains of yore passed on invaluable wisdom when they discovered the curative powers inherent in eating vitamin-rich fresh fruit. Even though my adventures on the high seas never last longer than a few hours on ferry crossings to Nantucket, Martha's Vineyard, or Block Island, I nonetheless crave a steady accent of fresh fruit in my diet as soon as New England's fresh summer vegetable bounty begins to wane. Mother Nature fortunately is quite kind and generous to

Seeking out secret places to pick pretty purple beach plums on sunny September days is an undertaking that I and fellow seaside foragers in southern New England look forward to.

Sandy Neck Beach Plum Chutney

This is a recipe of joy and sorrow. The joy comes from the fact that the chutney emerged as a result of a beach plum picking outing I was invited to participate in with my cherished Barnstable neighbors Judy and Walter Kaess. We left Barnstable Harbor in Walter's small Boston Whaler on a splendidly sunny September afternoon and made it across the Cape Cod Bay to the dunes of the Sandy Neck peninsula and Judy's top secret beach plum picking spot in a short twenty minutes. Beach plums abounded and we picked and swam the afternoon away with carefree abandon. Since Judy had long been the reigning queen of jam making on the Cape, I decided to make something other than jam with my beach plum bounty. I was very pleased with the results and the chutney even garnered the coveted seal of approval from Judy. The sorrow in the story comes from the sad fact that Judy lost a battle with cancer in December 2013. From here on forward everything beach plum for me personally will always carry memories of great times in Judy's uniquely ebullient company. MAKES 3½ TO 4 CUPS

2½ cups ripe beach plums, pits removed with a
    cherry or olive pitter

1 whole lemon, scrubbed

¾ cup dried cranberries

3 large cloves garlic, peeled and minced

2 tablespoons minced peeled fresh ginger

1¼ cups sugar

⅓ cup balsamic vinegar

1   Place the pitted beach plums in a heavy saucepan. Cut the lemon, skin included, into ¼-inch dice, removing and discarding the seeds. Add the lemon to the beach plums, stirring to combine.

her Yankees, for shortly after we have popped the last warm patio tomato or buttery kernel of corn into our mouths, it is time to go beach plum and/or apple picking and revel in local cranberry harvest festivals. I do all of the aforementioned with great enthusiasm and definitely keep scurvy at bay by cooking enough fruity chutneys, conserves, relishes, and sauces to tide me through until it is time to pick the first tender spears of asparagus in my garden in May.

Of course, my Thanksgiving spread is never complete without bowls of Baked Cranberry Conserve and Cranberry Citrus Relish gracing the table, but I am just as likely to serve the same accompaniments with a Cider-Braised Rack of Pork (page 225) in October or a Cast-Iron Skillet Roast Chicken (page 175) in January. And then there's the Valentine's Day treat of pairing the last little mason jar of my Sandy Neck Beach Plum Chutney with crispy servings of Speedy Duck Confit (page 186) and the fact that I'll happily simmer a stovetop pot of homemade applesauce both when the foliage is at its peak of autumnal color and again when those same trees are barren in the frigid depths of February.

2 Stir the dried cranberries, garlic, ginger, sugar, and balsamic vinegar into the beach plum mixture and let come to a boil over medium-high heat, stirring occasionally, Reduce the heat to low and let the chutney simmer, uncovered, stirring occasionally, until the fruit is quite soft and the juices have become concentrated and thickened, 30 to 40 minutes.

3 The chutney can be spooned into sterilized jars and sealed according to the manufacturer's instructions or simply stored in a covered container in the refrigerator for up to 3 weeks. It is excellent served as an accompaniment to a cheese tray or dolloped alongside roasted poultry, crispy duck, and pork.

Baked Cranberry Conserve

Lushly concentrated, this cranberry conserve has long been a star at my Thanksgiving table. Oddly enough, the recipe had originally been described to me at a luncheon I had been invited to attend in honor of Julia Child back in the 1980s in California (not Cape Cod!). Because I am now so Cape Cod crazed over cranberries and like to celebrate the late September/October harvest as much as possible, I often serve the conserve as a condiment to accompany my fall and winter poultry and pork dinners or cheese and charcuterie platters. I find the Baked Cranberry Conserve particularly wonderful dabbed on a slice of sharp cheddar or pungent blue cheese. **MAKES ABOUT 3 CUPS**

1 package (12 ounces) fresh cranberries

1 cup (packed) light brown sugar

1 cup coarsely chopped walnut halves, lightly toasted (see page 70)

2 tablespoons freshly squeezed lemon juice

1 cup orange marmalade, or other favorite citrus marmalade

Come autumn, on Cape Cod, I brake for the glistening ruby splendor of cranberry bogs. I snapped this photo a few miles from my home on a sunny October afternoon.

1 Preheat the oven to 350°F.

2 Place the cranberries in a colander and rinse them under cold running water. Discard any stray stems, leaves, or mushy cranberries. Drain the cranberries well.

3 Place the cranberries and brown sugar in a bowl and toss until evenly combined. Transfer the cranberry mixture to a medium-size glass or ceramic baking dish. Cover the dish tightly with aluminum foil and bake the cranberries until they pop and release their liquid, about 1 hour, stirring the mixture once after 30 minutes.

4 Add the walnuts, lemon juice, and orange marmalade to the baked cranberries, stirring to combine everything evenly. Bake the cranberry conserve, uncovered, until thickened and the flavors are well blended, about 15 minutes. Let the conserve cool to room temperature. The conserve tastes best when served at room temperature but can be refrigerated, covered, for 2 to 3 weeks.

Cranberry Citrus Relish

Several years ago my husband, Nigel, gave my mother a kumquat tree to plant in her backyard in Florida. The tree has been a prolific producer of fruit and we look forward to the kumquat care packages my mother sends to us on Cape Cod every year, just in time to add a handful to holiday batches of homemade cranberry relish. The kumquats impart an intriguing nuance to the basic cranberry-orange relish. MAKES ABOUT 2 CUPS

1 package (12 ounces) fresh cranberries

1 seedless orange, well washed

12 kumquats, well washed

¾ cup sugar

2 tablespoons orange liqueur

1   Place the cranberries in a colander and rinse them under cold running water. Discard any stray stems, leaves, or mushy cranberries. Drain the cranberries well.

2   Place the cranberries in a food processor. Cut the orange, including the rind, into ½-inch chunks and add it to the food processor. Cut the kumquats into quarters and, using the tip of a small paring knife, remove and discard the seeds. Add the kumquats to the food processor along with the sugar. Process until all the fruit is finely chopped but not pureed.

3   Transfer the cranberry relish to a bowl and stir in the orange liqueur. Cover the bowl and refrigerate the relish until ready to serve. The cranberry and citrus relish can be refrigerated, covered, for at least 1 week.

New England Applesauce

When I was growing up in Connecticut, one of my favorite after-school snacks was my mother's homemade applesauce, especially when it was served still warm immediately after being passed through the food mill. Recently, I went through a phase of trying all sorts of fancier applesauce recipes, adding ingredients like browned butter, fresh rosemary, bourbon, and crystallized ginger. In the end, my experimentation left me hankering for the straightforward applesauce of my childhood. It occurred to me that making applesauce should be similar to making wine in that it should express apple *terroir* in the way wine reflects the *terroir* of a particular grape or blend of grapes and the climate in which those grapes are grown. Since over forty varieties of apples grow in New England, there's a lot of fun to be had in creating different and distinctive *terroir*-driven batches of homemade applesauce.

I generally start with a dominant base of McIntosh apples because two-thirds of the apples grown in New England are McIntosh and these apples soften well when cooked and make great tasting applesauce. Like my mother, I always leave the skins on the apples during cooking because red-skinned apples impart an appealing rosy hue to the finished applesauce. Next, I'll usually add another variety of a New England red-skinned apple such as Macoun, Hampshire, Honeycrisp, or Northern Spy. Thirdly, I'll select a couple of yellow or green-skinned apples such as Golden Delicious, Ginger Gold, or Rhode Island Greenings. I personally prefer not to sweeten my applesauce with any sugar, but should you feel the need, two or three tablespoons of brown sugar added to the pot will be sufficient.

McIntosh may be the most commonly grown apple variety in New England, but this abundance in no way diminishes their elegant beauty and delightful flavor.

A bowl of warm applesauce is still for me a favorite afternoon pick-me-up, while I'll save the rest of the batch to serve warm, at room temperature, or cold as a de rigueur accompaniment to the pork roast and chop recipes I cook throughout the fall and winter. MAKES 4 TO 4½ CUPS

8 medium-large McIntosh apples, cored and cut into 1½-inch chunks

2 large red-skinned apples of another variety (see suggestions above), cored and cut into 1½-inch chunks

2 large yellow or green-skinned apples (see suggestions above), cored and cut into 1½-inch chunks

2 to 2½ cups freshly pressed apple cider

2 cinnamon sticks (each 3 to 4 inches long)

2 to 3 tablespoons light brown sugar (optional)

1   Place all of the apple chunks in a large, heavy pot and add 1½ cups of the cider, the cinnamon sticks, and brown sugar only if you must. Bring to a boil over medium-high heat, stirring occasionally. Reduce the heat to medium, and let simmer, stirring every 5 minutes, until the chunks begin to soften and turn to mush, 20 to 25 minutes for the McIntosh apples. Reduce heat to medium-low and continue cooking, stirring occasionally, until all of the apples have softened to a mushy consistency. Add more cider, as needed to keep the mixture moist and prevent it from sticking to the bottom of the pot. Depending on the apple varieties used, additional cooking time will vary from 20 to 30 minutes more and the total amount of cider used will be between 2 and 2½ cups.

2   Remove the cinnamon sticks from the pot and discard. Set a food mill over a medium-size bowl and pass the hot apple mixture through the food mill to separate the skins from the sauce. Savor the applesauce warm at once and then store the rest in the refrigerator until ready to use. The applesauce may be served cold, at room temperature, or reheated in a pot over low heat for a few minutes until warmed through. The applesauce will keep in the refrigerator, covered, for at least 5 days and may be frozen for up to 2 months.

Holy Cow! (& Other Meaty Matters)

"The only time to eat diet food is while you are waiting for the steak to cook." —Julia Child

My maternal grandparents were passionate about steak. Some of my fondest childhood memories from summer weeks spent at their kerosene-lit camp in Maine center around the evenings my grandfather seared thick steaks over a green alder wood fire in a rustically fashioned outdoor stone grill. My grandmother was even more particular about her steaks. If the steaks she had purchased at Merrill & Hinckley, the closest market in Blue Hill, didn't live up to her high expectations, she would think nothing of getting in her Lincoln Continental the following morning and driving for more than an hour to fashionable Bar Harbor in the quest to source better steaks to satisfy her exacting standards. As much as I sincerely celebrate New England seafood and agriculture, I would be remiss if I didn't also admit to having inherited a slightly modified strain of my grandparents' red meat loving genes. In fact, in my house a burger night can elicit as much excitement as a lobster feast.

The meat scene in New England has changed significantly since my grandparents' day. Should I have a hankering for lamb, Border Bay Junction Farm in West Barnstable is a mere two miles down the road from me. My husband is on a first name basis with the butchers at Cape Cod's finest meat market, twenty minutes east of us in Dennis. When we drive back from northwestern Connecticut, The Meat Market in Great Barrington, a treasure trove of superb, locally raised meat products, is an absolute must on our itinerary, as is Pineland Farms in New Gloucester, Maine. The latter is a five thousand acre cheese and natural meat operation that prides itself on representing more than two hundred farming families dedicated to raising cattle with dignity in order to ensure the best quality beef in New England.

While this chapter is devoted to meat recipes, it does not contain too many grand ones for showstopping chateaubriand or prime rib roasts simply because these expensive cuts are not the norm in my home-cooking rotation. Lavishing a lobster béarnaise sauce over a filet mignon or cooking a thick T-bone steak in my fireplace coals is about as fancy as I get because I find a pasta dinner with Meaty Bolognese Sauce or lamb shoulder chops topped with my cranberry bog *peperonata* just as gratifying.

In the coastal areas of New England, lobster and cod can jokingly be referred to as the "other white meat." However, pork truly deserves the

How could anyone not fall in love with a little rural farm named Truelove in Connecticut's lovely Litchfield Hills?

status of being regarded as so much more than the "other white meat" throughout New England because it pairs wonderfully with so many native New England fruits. In my neck of the woods, the Cape Cod Organic Farm sells heritage breed pork, and travels in northwestern Connecticut have led to the happy discovery of a pork farm called Truelove Farms in Morris, Connecticut.

A few years ago everyone in my brother's circle of Maine culinary buddies was bonding together to "go in on a pig" and then share the bounty once the pig had been processed. There was such a constant buzz at farmers' markets in the area about this that my husband and I decided to go in on a pig with my brother. Suffice it to say the undertaking was a learning experience because in our particular instance the pork tasted no better than average supermarket pork. I am convinced there must have been some sort of secret karma at work, in that one should never go in on a pig in the same place where E. B. White had lived and written *Charlotte's Web*.

The good news is that there is plenty of tasty pork being raised and sold in New England, preventing the need to go in on a pig in order to orchestrate memorable pork dinners. I take pleasure in seeking out rural pork breeders in travels hither and yonder and visits to farmers' markets. My curiosity never fails to deliver such bonuses as stellar sausage discoveries, too. These culinary dividends are all jam-packed into this chapter because when you bring home more than just the bacon, there is no better place to be than in your own kitchen brining pork chops in cider pressed at a local cider mill or stuffing a butterflied loin with apples, figs, and cranberries.

Finally, I would like to apologize to any Red Sox Nation New Englanders I may have offended by using Holy Cow!—an expression often associated with former New York Yankees shortstop and announcer Phil Rizzuto—in the title of this chapter. Much to the dismay of my Massachusetts cronies, I remain an avid Yankees fan, having been raised in Connecticut in an area where cheering for the Bronx Bombers was considered perfectly respectable. Mostly, however, I was imagining that Julia Child herself would have appreciated this title. In addition to getting a chuckle out of Julia's attitude toward dieting and steaks, I confess to admiring her inimitable fashion in having once quipped: "Personally, I don't think pure vegetarianism is a healthy lifestyle. I've often wondered to myself: Does a vegetarian look forward to dinner, ever?"

Filet Mignon with Lobster Béarnaise

During my catering years on Nantucket I learned, somewhat surprisingly, that tenderloin and filet mignon steaks tended to be just as popular a dinner entrée with my clients as native lobsters and seafood. This recipe is the ultimate surf and turf combination and covers all the bases in an indulgently rich albeit expensive manner. However, it is a dinner that never fails to delight and impress. Serve it at any celebratory occasion from small holiday gatherings to Father's Day, birthdays, and Valentine's Day. The preparation is crafted to allow the filets mignons to be seared in advance and finished in the oven since the lobster béarnaise will require your undivided attention at the last minute. SERVES 6

For the filets mignons

6 premium-quality filet mignon steaks (each 8 to 10 ounces and 1¾ to 2 inches thick)

Crunchy sea salt, such as fleur de sel, and freshly cracked black peppercorns

2 tablespoons canola or grape seed oil

For the lobster béarnaise

1¼ pounds freshly picked, cooked lobster meat (see page 120)

16 to 18 tablespoons (2 to 2¼ sticks) unsalted butter

1 teaspoon sweet paprika

2 to 3 tablespoons freshly squeezed lemon juice

2 tablespoons minced peeled shallots

1½ tablespoons minced fresh tarragon

1 scant teaspoon saffron threads

¼ cup white wine or Champagne vinegar

¼ cup dry white wine

3 large egg yolks

Fine sea salt and freshly ground black pepper

1 Prepare the filets mignons: Pat the filets mignons dry with paper towels. Season them generously all over with the crunchy sea salt and cracked peppercorns, pressing the seasonings gently onto the meat to help them adhere. Place the steaks on a platter and let stand at room temperature for 30 minutes.

2 Place a wire rack on a plate and set it aside. Place a large, heavy cast-iron or other ovenproof skillet over high heat and film it with the oil. When the skillet is very hot, using tongs, arrange the steaks in it without touching one another. Let the steaks sear, without

moving them, until the undersides are a crusted brown, 2 to 2½ minutes. Turn the steaks over and repeat with the second side. Finally, turn the steaks on their sides, rotating them 3 or 4 times to lightly sear them all around the edges. Transfer the steaks to the wire rack to catch any juices. Set the skillet aside. The steaks can stand at room temperature for 30 minutes to 1 hour while you prepare the rest of dinner.

3 Preheat the oven to 400°F.

4 Make the lobster béarnaise: Cut the lobster meat into large but bite-size chunks, leaving any smaller claw meat as intact as possible. Melt 6 tablespoons of the butter in a medium-size skillet over low heat. Add the lobster meat and sprinkle the paprika over it. Stir the lobster gently to coat it evenly with the paprika and butter. Let the lobster meat steep in the butter over very low heat for about 20 minutes. This will infuse the butter with the essence of the lobster's flavor. After the lobster has steeped for 20 minutes, stir 2 tablespoons of the lemon juice into the skillet.

5 Meanwhile, place water in the bottom pot of a double boiler and let it come to a gentle simmer. Place the shallots, 1 tablespoon of the minced tarragon, and the saffron, vinegar, and white wine in the top pot of the double boiler. Place the pot directly on the heat and let it come to a boil over medium-high heat, and continue cooking until only about 1 tablespoon of liquid remains, about 3 minutes. Place the top pot in the bottom pot of the double boiler; the water in the bottom pot should be barely simmering.

6 At this point, you are ready to finish cooking the filets mignons in the oven. Transfer them back to the skillet in which they were seared, along with any juices that may have accumulated on the plate. Place the skillet in the oven and cook the steaks until done to taste, 10 to 12 minutes for rare to medium-rare; an instant-read thermometer inserted in the thickest center part of a filet mignon will register between 125° and 130°F. If you prefer your meat more pink than rare, leave the steaks in the oven for about 3 minutes longer. Let the steaks rest for 4 to 5 minutes once they come out of the oven.

7 While the steaks are cooking, finish making the lobster béarnaise: Whisk the egg yolks into the shallot mixture in the double boiler until thoroughly blended and warm to the touch, 1½ to 2 minutes. Reduce the heat under the double boiler so that the water is still hot but no longer simmering. Add 10 of the remaining tablespoons of butter, 1 tablespoon at a time, whisking constantly until each has emulsified with the sauce before adding another, until all 10 tablespoons have been incorporated. Gently fold the lobster meat and its infused butter into the béarnaise sauce, stirring to incorporate the butter and make a silky, homogenous sauce. Taste for seasoning, adding salt and pepper to taste. Fold in the remaining ½ tablespoon of tarragon. Taste again. If the béarnaise sauce seems a bit too tart or acidic, add 2 more tablespoons of butter, 1 tablespoon at a time. Conversely, if the sauce is in need of a little tempering, add 1 more tablespoon of lemon juice.

8 Arrange the steaks on warmed dinner plates and lavishly spoon plenty of the lobster béarnaise over them. Indulge immediately.

Steak in the Coals with Anchovy and Caper Sauce

When I made one of my first of many pilgrimages to the famed Al Forno restaurant in Providence, Rhode Island, my husband, Nigel, was fortunate enough to be invited into the kitchen by chef-owner George Germon to watch him cook the restaurant's signature steak nestled into a pile of glowing wood coals—ashes and all. Over the ensuing years, Nigel has became rather obsessed with this technique and has managed to perfect his own version of the recipe, after eating a simple but magnificently memorable *bistecca alla fiorentina* during a vacation in Tuscany.

When cravings for hefty slabs of top-notch beef are at their greatest in the frigid depths of a nasty New England winter, we love to invite over a few fellow carnivores and cook the largest and thickest porterhouse or T-bone steaks we can find directly over the coals in our living room fireplace. Should you be a more modern New Englander with a gas-fired fireplace, the steaks may be cooked outside in fair weather in a charcoal kettle grill, as long as untreated hardwood charcoal is used for the fuel. The steaks could also be cooked over coals in an old-fashioned campfire, as long as the wood used to make the fire is of a flavor suitable for the food. Green alder, oak, maple, and fruitwoods are good New England choices.

The accompanying sauce is not your typical American steak sauce, but an anchovy and caper one that is sometimes paired with *bistecca* in the Arezzo area of Tuscany. We absolutely adore the sauce and it always tastes best when made with salted rather than brined capers. I usually buy my salted capers at one of the Italian grocery stores that line Atwells Avenue in Providence, Rhode Island. SERVES 4 TO 6

2 USDA Prime or dry-aged porterhouse or T-bone beefsteaks (each 24 ounces and 1½ to 2 inches thick)

¾ cup plus 3 tablespoons best-quality extra virgin olive oil

Sea salt and freshly cracked black peppercorns

6 oil-packed anchovy fillets, drained

2 cloves garlic

1½ tablespoons salted capers (not brine packed)

Crunchy sea salt, such as fleur de sel, for serving

Lemon wedges, for serving

1 Light a hardwood fire in an indoor fireplace or set up a charcoal kettle grill for grilling with hardwood charcoal and preheat it to high. The fire should initially

be a hot one and then over the course of 1 hour allowed to gradually die down to glowing red coals.

2 Lightly brush the steaks all over with 3 tablespoons of the olive oil. Season the steaks generously all over with salt and cracked peppercorns. Set the steaks on a platter and let stand at room temperature for 45 minutes to 1 hour.

3 Meanwhile, place the anchovies, garlic, and capers on a cutting board and, using a chef's knife, mince them together until finely chopped and pastelike. Transfer the anchovy paste to an attractive serving bowl and pour in the remaining ¾ cup of olive oil. Give the anchovy and caper sauce a good stir and let it stand at room temperature until ready to use.

4 When the coals in the fire are glowing red and all of the flames have subsided, nestle the 2 steaks directly in the glowing coals. Don't worry about the ashes, as they will fall away as the steaks cook and any remaining ones can be brushed off later. Cook the steaks for 8 to 9 minutes before turning them over. Continue cooking the steaks until they are well crusted on both sides and done to taste, 6 to 8 minutes longer for rare. An instant-read thermometer inserted in the thickest part of a steak, but not touching a bone, will register 125° to 130°F when done to rare. The length of time the steaks will need to cook in the coals will vary according to the thickness of the steaks and the heat of the coals. Plan on a total of at least 15 to 20 minutes.

5 Using long metal tongs, remove the steaks from the coals and shake off or brush away any ashes still clinging to the meat. Transfer the steaks to a carving board and let them rest for 7 to 8 minutes.

6 Cut the sirloin and fillet pieces away from either side of the center bones and then carve the meat into thick slices. Sprinkle a bit of crunchy salt lightly over the slices of steak. Arrange portions on warmed dinner plates and garnish each serving with a lemon wedge. Pass the anchovy and caper sauce at the table for spooning over the meat. Encourage a nice squeeze of the lemon juice over the meat as well.

Al Forno opened in 1980 and continues to thrill with its rustic but oh-so-seductive wood-fired cooking and choice of charming indoor and outdoor dining venues.

Summer Rib Eye Steaks with Fresh Rosemary, Lemon, and Garlic

Since I spend the greater portion of my summers in various coastal locales throughout New England, I relish eating the seasonal and local catch of the day wherever I may be. Yet, at least once a week, I do find myself needing a red meat fix to keep my strength up, if only to energize coping with the busier summer social calendar or battling infuriating traffic. When not succumbing to the allure of a great burger, I'll opt for a grilled rib eye steak to beef me up enough to handle the next wave of so-called summertime easy living. To my palate, this recipe is the perfect summer pick-me-up for an unscripted evening at home outside on the deck with just the immediate family or perhaps a friend or two. SERVES 4

1 tablespoon kosher salt

1½ teaspoons dry mustard

1½ teaspoons freshly cracked black peppercorns

3 garlic cloves, peeled and finely grated

6 tablespoons extra virgin olive oil

1½ lemons, sliced into thin rounds

16 small sprigs fresh rosemary

16 small sprigs fresh flat-leaf parsley

4 rib eye beefsteaks (each 10 to 12 ounces and about ¾ inch thick)

1 Place the salt, dry mustard, and cracked pepper-corns in a small bowl and stir to mix. Add the garlic and mix with a spoon to make a coarse paste.

2 Pour 3 tablespoons of the olive oil in a nonreactive baking dish large enough to hold the rib eye steaks in a single layer. Scatter half of the lemon slices, 8 of the rosemary sprigs, and 8 of the parsley sprigs over the olive oil. Smear the garlic paste lightly and evenly over both sides of the steaks. Place the steaks on top of the lemon slices and herbs in the baking dish and press down on the steaks to make the lemon slices and herb sprigs stick to them. Scatter the remaining lemon slices and rosemary and parsley sprigs over the top of the steaks. Drizzle the remaining 3 tablespoons of olive oil over the steaks. Press the lemon slices and herbs onto the steaks. Cover the baking dish tightly with plastic wrap and let the steaks marinate in the refrigerator for 3 to 6 hours. Remove the steaks from the refrigerator 30 to 45 minutes before grilling and let stand at room temperature.

3 Set up a charcoal or gas grill and preheat it to medium-high.

4 When ready to cook, place the steaks on the grill grate with the lemon slices and herbs still clinging to them. Grill the steaks until done to taste, 3½ to 4 minutes per side for medium-rare, turning them over carefully once with a large spatula to keep the charred herbs and lemons clinging to them. When done to medium-rare an instant-read thermometer inserted into the thickest part of a steak will register 125° to 130°F.

5 Transfer the steaks along with the charred lemons and herbs to 4 dinner plates. Let the steaks rest for at least 5 minutes before serving.

Pan-Seared Hanger Steaks with Red Wine and Shallots

As far as I am concerned the chewy texture and meaty flavor of hanger and skirt steaks cannot be beat. While these cuts of beef are frequently used for Tex-Mex style dishes like fajitas, I tend to cook them in a classic French bistro manner. Hanger steaks used to be difficult to come by in New England but their growing popularity has made them readily available in butcher shops and even in the larger supermarkets where I shop. I use hanger and skirt steaks interchangeably in this recipe. Because they are relatively inexpensive, easy and quick to cook, I'll often cook hanger steaks for a weeknight supper during the chillier months when good comfort food is all that is needed to end an inclement day on a satisfying note. Sometimes, I'll add some minced mushrooms to the shallots when making the red wine sauce. SERVES 4

The three brick houses that grace Main Street on Nantucket are symbolic of the prosperity that reigned during the nineteenth-century whaling era.

4 pieces hanger or skirt steaks
(each 6 to 7 ounces)

Sea salt and freshly cracked black peppercorns

1 tablespoon canola or grape seed oil

3 tablespoons unsalted butter

½ cup finely minced mushroom caps (optional)

3 tablespoons minced peeled shallots

1½ tablespoons red wine vinegar

½ cup robust red wine

2 tablespoons chopped fresh flat-leaf parsley

1   Season the steaks generously all over with salt and cracked peppercorns. Brush a large cast-iron skillet or other heavy skillet with the oil and heat it over high heat. Add the steaks and cook until thoroughly browned on the bottom, about 3 minutes. Turn the steaks over and cook them until done to taste, 2½ to 3½ minutes longer for medium-rare. Transfer the steaks to a platter and tent them with aluminum foil to keep warm while you make the sauce.

2   Melt 1 tablespoon of the butter in the skillet over medium heat. Add the mushrooms, if using, and the shallots and cook until softened but not browned, 3 to 4 minutes. Add the wine vinegar and cook until it is nearly evaporated, 45 seconds to 1 minute. Add the red wine, let it come to a boil, and continue cooking until reduced to about ¼ cup. Turn off the heat and swirl the remaining 2 tablespoons of butter into the skillet, stirring until it has melted and emulsified into the sauce.

3   Return the steaks to the skillet and spoon the red wine sauce over them. Sprinkle the parsley on top of the steaks and then transfer them to warmed dinner plates. Serve the steaks hot.

Nantucket Baked Steak

Almost every time I pop over to Nantucket for a visit, my close friend Toby Greenberg introduces me to some wonderful recipe culled from her *Mad Men* era collection of cookbooks. She'll claim she has been making the recipe for years and can't believe I have never had it. Recently she has taken to calling herself my VF, or vintage friend. Whether BF or VF, Toby's recipes, such as this uniquely retro baked steak, never cease to enthrall me. SERVES 6

1 center-cut sirloin beefsteak (3½ pounds and 3 inches thick)

Kosher salt and freshly cracked black peppercorns

1 clove garlic, peeled and finely minced

1 cup ketchup

3 tablespoons Worcestershire sauce

4 tablespoons (½ stick) unsalted butter, melted

1½ tablespoons freshly squeezed lemon juice

1 large red onion, peeled and sliced ¼ inch thick

1 Position a broiler rack 3 to 4 inches underneath the heat source and preheat the broiler to high.

2 Place the steak in a roasting pan and broil it until the side facing the heat source is browned, 4 to 5 minutes. Remove the steak and set the oven temperature to 450°F.

3 Season the browned side of the steak with salt and cracked peppercorns. Turn the steak over and season the second side with more salt and peppercorns and the minced garlic. Leave the steak in the roasting pan.

4 Place the ketchup, Worcestershire sauce, butter, and lemon juice in a small nonreactive mixing bowl and stir to mix. Spread the mixture evenly over the top of the steak. Top it with the red onion slices.

5 Bake the steak until medium-rare, about 45 minutes. An instant-read thermometer inserted into the thickest part of a steak will register 125° to 130°F. Let the steak rest for 8 to 10 minutes before carving it into ½-inch-thick slices. Serve hot.

Cape Cod Spoon Roast with Becky's Horseradish Sauce

Becky Overman is a longtime Cape Cod resident who came to the less hospitable North from Charleston, South Carolina. Her creative and culinary talents are many and it was Becky who introduced me to the Cape's best meat market, the Dennis Public Market or DPM, shortly after I moved from Nantucket to Cape Cod. One of the DPM's specialties is their "spoon roast," which for some reason they believe they have trademarked because it is always listed on their flyers and blackboards with a TM next to it. This is probably due to what I have come to refer to as a "CapeCododdity," because folks from other parts of the country sing the praises of spoon roasts all over the Internet.

Legalities aside, the Dennis Public Market's spoon roast is always superb, especially when served with a big dollop of Becky's horseradish sauce—so easy to make and the best horseradish sauce I have ever tasted—potent and palate clearing. The sauce is also excellent served with any leftover slices of cold spoon roast or tucked into a spoon roast sandwich. There are debates as to whether this type of well-marbled top butt slab of beef should be cooked at a high or a steady low temperature. I opt for a combination of the two. SERVES 8 TO 10

For the spoon roast

1 spoon roast (aka top butt or boned top sirloin; about 5 pounds), tied with kitchen twine (at the DPM the roasts are sold already tied by the butcher)

2 large cloves peeled garlic, 1 thinly sliced, 1 minced

8 sprigs (1 inch each) fresh rosemary, plus 1 tablespoon minced rosemary

3 to 4 bay leaves, preferably fresh

1 tablespoon kosher salt

1 teaspoon freshly cracked black peppercorns

2½ tablespoons extra virgin olive oil

For Becky's horseradish sauce

½ cup peeled and grated fresh horseradish

1½ tablespoons cider vinegar or white wine vinegar

2 teaspoons to 1 tablespoon sugar

Generous pinch of sea salt

1¼ to 1½ cups heavy (whipping) cream

1 Prepare the spoon roast: Pat the roast dry with paper towels and place it on a flat rack in a large roasting pan. Using the tip of a sharp paring knife, cut eight ½-inch slits, spacing them randomly but

somewhat evenly over the surface of the roast. Insert a slice of garlic and a rosemary sprig into each slit. Slide the bay leaves here and there underneath the kitchen twine holding the roast together. Combine the minced garlic and minced rosemary with the salt, cracked peppercorns, and olive oil in a small bowl, stirring to make a coarse paste. Smear the paste evenly all over the surface of the spoon roast and let it stand at room temperature for 30 to 45 minutes.

2 Place a rack in the center of the oven and preheat the oven to 450°F.

3 Roast the spoon roast until a brown crust starts to form, about 20 minutes, then reduce the oven temperature to 300°F. Continue roasting the meat to the desired degree of doneness, 2 to 2½ hours for medium (still pink inside). I like to cook my spoon roast until the internal temperature registers 140° to 145°F on an instant-read thermometer inserted in the center.

4 While the roast is in the oven, make Becky's horseradish sauce: Place the horseradish, vinegar, 2 teaspoons of sugar, and the salt in a food processor. Process for 30 seconds to combine. Add 1 ¼ cups of cream and process again until the sauce is thickened and somehow magically seems lightly whipped. Taste for seasoning, adding 1 more teaspoon of sugar if needed and a bit more cream if the texture doesn't seem quite to your liking and process again. (Becky is a very intuitive cook who never measures anything, so the sugar and cream are added until the sauce tastes and looks right.) Store the horseradish sauce in the refrigerator, covered, until ready to use. It keeps quite well for up to 2 weeks.

5 Let the roast rest for 10 to 15 minutes before removing and discarding the kitchen twine and bay leaves. Carve the spoon roast into large slices, as you would a roast beef.

The Best Brisket

This recipe comes from my friend Toby Greenberg's daughter Wendy, another good cook, although one destined to be overshadowed by the talents and enthusiasm of her daughter Zoe. Whenever my family gets together with Toby and members of Wendy's family on Nantucket, really tasty food, good times, and nonstop conversations abound. Wendy's brisket recipe ranks with almost all who are fortunate enough to be served it as the absolute "best brisket" in the world. When the top secret recipe was shared with me, I debated whether I could call for store-bought canned cranberry sauce in a cookbook devoted to sourcing fresh New England ingredients and Lipton's onion soup mix in any recipe whatsoever associated with me. Needless to say, I have concluded that superlative flavor must negate pride.

I take my cues from Toby and Wendy and cook the brisket a day ahead because it is easier to slice when cold. I then reheat the sliced brisket with the sauce remaining in the roasting pan. Since I can never resist toying with perfection, I am prone to use red wine in place of the water called for in the recipe and thereby bear the risk of being scolded with an oy vey. SERVES 8 TO 10

1 whole beef brisket (5 to 6 pounds), trimmed of some but not all fat

2 packages Lipton onion soup mix

2 cans (14 ounces each) jellied cranberry sauce, preferably Ocean Spray

1 cup water

1 Place a rack in the center of the oven and preheat the oven to 350°F.

2 Select a roasting pan that will contain the brisket rather snugly with only about ½ inch or so of space

around it. Rub the onion soup mix evenly all over the brisket and place it in the roasting pan, fat side facing up. Spread both cans of jellied cranberry sauce evenly over the top of the brisket. Pour the water into the bottom of the pan. Cover the pan tightly with aluminum foil.

3 Bake the brisket undisturbed in the oven for 3½ hours. The meat should become extremely tender. Let the brisket stand for at least 15 minutes before slicing it if you are serving it on the same day. Otherwise, let the brisket cool in the roasting pan for 45 minutes to 1 hour, then refrigerate it, covered, overnight.

4 Preheat the oven to 325°F.

5 Slice the cold brisket against the grain into ⅓- to ½-inch-thick slices and nestle them neatly back into the sauce remaining in the roasting pan. If the sauce seems a bit too thick, thin it with a splash of water or red wine. Cover the roasting pan and reheat the meat in the oven until warmed throughout, 25 to 30 minutes. Serve the brisket hot or warm.

Moxie-Braised Short Rib Beef Stew

I have long been a fan of Moxie (albeit Diet Moxie), a "distinctively different" tasting soda designated the official soft drink of the state of Maine in 2005. The soda reminds me a bit of a good cup of coffee in flavor and Moxie's unique and slightly bitter taste is attributed to gentian root extract. Famed Boston Red Sox player Ted Williams endorsed Moxie in the 1950s and E. B. White wrote: "Moxie contains gentian root, which is the path to the good life."

Since I've always liked both reading E. B. White and sipping Moxie, I swooned when I tasted chef Rich Hanson's Moxie-braised short ribs at the launch of the Maine Fare festival in Camden

a few years ago. I knew at once the recipe had to be in this book. Rich's original recipe has gone through a few necessary adaptations as he used to braise his ribs overnight in his now defunct Blue Hill restaurant, Table, in an oven that put out only two hundred degrees of heat. I have successfully braised the short ribs to delectable tenderness in a Dutch oven in a normal three-hundred-degree oven for around three hours. However, the short ribs do release quite a bit of fat. Refrigerating the ribs overnight allows you to skim off the excess fat easily. Since the meat becomes so tender that it falls off the bone, I end up just taking all the meat off the bones and serving it as a hearty, boneless stew, ladled atop a bed of mashed potatoes, egg noodles, or polenta. SERVES 4 TO 6

5 pounds meaty beef short ribs
    (each rib 4 to 5 inches long)

Kosher salt and freshly cracked black
    peppercorns

1 cup unbleached all-purpose flour

2 tablespoons vegetable or canola oil

1 cup peeled and diced carrots

1 cup diced celery

2 cups diced peeled yellow or white onions

4 bay leaves

1 cup beef stock or broth, homemade or
    store-bought

1 bottle Moxie (20 ounces), not diet,
    unfortunately

3 tablespoons blueberry jam, such as Stonewall
    Kitchen wild blueberry jam or Nervous
    Nellie's wild Maine blueberry preserves

¼ cup cider vinegar

Buttered egg noodles, mashed potatoes, or
    soft polenta, for serving

3 tablespoons minced fresh flat-leaf parsley

1 Preheat the oven to 300°F. Place a wire rack on top of a rimmed baking sheet.

2 Season the short ribs all over with salt and cracked peppercorns to taste. Place the flour in a shallow dish and dredge the ribs, shaking off any excess.

3 Heat the oil in a large Dutch oven or other large, heavy pot over medium heat. Working in batches so as not to overcrowd the pot, sear the short ribs on all sides until golden brown, 7 to 9 minutes. Place the browned short ribs on the prepared baking sheet to catch any juices.

4 Pour off all but 1 tablespoon of the fat in the pot and add the carrots, celery, onions, and bay leaves. Cook the vegetables over medium heat until they begin to soften, 8 to 10 minutes. Add the beef stock or broth and 1 ½ cups of the Moxie, scraping up any browned bits clinging to the bottom of the pot. Set the remaining 1 cup of Moxie aside. Return the ribs to the pot with the juices from the baking sheet and let come to a simmer. Cover the pot tightly, transfer it to the oven, and braise the ribs undisturbed for 3 hours.

5 Remove the pot from the oven and, using hinged metal tongs, carefully transfer the short ribs to a piece of heavy-duty aluminum foil, keeping the meat attached to the bones as best you can. Wrap the short ribs securely in the foil and refrigerate them overnight. Pour the liquid in the pot through a fine mesh strainer, pressing down on the vegetables to extract as much liquid and flavor as possible. Discard the vegetables. Refrigerate the liquid in a separate container overnight.

6 Skim the solidified fat from the surface of the strained liquid and discard it. Pour the liquid into a clean Dutch oven or other large, heavy pot and let come to a simmer over medium heat. Whisk in the blueberry jam, cider vinegar, and enough of the remaining 1 cup of Moxie to thin the sauce to a medium-thick consistency, whisking until the jam is completely dissolved. Taste for seasoning, adding salt and cracked peppercorns to taste if needed.

7 Remove all the meat from the short ribs, shredding it into 1-inch chunks, and add it to the simmering sauce. Cook the stew slowly over medium-low heat

until the meat is heated through, about 15 minutes. Ladle the hot stew over buttered egg noodles, mashed potatoes, or soft polenta. Sprinkle the top of each serving with the parsley and enjoy the stew hot.

Roasted Marrow Bones with a Small Herb Salad

One bleak winter day when I was perusing the rather barren and uninspiring aisles of a local supermarket, I came across some packages of caveman-like marrow bones at dirt-cheap prices in the meat section. I was ecstatic because on a trip to Boston I had recently dined on fabulous marrow bones at the Eastern Standard restaurant in the always welcoming Hotel Commonwealth. I immediately snatched up the packages and set to figuring out how best to prepare them as an unexpected dinner treat. I was so thrilled with the results that I ended up preparing the same recipe for 125 people when the Nantucket Wine Festival invited me to come up with a dish to pair with Au Bon Climat's 2006 La Bauge Au-dessus Pinot Noir at their annual May tasting event. The prep kitchen for the wine tasting was not on the premises and transporting huge and heavy roasting pans filled with the marrow bones on foot over Nantucket's one-way lanes to the site was not an undertaking I would wish to repeat.

Suffice it to say, I have since stuck to roasting smaller batches of marrow bones in the cozy familiarity of my own kitchen. I can happily make a decadent dinner out of two or three roasted marrow bones served with a small but invigorating herb and caper salad, a combination inspired by British chef Fergus Henderson. Otherwise, I serve a single marrow bone as an appetizer with a glass

of excellent pinot noir to friends adventuresome enough to appreciate it. SERVES 8 AS AN APPE-TIZER OR 3 OR 4 AS AN UNCONVENTIONAL BUT GREAT DINNER

2 shallots, peeled and thinly sliced

Ice water

8 center-cut beef marrow bones (each 2½ to 3 inches tall; about 4 pounds total weight)

3½ tablespoons extra virgin olive oil

Crunchy sea salt, such as fleur de sel and freshly cracked black peppercorns

1 cup chopped fresh flat-leaf parsley leaves

⅓ cup chopped fresh cilantro leaves

2 ounces (about 1 cup) fresh pea shoots (optional but a great addition when available)

1 tablespoon brine-packed capers, drained

1 tablespoon freshly squeezed lemon juice

8 slices (½ inch thick) crusty bread, such as ciabatta, toasted

1 Place the shallots in a bowl of ice water and let stand for 15 to 20 minutes to soften the sharpness of their raw flavor.

2 Preheat the oven to 425°F, preferably an oven with a convection setting. Line a rimmed baking sheet with heavy-duty aluminum foil.

3 Place the marrow bones in a mixing bowl, drizzle 1½ tablespoons of olive oil over them, and then toss to coat them lightly all over. Season the marrow bones all over with crunchy salt and cracked peppercorns. Arrange the marrow bones, marrow-side-up, on the prepared baking sheet. Roast the marrow bones until the marrow is soft and light golden brown, 15 to 20 minutes. Take care not to roast the bones too long or the marrow will begin to bubble out of the bones like lava from a volcano.

4 While the marrow bones are roasting, prepare the herb and caper salad: Drain the shallots and pat them

dry with paper towels. Place the shallots in a salad bowl, add the parsley, cilantro, pea shoots, if using, and capers and toss to mix. Just before serving, toss the salad with the remaining 2 tablespoons of olive oil and the lemon juice and season it with flaky sea salt to taste.

5 To serve, scatter a bit of the salad over each of 8 salad plates or 3 or 4 larger plates if you are serving the marrow bones as a main course. Center 1, 2, or 3 roasted marrow bones on top. Scatter more salad over the marrow bones and place 1 or 2 pieces of toast and a scant ½-teaspoon mound of crunchy salt on the edge of each plate. To savor, scoop out the marrow with a small spoon or palette knife and spread it on the toast. Season the marrow with a bit of the sea salt and top it with some of the herb salad. Enjoy immediately.

A Good Go-To Meat Loaf

Meat loaf is one of my all-time favorite comfort food dinners and I can happily lunch for long stretches of time on sandwiches made with leftover meat loaf. The Sicilian loaf, featured in my *Nantucket Open-House Cookbook*, has become the standard meat loaf recipe against which I judge all others and I am one who frequently tries different meat loaf recipes. Rarely do the results match or surpass that tried-and-true Sicilian loaf, with its interior spiraled roulade of smoky ham and melted cheese. Enter into the equation my son, Oliver, who still now at the age of seventeen claims he doesn't like cheese, much to the horror of his *fromage-ophile* parents. There's no sense trying to reason with the contradictory fact that pizzas and strombolis manage to be very high on my son's sustenance pyramid. Plan B has morphed into the quest to find a meat loaf recipe without cheese that I can covet as much as my Sicilian loaf and serve for a family dinner. This recipe has been years in the making and merges the merits of several different meat loaf experimentations. Please, just don't tell my son that a secret to the meat loaf's tenderness is the hidden addition of cottage cheese. The recipe has passed muster with him and what he doesn't know could actually nutritionally nourish him.

You can make the meat loaf with ground beef or a mix of ground beef, pork, and veal, often marketed as meat loaf mix. SERVES 6

1½ tablespoons extra virgin olive oil

1 large onion, peeled and minced

2 small ribs celery, minced

3 cloves garlic, peeled and minced

2 large eggs

3 tablespoons Dijon mustard, preferably imported

2 tablespoons Worcestershire sauce

⅔ cup cottage cheese (not low fat)

½ cup whole milk

1 teaspoon dried Italian seasoning

¼ teaspoon ground chipotle pepper or cayenne pepper

2 pounds ground beef sirloin or meat loaf mix

½ pound sweet Italian sausage, removed from its casing

1¼ cups fresh bread crumbs

2½ tablespoons minced fresh flat-leaf parsley

2½ tablespoons slivered fresh basil

2 teaspoons sea salt

½ teaspoon freshly ground black pepper

⅓ cup ketchup

1 tablespoon light brown sugar

6 slices apple wood-smoked bacon

1 Preheat the oven to 350°F. Line a large rimmed baking sheet with parchment paper.

When October skies cloud gray and marsh grasses turn to reddish brown, it's time to take my cooking indoors and make a really good meat loaf dinner.

2 Heat the olive oil in a medium-size skillet over medium heat. Add the onion, celery, and garlic and cook until softened, 6 to 8 minutes. Remove the skillet from the heat and let the vegetables cool for 10 minutes.

3 Place the eggs, 2 tablespoons of the mustard, and the Worcestershire sauce, cottage cheese, milk, Italian seasoning, and chipotle pepper in a medium-size bowl and beat until thoroughly combined.

4 Place the ground beef or meat loaf mix and sausage in a large mixing bowl. Pour the egg mixture over the meat and add the bread crumbs, parsley, basil, salt, and black pepper. Using your hands, mix and knead everything together until evenly combined. Transfer the meat mixture to the prepared baking sheet and form it into a large loaf shape.

5 Place the ketchup, brown sugar, and remaining 1 tablespoon of mustard in a small bowl and stir to mix. Spread the ketchup mixture evenly over the top and sides of the meat loaf. Arrange the bacon slices diagonally across the top and sides of the meat loaf.

6 Bake the meat loaf until it is nicely browned all over and an instant-read thermometer inserted into the center of the loaf registers 160°F, 70 to 75 minutes. Let the meat loaf rest for 5 to 7 minutes before slicing.

My Favorite New England Burger

When the burger craze was at its height of sophistication a few years ago, I was definitely on the bandwagon and had no qualms about paying outrageous sums of money and traveling great distances to try fancy concoctions garnering the media limelight. All that said, done, devoured, and gilded with foie gras, when I am having a burger night at home or on the road, I can still totally relish a classic old-fashioned New England burger topped with extra-sharp Vermont cheddar cheese and crisp bacon from a smokehouse in Vermont or New Hampshire. Sometimes I'll make my burgers with grass-fed beef from any one of several New England farms or splurge by ordering proprietary ground beef blends from Niman Ranch, Allen Brothers, or Pat LaFrieda. Other times, I'll even grind my own meat. However, the most important burger lesson I've learned is to make sure the beef used to form any burger is only 80 percent lean— a tip from Boston chef Michael Schlow, who also adds more fat in the form of olive oil to his famous Schlow burger.

For me personally, a burger is all about the burger and its toppings, like apple wood-smoked bacon from North Country Smokehouse in New Hampshire, and not about the bun. As a matter of fact, I don't like my burgers enveloped in buns and at home I serve the burgers I grill on top of toasted English muffin halves and eat them with a knife and fork. The nooks and crannies in the English muffin absorb the oozing burger juices beautifully and add the perfect minimal amount of carbohydrates to what I basically view as a carnivorous indulgence. SERVES 4

6 slices apple wood-smoked bacon

1½ to 1¾ pounds 80 percent lean ground beef

1 tablespoon extra virgin olive oil or melted bacon fat

2 teaspoons Dijon mustard, preferably imported

1½ teaspoons crunchy sea salt, such as fleur de sel

¾ teaspoon freshly cracked black peppercorns

Vegetable oil, for oiling the grill grate

4 ounces extra-sharp Vermont cheddar cheese, thinly sliced

2 sandwich-size English muffins, split with a fork and toasted

Ketchup, for serving

1 Set up a charcoal or gas grill for indirect grilling and preheat it to medium-high.

2 Place the bacon in a large, heavy skillet and cook over medium heat until nicely crisped, 7 to 9 minutes. Transfer the bacon to a paper towel–lined plate to drain. Set aside the bacon fat, if using.

3 Place the ground beef, olive oil or bacon fat, mustard, crunchy salt, and cracked peppercorns in a large mixing bowl and, using your hands, mix until evenly blended. Divide the ground meat mixture into 4 equal portions and shape each into a plump patty 1 to 1¼ inches thick.

4 When ready to grill, lightly brush the grate with vegetable oil. Place the burgers on the grate directly over the heat and cook until done to taste, 3 to 4 minutes per side for medium-rare.

5 Move the burgers so they are not above the heat, top each with sliced cheddar, close the lid of the grill, and wait for the cheese to melt, about 1 minute.

6 Cut each bacon slice in half crosswise. Perch each burger on top of a toasted English muffin half, top it with 3 pieces of bacon, and pass the ketchup. Serve the burgers with a knife and fork.

Meaty Bolognese Sauce

One of the most frequently requested meals in my house is pasta with Bolognese sauce. I have relied upon a husband-and-son pleasing, speedy Americanized version of the sauce for years, but decided I should change my recipe when my friend Elena Latici returned to Nantucket for a visit after living in Bologna. She invited me out to her parents' seaside shack in Madaket for a sunset supper of spaghetti with Bolognese sauce. The sunset was the most spectacular one I have ever witnessed, rivaled only by Elena's authentic Bolognese sauce and the spaghetti that she and her father had made by hand and draped over the dining room chairs to dry before cooking. Elena's Bolognese sauce was essentially a meat ragu with only a hint of tomato, whereas my speedy Bolognese sauce was much more of a tomato sauce enriched with some ground beef.

Haunted in a delightful way by the memory of this splendid evening, I decided to go back to the drawing board to create a somewhat more authentic Bolognese sauce. This is the result and my husband pronounced it the best Bolognese I have ever made. You can serve it over spaghetti or tagliatelle, but I also think it works particularly well with fusilli. MAKES ENOUGH SAUCE FOR 2 POUNDS OF PASTA; SERVES 8 TO 10

2 tablespoons extra virgin olive oil

2 ounces thinly sliced pancetta, diced (½ cup dice)

1 tablespoon unsalted butter

1 medium-size onion, peeled and minced

1 large carrot, peeled and finely diced

1 rib celery, finely diced

2 cloves garlic, peeled and minced

1 pound lean ground beef or a mixture of ground beef and ground veal

1 tablespoon coarsely chopped fresh oregano

Sea salt and freshly ground black pepper

½ cup dry white wine

3 tablespoons tomato paste

2 cups beef or veal stock or broth, homemade or store-bought

1 can (14½ ounces) crushed tomatoes, preferably San Marzano

⅓ cup heavy (whipping) cream

Your choice of pasta, for serving

1 Heat the olive oil in a large saucepan over medium heat. Add the pancetta and cook until beginning to crisp, 3 to 4 minutes. Add the butter and when it has melted, stir in the onion, carrot, celery, and garlic and cook until quite soft, 7 to 8 minutes. Add the ground meat and cook, breaking the meat into fine bits with the back of a wooden spoon, until nicely browned, about 10 minutes. Stir in the oregano and season the sauce with salt and pepper to taste.

2 Add the white wine to the pan, increase the heat to medium-high, and cook until almost evaporated, 4 to 5 minutes. Blend in the tomato paste and then pour in the beef or veal stock or broth. Let come to a simmer and simmer gently over medium to medium-low heat, stirring occasionally, for about 1 hour. Add the crushed tomatoes and cook until the flavors are blended, about 15 minutes. Stir in the cream and cook 2 to 3 minutes more. Taste for seasoning, adding more salt and pepper, if needed. Serve the sauce at once over the pasta of your choice. The sauce can be refrigerated, covered, for up to 5 days. Reheat it in a heavy saucepan over medium-low heat, stirring occasionally, about 15 minutes.

Yogurt and Pesto Marinated Butterflied Leg of Lamb

When I was growing up in Connecticut, my family cooked lamb far more often than beef and I guess this can account for my according lamb and beef equal red meat status in my cooking today. This is a recipe I like to make during the laziest, haziest days of summer because it is incredibly simple, requires very little prep, can rely on store-bought ingredients if need be, and delivers a huge amount of flavor and satisfaction for so little work. Did I mention it can easily feed unexpected guests and needs only to be rounded out with a fresh tomato, cucumber, or potato salad, or all three given the kitchen hours you'll be saving (and with a little luck the beach time you'll be gaining).

One of the secrets to imbuing tenderness throughout the grilled, butterflied leg of lamb is marinating it in yogurt, the enzymes of which work magic on transforming this often chewy cut. I specifically like to use the plain yogurt made by the Narragansett Creamery in Rhode Island. This yogurt has an especially appealing tang because it is made from unhomogenized milk. Simply combine the yogurt with some pesto, smear the mixture generously all over the butterflied lamb, and leave it to marinate peacefully in the refrigerator for twenty-four hours before grilling. Yes, there are only three ingredients in the recipe, if you don't count the salt and pepper. And, if I don't have a batch of my own homemade pesto on hand, I have no problem whatsoever using the freshly packaged Scarpetta Genovese pesto made outside of Boston by the folks at Sauces 'n Love, because theirs tastes just as good as my own. SERVES 8

1½ cups plain yogurt, preferably from Narragansett Creamery, or 2 percent Greek yogurt

½ cup pesto, homemade or fresh store-bought

1 butterflied leg of lamb (about 5 pounds), trimmed of excess fat

Coarse sea salt and freshly cracked black peppercorns

Vegetable oil, for oiling the grill grate

1 Place the yogurt and pesto in a small mixing bowl and stir until evenly mixed. Place the butterflied leg of lamb flat in a large nonreactive roasting pan or baking dish and smear the yogurt and pesto mixture evenly over both sides of the meat. Cover the pan tightly with plastic wrap and let the lamb marinate in the refrigerator for 18 to 24 hours.

2 When you are ready to cook, remove the lamb from the refrigerator and let it stand at room temperature for 30 to 45 minutes.

3 Set up a charcoal or gas grill for indirect grilling and preheat it to medium-high.

4 Scrape off any excess marinade from the lamb but do leave a thin layer of the yogurt mixture still filming the surface of the meat. Season the lamb generously on both sides with salt and pepper.

5 Brush the grill grate lightly with vegetable oil and place the lamb on the grate directly over the heat. Sear the lamb until nicely crusted on the underside, 5 to 7 minutes. Using 2 large spatulas, if necessary, turn the lamb over and grill it for another 5 to 7 minutes to crust the second side. Move the lamb so it is not above the heat, close the lid of the grill, and cook the lamb until done to taste, between 140° and 150°F for perfectly pink meat with a few well-done outer edges. To test for doneness, insert an instant-read thermometer in the thickest part of the meat.

6 Transfer the leg of lamb to a cutting board and let it rest for 10 to 15 minutes before carving it into thin or thick slices, as desired.

Lollipop Lamb Chops

For a good run of five to six years, these little grilled lamb chops were always my son Oliver's requested birthday dinner. The easy yet remarkably delicious recipe is actually very similar to a Roman specialty called *scottadito*, which translates into English as burn the finger. The name was bestowed because the lamb chops are intended to be snatched hot off the grill by the rib bone with one's fingers and eaten instantly with enough gusto and abandon to run the risk of fingers getting burned in the frenzy. I renamed the recipe Lollipop Lamb Chops to make it sound more kid-friendly and because Oliver at one point discovered that he liked to dip the little lamb chops into a pool of mint jelly and then lick them like a lollipop. With the passage of time and teen birthdays now being more about friends than food, the mint jelly component has fallen by the wayside. SERVES 4 TO 6

12 single-rib lamb chops (each 3 to 4 ounces and ½ to ¾ inch thick), trimmed of excess fat

⅓ cup extra virgin olive oil

⅓ cup freshly squeezed lemon juice

3 cloves garlic, peeled and minced

1½ tablespoons coarsely chopped fresh rosemary

Crunchy sea salt, such as fleur de sel, and freshly cracked black peppercorns

Vegetable oil, for oiling the grill grate

Lemon wedges, for serving

1 Arrange the lamb chops in a single layer in a shallow nonreactive baking dish and drizzle the olive oil and lemon juice over them. Scatter the garlic and rosemary on top. Turn the lamb chops to coat them on both sides with the marinade. Let the lamb chops marinate at room temperature for 45 minutes to 1 hour or in the refrigerator, covered, for up to 3 hours.

2 Set up a charcoal or gas grill and preheat it to high.

3 Season the chops with salt and cracked peppercorns to taste. Lightly brush the grill grate with vegetable oil. Grill the chops until done to taste, a quick 2 to 3 minutes per side for medium-rare. Serve the lamb chops hot off the grill with wedges of lemon to squeeze over the sizzling chops.

Broiled Lamb Shoulder Chops with Cranberry Bog *Peperonata*

Lamb shoulder chops are to lamb loin chops as hanger steaks are to filets mignons in that they are loaded with chewy, succulent flavor but carry little luxurious prestige. As would be expected, lamb shoulder chops are far less, and sometimes infinitely less, expensive than loin and rib chops and this is something that the Yankee thrift bred into my being cannot help but embrace. Besides, I daresay I find lamb shoulder chops to be quite fabulous and this is a recipe intended to convert skeptics into fellow aficionados.

I came up with the combination one autumn day on Cape Cod when I wanted the surrounding beauty of the crimson cranberry bogs and bright yellow and orange fall foliage to be somehow mirrored on my dinner plate. At the same time, I happened to find and buy my favorite arm cut of lamb shoulder chops at the market. I prefer arm chops to blade chops because arm chops sport a little off-center round bone like a miniature marrow bone, while blade chops have a maze of bones that is harder to navigate. Since at this time of year I almost always have a countertop basket filled with different colored bell peppers either from my garden or a local farm stand, I became inspired to make

Broiled Lamb Shoulder Chops with Cranberry Bog *Peperonata* »

a batch of Italian *peperonata* to accompany my lamb chops. SERVES 6

6 lamb shoulder arm chops (each about ½ inch thick and 10 to 12 ounces)

2½ tablespoons extra virgin olive oil

Sea salt and freshly cracked black peppercorns

2 teaspoons finely minced fresh rosemary

Cranberry Bog Peperonata (recipe follows), for serving

1 Position an oven rack about 4 inches underneath the heat source and preheat the broiler to high.

2 Arrange the lamb chops on top of a pan with a broiler rack. Brush each chop lightly all over with the olive oil and season it on both sides with salt and cracked peppercorns to taste. Scatter the rosemary over the top of the chops and let them stand at room temperature for about 10 minutes before placing them underneath the broiler.

3 Broil the lamb chops until medium, 3 to 4 minutes per side, turning them once. You want the chops to be crusted brown on the exterior and pink rather than bloody rare on the interior. Transfer the chops to dinner plates and top each with 2 to 3 tablespoons of the *peperonata*. Serve the chops at once.

Cranberry Bog *Peperonata*

I thought I should impart a Cape Cod spin to this vibrant stewed pepper condiment and hit upon the idea of replacing the traditional golden raisins in the recipe with dried cranberries. If only every experimental recipe I dream up could be this successful. MAKES ABOUT 3 CUPS

⅓ cup extra virgin olive oil

6 oil-packed anchovy fillets, drained and minced

1 red bell pepper, stemmed, seeded, and cut into ¼-inch-wide strips

1 yellow bell pepper, stemmed, seeded, and cut into ¼-inch-wide strips

1 orange bell pepper, stemmed, seeded, and cut into ¼-inch-wide strips

1 medium-size onion, peeled and cut lengthwise into ¼-inch-wide slivers

4 cloves garlic, peeled and cut into thin slivers

½ cup dried cranberries

2 tablespoons brine-packed capers, drained

¼ cup water

2½ tablespoons syrupy balsamic vinegar (see Note)

Sea salt, optional

3 tablespoons slivered fresh basil leaves

HEAT THE OLIVE oil in a large skillet over medium-high heat. Add the anchovies and cook, stirring, until dissolved, 45 seconds to 1 minute. Add the bell peppers, onion, and garlic and cook, stirring frequently, until softened and beginning to blister brown in spots, 10 to 12 minutes. Stir in the cranberries and capers and continue cooking, stirring occasionally, about 5 minutes. Reduce the heat to low and pour in the water and balsamic vinegar, stirring to combine. Cook the *peperonata* until the peppers are very tender and the juices are slightly thickened, about 10 minutes. Taste for seasoning; you may or may not wish to add a little salt. The *peperonata* can stand at room temperature for up to 4 hours before serving. Fold in the basil just before serving.

NOTE: *Many stores now carry bottles of balsamic glaze, a syrupy form of balsamic vinegar.*

Lamb Meatballs Simmered in a Tomato Eggplant Sauce

I suppose I could wax eloquent over this recipe but simply put, I am fond of ground lamb, meatballs, tomatoes, and eggplant, and this dish has them all. Serve this over pasta or polenta for a really tasty riff on spaghetti and meatballs. SERVES 6

For the lamb meatballs

1½ pounds lean ground lamb

5 tablespoons extra virgin olive oil

¾ cup panko bread crumbs

3 large egg yolks, lightly beaten

1 small onion, peeled and very finely minced

3 cloves garlic, peeled and finely grated

1 tablespoon fresh rosemary, very finely minced

1 teaspoon dried mint

1 teaspoon kosher salt

½ teaspoon freshly ground black pepper

For the tomato eggplant sauce

1 large eggplant

5 tablespoons extra virgin olive oil

3 cloves garlic, peeled and minced

1 can (14½ ounces) diced tomatoes

1 cup plain tomato sauce or tomato puree

¼ cup dry red wine

Pinch of ground cinnamon

Kosher salt and freshly ground black pepper

Pasta, such as tagiatelle or fettuccine, or polenta, for serving

Crumbled goat or feta cheese (optional), for serving

1 Preheat the oven to 350°F. Line a large rimmed baking sheet with parchment paper.

2 Make the meatballs: Place the ground lamb, 2 tablespoons of the olive oil, and the panko, egg yolks, onion, finely grated garlic, rosemary, and mint in a mixing bowl and season with salt and pepper. Using your hands, mix until thoroughly combined. Shape the lamb mixture into meatballs about 1½ inches in diameter. Arrange the meatballs on the prepared baking sheet, spacing them about ¾ inch apart. You should have 20 to 24 meatballs. Brush the meatballs all over with the remaining 3 tablespoons of olive oil. Bake the meatballs until nicely browned all over, about 30 minutes. If you are not using the meatballs within the hour, let them cool and then store them in the refrigerator, covered, until ready to use. The meatballs can be prepared up to 3 days in advance.

3 Preheat the oven or increase the temperature to 425°F. Line a 9-inch-square baking dish with aluminum foil.

4 Make the tomato eggplant sauce: Prick the eggplant all over with the tines of a fork or the tip of a sharp paring knife. Brush the skin with 2 tablespoons of the olive oil and place the eggplant in the prepared baking dish. Roast the eggplant until the skin has shriveled and collapsed and the flesh is tender, 35 to 45 minutes. Remove the eggplant from the oven and when it is cool enough to handle, cut off and discard the stem end, slit the eggplant open, and scrape all the flesh away from the skin. Discard the skin and coarsely chop the flesh. Set the eggplant aside.

5 Heat the remaining 3 tablespoons of olive oil in a large straight-sided skillet over medium heat. Add the minced garlic and cook until softened but not browned, about 2 minutes. Add the diced tomatoes, tomato sauce or puree, red wine, and cinnamon. Let come to a simmer and simmer, uncovered, for 15 minutes, stirring occasionally. Add the chopped eggplant and season the sauce with salt and pepper to taste. Let the sauce simmer until the eggplant blends into the sauce, about 10 minutes.

Winter beach scenes have a uniquely soulful allure that, for me, invokes cravings for the warmth of the kitchen and hearty, stick-to-your-ribs meals.

6　Add the lamb meatballs to the sauce, reduce the heat to medium-low, and let the meatballs simmer gently in the sauce, 20 to 30 minutes.

7　Ladle the meatballs and sauce over the pasta or polenta and top each serving with some crumbled goat cheese or feta cheese, if desired.

My Moussaka

Well over thirty years ago my aunt, Diane Madden, got me into making moussaka on Nantucket. Over the decades I have added different nuances to the recipe, like cooking the eggplant in the oven rather than frying it in a lot of oil and making the béchamel topping fluffier by folding ricotta cheese into it. Although my husband would prefer my tweaking energies be poured into making him a lasagna, moussaka and I go back too far for me to scratch it from my repertoire of top dishes to pack

for a ski getaway or bring to a large potluck gathering. SERVES 10 TO 12

For the eggplant and lamb sauce

3 large eggplants

Kosher salt

2 tablespoons extra virgin olive oil, plus olive oil for brushing the eggplant

1 large onion, peeled and minced

4 cloves garlic, peeled and minced

2 pounds lean ground lamb

1 tablespoon ground cinnamon

1 tablespoon dried oregano

½ teaspoon freshly grated nutmeg

1 can (28 ounces) plum tomatoes

¾ cup dry red wine

Freshly ground black pepper

¼ cup minced fresh flat-leaf parsley

For the béchamel sauce

3 cups whole milk

3 tablespoons unsalted butter

3 tablespoons unbleached all-purpose flour

½ teaspoon freshly grated nutmeg

Sea salt and freshly ground white pepper

1½ cups whole milk ricotta cheese, preferably from Rhode Island's Narragansett Creamery

3 large egg yolks, lightly beaten

4 cups freshly grated Greek Kasseri cheese

1　Prepare the eggplant and lamb sauce: Using a vegetable peeler, remove the skin from each eggplant in long strips, leaving a few narrow purple stripes of skin on each. Cut off and discard the stem ends. Cut the eggplant crosswise into ½-inch-thick rounds. Sprinkle each round with some salt and place all of the rounds in layers in a large colander. Place a weight such as a large can of beans or tomatoes on top and let stand in the sink for 1 hour to allow any bitter juices to drain off.

2 Meanwhile, heat the olive oil in a large, heavy skillet over medium-high heat. Add the onion and garlic and cook until softened, 5 minutes. Add the lamb and cook, breaking the meat into smaller pieces, until the meat begins to lose its pink color, 5 to 6 minutes. Add the cinnamon, oregano, and ½ teaspoon of nutmeg and cook until the flavors blend, about 2 minutes.

3 Working over the skillet, crush the plum tomatoes between your fingers into smaller pieces and add them to the lamb along with their juices. Stir in the red wine and season the lamb sauce with salt and black pepper to taste. Let the lamb sauce come to a simmer over medium heat and simmer, uncovered, stirring occasionally, until the flavors deepen, about 30 minutes. Remove the skillet from the heat and stir in the parsley.

4 Preheat the oven to 400°F. Line 2 large baking sheets with parchment paper.

5 Rinse the eggplant rounds under cold running water and then pat them dry with paper towels. Arrange the eggplant rounds on the prepared baking sheets, brushing each lightly on both sides with olive oil. Bake the eggplant, turning it over once, until the rounds are tender and lightly browned on both sides, 20 to 25 minutes. Remove the eggplant from the oven and reduce the oven temperature to 350°F.

6 Meanwhile, make the béchamel sauce: Warm the milk in a small saucepan over medium-low heat. Melt the butter in a heavy, medium-size saucepan over medium-low heat. Whisk the flour into the butter and cook, stirring constantly, until blended, about 2 minutes. Gradually whisk in the warm milk and let the sauce come to a boil by raising the heat to medium-high. Once boiling, reduce the heat to medium-low and let the sauce simmer until thick and creamy, 2 to 3 minutes. Season the sauce with the ½ teaspoon of nutmeg and salt and black pepper to taste and remove it from the heat. Place the ricotta cheese and egg yolks in a mixing bowl and whisk until thoroughly blended. Whisk the ricotta mixture into the hot béchamel sauce until thoroughly incorporated.

7 To assemble the moussaka, arrange half of the eggplant rounds in a baking dish that is about 18 by 12 inches. Spoon all of the lamb sauce over the eggplant and then sprinkle 2 cups of the Kasseri cheese on top. Arrange the remaining eggplant rounds on top of the cheese and then spread all of the béchamel sauce over the eggplant. Top the moussaka evenly with the remaining 2 cups of Kasseri cheese.

8 Bake the moussaka until the top is puffed and golden brown and everything is heated through, 45 minutes to 1 hour. Let the moussaka stand for about 10 minutes before serving. Moussaka will keep in the refrigerator, covered with aluminum foil, for up to 4 days. Let it come to room temperature before reheating in a 350°F oven.

Nigel's Lamb Shank Shepherd's Pie

During the elementary school years when my son was attending Cape Cod Academy the parents would get together once a year for a potluck dinner. The first year the theme for the gathering was comfort food and I was amazed when about 75 percent of those in attendance showed up bearing Pyrex dishes containing shepherd's pie.

Fast-forward several years later to a winter Sunday night during season four of *Downton Abbey*, with its downstairs rather than upstairs focus on the trials and tribulations of those inhabiting the Abbey. As a prelude to the 9 p.m. *Masterpiece* airing, my husband, Nigel, decided to make a British-inspired meal—the sort that Carson and crew would enjoy in the kitchen as opposed to Lord and Lady Grantham in their formal dining room. Nigel's Lamb Shank Shepherd's Pie was born, and the recipe is a really terrific comfort food keeper.

What makes this shepherd's pie exceptional is the time and care accorded to each of the casserole's three layers, so be sure to plan accordingly. The recipe can benefit from being made a day in advance and you may want to view it as a weekend project to assemble on a Saturday and serve for Sunday dinner. SERVES 6 TO 8

Braised Lamb Shanks (recipe follows)

For the vegetable layer

2 tablespoons extra virgin olive oil

1 medium-size onion, peeled and minced

3 cloves garlic, peeled and minced

2 carrots, peeled and cut into ¼-inch dice

2 ribs celery, trimmed and cut into ¼-inch dice

4 ounces button mushrooms, trimmed and quartered

2 tablespoons tomato paste

1¼ cups frozen peas

Sea salt and freshly ground black pepper

For the mashed potato topping

3 large Maine or russet potatoes, peeled and cut into ¾-inch chunks

1 large sweet potato, peeled and cut into ¾-inch chunks

2 tablespoons (¼ stick) unsalted butter, at room temperature

½ cup mascarpone, preferably from Vermont Creamery

Sea salt and freshly ground black pepper

3 ounces freshly shredded extra-sharp Vermont cheddar cheese

1 Prepare the lamb shanks.

2 Prepare the vegetable layer: Heat the olive oil over medium heat in a large skillet. Add the onion, garlic,

carrots, celery, and mushrooms. Cook, stirring frequently, until softened and almost tender, about 10 minutes. Stir in the tomato paste and cook, stirring, until incorporated, about 2 minutes. Add the peas, stirring to mix evenly with the other vegetables, and then remove the skillet from the heat. Season the vegetables with salt and pepper to taste.

3 Make the mashed potato topping: Place a steamer basket in a large pot and add enough water to come to the base of the basket. Layer the potato and sweet potato chunks in the steamer basket, cover the pot, and steam over medium-high heat until tender, 20 to 25 minutes. Transfer the hot potatoes to a large mixing bowl. Using a hand-held electric mixer on medium-low, beat the hot potatoes until coarsely mashed. Beat in the butter and mascarpone, increase the speed to medium-high, and continue to beat until the potatoes are smooth and fluffy, 1 to 1½ minutes. Season the mashed potatoes with salt and pepper to taste.

4 Place a rack in the center of the oven and preheat the oven to 350°F.

5 Assemble the shepherd's pie: Remove the meat from the lamb shanks, shred it into bite-size chunks, and discard the bones. Scatter the shredded lamb evenly over the bottom of a 13-by-9-inch casserole dish that is at least 2 inches deep. Spread the vegetable mixture evenly over the lamb. Skim any fat off the top of the reduced cooking liquid, then pour it over the vegetables and lamb. Spread the mashed potatoes evenly over the top. Scatter the cheddar over the mashed potatoes.

6 Bake the shepherd's pie until the juices are bubbling and the top is lightly browned and crusted, 40 to 45 minutes. Let the shepherd's pie stand for a few minutes before serving it in wide, shallow bowls.

NOTE: *You can make the shepherd's pie in advance; cover it with plastic wrap and refrigerate it overnight. Remove the shepherd's pie from the refrigerator 1 hour before baking it.*

Braised Lamb Shanks

Delicious in shepherd's pie or as is with a side of mashed potatoes or egg noodles. MAKES 4 BRAISED LAMB SHANKS

4 lamb shanks (about 1 pound each)

Sea salt and freshly cracked black peppercorns

2 tablespoons canola or grape seed oil

1½ cups robust red wine

8 to 9 cups beef or veal stock or broth, homemade or store-bought

1 medium-size onion, peeled and cut into sixths

4 cloves garlic, peeled

6 sprigs (3 inches long) fresh thyme

1 bay leaf

1 Season the lamb shanks all over with salt and pepper. Heat the oil over medium-high heat in a Dutch oven or other large, heavy pot and sear the lamb shanks on all sides, turning them to brown evenly, 8 to 10 minutes. Remove the lamb shanks from the pot, add ½ cup of the red wine, and scrape the bottom of the pot to release any browned bits clinging to it, 1 to 2 minutes. Return the lamb shanks to the pot and pour in enough beef or veal stock or broth to cover the shanks. Add the onion, garlic, thyme, and bay leaf. Let come to a simmer, cover the pot with a lid placed slightly ajar, and cook the lamb shanks at a gentle simmer over medium-low heat until the meat is falling-off-the-bone tender, 3 to 4 hours.

2 Remove the lamb shanks from the pot and set them aside. Strain the cooking liquid through a fine mesh sieve into a clean pot. Discard the solids. Add the remaining 1 cup of red wine, let come to a boil over medium-high heat, and continue to boil until reduced to 2 cups of liquid, about 30 minutes. If time allows, let the reduced braising liquid cool, then refrigerate it, covered so that the fat may be more easily skimmed off the top and discarded; cover the lamb shanks and refrigerate them separately. The lamb shanks will keep in the refrigerator, covered, for up to 3 days.

Nigel's Butterflied Pork Roast with Apple, Figs, and Cranberries

My husband, Nigel, has a habit of jumping in the car at any given time of the day and driving fifteen or so miles down Route 6A to his favorite meat market on Cape Cod, the Dennis Public Market, or DPM, as the locals refer to it. The butchers now know him by name and I usually don't voice any complaints because the dinners resulting from these increasingly frequent jaunts are almost always stellar, as was the case with this butterflied pork roast. SERVES 6

1 large Golden Delicious apple, peeled, cored, and cut into ¼-inch dice

8 dried Black Mission figs, stemmed and cut into ¼-inch dice

¾ cup fresh cranberries, coarsely chopped

¾ cup bourbon

2½ tablespoons unsalted butter, plus 3 to 4 tablespoons chilled unsalted butter

1¼ cups cubed (½ inch) ciabatta or sourdough bread

1 clove garlic, peeled and minced

1 center-cut pork loin (about 3 pounds), butterflied

Salt and freshly cracked black peppercorns

6 fresh sage leaves

2 sprigs fresh rosemary (each 4 inches long)

1½ tablespoons olive oil

½ cup chicken stock or broth, homemade or store-bought

½ cup apple cider

1 Place the apple, figs, and cranberries in a shallow dish, add ½ cup of the bourbon, and stir to mix. Let the fruit mixture stand until the figs are plumped, about 30 minutes.

2 Meanwhile, melt 2 tablespoons of the butter in a small skillet over medium-low heat, add the bread cubes and cook, turning frequently, until golden, about 10 minutes. Transfer the bread cubes to a medium-size mixing bowl.

3 Place a rack in the center of the oven and preheat the oven to 425°F.

4 Drain the fruit, setting aside the bourbon for the pan sauce. Melt ½ tablespoon of the butter over medium heat in the same skillet used to brown the cubed bread. Add the garlic and drained fruit and cook until softened, 5 to 7 minutes. Add the fruit mixture to the bread cubes and stir well to combine.

5 Place a piece of parchment paper on top of a work surface. Put the butterflied pork loin on top, butterflied side up, and season the top with salt and cracked peppercorns to taste. Pat the bread and fruit stuffing over the loin in a thin even layer. Scatter the sage leaves over the stuffing and arrange the sprigs of rosemary in a row lengthwise down the center. Starting with a long side, roll up the pork roast in a jelly roll fashion and tie it with kitchen twine at 4 evenly spaced intervals to secure it. Place the pork roast, seam side down, in a roasting pan. Brush the roast with the olive oil and season it with salt and cracked peppercorns to taste.

6 Roast the pork for 15 minutes. Reduce the heat to 350°F and continue roasting the pork until an instant-read thermometer inserted deep in the center registers between 160° and 165°F, 45 minutes to 1 hour longer (bear in mind Nigel is British and likes his

Cape Codders who are fans of the quality meats sold at the funky but fabulous Dennis Public Market often sport DPM bumper stickers on their cars.

roasts a bit more well done than is currently fashionable in America). Transfer the pork loin to a cutting board to rest for 15 minutes.

7 Discard all but 3 tablespoons of fat from the roasting pan. Pour in the remaining ¼ cup of bourbon and the bourbon drained from the fruit and carefully ignite it with a long match. Once the flames subside, place the roasting pan on a burner set to medium heat. Pour in the chicken stock or broth and cider, let come to a boil, and cook until reduced by half, about 5 minutes. Reduce the heat to low and whisk in the chilled butter, 1 tablespoon at a time, until the pan sauce is lightly emulsified (the more butter, the richer the sauce). Season the pan sauce with salt and cracked peppercorns to taste.

8 Remove and discard the kitchen twine from the pork loin. Carve the pork into ¾-inch-thick slices. Spoon a pool of the warm pan sauce on each dinner plate, arrange the slices of pork on top, and serve at once.

Cider-Braised Rack of Pork

By now it should be evident that I view pork as a vital part of cooking in New England and believe the more ways of roasting it the merrier because pork pairs so beautifully with native autumnal fruits. I like to accompany this spectacular looking rack of pork with Baked Cranberry Conserve (page 192) or New England Applesauce (page 193) and sometimes gild the lily with both. SERVES 8

1 center-cut 8-chop rack of pork
   (about 5 pounds), chine bone removed

2 teaspoons kosher salt

1½ pounds yellow onions, peeled, cut in half
   lengthwise, and then cut into thin crescents

1½ cups fresh apple cider

2 teaspoons lightly toasted caraway seeds
   (see Note)

1 Remove the rack of pork from the refrigerator and sprinkle the salt evenly all over it. Let the pork come to room temperature, 1 to 1½ hours.

2 Place a rack in the lower third of the oven and preheat the oven to 325°F.

3 Place a large piece of heavy-duty aluminum foil on a rimmed baking sheet (the piece of foil should be large enough to completely wrap around the rack of pork and be sealed with a crimped seam on the top). Place the onions on the foil and place the pork on top of the onions. Pull the edges of the foil up slightly and pour the cider over the pork. Sprinkle the caraway seeds on top, allowing some to fall into the onions. Tightly wrap the pork in the aluminum foil.

4 Braise the pork until an instant-read thermometer inserted into the thickest part of the meat, but not touching a bone, registers 145° to 150°F, about 1 hour and 45 minutes. (Open the foil slightly to insert the thermometer.) Remove the pork from the oven and increase the heat to 450°F.

5 Line a clean rimmed baking sheet with aluminum foil and transfer the pork onto it. Carefully pour the onion and cider mixture into a large bowl and set it aside. Return the pork to the oven, uncovered, and roast it until the meat is nicely browned on top, about 15 minutes. Remove the pork from the oven, loosely tent it with foil, and let it rest for about 20 minutes.

6 Meanwhile, skim the fat from the top of the onion and cider mixture and discard it. Place the onion and cider mixture in a saucepan over medium-low heat and let simmer until warmed through.

7 To serve, slice the pork to desired thickness or cut it into chops. Spoon some of the onion and cider mixture over the top of each serving and serve at once.

NOTE: *To toast caraway seeds, place them in a small skillet set over medium-high heat and cook, stirring constantly, until fragrant and beginning to color lightly, 1 to 1½ minutes. Remove from heat and transfer the caraway to a small bowl (so they do not continue to toast in the hot skillet).*

Sage Rubbed Pork Chops with Blue Cheese and Concord Grapes

The Concord grape season in New England lasts from about mid-September to mid-October and the instant I see the first Concord grapes, this is the recipe I want to make. I have substituted different grapes at other times of the year but the recipe really is best when made with Concord grapes. Seeding the grapes is a bit of a labor of love but there's no need to be super-meticulous since a few stray seeds won't hurt anyone and can be part of the personality of the dish. SERVES 4

For the pork chops

2 tablespoons finely slivered fresh sage leaves

1 tablespoon kosher salt

2 teaspoons freshly cracked black peppercorns

1½ tablespoons extra virgin olive oil

4 bone-in pork rib chops (12 to 14 ounces each and 1½ inches thick)

4 ounces creamy blue cheese, preferably a New England blue cheese such as Berkshire Blue, Blue Ledge Farm's Middlebury Blue, or Barley Hazen Blue

For the Concord grape sauce

1 tablespoon extra virgin olive oil

2 shallots, peeled and minced

2 teaspoons sugar

2 cups Concord grapes, cut in half and seeded as best you can

1½ tablespoons syrupy balsamic vinegar (see Note, page 216)

½ cup chicken stock or broth, homemade or store-bought

½ cup fruity red wine, such as Beaujolais or young chianti

Vegetable oil, for oiling the grill grate

1 Prepare the pork chops: Combine the sage, salt, cracked peppercorns, and the 1½ tablespoons of olive oil in a small bowl to make a coarse paste. Using a sharp knife, cut a slit 2 to 2½ inches deep and 3 inches wide into the side of each chop to form a stuffing pocket in the center of the chop. Stuff each pocket with about 2 heaping tablespoons of blue cheese. Rub the sage paste evenly over both sides of the pork chops, place them on a platter, and let stand for about 30 minutes.

2 Set up a charcoal or gas grill and preheat it to medium-high.

3 Make the Concord grape sauce: Heat the 1 tablespoon of olive oil in a large skillet over medium heat. Add the shallots and cook, stirring frequently, until beginning to brown, 8 to 10 minutes. Sprinkle the sugar on top and continue cooking the shallots until they are lightly caramelized, 2 to 3 minutes. Add the grapes, stir to combine them with the shallots, and cook until the grapes begin to release their juices, about 3 minutes. Add the balsamic vinegar and cook for 1 minute. Add the chicken stock or broth and red wine, raise the heat to medium-high, and let come to a boil. Cook until the liquid has reduced by half and the sauce is slightly thickened, 3 to 5 minutes. Keep the grape sauce warm over low heat.

4 When ready to grill, brush the grate with vegetable oil. Place the pork chops on the grate and grill them for 4 minutes, then rotate the chops a quarter turn for nice crosshatched grill marks and grill them for 4 minutes longer. Turn the chops over and repeat the process, grilling the chops until cooked through, 6 to 8 minutes more. An instant-read thermometer inserted into the thickest part of a chop, but not touching a bone, will register between 145° and 150°F.

5 Transfer the chops to the skillet with the grape sauce. Spoon some sauce over each chop and let the chops rest in the sauce for 5 to 7 minutes. Serve the chops with ample sauce spooned on top of and around them.

Cider-Brined Pork Chops with Spiced Coffee Rub

My brother worked behind the scenes at a fundraising event on Deer Isle, Maine, featuring the food of a few of the Northeast's most acclaimed chefs. Melissa Kelly, of Primo in Rockland, Maine, made a coffee-rubbed and slowly braised pork belly with wild apples and local ginger that was hands down the crowd's favorite dish of the evening. My brother began to fool around with components of the recipe and came up with this more humble rendition, which in turn ended up as the most popular main dish on his holiday season menu at his restaurant, Buck's, in Brooksville, Maine.

The recipe requires allowing 4 to 12 hours of brining time for the pork chops, followed by an initial grilling sear for the chops with the finishing cooking taking place in the oven. SERVES 6

5 cups fresh apple cider (slightly hard cider is okay)

4 cups water

⅓ cup sea salt

2 cloves garlic, peeled and crushed

2 tablespoons pure maple syrup

8 whole cloves

2 cinnamon sticks (each 3 to 4 inches long)

4 bay leaves

6 bone-in pork rib chops (each 10 to 12 ounces and 1¼ to 1½ inches thick)

4 tablespoons instant espresso powder

4 tablespoons ground ginger

Vegetable oil, for oiling the grill grate

4 tablespoons (½ stick) unsalted butter

3 medium-firm, tart apples, such as Macoun, Cortland, or Northern Spy, cored and sliced ½ inch thick

1 Place 4 cups of the apple cider and the water, salt, garlic, maple syrup, cloves, cinnamon sticks, and bay leaves in a small nonreactive saucepan and let come to a boil over medium-high heat. Reduce the heat to medium and let the cider brine simmer gently until it is infused with the flavors of the seasonings, about 10 minutes. Remove the pan from the heat and let the cider brine cool to room temperature.

2 Place the pork chops in a nonreactive container and cover them with the cooled brine, making sure that all of the chops are submerged in the liquid. Cover the container and refrigerate the chops for at least 4 or as long as 12 hours. Remove the pork chops from the brine and pat them dry on both sides with paper towels. Discard the brine.

3 Place the espresso powder and ginger in a small bowl and stir until well combined. Generously rub the espresso and ginger mixture over the pork chops, coating all sides. Let the chops stand at room temperature for about 30 minutes.

4 Meanwhile, set up a charcoal or gas grill and preheat it to medium. Preheat the oven to 350°F.

5 When ready to grill, lightly oil the grill grate. Grill the chops until seared, about 3 to 4 minutes on each side. Place the chops on a baking sheet and bake them until an instant-read thermometer inserted in the thickest part of a chop, but not touching a bone, registers 145° to 150°F, 12 to 15 minutes for chops with a slightly pink center. Remove the chops from the oven, cover them loosely with aluminum foil, and let them rest for 10 minutes.

6 Meanwhile, melt 2 tablespoons of the butter in a large skillet over medium heat. When the butter just begins to brown, add the apples and increase the heat to high. Move the apples around in the skillet so that they brown evenly. Add the remaining 1 cup of cider

and cook until the liquid is reduced by half, 3 to 4 minutes. Reduce the heat to low.

7 Arrange the chops on a serving platter. Swirl the remaining 2 tablespoons of butter into the cider and apple mixture, stirring to incorporate. Spoon the apples over the chops and serve.

Truelove Pork Blade Steaks

Truelove Farms in Morris, Connecticut, epitomizes everything I admire about small rural New England farms. They advertise the pork and beef they raise as being natural, ethical, and sustainable and sell their products out of a ramshackle garage filled on one side with personality, including pink Harley-Davidson motorcycles, and surrounded on all the other sides by beautiful grazing pastures. We discovered the farm after dropping our son off at the Rumsey Hall school. A delightful French woman, who had come from Paris to work on the farm during the summer months, talked us into purchasing pork blade steaks, raving that this shoulder cut was exceptionally flavorful when grilled. *Bien sûr*, she was right and Truelove Farms has been a must on our Connecticut itinerary ever since. SERVES 4

2 tablespoons freshly squeezed lemon juice

1½ teaspoons sea salt

⅓ cup extra virgin olive oil

4 cloves minced peeled garlic

1 tablespoon minced fresh flat-leaf parsley

1 tablespoon chopped fresh rosemary

1 teaspoon dried oregano

½ teaspoon lightly crushed fennel seeds

¼ teaspoon hot red pepper flakes

4 pork blade steaks (each 8 to 10 ounces and ¾ inch thick)

Vegetable oil, for oiling the grill grate

Crunchy sea salt, such as fleur de sel (optional), for serving

1 Set up a charcoal or gas grill and preheat it to medium-high.

2 Place the lemon juice and salt in a small nonreactive bowl and whisk to mix. Slowly whisk in the olive oil to make a light emulsion. Stir in the garlic, parsley, rosemary, oregano, fennel seeds, and hot red pepper flakes. The mixture will be more like an herb paste than a marinade.

3 Place the pork steaks on a platter and coat them lightly and evenly on both sides with the herb and olive oil mixture. Let the steaks stand at room temperature for 30 to 40 minutes before grilling.

4 When ready to grill, brush the grate with vegetable oil. Place the pork steaks on the grate and grill them, turning once, until nicely browned on both sides, 5 to 6 minutes per side. An instant-read thermometer inserted into the thickest part of a chop, but not touching the bone, should register 145° to 150°F. Serve with a sprinkle of crunchy sea salt, if desired.

Pork, Pepper, and Smashed Pumpkin Ale Stew

Every autumn food stores in New England seem to get more and more pumpkin crazed. While I'm not sure I really want to eat pumpkin-flavored Greek yogurt or pumpkin hummus, there is something to be said for cooking with and sipping the pumpkin ales being made by local New

England breweries. I've tasted several and am especially impressed by the Smashed Pumpkin Ale made in Portland, Maine, by the Shipyard Brewing Company. It adds terrific depth of flavor to this hearty and delicious stew. SERVES 6

1 cup unbleached all-purpose flour

Sea salt and freshly ground black pepper

2 pounds boneless pork shoulder,
    cut into 1-inch cubes

3 to 5 tablespoons canola oil

1 large onion, peeled and minced

1 large red bell pepper, stemmed, seeded, and
    cut into ½-inch pieces

1 large yellow bell pepper, stemmed, seeded,
    and cut into ½-inch pieces

4 cloves garlic, peeled and minced

½ teaspoon ground chipotle pepper
    (add more if you want a spicier stew)

2 teaspoons dried oregano

1 can (14½ ounces) diced tomatoes,
    preferably fire roasted

1 bottle (12 ounces) pumpkin ale,
    preferably Shipyard Brewing Company's
    seasonal Smashed Pumpkin Ale

1 cup beef stock or broth, homemade or
    store-bought

1 pound kielbasa or linguiça, sliced on the
    diagonal into ½-inch chunks

Cooked egg noodles, barley, or farro,
    for serving

1 Combine the flour, 2 teaspoons of salt, and 1 teaspoon of black pepper in a shallow dish. Dredge the cubed pork in the flour mixture, shaking off any excess. Heat 2 tablespoons of the canola oil in a Dutch oven or other large, heavy pot over medium-high heat. Working in batches, brown the pork well on all sides and transfer it to a shallow bowl once browned. Each batch will take 4 to 6 minutes. Add more oil to the pot as needed.

2 Once all of the pork has been browned, add the onion and red and yellow bell peppers to the pot and cook until quite soft, 8 to 10 minutes. Add the garlic, ground chipotle, and oregano and cook to soften the garlic, about 2 minutes. Add the tomatoes, 1½ cups pumpkin ale, and the stock or broth to the pot along with the browned pork. Let come to a boil over medium-high heat, reduce the heat to medium-low, and let the stew simmer, covered, stirring occasionally, until the pork is very tender, about 1½ hours. Alternatively, you can bake the pork for 1½ hours in an oven preheated to 325°F. Taste the stew for seasoning, adding more salt and black pepper if needed.

3 Stir the kielbasa or linguiça into the stew, cover the pot, and cook until heated through, 15 to 20 minutes. Serve the stew ladled over egg noodles, barley, or farro.

Portuguese-Style Pork and Clams

The recipes in this book have sometimes presented me with chicken and egg type dilemmas. For example, should this recipe go in the bivalve chapter or stay put here? Actually, when it comes down to it, the chapter choice is not as important as making certain this irresistible combination is included somewhere in the pages of this cookbook. The Portuguese and their large immigrant population in New England have long been on to something incredibly tasty with their habit of combining pork with shellfish, as illustrated by this stylized version of a classic dish often called *porco à alentejana*. Toasted slabs of country bread make a good accompaniment for sopping up the delectable juices and sauce. SERVES 4 TO 6

2 cups chopped peeled onion

6 cloves garlic, peeled and minced

Portuguese pride runs strong along the southeastern coast of New England where many Portuguese have immigrated. Here, costumed dancers revel at a festival in Stonington, Connecticut.

3 tablespoons sweet paprika

1 tablespoon kosher salt

2 cups full-bodied dry red wine, such as merlot, syrah, or zinfandel

3 tablespoons tomato paste

2½ pounds pork shoulder, cut into 1½-inch chunks

4 tablespoons vegetable or canola oil

1 pound Portuguese chouriço, cut in half lengthwise and then sliced into ¼-inch-wide half circles

1 can (28 ounces) whole peeled tomatoes

6 small red-skinned potatoes, scrubbed of any dirt

2 cups coarsely chopped fresh kale leaves

24 fresh littleneck clams in the shell

¼ cup fresh cilantro leaves

1 Place the onion, garlic, paprika, salt, red wine, and tomato paste in a large bowl and stir to mix well. Add the pork and stir to coat all of the pieces. Cover the bowl and refrigerate the pork for at least 6 hours or overnight.

2 Preheat the oven to 325°F.

3 Drain the pork in a colander, setting aside the marinating liquid.

4 Heat 2 tablespoons of the oil in a large skillet over medium-high heat. Add the *chouriço* and cook until lightly browned, 4 to 5 minutes. Using a slotted spoon, remove the *chouriço* from the skillet and set it aside.

5 Add another tablespoon of oil to the skillet. Add half of the pork and cook until browned on all sides, 4 to 6 minutes. Set the pork aside and repeat with the remaining 1 tablespoon of oil and pork. Add the reserved marinating liquid, scraping up any browned bits clinging to the bottom of the skillet. Transfer all of the pork and the marinating liquid to a Dutch oven or other large, heavy pot and add the *chouriço*. Working over the pot, squeeze the tomatoes between your fingers to crush them into smaller pieces and add them to the pot along with their juices. Cover the pot tightly and bake the pork until it is very tender and just beginning to fall apart, about 2 hours. The pork can be prepared to this point and kept covered in the refrigerator for up to 2 days in advance. Bring to room temperature before continuing with the recipe.

6 Put the potatoes in a small pot and add enough cold water to cover. Let come to a boil over medium-high heat, reduce the heat to medium-low, and simmer until barely tender, 15 minutes. Drain the potatoes and let them cool until easy to handle. Cut the potatoes into quarters and set them aside.

7 When ready to serve, let the pork mixture come to a simmer over medium heat. Stir in the potatoes and kale and let simmer until the kale wilts and the stew is heated through, about 10 minutes. Add the clams, let the stew come to a boil, then cover the pot tightly. Cook until the clams open up, 7 to 9 minutes. Discard any clams that have not opened.

8 Divide the clams among 4 to 6 large, shallow bowls. Ladle the pork mixture around the clams and garnish each bowl with cilantro leaves. Serve at once.

Stowe Mountain Lodge Pork Belly

Over the past five or six years pork belly preparations have been popping up everywhere on high-end restaurant menus. While I'm a big fan of pork belly, I wasn't going to include a recipe for it in this cookbook because I thought any recipe would be too chichi for the tone I was trying to establish throughout this recipe collection. I quickly changed my mind after eating an order of Vermont pork belly with balsamic vinegar and Lake Champlain honey late one après-ski winter afternoon at the Stowe Mountain Lodge. It took some time and persistence to catch up with and extract the recipe from Sean Buchanan, a very busy chap and the former chef at the Stowe Mountain Lodge. In the end, my persistence paid off because this has emerged as practically the only way I venture to cook pork belly at home. It is simple, really delicious, and swoonably aromatic as it braises away slowly in the oven for 4 hours.

The Alchemist Heady Topper Double IPA Sean calls for in the recipe is brewed year-round in Waterbury, Vermont, and marketed as a beer so loaded with hops that "it will put hair on your chest." MAKES ENOUGH FOR 12 APPETIZER/ TAPAS TYPE SERVINGS

2 pounds pork belly

Sea salt and freshly cracked black peppercorns

6 ounces (¾ cup) Alchemist Heady Topper Double IPA, or other hop-heavy ale

¼ cup cider vinegar

Peel from ½ lemon

Best-quality local honey

Syrupy balsamic vinegar (see page 216)

1 Preheat the oven to 350°F.

2 Season the pork belly generously with salt and cracked peppercorns and place it in a baking dish. Place the ale, cider vinegar, and lemon peel in a small nonreactive mixing bowl and stir to mix. Pour the ale mixture over and around the pork belly.

3 Cover the baking dish tightly with aluminum foil and bake the pork belly until it is partially cooked and a lot of fat has been rendered, about 2 hours. Turn the pork belly over, cover it, and bake until it is fully cooked, about 2 hours longer. Remove the baking dish from the oven, let the pork belly and liquid cool, and then refrigerate, covered, overnight.

4 When ready to serve, remove the pork belly from the liquid, cut it into ½-inch-thick baconlike strips, and panfry them in a skillet over medium heat, turning once, until crisp, 4 to 5 minutes per side. Center a slice of crisp pork belly on an appetizer plate and drizzle about 2 teaspoons of honey over it. Drizzle a tablespoon or so of balsamic vinegar around the edge of the plate. Repeat with the remaining slices of pork belly. To eat, slice the pork belly into bite-size morsels and dip these either in the honey or balsamic vinegar, or in a little of each. Savor slowly and be thankful you have cooked 2 pounds of pork belly. You will definitely be craving more.

Polish Kielbasa with Cottage Cheese Noodles

Believe it or not, this humble combination was one of my favorite meals when I was growing up in central Connecticut and a dinner I frequently requested my mother to serve. People like my husband can't understand my love for this type of Polish comfort food, so I'll make it for myself when I am home alone and I end up feeling like the happiest half Polish person in the world. Martin Rosol's was the brand of kielbasa I grew up eating, as it was made in New Britain, a town next to our hometown. New Britain still has a vibrant Polish neighborhood on Broad Street, and when I visit I've found, much to my amazement, that Polish is still the only language spoken by many of the shopkeepers. I usually end up pointing at the sausages I want and praying that I don't end up with less palatable Polish delicacies, like blood sausage. A safer bet is to pick up some Martin Rosol's kielbasa in a central Connecticut supermarket or else order it online. Another option for those living in the Chicopee area of Massachusetts is to buy the locally made Blue Seal kielbasa. Since the kielbasa merely needs to be simmered for this recipe, the better the provenance of the kielbasa, the better the result. SERVES 4

1 pound ring kielbasa

½ cup beer, such as Stella Artois (optional)

2½ tablespoons unsalted butter

1 medium-size onion, peeled, cut in half lengthwise and then cut into thin crescents

1½ tablespoons poppy seeds

8 ounces egg noodles

1 cup cottage cheese (I use Hood country-style cottage cheese)

½ cup sour cream

Sea salt and freshly ground black pepper

2 tablespoons thinly sliced scallions, both white and tender green parts

1½ tablespoons minced flat-leaf parsley

Polish or Dijon mustard, for serving

1 Place the kielbasa in a straight-sided skillet and add water to cover. (You can also add ½ cup beer if desired.) Let come to a simmer over medium-high heat, then reduce the heat to medium-low and let the kielbasa stay warm while you prepare the noodles.

2 Melt the butter in a medium-size pot over medium heat. Add the onion and cook, stirring occasionally,

until the onion is very soft and beginning to brown, about 15 minutes. Stir in the poppy seeds and cook until fragrant, 1 to 2 minutes.

3 Meanwhile, bring a large pot of water to a boil. Cook the egg noodles according to the package directions. Drain the noodles in a colander and immediately dump them into the pot with the onion and poppy seed mixture. Add the cottage cheese and sour cream and toss gently to combine well. Season with salt and pepper to taste, add the scallions and parsley, and toss gently to combine.

4 Remove the kielbasa from the skillet, slice it on the diagonal, and divide the kielbasa and cottage cheese noodles evenly among 4 dinner plates. Serve at once with a pot of Polish or Dijon mustard for the kielbasa.

Sausages with Broccoli Rabe, Peppers, and White Beans

I did not grow up eating broccoli rabe but once I discovered it while poking around Italian neighborhoods in Boston and Providence, I became a huge fan. This satisfying recipe is my own stylized combination of a few Italian-American favorites—sausages and peppers, sausages with white beans, and pasta with broccoli rabe and sausages. The DiLuigi company in Danvers, Massachusetts, makes a sweet Italian sausage with broccoli rabe and Romano cheese that I love using in this recipe for maximum broccoli rabe impact. However, any good sweet or hot Italian sausages alone or in combination may be used in the recipe. Bianco & Sons is another great brand of Italian sausages sold in New England. SERVES 4 TO 6

10 cups water

1 cup dry white wine

2 pounds fresh Italian sausages (8 links)

2½ tablespoons extra virgin olive oil

1 large onion, peeled, cut in half lengthwise, and cut into ½-inch-wide crescents

1 red bell pepper, stemmed, seeded, and cut into ¾-to-1-inch squares

1 yellow bell pepper, stemmed, seeded, and cut into ¾-to-1-inch squares

6 cloves garlic, peeled and coarsely slivered

¼ teaspoon hot red pepper flakes

1 large brunch broccoli rabe, tough lower stems trimmed and discarded

1 can (15½ ounces) cannellini beans, rinsed and drained

Sea salt and freshly ground black pepper

Freshly coarsely grated Pecorino Romano cheese, for serving

1 Pour the water and white wine into a Dutch oven or other large, heavy soup pot. Add the sausages and let them come to a boil over medium-high heat. Reduce the heat to medium-low and simmer the sausages until they lose their pink color, about 5 minutes. Then remove them from the pot. Set aside the sausage cooking liquid in the pot.

2 Heat the olive oil in a large, straight-sided skillet over medium heat. Add the sausages and cook, turning frequently, until nicely browned all over, 10 to 15 minutes. Remove the sausages from the skillet and set them aside. With the skillet still over medium heat, pour in ¼ cup of the sausage cooking liquid, and scrape up any browned bits clinging to the bottom. Add the onion, bell peppers, garlic, and hot red pepper flakes. Cook, stirring frequently, until the onion and bell peppers are tender and beginning to blister brown in spots, 15 to 20 minutes.

3 Meanwhile, bring the remaining sausage cooking liquid back to a boil over medium-high heat. Add the broccoli rabe and cook until it is wilted, about 3 minutes. Turn off the heat but leave the broccoli rabe in the pot.

4 Once the onion and bell peppers are tender, add the cannellini beans to the skillet, stirring to combine. Using tongs, transfer the broccoli rabe to the skillet along with any liquid clinging to it. Add ⅔ cup of the remaining sausage cooking liquid to the skillet. Cook over medium heat until the broccoli rabe is tender, 4 to 5 minutes. Season the broccoli rabe mixture with salt and black pepper to taste. Add the sausages to the skillet and cook over medium-low heat until the sausages are heated through, 4 to 5 minutes.

5 Serve in shallow bowls, allowing 1 to 2 sausages per person and surrounding the sausages with plenty of the vegetables and beans. Garnish each serving with a generous sprinkling of Pecorino Romano.

Cabin Fever Venison Meatballs

I am most definitely a gatherer and not a hunter, yet I feel compelled to acknowledge that deer hunting is quite a popular sport in New England. My brother, Jonathan, lives in one such area in Maine, where he has reported that the most common refrain among locals in the latter part of the fall is "Get your deer, yet?" I do know a few people who deer hunt on Nantucket, as well, but since hunting season is my least favorite time to be on the island, I decided to ask my brother for a venison recipe for this cookbook. I'm glad I did because the unusual but captivating recipe he created offers a strange kind of sweet revenge to the fact that my husband once suffered with three different deer tick induced illnesses at the same time.

These venison meatballs are in no way representative of what New England hunters do with their venison, but after Jonathan FedExed me a batch, I knew it would be a crime not to include the recipe, if only to shake up venison cookery in the Northeast. I surmise my brother must have been growing weary of Maine's long winter and dreaming of traveling to Sicily rather than driving through the neighboring town of Surry when he concocted these meatballs because the ingredients—golden raisins, ouzo, and capers—are those of the Mediterranean and not Maine. Nonetheless, the recipe stands as proof that cabin fever can be an inspirationally good thing. MAKES APPROXIMATELY 5 DOZEN SMALL MEATBALLS; SERVES 6 TO 8 AS A MAIN COURSE

For the meatballs

1 cup dried bread crumbs or panko bread crumbs

1 cup whole milk

¼ cup golden raisins

2 tablespoons ouzo or Pernod

¼ cup peeled minced red onion

1 tablespoon peeled minced garlic

1 pound ground venison

½ pound 80 percent lean ground pork

2 large eggs

¼ teaspoon ground cinnamon

⅛ teaspoon ground cloves

1 teaspoon sea salt

¼ cup brine-packed capers, drained and chopped

¼ cup pine nuts, lightly toasted (see page 70) and coarsely chopped

For the sauce

2 tablespoons extra virgin olive oil

2 tablespoons tomato paste

1 bottle (12 ounces) lager

⅔ cup chicken stock or broth, homemade or store-bought

1 cinnamon stick (3 to 4 inches)

Salt

Polenta or rice pilaf (optional), for serving

1 Make the meatballs: Place the bread crumbs and milk in a small bowl and stir to mix. Let the bread crumbs soak for about 10 minutes. Put the raisins in another small bowl and cover them with the ouzo or Pernod. Let the raisins soak for about 10 minutes.

2 Place the red onion, garlic, ground venison, ground pork, eggs, ground cinnamon, cloves, and 1 teaspoon of salt in a large bowl and mix until evenly combined. Drain the liquid from the raisins into the meat mixture. Chop the raisins and add them to the meat mixture along with the milk-soaked bread crumbs and the capers and pine nuts. Mix thoroughly.

3 Preheat the oven to 325°F. Line 2 large rimmed baking sheets with parchment paper.

4 Wet your hands and form the meat mixture into small walnut-size meatballs. Arrange the meatballs on the prepared baking sheets, leaving enough space in between so they do not touch. You should end up with about 60 meatballs. Bake the meatballs until they are very lightly colored, 15 to 20 minutes. Let the meatballs cool on the baking sheets.

5 Meanwhile, make the sauce: Heat the olive oil in a large skillet over low heat. Add the tomato paste and whisk to incorporate. Continue whisking, until the tomato paste takes on a rust color, about 2 minutes. Pour in the beer and chicken stock or broth and continue whisking until smooth. Let the sauce come to a boil over medium-high heat, then reduce the heat to medium-low. Add the cinnamon stick and season the sauce with salt to taste. Simmer gently to blend the flavors, 5 to 7 minutes.

6 Add the meatballs to the sauce and let simmer, covered, over very low heat until plumped and heated through, about 20 minutes. Serve the meatballs hot with toothpicks as an appetizer or serve them as an main course spooned over polenta or rice pilaf.

Farmstand Fever

"When you no longer care about fresh tomatoes and sweet corn, then death is near."— Garrison Keillor

When I attended my twenty-fifth college reunion at Harvard slightly over a decade ago, a silhouette of John Harvard dancing like John Travolta in his *Saturday Night Fever* role was chosen as the memory lane logo for our class. Since I had been more into Descartes than disco during my years at Harvard, I cannot honestly say I was thrilled by all the reunion paraphernalia I received emblazoned with disco embroidery. Yet, because one tends never to leave Harvard without learning one enduring lesson or another, I felt I departed Cambridge that June weekend with a valuable sense of what it means to embrace something at fever pitch. Hence the name of this hefty chapter, which has nothing to do with disco or Descartes.

I am not a vegetarian nor can I imagine ever becoming one. However, seasonal vegetables are what drive my passion for cooking in New England more than any other factor. Zucchini jokes don't offend me; brussels sprouts captivate me; there's no such thing as too many vine-ripened tomatoes; and yes, at one point I did take two days away from my computer in order to dig asparagus trenches in my backyard garden rather than write asparagus recipes for this chapter.

In New England we have been honoring that which springs from our soil ever since the Pilgrims orchestrated their first Thanksgiving in Plymouth, Massachusetts, not far from my Cape Cod home. Over the period of time I have been working on this cookbook I have borne witness to an exciting resurgence and pride in local farming, whether my travels take me just down the road to the Cape Cod Organic Farm or to the far reaches of Cape Rosier, Maine, to visit Eliot Coleman and Barbara Damrosh's Four Season Farm. In the end the bounty of recipes in this lengthy chapter merely begins to capture the highly contagious farmstand fever in which I and so many other like-minded New Englanders are reveling.

Grilled Baby Artichokes

For a long time all the artichokes I purchased and cooked came from California. Then, one summer I happened upon some locally grown artichokes at a vegetable stand out in the Hamptons on Long Island. The artichokes were tender baby ones and I bought a large bag of them. Once home, I steamed the artichokes, adding a little splash of Pernod to the cooking water. When the artichokes were crisp-tender I cut them in half, drizzled them with olive oil and lemon juice, and then grilled them over a hot hardwood charcoal fire. The artichokes tasted sensational. Still, I reasoned a recipe such as this was not appropriate for a New England cookbook because technically the artichokes had been grown close to New England but not in New England. I quickly changed my mind when I had the good luck of happening upon some locally grown baby artichokes at my very favorite farm stand in New England and perhaps the world—Chase's Daily in Belfast, Maine. SERVES 4 TO 6

16 baby artichokes, stems trimmed so the artichokes can sit upright and pointy outer leaves snipped straight

1½ tablespoons Pernod

½ cup extra virgin olive oil, plus oil for the grill grate

⅓ cup freshly squeezed lemon juice

1 teaspoon finely grated lemon zest

2 cloves garlic, peeled and finely minced or grated on a Microplane

Sea salt and freshly ground black pepper

Bagna Cauda (optional; recipe follows), for serving

1 Place a large steamer basket in a large pot. Arrange the baby artichokes upright in the steamer basket. Add enough water to the pot to come to just below the base of the steamer basket. Pour in the Pernod (the Pernod infuses the artichokes with a subtle but lovely hint of anise as they steam).

2 Cover the pot and let the water come to a boil over medium-high heat. Steam the artichokes until crisp-tender or just slightly undercooked, 6 to 8 minutes. Remove the artichokes from the pot. When cool enough to handle, slice each artichoke in half from top to bottom. Place the artichokes in a large mixing bowl and toss them with the olive oil, lemon juice, lemon zest, and garlic. Season the artichokes generously with salt and pepper and toss to mix well. Let the artichokes marinate at room temperature for at least 30 minutes and up to 1 hour.

3 Set up a charcoal grill and preheat it to medium-high. (You can use a gas grill but hardwood charcoal imparts a much better flavor.)

4 When ready to cook, oil the grill grate. Place the artichokes on the grate 5 to 6 inches above the coals. You can also place the artichokes in a grilling basket if you are worried about the artichokes falling through the bars of the grate into the fire. Turn the artichokes over once and grill each side until the leaves begin to char, blister, and crisp in random spots, 3 to 5 minutes per side. Serve the artichokes hot off the grill with the warm Bagna Cauda drizzled on top, if desired.

Bagna Cauda

Most of the time I serve artichokes hot off the grill as a vegetable accompaniment to our dinner. If I happen to have some homemade mayonnaise (page 129) or aioli (page 132) on hand, I'll offer that as a dip for the leaves but the artichokes do taste perfectly wonderful without further adornment. Once in a while, I'll drizzle the grilled artichokes with *bagna cauda*—a warm and garlicky Italian anchovy sauce that elevates tender and chokeless New

England–grown baby artichokes into the strato-sphere. ABOUT 1½ CUPS

12 oil-packed anchovy fillets, drained and
    coarsely chopped

6 cloves garlic, peeled and coarsely chopped

8 tablespoons (1 stick) unsalted butter,
    at room temperature

¾ cup extra virgin olive oil

⅓ cup heavy (whipping) cream (optional)

2 tablespoons minced fresh flat-leaf parsley

PLACE THE ANCHOVIES and garlic in a blender or mini food processor and process to a coarse paste. Add the butter and olive oil and process until evenly combined. Transfer the anchovy mixture to a saucepan and cook over low heat, stirring occa-sionally, until the flavors blend, about 15 minutes. The sauce may separate from time to time but will come back together when stirred. Add the cream, if using (the cream makes for a silkier sauce). Keep the sauce warm over very low heat until ready to use. The sauce can also be made to this point up to 3 days ahead, refrigerated covered, and reheated gently over low heat until warm to the touch, 5 to 7 minutes. Stir in the parsley just before serving.

Asparagus Gratinée

I love asparagus and have recently become an avid convert to eating locally grown New England asparagus nonstop during its late spring season. My aunt has been growing asparagus in Sandwich on Cape Cod for the past few years and after being invited over to pick my own asparagus directly from her garden, I became so envious that I went home and spent several backbreaking days dig-ging my own asparagus trenches in our backyard. When I'm lucky enough to have superfresh seasonal asparagus, I usually cook it very simply, placed in a skillet, covered with water, and boiled until crisp-tender. I coat the hot spears with butter or good olive oil and a squeeze of lemon, then season with sea salt and freshly ground pepper and sometimes top everything off with freshly grated Parmesan cheese.

I am also very fond of the dated but classic pair-ing of asparagus with hollandaise sauce, although I am not one to make hollandaise terribly often. When I'm in the market for an indulgent aspara-gus preparation that doesn't require much fussing, I make this Asparagus Gratinée and when I really want to splurge I substitute white truffle butter for the unsalted butter. SERVES 6 TO 8

2 pounds medium-thick fresh asparagus

2½ to 3 tablespoons unsalted butter or white
    truffle butter, at room temperature

Sea salt and freshly ground black pepper

2 ounces freshly grated Parmigiano-Reggiano
    cheese (about ¾ cup)

1 Cut or break off and discard the woody ends of the asparagus. Peel the bottom 2 inches of each stalk with a vegetable peeler. Place the asparagus in a sin-gle layer, if possible, in a large, shallow skillet and add water to cover. Bring to a boil and cook until the asparagus is al dente, 3 to 5 minutes.

2 Using tongs, remove the asparagus spears from the skillet, shaking off the excess water, and place them in a single layer in a large glass or ceramic gratin dish. Immediately toss the asparagus with the butter so it melts and coats the spears evenly. Season the aspar-agus with salt and pepper to taste and scatter the Parmigiano-Reggiano cheese over the top. You can prepare the recipe to this point up to 1 hour ahead of serving.

3 When ready to serve, preheat the oven to 450°F.

4 Bake the asparagus until the cheese has melted and is beginning to brown, about 5 minutes. Serve the asparagus at once.

Our Best Pizza Oven Pizza with Shaved Asparagus and Prosciutto

When we built a kitchen addition onto our home on Cape Cod my husband and I agreed that we wanted a Tuscan-style wood-burning oven to be the focal point. If I had it to do over again I would have had the oven installed outside because carting splits of wood through the kitchen is extremely messy and the 750°F temperature the oven reaches does little for my current "always hot" stage of life. We strive to make everything we cook in this domed oven memorable and worth all the trouble it takes to get the fire burning properly for roasting and/or sufficiently blazing hot enough to cook a pizza quickly in true Neapolitan fashion. Over the years, we have gone from hosting kid-friendly family pizza nights with everyone taking turns making a personal pizza to refining our pizza skills, with help and inspiration from Jim Lahey's cookbook *My Pizza: The Easy No-Knead Way to Make Spectacular Pizza at Home*, to achieving perfection in this unusual but totally irresistible white-sauce pizza topped with shaved asparagus, prosciutto, mozzarella, fried eggs, and fresh basil. You need not have a wood-burning oven to make this pizza successfully, as Jim Lahey's high temperature method using a pizza stone in a conventional oven works like a charm.

I like to make the pizza dough for this sophisticated pizza from scratch using a combination of specialty flours from the Vermont-based King Arthur Flour Company (these are available by mail order). However, if there's a good pizzeria in your town and you are able to talk them into selling you some of their dough, by all means feel free to go for it. An acceptable dough may also be made from scratch using only the King Arthur bread flour, commonly sold in many supermarkets. MAKES FOUR 10-TO-12-INCH PIZZAS

For the pizza dough

½ teaspoon active dry yeast

2 cups King Arthur Italian-style flour

About 3 cups King Arthur organic high-gluten flour

1½ teaspoons fine sea salt

1½ cups lukewarm water (100° to 110°F)

For the pizzas

12 thick asparagus spears, woody ends cut or broken off and discarded

6 ounces fresh mozzarella, sliced into thin rounds

4 to 5 ounces thinly sliced prosciutto, cut or ripped by hand into thin shreds

3 to 4 ounces thinly shaved Parmigiano-Reggiano cheese

8 large fresh eggs, preferably local organic ones

4 tablespoons slivered fresh basil leaves

Buttery Béchamel Sauce (recipe follows)

Cornmeal (optional)

1 **Make the pizza dough:** Early in the day combine the yeast, Italian-style flour, 2 cups of the high-gluten flour, and salt in a medium-size mixing bowl and stir to combine evenly. Add the water and continue mixing with a wooden spoon or your hands until the dough forms a sticky mass. Work in ¼ to ½ cup of the remaining high-gluten flour to make the dough less sticky to the point it pulls away from the side of the bowl and is smooth and satiny. Cover the dough with plastic wrap and let it rise at room temperature for at least 6 hours or up to 10 hours.

2 **Make the pizzas:** Position an oven rack 8 inches beneath the oven's broiler element. Place a 14-to-16-inch rectangular pizza stone that is at least ½ inch

thick on the rack and preheat the oven to 500°F and for a total of 30 minutes. If you do happen to have a wood-burning pizza oven, the pizza stone will not be needed but the wood in oven should burn long enough and hot enough so that the temperature is close to 750°F next to the flames.

3   Meanwhile, prepare the topping ingredients so everything can be quickly assembled after rolling out the pizza dough. Using a vegetable peeler, shave each asparagus spear lengthwise to make as many thin ribbons as possible and pile the ribbons into a shallow dish. Have the mozzarella rounds, prosciutto, Parmigiano-Reggiano, eggs, basil, and béchamel sauce ready to go.

4   Dust a large clean work surface with some of the remaining high-gluten flour. Punch down the pizza dough and turn it out onto the work surface. Divide the dough into 4 equal portions and shape each into a plump, bunlike round, sprinkling it with a bit more flour if needed to prevent sticking.

5   Crank the oven temperature up to broil for the last 10 minutes of preheating while you are rolling out and assembling the pizzas. Working with 1 round of dough at a time, roll it into a thin circle, 10 to 12 inches in diameter. If you feel confident and adept, you can lift the dough off the work surface and stretch it into a circular shape with your hands. Otherwise, I find using a heavy marble rolling pin works well. Transfer the dough to a well-floured pizza peel, if you have one. Otherwise, a large flat baking sheet without sides will do the trick. Just be sure to flour it or even dust with cornmeal to prevent sticking.

6   Spread ⅓ cup of the béchamel sauce evenly over the pizza dough, leaving about a ¾-inch rim on the outer edge bare. Scatter one quarter of the mozzarella rounds evenly over the pizza followed by one quarter of the asparagus ribbons and one quarter of the shredded prosciutto. Top off the pizza with one quarter of the Parmesan shavings. Slide the assembled pizza onto the piping hot pizza stone and cook it underneath the broiler for 2 minutes. Carefully slide out the pizza, crack 2 eggs, 1 on each half of the pizza,

taking care to keep the yolks intact. Continue broiling the pizza until the cheese is bubbling, the crust is impressively charred but not burnt, and the egg whites are set and the yolks are still semi-runny, 1 to 1½ minutes. Transfer the pizza to a serving platter and sprinkle 1 tablespoon of the slivered basil over it. Cut the pizza into 4 wedges, with each portion getting some runny yolk.

7   Repeat the process until all 4 of the pizzas have been assembled and cooked. It is easier to share each pizza as it emerges from the oven, rather than to try and serve each person an individual pizza. I am not usually a person who puts an egg on top of things, but the eggs truly work well on top of these fabulous pizzas. Omit them only if you must.

Buttery Béchamel Sauce

The béchamel sauce may be held at room temperature for up to 3 hours. Any extra sauce can be refrigerated, covered, for at least 5 days. MAKES ABOUT 2 CUPS

7 tablespoons unsalted butter

3½ tablespoons unbleached all-purpose flour

2 cups whole milk, at room temperature

Generous pinch of freshly grated nutmeg

Pinch of cayenne pepper

Fine sea salt and freshly ground white pepper

MELT THE BUTTER in a small saucepan over medium heat. Whisk in the flour and continue whisking constantly until well blended, about 2 minutes. Gradually pour in the milk, still whisking constantly, until all of the milk has been added and the béchamel sauce is thickened and smooth, 3 to 4 minutes. Reduce the heat to low and season the sauce with the nutmeg, cayenne pepper, and salt and white pepper to taste. Let the sauce cook, stirring occasionally, until the flavors mellow, 15 to 20 minutes.

At the Silo Cooking School in Connecticut, participants gather around a farmhouse table to savor the recipes prepared in class by both local and nationally known cookbook authors and chefs.

Roasted Broccolini and Baby Green Beans

I taught my first cooking class ever in life at Ruth Henderson's Silo cooking school at Hunt Hill Farm in New Milford, Connecticut. I have returned many times over the years both as a teacher and a guest and I never fail to learn something new on each and every visit to this beautiful rural farm. During one visit on a crisp autumn afternoon I was walking with Ruth by the cooking school's kitchen at the end of a class given by Susan Deborah Goldsmith, a longtime food editor for *Good Housekeeping* magazine. Susan's food smelled irresistible and was quite plentiful so Ruth and I decided to sit down with the class and enjoy an impromptu late lunch. I'm thrilled I did because Goldsmith's side dish vegetable recipe for roasted broccolini and baby green beans has been in regular rotation at my house ever since. Next time you don't know what to serve for a green vegetable try this adaptation and you won't

be disappointed. Sometimes when I am serving the preparation hot from the oven, I'll dust the roasted vegetables with a little freshly grated Parmesan. Other times, when I opt to serve the vegetables at room temperature, I'll scatter a few coarsely slivered pitted black olives over the top and add a squeeze of fresh lemon juice. SERVES 6

2 bunches (12 to 14 ounces each) broccolini, thicker lower stems trimmed off (about the bottom 2 inches)

1 pound thin green beans, often sold as haricots verts, stem ends trimmed, tails left intact

3 to 4 tablespoons extra virgin olive oil

¼ teaspoon hot red pepper flakes

Sea salt and freshly ground black pepper

1 Preheat the oven to 425°F.

2 Place the broccolini and green beans in a large mixing bowl. Add the olive oil and red pepper flakes, season with salt and black pepper to taste, and toss to coat evenly. Spread the vegetables out on a large rimmed baking sheet or shallow roasting pan. Bake the vegetables, stirring them 2 or 3 times, until they are tender and blistered brown in random spots, 20 to 25 minutes. Serve the vegetables hot, warm, or at room temperature.

Braised Broccoli Rabe

Often during the winter months when I was growing up in Connecticut, my mother would serve us frozen vegetables when there wasn't much else available. These days, when I find myself in a similar predicament, I'll cook fresh broccoli rabe and I'm sure my mother would have done the same had broccoli rabe been as easy to come by in markets as it is today. Perhaps we have Rhode Island's large Italian population to thank for helping broccoli

rabe become so much more mainstream. After all, author Linda Beaulieu noted in *The Providence & Rhode Island Cookbook*: "Without a doubt, broccoli rabe is a favorite vegetable in Rhode Island. It is often served on the side, affectionately known as an order of 'rabes' (pronounced rob-bees)."

My husband and I like broccoli rabe cooked in this traditional Italian manner so much that we eat it almost year-round. SERVES 3 OR 4

1 large bunch (1¼ to 1½ pounds) broccoli rabe

Sea salt

3 tablespoons extra virgin olive oil, plus a bit more for serving

4 cloves garlic, peeled and cut into thin slivers

¼ to ½ teaspoon hot red pepper flakes

2 tablespoons dry white or red wine (optional)

Freshly ground black pepper

1 Rinse the broccoli rabe and trim away the tough lower stems and any yellowed leaves. Bring a large pot of water to a boil, add salt and the broccoli rabe, and blanch it for about 3 minutes. Set aside ½ cup of the cooking water and then drain the broccoli rabe in a colander.

2 Heat the olive oil in a large skillet over medium heat. Add the garlic and hot red pepper flakes, using the larger amount if you want the broccoli rabe to be extra spicy, and cook until the garlic is fragrant but not browned, about 1 minute. Add the drained broccoli rabe and toss to coat with the olive oil and garlic. Add ¼ cup of the cooking water and the wine, if using. If you are not adding the wine, add 2 tablespoons more of the cooking water.

3 Reduce the heat to low, cover the skillet with a lid placed slightly ajar, and cook the broccoli rabe, stirring it occasionally, until tender, 10 to 12 minutes. Add a bit more of the cooking water if all the liquid has evaporated. Season the broccoli rabe with salt and black pepper to taste. Serve the broccoli rabe hot, warm, or at room temperature, drizzling a little olive oil over the top of each serving.

My Favorite Fall and Winter Brussels Sprouts

My doctor tells me every year when I go in for my annual physical that I have the highest "good cholesterol" he has even seen in a patient. Still, I can't currently quite bring myself to make what used to be my favorite brussels sprout recipe, which contains a cup and a half of heavy cream and a cup of light cream. So, here is my new favorite brussels sprout recipe that I make all fall and winter long. These brussels sprouts are often included in the extensive vegetable offerings in my family's Thanksgiving spread and they go with everything from chicken and salmon to roast pork and beefy grilled rib eye steaks. I vary the nuts and cheese in the recipe according to mood and menu. SERVES 4

12 ounces brussels sprouts, stems trimmed and any yellow outer leaves discarded, sprouts cut in half lengthwise

4 tablespoons extra virgin olive oil

Sea salt and freshly ground black pepper

1 tablespoon freshly squeezed lemon juice

⅓ cup coarsely chopped walnuts or pecans, toasted, or 2 tablespoons pine nuts, toasted (see Box, page 70)

1½ to 2 ounces Grana Padano, Parmigiano-Reggiano, Asiago, or Maine's Seal Cove Farm washed-rind "Olga" cheese, thinly shaved with a vegetable peeler

1 Preheat the oven to 425°F.

2 Place the brussels sprouts in a roasting pan just large enough to contain them in a single layer. Drizzle 2 ½ tablespoons of the olive oil over the brussels sprouts, season them with salt and pepper to taste, and toss well to coat.

3 Bake the brussels sprouts, stirring them once or twice, until some of the outer leaves have turned brown and crunchy and the centers of the brussels sprouts are tender when pierced with the tip of a paring knife, 20 to 25 minutes.

4 Remove the brussels sprouts from the oven and let them cool for 2 or 3 minutes. Toss the brussels sprouts with the remaining 1½ tablespoons of olive oil and the lemon juice and toasted nuts. Scatter the shaved cheese over the brussels sprouts and serve them hot or warm.

Uplands Glazed Carrots

My aunt, Diane Madden, has been serving these vibrant orange glazed carrots for as long as I can remember. Over the years, she has tweaked the recipe and this is the latest incarnation, which makes frequent appearances at the dinner gatherings she relishes in hosting at her lovely Cape Cod home, Uplands. SERVES 4 TO 6

4 tablespoons (½ stick) butter, preferably Kate's salted butter

8 to 10 large carrots, trimmed, peeled, and sliced ½ inch thick on a sharp diagonal

½ cup high-quality orange marmalade

Sea salt and freshly cracked black peppercorns

Finely grated zest of 1 orange

1 Melt the butter in a large skillet with a tight-fitting lid over medium heat. Add the carrots and stir to coat with the melted butter.

2 Cover the skillet, increase the heat to high, and cook the carrots, frequently shaking the pan back and forth, until they begin to blister, 3 to 4 minutes. Turn

off the heat and let the carrots stand, covered, for about 10 minutes.

3 Return the skillet to medium heat, stir in the marmalade, and cook, uncovered, stirring occasionally, until the carrots are crisp-tender and nicely glazed with the marmalade, 3 to 5 minutes. Season the carrots with salt and pepper to taste and sprinkle the orange zest over the top. Serve the carrots hot.

Chase's Daily Rainbow Carrots

The absolute prettiest and best-tasting carrots I have ever had are the rainbow carrots grown and sold by Chase's Daily in Belfast, Maine. The sublime flavor cries out for a simple preparation so I rely on the French method of waterless cooking. Try this recipe with the best locally grown carrots you can get your hands on. SERVES 4 TO 6

2 tablespoons (¼ stick) unsalted butter, or 2 tablespoons extra virgin olive oil

1 pound small, tender rainbow carrots (no more than ¾ inch in diameter and 5 to 6 inches long), scrubbed but not peeled, tops trimmed with the very tips of the green stems left intact

Sea salt and freshly ground black pepper

1½ tablespoons minced fresh flat-leaf parsley, chives, or dill

1 Melt the butter or heat the olive oil in a medium-size, straight-sided skillet over medium-low heat. Add the carrots and toss to coat with the butter or olive oil.

2 Cover the skillet with a tight-fitting lid and continue to cook over medium-low heat, shaking the pan

The recent craze for planting and growing pretty rainbow-colored carrots translates into a vegetable that brightens the plate as much as the palate.

2 pounds carrots, peeled and cut into ½-inch-thick slices

1½ pounds parsnips, peeled and cut into ½-inch-thick slices

3 to 5 tablespoons unsalted butter

Salt and freshly ground black pepper

1   Place the carrots in a large saucepan and add enough water to cover them by 4 inches. Let come to a boil over medium-high heat and let cook, 5 minutes. Add the parsnips and continue cooking at a low boil until both vegetables are tender, about 15 minutes. Remove from the heat and drain.

2   Return the vegetables to the pot, add 3 tablespoons of the butter, salt to taste, and lots of freshly ground pepper. Using a hand masher, mash the carrots and parsnips (no electric gadgets allowed) until the vegetables are mashed but not pureed. Add more butter if you feel like it. Serve the mash piping hot.

back and forth over the burner every now and again. The carrots are meant to cook by steaming slowly in their own moisture but not brown. Cook the carrots until they are crisp-tender, 15 to 20 minutes.

3   Season the carrots with salt and pepper to taste and then sprinkle the herb of your choice over them, tossing to coat evenly. Serve the carrots hot.

Mick's Mash

Mick Lahart is the Irish father of my son's best friend and the cook in their Irish/Polish family. The year we all celebrated Thanksgiving together at our house, Mick offered to make his favorite Irish mash—a recipe handed down in his family from his grandmother who may have gotten it from her grandmother. We were all so immediately smitten with the mash that we begged to have it handed down to us, too. SERVES 6 TO 8

Cauliflower Gratin with Vermont Cheddar

Whereas some people crave chocolate, I crave cauliflower. I have no idea why this is but I do know I make a cauliflower gratin for dinner at least once a month. I used to assemble the recipe in a French manner with finely shredded Gruyère cheese, but once I started working on this cookbook and had a refrigerator stocked with favorite Vermont ingredients, I switched out the Gruyère for extra-sharp Vermont cheddar and decided to introduce little bits of smoked Vermont ham into the mix. The gratin is decadently rich because mascarpone cheese is what binds everything together. I usually accompany this gratin with a simple green salad and a glass of good white wine. SERVES 4 AS A MAIN DISH OR 6 TO 8 AS A SIDE DISH

1 large head cauliflower, trimmed and broken into bite-size florets

12 to 16 ounces (1½ to 2 cups) mascarpone cheese, or more as needed, preferably from Vermont Creamery

4 ounces thinly sliced smoked ham, preferably from a Vermont smokehouse, cut into small ½-inch-long shards (optional)

¼ teaspoon freshly grated nutmeg

¼ teaspoon cayenne pepper or ground chipotle pepper

Sea salt and freshly ground white pepper

5 ounces aged extra-sharp Vermont cheddar cheese, freshly shredded (1½ cups)

1 teaspoon sweet paprika

1 Preheat the oven to 375°F.

2 Place a steamer basket in a medium-size pot and add enough water to come to just below the base of the steamer basket. Add the cauliflower florets, cover the pot, and let the water come to a boil over medium-high heat. Let the florets steam until almost tender, 5 to 7 minutes. Drain the cauliflower well.

3 Place the florets in a 1½- to 2-quart shallow baking dish. Add 1½ cups of the mascarpone, the ham, if using, and the nutmeg and cayenne or chipotle pepper. Season with salt and white pepper to taste. Use a flexible spatula to combine all the ingredients evenly. If the mixture seems to need additional binding and your conscience will allow it, add ¼ to ½ cup more mascarpone. Smooth the cauliflower mixture out in an even layer in the gratin dish. Scatter the cheddar evenly over the top and then dust the top with the paprika.

4 Bake the cauliflower gratin until it is bubbling irresistibly and golden brown on top, 40 to 45 minutes. Serve hot.

Cape Cod Corn Canoes

I created this sinfully rich and utterly delectable corn off the cob recipe fifteen years ago to accompany a Labor Day lobster bake my aunt and uncle were hosting at their Cape Cod home. Since I had just recently moved from Nantucket to Cape Cod, the recipe's alliterative name seemed like a natural. The "canoe" shape is fashioned from the corn husks, which house a colorful filling of corn kernels blended with sun-dried tomatoes, dried porcini mushrooms, and creamy mascarpone. The recipe's Labor Day debut seems apt, since making these canoes can indeed be a labor of love. Patience, however, will be rewarded as everyone who tastes these "canoes" begs for the recipe. I change the recipe a bit from time to time and will sometimes use lighter panko bread crumbs in place of the buttery and oh-so-New Englandy Ritz cracker crumbs. SERVES 8

12 sun-dried tomato halves

2 ounces dried porcini mushrooms

8 ears very fresh local corn, unhusked

4 tablespoons extra virgin olive oil

1 medium-size onion, peeled and minced

1 bunch scallions, trimmed, white and tender green parts minced

6 ounces (¾ cup) mascarpone cheese, preferably from Vermont Creamery

1½ cups freshly shredded Monterey Jack cheese

4 tablespoons slivered fresh basil

Sea salt and freshly ground black pepper

½ cup crushed Ritz crackers or panko bread crumbs

1 Place the sun-dried tomatoes and dried porcini mushrooms in 2 separate small saucepans. Add water to each pan to cover the sun-dried tomatoes and mushrooms by a couple of inches and let come just to a boil over medium-high heat. Reduce the heat to medium-low and let the tomatoes and mushrooms simmer until nicely plumped, about 10 minutes. Remove the pans from the heat and set them aside.

2 Pull off a strip of corn husk 1 to 1½ inches wide lengthwise from each ear of corn to expose a strip of kernels. Discard these strips of husk. Carefully peel back the remaining husks, keeping them attached to the stem ends of the cobs. Snap the stem ends off the cobs, making sure to keep the husks attached at that end. Remove and discard the corn silk clinging to the kernels and husks. Tear a thin strip from a tender inner portion of each husk and use it to tie the loose ends of that husk together to make a "canoe" shape. Arrange canoes on a large baking sheet.

3 Cut the corn kernels from the ears, discarding the cobs and setting the kernels aside. Drain the sun-dried tomatoes and porcini mushrooms, coarsely mince each, and set them aside.

4 Heat 3 tablespoons of the olive oil in a large skillet over medium heat. Add the onion and cook until softened, about 7 minutes. Add the scallions and cook until softened, about 3 minutes. Stir in the corn kernels, sun-dried tomatoes, and porcini mushrooms, and cook until the corn is crisp-tender, about 5 minutes, stirring occasionally. Remove the skillet from the heat.

5 Stir the mascarpone and Monterey Jack into the corn mixture, folding gently but thoroughly. Add the basil and season the filling with salt and pepper to taste. Spoon the filling carefully into the prepared husks, dividing it equally among them.

6 Combine the Ritz cracker crumbs or panko crumbs with the remaining 1 tablespoon of olive oil and sprinkle this mixture lightly over the top of each canoe. The corn canoes may be prepared to this point and refrigerated, loosely covered with plastic wrap, for up

to 12 hours before baking. Bring to room temperature before continuing with the recipe.

7 Preheat the oven to 375°F.

8 Bake the corn canoes until the husks are slightly charred and the filling is piping hot, 25 to 30 minutes. Serve the corn canoes hot.

Creamed Corn with Scallions and Buggy Whip Cheddar

A few summers ago, my brother, Jonathan, introduced me to Buggy Whip, a fabulously sharp cheddar cheese made in Maine. A little of this cheese goes a long way and I quickly learned that adding a mere ounce and half of it to creamed corn made for a most delicious creamed corn side dish. Once addicted, I subsequently discovered that Buggy Whip cheddar was hard to come by and began to fear that the makers may have gone out of business. After some sleuthing, I found out that Buggy Whip cheddar and several other cheese varieties are still being produced by Sonnental Dairy in Smyrna, Maine. The farm is part of an Amish community, hence the lack of advertising or website. Furthermore, I was told by a local Maine cheese store that Amish practices dictate that Sonnental can only take cheese orders over the phone for one hour each week. Consider yourself very lucky if you are able to score some Buggy Whip cheddar for this recipe. Otherwise, splurge on a wedge of Cabot Clothbound Cheddar from Vermont to produce creamed corn that runs a close second to the original Buggy Whip rendition. SERVES 4 TO 6

3 tablespoons unsalted butter

6 scallions, both white and tender green parts, trimmed and thinly sliced

Kernels from 5 ears very fresh local corn (2½ to 3 cups)

⅓ cup light or heavy (whipping) cream

1½ ounces very sharp and pungent cheddar, grated (scant ½ cup)

Sea salt and freshly ground black pepper

1   Melt the butter in a medium-size skillet over medium heat. Add the scallions and cook until just beginning to wilt, about 2 minutes. Add the corn kernels and continue to cook, stirring occasionally, until the corn is almost tender, 3 to 4 minutes.

2   Add the cream and cook until the corn is tender and the mixture lightly thickened, 2 to 3 minutes. Stir in the cheddar and continue cooking until the cheese has melted, about 1 minute. Season with salt and pepper to taste. Serve the creamed corn hot.

Embarrassingly Caloric Corn Pudding

The inspiration for this corn pudding comes from a Deen Brothers' recipe I ran in the weekly food column I write for Nantucket's *Inquirer and Mirror* newspaper. The time of the year was the middle of winter and my topic was "Caloric Consolation," a field in which both the brothers and their mother, Paula, excelled. The recipe was included in *The Deen Bros. Cookbook: Recipes From the Road*, where it was entitled Creamed Corn and Fried Onion Casserole. I was attracted to the recipe because Bobby and Jamie Deen claimed that the dish was "the one begged for at every potluck party" in the state of Texas. Furthermore, it contained only three ingredients: cream cheese, frozen corn, and a can of French's french fried onions.

My embarrassment quickly dissipated when one of Nantucket's foremost restaurateurs stopped me on the street and admitted to making the casserole for her family, who adored it! I mustered up the courage to try the recipe myself when I discovered that Trader Joe's carried interesting variations on the original ingredients, namely fire-roasted frozen corn and fried onions in a can labeled "gourmet fried onion pieces." I also substituted Vermont Creamery mascarpone for the cream cheese, certainly not to cut any calories but just because it made me feel better. So, here is my tweaked version of this embarrassingly rich but worth-it corn concoction. And yes, everyone does ask for the recipe, especially if it is being served on a bleak winter's night when summer's corn is a distant memory. 6 TO 8 VERY RICH SERVINGS

12 ounces (1½ cups) mascarpone, preferably from Vermont Creamery

1 bag (12 ounces; 1½ cups) frozen corn, fire-roasted if available, thawed

4 scallions, both white and tender green parts, trimmed and thinly sliced

⅓ cup minced fresh cilantro

Sea salt and freshly ground black pepper

1 to 1½ cups canned fried onions

1   Preheat the oven to 350°F.

2   Spread the mascarpone evenly over the bottom of a 1- to 1½-quart shallow baking or gratin dish.

3   Toss together the corn, scallions, and cilantro. Season with salt and pepper to taste. Spread the corn mixture evenly over the mascarpone, gently pressing the kernels into the mascarpone with the back of a spoon. Scatter the fried onions evenly over the top.

4   Bake the corn pudding until lightly browned and bubbly, 30 to 40 minutes. Serve hot.

Baby Eggplant, Tomato, and Cheese Gratin

Every time I make this superb vegetable gratin my husband says he would be happy eating just it for dinner, although I usually pair it with grilled lamb, beef, or chicken. While similar in flavor to eggplant Parmesan, the gratin is easier to make than the classic Italian eggplant "parm" and I think more visually attractive. I use (and now grow) the small, plump purple eggplants often labeled Italian eggplant and sometimes substitute Campari tomatoes for plum tomatoes. I also view the gratin as a great way to use up odds and ends of cheeses, with anything from creamy goat cheese to mozzarella and Manchego being fair game to layer under the tomatoes before the final flourish of grated Parmesan. The secret to the gratin's intoxicatingly intense flavor is its roasting in a hot oven, yielding lovely caramelization as well as crunch. SERVES 6 TO 8

4 plump baby Italian eggplants (about 6 ounces each), stems removed, eggplants cut in half lengthwise

½ cup extra virgin olive oil

Sea salt and freshly ground black pepper

2 tablespoons mixed, minced fresh herbs, such as rosemary, thyme, oregano, and parsley

8 large, whole fresh basil leaves

4 to 6 ounces good melting cheeses, such as goat cheese, mozzarella, or Manchego, either grated or crumbled into small pieces (1 to 1½ cups)

4 large, ripe plum tomatoes, cut in half lengthwise

2 ounces (heaping ½ cup) freshly grated Parmigiano-Reggiano cheese

1 Place a rack in the center of the oven and preheat the oven to 425°F.

2 Score the cut sides of the eggplant halves with a sharp paring knife in a ½-inch-deep crisscross pattern. Drizzle a bit of olive oil over the bottom of a 2-quart baking or gratin dish and arrange the eggplant halves, skin side down, snugly in the dish. Drizzle the eggplant halves with a couple more tablespoons of olive oil and then season them with salt and pepper to taste and the minced fresh herbs. Place a whole basil leaf in the center of each eggplant half and top them with the melting cheese or cheeses, dividing the cheese evenly among all the halves. Center the tomato halves, cut side down, on top of the cheese. Drizzle the rest of the olive oil evenly over the top.

3 Bake the gratin until the tomatoes are very soft and beginning to become richly caramelized, about 30 minutes. Reduce the heat to 375°F. Sprinkle the Parmigiano-Reggiano evenly over each eggplant half and return the gratin to the oven. Continue cooking until the Parmigiano-Reggiano is a crusty golden brown and the eggplants are very tender, 20 to 25 minutes. Let the gratin cool for at least 5 minutes, then serve it hot, warm, or at room temperature, allowing one eggplant half per person with the option of seconds for people like my husband.

Greek Eggplant Pudding

When I proudly transported the first crop of eggplant I had ever grown up to Maine to share with my family, my mother made this unusual and excellent pudding, based on a recipe she had clipped and saved some years ago. I could not wait to make the pudding again with the second crop of eggplant awaiting me in my garden when I returned home to Cape Cod. Never one to follow a recipe exactly or make something the same way every time, I decided to add a layer of tomatoes to the center of the pudding and am happy to pronounce this recipe a keeper any which way you choose to make it. Serve Greek Eggplant Pudding as a rich side dish to all manner of grilled fare or feature it on its own as a delicious vegetarian entrée. SERVES 6 TO 8 AS A SIDE DISH

2 medium-size eggplants, stems removed

Kosher salt

½ cup extra virgin olive oil, possibly a bit more

1 large onion, peeled and minced

4 cloves garlic, peeled and minced

6 large eggs

1½ cups crumbled feta cheese or creamy goat cheese

1½ teaspoons dried oregano, preferably Greek

Sea salt and freshly ground black pepper

2½ tablespoons coarsely slivered or torn fresh basil leaves

1 very large vine-ripened beefsteak tomato (optional), cored and cut into ⅓-inch-thick slices

1 Peel the eggplants and slice them into ⅓-inch-thick rounds. Layer the slices in a colander, sprinkling each layer with kosher salt. Place a weight such as a large can of beans or tomatoes on top and let stand in the sink for 45 minutes. Rinse the eggplant slices, drain them well, and dry them thoroughly with clean dish towels.

2 Preheat the oven to 375°F. Line 2 large baking sheets with parchment paper.

3 Arrange the eggplant slices on the prepared baking sheets and, using a pastry brush, brush the slices lightly all over with olive oil. Turn the slices over and brush the second sides lightly all over with some more of the olive oil. Bake the eggplant until tender, 35 to 45 minutes. Remove the eggplant from the oven but leave the oven on.

4 Meanwhile, heat the remaining olive oil (if there is not at least 2 tablespoons of olive oil, add enough more to measure 2 tablespoons) in a medium-size skillet, add the onion and garlic, and cook over medium heat until quite soft, 10 to 12 minutes.

5 Place the eggs in a medium-size mixing bowl and whisk them thoroughly. Stir in the cheese, oregano, and salt and pepper, to taste. Add the cooked onion and garlic and stir to mix.

6 Arrange one third of the cooked eggplant slices in a single layer in a 2-quart baking dish, such as a soufflé dish. Pour about one third of the egg mixture over the eggplant and scatter some of the basil on top. Repeat to make a second layer of eggplant, egg mixture, and basil, followed by the tomato, if using. Make a third layer with the remaining eggplant, egg mixture, and basil.

7 Bake the eggplant pudding until bubbling and set, 40 to 45 minutes. Serve it hot, warm, or at room temperature.

Baked Eggplant Puffs

As mentioned elsewhere in this book, my friend Toby Greenberg has legions of wonderful recipes she has been making for years in her Nantucket home. This eggplant recipe is but one of many memorable examples. Toby calls the recipe her easy "baked eggplant parmigiana," but I make a somewhat more elaborate flavored butter topping and my end result is more puffed than Parmesan-y. The same technique can also be applied to rounds of zucchini and summer squash, making the recipe one you will want to keep handy from midsummer through Indian summer.

Use either plump or skinny eggplants for the rounds: The fatter eggplants will yield impressive steaklike puffs and the thinner ones more diminutive coinlike puffs—both equally delicious. SERVES 4 TO 6

2 cloves garlic, peeled and coarsely chopped

2 tablespoons coarsely chopped fresh flat-leaf parsley, plus 1 tablespoon finely chopped parsley

1 tablespoon slivered fresh basil leaves

¼ cup freshly grated Parmigiano-Reggiano cheese

4 oil-packed sun-dried tomato halves, drained and coarsely chopped

5 tablespoons unsalted butter, at room temperature

1½ pounds eggplant, stems removed, eggplants cut into ¾-inch-thick rounds

3 to 4 tablespoons extra virgin olive oil

Sea salt and freshly ground black pepper

1 Preheat the oven to 400°F. Line 2 baking sheets with parchment paper.

2 Place the garlic, coarsely chopped parsley, basil, Parmigiano-Reggiano, and sun-dried tomatoes in a food processor. Pulse the machine on and off a few times to make a coarse paste. Add the butter and process until all the ingredients are evenly combined.

3 Arrange the eggplant slices on the prepared baking sheets. Brush the tops lightly all over with olive oil and season them generously with salt and pepper. Turn the eggplant slices over so the oiled sides are now facing down. Spread a layer of the flavored butter over the top of each eggplant slice and season it lightly with salt and pepper.

4 Bake the eggplant until tender and puffed to a light golden brown, 20 to 30 minutes, depending on the size of the rounds. Remove the puffs from the oven, sprinkle them with the finely chopped parsley, and serve hot or warm.

Growing eggplants doesn't seem to require much fuss and the harvest is alluringly purple and prolific, making the vegetable a summer staple in my cooking.

Frizzled String Beans

My son, Oliver, prefers to eat most of his vegetables raw, including string beans. However, I can entice him to eat cooked string beans when I frizzle them because the beans get very crispy and end up tasting almost as irresistible as french fries. In fact, I've yet to meet a kid who doesn't like these beans and the same goes for grown-ups, too.

For extra flavor, feel free to use an herb-infused sea salt blend in place of the plain sea salt. I often roast the string beans sprinkled with either the Mediterranean or Tuscan blend of sea salt from my husband's Coastal Goods line of seasonings. SERVES 6 TO 8

2 pounds garden-fresh string beans, stem ends trimmed

3 tablespoons extra virgin olive oil

Sea salt

1 Preheat the oven to 400°F.

2 Place the string beans in a roasting pan large enough to contain them in a slightly overlapping single layer (they'll shrink down to a single layer as they cook). Drizzle the olive oil over the string beans and season them generously with salt. Toss the beans until they are evenly coated with both the olive oil and salt.

3 Bake the string beans, shaking the pan back and forth a few times as they cook, until the string beans have become patched with brown spots and crisp, 25 to 30 minutes. Serve the string beans piping hot or warm.

Bacon Bundled Green Beans

This is my go-to recipe when I am asked to bring a green vegetable side dish to family gatherings. It works surprisingly well with Thanksgiving, Christmas, and even Easter menus. While green beans may not at first sound very exciting, once you bundle them into adorable individual servings secured by a strip of smoky bacon, everyone swoons over the presentation as well as the terrific flavor—grown-ups and children alike. Additionally, the recipe may be made a day in advance if desired. In other words, these bacon-bundled green beans can be a dream recipe for anyone designated with potluck vegetable duties at holiday time. SERVES 8 TO 10

12 ounces thinly sliced hardwood or cob-smoked New England bacon

Sea salt

1 pound tender green string beans, tail and stem ends trimmed

6 tablespoons (¾ stick) unsalted butter

1 clove garlic, peeled and grated on a Microplane or very finely minced

3 tablespoons pure maple syrup

1½ tablespoons freshly squeezed orange juice

1½ to 2 tablespoons soy sauce

1 teaspoon Worcestershire sauce

Freshly ground black pepper

1 Preheat the oven to 375°F. Line a baking sheet with parchment paper.

2 Arrange the slices of bacon on the prepared baking sheet. Bake the bacon until it is just beginning to brown but is not yet crispy, 12 to 15 minutes. Transfer the bacon to a paper towel-lined plate to drain. If you are serving the green beans after assembling the bundles, leave the oven on. Otherwise, turn it off.

3 While the bacon is cooking, bring a large pot of salted water to a boil. Add the green beans and blanch them until not quite crisp-tender, 2 to 3 minutes. Drain the beans, run them under cold tap water until cool, and then drain again. Pat the beans dry with a clean dish towel.

4 Gather the beans into groups of 10 to 12 beans and wrap a strip of bacon securely around the center of each grouping to make a bundle. Arrange the bundles with the ends of the bacon strip facing down, 1 to 1½ inches apart, in an attractive oven-to-table baking dish.

5 Melt the butter in a small saucepan over medium heat. Add the garlic and let cook until just fragrant, 30 to 45 seconds. Stir in the maple syrup, orange juice, 1½ tablespoons of soy sauce, and the Worcestershire sauce. Let the sauce come to a simmer, stir it, and let it bubble for 1 minute. Remove the sauce from the heat and taste it for seasoning, adding a few splashes of soy sauce if a saltier flavor is desired.

6 Brush or spoon the sauce generously over each green bean bundle. Grind some black pepper over the top of each bundle. The green bean bundles may be made up to this point and left to sit at room

temperature for up to 2 hours or stored, covered, in the refrigerator for as long as 24 hours. Let the green bean bundles return to room temperature before baking.

7 When ready to serve, bake the green bean bundles in a 375°F oven until the sauce is bubbling and the bacon is crispy, 15 to 20 minutes. Serve hot.

Parsnip *Brandade*

My brother, Jonathan, excels at making *brandade*—a rich French dish of pureed salt cod, garlic, and olive oil. I featured his recipe in my *Cold-Weather Cooking* cookbook. Now, I am pleased to share Jonathan's *brandade* innovation, using parsnips in place of the salt cod along with fresh goat cheese from Seal Cove Farm in neighboring Lamoine, Maine. While *brandade* is most often served as a hot appetizer spread on toast rounds, I like to feature this parsnip variation in place of mashed potatoes as an unusual winter accompaniment to roasts and steaks. SERVES 6 TO 8

1 medium-size head garlic

¼ cup plus 1 teaspoon extra virgin olive oil

1 pound parsnips, trimmed, peeled, and cut into 1-inch chunks

10 ounces creamy goat cheese, such as Seal Cove Farm's fresh chèvre, at room temperature

Sea salt

1 Preheat the oven to 375°F.

2 Cut off the top ¼ inch of the garlic head, taking care to leave all the cloves intact. Lightly rub the garlic all over with the 1 teaspoon of olive oil and place it in a small ovenproof dish. Roast until the garlic is very aromatic and the cloves are soft to the touch, 25 to 30 minutes. Take care not to let the garlic burn.

Remove the garlic from the oven and let it cool for a few minutes.

3 Meanwhile, place the parsnips in a saucepan and add enough water to cover by 1 inch. Let come to a boil over medium-high heat. Lightly salt the water, reduce the heat to medium, and let the parsnips simmer, uncovered, until very tender, 15 to 20 minutes.

4 Drain the parsnips and place them in a food processor. Separate the garlic cloves and squeeze the pulp from each clove into the food processor; discard the skins. Crumble the goat cheese into the food processor and pulse the machine several times to partially blend the ingredients.

5 With the machine running, slowly pour the remaining ¼ cup of olive oil through the feed tube and process until smooth, 10 to 15 seconds. Season the *brandade* with salt to taste and process again. At this point, the *brandade* may be refrigerated, covered, for up to 2 days. Let it return to room temperature before using.

6 When ready to serve, preheat the oven to 375°F.

7 Butter a single 1½-quart baking or gratin dish or 6 to 8 individual ramekins and fill with the *brandade*. Bake the *brandade* until the top just begins to blister brown, anywhere from 15 to 25 minutes, depending on the size of the dish or dishes. Serve the *brandade* hot.

Zee Peas

For years, we have spent the Fourth of July partaking in or simply watching the patriotic hometown parade that moves through our village of Barnstable. Now that our son is too old to ride his bicycle in the parade, or even to consider marching with our feisty and uncooperative Jack Russell Terrier, or muster the determination to

A very rare quiet and traffic-less moment on Nantucket's cobblestoned Main Street before the onslaught of the Fourth of July parade and other festivities.

3 tablespoons unsalted butter

4 scallions, both white and light green parts, trimmed and thinly sliced

1 cup shredded butter or Boston lettuce

2 cups freshly shelled peas

½ cup chicken or vegetable stock or broth, homemade or good-quality store-bought

Sea salt and freshly ground black pepper

1   Melt the butter in a saucepan over medium heat. Add the scallions and cook until softened, about 2 minutes. Stir in the shredded lettuce and cook until wilted, about 1 minute.

2   Add the peas and broth. Let come to an energetic simmer and continue cooking, uncovered, until the peas are crisp-tender, French, not British style, 5 to 7 minutes. Season the peas with salt and pepper to taste and serve hot.

wait in a long line of kids to climb a greased pole in an attempt to grab a stash of cash during the games that follow the parade, we are free to make more spontaneous plans. This is how we recently found ourselves on Nantucket surrounded by old friends, fireworks, lots of laughs and eating *Zee* Peas as part and parcel of a most memorable Fourth.

Our hosts were Marina and Michel Becaas. Michel is French and was once the chef at the island's renowned Opera House restaurant. We quickly gleaned that Michel runs the kitchen in his own Nantucket home as if he were still head chef and while I was allowed to shell the fresh garden peas I had contributed, there was no way I was going to be allowed to cook them. My husband, Nigel, had to kiss his British predisposition for mushy peas au revoir for no French cook would ever prepare them to a stage certain members in my family would consider tender. Nonetheless, Michel's method is how I have now taken to cooking fresh garden peas if it is Bastille Day or I am just in the memory lane mood for a chuckle. SERVES 4

Mascarpone Mashed Potatoes

This is the one dish that is always on my Thanksgiving menu, and often on my Christmas menu as well. While these may well be the best mashed potatoes I have ever tasted, they garner even more accolades because the recipe can be made ahead up to two days in advance of serving. At Thanksgiving, I like to use white potatoes grown in Maine, but at other times of the year I opt for the buttery color of Yukon Gold potatoes. Speaking of butter, substituting white truffle butter for the unsalted butter called for in the recipe makes for the ne plus ultra of mashed potatoes and is an option I confess has morphed into habit with me. SERVES 8 TO 10

3½ to 4 pounds all-purpose potatoes, peeled and cut into 2-inch chunks

4 tablespoons (½ stick) unsalted butter or white truffle butter, at room temperature

12 ounces (1½ cups) mascarpone cheese, preferably from Vermont Creamery, at room temperature

½ cup snipped fresh chives

Sea salt and freshly ground white or black pepper

1 cup freshly grated Parmesan cheese

1 teaspoon sweet paprika

Pinch of freshly ground nutmeg

1 Place a steamer basket in a large pot and add enough water to come to just below the base of the steamer basket. Add the potatoes, cover the pot, and let the water come to a boil over medium-high heat. Let the potatoes steam until very tender, 25 to 30 minutes.

2 Drain the potatoes well and transfer them to a large mixing bowl. Using a hand-held mixer beat the butter into the hot potatoes until melted and incorporated. Add the mascarpone and continue beating until the potatoes are thoroughly mashed and the entire mixture is smooth and fluffy, 1½ to 2 minutes. Fold in the chives and season the potatoes with salt and pepper to taste.

3 Transfer the mashed potatoes to a lightly buttered shallow 2-quart baking or gratin dish. Sprinkle the Parmesan cheese evenly over the top and then dust the potatoes lightly with the paprika and a sprinkle of freshly grated nutmeg. At this point, the potatoes may be covered with plastic wrap and refrigerated for up to 48 hours before baking. When ready to cook the mashed potatoes, let them come to room temperature.

4 Preheat the oven to 350°F.

5 Bake the mashed potatoes until puffed and golden brown on top, 40 to 45 minutes. Serve hot.

Crispy Potatoes with Garlic and Rosemary

I make this potato recipe more than any other because it is easy, delicious, and everyone in my family loves it. All sorts of potatoes can be used, running the gamut from Red Bliss and russet to Yukon Gold. However, I am most partial to making the recipe with fingerling and other small tender-skinned potatoes because, once quartered, their shapes are less uniform and more interesting than those that result from cutting larger potatoes into bite-size pieces. Soaking the potatoes in cold water before cooking removes much of the starch, allowing for better crisping in a minimal amount of fat. Most of the time, I sauté my potatoes in olive oil but every once in a while I'll use duck fat instead if I happen to have it on hand. SERVES 4

1 to 1¼ pounds fingerling or other small potatoes, scrubbed of any dirt, cut in half lengthwise and then crosswise to make 4 bite-size quarters per potato

1½ tablespoons extra virgin olive oil

8 to 12 whole cloves garlic, unpeeled

1 tablespoon coarsely chopped fresh rosemary

Sea salt and freshly ground black pepper

1 Place the quartered potatoes in a large bowl and fill it with cold water to cover. Let the potatoes stand for 2 minutes, then discard the water and fill the bowl again with fresh cold water. Let the potatoes stand for 5 minutes and then drain them in a colander, rinsing them one last time with more cold running water. Drain the potatoes again and then pat them as dry as possible with a clean cloth dish towel.

2 Heat the olive oil in a medium-size skillet over medium heat. Add the potatoes, garlic, and 2 teaspoons of the rosemary. Season the potatoes generously with salt and pepper and spread them out in a single layer

with most of the cut sides facing down. Cook the potatoes, resisting the temptation to stir them, until the undersides are golden, 6 to 8 minutes. Stir the potatoes to turn them, reduce the heat to medium-low, and continue cooking, stirring and turning occasionally, until the potatoes are browned and crisp all over, 20 to 25 minutes longer. The garlic cloves should also be tender so they may be squeezed from their skins if desired to further flavor the potatoes when served. The potatoes may be kept warm in the pan over very low heat for up to 30 minutes.

3 Sprinkle the potatoes with the remaining 1 teaspoon of rosemary just before serving. Serve the potatoes hot or warm, making sure there are a few garlic cloves in each serving.

Salt Potatoes

I first tasted a regional specialty called boiled salt potatoes at Lenny & Joe's Fish Tale, a no-frills but popular seafood restaurant with a couple of locations along the Connecticut shoreline. Although Salt Potatoes are usually associated with Syracuse, New York, having them for the first time at Lenny & Joe's Fish Tale made me realize that potatoes could make an excellent accompaniment to many New England seafood dishes.

When small red-skinned new potatoes are cooked simply in heavily salted water the salt causes the water to boil at a higher temperature, which in turn allows the starch in the potatoes to cook more thoroughly, and produce a creamier interior texture. At the same time the potato skins develop an attractive white crusting from the salt. Melted butter or olive oil, a sprinkling of fresh parsley or dill, and a grinding of black pepper suffice as finishing touches. SERVES 4 TO 6

6 cups water

¾ cup kosher salt

2 pounds small red-skinned potatoes (about 2 inches in diameter), scrubbed of any dirt

3 tablespoons unsalted butter or extra virgin olive oil

1½ tablespoons minced fresh parsley or dill

Freshly ground black pepper

1 Pour the water into a medium-size saucepan and swirl in the salt. Let come to a boil over medium-high heat and then add the potatoes. Reduce the heat to medium and let the potatoes cook at a gentle boil until tender, 20 to 25 minutes.

2 Drain the potatoes well in a colander. Return the potatoes to the saucepan over medium heat and add the butter, if using, tossing until melted. If using olive oil, toss the potatoes until they are evenly coated. Add the parsley or dill and season with pepper to taste. Toss the potatoes again and serve hot.

Sage Potatoes

In Italy, a popular hors d'oeuvre I adore is fried anchovies sandwiched between fresh sage leaves. At home, I can't seem to generate the same enthusiasm for this snack, so I have taken to sandwiching sage leaves from my herb garden between potato slices and then baking the slices to pretty and crispy irresistibility in a hot oven. It is a win-win for everyone as well as a much sought-after accompaniment for roast chicken or pork dinners. Better yet, replace the *frites* in the beloved steak/ *frites* combo with Sage Potatoes, and rest assured the choice will be a devoured one. SERVES 4 TO 6

The picture-perfect Dexter Grist Mill in Sandwich on Cape Cod was restored to working order and opened to the public as a historic attraction in 1962.

4 medium-size baking potatoes, peeled

8 to 10 tablespoons (1 to 1¼ sticks) unsalted butter, melted

14 to 18 whole fresh sage leaves

Fine sea salt and freshly ground black pepper

Garlic powder

1 Preheat the oven to 350°F. Line 2 large baking sheets with parchment paper.

2 Using either a mandoline or a sharp knife, slice the potatoes as thinly as possible, preferably slightly less than ⅛ inch thick. Match up the potato slices in pairs to make as many similarly sized sandwiches as possible; you should have between 14 and 18 sandwiches.

3 Arrange the bottom slices from each potato sandwich on the prepared baking sheets. Brush each slice lightly with some melted butter. Place a whole sage leaf in the center of each potato and then top it with the potato's sandwich mate, pressing them together gently. Lift up each sandwich and brush more melted butter on the outside of the potatoes. Season the sandwiches all over with a little salt, pepper, and garlic powder.

4 Bake the sandwiched potatoes until golden on both sides, about 15 to 20 minutes per side, turning them over halfway through the baking time. Serve the potatoes hot. The potatoes may be baked a few hours ahead and then placed back in a hot 350°F oven for a few minutes to reheat.

Easy Creamed Spinach

Almost everyone loves creamed spinach but not the labor of making it from scratch. Since I personally think of creamed spinach as the ultimate vegetable comfort food, I decided I needed to find a way to make the preparation less burdensome without sacrificing any flavor. Modesty aside, I am thrilled with the results of this recipe, which doesn't skimp on fresh spinach but cheats by using a garlic and herb flavored cheese to make the cream sauce. You can't go wrong using luscious French Boursin cheese to create the sauce. However, if you want to keep the recipe local and live where you can purchase Narragansett Creamery's version of Boursin—garlic and herb Angelito—by all means go for it. SERVES 4 TO 6

3 pounds fresh baby spinach, preferably organic

1½ tablespoons unsalted butter

1 bunch scallions, both white and tender green parts, trimmed and thinly sliced

1 package (5.2 ounces) garlic and fine herbs Boursin cheese, or ¾ cup other similar cheese

2 to 3 tablespoons light or heavy (whipping) cream

¼ teaspoon freshly grated nutmeg

Sea salt and freshly ground white or black pepper

1 Rinse the spinach under cold running water. Remove and discard any tough stems from the spinach and shake the leaves with tongs over a sink until only a few droplets of water remain clinging to the leaves. Set the spinach aside.

2 Melt the butter in a medium-size skillet with straight sides over medium heat. Add the scallions and cook until softened, 2 to 3 minutes. Crumble the Boursin cheese into small pieces and add them to the skillet. Reduce the heat to low and cook, stirring, until the cheese is melted and very smooth. Keep the cheese mixture warm over very low heat.

3 Place the spinach in a steamer basket and place it in a large pot filled with water to a depth of 2 inches. Cover the pot, place it over medium-high heat, and let the spinach steam until wilted, 2 to 3 minutes, shaking the pot from time to time. Using metal tongs and shaking off any excess liquid as you work, transfer the wilted spinach to a food processor. Pulse the machine on and off several times to chop the spinach and make a coarse puree.

4 Add the chopped spinach to the cheese mixture in the skillet, stirring to coat it evenly. Increase the heat to medium and cook the spinach mixture until it is heated through, 4 to 5 minutes. Add enough cream to thin the creamed spinach slightly. Add the nutmeg and season the creamed spinach with salt and pepper to taste. Serve the creamed spinach hot.

Really Rich Polenta with Butternut Squash and Cheddar

There are picturesque grist mills scattered throughout New England and the one closest to my home is Dexter's in Sandwich on Cape Cod.

Stone-ground cornmeal makes superior polenta and this rich concoction is inspired by a recipe for grits that appeared in a Vermont cookbook aptly name *The Mist Grill*. While the Mist Grill no longer exists as a restaurant, having been replaced by the equally fabulous Hen of the Wood, the former restaurant cookbook is one of my favorites. It is here that owner Stephen Schimoler tells his story of stumbling across an abandoned two-hundred-year-old building perched at the edge of a waterfall in Waterbury, Vermont. Schimoler had mistakenly read the sign on the building as "Mist Grill" rather than "Grist Mill," and the dyslexic lapse led to his turning the building into the rustic bistro of his dreams.

In the Mist Grill cookbook, Schimoler had described his Aged Cheddar and Heavy Cream Grits as "the consummate rustic, country side dish for many of our main dishes." I don't cut back on any of the calories in this heavenly recipe but I do use stone ground cornmeal in place of the quick grits Schimoler had called for and further enliven the color and flavor of the polenta with a fresh puree of butternut squash. SERVES 6 TO 8

3 cups peeled and cubed butternut squash (about 1 pound)

2 cups heavy (whipping) cream

3 cups 2 percent or whole milk, divided

1 cup yellow stone ground cornmeal

Salt and freshly ground black pepper

6 ounces extra-sharp Vermont cheddar cheese, shredded on a box grater (about 2 cups)

5 scallions, both white and light green parts, trimmed and thinly sliced

1 Place a steamer basket in a medium-size pot and add enough water to come to just below the base of the steamer. Add the butternut squash, cover the pot, and let the water come to a boil over medium-high heat. Let the squash steam until it is very tender, about 15 minutes. Drain the squash and let it cool for about 5 minutes. Transfer the squash to a food

processor and process to make a smooth puree. Set the squash puree aside.

2   Place the cream and 2 cups of the milk in a Dutch oven or other large, heavy pot and let come to a boil over medium-high heat. Reduce the heat to medium and slowly pour the cornmeal into the hot liquid, whisking constantly until all the cornmeal has been absorbed and the mixture is smooth.

3   Reduce the heat to low and cook the polenta about 50 minutes, giving it a good stir with a wooden spoon every 10 minutes or so. The polenta should have the consistency of firm mashed potatoes and you'll need to add most or all of the remaining 1 cup of milk to the mixture in ¼ cup increments to maintain the consistency. Stir in the butternut squash puree and continue cooking and stirring the mixture until the squash is thoroughly incorporated and hot. Season the polenta with salt and pepper to taste.

4   Add the cheddar and stir until melted. Fold in most of the scallions reserving a few to sprinkle over the top of each serving. Serve the polenta hot, mounded as a side onto dinner plates. Top each serving of polenta with a few sliced scallions.

Roasted Acorn Squash with Blue Cheese and Sage

While I am an avid collector of anything with an acorn theme, I had never really warmed up to acorn squash preparations until I discovered this enticing savory, rather than sweet, method of cooking the squash. SERVES 6

2 medium-size acorn squashes

⅓ cup extra virgin olive oil

Sea salt and freshly ground black pepper

5 ounces creamy blue cheese, coarsely crumbled (about 1 cup)

8 large fresh sage leaves, coarsely slivered

1   Preheat the oven to 400°F.

2   Cut each squash lengthwise in half and scoop out the seeds. Cut each half into 3 crescent wedges and then arrange all 12 wedges in a roasting pan or baking dish just large enough to contain them in a single layer. Drizzle the olive oil evenly over the squash wedges and season them with salt and pepper to taste. Scatter some of the crumbled blue cheese and slivered sage into the hollow of each wedge.

3   Roast the acorn squash until the edges of the wedges are caramelized, the flesh is tender, and the blue cheese is very melted, 50 minutes to 1 hour. Serve the acorn squash hot.

Caramelized Tomatoes

When I first started going to Nantucket in the 1970s, there was a restaurant known for serving great grilled lamb chops with a baked tomato half—whether it was the height of summer or the dead of winter. Even though the tomatoes were pretty pathetic tasting during the winter, I have always liked the idea of serving tomato halves as an accompaniment to grilled fare and this is my updated version. Because we now have better quality tomatoes available year-round and the tomato's flavor ends up being heightened by caramelization, I do sometimes make this dish in the winter, but the recipe is always best when made with locally grown, vine-ripened tomatoes in season. SERVES 6

¼ cup extra virgin olive oil

6 firm but ripe, medium-size tomatoes,
  cut in half crosswise

Sea salt and freshly ground black pepper

2 teaspoons minced fresh rosemary or oregano

2 tablespoons finely slivered fresh basil leaves

¾ cup freshly grated Parmesan or Asiago
  cheese

1 Preheat the oven to 375°F.

2 Heat the olive oil in a large skillet over medium-high heat. When quite hot, place the tomatoes in the skillet, cut side down. Sear the tomatoes without turning or moving them until the cut surfaces are caramelized and blistered brown, 5 to 6 minutes. Carefully transfer the tomatoes to a baking dish, arranging them seared sides facing up in a snug single layer.

3 Season the tomatoes generously with salt and pepper. Toss the rosemary or oregano, basil, and grated cheese together in a small bowl and then sprinkle the mixture evenly over the tomato halves. Drizzle any cooking juices remaining in the skillet over the top of the tomatoes.

4 Bake the tomatoes, uncovered, until they are hot and the cheese is crusted a light brown, 20 to 30 minutes. Serve the tomatoes hot, warm, or at room temperature, allowing 2 halves per person.

Fresh Tomato Butter Sauce

For many years Giuliano Hazan's *The Classic Pasta Cookbook* has been one of my most reliable sources for all things pasta. One summer I decided to play around with a tomato sauce recipe Hazan had referred to as "the simplest of all pasta sauces"

and one that would "evoke childhood memories for many an Italian." What immediately struck me as unusual about this recipe was that it used butter rather than olive oil, but once I tasted the sauce I wondered no more. The sauce proved to be a true epiphany in my many years of experimenting with a vast variety of different fresh tomato sauce recipes.

Hazan also cautioned to use fresh tomatoes, if you can, but that good canned tomatoes were a far better choice than poor fresh ones. I have discovered that I like the combination of both good fresh tomatoes and good canned ones when I make this sauce in the summer months, and I tend not to go through the fuss of peeling my fresh tomatoes. I also prefer not to discard the onion halves Hazan called for in his original recipe and instead use chopped onions as a base for the sauce. Recently, I happened to read that Giuliano Hazan's tomato butter sauce recipe had become the most sought-after tomato sauce recipe on Google, a tidbit that amused me because I had been making the sauce from his book some years before Google was invented. The following is my version. It makes enough to feed a small crowd—perfect for summer entertaining. If you prefer to follow Giuliano Hazan's original recipe, I am sure you can Google it. MAKES ENOUGH SAUCE FOR 2 POUNDS OF PASTA; SERVES 8 TO 12

6 tablespoons (¾ stick) unsalted butter

1 medium-size onion, peeled and minced

1 can (28 ounces) best-quality crushed
  tomatoes, such as San Marzano

1 pound flavorful vine-ripened tomatoes,
  seeded and coarsely chopped

Sea salt and freshly ground black pepper

2 pounds fresh or dried pasta of your choice

Fresh basil leaves, for serving

Freshly grated Parmigiano-Reggiano cheese,
  for serving

1 Melt the butter in a large, straight-sided skillet over medium heat. Add the onion and cook until quite soft, 7 to 8 minutes. Stir in the canned crushed

tomatoes and fresh chopped tomatoes. Season the sauce with salt and pepper to taste and let simmer, uncovered, until the fresh tomatoes break down and blend into the canned tomatoes, 30 to 40 minutes, stirring occasionally. Taste for seasoning, adding more salt and/or pepper as needed. The sauce may be used immediately or can be refrigerated, covered, for 3 to 4 days. Reheat as needed.

2   When ready to serve, bring a large pot of water to a boil. Add salt and the pasta and cook according to the package directions until al dente. Drain the pasta well in a colander. Toss the cooked pasta with enough sauce to coat it generously and scatter a few fresh basil leaves and some Parmigiano-Reggiano over the top of each serving. Pass more Parmigiano-Reggiano at the table.

Summer Spaghetti Puttanesca

Pasta with the classic Italian puttanesca sauce never fails to delight me and is a dinner I enjoy at any time of the year. In the summertime, when I have an abundance of small varieties of cherry tomatoes growing in my garden and patio planters, I like to exercise a bit of poetic license and use the bounty to make this stylized, slow-roasted version of puttanesca sauce. While Italians would never dream of adding goat cheese to a puttanesca, for me the strong sauce flavors of olives, capers, and anchovies cry out for a bit of counterbalance in the form of a contrasting crumble of creamy goat cheese, such as the fresh goat cheese made by Vermont Creamery. SERVES 4

½ cup extra virgin olive oil

5 large cloves garlic, peeled and thinly sliced

½ teaspoon hot red pepper flakes

2 pounds cherry, grape, or other small tomatoes, cut in half

Sea salt

1½ teaspoons sugar

⅓ cup tomato juice or V8 juice

½ cup pitted kalamata olives, coarsely chopped

6 oil-packed anchovy fillets, drained and minced

1½ tablespoons brine-packed capers, drained

1 pound dried spaghetti

4 tablespoons slivered fresh basil leaves

2 tablespoons minced fresh flat-leaf parsley

4 ounces creamy white goat cheese, coarsely crumbled and at room temperature

1   Preheat the oven to 275°F.

2   Place the olive oil, garlic, and hot red pepper flakes in a small skillet over medium heat and cook just until the garlic is somewhat softened and aromatic, about 3 minutes. Remove the skillet from the heat.

3   Place the tomatoes in a nonreactive baking or gratin dish large enough to hold them snugly in a single layer. Toss the tomatoes with 1 teaspoon of salt and the sugar to coat the tomatoes lightly and evenly. Pour the warm olive oil mixture and tomato juice evenly over the tomatoes. Bake the tomatoes, stirring once or twice, until quite tender, about 2 hours. Stir in the olives, anchovies, and capers and bake until the flavors are blended, about 30 minutes.

4   Meanwhile, bring a large pot of water to a boil. Add salt and the spaghetti and cook according to package directions until al dente. Drain the spaghetti well in a colander. Stir the basil and parsley into the slow-roasted tomato mixture and then combine the mixture with the spaghetti in a large pot or bowl, tossing well. Divide the spaghetti puttanesca among 4 shallow, wide serving bowls and sprinkle some crumbled goat cheese over the top of each serving. Serve at once.

The Pitcher Inn
Turnip Gratin

This is the sort of rich and comforting gratin that makes you want to spend the entire day outside doing rigorous winter activities just so you can guiltlessly savor every delicious calorie while dining fireside at the pampering Pitcher Inn in Warren, Vermont. Chef Susan Schickler uses several of my favorite Vermont ingredients in her creation capturing the rural regional flavors of Vermont spectacularly. SERVES 6 TO 8

1 slab (8 ounces) smoked bacon, cut into lardons (1 inch long by ¼ inch wide)

1 medium-size white onion, peeled

4 purple top turnips, peeled

4 Yukon Gold potatoes (each 5 to 6 ounces), peeled

2 tablespoons (¼ stick) unsalted butter

Kosher salt

Aleppo pepper or other mildly hot red pepper flakes

6 ounces Cabot Clothbound Cheddar cheese, grated (about 2 cups)

2 cups heavy (whipping) cream

1 cup crème fraîche, preferably from Vermont Creamery

1 Preheat the oven to 350°F. Line a plate with paper towels.

2 Place the bacon lardons in a skillet over medium heat and cook until crispy, 7 to 8 minutes. Transfer the lardons to the prepared plate to drain.

3 Using a mandoline or by hand, slice the onion as thinly as possible. Cut the turnips and potatoes into ¼-inch-thick slices. Spread the butter over the bottom and sides of a large baking or gratin dish.

Assemble the gratin by making a bottom layer of the potato slices, arranging them in a slightly overlapping pattern. Season the layer with a sprinkling of salt, Aleppo pepper, and grated cheddar. Arrange a layer of turnips on top of the potatoes, seasoning it with salt, Aleppo pepper, and cheddar. Continue alternating layers of the potatoes and turnips, topping only 1 or 2 layers with a combination of the onion and lardons. Once all the ingredients have been layered, gently pour the cream over the dish.

4 Bake the gratin until the potatoes and turnips are tender when pierced with a toothpick, about 1 hour. Stir the crème fraîche to loosen it and spread it in a thin layer over the top of the gratin. Return the gratin to the oven and bake it until the top is lightly browned and bubbling, about 10 minutes. Let the gratin rest for 5 to 10 minutes before serving. Serve the gratin hot.

Eastham Turnip Puree

The Cape Cod town of Eastham is locally famous for its sweet white turnips. Not to be outdone by the neighboring village of Wellfleet and its popular OysterFest, Eastham stages its own turnip festival every November. Though I have never had the opportunity to attend this festival, I am an avid fan of Eastham white turnips, also sometimes called Cape white turnips. I decided the greatest way I could personally honor this local specialty was to prepare the turnips in the brilliant and butter-laden manner of Joël Robuchon's renowned potato puree. Aided and abetted by watching a video of Robuchon expound on the recipe during an Air France flight, I returned home from Paris and immediately went to work on making Eastham Turnips Puree in the style of Robuchon—a dish to savor when you are taking a break from cholesterol worries. 6 TO 8 VERY RICH SERVINGS

1 large white turnip (about 1 pound), peeled
   and cut into 1-inch chunks

1 very large white potato (about 1 pound),
   peeled and cut into 1-inch chunks

Fine sea salt

12 ounces (3 sticks) unsalted butter, chilled
   and cut into tablespoons

¼ cup milk or light cream (optional),
   at room temperature

Freshly ground white pepper

1   Place the turnip and potato in a saucepan, add
water to cover, and 1½ teaspoons of salt. Let come to a
simmer over medium heat, and cook, uncovered, until
the turnip and potato are tender, 20 to 25 minutes.
Drain very well.

2   Place the turnip and potato in a food mill set over
a large saucepan and pass them through the food mill
into the pan. Cook the puree over medium-low heat,
stirring it with a silicone spatula, for 1 to 2 minutes to
evaporate any excess moisture.

3   Reduce the heat to low. Whisk in the chilled butter, 1 tablespoon at a time, waiting for each tablespoon
to be incorporated before adding another and whisking all the while to achieve a creamy texture. Whisk
in the milk or cream if you want the consistency to be
slightly silkier. Season the puree with salt and white
pepper to taste. Serve the puree at once or keep it
warm until ready to serve by placing the pot, covered,
in a larger pot of warm water set over low heat.

Martha's Vineyard–Style Zucchini Casserole

One summer when I was on a serious quest to
find a good recipe for a zucchini casserole
that didn't call for a can of condensed soup, I came
across this recipe while accompanying my son to a
baseball game on Martha's Vineyard. The day was
brutally hot and I managed to sneak away briefly in
an air-conditioned vehicle to buy a just-published
copy of the *Morning Glory Farm and the Family that
Feeds an Island* cookbook at the Bunch of Grapes
Bookstore in Vineyard Haven. I never make the
Morning Glory's zucchini casserole exactly as it is
written in their cookbook but do rely on the recipe
as a trustworthy guide. I decided to write down my
latest zucchini casserole rendition after my dog sit-
ter, who is a vegetarian, told me the leftovers I had
left for her in my refrigerator were one of the best
things she had ever tasted. SERVES 6 TO 8

3 tablespoons extra virgin olive oil

1 medium-size onion, peeled lengthwise,
   cut in half and then cut into ¼-inch-wide
   crescent slices

1 yellow bell pepper, stemmed, seeded, and
   cut into ½-inch-wide strips

1 red bell pepper, stemmed, seeded, and
   cut into ½-inch-wide strips

3 cloves garlic, peeled and minced

2 medium-size zucchini, trimmed and cut into
   ¼-inch-thick rounds

2 medium-size yellow summer squash,
   trimmed and cut into ¼-inch-thick rounds

3 ripe medium-size tomatoes, seeded and cut
   into ½-inch dice

3 tablespoons slivered fresh basil

Sea salt and freshly ground black pepper

4 ounces smoked mozzarella or sharp cheddar
   cheese, shredded (about 1 heaping cup)

1   Preheat the oven to 350°F.

2   Heat the olive oil in a large skillet over medium-
high heat. Add the onion and bell peppers and cook
until softened, 5 to 7 minutes. Stir in the garlic and
cook until slightly softened, about 1 minute. Add the
zucchini, summer squash, and tomatoes, reduce the
heat to medium, and cook, stirring frequently, until

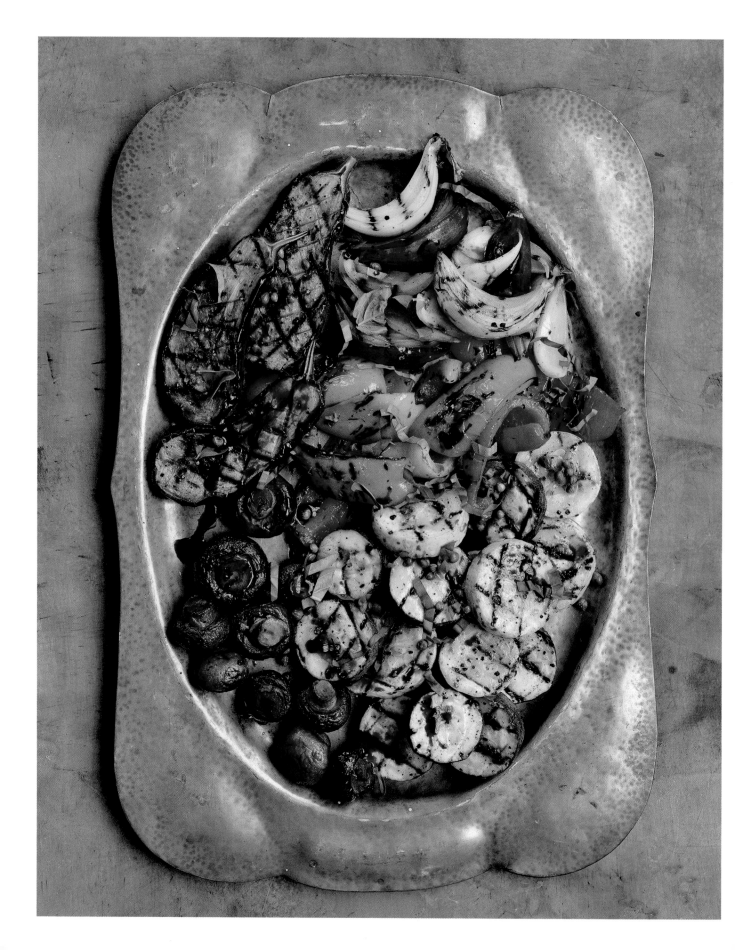

the squash are almost tender, 12 to 15 minutes. Stir in the basil and season the vegetables with salt and pepper to taste.

3 Transfer the vegetables to a 13-by-9-inch baking dish. Top them with the shredded cheese. Bake the casserole until it is bubbly and the cheese is lightly browned, about 30 minutes. Serve the casserole hot or warm.

Grilled Cornucopia of Summer Garden Vegetables

At the height of the summer growing season when every night calls for firing up the outdoor grill and you can't decide which vegetable to cook from the backyard garden or local farmers' market, this grilled cornucopia of vegetables is your answer. If looking svelte on the beach is a top priority, you may want to skip grilling any accompanying protein and simply feast on this beautiful and bountiful platter of colorful and tasty vegetables. Otherwise, the grilled array of vegetables is perfect to pair with everything from the catch of the day to succulent rib eye steaks. SERVES 8 TO 10 AS A SIDE DISH, 4 TO 6 AS A MAIN DISH

6 baby eggplants, stems removed, eggplants cut in half lengthwise

1 large yellow summer squash, trimmed and cut into ½-inch-thick rounds

1 large zucchini, trimmed and cut into ½-inch-thick rounds

1 large yellow onion, peeled and cut into ½-inch wedges

1 large red onion, peeled and cut into ½-inch wedges

3 bell peppers, preferably an assortment of colors, stemmed, seeded, and cut into ¾-inch-wide strips

12 ounces mushrooms, preferably shiitake or cremini, stems trimmed or removed

3 tablespoons vegetable oil

Sea salt and freshly ground black pepper

6 tablespoons extra virgin olive oil

2 tablespoons balsamic vinegar

2 tablespoons drained brine-packed capers

½ cup slivered fresh basil leaves

1 Combine the eggplants, yellow squash, zucchini, yellow and red onions, bell peppers, and mushrooms in a large mixing bowl and toss with the vegetable oil. Season with salt and pepper to taste and toss to coat evenly.

2 Set up a charcoal or gas grill and preheat it to medium-high.

3 Arrange the vegetables, working in batches if necessary, in a hinged wire grill basket or place them on top of a small-mesh grilling rack. Grill the vegetables a few inches above the heat, turning them frequently, until crisp-tender. Some vegetables will take longer to cook than others, so you want to tend them carefully and transfer them to a large and attractive serving platter as they become crisp-tender.

4 Once all of the vegetables have been grilled and placed on the platter, drizzle the olive oil and balsamic vinegar over them. Scatter the capers and basil over the top. Serve the vegetables warm or at room temperature.

Picnic Pastimes & Tailgating Traditions

> "Yes, one of the brightest gems in the New England weather is the dazzling uncertainty of it. There is only one thing certain about it, you are certain there is going to be plenty of weather. A perfect grand review; but you can never tell which end of the procession is going to move first."
> —Mark Twain

An appetite and ardor for making and eating picnic-friendly foods sparked the early stages of my culinary career. My Que Sera Sarah food shop on Nantucket was devoted to selling a creatively eclectic array of portable comestibles to savor wherever one pleased—porch, parlor, patio, park bench, pasture, pool, bike path, beach blanket, sand dune, sailboat, or steamship crossing. I grew up in a family who valued picnicking over stopping at fast food joints whenever we traveled. In fact, I still shiver as I recall the sound of the Styrofoam ice chest my mother packed for summer vacations or ski trips squeaking in the back of our station wagon the entire way from our home in Connecticut to the rocky Penobscot coast of Maine or the snow-capped mountains of Vermont. Needless to say, I am grateful for all the advances that have transpired over the years to keep food safely and stylishly chilled or heated. My travels throughout New England these days almost always find me with a state-of-the-art, nonsqueaking cooler tucked accessibly into our SUV.

My family also occasionally engaged in tailgating on warm summer evenings before Boston Symphony Orchestra outdoor concerts at Tanglewood, although our most cherished tailgating expeditions were reserved for November to attend the Harvard-Yale football game in either New Haven or Cambridge.

In recent years, most of my picnicking energies have gone into preparing foods for Nantucket's annual Daffodil Weekend picnic event, beach and boating excursions on Cape Cod or in Maine, and the occasional New England Patriots or college football tailgating outing to modern Gillette Stadium or historic Harvard Stadium. Mind you, attending the football game itself is never really my

Nantucket's annual Daffodil Festival picnic extravaganza takes place in the village of Siasconset, or Sconset as the islanders call it, on the last Saturday of April.

source of motivation. Rather, when you just so happen to have a gregarious friend, as my husband and I do, who lives to tailgate and has hosted his own tailgating food show on cable TV, you pretend to know NFL stats for the sake of being welcomed as a contributor to an amazing tailgating extravaganza. Likewise, when it comes to packing a picnic that will be judged for coveted honors at Nantucket's Daffodil Festival, you want to be on your toes with a pretty Smoked Salmon Mousse, big bowl of Pickled Shrimp, or chicken salad curried as yellow as the daffodils it is intended to celebrate.

The one pesky and perennial problem with planning and packing picnics and tailgates in New England is unpredictable weather. I try not to let forecasts bother me terribly much, because the type of food in this chapter is for the most part casual and indulgent comfort food that tastes just as delicious in your own home, watching the game on TV cozied next to the fireplace or relying on the familiarity of your own kitchen, rather than fussing over portable grills, smokers, burners, and what not under inclement conditions. Whenever Mother Nature disappoints, I try to counter with optimism

by insisting that the "B" in Plan B stands for best-case scenario and bounty unfettered by "neither snow nor rain nor heat nor gloom of night."

Smoked Salmon Mousse

Sue Lingeman, a longtime Nantucket summer resident and talented artist, shared this recipe with me many moons ago. I like it for its pretty pale pink color, delicious savor, and ease of assembly. The mousse imparts the elegance of smoked salmon to a picnic without having to go through the fuss of arranging a platter of sliced smoked salmon with all the individual fixings. MAKES ABOUT 2 CUPS

⅓ pound, sliced smoked salmon, coarsely
  chopped

1 container (8 ounces) whipped cream cheese
  with chives, at room temperature

2 scallions, both white and tender green parts,
  trimmed and minced

2 tablespoons minced fresh dill

¼ teaspoon ground cumin

2 tablespoons lemon-flavored or plain vodka

1 tablespoon freshly squeezed lemon juice

A couple shakes of Tabasco sauce

Fine sea salt and freshly ground black pepper

Crackers, capers, and minced red onion, for
  serving

1 Place the smoked salmon, cream cheese, scallions, dill, cumin, vodka, lemon juice, and Tabasco sauce in a food processor or blender and puree until smooth. Taste for seasoning, adding salt and pepper as needed. Transfer the salmon mousse to a decorative serving dish and refrigerate it, covered, overnight for the

flavors to meld. It will keep in the refrigerator for up to 5 days.

2   When ready to serve, let the mousse stand at room temperature for at least 20 minutes, then surround it with crackers and small dishes of capers and chopped red onion.

Smoked Mackerel Rillettes

The most extravagant tailgate gathering I have ever attended was orchestrated by Joshua Smith at Gillette Stadium prior to a New England Patriots and New Orleans Saints football game. Smith had decided upon a theme of giving famed New Orleans dishes like po'boys and beignets a New England twist but kicked off the bountiful spread with a splendid and swoon-inducing array of his own, signature New England Charcuterie products. After reveling in pork galore, I in turn became inspired to think of including seafood-based charcuterie in future picnic and tailgate events, reasoning that such preparations would be easier for home cooks to prepare than pork-based charcuterie. My brother, Jonathan, frequently makes smoked mackerel rillettes in Maine and his recipe for this butter-rich, French pâté-like spread perfectly illustrates my point and inclinations. If you have not caught and smoked your own mackerel fillets, feel free to use packaged smoked mackerel fillets from a smokehouse such as Ducktrap River of Maine. MAKES 3 ½ CUPS

16 tablespoons (2 sticks) unsalted butter

¼ cup peeled minced onion

1 pound smoked mackerel fillets, skinned

1¼ cups dry white wine

Grated zest of 1 lemon

½ teaspoon freshly ground black pepper

1 teaspoon or less sea salt

Toasted baguette slices rubbed with fresh garlic cloves or crackers, for serving

1   Melt the butter in a medium-size saucepan over low heat. Add the onion and cook until quite soft but not browned, about 8 minutes.

2   Using your hands, shred the mackerel flesh into flakes and add it to the saucepan with the butter and onion mixture. Mix well with a wooden spoon, pressing the fish against the side of the saucepan. Continue stirring and pressing until the mixture is heated through. Add the white wine, mix well, continuing occasionally to stir and press until the wine is mostly absorbed into the fish, about 20 minutes. Add the lemon zest and pepper and mix well. Remove from the heat.

3   Taste the rillettes and season with salt to taste. Depending on the smoking technique employed, little or no salt may be necessary. Transfer the rillettes to a ceramic crock or large ramekin and cover with plastic wrap. Press on the plastic wrap so that it is in direct contact with the surface of the rillettes (there should be no air space between the rillettes and the plastic). Refrigerate the rillettes for at least 6 hours for the flavors to meld. They will keep for 1 week in the refrigerator.

4   To serve, let the rillettes come to a "cool" room temperature, removing them from the refrigerator about 45 minutes before serving. Serve the rillettes with toasted slices of baguette rubbed with fresh garlic cloves or your favorite crackers.

Pickled Shrimp

Pickled shrimp isn't a pickle like other pickles in the New England larder. Rather it is a showstopping variation on the ubiquitous shrimp cocktail and benefits from being made two or three days in advance of serving. Using peeled and deveined shrimp will take the arduous work out of the shrimp preparation and the recipe looks terrific piled into an earthenware crock. Serve Pickled Shrimp as a kickoff to an upscale tailgate or as a main salad at a picnic. SERVES 10 TO 12 AS A STARTER, 6 TO 8 AS A MAIN DISH

½ cup freshly squeezed lemon juice

3 tablespoons white wine vinegar

1½ tablespoons Dijon mustard

3 cloves garlic, peeled and minced

1½ teaspoons sea salt

¾ cup extra virgin olive oil

1 jar (4 ounces) diced pimiento

½ cup pitted black olives, such as kalamata, coarsely chopped

1 small red onion, peeled and thinly sliced

1 large lemon, thinly sliced and slices then cut in half

1 small bunch fresh dill, cilantro, parsley, or mint, minced (½ to ⅔ cup)

2 tablespoons Old Bay or other shrimp boil seasoning

4 pounds (16 to 20 count) shrimp, peeled and deveined

1　Place the lemon juice, wine vinegar, mustard, garlic, and salt in a large bowl and whisk to mix. Slowly whisk in the olive oil. Stir in the pimiento, olives, red onion, lemon slices, and dill or other herb. Set the pickling marinade aside.

2　Fill a large pot with water and add the shrimp boil seasoning. Let come to a boil over high heat. Add the shrimp and cook until just cooked through the centers, 2 to 4 minutes. Drain the shrimp in a colander. Immediately toss the hot shrimp in the pickling marinade. Let cool to room temperature, stirring occasionally.

3　Store the shrimp in the refrigerator, covered, for 2 to 3 days (and no longer than 5 days), stirring occasionally. Serve chilled.

Chicken Liver Pâté with Ruby Port and Dried Cranberries

A well-made chicken liver pâté can taste almost as indulgent as far pricier and much more controversial foie gras. This recipe combines favorite elements of various memorable chicken liver pâtés I have tasted over the years. Soaking the chicken livers in milk is a technique originally suggested by Julia Child to remove any bitterness and make for an all-around smoother flavor. While some find this step unnecessary, I have come to swear by it. As with many things Julia, lots of butter helps make this extra delicious. I find it to be the perfect initial offering to set the stage for a fancy picnic or tailgate party. MAKES ABOUT 2 CUPS

1¼ pounds fresh chicken livers

1 cup milk

½ cup dried cranberries

½ cup ruby port

12 tablespoons (1½ sticks) unsalted butter, at room temperature

2 large shallots, peeled and minced

Sea salt and freshly ground black pepper

1 teaspoon fresh thyme leaves, coarsely chopped

1 teaspoon fennel seeds, ground as finely as possible in a mortar with a pestle or in a coffee grinder dedicated as a spice mill

¼ cup finely minced fresh flat-leaf parsley

2½ tablespoons melted duck or chicken fat or unsalted butter

¼ cup shelled, dry roasted pistachio nuts, coarsely chopped

Toast rounds or crackers, for serving

1   Place the chicken livers in a colander, rinse them under cold running water, and drain them. Take meticulous care to cut away and discard any connective membranes and fat deposits clinging to the livers (this ranks up there among my least favorite but absolutely necessary culinary chores). Place the cleaned livers in a shallow bowl and pour the milk over them. Cover and refrigerate the chicken livers for at least 2 hours or as long as overnight. Drain the chicken livers well when you are ready to make the pâté.

2   Place the cranberries and ¼ cup of the ruby port in a small saucepan and let come to a simmer over medium heat, 3 to 4 minutes. Remove from the heat and let the cranberries stand for at least 15 minutes before using.

3   Melt 4 tablespoons of the butter in a medium-size skillet over medium-low heat. Add the shallots and cook until quite soft but not browned, 7 to 8 minutes. Add the drained chicken livers to the skillet, season with salt and pepper to taste, and increase the heat to medium-high. Cook the chicken livers, stirring frequently, until nicely browned, about 5 minutes. Add the remaining ¼ cup of ruby port to the skillet, let come to a simmer, and simmer until the chicken livers are cooked but still a bit pink in the centers, about 2 minutes. Remove the skillet from the heat and set it aside to cool for 10 minutes.

4   Transfer the contents of the skillet to a food processor. Add the thyme and fennel seeds and process everything until smooth. Add the remaining 8 tablespoons of butter and process again until smooth, scraping down the side of the work bowl as necessary. Taste the pâté for seasoning, adding more salt and/or pepper if needed. Add the parsley and all but 1 tablespoon of the macerated dried cranberries. Pulse the

machine on and off a few times to incorporate them evenly throughout the pâté. Transfer the pâté to a 2-to-3-cup ramekin or divide it among a few smaller ramekins if preferred.

5   Pour the melted duck or chicken fat, or butter, over the top of the pâté to make a thin, sealing layer. Place the pâté in the refrigerator for 15 minutes to chill and coagulate the fat. Sprinkle the remaining cranberries and the pistachio nuts over the hardened fat on the pâté. Cover and refrigerate the pâté for at least 6 hours for the flavors to meld. It will keep in the refrigerator for 1 week. Allow the pâté to sit at room temperature for at least 20 minutes before serving. Serve with toast rounds or favorite crackers.

Whipped Feta Cheese Dip

Initially, whipped feta cheese may sound like a treat to be consumed on Mykonos during a hot yachting day rather than in Maine on a bustling, tourist-filled summer evening, but I did in fact experience my first taste of this addictive dip at the restaurant Cleonice in downtown Ellsworth, Maine. Cleonice bills itself as a Mediterranean bistro but has always relied heavily on local Maine ingredients to create its internationally flavored menus. Over the years, Cleonice chef/owner Rich Hanson has been at the helm of many Maine culinary undertakings and his creativity never fails to inspire me and weave its way into my own New England culinary creations. Rich's version of whipped feta is redolent of fruity olive oil and given a spicy kick via the addition of minced pepperoncini. Serve this perfect picnic dip with assorted raw vegetables and/or toasted pita triangles. MAKES ABOUT 2½ CUPS

It is easy to understand why Acadia National Park on Maine's breathtakingly scenic Mount Desert Island, or MDI as the locals abbreviate it, attracts well over 2 million visitors a year.

12 ounces soft and creamy feta cheese, crumbled (about 2 cups)

½ cup extra virgin olive oil

3 tablespoons freshly squeezed lemon juice

1 teaspoon grated lemon zest

2 to 3 tablespoons slivered fresh mint leaves

1 to 2 whole pepperoncini (adjust to suit pepper preferences), drained and finely minced

Baby carrots, sliced cucumbers, bell pepper wedges and/or toasted pita triangles, for serving

1 Place the feta in a food processor and process until smooth. With the machine running, add the olive oil to make a very smooth and creamy spread. Add the lemon juice, zest, mint, and pepperoncini and pulse to combine.

2 Transfer the whipped feta to a decorative serving bowl and refrigerate it, covered, for a few hours to firm it up. Serve the feta on a platter surrounded by the dippers of your choice.

Roasted Red Pepper and Feta Cheese Spread

Oddly enough, this is another feta cheese spread/dip recipe with Maine roots, in this case a spread my brother, Jonathan, makes to sell in the market he manages in Buck's Harbor, Maine. It is a favorite with boating folks who anchor in the harbor for provisions while sailing the coast. Whenever I go up to Maine in the summer, I immediately have to obtain a container of this spread because I absolutely adore it and smear it on crackers and picnic sandwiches of all sorts and sometimes use it as a dip with pita chips, olives, and vegetable crudités. The recipe here is a scaled down version of the large batches Jonathan makes for the market. It is perfectly acceptable to use store-bought roasted red peppers as my brother does, favoring the Mancini brand. MAKES ABOUT 3 CUPS

12 ounces (1½ packages) cream cheese, at room temperature

1 jar (7 ounces) roasted red peppers, well drained

¾ pound soft and creamy feta cheese, crumbled into small pieces

PLACE THE CREAM CHEESE and roasted peppers in a food processor and process until smooth. Add the feta cheese and pulse the machine on and off to incorporate the feta evenly throughout the spread but not puree it into the mixture. Transfer the feta spread to a container, cover it, and store it in the refrigerator until ready to use. The spread will keep for a week.

RSVP Gazpacho

RSVP, in tiny West Cornwall, Connecticut, is one of those extraordinarily special, one of a kind restaurants. Guy is French and the lone chef in the open kitchen fringing the eclectic and cramped seven- to-eight-table dining area. Guy's partner Charles is RSVP's maître d' and waiter, pouring lots of high-end BYOB wine and masterfully serving the six refined courses Guy has prepared for the evening's menu. The restaurant has no website and enjoys a well-deserved word-of-mouth cult following. I have only had the great pleasure of dining at RSVP once, on a mild evening in May, and this unique rendition of gazpacho hit just the right chord of garden freshness when it was brought to our table as a second course.

I don't often pack soups for picnics, but gazpacho is the one exception because I think of it as a salad that's easy to drink and does not require the fuss of soup bowls and spoons. Guy served his gazpacho with slices of spicy sautéed *merguez* sausages as a garnish, but for picnic purposes I offer the gazpacho in cups to accompany a charcuterie board laden with various sliced sausages. SERVES 6 TO 8

3 small cucumbers, peeled, seeded, and diced meticulously fine

½ large red bell pepper, stemmed, seeded, and diced meticulously fine

½ large green bell pepper, stemmed, seeded, and diced meticulously fine

½ large Vidalia or other sweet onion, peeled and diced meticulously fine

4 to 5 cups tomato juice (Guy uses Italian tomato juice)

1 slice day-old country-style white bread

6 tablespoons sherry vinegar

6 tablespoons extra virgin olive oil

Sea salt and freshly ground black pepper

⅓ cup finely minced fresh flat-leaf parsley

Croutons (optional; recipe follows), for garnish

1 Place the cucumbers, red and green bell peppers, and onion in a large mixing bowl and stir to combine the vegetables evenly.

2 Put 4 cups of the tomato juice and the slice of bread, sherry vinegar, and olive oil in a blender and puree until smooth. Pour the tomato juice mixture over the vegetables and stir to combine well. If the soup seems too thick, thin it to the desired consistency with additional tomato juice.

3 Season the gazpacho with salt and black pepper to taste and then stir in the parsley. Refrigerate the gazpacho, covered, for at least 3 hours for the flavors to meld. It will keep in the refrigerator for up to 2 days. Serve the gazpacho chilled in cups for sipping or in bowls with spoons if you are not packing it for a picnic. If desired, garnish each serving with a couple of the crunchy croutons.

Croutons

Freshly made croutons give an added crunch to soups and salads. MAKES 2 CUPS

3 tablespoons extra virgin olive oil

2 cups ciabatta or other rustic country white bread cut into ½-inch cubes

HEAT THE OLIVE oil in a medium-size skillet over medium heat. Add the cubed bread and toss it to coat on all sides with the oil. Reduce the heat to medium-low and cook, stirring and turning occasionally, until the bread is golden on all sides, about 20 minutes. Remove the skillet from the heat and keep the croutons in a dry place, such as a cold oven with the door shut, until ready to use. They are best eaten within 24 hours.

Chicken Salad 101

I am one who believes you can never have too many chicken salad recipes, as long as they are all excellent. Mention the word "picnic" and chicken salad is the first thing that pops into my mind. When I had my Que Sera Sarah take-out food shop on Nantucket, the store's signature chicken and grape salad was always in demand. My son, Oliver, was happy eating it for years until he discovered he liked chicken salad sandwiches with potato chips crushed on top of the salad.

Grapes and potato chips don't go together particularly well, so I came up with this straightforward, kid-friendly chicken salad and must admit I really like it, too, especially when embellished with those crushed potato chips and sandwiched between superfresh slices of very fresh white bread from a good local bakery. I don't put green peppers in many recipes I make, but I do feel they work well in this one without being overpowering. Omit them if you wish. MAKES ENOUGH FOR 4 SANDWICHES

3 skinless, boneless chicken breast halves (1½ to 2 pounds)

2 thin ribs celery, cut into ¼-inch dice

½ cup diced green bell pepper or green Italian frying pepper (⅛-inch dice)

3 scallions, both white and tender green parts, trimmed and minced

½ to ⅔ cup mayonnaise, Hellmann's or homemade (page 129)

2 tablespoons light or heavy (whipping) cream

Sea salt and freshly ground black pepper

8 very fresh sandwich-size slices white bread

Crushed potato chips, preferably Cape Cod Potato Chips (optional)

Nantucket is a dog lover's paradise and creatively festooned canines are a welcome part of many island events, including the annual April Daffodil Festival.

1 Place the chicken breasts in a medium-size, straight-sided skillet. Add enough cold water to cover the chicken breasts amply. Let come to a full boil over medium-high heat then, cover the skillet and remove it from the heat. Let the skillet stand, covered, for 30 minutes to let the residual heat finish cooking the chicken. Drain the chicken breasts.

2 Cut the chicken breasts into ½-inch dice, removing any tough tendons as you chop. Place the chicken in a mixing bowl, add the celery, bell pepper, and scallions, and toss to mix. Add enough mayonnaise to bind the ingredients moistly together and then thin the salad slightly with the cream. Season the chicken salad with salt and black pepper to taste. The chicken salad can be refrigerated, covered, for 3 days.

3 To make the sandwiches, pile a ½-inch-thick layer of the chicken salad onto 4 of the slices of bread. If desired, coarsely crush 3 or 4 potato chips evenly over the filling on each sandwich. Top with the remaining 4 slices of bread and then slice the sandwiches in half on the diagonal. Enjoy at once or wrap for a picnic.

Daffodil Picnic Curried Chicken Salad

The Daffodil Festival takes place on Nantucket during the last weekend in April and is anchored by a parade of antique cars festooned with artfully arranged daffodils. These cars are parked for viewing throughout the morning on the town's cobblestoned Main Street before parading at noon out to the village of 'Sconset along a road planted with thousands and thousands more daffodil bulbs. Once all the antique cars and everyone else on the island have arrived in 'Sconset, a grand daffodil-themed picnic takes place in which yellow-hued foods hold the highest place of honor. This is the chicken salad I make every April in honor of the event. MAKES 6 SERVINGS

2½ to 3 pounds skinless, boneless chicken breasts

½ cup dried cranberries

½ cup cream sherry

¾ cup dry roasted cashew halves

¼ cup minced crystallized ginger

1 bunch scallions, both white and tender green parts, trimmed and thinly sliced

⅓ cup minced fresh cilantro

1 cup mayonnaise, Hellmann's or homemade (page 129)

3 tablespoons mango chutney, large pieces of fruit minced

1 tablespoon Dijon mustard

1½ tablespoons freshly squeezed lime juice

1 to 1½ tablespoons best-quality curry powder

Salt

1   Place the chicken breasts in a large, straight-sided skillet. Add enough cold water to cover the chicken breasts amply. Let come to a full boil over medium-high heat, then cover the skillet and remove it from the heat. Let the skillet stand, covered, for 30 minutes to let the residual heat finish cooking the chicken. Drain the chicken breasts. Cut the chicken breasts into ½-inch dice, removing any tough tendons as you chop.

2   Place the cranberries and sherry in a small saucepan and stir to mix. Let come to a boil over medium-high heat, then reduce the heat to medium and simmer until the cranberries plump, 4 to 5 minutes. Remove the pan from the heat and let the cranberries cool for a few minutes. Place the chicken, cashews, crystallized ginger, scallions, cilantro, and cranberries including any remaining liquid in a large mixing bowl and toss to mix.

3   Place the mayonnaise, chutney, mustard, and lime juice in a small bowl and whisk to mix. Season with 1 tablespoon curry powder and salt to taste. Combine the mayonnaise mixture and chicken salad, stirring to coat it evenly with the mayonnaise. Taste for seasoning, adding more curry powder and salt as needed. Refrigerate the chicken salad for at least 1 hour to blend the flavors. It will keep in the refrigerator for up to 3 days.

Cranberry Chicken Salad

As popular as chicken salad is across the country, it can be hard to find establishments where the chefs make and sell really good versions. I prided myself on this when I ran Que Sera Sarah on Nantucket and was happy to discover years after I had closed shop that another Nantucket shop—Cowboy's Meat Market & Deli—was making a chicken salad worthy of its somewhat expensive per pound purchase price. Whenever I don't have any of my own homemade chicken salad on hand, a half pound of Cowboy's delicious cranberry chicken salad is one of my favorite lunches to grab on the go.

This is my slight adaptation of Cowboy's recipe, using my preferred commercial brand of mayonnaise. The salad's winning appeal is due to an abundance of meaty white chunks of chicken, exceptionally moist dried cranberries, and the addition of a rich dollop of sour cream to the mayonnaise for binding everything together. While moist dried cranberries may sound like an oxymoron, I have found dried cranberries vary in texture and plumpness according to brand and age. I have specifically found that Ocean Spray's Craisins work well in the recipe. SERVES 6 TO 8

3 pounds white meat chicken, either tenders or skinless, boneless chicken breasts

3 ribs celery, trimmed and diced

1 cup plump dried cranberries

¾ cup mayonnaise, Hellmann's or homemade (page 129)

⅓ to ½ cup sour cream

Sea salt and freshly ground black pepper

1 Place the chicken in a medium-size, straight-sided skillet. Add enough cold water to cover the chicken amply. Let come to a full boil over medium-high heat, then cover the skillet and remove it from the heat. Let the skillet stand, covered, for 30 minutes to let the residual heat finish cooking the chicken.

2 Drain the chicken and cut it into ¾-inch chunks, removing any tough tendons as you chop. Place the chicken in a large mixing bowl, add the celery and cranberries, and toss to mix. Add the mayonnaise and enough sour cream to moistly bind the ingredients together. Season the salad with salt and pepper to taste. Transfer the chicken salad to a decorative serving bowl and refrigerate it, covered, for at least 1 hour before serving. The chicken salad will keep for 3 days in the refrigerator.

Fruited Turkey Salad with Poppy Seed Dressing

This salad has so much sumptuous pizzazz that you may find yourself roasting a turkey solely for salad-making purposes. The turkey meat is coarsely shredded and combined with sharp cheddar cheese and toasted pecans, then bathed in a sweet-and-savory poppy seed dressing laced with slivered apricots and dried figs. It's a terrific salad perfectly suited for serving at fall and winter luncheons and always a hit at tailgate gatherings. SERVES 6 TO 8

¼ cup freshly squeezed lemon juice

¼ cup white wine vinegar

2 tablespoons honey

2 tablespoons Dijon mustard

⅔ cup vegetable oil

3 tablespoons finely minced peeled red onion

3 tablespoons poppy seeds

Grated zest of 1 orange

½ cup thinly slivered dried apricots

½ cup thinly slivered dried figs

5 to 6 cups coarsely shredded roasted turkey meat

⅓ pound sharp cheddar cheese, cut into 1½-inch matchsticks (about 1¾ cups)

4 ribs celery, coarsely chopped

¾ cup pecan halves, lightly toasted (see page 70) and coarsely chopped

Sea salt

Salad greens, for serving

1   Place the lemon juice, wine vinegar, honey, and mustard in a small mixing bowl and whisk to mix. Slowly whisk in the oil to make an emulsion. Stir in the red onion, poppy seeds, and orange zest. Add the slivered apricots and figs. Set the dressing aside for 30 minutes for the flavors to meld.

2   Combine the turkey, cheddar, celery, and pecans in a large mixing bowl. Pour the poppy seed dressing over all, tossing to coat well. Season the turkey salad with salt to taste. Refrigerate the salad, covered, for a few hours to mellow the flavors. Serve the turkey salad mounded on top of a bed of your favorite greens.

Fully Loaded Potato Salad

This is another great picnic salad sold at Cowboy's Meat Market on Nantucket. While the over-the-top potato salad harkens back to owner Laura McClosky's Texas roots, I add my own New England spin by using apple wood-smoked bacon from North Country Smokehouse in New Hampshire and sharp cheddar cheese from Vermont. SERVES 10 TO 12

5 pounds red new potatoes

1 pound apple wood-smoked bacon

4 ounces freshly shredded sharp cheddar cheese (about 2 cups)

1 bunch scallions, both white and tender green parts, trimmed and thinly sliced

2 cups mayonnaise, Hellmann's or homemade (page 129)

1 cup sour cream

Sea salt and freshly ground black pepper

⅓ cup minced fresh flat-leaf parsley

1   Scrub the potatoes if they are dirty. Put the potatoes in a large pot and add enough cold water to cover them amply. Let come to a boil over medium-high heat, reduce the heat to medium, and simmer the potatoes until fork tender but not mushy, 25 to 30 minutes. Drain the potatoes and let them cool until easy to handle but still quite warm, about 10 minutes.

2   While the potatoes are cooking, place the bacon in a large, heavy skillet and cook over medium heat until nicely crisped, 10 to 12 minutes. Transfer the bacon to a paper towel-lined plate to drain.

3   Cut the potatoes into large bite-size chunks and place them in a large mixing bowl. Crumble the bacon and add it, plus the cheddar, and scallions and toss to mix. Add the mayonnaise and sour cream, stirring to bind the salad together. Season the potato salad with salt and pepper to taste.

4   Transfer the potato salad to a decorative serving bowl and sprinkle the parsley over the top. Serve the salad at once or refrigerate it, covered, until ready to serve. The salad is best when consumed within a day or so of making; otherwise the bacon loses its crispness.

Herb-Bathed New Potato Salad

This winning potato salad, which contains no mayonnaise, is a riff on a recipe I learned years ago while working on *The Silver Palate Good Times Cookbook*. I've been making it for picnic and pot-luck gatherings ever since to rave reviews. It is especially flavorful when made in the summertime with locally grown potatoes and herbs. SERVES 10 TO 12

Herb-Bathed New Potato Salad »

Roy's Corn Bar

New England has its oyster bars, Bloody Mary brunch bars, and even burger bars. And then there is the unique and irresistibly indulgent corn bar invented by the affable and party-loving Roy Roberts as a signature component to many of the tailgating events Roy excels at staging.

Roy is definitely among the foodiest of all my foodie friends. When I was beginning to do research for this cookbook, Roy invited my family to his vacation home in New Hampshire and proceeded to take me on a customized tour of every worthy dining, drinking, and provisioning stop within a seventy-five mile radius of Mount Sunapee. Roy can just as readily reel off a wealth of insider tips should your appetite take you merely around the corner from his Boston home to Newbury Street or farther afield to New York, New Orleans, or Napa. You name it, and Roy will have most likely been there and eaten memorably somewhere in the environs.

But I digress and must return to waxing eloquent over Roy's tailgating corn bar setups. Roy begins by cooking a plethora of freshly shucked ears of local corn in a huge pot of water set over a portable propane burner. The idea is for guests to grab a hot ear of corn from the pot and head over to a table laden with a vast assortment of corn-on-the-cob embellishments that Roy categorizes as slathers (butters, compound butters or liquids like lime juice that either melt or seep into the kernels of corn), sprinkles (ground spices, salts, sugars, finely grated cheeses and anything else that can be sprinkled or shaken onto the ear of corn), and crumbles (coarser toppings that add texture to the corn, such as crumbled crispy bacon, crumbled gorgonzola and feta cheeses, chopped olives, slivered fresh herbs, toasted pine nuts, and shaved truffles).

The semantics surrounding his corn bar toppings are of particular importance to Roy and he is quick to make distinctions like: "Grated Parmigiano-Reggiano cheese is a sprinkle, but shaved Parmigiano-Reggiano cheese is a crumble." If you don't possess an imagination as vibrant as Roy's, he offers the following slather/sprinkle/crumble combinations to nudge you down the path to your own special tailgating cornucopia:

SIMPLE KETTLE CORN: butter slather followed by sprinkles of sea salt and sugar

PESTO CORN: basil butter slather, sprinkles of grated Parmesan, pine nut crumble

CARBONARA CORN: garlic butter slather, sprinkles of grated Parmesan, crispy bacon crumble

MEXICAN CORN: lime butter slather, chili powder sprinkle, shaved Manchego cheese crumble

---

4 pounds small new potatoes, no larger than a small egg

6 cloves garlic, peeled and minced

1 to 1¼ cups extra virgin olive oil

1 bunch fresh mint, stemmed and minced (at least ¾ cup)

1 bunch fresh cilantro, stemmed and minced (at least ¾ cup)

1 bunch fresh flat-leaf parsley, stemmed and minced (at least ¾ cup)

Coarse sea or kosher salt and freshly ground black pepper

1 Preheat the oven to 375°F.

2 Scrub the potatoes if they are dirty and arrange them in a single layer in a large roasting pan. Bake the potatoes until they are tender when pierced through

the center with the tip of a sharp paring knife, 1 to 1¼ hours.

3 Meanwhile, combine the garlic with 1 cup of the olive oil in a large mixing bowl. Add the mint, cilantro, and parsley, stirring to coat them with the olive oil. Season the herbed olive oil with salt and pepper to taste.

4 Cut the hot roasted potatoes into uneven bite-size chunks and immediately toss them with the herbed olive oil. Add more olive oil if the salad seems a bit too dry. Serve the salad hot, warm, or at room temperature. The salad is best consumed within a few hours of being made.

Farro Tabbouleh

My husband, Nigel, knows that he should eat more grains but tends to have a mild fit every time I try to sneak bulgur wheat, couscous, or quinoa into our diet. I have limited success with farro because we tasted farro for the first time in Tuscany and Nigel likes Tuscany a lot and farro far more than bulgur.

I thought my tabbouleh-making-days were over when I married Nigel but now that farro is in vogue and easy to find in America, I can get away with sneaking the occasional container of Farro Tabbouleh into a family picnic basket and have personally come to like this poetically licensed tabbouleh more than authentic bulgur-based recipes.

The recipe is written using farro that needs to be soaked before cooking. Farro labeled as "pearled" often does not need soaking, so be sure to look at the directions on the package of farro you purchase and follow them before proceeding with the recipe. SERVES 6 TO 8

1 cup farro

Kosher salt

¼ cup extra virgin olive oil

¼ cup sherry vinegar

2 cups unwaxed, seeded and diced cucumber (¼-inch dice)

1½ cups seeded and chopped ripe tomatoes, or 1½ cups multicolored grape or cherry tomato quarters

1 cup peeled and diced red onion (¼-inch dice)

1 cup minced fresh flat leaf parsley

¾ cup crumbled feta or mild blue cheese

Freshly ground black pepper

1 Soak the farro in a bowl of cold water for at least 1 hour and up to 3 hours, following the directions on the package. Drain the farro and rinse it with cold water. (If the directions do not call for soaking, proceed directly to Step 2.)

2 Place the farro in a 2-quart saucepan and add water to cover it by at least 2 inches. Add 1 tablespoon of salt and let come to a boil over medium-high heat. Skim off the foam that accumulates on the surface and discard it. Reduce the heat to medium and let the farro simmer until the grains are tender, 25 to 30 minutes. Drain the farro thoroughly and place it in a large bowl.

3 Add the olive oil and sherry vinegar to the farro while it is still hot and mix well. Let the farro cool to room temperature.

4 Add the cucumber, tomatoes, red onion, parsley, and crumbled cheese. Mix well and season with salt and pepper to taste. Refrigerate the farro mixture for 2 hours for the flavors to meld. It will keep in the refrigerator for up to 3 days. Serve chilled or at room temperature.

Ziti Picnic Salad

This is one of the first pasta salads I learned to make and one of the few pasta salads I continue to make. I originally came across the recipe when I cooked almost exclusively from Bert Greene's terrific cookbooks in the early 1980s. I've changed it a bit over the years but find its retro appeal to be still more satisfying than any new-fangled pasta salad I have ever made or tasted. SERVES 8 TO 10 AS A SIDE SALAD

Sea salt

1 pound ziti pasta

1 medium-size red onion, peeled and minced

1 bunch scallions, both white and tender green parts, trimmed and minced

2 large ripe tomatoes, seeded and diced

1 red bell pepper, stemmed, seeded, and diced

1 yellow bell pepper, stemmed, seeded, and diced

1 orange bell pepper, stemmed, seeded, and diced

8 dill pickle spears, cut into ¼-inch dice

½ cup minced fresh dill

1 cup mayonnaise, Hellmann's or homemade (page 129)

⅔ cup sour cream

2 tablespoons dill pickle juice

Freshly ground black pepper

1. Bring a large pot of water to a boil. Add salt and the ziti and cook according to package directions until al dente. Drain the ziti well in a colander.

2. Place the red onion, scallions, tomatoes, red, yellow, and orange bell peppers, pickles, and dill in a large mixing bowl and toss to mix. Add the cooked and drained ziti and toss again.

3. Place the mayonnaise, sour cream, and pickle juice in a smaller bowl and whisk to mix. Add the mayonnaise mixture to the ziti salad and toss gently with a rubber spatula to coat and bind the salad loosely together. Season the salad with salt and pepper to taste. Transfer the salad to a decorative serving bowl and refrigerate it, covered, for at least 2 hours before serving for the flavors to meld. It will keep in the refrigerator for up to 3 days.

Reuben Roulades

While most people associate Maine with lobsters and wild blueberries, the state's sauerkraut and mustards are so good that someone like me can't help but think of making a mighty tasty Reuben sandwich. My only problem was that I wanted to make a Reuben that could be easily transported to a tailgate party, so I had to think outside the sandwich. These savory puff pastry–based swirls are the happy outcome.

At first glance the roulades may look like a cross between a sweet cinnamon bun and an elephant ear but the taste is most definitely that of the Reuben of my Maine and New York delicatessen dreams. While you need not make these with Morse's Sauerkraut or Raye's Old World Gourmet Mustard, they will be even more delicious if you do. The sauerkraut has been produced in Waldoboro since 1918 from Maine-grown cabbage brined without preservatives and then hand-packed directly from the fermenting barrel. Raye's Mustard hails from Eastport, Maine, where it is ground in a mustard mill set on the Bay of Fundy. The mill is the last operating stone mill in America and the Old World Gourmet variety is a grainy and robust Dijon-style mustard that has garnered awards at international competitions. MAKES 6 ROULADES

1 teaspoon vegetable oil or vegetable oil cooking spray

2 teaspoons caraway seeds

1 cup Morse's Sauerkraut or other good-quality sauerkraut, drained

All-purpose unbleached flour, for dusting the work surface

1 package (2 sheets) puff pastry, thawed according to package directions

4 teaspoons Raye's Old World Gourmet Mustard or grainy Dijon mustard

6 ounces thinly sliced lean corned beef

8 thin slices Swiss cheese

1 large egg

2 tablespoons water

Eastport, Maine, is the easternmost town in the U.S. and is best known as home to Raye's Mustard Mill & Museum and for hosting Maine's annual Salmon Festival in September.

1 Preheat the oven to 400°F. Line a baking sheet with parchment paper. Evenly brush the prepared baking sheet with the oil, covering the entire surface. Alternatively, you can spray the prepared baking sheet with vegetable oil cooking spray.

2 Place the caraway seeds in a dry skillet set over medium heat. Toss the seeds until they begin to darken in color and become very aromatic, about 90 seconds. Add the sauerkraut to the skillet, reduce the heat to low, and stir to distribute the caraway seeds evenly throughout the sauerkraut. When warmed through, 4 to 5 minutes, remove the skillet from the heat and let the sauerkraut cool to room temperature.

3 Dust a work surface with flour, then place 1 sheet of the puff pastry on it. Spread 2 teaspoons of the mustard evenly over the surface of the puff pastry. Arrange half of the corned beef on the puff pastry, starting at the borders and working toward the center. Top the corned beef with 4 slices of the Swiss cheese.

4 Place the second sheet of puff pastry on top of the Swiss cheese. Arrange the remaining corned beef on top of the puff pastry, working in from the borders. Spread the sauerkraut mixture evenly on top of the corned beef, working in from the borders. Top the

sauerkraut with the remaining 4 slices of Swiss cheese. Spread the remaining 2 teaspoons mustard over the Swiss cheese.

5 Carefully roll the layered puff pastry into a compact jelly roll, starting from the short end of the rectangle.

6 Beat the egg with the water. Make sure the roll of puff pastry is positioned on the work surface with the seam side down. Brush some of the egg mixture evenly all over the roll. Using a sharp knife, cut the roll crosswise into 6 even rounds. Arrange the roulades flat on the prepared baking sheet, leaving 1 inch between each round. Secure each roulade at the seam with a toothpick. Brush the tops of the roulades lightly with the remaining egg wash.

7 Bake the roulades until golden brown, 30 to 35 minutes. Remove the roulades from the oven and transfer them to a wire rack to cool. The roulades taste best when still a bit warm. If you are transporting them to a tailgate, wrap each in aluminum foil and reheat them briefly on top of a portable grill.

Prize-Winning Grilled Brie, Cranberry, and Almond Sandwiches

This luscious grilled cheese sandwich is the invention of Barbara Gookin, who won first prize with it in a grilled cheese competition staged by Bartlett's Farm on Nantucket to enliven the bleak month of March on the island. Barbara says her inspiration was to try to deconstruct the popular *Brie en croûte* recipe often made on the island with a layer of fruit preserves or cranberry sauce. The sandwich exudes plenty of crunch from the sliced almonds and the bread slowly toasted in butter in a frying pan, a contrast to the gooey ooze of creamy melted Brie. Dried cranberries add a bright ruby and tart note, in turn balanced by the sweetness of dark brown sugar.

The sandwich is incredibly rich and quite obviously not picnic portable. However, it is the perfect consolation sandwich to make at home during those times when bad weather has canceled your outdoor plans. In fact, you may even find yourself pining for rain in the forecast. SERVES 2 TO 4

4 large slices country-style oat bread

3 to 4 tablespoons unsalted butter, at room temperature

5 ounces double or triple cream Brie

2 tablespoons dried cranberries

2 tablespoons dark brown sugar

3 tablespoons lightly toasted sliced almonds (see page 70)

1 Generously spread the slices of bread on one side with about 2 tablespoons of the butter. Place the slices of bread, buttered side down, on a griddle or in a large skillet and cook slowly over medium-low heat until toasted light golden brown, about 4 minutes.

Remove the bread from the skillet and place the slices, toasted side up, on a work surface.

2 Score the rind of the Brie in a crosshatch pattern and then break it into ½-inch chunks. Scatter the chunks evenly over the toasted surface of 2 of the slices of bread. Scatter the cranberries, brown sugar, and almonds evenly on top of the Brie. Place the remaining 2 slices of bread, toasted side down, on top of the filling. Butter the outside of the sandwiches on both sides with as much of the remaining butter as your conscience and cholesterol count will allow.

3 Place the sandwiches in the griddle or skillet and cook them slowly over medium-low heat, turning once, until both sides are toasted a golden brown and the cheese is melted, 10 to 12 minutes. Cut the sandwiches in half on the diagonal and serve hot.

Café Chew's "Pilgrim" Turkey Sandwiches

While many have the tradition of making a day-after-Thanksgiving turkey sandwich with leftover stuffing and cranberry sauce, this combination is often served in New England sandwich shops year-round. One of the best renditions is at Café Chew in Sandwich on Cape Cod. The breakfast and lunch café is run by Bob King and Tobin Wirt, animated members of my Cape Cod food and travel book club. If you ever need the up-to-the-minute scoop on the newest restaurant to open between Provincetown and Boston, Bob and Tobin will have it. At the same time, if you just need to scoop something good to eat or pack for a beach picnic or other excursion around Cape Cod, head to Café Chew.

Café Chew's "Pilgrim" is made on a fabulous cranberry-nut bread, a specialty of the Pain

D'Avignon bakery in Hyannis. You can substitute another nut bread or your favorite sandwich bread from a local bakery. MAKES 4 SANDWICHES

4 tablespoons (½ stick) unsalted butter

3 ribs celery, trimmed and diced

1 medium-size onion, peeled and minced

4 cups crumbled day-old white or wheat bread, lightly toasted

1 tablespoon Bell's poultry seasoning

Sea salt and freshly ground black pepper

¼ to ½ cup turkey or chicken stock or broth, homemade or good-quality store-bought

½ cup Baked Cranberry Conserve (page 192) or whole cranberry sauce

½ cup mayonnaise, Hellmann's or homemade (page 129)

8 large slices cranberry-nut bread or other favorite sandwich bread

12 ounces sliced roasted turkey (12 to 16 slices)

Lettuce or baby arugula leaves

1 Melt the butter in a large skillet over medium-high heat. Add the celery and onion and cook until soft and beginning to brown, 5 to 7 minutes. Add the crumbled toasted bread and Bell's seasoning and season with salt and pepper to taste. Cook the stuffing mix, stirring to blend, 2 to 3 minutes. Add enough stock or broth to moisten and bind the stuffing loosely together. Remove the skillet from the heat.

2 Place the cranberry conserve or sauce and mayonnaise in a blender or food processor and process until thoroughly combined.

3 Pat a ½-inch-thick layer of the stuffing onto 4 slices of the bread. Top the stuffing with 3 or 4 slices of roast turkey and season it lightly with salt and pepper. Place lettuce or arugula leaves on top of the turkey. Smear the remaining 4 slices of bread with the cranberry mayonnaise and place them on top of the sandwiches, mayonnaise side down. Slice the

sandwiches in half on the diagonal and wrap them to pack for a picnic or enjoy them immediately. Any leftover stuffing and cranberry mayonnaise can be refrigerated, covered, for 3 to 4 days.

Truffled Egg Salad Tartines

I am fortunate to live only a few miles from Cape Cod's very popular Pain D'Avignon bakery and café. While I covet many things made at the bakery, the Truffled Egg Salad Tartines are probably my favorite indulgence of all. I'll dash into the bakery at least once a week to grab one for a lunch on the go while doing errands around town. One day I finally decided to make my own. After all, Truffled Egg Salad Tartines are the perfect fashionably yellow fare to pack for the umpteenth Daffodil Festival picnic on Nantucket, although they are also irresistible at any time of the year.

At Pain D'Avignon the truffled egg salad is smeared atop thin, wide slabs of toasted day-old baguettes. You can also use toasted slabs of a good sliced country-style peasant bread, as I often do. MAKES 6 TARTINES

9 large eggs, preferably organic

Ice

1 heaping tablespoon black or white truffle butter, at room temperature (see Note)

2 tablespoons minced fresh chives

Fleur de sel or other crunchy sea salt and freshly ground black pepper

⅓ cup mayonnaise, Hellmann's or homemade (page 129)

6 wide thin baguette slices (each about 3 by 6 inches), toasted, lightly buttered if desired

1 Place the eggs in a single layer in a saucepan and add enough cold water to cover them amply. Let come to a boil over high heat. Once the water is rapidly boiling, cover the pan and remove it from the heat. Let the eggs stand undisturbed for 15 to 17 minutes.

2 Meanwhile, fill a large bowl with ice water. Drain the cooked eggs and immediately plunge them into the bowl of ice water to cool completely. Peel the eggs. Remove 2 of the yolks and mash them with the truffle butter in a small dish until thoroughly combined.

3 Finely chop the remaining whites and yolks and place them in a mixing bowl. Add the chives and mashed egg yolks and season with *fleur de sel* and pepper to taste. Toss gently with a rubber or silicone spatula to combine. Fold in the mayonnaise to bind the egg salad together. The salad should be more pastelike than mayonnaisey. Refrigerate the egg salad, covered, if you are not using it right away. It will keep in the refrigerator for up to 4 days.

4 Spread a thin layer of the truffled egg salad evenly over each toasted slab of bread. Enjoy at once or wrap to pack for a picnic.

NOTE: *D'Artagnan and Urbani make excellent truffle butter. Both brands can be found at Whole Foods as well as specialty food stores.*

Top Dogs

From time to time in my life, when I have grown weary of too much preciousness in the food world, I have dreamed of opening a hot dog stand and calling it either Chien Lunatique or Franks for the Memory. While it is fun to dream, it is even better to sneak a really good hot dog every once in a while, especially at a Fourth of July picnic or fall football tailgate. People throughout New England have regional loyalties to brands of hot dogs. In Rhode Island, Saugy frankfurters reign supreme and they are often topped with a Coney Island–inspired beef chili sauce. Wasses hot dogs have legions of fans in the midcoast area of Maine. My favorite New England hot dog is an oversize frankfurter made by Pearl Meat in Randolph, Massachusetts, and sold as Pearl Kountry Klub beef frankfurters.

I do like to gild the dog by slitting it down the center and stuffing it with a few matchsticks of extra-sharp Vermont cheddar cheese and then wrapping the dog in a strip of smoked bacon. Once the hot dog is grilled to crispy bacon and melting cheese perfection and tucked into a toasted bun, caviar can pale by comparison as an indulgence. Finish the dog off simply with a squirt of Maine-made Raye's Top Dog Mustard or your favorite sharp Dijon mustard. Accompany with Polish Bread and Butter Pickles and savor a really excellent and unpretentious "franks for the memory" moment. SERVES 8

8 Pearl Kountry Klub beef frankfurters or other good-quality all-beef hot dogs

4 ounces extra-sharp Vermont cheddar cheese, cut into ¼-inch-wide strips

8 slices apple wood- or cob-smoked bacon

8 New England-style, top-split hot dog buns, lightly buttered and toasted on the grill

Polish Bread and Butter Pickles (recipe follows)

Mustard and any other favorite hot dog toppings, if desired

You'll also need

Small metal trussing skewers or wooden toothpicks that have been soaked in water for 20 minutes to prevent burning

1 Set up a regular charcoal or gas grill or a portable grill and preheat it to medium-high.

2 Cut a slit down the center of each hot dog to create a pocket for the cheese but take care not to cut all the way through the hot dog and split it in half. Insert strips of cheddar into the slit of each hot dog to fill it.

Those who make it through mud season in Connecticut's Litchfield Hills are rewarded with the splendor of spring blossoms and scenic spots for first-of-the season picnicking.

Wrap each hot dog on the diagonal from end to end with a slice of bacon and secure the bacon in place with the small metal trussing skewers or toothpicks.

3 Place the hot dogs on the grill and cook, turning frequently, until the bacon is crisped all over and the cheese has melted and is beginning to ooze out of the hot dogs, 6 to 8 minutes. Tuck the grilled hot dogs into the toasted buns and serve at once with the bread and butter pickles, mustard, and any other toppings you wish. Don't forget to remove the skewers or toothpicks from the hot dogs before munching.

Polish Bread and Butter Pickles

This cherished recipe was shared with me by my second cousin Henry "Skipper" Gwiazda and his wife, Suzanne. The recipe is more than a century old and Skipper, who is an accomplished archivist, has traced the recipe's origins back to Julianna Smigel. Julianna was born in 1885 in Ostrołęka, Poland, and immigrated to the large Polish community settled in New Britain, Connecticut, at the age of fifteen. She married Ignacy Gwiazda in 1901 and began cooking and making preserves to sustain her growing family during lean times. Julianna's bread and butter pickle recipe has been passed down through the generations and continues to be a source of family pride and anticipatory joy every year when the annual batch is made.

We love these pickles so much in my immediate family that I have to hide jars from my husband to keep them from being devoured too rapidly. Serve them alongside sandwiches, hot dogs, and burgers, or add them to a charcuterie assortment in place of the more traditional cornichons. MAKES 10 TO 12 PINTS

10 pounds large pickling (Kirby) cucumbers

3 pounds yellow or white onions, peeled

Kosher salt

Ice cubes

8 cups sugar

8 cups distilled white vinegar or cider vinegar

1 tablespoon whole mustard seeds

1½ teaspoons whole cloves

2 teaspoons celery seeds

2 teaspoons dill seeds

2½ teaspoons ground turmeric

You'll also need

10 to 12 canning jars (each 1 pint)

1 Outfit a food processor with the slicing disk. Feed the cucumbers and onions into the food processor, emptying the bowl as necessary, until all have been sliced. Alternatively, you can laboriously slice everything by hand into ¼-inch-thick slices.

2 Layer the cucumbers and onions into a large bowl or roasting pan, sprinkling each layer with a fine layer of salt. Cover the mixture with ice cubes and replenish as necessary when they melt. The salt drains excess moisture from the cucumbers and onions and the melting ice distributes the salt. Let the cucumbers and onions stand for 4 hours, then pour off all the liquid,

rinse the cucumbers and onions under cold running water, and drain them.

3 Combine the sugar, vinegar, mustard seeds, cloves, celery seeds, dill seeds, and turmeric in a very large pot and let come to a boil over high heat. Add the drained cucumbers and onions. When the liquid returns to a boil, immediately remove the pot from the heat. This will ensure crisp pickles.

4 Have ready the canning jars that have been sterilized according to the manufacturer's directions. Fill the jars with the warm pickles, taking care to add enough brine to come to the top of each jar. Seal the jars according to the manufacturer's instructions. If you opt not to seal the jars, the pickles may be stored in the refrigerator covered in their brine for at least 2 weeks.

Barbecued Ribs with Moose-a-maquoddy Molasses Mustard

I don't have a ton of experience when it comes to barbecuing ribs, but the guys in my family love them and I knew no tailgating chapter in a book of mine could fly without a really good rib recipe. I lucked out when I experimented with this recipe because I happened to score some really terrific ribs at a locavore-driven butcher shop called The Meat Market in Great Barrington, Massachusetts, and had simultaneously received a shipment of mustards from Raye's in Maine. Raye's Moose-a-maquoddy Molasses mustard beckoned by name alone; now I can't imagine making these finger-licking ribs with anything else. SERVES 6

3 pounds St. Louis-style spareribs (see Note)

2½ cups fresh apple cider

5 to 6 tablespoons Raye's Moose-a-maquoddy Molasses mustard

2 tablespoons turbinado sugar

1 tablespoon kosher salt

1 tablespoon chili powder

1 tablespoon sweet paprika

1 teaspoon freshly cracked black peppercorns

½ teaspoon garlic powder

1 cup your favorite store-bought hickory flavored barbecue sauce

2 tablespoons pure maple syrup

Vegetable oil, for oiling the grill grate

1 Preheat the oven to 300°F. Place a large sheet of heavy-duty aluminum foil in the center of a large roasting pan.

2 Place the ribs in the center of the prepared roasting pan. Bring up the sides of the foil to enclose the ribs, leaving an opening in the top. Pour the cider over the ribs, then loosely seal the foil to enclose the ribs.

3 Bake the ribs until very tender, about 1 hour and 45 minutes to 2 hours. Carefully open the foil packet to allow any steam to escape, remove the ribs from the foil, and transfer the ribs to a large baking sheet. Discard the foil and cider. Smear the ribs all over with 3 to 4 tablespoons of the mustard.

4 While the ribs are braising, combine the turbinado sugar, salt, chili powder, paprika, peppercorns, and garlic powder in a small bowl, stirring to blend evenly. Sprinkle the spice mixture evenly all over the mustard-coated ribs. The mustard will help the spices adhere. The ribs may be prepared up to this point, covered with foil, and refrigerated for up to 2 days, if you plan on transporting them to a tailgate event.

5 Set up a charcoal or gas grill and preheat it to medium-high.

6 Place the barbecue sauce, 2 tablespoons of mustard, and the maple syrup in a small mixing bowl and stir until well combined.

7 When ready to grill, brush the grill grate with oil. Place the seasoned ribs on the grate meaty side down. Cover the grill and cook the ribs until beginning to brown, about 15 minutes. Turn the ribs over and grill them for 10 to 15 minutes longer. Then, baste the ribs with about one third of the barbecue sauce mixture. Continue grilling the ribs, turning them and basting them with the sauce, watching carefully so the sauce does not burn, until the ribs are lightly charred and very tender, 15 to 20 minutes longer. Serve the ribs hot or warm, cut into serving portions. Accompany the ribs with any remaining barbecue sauce for dipping and plenty of napkins.

NOTE: *St. Louis-style ribs are pork ribs trimmed rectangularly.*

Lemonade Chicken Drumsticks

The last time I was at Gillette Stadium for a tailgate prior to a New England Patriots game I noticed that almost every tailgate gathering (there were well over a hundred!) featured chicken wings being cooked over a portable grill. Personally, I find chicken wings difficult to eat and have always preferred meatier and easier to hold drumsticks. I'm willing to risk a modicum of flack for opting to include this tasty drumstick recipe instead of wings in this chapter. The drumsticks are equally tasty hot off the grill or cooked in advance and served slightly chilled or at room temperature. SERVES 6

½ can (6 ounces; ½ cup) frozen lemonade
    concentrate, thawed

¼ cup soy sauce

1½ tablespoons minced peeled fresh ginger

3 cloves garlic, peeled and minced

½ teaspoon sea salt

½ teaspoon sweet paprika

Finely grated zest of 1 lemon

3 pounds chicken drumsticks (12 to 16
    drumsticks)

⅓ cup minced fresh cilantro

Vegetable oil, for oiling the grill grate

1 Place the lemonade concentrate, soy sauce, ginger, garlic, salt, paprika, and lemon zest in a mixing bowl and stir to mix.

2 Place the drumsticks in a nonreactive baking dish such as a 13-by-9-inch glass or ceramic dish. Pour the marinade over the drumsticks, turning them to coat, and sprinkle the minced cilantro on top. Cover the baking dish and let the drumsticks marinate for at least 6 hours in the refrigerator or overnight.

3 When ready to grill, set up a charcoal or gas grill and preheat it to medium-low heat.

4 Remove the drumsticks from the marinade and discard the marinade. Brush the grill grate with oil, place the drumsticks on the grate, and grill them, until cooked through, 45 to 50 minutes, turning them every 7 to 10 minutes to brown them evenly all over. (Grilling the drumsticks slowly over low heat makes them very tender and tasty.) Serve the drumsticks hot off the grill or prepare them ahead and serve them slightly chilled or at room temperature. They will keep, covered, in the refrigerator for up to 1 day.

Parke's Picnic Chicken

My cousin Parke Madden runs The Weather Store in Sandwich on Cape Cod, just down the street from his mother's home. He has a tradition of eating lunch often with her and he and his young family are also frequent dinner guests. This simple chicken thigh recipe is one of Parke's favorite

« Barbecued Ribs with Moose-a-maquoddy
    Molasses Mustard

dinners and my aunt, Diane Madden, apologetically explains it was originally created as a winter dinner using dried herbs when Parke was growing up on Nantucket. However, the first time I tasted the recipe was on a warm September evening in Sandwich when my aunt served it with sliced garden tomatoes and corn on the cob. It was love at first bite and I decided she needed to stop feeling embarrassed about calling for dried herbs when fresh were in season. I now have taken to making the recipe solely for picnicking purposes.

A key seasoning in this recipe and many others that my aunt makes is what she calls her house seasoning: McCormick California Style Garlic Pepper containing both red bell peppers and black peppercorns. The blend is sold in many supermarkets. SERVES 6

1 tablespoon McCormick's California Style Garlic Pepper

1 teaspoon sea salt

1 teaspoon crumbled dried tarragon

½ teaspoon crumbled dried oregano

¼ teaspoon dried thyme

½ teaspoon sweet paprika

10 to 12 skin-on, bone-in chicken thighs (4½ to 5 pounds)

3 tablespoons extra virgin olive oil

1 Preheat the oven to 325°F. Line a large rimmed baking sheet with heavy-duty aluminum foil.

2 Place the garlic pepper, salt, tarragon, oregano, thyme, and paprika in a small bowl and stir to blend.

3 Trim any excess fat from the chicken thighs and discard it. Brush the chicken thighs evenly all over with the olive oil and place them on the prepared baking sheet. Season each thigh with a generous sprinkling of the seasoning blend. Bake the thighs for 45 minutes. Take the baking sheet out of the oven and carefully pour off any fat that has accumulated in the pan. Return the chicken to the oven and continue baking until crispy and golden brown, 45 minutes longer.

4 Serve the chicken thighs hot, warm, or at room temperature. They will keep in the refrigerator, covered, for up to 3 days.

Catcher in the Rye Bread

When I was assigned to write a magazine article on Home Hill Inn in Plainfield, New Hampshire, I became instantly enamored of this picturesque, rural area and particularly intrigued with the neighboring town of Cornish, famous as the place where writer J. D. Salinger lived as a recluse. At the time, I had yet to read Salinger's *The Catcher in the Rye* and only did so after it was required reading for my son in his ninth grade English class. Suffice it to say, I immediately understood why the book had never been required reading for me when I was that age, attending an all-girls boarding school in Connecticut. I have subsequently done a lot of additional reading about Salinger and his confounding idiosyncrasies, making me even less of a literary fan.

Even though my Salinger research has made me aware that the writer's bizarre dietary practices would never have permitted him to eat this bread, I could not resist naming it as I have because I can actually picture myself tearing into a loaf and enjoying it with a hunk of cheese and/or some sausages on a picnic excursion in the truly beautiful New Hampshire countryside that was home to J. D. Salinger for many decades. MAKES TWO 1-POUND LOAVES

½ cup lukewarm water (105°F)

2 teaspoons active dry yeast

4 cups unbleached all-purpose flour, plus flour for kneading

1⅓ pounds rye flour

2 tablespoons plus 1 teaspoon cornmeal

2 tablespoons caraway seeds

1½ teaspoons sea salt

1 teaspoon sugar

1 bottle (12 ounces) ale or other amber beer

2 tablespoons molasses

2 tablespoons vegetable oil, plus 1 teaspoon

1 Place the lukewarm water in a small bowl and sprinkle the yeast over it. Stir to mix and allow to stand until the yeast is foamy and bubbly, 5 to 10 minutes.

2 Place the all-purpose flour, rye flour, 2 tablespoons of cornmeal, caraway seeds, salt, and sugar in a large bowl and thoroughly stir to mix.

3 Place the beer in a saucepan, let it come to a boil, and then remove it from the heat. Stir in the molasses and 2 tablespoons of the vegetable oil. Let the beer mixture cool to lukewarm, approximately 95° to 105°F on an instant-read thermometer. Stir the proofed yeast into the beer mixture.

4 Make a well in the center of the flour mixture. Pour the beer mixture into the well and slowly stir with a wooden spoon to combine and form a rather firm dough. Turn the dough out onto a lightly floured work surface and knead it until smooth and satiny, 6 to 8 minutes. Grease the inside of a large clean bowl with the remaining 1 teaspoon of oil. Place the dough in the bowl and cover it tightly with plastic wrap. Place the dough in a relatively warm, draft-free location and let it rise until doubled in bulk, about 1½ hours. Punch down the dough, cover it again with plastic wrap or a clean dish towel, and let it sit for 30 minutes.

5 Position a rack in the center of the oven and place a pizza stone on it. Place a rack in the bottom of the oven. Place a cake pan filled almost to the top with water on the bottom rack of the oven. Preheat the oven to 450°F.

The historic gardens, pathways, outdoor concerts, country fairs, art exhibits, and abundant hiking and canoeing opportunities make Cornish, New Hampshire, a delightful destination.

6 Meanwhile, divide the dough in half and shape it into 2 round loaves. Lightly dust a pizza peel or large baking sheet with the remaining 1 teaspoon of cornmeal and place the loaves on top, making sure they are several inches apart. Cover the loaves with a clean dish towel and let them rise for an additional 45 minutes.

7 Using a very sharp knife, razor, or serrated knife, make a ½-inch-deep slash across the top of each loaf. Slide the loaves onto the heated pizza stone, spacing them a few inches apart. Bake the loaves for 15 minutes and then reduce the heat to 400°F. Continue baking until the bread makes a hollow sound when tapped with your knuckles, 20 to 25 minutes longer.

8 Transfer the loaves to a wire rack and let them cool before slicing. Since making this delicious rye bread is a labor of love, you may want to freeze one of the loaves for a future picnic or to have on hand for making sandwiches. To freeze, place the loaf in a large plastic bag, removing any air pockets. Freeze for up to 2 months. It will take 2 to 3 hours to thaw at room temperature.

Pumpkin Corn Bread with Maple Pecan Butter

Baking this moist corn bread in a cast-iron skillet makes it easy and attractive to transport to a tailgate picnic. The flavors say fall and if you have a portable grill going at your gathering, you can place the skillet on it for a few minutes to rewarm the corn bread before slathering it with the maple pecan butter. MAKES ONE 12-INCH-ROUND CORN BREAD; SERVES 8 TO 10

For the pumpkin corn bread

6 tablespoons (¾ stick) unsalted butter

2 cups yellow cornmeal

1 teaspoon baking powder

1 teaspoon baking soda

1 tablespoon sugar

¾ teaspoon salt

¾ cup buttermilk

1 cup (8 ounces) sour cream

¾ cup canned unsweetened pumpkin

1 large egg, lightly beaten

For the maple pecan butter

6 tablespoons (¾ stick) unsalted butter, at room temperature

¼ cup pure maple syrup

⅓ cup chopped pecans, lightly toasted (see page 70)

1 Preheat the oven to 350°F.

2 Make the pumpkin corn bread: Place 2 tablespoons of the butter in a 10- to 11-inch cast-iron skillet and place the skillet in the oven until the butter is melted. Brush the melted butter evenly over the bottom and up the side of the skillet. Melt the remaining 4 tablespoons of butter in a separate small saucepan and set it aside briefly.

3 Combine the cornmeal, baking powder, baking soda, sugar, and salt in a mixing bowl. Place the buttermilk, sour cream, pumpkin, egg, and melted butter in a second mixing bowl and whisk until thoroughly combined. Add the pumpkin mixture to the cornmeal mixture and stir until evenly combined.

4 Scrape the batter into the prepared skillet and bake the corn bread until a toothpick inserted into the center of the corn bread comes out clean, about 25 minutes. Let cool a few minutes before serving.

5 Make the maple pecan butter: Place the 6 tablespoons of room temperature butter and the maple syrup in a small mixing bowl and mash them with the back of a spoon until thoroughly combined. Fold in the pecans and transfer the maple pecan butter to a small, decorative crock. Serve the butter with the warm pumpkin corn bread, slathering it over the top of each piece.

Early to Rise

"Early to bed, and early to rise,
Makes a man healthy, wealthy, and wise."
—Benjamin Franklin

The "early to rise" proverb, often attributed to Ben Franklin, may not be infallible advice for navigating today's complex and turbulent economy, and I have read that statesmen and writers have been poking fun at the proverb for centuries. George Washington was said not to believe it and Mark Twain claimed he became "poorer and poorer" whenever he got up early. In 1939, James Thurber wrote in *The New Yorker*: "Early to rise and early to bed makes a male healthy and wealthy and dead."

Since I am not male and my late-night partying days scarcely ever existed and ceased long ago, I still happen to believe in the merit of rising early—if only to glimpse a fleeting pink sunrise outside my bedroom window, hear wild birds chirping symphonically in my backyard, revel in rare minutes of tranquillity, or take time to savor the breakfast treats in this chapter. Since my son is at an age where sleep is a paramount priority, he is far more annoyed than overjoyed when I brake during family travels to hunt down exceptional bagels to use in assembling the smoked salmon breakfasts

my husband and I so adore. Of course, those who snooze, lose. Some may bat a groggy eyelid at a few of my less mainstream breakfast rituals, as I have long relished in the odd habit of mashing avocado onto toast, and scrambling my eggs with cottage cheese. I tend to throw caloric care to the wind when it comes to indulging in baked breakfast goodies, pancakes, and French toast. Furthermore, I'll never say no to a slice (more accurately, slices) of crispy New England bacon and on rare occasions (occasions that readily rouse my son from slumber) will serve a fruit-based dessert like plum crunch for breakfast or brunch. In general, my morning fare is not as unusual or indulgent as I may make it sound since I am quite happy eating Greek yogurt mixed with granola most days of the week, especially when rhubarb is in season and I can further lavish the combination with a couple of tablespoons of Oven-Roasted Rhubarb.

My bank balance may not reflect it, but I wholeheartedly believe I am at least metaphorically richer and most certainly gastronomically richer for rising early.

Pickett Street Cafe Inspired Breakfast Bagels with Smoked Salmon

The 158 Pickett Street Cafe in South Portland, Maine, offers a terrific breakfast and lunch menu centered around homemade bagel sandwiches, running the gamut from the classic New England bacon, egg, and cheddar to the "Hippie" with hummus, cucumbers, carrots, greens, and seeds. All are served in a wonderfully clever yet basic Maine fashion—artfully arranged in a pie tin rather than on a regular plate. My husband's favorite breakfast has long been a toasted bagel with cream cheese and smoked salmon, so it is no surprise that this is our favorite combination to order at the Pickett Street Cafe, no matter what the time of day.

Pickett Street Cafe gussies up its bagel and smoked salmon presentation with thinly sliced cucumbers, red onion, capers, and sprigs of fresh dill, garnishes we now love to use at home as well. I have even gone so far as to buy a couple of old pie tins so we can totally relive the Pickett Street Cafe experience when in our Cape Cod kitchen. Plain or whipped Philadelphia cream cheese is absolutely fine to spread on the bagels, but if you are feeling extra energetic you may want to stir up a batch of my Preppy Cream Cheese, a family favorite. Needless to say, high-quality smoked salmon is a must to serve with the bagels and the hardwood-smoked salmon from Sullivan Harbor Farm in Hancock Village, Maine, is an excellent choice to use here. SERVES 2 TO 4

2 top-quality sesame, poppy, or everything
 bagels, cut in half crosswise

The food served at 158 Pickett Street Cafe in South Portland, Maine—trust me—is fabulous. The bagels are made on the premises and are some of the best I have ever eaten.

4 to 6 tablespoons Preppy Cream Cheese (recipe
 follows) or plain or whipped Philadelphia
 cream cheese

4 to 6 ounces thinly sliced top-quality smoked
 salmon

4 thinly sliced rounds of cucumber, peeled if
 waxed, slices cut in half

¼ cup thinly sliced peeled red onion

1½ teaspoons drained brined capers

12 small sprigs fresh dill

Coarsely cracked black peppercorns

1 Toast the bagels to your desired degree of brownness. Immediately spread the cut side of each toasted bagel half with a thin smear of Preppy Cream Cheese or plain cream cheese (I tend to use far less cream cheese than traditional Jewish delis).

2 Top each bagel half with a slice or a bit more of the smoked salmon. Place 1 cucumber round (i.e., two halved slices) on top of each salmon-topped bagel half. Scatter the red onion and capers evenly over the

Braking for Bagels

My husband and I consider ourselves to be very fussy bagel aficionados and therefore will go to great lengths to brake for really good bagels wherever our travels take us. In the Cape Cod area both Pain D'Avignon in Hyannis and Iggy's Bread in Cambridge supply select stores with decent bagels. However, the most exceptional bagels (yes, even better than those at the now defunct H&H Bagels in New York City) we have ever enjoyed come from two neighboring sources in an unlikely spot—South Portland, Maine—the 158 Pickett Street Cafe and the Scratch Baking Co. South Portland's 158 Pickett Street is a totally funky café across the street from a community college and it is staffed by various body-pierced employees who aspire to and in fact deserve to earn tips for "counter intelligence."

Scratch Baking Co. is located in a quiet little town square less than a mile from the 158 Pickett Street and everything I have bought at this neighborhood bakery has been sensational, although the bagels are always my primary reason for factoring a thirty-minute detour into my Down East travels. Both places limit the number of bagels any one person can purchase at one time and both quickly sell out of bagels on busy summer weekends and holidays. After so many Scratch Baking Co. customers asked Scratch baker Sonja Swanberg, "Why don't you just make more bagels?" she featured the bakery's bagel recipe in the company's excellent *Baker's Notes* publication, making it clear to customers how time-consuming and labor-intensive a process crafting extraordinary bagels from scratch really is. I don't think too many people have taken to following the recipe and making their own bagels—Scratch Baking Co. had already sold out of bagels on my last pre-Labor-Day weekend morning visit.

Should New England travels take you to the Berkshires in Western Massachusetts, The Great Barrington Bagel Company is a recent "braking" find, instantly worthy of garnering a permanent listing in our car's GPS system.

bagels, then top each with 3 dill sprigs. Season the bagels with coarsely cracked peppercorns to taste. Serve 1 or 2 bagel halves per person in a pie tin, if desired, for a memorable Pickett Street Cafe–style breakfast or brunch.

Preppy Cream Cheese

Bagel shops often sell a variety of flavored cream cheese spreads or "schmears" to pair with their bagels, but it is a cinch to make your own cream cheese spread and I always find homemade spreads taste superior to purchased ones. I dub this particular spread "preppy" because the pink and green flecks from the radishes and scallions make the cream cheese look like something Lilly Pulitzer would have invented. MAKES 1½ CUPS

1 package (8 ounces) full fat cream cheese, at room temperature

½ cup finely minced scallions

½ cup finely chopped red radishes

PLACE THE CREAM cheese, scallions, and radishes in a mixing bowl and beat them with a hand-held electric mixer until the cream cheese is fluffy and the scallions and radishes are evenly distributed. Refrigerate the cream cheese mixture, covered, until ready to use. The cream cheese will keep for at least 1 week.

Avocado on Toast

While this may sound like an odd morning combination, it has actually been my mother's and my favorite breakfast for almost as long as I can remember. I think the family tradition began when my mother's parents would drive their Winnebago camper up from their home in Florida to New England for the summer and pack it full of mangoes and avocados harvested from their fecund backyard. We had to do something with all the ripening bounty and mashing slices of ripe avocado onto hot toast for breakfast was born.

These days, the toast selection is far more exciting than it was decades ago and I now find it de rigueur to season the mashed avocado with French *fleur de sel*. When I really want to gild the lily, I'll sprinkle bits of crispy bacon or smoked salmon on top of the mashed avocado or even go off on a Mexican bent by garnishing with sprigs of fresh cilantro, a squeeze of lime juice, and a sprinkle of hot pepper flakes. Recently I discovered that drizzling really good extra virgin olive oil sparingly over the mashed avocado is simply divine. Meanwhile, my mother has started smearing a bit of coconut oil on her toast before topping it with mashed avocado. Tailor the toast to suit your own personal preferences, as slices of rye, multigrain, sourdough, ciabatta, olive, or rustic country bread are all very tasty when topped with mashed avocado. Savory toasted bagels can also work well. SERVES 1

For the toasts

1 large sandwich-size slice of any good savory bread

½ of a ripe Hass avocado, pitted

Crunchy sea salt, such as fleur de sel

Coarsely cracked black peppercorns

For embellishments (optional)

Crispy crumbled bacon

Smoked salmon

Fresh cilantro sprigs, freshly squeezed lime juice, and hot red pepper flakes

Extra virgin olive oil

Coconut oil

TOAST THE BREAD until lightly golden. Halve and peel the avocado and cut the flesh into slices. Arrange the avocado slices on top of the toast and, using a fork, mash the avocado evenly over the top of the warm toast. Season the avocado with salt and cracked peppercorns to taste and enjoy at once as is, or gild the avocado with embellishments as desired.

Peanut Butter, Banana, and Nutella

Yes, it is true that everyone in my family has a different favorite breakfast and this combination has been my son's favorite breakfast and sometimes lunch, too. Oliver likes this indulgent sandwich to be made with Pepperidge Farm cinnamon swirl raisin bread, preferably untoasted, although I personally think the bread should be toasted so that the warmth can partially melt the peanut butter and Nutella—the hazelnut and chocolate spread. For the ultimate rendition of this kid-friendly treat, try to find Nutella that has been imported from Italy rather than the Canadian-made Nutella sold throughout North America. A few Italian specialty stores in Boston's North End take pride in selling only Nutella imported from Italy. The Italian Nutella has a more pronounced hazelnut flavor than the North American version. MAKES 1 GROWING BOY VERY HAPPY

2 slices Pepperidge Farm cinnamon swirl
    raisin bread

2 tablespoons smooth peanut butter

½ of a ripe banana, peeled and sliced into
    ⅓-inch-thick rounds

1½ tablespoons Nutella

TOAST THE BREAD, if desired, until lightly
golden. Spread 1 slice with the peanut butter and top
it with the banana slices. Spread the second slice of
bread with the Nutella and lightly smush the Nutella
side into the bananas to make a sandwich. Cut the
sandwich in half on the diagonal and serve with plenty
of napkins.

Classic New England Breakfast Sandwich

When I first moved off Nantucket to mainland Cape Cod, I found being able to order
a breakfast sandwich at drive-through places like
Dunkin' Donuts to be an irresistible novelty since
nothing like that existed on Nantucket. When faced
with a morning rush I can still succumb to the lure
of these commercial premade sandwiches, but the
truth is that a breakfast sandwich is always much
better when made from scratch at home with top-
notch New England ingredients.

Breakfast sandwiches can of course be crafted
with all sorts of esoteric or gourmet add-ons but
why make things complicated when the combination of a properly fried local egg topped with a few
slices of crispy top-notch bacon and melted sharp
cheddar cheese is so perfectly delicious! A fork-
split toasted English muffin is usually my preferred
bread enclosure, but sometimes I'll opt to make
an open-faced breakfast sandwich on top of half a
toasted sesame or poppy seed bagel.

Still another option I like when I end up with
a loaf of artisanal bread punctuated with annoy-
ing air pockets is to panfry a thick slice in butter
with an egg plopped into the largest hole. Once the
egg has set, I place the cheddar on top to melt and
coarsely crumble the bacon over the melted cheese.
Transferred to a plate, I eat it with a knife and fork.
In my house we call this toad in a hole, although true
toad in a hole is a terrific British dish of browned
sausages, or bangers, baked in a popover-type batter and is an indulgence my husband often makes
on Christmas morning. MAKES 1 BREAKFAST
SANDWICH

2 slices top-quality bacon, such as Vermont
    Smoke and Cure or North Country
    Smokehouse Applewood Smoked

1 tablespoon unsalted butter

1 very fresh large or extra-large egg,
    preferably organic

Sea salt and freshly ground black pepper

1 fork-split English muffin, or 2 slices your
    choice of bread

1 ounce thinly sliced or coarsely shredded
    sharp or extra-sharp Vermont cheddar
    cheese

1   Place the bacon in a large, heavy skillet and cook
over medium heat until nicely crisped, 5 to 6 minutes. Transfer the bacon to a paper towel–lined plate
to drain.

2   Melt the butter in a small skillet over low heat.
Carefully break the egg into the skillet, add salt and
pepper to taste, increase the heat to medium-low, and
cook the egg slowly until the white has just set and
the yolk is cooked to the degree of doneness you prefer, 3½ minutes for a runny yolk to 5 minutes for a
completely set yolk.

3   While the egg is cooking, toast the English muffin halves. Transfer the fried egg to 1 of the toasted
English muffin halves and top it with the bacon. Dip

the other English muffin half, cut side down, into the skillet in which the egg was cooked to absorb any remaining butter. Top that English muffin half with the cheddar cheese and place it in a microwave oven set on high power for 20 to 30 seconds to melt the cheese.

4 Plop the melted cheese side of the muffin on top of the bacon and egg and press gently to sandwich everything together. Enjoy at once.

Blueberry Pancakes

While pancakes are not a mainstay in my own breakfast routine, I believe every home cook in New England wants to have a good go-to recipe that doesn't rely on a prepackaged mix. This is mine. You do not have to add the blueberries if they are not in season or if you prefer plain pancakes, but blueberry pancakes seem to be a big draw wherever I travel in New England. Feel free to substitute other seasonal fruits for the blueberries, bearing in mind that it is always best to scatter the fruit on top of the pancake batter once it has hit the griddle or frying pan rather than mix it into the batter. That way you can control how the fruit is dispersed in the batter.

While I insist on panfrying my pancakes in butter, I tend not to top the cooked pancakes with additional butter, preferring to drizzle some real New England maple syrup artfully over the top of each serving. Try not to drench the pancakes in excessive syrup, as the flavor of all the from-scratch pancake components shines brighter when syrup constraint is exercised. MAKES 8 TO 10 PANCAKES; SERVES 4

1 cup unbleached all-purpose flour

2 tablespoons sugar

½ teaspoon baking powder

½ teaspoon baking soda

1 cup plain yogurt (use whole milk variety) or sour cream

2 large eggs, lightly beaten

4 tablespoons (½ stick) unsalted butter, melted and cooled for at least 5 minutes, plus butter for cooking the pancakes

⅓ cup whole milk

½ teaspoon pure vanilla extract

⅔ cup fresh highbush or wild Maine blueberries, carefully sorted for stem, leaves, and mushy berries

Pure maple syrup, for serving

1 Preheat the oven to 200°F (optional).

2 Place the flour, sugar, baking powder, and baking soda in a medium-size mixing bowl and stir to combine evenly. Make a well in the center and add the yogurt or sour cream, eggs, melted butter, milk, and vanilla. Whisk the liquid ingredients until blended and then stir them into the dry ingredients to make a smooth batter.

3 Melt 2 tablespoons of butter in a large, heavy skillet or on a griddle over medium heat. When the butter begins to sizzle, working in batches, drop the pancake batter by about 3 tablespoonfuls into the hot skillet. Once the batter has spread to 3- to 4-inch pancakes, scatter a small handful of blueberries over the surface of each.

4 Cook the pancakes until several bubbles start to form on the top and the bottom is a light golden brown, 2 to 2 ½ minutes. Turn the pancakes over and continue cooking them until the second side has browned, 2 to 2 ½ minutes longer. Serve the pancakes at once or keep them warm in the oven while you cook the rest of the pancakes. Repeat with the remaining batter and blueberries, adding more butter to the skillet as needed, until all of the pancakes have been cooked. Serve the pancakes with maple syrup drizzled on top.

Pumpkin and Ricotta Pancakes with Maple Pecan Browned Butter and Dried Cranberries

My attitude toward cooking with store-bought ricotta cheese changed once I discovered the kettle-heated, hand-dipped, unhomogenized tubs of ricotta being made in Providence, Rhode Island, by Narragansett Creamery. While I have on occasion made my own ricotta cheese, it tends to be too delicate to cook with and I usually end up eating it as is sprinkled with fresh herbs and olive oil or topped with fruit and honey. The creamery's Renaissance Ricotta offers the best of both worlds—a fluffy textured, cloudlike cheese that is delicious spooned directly from its tub yet sturdy enough to be used in cooking. These tender pumpkin pancakes are a great way to experience the romance of the creamery's philosophy of promising to deliver the savor of Rhode Island's "salty sea meeting the rocky shore." The maple pecan browned butter and dried cranberry topping is pretty terrific, too. MAKES 12 PANCAKES; SERVES 6

For the maple pecan browned butter

8 tablespoons (1 stick) salted butter, preferably Kate's salted butter

½ cup pure maple syrup

½ cup coarsely chopped pecans, toasted (see page 70)

⅓ cup dried cranberries

For the pumpkin pancakes

1½ cups unbleached all-purpose flour

3 tablespoons (packed) light brown sugar

2 teaspoons baking powder

¾ teaspoon pumpkin pie spice

½ teaspoon fine sea salt

2 large eggs

1⅓ cups whole milk

¾ cup canned unsweetened pumpkin

½ cup ricotta cheese, preferably Narragansett Creamery's Renaissance Ricotta

Unsalted butter, for cooking the pancakes

1 Preheat the oven to 200°F (optional).

2 Make the maple pecan browned butter: Melt the butter in a small, heavy saucepan over medium heat, stirring. Cook the butter, stirring it occasionally and watching it carefully, until the butter has turned to a fragrant nutty brown color, 3 to 5 minutes. Remove the pan from the heat and stir in the maple syrup, pecans, and cranberries. Keep the browned butter warm over very low heat.

3 Make the pumpkin pancakes: Place the flour, brown sugar, baking powder, pumpkin pie spice, and salt in a mixing bowl and stir until evenly combined. Place the eggs, milk, pumpkin, and ricotta cheese in another mixing bowl and whisk until well combined. Add the dry ingredients to the pumpkin mixture and stir until just combined and smooth.

4 Melt 2 tablespoons of butter in a large, heavy skillet or on a griddle over medium heat. When the butter begins to sizzle, working in batches, drop the pancake batter by ¼ cupfuls into the hot skillet. Cook the pancakes until they are covered with bubbles on the top and golden brown on the bottom, 2 to 2½ minutes. Turn the pancakes over and continue cooking them until the second side is golden, 2 to 2½ minutes longer. Serve the pancakes at once or keep them warm in the oven while you cook the rest of the pancakes. Repeat with the remaining pancake batter, adding more butter to the skillet as needed until all of the pancakes have been cooked. Serve 2 hot pancakes per person with the warm maple pecan browned butter spooned over the top.

Being taken to the woodshed is not punitive when that woodshed is part of the pastoral landscape of Rhode Island's beautiful Block Island.

Rhode Island Johnnycakes

For the longest time, I couldn't muster up much enthusiasm for Rhode Island's beloved version of pancakes, called johnnycakes, made from stone ground white cornmeal and boiling water. I'd look at the traditional 1886 recipe printed on the blue and white box of Kenyon's johnnycake white cornmeal, the product most people use to make johnnycakes, be less than enthusiastic about its four ingredients, and let the box sit in the back of my refrigerator for another year, since the package had promised: "Kenyon's Johnny Cake Corn Meal will last indefinitely when refrigerated." Well, let's just say since I found this advertising to be truthful, I decided to read all the fine print on the Kenyon's box more carefully and was reinvigorated when I read that: "All Rhode Islanders will agree, there's only one correct Johnny Cake recipe—and that's their own!"

I set out to make my own johnnycake recipe and was pleasantly surprised to find that thinning the traditional johnnycake batter with half-and-half did the trick for me and soon I found myself eating johnnycakes unadorned directly from the skillet, topping them with smoked salmon and crème fraîche, and using them as an absorbent accompaniment to Finnan Haddie. When all is said and done, if you are a fan of polenta and/or grits, you most likely will be happy to join Rhode Islanders in enjoying johnnycakes for breakfast.

Boxes of Kenyon's johnnycake cornmeal are sold all over Rhode Island and are increasingly being stocked in New England supermarkets. It is also easy to order from the Kenyon website: Kenyonsgristmill.com MAKES 10 TO 12 JOHNNYCAKES; SERVES 4 TO 6

1 cup Kenyon's stone ground johnnycake white cornmeal

1 teaspoon sugar

½ teaspoon fine sea salt

1½ cups boiling water

½ cup half-and-half

2 tablespoons (¼ stick) unsalted butter

1 tablespoon olive oil

Smoked salmon and crème fraîche, Roasted Sausages and Pears (page 214), or Down East Finnan Haddie (page 313), for serving (optional)

1 Combine the cornmeal, sugar, and salt in a heatproof mixing bowl. Pour in the boiling water and stir well to make a thick batter. Mix in the half-and-half.

2 Melt the butter in the olive oil in a large skillet over medium-high heat. Drop the johnnycake batter by heaping tablespoonfuls into the hot skillet and let cook undisturbed until the bottom is golden brown, 5 to 6 minutes. Turn the johnnycakes over and continue cooking them until the second side is crisp and golden brown, 4½ to 5 minutes. Serve the johnnycakes hot, either plain or with your choice of accompaniments.

Scrambled Eggs with Cottage Cheese

When I was growing up in Connecticut, Bob Steele was the best-known personality on our local Hartford radio station, WTIC. Bob Steele had started broadcasting for the station in 1936 and stayed with WTIC for his entire sixty-six year career, until he passed away in 2002. He was totally revered by my family and my father always had Bob Steele's show on the radio every morning as he drove me and my siblings to Mooreland Hill School in Kensington on his way to his dentistry office in New Britain, Connecticut.

Bob Steele had a special way of scrambling eggs with cottage cheese and he often talked about the recipe on the radio. Naturally, my mother took to scrambling her eggs in Bob Steele's manner and to this day everyone in my family still loves eggs scrambled with cottage cheese. The cottage cheese adds an extra boost of protein as well as a creamy texture to the eggs. I prefer to use either Hood Country Style cottage cheese or Cabot Vermont-style 4 percent milk fat cottage cheese in the recipe. Since I usually have a pot of chives growing on my deck, I like to top off the scrambled eggs with a generous smattering of freshly snipped chives. SERVES 2 (THE RECIPE CAN BE EASILY DOUBLED OR TRIPLED)

4 extra-large eggs, preferably organic

⅔ cup cottage cheese, preferably not low-fat or fat-free

1 tablespoon unsalted butter

Sea salt and freshly ground black pepper

1 tablespoon snipped fresh chives (optional)

1 Crack the eggs into a small mixing bowl. Add the cottage cheese and whisk vigorously for about 1 minute until very well combined.

2 Melt the butter in a medium-size skillet over medium heat. When the butter begins to sizzle, pour in the scrambled egg mixture and reduce the heat to low. Let cook undisturbed for about 1 minute. Using a silicone spatula, fold the cooked portion of the eggs at the edge of the skillet into the center, stirring gently but constantly. Once the eggs have begun to form fluffy curds, 2 to 3 minutes, season them with salt and pepper to taste. Continue cooking the eggs to the desired consistency, 1 to 2 minutes more; they should be moist and creamy and still slightly runny.

3 Serve the scrambled eggs at once and top each serving with a generous sprinkling of chives, if desired.

New Hampshire-Style Egg Scramble

The Friendly Toast, a kitschy fifties-style diner with locations in Portsmouth, New Hampshire, and Cambridge, Massachusetts, gets tons of rave reviews and some reviewers claim that it serves "the best breakfast in America." Both Friendly Toast locations serve eggs that are scrambled with asparagus, bacon, and goat cheese and the dish is listed on the menu as "New Hampshire's Finest."

What I like best about the preparation is the way the goat cheese is added at the end of the cooking, allowing the crumbles to stay intact but warmed just enough to begin to melt. Having gone through all the hard labor digging trenches to plant my own asparagus patch, I find it a sacrilege to add asparagus to scrambled eggs and instead make my New Hampshire-style scramble with colorful strips of bell peppers. The Friendly Toast accompanies their scrambled eggs, in fine New England fashion, with toasted anadama bread, made from cornmeal, rye flour, and molasses. SERVES 4

4 slices top-quality New England smoked bacon

2 tablespoons extra virgin olive oil

½ small red bell pepper, stemmed, seeded, and cut into strips 1½ inches long and ½ inch wide

½ small yellow or orange bell pepper, stemmed, seeded, and cut into strips 1½ inches long and ½ inch wide

4 scallions, both white and tender green parts, trimmed and thinly sliced

7 extra-large eggs, preferably organic

Sea salt and freshly ground black pepper

4 ounces creamy goat cheese, preferably from a New England cheese maker (see Note), crumbled

1 Place the bacon in a large, heavy skillet and cook over medium heat until nicely crisped, 7 to 9 minutes. Transfer the bacon to a paper towel–lined plate to drain. Wash out the skillet.

2 Heat the olive oil in the cleaned skillet over medium-high heat. Add the bell pepper strips and cook until softened, about 5 minutes. Stir in the scallions and cook a minute or two more. Reduce the heat to medium-low.

3 Crack the eggs into a mixing bowl and whisk vigorously. Pour the eggs into the skillet with the vegetables. Using a silicone spatula, fold the cooked portion of the eggs at the edge of the skillet into the center, stirring gently but constantly until the eggs are almost set but still a little wet, 3 to 4 minutes. Season the eggs with salt and black pepper to taste, then crumble the bacon and sprinkle it and the goat cheese evenly over the top. Cook 30 seconds longer.

4 Remove the skillet from the heat and let the scrambled eggs stand for 1 to 2 minutes to finish cooking while the goat cheese crumbles warm. Serve the scrambled eggs at once.

NOTE: *New Hampshire's Heart Song Farm, Vermont Creamery, and Maine's Seal Cove Farm are but a few very good sources for New England goat cheese.*

Vermont Breakfast Puff with Crisp Bacon, Cheddar Cheese, and Maple Syrup

I believe that puffy Dutch baby pancakes first came into vogue in this country when Craig Claiborne published a recipe in *The New York Times* in 1966 called David Eyre's pancake. The recipe went on to become wildly popular and now numerous variations abound, most calling for the addition of sweetened fruit. Since fruit recipes already share much of the limelight in my breakfast repertoire, I decided to play around with a savory version of a Dutch baby pancake in the hopes the result would taste something like a quiche lorraine but be less fussy to make. My experimentation was not only rewarded but also ended up as a tasty tribute to a few of my favorite Vermont products. Be sure to plan ahead, as the batter works best when whisked together the night before and refrigerated overnight. MAKES 1 PUFF; SERVES 4 TO 6

For the batter

6 large eggs, preferably organic

1 cup whole milk

1 cup unbleached all-purpose flour

¼ teaspoon fine sea salt

2½ tablespoons unsalted butter

For the toppings

6 slices top-quality thick-cut maple smoked bacon, cooked until crisp, then drained on paper towels

1 cup grated sharp Vermont cheddar cheese

2 scallions, both white and light green parts, trimmed and thinly sliced on the diagonal

Pure maple syrup, for serving

1   Make the batter: The night before you plan on baking the breakfast puff, beat the eggs in a medium-size mixing bowl with a hand-held mixer at high speed until frothy, about 1½ minutes. Add the milk, flour, and salt and continue beating until the batter is very smooth and creamy, about 3 minutes. Cover the bowl and refrigerate the batter overnight. Remove the batter from the refrigerator at least 15 minutes before you plan on baking the puff.

2   Place a rack in the center of the oven and preheat the oven to 425°F. Place a medium-size cast-iron skillet or other heavy skillet, in the oven to preheat.

3   Remove the hot skillet from the oven and add the butter, swirling the skillet to melt it. Give the batter a quick whisk and pour it into the skillet. Bake the puff until it has risen in a dramatic fashion and the edges are golden brown, about 25 minutes.

4   Add the toppings: Crumble the bacon into pieces and scatter it and the cheddar evenly over the top of the puff. Return the skillet to the oven and cook the puff until the cheese has melted, 4 to 5 minutes.

5   Remove the puff from the oven and scatter the scallions over the top. Cut the puff into wedges and serve it at once with a scant drizzling of maple syrup (the syrup may sound like an odd addition but it adds a really compelling contrast to the savory ingredients).

Castle Hill Inn's Signature Breakfast Hash

Of all the places I have stayed during the process of researching this cookbook, Castle Hill Inn—a Relais & Châteaux property on a splendidly picturesque and tranquil forty acre peninsula in Newport, Rhode Island, has to be the most magically restorative. Castle Hill Inn's spectacular ocean views and nature trails soothe away the stresses of our modern world. And, its food is some of the finest I have ever enjoyed, as chef Karsten Hart's absolute passion for cooking shines through in every dish.

Hart is a highly personable half-German and half-Sicilian chef who grew up cooking in New Orleans and now has the challenge of applying his culinary sensibilities to New England cooking. Don't worry—the combination is truly a winning one! Witness Castle Hill's indulgent signature breakfast hash made with native lobsters and potatoes. At Castle Hill this hash is served topped with two poached eggs, but I usually opt for one when I make it at home. I considered skipping the poached egg altogether but discovered that the hash is really best when the egg yolk oozes between the crevices of the succulent lobster meat and crispy potatoes. SERVES 6

3 large white potatoes, peeled and cut into
    ½- to ¾-inch dice

Sea salt

1 pound freshly cooked lobster meat (see page
    120), coarsely chopped

1 bunch scallions, both white and tender green
    parts, trimmed and finely diced

4 cloves garlic, peeled and minced

1½ tablespoons minced fresh tarragon

½ cup crème fraîche

½ cup panko bread crumbs, or more as needed

Freshly ground white or black pepper

Freshly squeezed lemon juice

½ cup yellow cornmeal

¼ cup canola or grape seed oil

6 large eggs, preferably organic, poached (see
    Box)

1   **Place the diced potatoes in a pot of cold salted**

water and cook over medium heat until just fork tender, about 20 minutes. Take care not to let the potatoes boil while cooking (says Hart). Drain the potatoes very well and transfer them to a large mixing bowl. Let the potatoes cool to room temperature.

2 Add the lobster meat, scallions, garlic, and tarragon to the cooled potatoes and toss to combine. Add the crème fraîche and panko, stirring to bind the ingredients together. The lobster hash should be somewhat wet but still hold its shape when formed into a patty. Add more panko if necessary to bind. Season the hash with salt, pepper, and lemon juice to taste.

3 Form the hash into plump patties, approximately 3 inches in diameter. Place the cornmeal in a wide shallow dish or on a plate and dredge the hash patties in the cornmeal, turning them to coat both sides and then shaking off any excess.

4 Heat the oil in a large skillet over medium heat. Gently place the hash patties into the hot oil. Panfry the patties until golden on both sides, 3 to 4 minutes per side. Serve 2 lobster hash patties per person topped with a poached egg.

Down East Finnan Haddie

I have been to lots of places in coastal New England where it is common to serve fish for breakfast, as peculiar as the practice may sound to inland folks. The tween boys in one neighborhood where we lived on Nantucket told me they loved fried bluefish cheeks for breakfast and lots of popular breakfast joints up and down the rocky coast of Maine feature fish cakes on both their breakfast and lunch menus. Finnan haddie is an old-fashioned Scottish breakfast of smoked haddock poached in milk that seems currently to be enjoying a mini revival, probably

Poaching Coaching

Although poaching an egg requires only two ingredients, the egg itself and water, accomplishing the task can be both a bit tricky and intimidating. Here are a few tips and tricks for poaching perfection.

Begin by filling a straight-sided skillet with water to a depth of 2 to 2 ½ inches. Bring the water to a very faint simmer over medium heat. You definitely do not want the water to boil and the most surefire way to know the water is at the proper temperature for poaching is to use an instant-read thermometer and aim for a reading between 180° and 185°F.

While the water is heating, crack as many really fresh organic (if possible) eggs as needed individually into separate coffee cups or small bowls. When the poaching water is ready, tip an egg from the cup into a fine mesh strainer with a rounded bottom set over another mixing bowl and swirl it in the strainer to drain off any loose and excess egg white. This extra step is key to avoiding unsightly stray strands of egg whites surrounding the poached egg and maintaining a pleasantly rounded poached egg shape. Ease the egg from the strainer directly into the pan of barely simmering water. Repeat the process with each egg you wish to poach. Using a slotted spoon, swirl the eggs gently about while poaching to ensure even cooking.

Poach the eggs until the whites are set but the yolks remain as runny as your particular preference dictates, usually 3½ to 4 minutes. Remove each poached egg from the skillet with the slotted spoon, letting any excess water drain back into the pan and serve the eggs as desired atop hash, toast, or English muffins.

due to the superior reputation of the haddock a man named Richard Penfold smokes exclusively for Stonington Seafood on Deer Isle, Maine. Check out the website in the Note if you want to keep up with all the latest buzz and purchase this exceptional smoked haddock.

My brother, Jonathan, has long been a fan of Penfold's smoked seafood and adapted this recipe for finnan haddie from tips Rich shared with him. Jonathan says the dish will always have extra sauce because of the amount of milk required to poach the smoked haddock and he likes to add the extra smoky liquid to a pot of fish chowder. Now that I have come around to embracing Rhode Island Johnnycakes (page 308), I like the notion of arranging leftover johnnycakes in a small dish and baking them with the extra sauce spooned on top to make a quirky but very comforting Down East gratin. SERVES 4

1 piece smoked haddock (1 to 1¼ pounds), preferably from Stonington Seafood (see Note), skin removed

2 cups whole milk

2 tablespoons (¼ stick) unsalted butter

1½ tablespoons unbleached all-purpose flour

½ teaspoon freshly ground black pepper

½ teaspoon ground turmeric

1 tablespoon Dijon mustard, preferably imported

1 cup frozen baby peas, thawed

4 square slices toasted white bread, crusts removed, toast cut into triangles

1 Preheat the oven to 350°F.

2 Cut the smoked haddock into 4 equal pieces. Place the fish in a straight-sided skillet and cover it with the milk. Let come to a simmer over medium heat and cook, uncovered, until the milk has become infused with the smoky flavor of the fish, about 5 to 6 minutes. Remove the fish from the milk and place it in a nonreactive baking dish large enough to comfortably hold it. Set aside the warm milk.

3 Melt the butter in a small saucepan over medium-low heat. Whisk in the flour, and cook, whisking constantly, until well blended, about 2 minutes. Do not allow the flour mixture to brown. Stir in the pepper and turmeric and cook until blended, about 30 seconds. Slowly whisk in the reserved milk. Add the mustard and cook until the sauce thickens, 2 to 3 minutes. Stir in the peas, let cook until they are cooked through, 1 minute, then remove the sauce from the heat.

4 Pour the sauce over the smoked haddock, cover the dish with aluminum foil, and bake until the sauce is just beginning to bubble, 15 to 20 minutes.

5 To serve, place one portion of finnan haddie on each of 4 warmed plates. Spoon ⅓ to ½ cup of the sauce over each serving and surround the finnan haddie with 4 toasted bread triangles.

NOTE: *Smoked haddock can be ordered by mail from Stonington Seafood at stoningtonseafood.com.*

Roasted Sausages and Pears

I first became a fan of roasting sausages with fruit when I roasted sausages with white wine and grapes as a recipe for my *Pedaling Through Burgundy Cookbook*. Closer to home, Rhode Island restaurateurs Johanne Killeen and George Germon are quite well known for their recipe for roasted sausages and grapes made with equal amounts of hot and sweet Italian sausage.

One yuletide season when I had a surfeit of pears on hand, I decided to tinker with the concept and try roasting sausages with pears as part of a New Year's Day brunch buffet I was hosting for family. I was thrilled with the results and so was everyone else. SERVES 8 TO 10

Nantucket tends to get less winter snow than many other places in New England. However, when it does snow, the island takes on an especially enchanting and peaceful aura.

3 Meanwhile, combine the pears, balsamic vinegar, and port in a large, shallow bowl. Let the pears marinate for at least 15 minutes.

4 Add the pears, marinade, and rosemary sprigs to the roasting pan with the sausages and onion, stirring to distribute the pears evenly. Bake the pears until they have softened and the sausages and onions have browned even further, 12 to 15 minutes. Serve the sausages and pears hot or warm, preferably straight from the roasting pan.

8 high-quality fresh sweet Italian sausages (about 2 pounds), preferably made with fennel seeds

1 large red onion, peeled and cut into 1-inch chunks

3 large ripe but still firm pears, peeled, cored, and each cut into 6 to 8 chunky slices

½ cup good-quality balsamic vinegar

3 tablespoons port

8 sprigs fresh rosemary

1 Preheat the oven to 425°F.

2 Place the sausages in a pot and add water to cover. Let come to a simmer over medium heat, and cook until just barely cooked through, 12 to 15 minutes. Remove the sausages from the pot, setting aside the cooking water. Cut the sausages in half crosswise and arrange them in a large roasting pan. Scatter the onion chunks in between the pieces of sausage. Pour the cooking water into the roasting pan to a depth of about ⅛ inch. Bake the sausages, tossing them occasionally, until the liquid has evaporated and the sausages are beginning to brown nicely, 20 to 25 minutes.

Smashed Potatoes

I've never been one to make home fries for breakfast in the morning, but I inadvertently discovered these wonderful smashed potatoes make an easy and excellent alternative when I reheated leftover potatoes from a dinner the night before for breakfast. As with several of my New England recipes, it is the use of the Maine-made Kate's sea salted butter that makes the taste of even the simplest recipes extra special. You can make the potatoes ahead, refrigerate them, and then reheat them in the morning either in a skillet or hot oven. Serve these potatoes with any breakfast dish you would normally accompany with home fries. My family and friends, who have tasted these smashed potatoes, love them so much that the recipe has become a much requested dinner side dish as well. SERVES 4 TO 6

16 small new or fingerling potatoes, about 1 inch in diameter, scrubbed of any dirt

4 tablespoons (½ stick) salted butter, preferably Kate's salted butter

Sea salt and freshly ground black pepper

1 tablespoon minced fresh flat-leaf parsley or chives

1   Place the potatoes in a saucepan and add enough cold water to cover them. Let come to a boil over medium-high heat, then reduce the heat to medium and simmer until just barely tender, 15 to 20 minutes. Drain the potatoes well. Place them on a clean cutting board and smash each one squat (about ½ inch thick) with a potato masher. If you don't have a potato masher, you can use the palm of your hand or the bottom of a small, heavy skillet. The potatoes should split apart but remain intact as a round or oblong patty because of their skins.

2   Melt 2 tablespoons of the butter in a large cast-iron skillet or other heavy skillet over medium heat. Add the smashed potatoes and cook, without stirring, until crisp and brown on the bottom, 5 to 7 minutes. Using a thin metal spatula, turn the potatoes over, add the remaining 2 tablespoons of butter to the skillet and continue cooking the potatoes, without stirring, until the second side is crisped and brown, about 5 minutes more. Season the potatoes with salt and pepper to taste and sprinkle the parsley or chives on top just before serving.

Debbie's Blue Ribbon Maine Muffins

Debbie bakes these prize-winning muffins daily for the rural market my brother, Jonathan, runs in the beautiful inlet of Buck's Harbor in Brooksville, Maine. Loyal fans of the muffins secretly entered them a few years ago in the neighboring Blue Hill Fair, held annually over the Labor Day weekend. The muffins garnered a top prize and deservedly so. The secret to the muffin's tenderness is the addition of sour cream to the batter. In the summer months Debbie makes the muffins with either Maine blueberries or raspberries. I am particularly partial to the raspberry muffins and if you don't happen to have a prolific raspberry patch in your backyard, you can use frozen berries as long as they are IQF ones—that is individually quick frozen berries. In the fall and winter, Debbie uses the same batter to make cranberry orange or apple cinnamon muffins. For the cranberry variation, you'll need to substitute orange juice for the milk and dried cranberries for the blueberries or raspberries. For apple muffins, replace the berries with one cup of peeled and diced Granny Smith apples and add one half teaspoon of ground cinnamon to the batter along with the flour and baking powder. MAKES 1 DOZEN MUFFINS

Vegetable oil cooking spray

⅓ cup vegetable oil

¾ cup plus 1 tablespoon sugar

1 large egg

½ cup sour cream

2¼ cups unbleached all-purpose flour

4½ teaspoons baking powder

½ teaspoon fine sea salt

1 cup whole milk

1 cup raspberries or Maine blueberries, fresh or individually frozen

1   Place a rack in the center of the oven and preheat the oven to 375°F. Lightly coat a muffin tin that has 12 standard-size ½-cup muffin cups with vegetable oil cooking spray.

2   Place the vegetable oil, ¾ cup of the sugar, and the egg in a medium-size mixing bowl and, using a large spoon or wire whisk, whisk to mix, stirring well until nicely blended. Add the sour cream and mix well.

3   Place the flour, baking powder, and salt in a small bowl and stir until evenly combined. Add the dry ingredients to the egg mixture along with the milk and stir gently but thoroughly until a smooth batter forms. Gently fold in the berries. If you are using frozen berries do not thaw them before adding them to the batter.

4 Divide the muffin batter evenly among the 12 prepared muffin cups, filling each about three quarters full. Sprinkle the remaining 1 tablespoon of sugar evenly over the muffin tops.

5 Bake the muffins until a toothpick inserted in the center of a muffin comes out clean, 30 to 35 minutes. Let the muffins cool in the muffin tin for a few minutes, then transfer the muffins to a wire rack to cool completely—that is if you can resist eating them hot or warm.

Morning Glory Muffins

Pam McKinstry was the great talent behind a variety of food enterprises on Nantucket when I was just beginning my culinary career on the island. While I have never encountered a Pam McKinstry recipe I didn't adore, Pam herself would tell you her reputation was made with these muffins, a recipe she developed in 1978 for her first restaurant, the Morning Glory Café, situated at the end of a wharf on Nantucket's busy summer waterfront. Over the years I have seen this recipe reprinted innumerable times, often with ingredient changes, and rarely with credit given where credit is due—to Pam. However, Pam did garner the honor in 1991 of having her recipe chosen as one of *Gourmet* magazine's twenty-five favorite recipes from the past fifty years. Skip trying to figure out the math and/or reasoning guiding the award selection and instead spend your time making these beloved muffins.

Pam notes that it is the combination of fruits and carrots that keeps the muffins moist and that they actually taste better a day or two after baking, magically mellowing like a fruitcake. Pam also once revealed that she personally liked to eat her muffins with cream cheese and honey. MAKES 16 MUFFINS

2¼ cups unbleached all-purpose flour

1¼ cups sugar

1 tablespoon ground cinnamon

2 teaspoons baking soda

½ teaspoon fine sea salt

½ cup sweetened or unsweetened shredded coconut

½ cup golden raisins

1 apple, peeled and shredded over the large holes of a box grater

1 can (8 ounces) crushed pineapple, drained

2 cups shredded peeled carrots (about 4 carrots)

½ cup chopped pecans or walnuts

3 large eggs

1 cup canola or vegetable oil

1 teaspoon pure vanilla extract

1 Place a rack in the center of the oven and preheat the oven to 350°F. Line 16 standard-size ½-cup muffin cups with double-lined aluminum foil and paper muffin cup liners (see Note).

2 Sift the flour, sugar, cinnamon, baking soda, and salt together into a large mixing bowl. Add the coconut, raisins, apple, pineapple, carrots, and nuts and stir to combine.

3 Place the eggs, oil, and vanilla in a small bowl and whisk until well combined. Pour the egg mixture into the bowl with the dry ingredients and fruit and mix well.

4 Divide the muffin batter evenly among the 16 prepared muffin cups, filling each to the brim. Bake the muffins until a toothpick inserted in the center of a muffin comes out clean, about 35 minutes.

5 Let the muffins cool in the muffin tins for about 10 minutes, then transfer the muffins to a wire rack to finish cooling. Store the muffins at room temperature in an airtight container, letting them "ripen" for at least 24 hours before enjoying. The muffins will keep

for up to 3 days and may also be frozen for up to 2 months in zipper-top bags. If frozen, thaw the muffins in the refrigerator overnight and then let come to room temperature before serving.

NOTE: *These double-lined muffin cup liners are available in the supermarket.*

Highbush Blueberry Muffins

Awhile ago I was reading Jason Epstein's culinary memoir entitled *Eating*. While the chapters include several recipes, Mr. Epstein happened to mention but not print a recipe for Devon Fredericks's blueberry muffins, stating that they were far too rich for him to consider making any longer. The comment piqued my curiosity since I reasoned that something too rich for this legendary editor might in fact be right up my alley.

I knew my friend Ina Garten was a close friend of Devon's and that they were neighbors out in East Hampton so I asked her if she knew of the recipe. Ina was able to trace the recipe immediately to the great little *Loaves and Fishes* paperback cookbook Devon had written with Susan Costner back in 1980. As Ina rattled off the recipe to me, I realized that it was this very recipe that had inspired the tri-berry muffins I had made every summer morning in the 1980s in my Nantucket food shop, Que Sera Sarah. The tri-berry recipe was published in my *Nantucket Open-House Cookbook* and has lived on to become my son's favorite muffin and a recipe that I am frequently asked to bake for various school functions.

The recipe here revisits both Devon's blueberry muffin and my tri-berry muffin recipes but places an exclusive taste emphasis on the plump and juicy highbush blueberries that are most prevalent in New England from late June through July. I love the combination of blueberries and lemon and have thus chosen to lace these muffins with grated lemon zest, though blueberry purists and young children might prefer having the zest left out. If you are looking for a truly great blueberry muffin recipe that is easy to make and feeds a crowd, look no further. Just don't count the calories. MAKES 18 TO 20 MUFFINS

3½ cups unbleached all-purpose flour

1½ cups sugar

4½ teaspoons baking powder

½ teaspoon baking soda

½ teaspoon fine sea salt

1 tablespoon ground cinnamon

2 large eggs, beaten

1½ cups whole milk

16 tablespoons (2 sticks) unsalted butter, melted and cooled for at least 5 minutes

2 teaspoons finely grated lemon zest (optional)

2 to 2½ cups fresh blueberries, rinsed and carefully sorted for stems, leaves, and mushy berries

1 Place a rack in the center of the oven and preheat the oven to 375°F. Line 18 to 20 standard-size ½-cup muffin cups with double-lined aluminum foil and paper muffin cup liners (see Note, this page).

2 Place the flour, sugar, baking powder, baking soda, salt, and cinnamon in a large mixing bowl and stir to mix. Make a well in the center of the dry ingredients. Pour the eggs, milk, and melted butter into the well and stir quickly until all of the ingredients are just combined and the batter is almost smooth. A little lump here or there is fine. Gently fold in the lemon zest, if using, and the blueberries until evenly distributed.

3 Divide the muffin batter evenly among the prepared muffin cups, filling each almost to the brim. Bake the muffins until they are puffed and lightly golden on top, about 25 minutes. Let the muffins cool

in the muffin tins for at least 10 minutes, then enjoy them hot, warm, or at room temperature. The muffins taste best the day they are baked but are still quite tasty the following day. They may also be frozen for up to 2 months in zipper-top freezer bags. If frozen, thaw the muffins in the refrigerator overnight and then let come to room temperature before serving.

Maple Pear Muffins with Walnut Streusel

My friend John Boyajian's Massachusetts company, Boyajian Inc., sells an extraordinary line of intensely flavored oils, vinegars, and baking extracts. Its Natural Maple Flavor extract is one of my favorite products and it adds a distinctive yet not overpowering maple flavor to the spice and fruit melodies at play in this autumnal muffin recipe. MAKES 12 TO 14 MUFFINS

For the muffin batter

8 tablespoons (1 stick) unsalted butter, at room temperature

4 ounces cream cheese, at room temperature

½ cup granulated sugar

½ cup (packed) light brown sugar

3 large eggs

1 teaspoon pure maple flavor extract, preferably Boyajian's Natural Maple Flavor extract (see Note)

2 cups unbleached all-purpose flour

1½ teaspoons baking soda

½ teaspoon fine sea salt

1½ teaspoons ground cinnamon

¼ teaspoon freshly grated nutmeg

1 large ripe but still firm green or red Anjou pear, peeled, cored, and cut into ¼-inch dice

For the walnut streusel

¼ cup unbleached all-purpose flour

⅓ cup (packed) light brown sugar

¼ cup walnuts, chopped into small pieces

½ teaspoon ground cinnamon

3 tablespoons unsalted butter, at room temperature and cut into small pieces

1 Place a rack in the center of the oven and preheat the oven to 375°F. Line 12 to 14 standard-size ½-cup muffin cups with double-lined aluminum foil and paper muffin cup liners (see Note, page 319).

2 Make the muffin batter: Place the 8 tablespoons of butter, the cream cheese, granulated sugar, ½ cup of brown sugar, eggs, and maple extract in a large mixing bowl and, using a hand-held electric mixer, beat at medium speed until smooth and creamy.

3 Place the 2 cups of flour and the baking soda, salt, the 1½ teaspoons of cinnamon, and the nutmeg in a smaller mixing bowl and stir to mix. Stir the dry ingredients into the bowl with the butter mixture until just blended, taking care not to overmix and toughen the batter. Gently fold the diced pear into the muffin batter until evenly distributed. Divide the muffin batter evenly among the prepared muffin cups, filling each about three-quarters full.

4 Make the walnut streusel: Combine the ¼ cup of flour, ⅓ cup of brown sugar, the walnuts, and the ½ teaspoon of cinnamon in a small bowl. Scatter the pieces of softened butter over the top and, using the tips of your fingers or the tines of a fork, blend them in until the mixture forms small clumps. Sprinkle the streusel evenly over the muffin tops.

5 Bake the muffins until the streusel topping is a light golden brown, about 20 minutes. Let the muffins cool in the muffin tin(s) for at least 10 minutes, then enjoy them hot, warm, or at room temperature.

NOTE: *Boyajian extracts are available from the company. Visit their website at boyajian.com.*

Banana Bundt Bread

For reasons I have yet to fathom, my son, Oliver, refuses to eat bananas that have any light or dark spots on their peels. After becoming exasperated trying to keep spotless bananas on hand for healthy round-the-clock snacking, I took to making banana bread at least once a week.

Over the years, I have tried numerous banana bread recipes and my search for the best banana bread finally ended when I discovered the absolutely delicious cakelike banana bread made at the acclaimed Flour Bakery in Boston, run by fellow Harvard alumna Joanne Chang. This banana bread has so many diehard fans that it has become known as Flour's Famous Banana Bread, and I soon discovered that the Internet is abuzz with people weighing in on the merits of the bread. Like everyone else, I had to try the recipe and then tweak it to suit my own and especially Oliver's finicky tastes. The best tip I picked up in the process was to bake the bread in a twelve-cup Bundt pan rather than the nine-by-five-inch loaf pan stipulated in Chang's original recipe, since numerous reviewers had complained about the bread batter flowing out of the loaf pan or taking forever to bake.

Chang's technique in making the batter is different from what you will encounter in any other banana bread recipe. She beats the eggs and sugar together for at least five minutes in a stand mixer using the whip attachment. Next, she incorporates the oil, drizzling it in at low speed, almost as if she were making a mayonnaise. Chang explains the oil needs to be incorporated into the eggs gradually so as not to deflate them, especially after you have taken all that time to whip air into them in the initial step. I follow Chang's technique to the letter but use slightly less oil than she calls for in her recipe and omit the walnuts because I find their crunch a distraction to the uniquely light texture of the bread and also figure Oliver would probably object to the addition of nuts. I add a bit more

spice to the bread, replace some of the white sugar with brown, and sneak in just a little splash of rum, which I really like and which somehow has managed not to be picked up by the discerning palate of you know who. The recipe makes a big banana bread but it keeps well for at least four days when stored properly. If your family is larger than mine, this superior banana bread will certainly not last that long. MAKES 1 BANANA BREAD; SERVES 10 TO 12

Unsalted butter or vegetable oil cooking spray, for greasing the Bundt pan

1¼ cups unbleached all-purpose flour

1 teaspoon baking soda

½ teaspoon ground cinnamon

¼ tablespoon freshly grated nutmeg

½ teaspoon fine sea salt

½ cup granulated sugar

½ cup (packed) light brown sugar

2 large eggs

⅓ cup canola oil

4 very ripe medium-size bananas, peeled and mashed with a potato masher

3 tablespoons sour cream

1 teaspoon pure vanilla extract

1 tablespoon golden rum (optional)

1 Preheat the oven to 325°F. Lightly butter a 12-cup Bundt pan or coat it lightly with vegetable oil cooking spray.

2 Sift the flour, baking soda, cinnamon, nutmeg, and salt into a medium-size mixing bowl and set aside.

3 Using a stand mixer fitted with the whip attachment, beat the granulated sugar, brown sugar, and eggs together at medium speed until very light and fluffy, 5 to 7 minutes. Beating on low speed, gradually drizzle in the oil in a very light and thin stream. Take extra care to add the oil very slowly so that it is incorporated into the eggs gradually without

deflating them; this should take at least 1 minute. Add the mashed bananas, sour cream, vanilla, and rum, if using. Continue to beat on low speed just until all the ingredients are evenly combined, 45 seconds to 1 minute.

4   Using a rubber spatula, fold in the dry ingredients until just combined. No streaks of flour should be visible. Scrape the batter into the prepared Bundt pan, smoothing the top. Bake the banana bread until the top is golden brown and the bread springs back when gently pressed in the center with your finger, 45 to 55 minutes.

5   Let the banana bread cool in the Bundt pan for at least 30 minutes and then invert it onto a wire rack to cool completely. Cut the bread into 1-inch-thick serving slices. I like to store the bread on a plate at room temperature with the Bundt pan inverted back over it to keep it airtight and moist. The bread will keep for at least 4 days.

Apple Walnut Coffee Cake

This is another one of my friend Toby Greenberg's retro but terrific fruit recipes. Toby usually serves this delightful apple cake as a dessert to cap off one of her many comfort food autumn dinner gatherings, but in my house we tend to delight in the cake for breakfast since my son has a morning (noon and night, too) sweet tooth and we often skip dessert in the evening if we are not entertaining. Serve the cake with a dollop of Greek yogurt and your day will be off to a tasty start. MAKES 1 COFFEE CAKE; SERVES 6 TO 8

8 tablespoons (1 stick) unsalted butter, melted and cooled, plus butter for greasing the baking pan

1¼ cups unbleached all-purpose flour, plus flour for dusting the baking pan

2 tart apples, peeled, cored, and cut into ½-inch dice

1 cup sugar

1 large egg

1 teaspoon ground cinnamon

1 teaspoon baking soda

½ teaspoon fine sea salt

½ cup coarsely chopped walnuts

1   Preheat the oven to 375°F. Butter and lightly flour an 8-by-8-by-2-inch baking pan.

2   Place the apples, sugar, melted butter, and egg in a medium-size mixing bowl and stir to combine.

3   Combine the flour, cinnamon, baking soda, and salt in a fine mesh sieve and sift over the apple mixture. Add the walnuts and stir to mix thoroughly. Scrape the batter into the prepared baking pan.

4   Bake the coffee cake until it is golden on top and a toothpick inserted in the center comes out clean, about 45 minutes. Let the coffee cake cool in the baking pan and then serve it, cut into squares, at room temperature.

The Original September Prune Plum Crunch

Over the years, my husband and I have rented many cabins and camps in Maine on the Blue Hill peninsula in order to have our own space while visiting family. All our rentals prove to be great adventures but hands-down the most spectacular Maine experience was at the nearly century-old Kill Kare Kamp, built smack-dab on top of waterfront boulders edging Walker Pond in Sedgwick.

Despite the age of the property, the kitchen was extremely well equipped and most conducive to planning evening dinner events. So, most nights friends and family joined us on Kill Kare's wraparound porch to feast and take in the magnificent sunsets.

On our final post-Labor Day evening, I decided to make a plum crunch for dessert. The Tradewinds supermarket in Blue Hill had a surprisingly enticing supply of September prune plums and having a crunch at this time of the year had been a long-standing family tradition. When I consulted the recipe, which I had published long ago in my *Nantucket Open-House Cookbook*, I realized I didn't have certain key ingredients like oatmeal and walnuts on hand. I phoned my mother in Blue Hill to see if she had the ingredients I was lacking and she said, "You know my recipe for plum crunch never called for oatmeal and walnuts in the topping but it does have a really good topping made with an egg and melted butter." I decided it was both easier and more diplomatic to make my mother's original recipe and I must say I'll be making this recipe every September from here on in. The undertaking also reminded me that my father's once common refrain of "if there's a hard way to do something, Sarah will find it" had probably been quite accurate.

The reason this recipe is in my breakfast chapter is because we enjoyed the leftovers of the plum crunch so much the following morning that in my house we now plan to continue to enjoy plum crunch as a morning treat. It should come as no surprise that I love the crunch in the a.m. dolloped with Greek yogurt as opposed to the ice cream that is recommended for the p.m. MAKES 1 CRUNCH; SERVES 6 TO 8

3 pounds prune plums, pitted and quartered

¼ cup (packed) light brown sugar

1 cup unbleached all-purpose flour

1 cup granulated sugar

1 teaspoon ground cinnamon

½ teaspoon fine sea salt

1 large egg, beaten

8 tablespoons (1 stick) unsalted butter, melted

1   Preheat the oven to 375°F.

2   Combine the plums and brown sugar in a 1 ½- to 2-quart baking dish and toss to coat the plums with the brown sugar.

3   Sift the flour, granulated sugar, cinnamon, and salt together into a medium-size mixing bowl. Add the egg and, using your fingertips or a fork, mix until moistened enough to form clumps. Scatter the clumps of flour mixture evenly over the plums. Drizzle the melted butter evenly over the top.

4   Bake the plum crunch until the plums are bubbling and the topping is golden, about 45 minutes. Serve warm or at room temperature. Keep leftovers at room temperature covered with plastic wrap. The crunch will keep for up to 3 days.

Thanksgiving 2010 Granola

When my son was attending school on Nantucket in 2010, we celebrated Thanksgiving with our friends Bill and Christy Camp and assorted guests at the Camp's lovely island home on upper Main Street. The Camps hail from Houston and have long been known for their warm, Texas size and style hospitality. Christy spent weeks putting together custom-printed goodie bags for all her guests and one of the guests, Diane Zuckerman, contributed her special granola to the endeavor. This granola really hit the spot in the days following all the excesses of the Thanksgiving feast and I became so haunted by the memory of its healthful delectability that I finally asked Diane to share the recipe; she graciously obliged.

I now realize why this is some of the best granola I have ever tasted. It is laden with great ingredients and Diane's method for making her granola is unlike any other granola recipe I have ever seen. Diane says if you can't find an ingredient like dried mango that it is okay to substitute another dried fruit, noting that using a minimum of four different dried fruits always makes for the tastiest granola. This recipe makes a huge batch—a whopping three gallons! However, if you give granola care packages away to friends, I am certain the recipients will be as delighted as I was to receive my Thanksgiving allotment. Otherwise, if you are adept with fractions, feel free to cut Diane's recipe in half. MAKES 3 GALLONS

½ cup coconut oil

2 pounds rolled oats (Diane likes to use the Bob's Red Mill brand)

24 ounces (3 cups) flaxseeds

16 ounces (2 cups) unsweetened coconut

16 ounces (2 cups) hulled sunflower seeds

16 ounces (2 cups) pumpkin seeds (pepitas)

16 ounces (2 cups) sliced almonds

16 ounces (2 cups) dried apricots, cut into bite-size pieces

16 ounces (2 cups) dried cranberries

12 ounces (1½ cups) pitted dried prunes, cut into bite-size pieces

7 ounces (scant 1 cup) dried mango, cut into bite-size pieces

24 ounces (3 cups) amber agave nectar or honey

1 Preheat the oven to 325°F.

2 Heat ¼ cup of the coconut oil in a large skillet over medium heat. Add half of the rolled oats and toast them, stirring frequently, until lightly golden, about 10 minutes. Transfer the toasted oats to a very large mixing bowl. Repeat with the remaining ¼ cup of coconut oil and rolled oats. Transfer the second batch of toasted oats to the mixing bowl.

3 Cooking each ingredient separately, add the flaxseeds, coconut, sunflower seeds, pumpkin seeds, and almonds to the same skillet and cook until each is dry roasted, about 5 minutes per ingredient. As each ingredient is finished, add it to the bowl with the toasted oats. Add the apricots, cranberries, prunes, and mango to the bowl and toss to combine. Pour in the agave nectar or honey and toss again to coat all of the ingredients evenly.

4 Spread the granola in a layer no more than ½-inch thick on rimmed baking sheets and bake until the agave nectar or honey is hot and beginning to glisten, 12 minutes. Using a spatula, toss the granola, then continue baking it until it reaches a slightly richer shade of golden brown, 3 to 5 minutes longer.

5 Let the granola cool on the baking sheets, stirring it occasionally. Store the granola in the refrigerator in three 1-gallon refrigerator or freezer bags or divide it into smaller bags to share with friends. The granola may be refrigerated for up to 2 weeks and frozen for up to 4 months. Thaw overnight in the refrigerator.

Oven-Roasted Rhubarb

My Nantucket friend Toby Greenberg, of blueberry cheesecake fame (see page 347) and many other delights in this book, has a knack for making the very best fruit recipes. Anyone who has ever baked the recipe for Toby's cranberry pie featured in my *Cold-Weather Cooking* cookbook makes it again and again. Every spring, when the first rhubarb hits the market, Toby makes a batch of this Oven-Roasted Rhubarb and personally delivers a container to me. I immediately spoon it over Greek yogurt sprinkled with granola and look forward to having the very same breakfast, come April showers or May flowers, every single day of the week. Toby tells me that she discovered this method for cooking rhubarb in a 1951 edition of a cookbook entitled *The Way to a Man's Heart: The Settlement Cookbook*— the very same cookbook that first taught her how to bake a potato when she was a newlywed. MAKES ABOUT 4 CUPS

2 pounds rhubarb, trimmed and cut into ¾-inch slices

1¾ cups sugar

Greek yogurt and Thanksgiving 2010 Granola (page 324), for serving (optional)

1 Preheat the oven to 350°F.

2 Place the rhubarb in a 13-by-9-inch baking dish, add the sugar, and toss well. Cover the baking dish tightly with heavy-duty aluminum foil. Bake the rhubarb for 25 minutes, then uncover the baking dish and stir the rhubarb. Replace the foil and continue baking the rhubarb until it is tender, about 20 minutes longer.

3 Let the rhubarb cool to room temperature and then store it in the refrigerator, covered. It will keep for up to 10 days. Serve the rhubarb plain in a bowl or mix it with Greek yogurt and granola for breakfast.

Weekend Orange Juice

When I was growing up in Connecticut, my mother often whizzed bananas and orange juice together in the blender to kick off our weekend breakfasts. The combination is far more delicious than its simplicity would suggest and the frothy texture is most appealing. I now make this all the time for my son for breakfast, sometimes tossing in a few strawberries or raspberries, because he loves it and it is a clever way for me to use up bananas with pesky little spots on their peels that he would not otherwise eat. SERVES 4

2½ cups good-quality orange juice

1 large ripe banana, peeled and cut into 1-inch chunks

PLACE THE ORANGE juice and banana in a blender. Blend on high speed until smooth and frothy, about 45 seconds. Immediately pour the banana/orange juice into juice glasses and serve.

Newport Summer Berry Smoothies

Mornings at Castle Hill Inn in Newport, Rhode Island, kick off in the scenic ocean-view dining room with a small complimentary fruit smoothie brought to your table after the first pour of rich hot coffee. This deep blue and delicious berry smoothie was served to me one sunny August morning and it was love at first and last sip. SERVES 6

1 pint fresh blueberries, rinsed and carefully sorted for stem, leaves, and mushy berries

4 large ripe strawberries, rinsed, hulled, and sliced

1 cup diced pineapple

1 cup diced cantaloupe

2 tablespoons honey

1 cup plain yogurt

½ cup ice cubes

1 teaspoon finely slivered fresh mint, plus mint sprigs for garnish

PLACE THE BLUEBERRIES, strawberries, pineapple, cantaloupe, honey, yogurt, ice cubes, and slivered mint in a blender and blend on medium speed until smooth, about 1 minute. Immediately pour the smoothies into juice glasses and serve garnished with small sprigs of fresh mint.

A Baker's Dozen
and Then Some

"We must have a pie. Stress cannot exist in the presence of a pie." —David Mamet, *Boston Marriage*

When I think of baked goods that exude New England flavor, I think first and foremost of pies. While I cannot understand the gluttonous allure of pie-eating contests that are part and parcel of many a local town's Fourth of July festivities, I am a tuned-in fan of the pie-baking competitions that take place annually at country fairs and other community events throughout New England. My stance is rooted in the classic theory of less being more and a resounding preference for superb quality over inferior quantity.

Having grown up in a family that enjoyed a slice of homemade pie not only for dessert after dinner but for breakfast the following morning, I don't undertake the baking of my homemade pies lightly and you will find the carefully selected and crafted pie recipes in this chapter are as fruity in filling—think abundant autumn apples, wild Maine blueberries, and summer strawberries—as they are flaky in crust. Since most New Englanders top slices of pie with vanilla ice cream or whipped cream, those options are prevalent throughout this chapter and should you be feeling extra ambitious there's a recipe for Super-Rich Homemade Vanilla Ice Cream that can immediately elevate a pie and many another New England dessert to the "to die for" category.

New Englanders are also quite fond of cookies and bars as sweet pick-me-ups and both my grandmother and mother taught me by example about the welcoming gesture of hospitality inherent in keeping a pretty glass cookie jar on a kitchen counter—stocked, of course—with really good chocolate chip or ginger cookies, brownies, or lemon bars.

My husband sometimes laments that I do not frequently bake desserts for our weeknight family dinners. I in turn believe his waistline should thank me. After all, we can look forward all the more to the fact that I do set aside ample time to make desserts whenever we have company and host dinner parties. Then, I seize the occasion to whip up some of my very favorite desserts, such as Toby's Blueberry Cheesecake, Chocolate Amaretti Torte, Snowy White Coconut Cake, and Transplanted Tiramisu.

Northern Spy Apple Pie

My family would disown me if I didn't make an apple pie for dessert on Thanksgiving. Yes, they love pecan and pumpkin pies, too, but it is my apple pie that gets the highest priority ranking. Actually, I tend to make my pies a little differently each year, usually piling the crust high with a willy-nilly mix of Macoun, Empire, McIntosh, Golden Delicious, and a Granny Smith apple or two for good measure. My father had long insisted that Rhode Island Greenings were the best pie apple, but I never seemed to be able to find any when Thanksgiving rolled around, thereby inducing a tinge of guilt for never having personally decided upon a favorite pie apple.

This all changed one autumn day when I came across a sumptuous display of Northern Spy apples at Crow Farm in Sandwich, Massachusetts. Because I had never seen these apples in New England supermarkets, I did some research and learned Northern Spy apples are nicknamed the "Pie Apple" and are native to the American Northeast. How fortuitous—what more could I ask for?

For the first time ever, I put together a pie with a single variety of apples and nary a complaint was heard. Some even crowned it the best apple pie they had ever tasted. Should you not be able to find Northern Spy apples, you can go back to my old method of mixing different apple varieties together for the filling. However, if you can find Northern Spys you'll be in for a treat and a pie worthy of topping with Super-Rich Homemade Vanilla Ice Cream. MAKES 1 PIE; SERVES 8 TO 10

9 or 10 Northern Spy apples (4 to 4 ½ pounds)

¾ cup, plus 2 tablespoons sugar

¼ cup unbleached all-purpose flour, plus flour for dusting the work surface

2 teaspoons ground cinnamon

½ teaspoon freshly grated nutmeg

Pinch of fine sea salt

½ cup plus 2 tablespoons heavy (whipping) cream

Cream Cheese Pie Crust (recipe follows)

Super-Rich Homemade Vanilla Ice Cream (page 354) or another vanilla ice cream (optional), for serving

Aged Vermont cheddar cheese (optional), for serving

1 Place a rack in the center of the oven and preheat the oven to 375°F. Line a baking sheet with aluminum foil.

2 Peel and core the apples and then cut them into a combination of ½-inch-wide slices and chunks. You should have 11 to 12 cups of apples. Place the apples in a large mixing bowl, add the ¾ cup of sugar and the flour, cinnamon, nutmeg, and salt and toss to coat evenly. Pour in ½ cup of the cream and toss again.

3 Lightly flour a work surface. Roll 1 pastry disk into a 12-inch circle. Ease the pastry into a 10-inch deep-dish pie pan, letting the extra overhang the edge. Mound the apple filling into the pie crust.

4 Roll out the remaining pastry disk into a 12-inch circle. Place this circle of pastry over the top of the pie. Trim the edge of the pie crust and crimp it decoratively to seal the crust together. Any excess pastry can be used to make decorations on the top of the pie if you wish to get fancy. Brush the top of the pie lightly all over with the remaining 2 tablespoons of cream and then sprinkle it evenly with the remaining 2 tablespoons of sugar. Using a small sharp knife, cut several slits in the top of the pie crust to serve as vents for steam while the pie bakes. Place the pie on the prepared baking sheet to catch any drips during baking.

5 Bake the pie until the crust is golden and the apples are tender and surrounded by bubbling

juices, 1¼ to 1½ hours. If the crust seems to be getting too brown before the filling is tender, cover the top of the pie loosely with aluminum foil and continue baking.

6 Let the pie cool for several hours or overnight. This pie is much easier to serve and is even tastier when allowed to stand for at least 12 hours. If you must have the pie warm, you can always reheat it in a 325°F oven for about 10 minutes. Serve the pie cut into wedges topped with a small scoop of Super-Rich Homemade Vanilla Ice Cream, if desired. The pie may also be served in true New England fashion with a wedge of crumbly aged Vermont cheddar cheese.

Cream Cheese Pie Crust

For my apple pie, I like this cream cheese crust that I adapted from a Rose Levy Beranbaum recipe. MAKES 2 PIE CRUSTS (EACH 10 INCHES IN DIAMETER)

1⅔ cups unbleached all-purpose flour, plus flour for dusting the work surface

⅓ cup plus 2 tablespoons cake flour

Pinch of salt

¼ teaspoon baking powder

12 tablespoons (1½ sticks) unsalted butter, well-chilled and cut into small pieces

4 ½ ounces cream cheese, well-chilled, cut into small pieces

2 tablespoons ice water

1 tablespoon distilled white vinegar or cider vinegar

PLACE THE ALL-PURPOSE flour, cake flour, salt, and baking powder in a food processor. Pulse to combine. Add the butter and cream cheese all at once and process until the mixture resembles coarse crumbs. Add the ice water and vinegar and pulse the machine just until the dough begins to

form a ball. Divide the pastry dough in half and, working on a lightly floured work surface, shape each half into a flat disk. Wrap each disk in plastic wrap and refrigerate the disks for at least 1 hour and up to 24 hours. The pastry is now ready to roll out and bake.

Pain D'Avignon's Pumpkin Pie

In my family, Thanksgiving tradition has long dictated that the feast conclude with at least three different types of pies in the dessert line-up, with apple and pumpkin being non-negotiable. However, to be honest, I personally was never a great fan of pumpkin pie until I tasted the version baked at Pain D'Avignon in Hyannis, a bustling café and our go-to bakery on Cape Cod. Pain D'Avignon's executive pastry chef, Else Rhodes, enthusiastically shared her prized recipe with me, along with the added option of topping the pie with a candied ginger and pecan crumble. Else elaborated: "I developed this recipe for the bakery to be a cross between a custard and a regular pumpkin pie. The ginger crumble topping is optional but adds a little bit of zing to the pie." SERVES 8

For the ginger crumble topping

¾ cup unbleached all-purpose flour

½ teaspoon kosher salt

½ cup granulated light brown sugar

¼ cup chopped pecans

1 tablespoon candied ginger, very finely minced

6 tablespoons (¾ stick) cold unsalted butter, cut into ½-inch cubes

For the pastry crust and pumpkin custard filling

Pastry Crust (recipe follows)

2 large eggs

1 can (15 ounces) unsweetened pumpkin

2 tablespoons light corn syrup

1 tablespoon unbleached all-purpose flour

½ teaspoon ground cinnamon

1 teaspoon freshly grated nutmeg

1 teaspoon ground ginger

½ teaspoon ground cloves

1 teaspoon kosher salt

½ cup plus 2 tablespoons (packed) light brown sugar

1¼ cups whole milk

1 Make the ginger crumble: Place the flour, salt, brown sugar, pecans, and candied ginger in the bowl of a stand mixer fitted with the paddle attachment. Add the cubes of cold butter and mix at medium-low speed until small- to medium-size clumps form, 1 to 1½ minutes. Transfer the crumble to a small bowl, cover with plastic wrap, and refrigerate until ready to use. The crumble can be made up to 3 days in advance.

2 When ready to bake the pie, arrange a rack in the bottom third of the oven and preheat the oven to 350°F. Line a baking sheet with parchment paper.

3 On a lightly floured surface, roll the pastry out to a thickness of about ⅛ inch to form an 11- to 12-inch circle. Ease the pastry into a 9½-inch pie pan, crimp the edges decoratively, trimming away any excess pastry. Chill the pastry shell in the refrigerator until firm, about 30 minutes.

4 Meanwhile, make the pumpkin filling: Whisk the eggs until blended in a large mixing bowl. Whisk in the pumpkin, corn syrup, flour, cinnamon, nutmeg, ginger, cloves, salt, and brown sugar until thoroughly combined and smooth. Add the milk and whisk until thoroughly incorporated into the filling.

5 Set the chilled pastry shell on the prepared baking sheet. Pour the pumpkin filling into the shell. Scatter the ginger crumble evenly over the top. Bake the pie, rotating the sheet pan about two-thirds of way through, until the crust is golden brown and the custard has set to the point where a toothpick inserted into the center comes out clean, 55 to 60 minutes. Transfer the pie to a wire rack to cool to room temperature. Serve the pie at room temperature. The pie may be stored at room temperature, covered with aluminum foil or plastic wrap, for up to 2 days.

Pastry Crust

This is an all-purpose, sure-to-please pie crust.

MAKES 2 PIE CRUSTS (EACH 9 INCHES IN DIAMETER)

2 cups unbleached all-purpose flour, plus extra for dusting the work surface

½ teaspoon kosher salt

2 teaspoons sugar

4 tablespoons (½ stick) cold unsalted butter, cut into ½-inch cubes

4 tablespoons solid vegetable shortening, such as Crisco

3½ to 4 tablespoons ice water

SIFT THE FLOUR, salt, and sugar into the bowl of a stand mixer fitted with the paddle attachment. Add the butter and shortening to the bowl and run the mixer at medium speed until the mixture resembles coarse crumbs. Add 3½ tablespoons of the ice water, reduce the speed to medium-low, and continue mixing until the mixture binds together to form a ball. Add another ½ tablespoon of ice water if needed to make the dough form a ball. Flatten it into a disk, wrap in plastic, and refrigerate for at least 2 hours or as long as overnight. The pastry is now ready to roll out and bake.

These old-fashioned wooden blueberry rakes and baskets have been handed down in my family and we continue to use them to gather wild Maine blueberries.

Not Quite My Mother's Maine Blueberry Pie

Every summer when my family goes up to visit my mother in Blue Hill, Maine, our food requests are simple and consistent. We look forward to local lobsters and my mother's potato and cucumber salads, followed by her homemade blueberry pie for dessert. Now, my mother makes a superb classic Maine blueberry pie, almost always with wild blueberries she has painstakingly picked herself since she has long had the reputation of being the most impeccable blueberry picker in the family.

However, I got the urge to tinker slightly with my mother's recipe when a foodie friend enlightened me to the buzz surrounding a *Cook's Illustrated* foolproof pie crust recipe using chilled vodka for some of the pastry's binding liquid. This in turn gave me the idea to use Maine's Cold River Blueberry Flavored Vodka in the crust of my mother's blueberry pie. I also added more berries than

my mother usually uses. The results were truly memorable. MAKES 1 PIE; SERVES 6 TO 8

5½ to 6 cups wild Maine blueberries, carefully sorted for stems, leaves, and mushy berries

¾ cup sugar

2½ tablespoons unbleached all-purpose flour

1½ tablespoons freshly squeezed lemon juice

½ teaspoon ground cinnamon

⅛ teaspoon freshly grated nutmeg

Vodka Pie Crust (recipe follows)

2 tablespoons (¼ stick) unsalted butter, cut into small pieces

Super-Rich Homemade Vanilla Ice Cream (page 354), for serving (optional)

1 Place a rack in the center in the oven and preheat the oven to 400°F. Line a baking sheet with aluminum foil.

2 Make the blueberry pie filling: Place the blueberries, sugar, and flour in a mixing bowl and toss gently until the berries are evenly coated. Stir in the lemon juice, cinnamon, and nutmeg and toss gently again.

3 Flour a work surface well. Roll out 1 pastry disk into an 11- to 12-inch circle. Ease the pastry into a 9½-inch glass pie pan, letting the extra pastry hang over the rim of the dish. Mound the blueberry filling into the pie crust and dot with the butter. Roll out the remaining pastry disk into another 11- to 12-inch circle. Place this circle of pastry over the top of the pie. Trim the edge of the pie crust and crimp it decoratively to seal the crust together. Using a sharp knife, cut several slits in the top of the pie to serve as vents for steam while the pie bakes.

4 Place the pie on the prepared baking sheet and bake the pie until the crust is golden brown and the filling is bubbling, 55 minutes to 1 hour. Let the pie cool for at least 30 minutes. Serve warm or at room temperature with a big scoop of ice cream, if desired.

Vodka Pie Crust

Cold River Blueberry Flavored Vodka is quite pricey and should the expense rankle a thrifty Yankee conscience, less expensive plain vodka may be substituted. On the other hand, Cold River's vodka imparts the aroma of picking wild Maine blueberries in a barren and truly raises the bar on complete Maine blueberry bliss. MAKES 2 PIE CRUSTS (EACH 9 INCHES IN DIAMETER)

2½ cups unbleached all-purpose flour, plus flour for dusting the work surface and pastry disks

2 tablespoons sugar

1 teaspoon fine sea salt

12 tablespoons (1½ sticks) cold unsalted butter, cut into small pieces

8 tablespoons (1 stick) cold unsalted margarine (I always use Fleischmann's), cut into small pieces

¼ cup chilled Cold River Blueberry Flavored Vodka or plain vodka

3½ tablespoons ice water

1 Place 1½ cups of the flour, the 2 tablespoons of sugar, and the salt in a food processor and pulse a couple of times to combine evenly. Add the cold butter and margarine and process until the dough begins to ball up into uneven clumps, 15 to 20 seconds. Using a rubber spatula, scrape down the side of the processor bowl to redistribute the flour mixture evenly. Add the remaining 1 cup of flour and pulse the machine until the mixture resembles coarse crumbs.

2 Drizzle the chilled vodka and ice water on top and continue pulsing the machine until the dough sticks together in a somewhat moist and tacky ball. (The dough will be significantly moister than that of most other pie crusts.) Divide the pastry dough in half, and working on a lightly floured work surface, shape each half into a flat disk. Coat the disks lightly all over with flour, wrap them in plastic wrap, and refrigerate them for at least 4 hours or overnight.

Old-Fashioned Strawberry Pie

Strawberry shortcake may be New England's favorite strawberry dessert, but I have to confess I have never really liked shortcake biscuits and am not crazy about whipped cream. This admission may be surprising, seeing that when I was growing up in Connecticut, my mother designated one night every June when we would just have an entire strawberry shortcake dinner in celebration of native strawberries grown at a farm down the road from our house. A few years ago, at a fusion restaurant on Nantucket, I had a version of strawberry shortcake I actually adored. It featured sugared fresh strawberries spooned over a fabulous piece of *tres leches* cake. I have tried to figure out a way to justify putting a similar recipe in this book, but in the end have failed to justify any credible New England connection.

The one strawberry dessert that always sends me into orbit, however, is a strawberry pie recipe I got in Camden, Maine, from food writer Nancy Harmon Jenkins's then nonagenarian aunt back in the early 1990s, when I was researching my *Saltwater Seasonings* cookbook. The recipe appears in the cookbook as Doris Henderson's Strawberry Pie, and it is so wonderful that I am still willing to include strawberry-flavored Jell-O in the ingredient list since it's vital to the success of the pie. Why strawberry Jell-O? It's the secret that heightens the deep red strawberry color of the pie. MAKES 1 PIE; SERVES 8

For the pie crust

1 cup unbleached, all-purpose flour, plus flour for dusting the work surface

⅓ cup solid vegetable shortening, such as Crisco

½ teaspoon sugar

½ teaspoon fine sea salt

½ teaspoon cider vinegar

2 to 3 tablespoons ice water

For the strawberry pie filling

1 cup sugar

¾ cup boiling water

½ teaspoon fine sea salt

3 tablespoons cornstarch dissolved in ¼ cup cold water

2 tablespoons strawberry-flavored Jell-O

1½ quarts fresh local strawberries, rinsed, hulled, and cut in half

2 cups lightly sweetened whipped cream, for serving (optional; see Note)

1 Make the pie crust: Combine the flour, vegetable shortening, ½ teaspoon of sugar, and ½ teaspoon of salt in a mixing bowl. Using a pastry cutter, blend the mixture until it resembles coarse crumbs. Add the vinegar and enough ice water to hold the dough together. Working on a lightly floured work surface, shape the dough into a flat disk, wrap it in plastic wrap, and refrigerate it for at least 1 hour or as long as 24 hours.

2 Place a rack in the center of the oven and preheat the oven to 375°F.

3 Lightly flour a work surface. Roll out the pastry disk to form an approximately 11-inch circle. Ease the pastry into a 9-inch pie pan and crimp the edge decoratively, trimming away any excess dough. Line the pie crust with aluminum foil or parchment paper and then fill it with ceramic pie weights or dried beans. Bake the shell until light golden brown, 20 to 25 minutes.

Remove the weights and liner and let the pie crust cool completely.

4 Meanwhile as the pie crust bakes, make the strawberry pie filling: Combine the 1 cup of sugar, the boiling water, ½ teaspoon of salt, and dissolved cornstarch in a saucepan. Let come to a boil over medium heat, stirring constantly, and cook until the mixture is thickened and clear, 5 to 6 minutes. Remove the cornstarch mixture from the heat, add the strawberry Jell-O, and stir until it dissolves. Add the strawberries, stir gently to coat, and then pile the filling into the cooled pie crust. Refrigerate until cold, 3 or so hours.

5 When ready to serve, cut the pie into wedges and dollop them liberally with whipped cream if desired.

NOTE: *For 2 cups of lightly sweetened whipped cream, you'll need 1 cup of heavy (whipping) cream mixed with 1½ tablespoons confectioners' sugar. Beat with a hand mixer until soft peaks form. A ¼ teaspoon of vanilla extract may also be added.*

Jennifer's Cranberry Date Pie

Jennifer Madden is married to my cousin Parke and she came to Cape Cod from Rochester, Minnesota, an area deeply steeped in baking traditions. When Jennifer isn't working hours on end as the director of collections and exhibitions at the acclaimed Heritage Museums & Gardens in Sandwich, she is home baking sweet treats, much to the delight of her friends and family.

While Jennifer may be most renowned for the coconut cake she makes every year for her husband's birthday in January, I am especially fond of this far less elaborate but very unique and tasty cranberry date pie, a lovely autumn Cape Cod

Before environmental advances came to the cranberry industry, wooden booms were used to contain the berries after they had been harvested from their bogs.

dessert and welcome addition to Thanksgiving dessert offerings. MAKES 1 PIE; SERVES 8

3 cups fresh cranberries

1¾ cups sugar

¼ cup unbleached all-purpose flour

½ cup water

1 cup chopped pitted dates

Jennifer's Grandmother's Crust (recipe follows)

Lightly sweetened whipped cream (see Note, page 334) or Super-Rich Homemade Vanilla Ice Cream (page 354), optional, for serving

1 Place the cranberries in a colander and rinse them under cold running water. Discard any stray stems, leaves, or mushy cranberries. Drain the cranberries well.

2 Place the cranberries, sugar, and flour in a medium-size saucepan and toss to mix. Stir in the water and let come to a boil over medium-high heat, stirring occasionally. Reduce the heat to medium-low so the cranberries are barely simmering, cover the pan, and cook until almost all of the cranberry skins have popped, 7 to 9 minutes. Remove the pan from the heat and stir in the dates. Let the filling cool to room temperature.

3 Place a rack in the center of the oven and preheat the oven to 375°F.

4 Lightly flour a work surface. Roll out 1 pastry disk to form an 11- to 12-inch circle. Ease the pastry into a 9-inch pie pan and crimp the edge decoratively, trimming away any excess dough. Mound the cooled cranberry and date filling into the unbaked pie crust. Shield the crimped edge of the pie by covering it with aluminum foil. Bake the pie for about 25 minutes. Remove the foil from the edge and continue baking until the crust is golden, 20 to 25 minutes more.

5 Transfer the pie to a wire rack to cool and serve at room temperature. Embellish the slices of pie with whipped cream or vanilla ice cream, if desired.

Jennifer's Grandmother's Crust

Like many life-long bakers, Jennifer sticks to using her grandmother's tried-and-true pie crust recipe. Jennifer stashes the extra pastry dough in the freezer so it will be on hand for the next time she is asked to bring a cranberry date pie to a family gathering. MAKES 2 PIE CRUSTS (EACH 9 INCHES IN DIAMETER)

4 cups unbleached all-purpose flour, plus flour for dusting the work surface

1¾ cups solid vegetable shortening, such as Crisco

1 tablespoon sugar

2 teaspoons fine sea salt

1 teaspoon freshly squeezed lemon juice

1 large egg

½ cup ice water

1 Place the flour, vegetable shortening, sugar, and salt in a food processor and pulse the machine until the mixture resembles coarse crumbs.

2 Place the lemon juice, egg, and ice water in a mixing bowl and whisk to mix. Pour the lemon juice mixture over the flour mixture and pulse the machine several times until the mixture begins to form a ball. Divide the pastry dough in half and, working on a lightly floured work surface, shape each half into a flat disk. Wrap each pastry disk in plastic wrap and refrigerate the disks for at least 45 minutes and up to 24 hours. Or freeze them for up to 3 months. Let a disk of dough thaw overnight in the refrigerator before using.

Fresh Fruit Tart with Lemon Mascarpone Cream Filling

My enthusiasm for baking increased significantly when the Vermont Creamery began selling good domestic mascarpone cheese, meaning I no longer had to go to great lengths to purchase the highly perishable mascarpone imported from Italy. As a result, this fruit tart with its lemon mascarpone cream filling has become my new gold standard summer fruit tart. More often than not, I make it with fresh raspberries but feel free to substitute any ripe summer fruits that tickle your own personal fancy—strawberries, blackberries, blueberries, sliced peaches, and figs, alone or in combination are all worthy candidates. MAKES 1 TART; SERVES 6 TO 8

Tart Crust (recipe follows)

3 large eggs

5 tablespoons freshly squeezed lemon juice

1 tablespoon finely grated lemon zest

5 ounces (⅔ cup) mascarpone

⅓ cup heavy (whipping) cream

¼ cup sugar

Pinch of fine sea salt

3 cups fresh raspberries or other fresh fruit of choice

1 cup seedless berry or red currant jelly

⅓ cup cassis (black currant liqueur)

1 Lightly flour a work surface. Roll out 1 pastry disk to form an approximately 11-inch circle. Ease the pastry into a 9-inch tart pan with a removable bottom. Crimp the edge decoratively, trimming away any excess dough. Refrigerate the tart crust for about 30 minutes before baking it.

2 Place a rack in the center of the oven and preheat the oven to 350°F.

3 Line the chilled tart crust with aluminum foil or parchment paper and then fill it with ceramic pie weights or dried beans. Bake the tart crust until the edges begin to brown, about 15 minutes. Remove the weights and liner and continue baking the tart crust until the bottom is a light golden brown, 12 to 15 minutes. Transfer the tart crust to a wire rack and reduce the oven temperature to 325°F.

4 Meanwhile as the tart crust bakes, make the filling: Combine the eggs, lemon juice, lemon zest, mascarpone, cream, sugar, and salt in a mixing bowl and beat with a hand-held electric mixer at medium speed until smooth and creamy. Pour the filling into the baked tart crust.

5 Bake the tart until the filling is set, 20 to 25 minutes. Let the tart cool completely on the wire rack.

6 Arrange the raspberries or other fruit in tight and attractive concentric circles over the top of the cooled tart. Place the jelly and cassis in a small saucepan, stir to combine, and heat over medium-low heat until melted and smooth. Using a pastry brush, brush the

Fresh Fruit Tart with Lemon Mascarpone Cream Filling »

Simply stated, Vermont Creamery's topnotch dairy products make me delirious, whether I'm baking, cooking, or just grazing.

warm jelly mixture gently over the fruit to glaze it. Serve the tart the same day it is made, preferably within a few hours of making it. Refrigerate it until ready to serve.

Tart Crust

This pastry recipe makes enough for two nine-inch tarts and half the pastry can be stored in the freezer ready to thaw to make another tart whenever the urge, craving, or berry bounty strikes.

3 cups unbleached all-purpose flour, plus flour for dusting the work surface

2 tablespoons sugar

Pinch of fine sea salt

24 tablespoons (3 sticks) chilled unsalted butter, cut into small pieces

About 3 tablespoons ice water

MAKE THE PASTRY CRUST: Place the flour, sugar, pinch of salt, and butter in a food processor and pulse the machine until the mixture resembles coarse crumbs. With the machine running, drizzle in enough ice water to make the dough begin to form into a ball. Divide the pastry dough in half and, working on a lightly floured work surface, shape each half into a flat disk. Wrap each pastry disk in plastic wrap and refrigerate the disks for at least 45 minutes and up to 24 hours or freeze them for up to 3 months.

Snowy White Coconut Cake

While coconut may seem like a tropical ingredient, the pristine whiteness of this lovely cake reminds me of the snow-capped mountains and trees that make up the winter landscape at some of our favorite ski resorts in Vermont, New Hampshire, and Maine. I used to feature this recipe in my cooking classes and to this day I continue to get requests from people who have lost or misplaced their copy and just have to make it for a special birthday celebration. For a total nor'easter effect, the coconut cake may be served without the accompanying raspberry coulis, but I usually serve it with the deep red coulis from Valentine's Day on. MAKES 1 LAYER CAKE; SERVES 12 OR MORE

For the sponge cake

1 cup cake flour

⅔ cup sugar

1¼ teaspoons baking powder

Pinch of fine sea salt

¼ cup vegetable oil

1 large egg

¼ cup water

½ teaspoon pure almond extract

4 large egg whites

For the coconut cream

1½ cups whole milk

2 teaspoons pure vanilla extract

½ cup sugar

¼ cup unbleached all-purpose flour

4 large egg yolks

3 cups sweetened shredded coconut

1½ cups heavy (whipping) cream

For the raspberry coulis

2½ cups fresh or frozen unsweetened raspberries, thawed if frozen

¾ cup sugar

2 tablespoons freshly squeezed lemon juice

3 tablespoons cassis (black currant liqueur)

1 Place a rack in the center of the oven and preheat the oven to 350°F.

2 Make the sponge cake: Place the cake flour, ⅓ cup of the sugar, and the baking powder and salt in a large mixing bowl and stir to combine. Place the oil, egg, water, and almond extract in a small bowl and whisk to mix. Add this mixture to the flour mixture, stirring to make a smooth batter. Place the egg whites in a medium-size bowl and, using an electric mixer, beat them on medium-high speed until they begin to hold soft peaks. Slowly beat in the remaining ⅓ cup of sugar, 1 tablespoon at a time, until all has been added. Continue beating until the meringue is glossy and holds stiff peaks, 2 to 3 minutes longer. Fold one fourth of the meringue into the cake batter to lighten it and then gently fold the rest into the batter until just evenly incorporated.

3 Pour the batter into an ungreased 9-inch spring-form pan. Bake the cake until a toothpick inserted into the center comes out clean, about 20 minutes. Run a knife around the edge of the springform pan, release the clasp to remove the side of the pan, and invert the cake onto a wire rack to cool. Ease the bottom of the pan off the cake after inverting it onto the rack.

4 Make the coconut cream: Place the milk and vanilla in a medium-size saucepan and let come to a boil over medium-high heat, then remove the pan from the heat. Place ¼ cup of the sugar and the flour and egg yolks in a small bowl and whisk until blended. Whisk ⅓ cup of the hot milk mixture into the egg yolk mixture, whisking until smooth. Whisk the egg yolk mixture into the saucepan and return it to the stove. Let the mixture come to a boil over medium heat, stirring constantly, and continue cooking and stirring until the mixture thickens to a custard, 2 to 3 minutes. Remove the pan from the heat and transfer the custard to a clean medium-size mixing bowl, stirring every now and again, until cooled to room temperature. Once cooled, stir in 1 cup of the coconut. Chill the custard in the refrigerator until cold, at least 1 hour and up to 24 hours.

5 Place the cream and the remaining ¼ cup of sugar in a mixing bowl and, using an electric mixer, beat the cream on medium-high speed until it holds stiff peaks. Fold 1 cup of the whipped cream into the cold custard and set the remaining whipped cream in the refrigerator, covered, until you are ready to assemble the cake.

6 To assemble the cake, slice the cake horizontally into 3 equal layers. Place the bottom layer, cut side up, on a large round serving plate. Spread half of the coconut cream over the cake and top it with the middle layer. Spread the rest of the coconut cream over this layer and top it with the remaining layer, cut side down. Spread the reserved whipped cream on top and around the side of the cake. Sprinkle and press the remaining 2 cups of coconut onto the top and side of the cake. Store the cake in the refrigerator, loosely covered with plastic wrap, until ready to serve (see Note).

7 Make the raspberry coulis: Place the raspberries, ¾ cup of sugar, lemon juice, and cassis in a blender and puree until smooth. Strain the seeds from the coulis by passing the puree through a fine sieve. Store the coulis in the refrigerator, covered, for up to 5 days.

8 To serve, cut the cake into wedges, place them on serving plates, and surround each with a pool of the raspberry coulis. The cake is best when served the same day it has been assembled.

NOTE: *I usually stick 4 to 6 toothpicks partially into the top of the cake, letting the plastic wrap be propped up by the toothpicks so it doesn't cling to the cake.*

Chocolate Amaretti Torte

When I first visited Nantucket as a young teenager in the 1970s, the island's most fashionable set used to end evenings on the town on a sweet note by crunching on colorfully wrapped Italian cookies packaged in stunning bright red and orange tins. After eating these Lazzaroni Amaretti di Saronno cookies, the decorative pastel wrappers would be set on fire and wishes would be made as they burned, a custom I saw as a chic Italian spin on making a wish while blowing out the candles on a birthday cake.

So began my fascination with these quintessentially Italian cookies, which back then could only be procured in specialty Italian markets in Boston's North End or Providence's Federal Hill. Once they began to become more widely available, I started making this Chocolate Amaretti Torte. While not fancy looking, I daresay it is my very favorite dessert in the world. This declaration shouldn't be taken lightly, considering I have never been a great chocolate aficionado. It must be the beguilingly bitter taste of the ground almonds in the Italian amaretti that strikes my fancy.

I like to serve the torte slightly warm, dusted with confectioners' sugar, and accompanied by a scoop of good coffee ice cream (such as Gifford's Camp Coffee, made in Maine) or hazelnut gelato (Giovanna hazelnut gelato, from Malden, Massachusetts, is heaven). Feature the torte as a finale to one of New England's great Italian-American feasts or to end any meal—just because it is that good. I try to save a sliver of the cake after I present it as an evening dessert because I have discovered the leftover cake is sheer bliss when nibbled while sipping a strong cup of coffee the following morning. MAKES 1 CAKE; SERVES 8

16 tablespoons (2 sticks) unsalted butter, at room temperature, plus butter for greasing the cake pan

½ cup unbleached all-purpose flour, sifted, plus flour for dusting the cake pan

1 cup granulated sugar

5 large egg yolks

⅔ cup finely crushed amaretti crumbs (be sure to use authentic Italian amaretti)

6 ounces bittersweet (70 percent cocoa content) chocolate, chopped

6 large egg whites

Confectioners' sugar, for dusting the cake

Fresh raspberries (optional), for serving

Coffee ice cream or hazelnut gelato (optional), for serving

1 Place a rack in the center of the oven and preheat the oven to 350°F. Lightly butter a 9-inch round cake pan. Line the cake pan with a parchment paper circle, and butter and lightly flour the parchment paper, shaking out any excess flour.

2 Place the butter and granulated sugar in a large mixing bowl and, using a hand-held electric mixer, beat on medium-high speed until very fluffy and almost white in color, 3 to 4 minutes. Beat in the egg yolks, one at a time, beating well after each addition. At low speed, gradually beat in the amaretti crumbs and the flour. Using a rubber spatula, gently fold in the chocolate. The batter will seem rather dense.

3 Beat the egg whites in a separate bowl until quite stiff but not dry. Using the rubber spatula, gently fold one quarter of the whites into the cake batter to begin to lighten it. Then fold in the remaining egg whites, gently but thoroughly. Spread the batter evenly in the prepared cake pan.

4 Bake the cake until it springs back when touched lightly in the center, 30 to 35 minutes. Let the cake cool for 10 to 15 minutes and then invert it onto a decorative serving plate. (Yes, the bottom of the cake is now the top.) Just before serving, sift a dusting of confectioners' sugar over the top and rim raspberries around the edge of the cake, if desired. Try to serve the cake while it is still slightly warm, accompanied by a scoop of coffee ice cream or hazelnut gelato, if desired.

Apple Carrot Cake

During the years I ran my Que Sera Sarah food shop and catering business on Nantucket, carrot cake was all the rage. The Silver Palate's famous carrot cake was my go-to recipe and once I even fashioned it into a wedding cake when I was hired to cater actress Glenn Close's intimate wedding reception on a chartered private yacht on Nantucket Sound. The marriage didn't last long and carrot cake gradually began to fade from vogue. For several years I simply never thought of making carrot cake until Debbie Hensler, the wife of one of my husband's closest Nantucket buddies, introduced us to her apple and carrot cake. Now, I am especially fond of serving this cake at Easter as a subtle nod to carrot-loving bunnies, real or fictitious.

Debbie's cream cheese frosting recipe called for margarine, but I use butter when I make it. MAKES 1 CAKE; SERVES 12 TO 14

For the cake

Unsalted butter, for greasing the baking pans

1½ cups granulated sugar

1½ cups vegetable oil

3 large eggs

2 teaspoons pure vanilla extract

2 cups unbleached all-purpose flour

2 teaspoons ground cinnamon

1 teaspoon baking soda

1 teaspoon baking powder

1 teaspoon kosher salt

2 cups shredded peeled carrots (4 medium-size carrots)

1 cup coarsely diced peeled apple (1 large apple)

1 cup chopped walnuts

For the cream cheese frosting

2 packages (8 ounces each) cream cheese, at room temperature

8 tablespoons (1 stick) unsalted butter, at room temperature

1 to 2 cups confectioners' sugar

1 teaspoon pure vanilla extract

1 Make the cake: Place a rack in the center of the oven and preheat the oven to 350°F. Grease two 9-inch round cake pans, line them with parchment paper circles, and grease the parchment paper as well.

2 Place the granulated sugar, vegetable oil, eggs, and 2 teaspoons of vanilla in the bowl of a stand mixer fitted with the paddle attachment. Beat at medium speed until well blended, 1½ to 2 minutes. Sift together the flour, cinnamon, baking soda, baking powder, and salt. Add the dry ingredients to the mixer bowl and beat at low speed until incorporated. Using a wooden spoon, stir in the carrots, apple, and walnuts until evenly distributed throughout the batter. Divide the batter evenly between the 2 prepared cake pans.

3 Bake the cake layers until the centers spring back when gently pressed with a finger and the edges have begun to pull away from the side of the pans, 35 to 40 minutes. Transfer the cake layers in their pans to a wire rack to cool completely, 2 to 3 hours.

4 Make the frosting: Place the cream cheese and butter in a medium-size mixing bowl and, using a hand-held electric mixer on medium-high speed, beat until smooth. Slowly sift in 1 cup of the confectioners' sugar, beating until smooth. Add enough of the remaining 1 cup of confectioners' sugar to suit your taste. The frosting should not be cloyingly sweet. Beat in the 1 teaspoon of vanilla.

5 Invert one cake layer (the bottom is now the top) onto a serving plate and spread frosting over the top and side of the bottom layer. Place the second layer on top of the first and use the rest of the frosting to completely cover the cake. Store the cake in the refrigerator, covered in plastic wrap (see Note, page 341), if you are not serving it within 30 to 45 minutes. It will keep up to 4 days.

Blue Hill
Blueberry Bliss

From the time I began working on this cookbook I was on the lookout for the perfect rendition of the simple, almost muffinlike, blueberry cakes served frequently at B&Bs and tucked into the recipe boxes of many old-time New Englanders. My search ended in August 2011 when my mother took me to a special barbecue night at the Blue Hill Country Club in Maine. While I always enjoy going to this exceptionally picturesque club because my husband and I had had our wedding reception there, I was in for an extra special treat when the blueberry cake of my dreams was served for dessert.

When the kitchen willingly obliged me with their recipe, I was surprised to learn that they considered it a blueberry buckle and that the recipe contained nectarines, which I hadn't detected. There's no reason to quibble over semantics or ingredient inclusions when perfection is the result! The nectarines add a moistness to the cake and peaches can be substituted for the same effect. MAKES 1 CAKE; SERVES 6 TO 8

For the topping

4 tablespoons (½ stick) chilled unsalted butter, cut into small pieces

½ cup sugar

⅓ cup unbleached all-purpose flour

¾ teaspoon ground cinnamon

¼ teaspoon freshly grated nutmeg

For the cake

12 tablespoons (1½ sticks) unsalted butter, at room temperature, plus butter for greasing the baking pan

¾ cup sugar

1 teaspoon pure vanilla extract

1⅓ cups unbleached all-purpose flour

½ teaspoon fine sea salt

¼ teaspoon baking soda

3 large eggs

2 cups wild or highbush blueberries, rinsed and carefully sorted for stems, leaves, and mushy berries

2 large ripe peeled nectarines or peaches, pitted and cut into ½-inch chunks

Sweetened whipped cream (see Note, page 334) or Super-Rich Vanilla Ice Cream (page 354), optional, for serving

1 Make the topping: Place the 4 tablespoons of butter, ½ cup of sugar, ⅓ cup of flour, and the cinnamon and nutmeg in a small bowl and mix them together with your fingertips, a fork, or pastry blender until the

taying outdoors in the sun and fresh air all afternoon to pick berries is . . . a useful chore justified by tangible results and some discomfort in the form of scratched hands and a lame back. The discomfort is important to the Conscience, which is to the Down-easter as real and painful as an inflamed sciatic nerve and requires equally delicate treatment.

—Louise Dickinson Rich, *State O'Maine*

mixture resembles coarse crumbs. Place the topping in the refrigerator to chill while you make the cake batter.

2   Place a rack in the center of the oven and preheat the oven to 350°F. Lightly butter a 10-by-2-inch round or 9-inch-square baking pan.

3   Make the cake: Place the 12 tablespoons of butter, ¾ cup of sugar, and the vanilla in a large mixing bowl and, using a hand-held electric mixer, cream them on medium speed until smooth and well blended. Place the 1⅓ cups of flour and the salt and baking soda in a separate small bowl and stir to mix. Beat the dry ingredients into the batter alternately with the eggs, adding 1 egg at a time and beating well after each addition. Fold the blueberries and nectarines or peaches into the batter.

4   Spread the batter evenly in the prepared baking pan. Sprinkle the chilled topping evenly over the top of the batter. Bake the cake until a toothpick inserted into the center comes out clean and the topping is golden, 45 to 50 minutes. Serve the cake warm or at room temperature with whipped cream or vanilla ice cream, if desired. I personally prefer to eat my cake unadorned.

Mums and pumpkins are the words and colors of the season at farmstands, garden centers, and front door stoops across New England come October.

Halloween Pumpkin Spice Cake with Broiled Coconut Pecan Frosting

My son, Oliver, was throughout his now seemingly fleeting youth a huge fan of Halloween and would spend months researching his yearly costume options in stores and online. This ardor did not exactly thrill me and I often found myself exasperated by the process when Halloween finally rolled around. Oliver was also quite skilled at unearthing elaborate scary designs for jack-o'-lanterns and I was destined to carve these into at least three major pumpkins every Halloween.

Thankfully now that Oliver has outgrown the trick-or-treating stage, I can return to focusing on the Halloween-inspired activities I used to enjoy most—coming up with creative and tasty orange-and-black-themed food. As much as I love accenting my home with an eclectic, autumnal variety of locally grown pumpkins, gourds, and squashes, I now definitely know it to be far more rewarding to make this crowd-pleasing cake than to spend hours altering flimsy costumes, monitoring candy intake, or carving jack-o'-lanterns in patterns that only look compelling and do-able on the pages of glossy magazines. MAKES 1 CAKE; SERVES 12 TO 15

For the cake

16 tablespoons (2 sticks) unsalted butter, at room temperature, plus butter for greasing the baking pan

2 cups unbleached all-purpose flour, plus flour for dusting the baking pan

⅔ cup unsweetened cocoa powder

1 cup quick-cooking oats

2 teaspoons baking powder

1 teaspoon baking soda

¼ teaspoon fine sea salt

1 tablespoon ground cinnamon

½ teaspoon ground cloves

2 cups granulated sugar

4 large eggs

1 can (15 ounces) unsweetened pumpkin

1 can (8 ounces) crushed pineapple in unsweetened juice

1 teaspoon pure almond extract

For the broiled coconut frosting

8 tablespoons (1 stick) unsalted butter

1 cup (packed) dark brown sugar

½ cup light cream

1½ cups sweetened shredded coconut

1½ cups pecan halves

1 Place a rack in the center of the oven and preheat the oven to 350°F. Lightly butter and flour a 13-by-9-inch baking pan.

2 Make the cake: Place the flour, cocoa, oats, baking powder, baking soda, salt, cinnamon, and cloves in a large mixing bowl, stir to mix, and set aside.

3 Place the 16 tablespoons of butter and the granulated sugar in a mixing bowl and, using an electric mixer, beat them on medium speed until light and fluffy. Beat in the eggs, 1 at a time, beating well after each addition. Beat in the pumpkin, pineapple, and almond extract on medium-low speed until thoroughly combined; the mixture may look a bit curdled at this point, but don't worry. Using a wooden spoon, gradually stir the dry ingredients into the pumpkin mixture until a thick batter forms. Spread the batter evenly in the prepared baking pan.

4 Bake the cake until a toothpick inserted in the center comes out clean, 40 to 45 minutes.

5 Meanwhile, make the frosting: Melt the 8 tablespoons of butter in a medium-size saucepan over low heat. Add the brown sugar and cream and stir until the sugar is dissolved and the mixture is smooth. Stir in the coconut and pecans and remove from the heat.

6 Once the cake is out of the oven, position a broiler rack 4 to 5 inches underneath the heat source and preheat the broiler to high.

7 Spread the frosting evenly over the top of the warm cake. Place the cake under the broiler and broil it until the frosting is golden and bubbling, 4 to 5 minutes. Let the cake cool to room temperature on a wire rack before cutting it into squares.

Toby's Blueberry Cheesecake

This is a legendary Nantucket summer recipe from my beloved friend Toby Greenberg. Toby has lost count of just how many of these fabulous cheesecakes she has made for numerous dinner parties. I make at least one every Fourth of July and then continue to bake and bring this always devoured cheesecake to friends until the last of summer's plumpest blueberries fade away. The blueberries, which must be large and juicy highbush ones as opposed to tiny wild ones, are folded right into the magically light filling, making it unlike any other cheesecake I have ever tasted. MAKES 1 CHEESECAKE; SERVES 8 TO 10

For the graham cracker crust

1½ cups graham cracker crumbs

3 tablespoons sugar

Pinch of ground cinnamon

6 tablespoons (¾ stick) unsalted butter, melted

For the filling

12 ounces cream cheese, at room temperature

½ cup sugar

2 large eggs

½ teaspoon pure vanilla extract

1 pint (2 cups) fresh, plump highbush blueberries, rinsed and carefully sorted for stems, leaves, and mushy berries

For the topping

1 pint (2 cups) sour cream

3 tablespoons sugar

1 teaspoon pure vanilla extract

Fresh raspberries or strawberries (optional), for garnish

1 Place a rack in the center of the oven and preheat the oven to 375°F.

2 Make the crust: Combine the graham cracker crumbs, 3 tablespoons of sugar, and the cinnamon in a small mixing bowl. Drizzle the melted butter on top, stirring to coat the crumbs evenly. Pat the crust into the bottom and 2 inches up the side of a 9-inch springform pan. Bake in the oven until just beginning to brown, about 10 minutes. Set aside to cool while making the filling. Leave the oven on.

3 Make the filling: Place the cream cheese and ½ cup of sugar in a mixing bowl and, using an electric mixer, beat on medium-high speed until creamy and smooth. Add the eggs and the ½ teaspoon of vanilla and beat until well combined. Gently fold the blueberries into the batter and pour it into the springform pan.

4 Bake the cheesecake until just firm to the touch in the center, about 25 minutes.

5 Meanwhile, make the topping: Place the sour cream, 3 tablespoons of sugar, and 1 teaspoon of vanilla in a bowl and whisk until smooth. Remove the cheesecake from the oven and spread the sour cream mixture evenly over the top. Return the cheesecake to the oven and bake it until the sour cream begins to set, about 5 minutes. Let the cheesecake cool in the pan, then refrigerate it for 4 hours before unmolding and serving it. If desired, you can decorate the top with fresh raspberries or strawberries.

Rhubarb Pudding Cake

Come springtime, I can eat rhubarb every single day and never tire of it. In fact, rhubarb is the only food I remember craving when I was pregnant. I came across a recipe for a strawberry rhubarb pudding cake on the *Gourmet* website and it gave me the idea of doing a springtime version of my friend Toby Greenberg's Cranberry Pie recipe featured in my *Cold-Weather Cooking* cookbook. It took a couple of tries to get this recipe just right, but I am now pleased with the results, and imagine other lovers of both rhubarb and Toby's original pie will be, too. MAKES 1 CAKE; SERVES 6 TO 8

8 tablespoons (1 stick) unsalted butter, melted, plus butter for greasing the pie pan

1½ tablespoons cornstarch

3 tablespoons freshly squeezed orange juice

3 cups diced rhubarb (½-inch dice; 5 to 6 stalks)

½ cup (packed) light brown sugar

1¼ cups granulated sugar

1 tablespoon finely grated orange zest

2 extra-large eggs

½ cup sour cream

1 teaspoon pure vanilla extract

1 cup unbleached all-purpose flour

1 Place a rack in the center of the oven and preheat the oven to 325°F. Lightly butter a 9 ½-inch glass pie pan.

2 Place the cornstarch and orange juice in a small bowl and stir until the cornstarch dissolves.

3 Place the rhubarb, brown sugar, and ¼ cup of the granulated sugar in a large mixing bowl and toss to coat the rhubarb with the sugars. Add the orange zest and cornstarch and orange juice mixture and stir to combine. Scrape the rhubarb mixture into the prepared pie pan.

4 Place the eggs in a medium-size mixing bowl and, using a wire whisk, whisk until blended, 20 to 30 seconds. Whisk in the melted butter, the remaining 1 cup of granulated sugar, and the sour cream and vanilla until evenly blended and smooth. Gradually stir in the flour until fully incorporated. Spread the batter evenly over the rhubarb.

5 Bake the cake until it is lightly golden on top and the center springs back when pressed gently with a finger, 50 minutes to 1 hour. Let the cake cool in the pan for at least 15 minutes before serving. Serve the cake warm or at room temperature as a coffee cake at breakfast, an afternoon snack, or a simple but satisfying evening dessert.

Cape Cod Chocolate Chip Cookies

Toll House chocolate chip cookies, invented in the late 1930s by Ruth Wakefield at the family-owned Toll House Inn located in Whitman, Massachusetts, are undoubtedly New England's, if not America's, most famous cookie. Ruth Wakefield's recipe still appears on the back of all packages of Nestlé's chocolate chips, but numerous variations and refinements of the recipe abound. While I have made and enjoyed the original recipe countless times, this variation has become a new favorite.

The recipe came my way via professional baker Jackie Moy, the aunt of twins who were in my son's elementary classes when he attended Cape Cod Academy in Osterville. During this time the schools's founding headmaster, Tom Evans, decided to retire after three decades of shepherding the institution through struggling early years on to successful later years with K through 12 classes and a large and beautiful campus. I was on the committee organizing his retirement gala and proposed that all attendees should have a favor to take home from the celebration that represented the headmaster's admirable common sense values.

When we couldn't come up with a way to use Tom's favorite ice cream flavor—vanilla—as a favor without it melting, we turned to Plan B—chocolate chip cookies. Jackie offered her recipe and the two of us mixed huge batches of the batter in a commercial kitchen and then distributed the cookie dough to various parent volunteers for baking and special packaging. We used premium, chopped Valrhona chocolate in place of the usual supermarket chocolate chips and ever since I have never been able to go back to following the original Toll House cookie recipe.

Jackie's recipe is written to produce large cookies using a standard ice cream scoop for sizing but she encourages those who wish to get a lot more cookies to use a smaller scoop. MAKES 2 DOZEN COOKIES

20 tablespoons (2½ sticks) unsalted butter, at room temperature

1 cup (packed) light brown sugar

1 cup granulated sugar

3 extra-large eggs

3½ teaspoons top-quality pure vanilla extract (Jackie suggests Nielsen-Massey)

4 cups unbleached all-purpose flour

1½ teaspoons baking soda

½ teaspoon baking powder

½ teaspoon fine sea salt

12 ounces top-quality semisweet or bittersweet chocolate, such as Valrhona or Callebaut, chopped into small chunks (about 2 cups loosely packed pieces)

1   Place 2 oven racks as centrally located as possible and preheat the oven to 350°F. Line 2 large rimmed baking sheets with parchment paper.

2   Place the butter, brown sugar, and granulated sugar in the bowl of a stand mixer fitted with the paddle attachment and beat at medium speed until light in color, 2 to 3 minutes. Beat in the eggs and vanilla, mixing only until the eggs are just broken (Jackie cautions that mixing the eggs more thoroughly into the batter at this point toughens the dough).

3   Place the flour, baking soda, baking powder, and salt in a large mixing bowl and whisk to blend. Add the chocolate chunks to the flour mixture, tossing gently to coat, and then add the entire mixture to the bowl with the wet ingredients. Beat on medium-low speed until evenly incorporated, about 1 minute, scraping down the side of the bowl as necessary.

4   Using a 2¼-inch-wide ice cream scoop, arrange balls of the batter on the prepared baking sheets, spacing them about 1½ inches apart. Bake the cookies until golden brown, 10 to 15 minutes. The baking time will be influenced by the size of the cookies and the quirks of your oven. Let the cookies cool for 1 to 2 minutes on the baking sheets, then transfer them to a wire rack to cool completely. The cookies will keep for 4 days when stored in an airtight container but are tastiest if devoured the day they are baked.

Chocolate Buttercrunch Cookies

Sweet Inspirations is a fine chocolate shop on Nantucket, best known for its chocolate-covered cranberries. They also make a premium version of an English toffee brickle, which they call Buttercrunch. These types of confections aren't normally on my radar, but one evening when I was dining with friends at Le Languedoc restaurant, located just around the corner from Sweet Inspirations, I was given a bite of the restaurant's signature sundae made with Sweet Inspirations' Buttercrunch. My friend loves this dessert and I instantly became a fan as well and couldn't wait to find more uses for the Buttercrunch. These decadent cookies are the result.

Many other New England chocolatiers make excellent versions of English toffee-style brickles.

Salem-based Harbor Sweets Sweet Sloops ice cream topping comes to mind immediately, and you should feel free to experiment with similar products you may come across in your neck of the woods. In a pinch, you can always chop English toffee into small bits or even use the Heath English toffee bits sold in the baking aisle of most supermarkets. MAKES ABOUT 30 COOKIES

½ cup unbleached all-purpose flour

1 teaspoon baking powder

¼ teaspoon fine sea salt

1 pound bittersweet chocolate, chopped

4 tablespoons (½ stick) unsalted butter

1½ cups (packed) light brown sugar

4 large eggs

3 teaspoons pure vanilla extract

¼ teaspoon pure almond extract

8 ounces Sweet Inspirations Buttercrunch or other English toffee-style brickle bits

1 cup lightly toasted pecans, walnuts, or skinned hazelnuts (see Box, page 70), chopped

1 Place the flour, baking powder, and salt in a small mixing bowl and stir to blend.

2 Place the chocolate and butter in the top of a double boiler set over simmering water and cook, stirring occasionally, until melted and smooth, 6 to 8 minutes. Remove the chocolate mixture from the heat and let it cool for about 15 minutes.

3 Place the brown sugar and eggs in a large mixing bowl and, using an electric mixer, beat on medium-high speed until thick and light in color, 3 to 4 minutes. Reduce the speed to medium-low and beat in the melted chocolate mixture and vanilla and almond extracts. Using a wooden spoon, stir in the flour mixture, followed by the toffee bits and nuts. Chill the batter, covered, in the refrigerator for at least 1 hour and up to 24 hours to firm up.

4 Place 2 oven racks as centrally located as possible and preheat the oven to 350°F. Line at least 2 large rimmed baking sheets with parchment paper.

5 Drop heaping 2-tablespoon mounds of the cookie batter on the prepared baking sheets, spacing them about 2 inches apart. Bake the cookies until the edges have browned but the centers are still slightly soft to the touch, 13 to 15 minutes. Let the cookies cool long enough to transfer to wire racks, then line the baking sheets with fresh parchment and repeat the process until all the cookies are baked. Once cooled, store in an airtight container. The cookies will stay fresh for 3 to 4 days.

Castine Ginger Cookies

My mother is especially fond of ginger and she raved about this cookie recipe, which had appeared in Allene White's column in Maine's *Ellsworth American* newspaper a few years ago. Allene lives in Brooklin, the next town over from my mother, and happens to be the daughter-in-law of E. B. White, whose beautifully landscaped former house and barn continues to make everyone in our *Stuart Little* and *Charlotte's Web* loving family awestruck each and every time we have occasion to pass by.

This recipe is not Allene's. She credits Hildy Whitaker of Castine, Maine, as the creator of the recipe. Allene noted in the column that she rarely comes across cookies she finds truly exceptional and this particular cookie made her list as her "third-all-time favorite," further adding that the recipe had not been "widely shared."

Gingerbread in cake form has long been a very popular dessert throughout New England, but personally I'd rather munch on a batch of Hildy Whitaker's ginger cookies any day of the week. The cookies are a perfect candidate for cookie jars but are also nice to pack for boating excursions since ginger is reputed to combat seasickness. MAKES ABOUT 2 DOZEN COOKIES

8 tablespoons (1 stick) unsalted butter, at room temperature

1½ cups (packed) dark brown sugar

½ cup granulated sugar

1 large egg

1 teaspoon pure vanilla extract

1 cup unbleached all-purpose flour

1 teaspoon baking powder

½ teaspoon fine sea salt

¾ cup old-fashioned rolled oats

¾ cup lightly toasted pecans (see Box, page 70), chopped

¾ cup crystallized ginger, finely minced

1 Place 2 oven racks as centrally located as possible and preheat the oven to 325°F. Line 2 large rimmed baking sheets with parchment paper.

2 Using an electric mixer on medium-high speed, cream together the butter, brown sugar, and granulated sugar in a medium-size mixing bowl until very smooth. Reduce the speed to medium-low and beat in the egg and vanilla.

3 Place the flour, baking powder, and salt together in a small bowl and stir to mix. Beat the dry ingredients into the butter mixture on low speed until thoroughly combined. Stir in the oats, pecans, and crystallized ginger until evenly distributed.

4 Drop rounded tablespoons of the batter onto the prepared baking sheets, spacing the cookies about 1 inch apart. Bake the cookies until they are lightly browned, 12 to 13 minutes. Let the cookies cool for about 2 minutes on the baking sheets, then transfer them to a wire rack to cool completely. The cookies can be stored in an airtight container for up to 1 week.

Daffodil Lemon Squares

In well over 20 years of celebrating Daffodil Festival Weekend on Nantucket, I thought I had exhausted my repertoire of yellow-hued food to serve at the Saturday picnic that follows the antique car parade through town. At a recent picnic I was hosting, my cousin Parke's wife, Jennifer Madden, contributed these delicious lemon squares. Of course, lemon squares are an obvious dessert choice for a daffodil-themed picnic, but one so obvious that they had never occurred to me. I am now convinced there is no better way to cap off a picnic, daffodil or otherwise, than with these fast-to-disappear lemon squares. Jennifer says the recipe was handed down to her from her mother in Minnesota. MAKES 16 TO 20 BARS OR SQUARES (DEPENDING ON HOW GENEROUS YOU ARE IN THE CUTTING)

For the base

8 tablespoons (1 stick) unsalted butter, at room temperature

1 cup unbleached, all-purpose flour

¼ cup confectioners' sugar

For the filling

2 large eggs

1 cup granulated sugar

2 tablespoons unbleached all-purpose flour

½ teaspoon baking powder

3 tablespoons fresh lemon juice

1 tablespoon finely grated lemon zest

For the icing

2 tablespoons plus 2 teaspoons unsalted butter, at room temperature

1½ cups confectioners' sugar

Approximately ½ tablespoon lemon juice

1 Place a rack in the center of the oven and preheat the oven to 350°F.

2 To make the crust: In a small bowl, blend together the 8 tablespoons butter, 1 cup flour, and ¼ cup confectioners' sugar with a fork, your fingers, or a pastry blender, until the flour is absorbed into the butter and coarse clumps have formed. Transfer the mixture to a 9-inch-square baking pan and pat it down with your fingers to form an even layer over the bottom of the pan. Bake until the crust is just beginning to color, about 15 minutes.

3 Meanwhile make the filling: Whisk together the eggs, granulated sugar, 2 tablespoons flour, baking powder, 3 tablespoons lemon juice, and lemon zest until well combined. Pour the filling over the partially baked crust and continue baking until the filling is set, about 25 minutes longer. Remove the pan from the oven and let the bars cool completely.

4 To make the icing: Beat the 2 tablespoons plus 2 teaspoons butter and 1½ cups confectioners' sugar together until smooth. Add enough lemon juice to make the icing into a desirable spreading consistency.

5 Spread the icing over the bars once they are cool. Let the icing set up for at least 1 hour before cutting the bars into bars or squares. Cover the pan with plastic wrap and store at room temperature for up to 2 days.

Four Seas is a Cape Cod institution that began making and serving its terrific ice cream in 1934. The small shop always has summer lines that spill out the door.

Connecticut Saucepan Brownies

When I was growing up in Connecticut, there was not the craze for decadent and newfangled brownies that exists today. As much as I now adore the creative goods made by New England companies like the Vermont Brownie Company (think maple toffee crunch and apple blondies), families in the time of my childhood usually had one choice brownie recipe they made over and over again. This is our family's favorite recipe, one that my mother could easily teach her three daughters to whip up because the entire batter is made in a single saucepan.

Brownie sleuths will quickly recognize that the recipe is one and the same as Katharine Hepburn's famed brownie recipe, and I imagine this may have been part of its original appeal to my mother since Hepburn was one of Connecticut's most famous, glamorous, and reclusive residents. Movie star connections aside, I am always amazed to this brownie-obsessed day how utterly delicious these brownies are for such a simple recipe without any extraordinary ingredients. Because the brownies are so easy to make, I'll frequently stir up a batch before dinner to bake while we eat dinner and then serve them warm from the oven with some ice cream from our favorite local Cape Cod creamery,

Four Seas in Centerville. For an over-the-top, old-fashioned treat drizzle my friend Becky's hot chocolate sauce (page 355) over the brownies à la mode. MAKES 16 BROWNIES

8 tablespoons (1 stick) unsalted butter, plus butter for greasing the baking pan

2 squares unsweetened chocolate

1 cup sugar

2 large eggs, beaten

½ teaspoon pure vanilla extract

¼ cup unbleached all-purpose flour

¼ teaspoon fine sea salt

1 cup chopped walnuts

1　Place a rack in the center of the oven and preheat the oven to 325°F. Lightly butter an 8-inch-square baking pan.

2　Melt the chocolate and the butter in a medium-size saucepan over medium-low heat, stirring until smooth. Remove the saucepan from the heat and stir in the sugar. Add the eggs and vanilla and stir well to incorporate. Fold in the flour, salt, and walnuts, stirring just until incorporated.

3　Pour the batter into the prepared baking pan and bake until the center springs back when touched lightly with the tip of a finger, 35 to 40 minutes. Let the brownies cool in the pan on a wire rack for at least 10 minutes before cutting them into 2-inch squares. The brownies will keep for a couple of days (see Note), but ours rarely last for more than 3 or 4 hours after emerging from the oven.

NOTE: *I cover the pan with plastic wrap and hide them in our oven (obviously turned off) and hope no one will find them there.*

Transplanted Tiramisu

My husband and I met at a Burgundy wine-tasting dinner on Nantucket, got married in Maine, and then honeymooned in Rome and Tuscany, where we inevitably succumbed to the pleasures of the exquisite and wildly popular Italian dessert, tiramisu. Savoring tiramisu in its place of origin was an enlightening experience and I vowed never to splurge on all those calories again unless an authentic tiramisu was in the offering. Once the Vermont Creamery began marketing a reasonable facsimile of Italian mascarpone cheese (very good, although not quite the same as Italian mascarpone), I decided to undertake making the tiramisu of our memories with ingredients I could readily find in New England. I'm thrilled with the result and most people who partake of it are, too. When we served this rendition of tiramisu to celebrate our son's christening on Nantucket, my husband decided the dessert would be better translated from the Italian not as "pick me up" but as "fatten me up!" SERVES 10 TO 12

3 cups extra-strong brewed espresso coffee

¼ cup coffee-flavored liqueur, such as Kahlúa

24 to 30 Savoiardi biscuits (dry Italian ladyfingers)

6 large egg yolks

½ cup sugar

3 tablespoons sweet Marsala wine

1½ pounds (3 cups) mascarpone

2 cups heavy (whipping) cream

4 ounces best-quality bittersweet chocolate, coarsely chopped

Unsweetened cocoa powder, for dusting the tiramisu

1 Combine the espresso and coffee-flavored liqueur in a shallow dish such as a pie pan. Quickly dip 12 to 15 of the Savoiardi biscuits into the coffee mixture to moisten them but not saturate them. Line the bottom and side of a 2½- to 3-quart decorative serving bowl with the moistened biscuits. Set the dish with the espresso mixture aside.

2 Whisk together the egg yolks, sugar, and Marsala in the top of a double boiler set over simmering water, whisking constantly until the mixture has thickened, tripled in volume, and is hot to the touch, about 5 minutes. Remove the egg mixture from the heat.

3 Place the mascarpone in a medium-size bowl and, using an electric mixer on medium speed, beat until soft and fluffy, 1 to 2 minutes. Beat in the warm egg mixture until well combined. Clean the beaters, pour the cream into a clean bowl, and beat it on medium-high speed until stiff. Gently but thoroughly fold the whipped cream into the mascarpone mixture.

4 Spoon half of the mascarpone mixture into the Savoiardi-lined bowl. Sprinkle half of the chopped chocolate over the top. Dip enough of the remaining Savoiardi into the coffee to make a single layer over the mascarpone. Top these with the remaining mascarpone mixture and sprinkle the rest of the chopped chocolate over the top. Cover the tiramisu with plastic wrap and refrigerate it for at least 6 hours and up to 2 days. When ready to serve, dust the top with a thin layer of sifted cocoa powder. Using a large serving spoon, scoop portions onto individual serving plates or into shallow bowls.

Super- Rich Homemade Vanilla Ice Cream

So many New England desserts are best when served with a scoop of vanilla ice cream. While there are plenty of terrific ice cream companies throughout New England, nothing can compare with the flavor and texture of this homemade vanilla ice cream. The recipe comes from my friend and fellow cookbook writer Ann Hodgman who lives in Washington, Connecticut. Ann wrote two of my favorite cookbooks back in the 1990s: *Beat This!* followed by *Beat That!* She was kind enough to bestow top honors on a Thanksgiving stuffing recipe of mine in *Beat This!* and in exchange said I could have lifetime rights to her vanilla ice cream recipe, which appeared in the same book. Thank you, Ann!

I usually make this ice cream with my son, Oliver, and only for the most special occasions—to accompany Thanksgiving pies or at the height of the summer berry season—so as not to become too accustomed to it or spoiled by its sublimity. The ice cream takes a couple of days to make and a fair amount of conscientious labor, so plan accordingly. MAKES 1 QUART

4 cups heavy (whipping) cream

2 whole vanilla beans

Ice cubes

8 large egg yolks

⅔ cup superfine sugar

Pinch of fine sea salt

1 At least 2 days before you plan on serving the ice cream pour the heavy cream into a medium-size heavy saucepan. Cut the vanilla beans in half lengthwise and, using the tip of a sharp paring knife, scrape the seeds into the cream. Drop the pods into the cream, cover the pan, and refrigerate it overnight.

2 Fill a large shallow pan with ice water.

3 Remove the vanilla infusion from the refrigerator and scald it (bring it almost to a boil—the surface of the cream will just begin to quiver, as opposed to bubble) over medium-high heat, about 5 minutes. While the cream is heating, place the egg yolks, sugar, and salt in a medium-size mixing bowl and whisk until light, 2 to 3 minutes. Once the cream has scalded,

remove the vanilla pods (but not the seeds) from it and very gradually whisk the hot cream into the egg yolk mixture to combine (go slowly so the eggs don't curdle). The mixture should be silky smooth but not foamy from too much whisking.

4 Transfer the mixture to a large clean saucepan and cook over low heat, stirring constantly, until thickened into a light custard, 6 to 8 minutes. I usually do this visually but if you want to be precise, the custard should register between 170° and 180°F on a candy thermometer. Remove the custard from the heat and cool it by placing it in the pan of ice water. until cold, 20 to 25 minutes. (Making great vanilla ice cream takes work!)

5 Transfer the custard to an ice cream maker and freeze it into ice cream by following the manufacturer's directions. Transfer the ice cream to 2 pint containers or 1 quart container; seal, and store the ice cream in the freezer overnight for the flavor to mellow and the texture to become firmer. Serve small scoops of the ice cream as an indulgence with anything improved by great vanilla ice cream.

Becky's Harwich Hot Chocolate Sauce

I met Becky Overman through my aunt and uncle shortly after we moved from Nantucket to Cape Cod at the onset of the millennium. Becky originally hailed from Charleston, South Carolina, and her Southern charm combined with her extraordinary creative talent and resourcefulness has enriched my family's life on Cape Cod in ways far too numerous, delicious, and dramatic to count. While she bravely introduced my husband, Nigel, to travel in India on her sixty-ninth business trip to the country, I am equally awed by the far less

exotic but nonetheless exemplary hot chocolate sauce she makes to spoon over vanilla ice cream in her Harwich kitchen on Cape Cod. I have loved peppermint stick ice cream ever since I was a little girl and once a summer I like to treat myself to this sauce spooned over the excellent peppermint stick ice cream churned by Four Seas in Centerville, Massachusetts. MAKES ABOUT 2 CUPS

8 tablespoons (1 stick) unsalted butter

2½ cups confectioners' sugar

1 can (5 ounces; ⅔ cup) evaporated milk

6 squares (6 ounces) unsweetened chocolate

PLACE THE BUTTER, confectioners' sugar, evaporated milk, and chocolate in a medium-size, heavy saucepan and heat over medium-low heat. Cook the chocolate sauce until the butter and chocolate have melted and the flavors have had time to blend, about 30 minutes without stirring. (I always find it hard to resist the temptation to stir but Becky insists this is part of the secret to the recipe.) After 30 minutes, remove the pan from the heat and whisk the chocolate sauce vigorously with a wire whisk or, using a hand-held electric mixer, beat it at medium speed until smooth and creamy, about 2 minutes. Keep the chocolate sauce warm over very low heat until ready to use (see Note).

NOTE: *I do not encourage making the sauce ahead. It can be held over very low heat for a good hour. If there are leftovers, they should be stored in a covered heavy glass jar in the refrigerator. To reheat: Remove the cover and place the jar in a small saucepan filled with enough water to come halfway up the side of the jar. Heat over medium heat, stirring the chocolate sauce as it melts. Once melted and smooth, turn off the heat but keep the jar warm in the hot water in the saucepan until ready to use.*

Attitude Adjusters

> "There can't be good living where there is not good drinking."—Benjamin Franklin

Years ago when I was conducting research for my Maine cookbook, *Saltwater Seasonings*, I had the great pleasure of interviewing a lobsterman in Buck's Harbor named Dana Holbrook, who, as promised, proved to be quite the colorful character.

I was scheduled to meet with Dana at four in the afternoon on a beautiful summer day and went to find him at the rocky cove where he kept his lobster boat, *Shady Lady*. Dana was just pulling in to anchor after a long day on the water, a typical one that had begun at sunrise. Nonetheless, he was in a chipper mood and invited me into his shanty to chat and join him in imbibing an "attitude adjuster." Dana's attitude adjuster consisted of a crude mix of Diet Pepsi and vodka poured from half-gallon jugs into oversize plastic cups. While I have refrained from including Dana's cocktail recipe in this chapter, I have forever after embraced his attitude adjuster terminology and such has led to many memorable New England–inspired happy hours sipping somewhat more sophisticated libations than the one that prompted the title of this chapter. In fact, wineries, distilleries, and breweries have become so prevalent throughout New England, and are producing enough noteworthy products, that an entire book could be devoted to the topic.

Not all attitude adjusters are geared to improve the moods of the over twenty-one set. Parenthood has taught me that a pretty pitcher of homemade Watermelon Lemonade or fragrant pot of mulled cider can work miracles to improve the dispositions of cranky youngsters, too.

Sun Tea

One of the most popular bumper stickers on Nantucket Island is "Fog Happens." However, I happen to think that the thickest fog I have ever experienced in New England occurs around the Penobscot Bay area of the Maine Coast. Because fog, during certain summers, can be overwhelming along Maine's rocky coastline, it is easy to imagine how sunny days might become so cherished and celebrated. During Down East stretches of sunny summer weather, my mother is usually quick to seize the moment to make Sun Tea, New England's answer to the South's sweet tea.

When Life Gives You Lemons . . .

Del's Lemonade, and especially Del's Soft-Frozen Lemonade, is arguably New England's most famous lemonade. The Rhode Island-based company has a romantic story behind its founding, telling of Great-Grandfather DeLucia inventing the prototype recipe back in Naples, Italy, in 1840, when he decided to store winter snow insulated in straw in a nearby cave. Come summertime, Grandfather DeLucia squeezed juice from a crop of ripe local lemons and then returned to the cave with the juice and some sugar to mix together with the stored snow, and thus frozen lemonade came into being.

Del's is still run in Cranston, Rhode Island, by descendents of Grandfather DeLucia. Personally, I have always found the Del's story more appealing than their lemonade products, but it is worth noting that Del's almost managed to make lemonade the official drink of the state of Rhode Island, ultimately losing the honor to another favorite Rhode Island oddity—coffee milk.

The recipe is simple and epitomizes Yankee thriftiness, because the tea is steeped outside using the power of the sun, thereby avoiding utility expense and the possibility of having the stove further heat up the kitchen on an already hot summer day. Tea that is slowly steeped by the heat of the sun as opposed to brewed has slightly different flavor nuances and does not tend to keep as well as traditionally brewed tea.

Sun Tea should be consumed within two days of making, never a problem in our ice tea loving family. We always pour the tea into tall glasses over lots of ice, sweeten it sparingly with sugar, add lemon wedges and fresh mint, and sometimes a splash or two of fresh orange juice. Use your favorite traditional, fruit, or herbal tea bags to make Sun Tea. MAKES 2 QUARTS

5 tea bags

2 quarts good tap water or unflavored bottled still water

Ice cubes, for serving

Sugar, fresh mint, and lemon wedges, for serving

PLACE THE TEA bags in a 2-quart glass jar with a lid and fill it with the water. Put the lid on the jar and place it outside in a hot and sunny location. Let the tea steep until it reaches the desired strength, 3 to 5 hours. Move the jar, if necessary, to keep it in direct sunlight. Remove and discard the tea bags and store the jar of Sun Tea in the refrigerator; it will keep for 2 days. Serve the tea in tall, ice-filled glasses, letting each person doctor the tea to his or her liking with sugar, fresh mint, and lemon.

Watermelon Lemonade

As far as I am concerned the very best lemonade is made from scratch at home on hot summer afternoons. This lemonade, flavored with watermelon and strawberries, was invented back in 2003 when I was asked to write an article on summer drinks for *Nantucket Today* magazine. My friend Cary Hazlegrove was photographing the story and her daughter, Virginia, was close in age to my son, Oliver, six years old at the time. Oliver and Virginia had somehow managed to be engaged in friendly rivalries almost from birth and I ended up having to make his and her lemonade recipes to satisfy the egos and thirsts of the two. Cary photographed Virginia and Oliver in a rare moment of truce seated sipping their lemonades together on a weathered outdoor bench and the photo ended up

gracing the cover of the magazine. This lemonade is still a favorite summer drink of Oliver's. MAKES ABOUT 1 QUART

3 heaping cups seeded and diced watermelon (about 1 inch dice), plus watermelon wedges (optional), for garnish

1½ heaping cups hulled and quartered fresh strawberries, plus strawberries (optional), for garnish

½ cup superfine sugar

½ cup freshly squeezed lemon juice

1 cup good tap water or your favorite unflavored bottled still water

Ice cubes, for serving

1   Place half of the diced watermelon and quartered strawberries and ¼ cup of the superfine sugar, ¼ cup of the lemon juice, and ½ cup of the water in a blender and puree until smooth. Strain the juice mixture through a fine mesh strainer to remove the strawberry seeds. Pour the juice mixture into a large pitcher. Repeat with the remaining diced watermelon and quartered strawberries and ¼ cup of superfine sugar, ¼ cup lemon juice, and ½ cup of water. Refrigerate the lemonade until ready to serve—it will keep for up to 3 days; stir before serving.

2   Pour the lemonade into ice-filled glasses and garnish the rim of each glass with a watermelon wedge or fresh strawberry, or both, if desired.

Cranberry Orange Lemonade

This is the lemonade recipe I created for photographer Cary Hazlegrove's daughter, Virginia. Sparkling water can be added to the lemon base in place of still water, if desired, to impart a slight effervescence, much like Virginia's personality. MAKES 1 QUART OF JUICE MIXTURE

2 cups freshly squeezed orange juice

¾ cup freshly squeezed lemon juice

¾ cup superfine sugar

½ cup cranberry juice

Ice cubes, for serving

1½ to 2 cups good tap water or your favorite unflavored bottled still or sparkling water, for serving

Orange slices (optional), for garnish

1   Combine the orange juice, lemon juice, superfine sugar, and cranberry juice in a blender and puree until smooth. Pour the juice mixture into a large pitcher and refrigerate it until ready to serve—it will keep for up to 3 days; stir before serving.

2   Pour the juice mixture into ice-filled glasses, filling them three quarters full. Top off the glasses with still or sparkling water and stir. Garnish the rim of each glass with an orange slice, if desired.

Mulled Cider With or Without Hurricane Rum

My husband and I spent a period of time over the course of several fall weekends driving our son all over New England to youth soccer tournaments. While I surprised my nonsport-spectating self with the ferocity of my cheering, soccer mom was never a title that made me feel comfortable. In fact, I should be honest and admit that sometimes the saving grace of these time-consuming, hundred-mile-plus jaunts was stumbling upon a local cider mill and scoring a great jug of freshly pressed cider. Hours spent watching matches in inclement weather often meant returning home in an uncomfortably damp and frozen state, which I soon discovered could best be alleviated by mulling a pot of hot cider.

This is a recipe that I have tinkered with over the years, after I realized that cranberry juice added quite the complementary tang and blush to the mulled cider. The concoction was further aided, abetted, and advanced by having a husband in the spice business. The resulting hot tonic, with its combination of honey and spices, is always soothing and restorative for all family members. Depending on the circumstances, adding a generous splash of Hurricane Rum, produced by the talented team at Nantucket's Triple Eight Distillery, can impart welcome magical wonders for the ever-growing coterie of beleaguered soccer moms and dads.

Hurricane Rum was added to the Triple Eight Distillery product line during an especially intense Northeast hurricane season in 2003. The rum is aged in bourbon casks to impart both a golden color and a subtle whiskey flavor and then purposely overproofed to match the strength of the major hurricanes that have hit the New England coast over the years. Another golden-hued rum can be substituted but it is hard to resist the poetic allure of Hurricane Rum, if you are fortunate enough to have a bottle on hand. SERVES 8

5 cups apple cider, preferably freshly pressed from a New England cider mill

3 cups cranberry juice

½ cup (packed) light brown sugar

3 tablespoons honey, preferably a cranberry bog honey from New England

4 cinnamon sticks (each 4 inches long), plus additional cinnamon sticks (optional), for garnish

2 slices (½ inch thick) peeled fresh ginger

12 whole cloves

1 large navel orange, cut in half lengthwise

1 star anise (optional, but wonderful)

Hurricane Rum or other golden rum (optional)

1 Combine the cider, cranberry juice, brown sugar, honey, cinnamon sticks, and ginger in a large non-reactive saucepan. Stick 6 cloves in a row down the outside of each orange half as if you were fashioning a clove Mohawk hairdo, spacing the cloves about ¼ inch apart. Slice the orange halves into half-moon semicircles in between the cloves and add them to the saucepan. (Doing it this way is easier than sticking the cloves into the orange after it is sliced and prevents loose cloves from floating around in the cider, which could be a choking hazard.) Add the star anise, if using.

2 Let the cider mixture come to a boil over medium-high heat, stirring to dissolve the brown sugar and honey. Reduce the heat to medium-low and let the cider mixture simmer until the flavors meld, about 30 minutes.

3 Ladle the hot cider into mugs or punch cups and garnish each cup with a fresh cinnamon stick, if desired. Also if desired, spike each serving of the mulled cider with 1 to 2 ounces of rum.

Mount Mansfield Mulled Wine

Stowe is my family's favorite ski area in New England. My son honed his skiing skills at Stowe's excellent ski school and now enjoys schuss-booming down black diamond trails far more challenging than his more cautious parents would dare to tackle. Stowe's many amenities are what make the mountain a top choice for my husband and me and the highlight of our skiing day is always a

lunch or late afternoon stop at the Cliff House restaurant, offering breathtaking panoramas from its precarious perch near the top of Mount Mansfield.

Perhaps anything would taste good in frigid weather at an elevation of 3,625 feet, but we never cease to be awed by the quality and freshness of the rustic fare served in the alpine-style restaurant. The Cliff House's mulled wine is my go-to après-ski warmer and thanks are due to chef Matthew Reeve for sharing his recipe, as I never would have guessed that blackberry brandy is the secret to making the libation extra warming. SERVES 4

1 bottle (750 milliliters) merlot

6 whole cloves

1 small navel orange

1 cinnamon stick, plus 4 cinnamon sticks
  (each 4 inches long; optional), for garnish

3 ounces blackberry brandy

POUR THE MERLOT into a medium-size saucepan. Stick the cloves into the orange and add it to the saucepan along with the cinnamon stick. Add the blackberry brandy. Let the wine mixture come to a simmer over medium heat and continue to simmer until the flavors meld, about 10 minutes. Ladle the hot wine into glass mugs. Garnish each mug with a fresh cinnamon stick, if desired. Serve at once.

Blueberry Sangria

I learned to appreciate well-made fruit wines, more than two decades ago when my brother introduced me to Kathe and Bob Bartlett, proprietors and vintners at the Bartlett Maine Estate Winery in Gouldsboro, Maine. While the Bartletts knew they had a calling for winemaking, they also knew that wine grapes could not thrive in Maine's cool climate. They explain, "Inspiration hit with the low-bush blueberries that cover our coastline. Rich in tannins and bursting with flavor, we knew they would be an ideal fruit for making wine."

Over the years, Bartlett wines have expanded beyond blueberries to being distilled from apples, pears, and peaches in dry, semidry, and sweet dessert bottlings. The Bartletts also make a potent pear eau-de-vie and an apple brandy.

While there are other wineries in New England making fruit-based wines, the Bartlett wines have always been my gold standard in this niche market. Since I love sangria but find most restaurant renditions to be overly sweet, I came up with the idea of showcasing some of the Bartlett semidry wines as a natural fruity base for my house-made sangria since they require no added sugar. Modesty aside, this is one of the best sangrias I have ever tasted and it is the perfect way to introduce neophytes or doubters to the pleasures of Bartlett Maine Estate Winery's fruit wines. SERVES 4 TO 6

1 bottle (750 milliliters) Bartlett semidry
  Wild Blueberry wine

2 cups premium lemonade, such as Odwalla

2 cups freshly squeezed orange juice

½ cup brandy or orange liqueur, such as Grand
  Marnier

¾ cup highbush blueberries (wild blueberries
  are too small and could be a choking hazard)

1 navel orange, cut in half and then cut into
  thin slices

1 lemon, cut in half and then cut into thin
  slices, seeds removed

1 lime, cut in half and then cut into thin slices

Ice cubes, for serving

Club soda or ginger ale

1   Pour the blueberry wine, lemonade, orange juice, and brandy or orange liqueur into a large clear glass serving pitcher. Stir in the blueberries and orange, lemon, and lime slices. Chill the sangria in the refrigerator for at least 3 hours and as long as overnight.

2 When ready to serve, fill balloon-style wine glasses half full with ice cubes. Pour the chilled sangria over the ice, making sure to include some of the fruit. Do not fill the glasses completely. Top off the sangria with a generous splash of club soda or ginger ale. Enjoy, preferably on an outdoor deck or porch on a hot summer day.

Peach Sangria

Every once in a while, I like to concoct a white-wine based pitcher of sangria and the Bartlett Maine Estate Winery semidry peach wine makes an ideal base for this very fruity and pretty summer sangria. SERVES 4 TO 6

1 cup hulled and thickly sliced fresh strawberries

2 ripe peaches, pitted and cut into ½-inch-wide wedges

¾ cup green grapes, cut in half

½ cup orange liqueur, such as triple sec

2 tablespoons brandy

1 bottle (750 milliliters) Bartlett semidry peach wine

½ cup freshly squeezed orange juice

½ cup chilled bottled sparkling lemonade or limeade

Ice cubes, for serving

Fresh mint sprigs, for garnish

1 Place the strawberries, peaches, and grapes in a large, clear glass serving pitcher. Add the orange liqueur and brandy and toss gently to mix. Let the fruit macerate at room temperature for about 45 minutes.

2 Add the peach wine and orange juice, stir, and refrigerate the sangria for at least 1 hour and up to 4 hours.

3 When ready to serve, add the sparkling lemonade or limeade to the pitcher of sangria and stir well to mix. Fill balloon-style wine glasses half full with ice cubes and pour the sangria over the ice, making sure to include some of the fruit. Garnish each glass with a mint sprig and serve at once.

New England Kir

I learned to appreciate the French aperitif known as a kir, a combination of dry white wine (traditionally Burgundian aligoté) and black currant liqueur (cassis) in Burgundy, the very place where the drink originated and where it remains wildly popular. I never imagined having a variation on this quintessentially French drink in a New England cookbook until I met Tim Dempsey, the knowledgeable and innovative bartender at The Pitcher Inn in Warren, Vermont.

Tim had many libations unfamiliar to me tucked into the nooks and crannies of his bar and sent me home with a bottle of his favorite New England sparkling cider—Farnum Hill Farmhouse cider distilled in Lebanon, New Hampshire, from cider apples grown in the company's Poverty Lane Orchards. Tim encouraged me to use this sparkling cider to make a kir, an idea that in turn immediately inspired me to whip up a batch of Cheddar *Gougères* (find them on page 18), since *gougères* made with the French Gruyère cheese are traditionally served with kirs in Burgundy.

As I played around with the proportions of the aperitif, it struck me that cassis was not the best flavor match with the Farmhouse cider's taste elements of citrus, pineapple, bittersweet apple, and slightly funky barnyard. I found that I preferred cranberry as a flavor enhancer and now opt to make my New England version of kir with a couple of tablespoons of the cranberry syrup my husband uses in his Cape Codder (page 364) or the cranberry liqueur made by Flag Hill in Lee, New Hampshire. In a pinch, even a generous splash of cranberry juice will work and make for a low alcohol drink since the alcohol in Farnum Hill Farmhouse cider is only 6.5 percent by volume. SERVES 4

6 tablespoons Nigel's Cranberry Syrup (page 366) or Flag Hill cranberry liqueur

1 bottle (750 milliliters) Farnum Hill Farmhouse cider, well chilled

SPOON 1½ TABLESPOONS of cranberry syrup or cranberry liqueur into each of 4 champagne flutes. Fill each flute with chilled sparkling cider. Swirl each drink with a swizzle stick to blend and serve at once.

Strawberry Rhubarb Bellini

Ever since I tasted my first Bellini at Harry's Bar in Venice on a post high school graduation bicycle trip around Europe, I have yearned to create the same drink back home, to no avail. After years of sipping trial homemade Bellinis that inevitably disappointed, I decided to wipe the slate clean and stop trying to perfect the Italian white peach puree that goes into making the Harry's Bar Bellini so memorable and instead highlight one of my favorite fruity New England combinations—strawberry and rhubarb. This drink is definitely the "attitude adjuster" any adult commuter to the Cape deserves after braving the infuriating traffic jams that so often back up for miles when that commuter is trying to drive over the dated two-lane Bourne and Sagamore bridges that span the canal separating the Cape from the mainland. SERVES 8 TO 10, DEPENDING ON THE SIZE OF THE FLUTED GLASSES

1 pint fresh strawberries, hulled and cut into ½-inch dice, plus strawberries (optional), for garnish

1 cup sliced fresh rhubarb (2 plump stalks; ½-inch-thick slices), stalk ends trimmed

¾ cup sugar

½ cup water

2 tablespoons cassis (black currant liqueur)

2 bottles (each 750 milliliters) prosecco or other dry sparkling white wine, well chilled

1 Place the diced strawberries and rhubarb in a medium-size saucepan, add the sugar, and toss to mix. Add the water and cassis and let come to a boil over medium-high heat. Reduce the heat to medium-low, and let simmer, stirring occasionally, until the rhubarb is very tender, about 15 minutes. Remove the pan from the heat and let the strawberry and rhubarb mixture cool for at least 15 minutes.

2 Transfer the cooled strawberry and rhubarb mixture to a blender and puree until very smooth. Store the puree in an airtight container in the refrigerator until ready to make the Bellinis. The puree can be refrigerated for at least 1 week.

3 When ready to make the Bellinis, spoon 2 tablespoons of the chilled strawberry rhubarb puree into the bottom of each champagne flute. Fill each flute with chilled prosecco and swirl with a swizzle stick to blend. Garnish each flute with a strawberry perched on the rim, if desired, and serve at once.

Nigel's Cape Codder

Whenever we entertain, Nigel prides himself on inventing a special, welcoming cocktail to suit the occasion. At some point I suggested that I would love for him to create a straightforward

I love visiting Newport, Rhode Island, at any time, but the yachting and sailing scene is at its height during the summer, when excellent dining choices abound along the waterfront.

Cape Codder cocktail but find a way to make it better than any he had ever been served. Nigel took to the task with far more speed and relish than my more frequent culinary requests of peeling substantial amounts of garlic or seeding tomatoes and jalapeño peppers. Suffice it to say, there was nothing menial to bog (pun intended) him down and the task was accomplished with exemplary craft-cocktail expertise. SERVES 1

Generous 2 ounces vodka

4 ounces cranberry juice

2 ounces Nigel's Cranberry Syrup
  (recipe follows)

Ice cubes, for serving

1 lime wedge, for garnish

PLACE THE VODKA, cranberry juice, and cranberry syrup in a tall mixing glass or beaker and stir to mix. Pour the cocktail into an ice-filled highball glass and garnish with a wedge of lime.

Nigel's Cranberry Syrup

The popular Cape Codder cocktail usually consists of three ingredients: vodka, cranberry juice, and a squeeze of lime. Nigel decided to make a homemade cranberry syrup to replace some of the standard cranberry juice and the resulting cocktail was elevated to a whole new stratosphere. MAKES 1¾ CUPS

1 cup whole fresh or frozen cranberries

1 cup cranberry juice

⅓ cup sugar

2 tablespoons freshly squeezed lime juice

1 teaspoon finely grated lime zest

1 Place the cranberries, cranberry juice, sugar, lime juice, and lime zest in a small nonreactive saucepan and cook over medium heat, stirring occasionally, until the cranberries have softened and burst open, 10 to 12 minutes. Remove the cranberry mixture from the heat and let it cool for at least 10 minutes.

2 Transfer the cranberry mixture to a blender and puree until smooth. Store the syrup in the refrigerator, covered, until ready to use. The syrup will keep for at least 1 week.

Cape Cod Cosmopolitan

Cranberries were never considered to be particularly chic until the pretty pink cosmopolitan tinged with cranberry juice became Carrie Bradshaw's cocktail of choice on TV's *Sex and the City* series. Since then, the cosmopolitan or cosmo has risen to become one of the most ordered cocktails in bars across America. The downside is that this popularity has led to many cosmopolitans being made with inferior or compromised ingredients. If there were ever a place to make a really good cosmo, it is on Cape Cod and the addition of my husband's homemade cranberry syrup makes this cosmopolitan soar above most others. SERVES 1

Ice cubes

2 ounces top-quality orange-infused vodka

½ ounce orange liqueur, preferably
  Grand Marnier

½ ounce Nigel's Cranberry Syrup (page 366)

½ ounce freshly squeezed lime juice

FILL A COCKTAIL shaker half full with ice cubes. Add the orange-infused vodka, orange liqueur, cranberry syrup, and lime juice. Cover the shaker and shake well and then strain the cocktail into a chilled martini glass.

Blueberry Pi

During the years our son, Oliver, attended the Lighthouse School on Nantucket, Evan and Maria Marley's Pi Pizzeria restaurant was hands down our favorite family restaurant. Not only is the Neapolitan-style, wood-fired pizza perfection, but so too is everything else on the stylized Italian menu. Evan and Maria were kind enough to give Oliver, at the age of thirteen, a glimpse into what it was like to work in a bustling restaurant kitchen and my guess is that the Friday-night shift challenged Evan more than Oliver. While Oliver's calamari cleaning and pizza box folding days are behind him, Nigel and I still, as always, enjoy dinner seated at Pi's intimate and lively bar whenever we're on the island.

Pi prides itself, rightfully so, on its bartenders who are described on the restaurant's website as "experienced cocktailians with a passion for the art of mixology." The Blueberry Pi cocktail, made with Nantucket's deep blue Triple Eight Blueberry Vodka, is as delicious as it is unique in flavor and clever in title, its creation attributed to bartender Chris Perone. At home we garnish our cocktails by skewering fresh blueberries and mint leaves on bamboo toothpicks. SERVES 2

Crushed ice

4 ounces Triple Eight Blueberry Vodka

2 ounces orange liqueur, preferably Cointreau

1 ounce freshly squeezed lemon juice

1 ounce freshly squeezed lime juice

Ginger ale

2 small lime wedges or twists of lime peel,
  for garnish

FILL A COCKTAIL shaker half full with crushed ice. Add the blueberry vodka, orange liqueur, lemon juice, and lime juice. Cover the shaker and shake vigorously for at least 30 seconds. Strain the cocktail into 2 chilled martini glasses. Top off each cocktail with a generous splash of ginger ale and garnish it with a small lime wedge or twist.

Smoked Salt–Rimmed Bloody Mary

Bloody Marys never go out of fashion, continuing to be extremely popular with New England's nautical set and Sunday brunch goers. Opinions as to what makes a perfect Bloody Mary vary widely and as of late garnishes have morphed from the classic celery stick to the likes of crisp bacon strips, jumbo shrimp, and lobster tails.

Many people rely on the convenience of bottled Bloody Mary bases and some favorites include the Triple Eight Bloody Mary mix, the Farmer's Bloody Mary mix made by Waldingfield Farm in Litchfield County, Connecticut, and (nepotism aside) my husband's Nantucket Speakeasy Bloody Mary Spiced Tomato Mixer. On the other hand, my brother, Jonathan, swears by the nationally distributed Zing Zang product for the Bloody Marys he serves at his restaurant's bar in Bucks Harbor, Maine. On still yet another hand, there's the Bloody Mary my Barnstable neighbors Alice Pitcher and Tom Dott made famous when they ran Old Drovers Inn, just over the Connecticut border in Dover Plains, New York. The secrets to this include using Sacramento brand tomato juice and rimming the glass with a specially made hickory-smoked sea salt. Should you wish to make a virgin version of this Bloody Mary, be sure to call it by its former Old Drovers name—Bloody Shame.

The hickory-smoked sea salt used to be made exclusively for Old Drovers Inn but over this past salt-crazed decade smoked sea salts have become far more readily available. My husband sells a smoked sea salt called Sea Smoke under his Coastal Goods label and the Maine Sea Salt Company has an enticing variety of hickory, apple, and alder wood smoked sea salts. The crystals in these New England smoked sea salts tend to be on the large size, so they will need to be ground fine in a spice mill in order to be able to adhere to the rim of a Bloody Mary glass.

Should you want to venture into garnishing your Bloody with more than a celery stick, I'm fond of my husband's garden fresh tiny tomatoes speared on a toothpick with fresh basil leaves. SERVES 1

3 ounces tomato juice, preferably
   Sacramento brand

1 tablespoon Worcestershire sauce

1 teaspoon potent prepared horseradish,
   preferably Gold's or Heluva Good

3 "healthy" shakes celery salt

2 shakes Tabasco sauce

3 ounces vodka

Juice of 1 lemon, plus a lemon wedge for
   priming the glass

Ice cubes

Freshly ground black pepper

Finely ground smoked sea salt

1 Combine the tomato juice, Worcestershire sauce, horseradish, celery salt, Tabasco sauce, vodka, and lemon juice in a tall mixing glass or beaker. Add a couple of handfuls of ice cubes and stir well. Season with pepper to taste.

2 Spread a thin layer of smoked salt on a small plate. Run a small wedge of lemon around a highball glass and invert the glass into the salt, giving it a twist or two to make the salt adhere to the rim. Fill the glass with the Bloody Mary and ice cubes and serve at once.

The Englishman's Breakfast

My husband is quintessentially British in his love of a breakfast of tea and marmalade on toast. When our next door neighbor Judy Kaess presented us with a jar of calamondin marmalade she had made from fruit harvested in her greenhouse, Nigel somehow got the notion to mix it into a cocktail rather than spread it on toast. Thus, this wonderfully brilliant cocktail was born.

Calamondins are small, round, and very tart citrus fruits with delicate, thin skins that are sweeter than the interior fruit. The trees are commonly grown in Florida backyards, but it is unusual to find fresh calamondins or calamondin products in New England, so feel free to substitute traditional orange marmalade or any other marmalade that tickles your fancy. Should calamondin curiosity get the better of you, do consider checking out the terrific mail-order products from the Calamondin Café (calamondincafe.com) in Fort Myers, Florida. Their Calamondin Jam would be an excellent choice to use in making The Englishman's Breakfast cocktail. SERVES 1

1 orange

2 tablespoons sugar

Ice cubes

2 ounces freshly squeezed orange juice

2 ounces orange-infused vodka

1 ounce freshly squeezed lime juice

¾ ounce orange liqueur, preferably Grand Marnier

1 tablespoon orange or other citrus marmalade

1 small orange or lime wedge

1 Using a Microplane, grate the zest of the orange as finely as possible. Spread the orange zest out on a small microwave-safe plate and microwave it on high power until the zest is dried out, 1 to 2 minutes, depending on the wattage of your microwave oven. Let the zest cool about 5 minutes, then add the sugar to the orange zest and toss to combine evenly on the plate. Set the plate with the orange zest mixture aside.

2 Fill a cocktail shaker halfway with ice cubes. Add the orange juice, orange-flavored vodka, lime juice, orange liqueur, and marmalade. Cover the cocktail shaker and shake vigorously for at least 30 seconds.

3 Run a small wedge of orange or lime around the rim of a chilled martini glass and invert the glass into the orange zest mixture, giving it a few twists to coat the rim. Strain the shaken cocktail into the glass and serve at once.

New Hampshire Mudslide

New England's mud season in late March and early April is not the stuff of tourist marketing dreams and Vermont, New Hampshire, and Maine tend to be worse off than their neighboring states to the south. The only redeeming feature to this dreaded time of the year is the fact that it inspired this terrific cocktail during a visit to friends in Grantham, New Hampshire.

Grantham is not far from my favorite New England dairy, McNamara Dairy in Plainfield and we had made a point of provisioning for our stay with an array of the dairy's superior creams, sold in old-fashioned thick glass bottles. To stave off cabin fever we took to mixing up batches of a most memorable frozen mudslide—incredibly rich but irresistible. SERVES 2

2 ounces vodka

2 ounces Baileys Irish cream liqueur

2 ounces Kahlúa

2 large ice cubes

1 cup premium coffee ice cream

2 ounces light cream

Bittersweet chocolate

PLACE THE VODKA, Baileys Irish cream, Kahlúa, ice cubes, ice cream, and cream in a blender and blend to the consistency of a milk shake. Divide the frozen mudslide between 2 old-fashioned glasses and shave or grate a few shards of bittersweet chocolate over the top of each drink. Serve at once.

Shandy Gaff

This is one of the first cocktails I learned to make and I still find it to be one of the most refreshing. You simply pour equal amounts of beer and ginger beer into a pitcher filled with ice, though nuances of the drink can be numerous now that there are so many microbreweries throughout New England and so many artisanally made ginger beers. Sometimes I even make a "lite" version by using light beer and diet ginger ale. However, the best Shandy Gaffs are made with a good lager-type beer and an intensely flavored ginger beer.

I find that the drink is most enjoyable when served in the late afternoon after returning home from a day at the beach or on the water. If you are a golfer, you may want to follow in my father's footsteps and make a Shandy Gaff your 19th hole libation of choice. SERVES 2 TO 4

Ice cubes

2 bottles or cans (each 12 ounces) your favorite local lager-style beer

2 cans ginger beer (each 12 ounces), such as Reed's Extra Ginger Brew or Gosling's Ginger Beer

A porch swing need not have a seaside vista to beckon as a breezy spot to sip an attitude adjuster in the late afternoon on a lazy summer day.

FILL A LARGE PITCHER halfway with ice cubes. Pour 1 bottle of beer and 1 bottle of ginger beer simultaneously over the ice. Repeat with the remaining bottles of beer and ginger beer. Stir and serve at once poured into chilled pilsner glasses or tankards.

Conversion Tables

Please note that all conversions are approximate but close enough to be useful when converting from one system to another.

Oven Temperatures

FAHRENHEIT	GAS MARK	CELSIUS
250	½	120
275	1	140
300	2	150
325	3	160
350	4	180
375	5	190
400	6	200
425	7	220
450	8	230
475	9	240
500	10	260

Note: Reduce the temperature by 20°C (68°F) for fan-assisted ovens.

Approximate Equivalents

1 stick butter=8 tbs=4 oz=½ cup=115 g

1 cup all-purpose presifted flour=4.7 oz

1 cup granulated sugar=8 oz=220 g

1 cup (firmly packed) brown sugar=6 oz=220 g to 230 g

1 cup confectioners' sugar=4½ oz=115 g

1 cup honey or syrup=12 oz

1 cup grated cheese=4 oz

1 cup dried beans=6 oz

1 large egg=about 2 oz or about 3 tbs

1 egg yolk=about 1 tbs

1 egg white=about 2 tbs

Liquid Conversions

U.S.	IMPERIAL	METRIC
2 tbs	1 fl oz	30 ml
3 tbs	1½ fl oz	45 ml
¼ cup	2 fl oz	60 ml
⅓ cup	2½ fl oz	75 ml
⅓ cup + 1 tbs	3 fl oz	90 ml
⅓ cup + 2 tbs	3½ fl oz	100 ml
½ cup	4 fl oz	125 ml
⅔ cup	5 fl oz	150 ml
¾ cup	6 fl oz	175 ml
¾ cup + 2 tbs	7 fl oz	200 ml
1 cup	8 fl oz	250 ml
1 cup + 2 tbs	9 fl oz	275 ml
1¼ cups	10 fl oz	300 ml
1⅓ cups	11 fl oz	325 ml
1½ cups	12 fl oz	350 ml
1⅔ cups	13 fl oz	375 ml
1¾ cups	14 fl oz	400 ml
1¾ cups + 2 tbs	15 fl oz	450 ml
2 cups (1 pint)	16 fl oz	500 ml
2½ cups	20 fl oz (1 pint)	600 ml
3¾ cups	1½ pints	900 ml
4 cups	1¾ pints	1 liter

Weight Conversions

US/UK	METRIC	US/UK	METRIC
½ oz	15 g	7 oz	200 g
1 oz	30 g	8 oz	250 g
1½ oz	45 g	9 oz	275 g
2 oz	60 g	10 oz	300 g
2½ oz	75 g	11 oz	325 g
3 oz	90 g	12 oz	350 g
3½ oz	100 g	13 oz	375 g
4 oz	125 g	14 oz	400 g
5 oz	150 g	15 oz	450 g
6 oz	175 g	1 lb	500 g

Index

C

sauce, 154–55

and tomato salad, summer, 58

Curried chicken salad, Daffodil picnic, 279

D

Date cranberry pie, Jennifer's, 334–36

Desserts, 327–55

brownies, Connecticut saucepan, 352–53

fresh fruit tart with lemon mascarpone cream filling, 336–38, *337*

lemon squares, Daffodil, 351–52

prune plum crunch, the original September, 323–24

tiramisu, transplanted, 353–54

vanilla ice cream, super-rich homemade, 354–55

see also Cakes; Cookies; Pies

Dill mustard sauce, 152–53

Dilly beans, refrigerator, *9*, 10–11

Dips:

carrot, Woodstock Farmers' Market, 2–3, *9*

crabmeat, hot, 4–5

crabmeat, my mother's, 3–4

crab spread, community cookbook, 5

cranberry salsa, fresh, 5–6

feta cheese, whipped, 275–76

guacamole, seaside, *6*, 7–8

Dressing, oyster and Swiss chard, 190

Dressings (for salads):

blue cheese, 66

Niçoise, 136

poppy seed, 280–82

see also Vinaigrette

Drinks. *See* Beverages

Duck:

breasts, seared, à l'orange, 184–85

breasts with fennel and rosemary, 185–86

confit, speedy, 186–87

E

Egg(s):

breakfast hash, Castle Hill Inn's signature, 312–13

classic New England breakfast sandwich, 304–5

lobster omelet, 134–35

our best pizza oven pizza with shaved asparagus and prosciutto, 240–41

poaching, 313

salad tartines, truffled, 289–91, *290*

scramble, New Hampshire–style, 309–11, *310*

scrambled, with cottage cheese, 309

Eggplant:

baby, tomato, and cheese gratin, 251

grilled cornucopia of summer garden vegetables, *268*, 269

my moussaka, 218–19

pudding, Greek, 251–52

puffs, baked, 252–53

"sandwiches," 24–25

tomato sauce, lamb meatballs simmered in, 217–18

Englishman's breakfast, 368–69

F

Farro tabbouleh, 285

Fennel:

and coriander crusted tuna steaks with red wine béarnaise, 164–65

mountaintop mussels with tomatoes and, 99

Feta cheese:

chopped kale with cranberries and, 66–69, *68*

dip, whipped, 275–76

Greek eggplant pudding, 251–52

heirloom tomato and watermelon salad, 59

and roasted red pepper spread, 276

warm, Greek salad with, 171

Figs:

butterflied pork roast with apple, cranberries and, Nigel's, 222–23

"fig n pig," 13–15, *14*

Filet mignon with lobster béarnaise, 196–98

Finnan haddie, Down East, 313–14

Fish:

chowder, 36–37

halibut pan roast with clams and *linguiça*, 150–51

mackerel, campfire, 151–52

mackerel, smoked, rillettes, 273

salt cod salad, "almost Italian," 144–46

sandwiches, Down East, 149–50

scrod, baked, beyond Boston, 146

G

P

Prosciutto:

    pizza with shaved asparagus and, our best pizza oven, 240–41

    -wrapped sea scallops, rosemary skewers with, 106–8

Prosecco, in strawberry rhubarb Bellini, 364

Provolone cheese, in "eggplant sandwiches," 24–25

Prune plum crunch, the original September, 323–24

Pudding cake, rhubarb, 347–48

Puddings (savory):

    corn, embarrassingly caloric, 250

    eggplant, Greek, 251–52

Puff pastry, in Reuben roulades, 286–87

Pumpkin:

    corn bread with maple pecan butter, 298

    October chili, 53

    pie, Pain D'Avignon's, 330–31

    and ricotta pancakes with maple pecan browned butter and dried cranberries, *306*, 307

    spice cake, Halloween, with broiled coconut pecan frosting, 345–46

Pumpkin seed(s) (*pepitas*):

    pesto, 26

    Thanksgiving 2010 granola, 324–25

Puttanesca, summer spaghetti, 265

Q, R

Quahogs, in Sal's stuffies, 90–91

Quesadillas with smoked Vermont Cheddar and pumpkin seed pesto, 25–26

Ragu, calamari, 171–72

Raspberry(ies):

    coulis, 339

    Debbie's blue ribbon Maine muffins, 316–17

    fresh fruit tart with lemon mascarpone cream filling, 336–38, *337*

Red wine:

    béarnaise, 164–65

    mulled, Mount Mansfield, 360–62, *361*

    Rhode Island, swordfish baked in, 162–63

Relish, cranberry citrus, 193

Reuben roulades, 286–87

Rhubarb:

    oven-roasted, 325–26

    pudding cake, 347–48

    strawberry Bellini, 364

Rib(s):

    barbecued, with Moose-a-maquoddy molasses mustard, 293–95, *294*

    short, beef stew, Moxie-braised, 205–6

Rib eye steaks, summer, with fresh rosemary, lemon, and garlic, 199–201, *200*

Ricotta and pumpkin pancakes with maple pecan browned butter and dried cranberries, *306*, 307

Rillettes, smoked mackerel, 273

Romaine hearts:

    grilled, with blue cheese and bacon, 66, *67*

    mood-enhancing winter salad, 65

    winter chopped salad, 64–65

Rosemary skewers with prosciutto-wrapped sea scallops, 106–8

Rum, Hurricane, mulled cider with or without, 359–60

Rye flour, in Catcher in the Rye bread, 296–97

S

Sage:

    brown butter, bay scallops with spaghetti squash and, 110

    potatoes, 258–60, *259*

    -rubbed pork chops with blue cheese and Concord grapes, *224*, 225–26

Salads, 56–75

    beet tartare, Broad Street, 72–73

    broccoli, with dried cranberries and toasted almonds, 62–63

    Brussels sprout Caesar, The Pitcher Inn's, 69–71

    chicken, 101, 278

    chicken, cranberry, 279–80

    chicken, curried, Daffodil picnic, 279

    coleslaw, poppy seed, 63–64

    corn, fresh, 62

    croutons for, 277

    cucumber, my mother's, 57

    cucumber and tomato, summer, 58

    farro tabbouleh, 285

    goat cheese, warm, with beach plum balsamic glaze, 71–72

    Greek, with warm feta, 171

    herb and caper, small, 206–8, *207*

    kale, chopped, with cranberries and feta, 66–69, *68*

    lobster Niçoise, 135–36

T

Additional stock photography:

Alamy: age fotostock Spain, S.L pp. 97, 118; Aurora Photos p. 90; Pat & Chuck Blackley p. 150; Wayne Bruzek p. 141; Norman Eggert p. 287; Aaron Flaum p. 231; Blaine Harrington III p. 178; Image Collective p. 169; Henk Meijer p. 148; Mira p. 260; Susan Pease p. 191. **Fotolia:** 14ktgold p. 57; Berlin85 p. 276; ermess p. 145; Kseniya Ragozina p. 345; sarsmis p. 253. **Getty Images:** Brian T. Evans/Moment Open p. 29; Peter Johansky/Photodisc p. 308; Ochand Courtney Lee/Chad Pierre/Moment Open p. 315; Ron and Patty Thomas Photography/E+ p. 158; Gail Shotlander/Moment Open p. 297; Tara Shannon Thayer/Moment Open pp. 44, 246; Kenneth Wiedemann/E+ p. 154; Betty Wiley/Moment Open p. 64. **NantucketStock:** © Cary Hazlegrove pp. 39, 54, 63, 74, 78, 83, 100, 111, 124, 130, 147, 165, 194, 209, 218, 256, 271, 332, 335; © Greg Hinson p. 153; © Kit Noble pp. 73, 202. **Newscom:** Edwin Remsberg/VWPics p. 186; **Terry Pommett:** p.TK (author photo); **Christopher Taylor:** p. 177. **Thinkstock:** Albert51Photo/iStock p. 48; ArtPhaneuf/iStock p. 34; DepthofField/iStock p. 366; DonLand/iStock p. 53; Genfirstlight/iStock p. 162; ISnap/iStock Editorial p. 136; JuliScalzi/iStock p. 134; Jupiterimages/iStock p. 370; Kenneth Keifer/iStock p. 51; mchebby/iStock p. 87; Kara Parlin/iStock p. 292.

Special thanks to the following contributors:

158 Pickett Street Café: p. 301; **Al Forno Restaurant:** p. 199; **Sarah Chase:** p. 192; **Dennis Public Market:** p. 223; **Farnum Hill Ciders:** p. 19; **Four Seas Ice Cream:** p. 352; © **Michael Galvin:** p. 278; **Hunt Hill Farm:** © Tim Lindaburg p. 242; **Trenton Bridge Lobster Pound:** p. 116; **Truelove Farms:** © Thomas Truelove p. 196; **Vermont Creamery:** p. 338, © Becky Luigart-Stayner, Sunny House Studio p. 24; **Woodstock Farmers' Market:** p. 2.